IFIP Advances in Information and Communication Technology 515

IFIP – The International Federation for Information Processing

IFIP was founded in 1960 under the auspices of UNESCO, following the first World Computer Congress held in Paris the previous year. A federation for societies working in information processing, IFIP's aim is two-fold: to support information processing in the countries of its members and to encourage technology transfer to developing nations. As its mission statement clearly states:

> *IFIP is the global non-profit federation of societies of ICT professionals that aims at achieving a worldwide professional and socially responsible development and application of information and communication technologies.*

IFIP is a non-profit-making organization, run almost solely by 2500 volunteers. It operates through a number of technical committees and working groups, which organize events and publications. IFIP's events range from large international open conferences to working conferences and local seminars.

The flagship event is the IFIP World Computer Congress, at which both invited and contributed papers are presented. Contributed papers are rigorously refereed and the rejection rate is high.

As with the Congress, participation in the open conferences is open to all and papers may be invited or submitted. Again, submitted papers are stringently refereed.

The working conferences are structured differently. They are usually run by a working group and attendance is generally smaller and occasionally by invitation only. Their purpose is to create an atmosphere conducive to innovation and development. Refereeing is also rigorous and papers are subjected to extensive group discussion.

Publications arising from IFIP events vary. The papers presented at the IFIP World Computer Congress and at open conferences are published as conference proceedings, while the results of the working conferences are often published as collections of selected and edited papers.

IFIP distinguishes three types of institutional membership: Country Representative Members, Members at Large, and Associate Members. The type of organization that can apply for membership is a wide variety and includes national or international societies of individual computer scientists/ICT professionals, associations or federations of such societies, government institutions/government related organizations, national or international research institutes or consortia, universities, academies of sciences, companies, national or international associations or federations of companies.

More information about this series at http://www.springer.com/series/6102

Arthur Tatnall · Mary Webb (Eds.)

Tomorrow's Learning: Involving Everyone

Learning with and about Technologies and Computing

11th IFIP TC 3 World Conference
on Computers in Education, WCCE 2017
Dublin, Ireland, July 3–6, 2017
Revised Selected Papers

Springer

Editors
Arthur Tatnall
Victoria University
Melbourne, VIC
Australia

Mary Webb
King's College London
London
UK

ISSN 1868-4238 ISSN 1868-422X (electronic)
IFIP Advances in Information and Communication Technology
ISBN 978-3-319-74309-7 ISBN 978-3-319-74310-3 (eBook)
https://doi.org/10.1007/978-3-319-74310-3

Library of Congress Control Number: 2018930742

Printed on acid-free paper

This Springer imprint is published by Springer Nature
The registered company is Springer International Publishing AG
The registered company address is: Gewerbestrasse 11, 6330 Cham, Switzerland

Preface

Every four years, Technical Committee 3 (Education) of the International Federation for Information Processing (IFIP) presents a major international conference: the World Conference on Computers and Education (WCCE). WCCE 2017 was held at Dublin Castle in Dublin, Republic of Ireland.

This book contains research papers relating to education and information technologies from authors around the world. It contains research papers from Greece, Germany, Denmark, Portugal, Ireland, The Netherlands, Austria, Canada, Malaysia, Australia, UK, Kenya, Finland, South Africa, France, Italy, Japan, USA, Slovakia, Czech Republic, Croatia, New Zealand, Israel, Poland, Cyprus, Morocco, and Slovenia.

The papers in the book were selected from those accepted for presentation at WCCE 2017. All papers submitted to the conference were double-blind peer reviewed and only the best were accepted. Of these, a further selection was made after the conference for publication. Based on conference feedback, each author was given the opportunity to improve their paper, and these papers were again peer reviewed before inclusion in this book.

The book is organized into the following sections:

1. Futures of Technology for Learning and Education
2. Innovative Practices with Learning Technologies
3. Computer Science Education and Its Future Focus and Development

Futures of Technology for Learning and Education

What is the future of education and ICT? Papers in this section attempt to offer some possible suggestions and answers for this question. The first paper by Kennewell compares presentations from the WCCE 1995 and WCCE 2017 conferences and suggests that a shift can be seen from "liberation" to "involvement." Two papers (by Dabner) look at ICT and education in New Zealand in relation to digital safety and to future citizens. Following is a discussion (by Akoh) of mobile learning in Canadian First Nations.

From Greece, Nikolopoulou reports on a study of adolescent Internet attitudes, which found that almost all adolescents believe that the Internet allows for more interesting and imaginative work.

Several papers then discuss computer-based gaming. Holvikivi and Toivanen-Labiad investigate health-game development, while Alghamdi and Holland report on how online gaming effects the dispositions, abilities, and behaviors of primary school students. Economides looks at alternate reality gaming as it relates to higher education.

Fluck, Ranmuthugala, Chin, Penesis, Chong, and Yang discuss two computer-based interventions in Year 6 classrooms that used sophisticated software alongside multimedia learning materials to teach topics from curriculum objectives many years ahead of these students' chronological ages. Grandbastien describes e-Fran, an on-going French initiative for linking academics from various disciplines and practitioners to design and test innovative ways of using digital technologies to improve learning outcomes.

Four papers then consider the use of mobile technologies. Firstly, Symons, Redman, and Blannin report on how these technologies can support pre-service teacher STEM education. Lopez-Fernandez and Nikolopoulou discuss mobile phone dependence in Spanish and Greek high school students. Learning in vocational training for mechanical engineering involves theoretical knowledge and practical activities, and how mobile technologies can assist is described by Wilke. Tablets have become very popular and Drossel and Eickelmann look at the how these relate to computer literacy.

From Africa, Maina (Kenya), Mavengere (Finland), Manzira (South Afrrica), Kihoro (Kenya), and Ruohonen (Finland) describe a multicultural remote collaborative learning environment. Manzira and Munyoka then present a South African case study of higher education collaborative postgraduate education.

MOOCS have become an important aspect of education and Butler, Leahy, Hallissy, and Brown look at how they can be used in teacher professional learning to recreate deep learning conversations. Investigating how teachers can be supported and guided in the planning of Web-based learning scenarios, Hofmann offers a connection of didactical aspects and ontological structures.

In the last three papers in this section, Jugo, Balaban, Pezelj, and Redjep discuss the development of a model to assess digitally mature schools in Croatia. Frankl, Schartner, and Jost look at a secure exam environment and Brites-Pereira, João Almeida and Osório investigate acceptance of motion detection devices by the elderly.

Innovative Practices with Learning Technologies

New technologies of all types offer novel innovative learning practices. This was true of the movie projector, video-tape recorder, DVD player, and other multimedia devices, and of course ICT. This section examines the wide range of some of these innovative practices.

We begin with an article by Masters on a project on Tasmania's King Island for extending children's literacies through developing digital stories. This is followed by Tosato and Banzato's discussion of gender difference in handmade robotics for children.

Blended learning is an important concept and Webb, Hatzipanagos, San Diego, Khan, and Goral offer a decision support tool to assist with assessment design. Sen, Chuen, Harn Liew, and Zay Hta next offer the concept of using augmented reality as a tool for learning of clinical skills in the early years of medical training. Soonja Yeom, Fluck, and Sale describe use of the technology acceptance model (TAM) to investigate students' acceptance of a haptic learning resource in anatomy education. Holmes, Latham, Crockett, and O'Shea then present a conversational intelligent tutoring system.

In terms of professional education, Lecomber and Tatnall describe how project management education can be of great value to IT professionals. Andresen then deals with teacher-driven learning analytics in primary and secondary education. It is seen as challenging for teachers to select the most suitable educational app to support students' learning, and Bano, Zowghi, and Kearne offer an innovative technique for evaluating educational mobile apps. Jakab and Redman address science concepts for young children with the use of ICT interactives.

Kolbæk and Nortvi describe student interactions with online problem-based learning. Selcuk investigates student perceptions of peer affective factors during a Facebook-based collaborative writing activity, while Araújo, Osório, and Martins discuss writing opinion essays using ICT. Donkor and Toplis investigate virtual learning environments in relation to the importance of emotional intelligence. Virtual environments and different learning modes is the topic of a paper by Mavengere, Ruohonen, and Vartiainen.

The first of three more papers relating to teacher education comes from Niess, who presents a case study on the design of online learning educational environments. McLeod and Carabot next look at the best way to embed ICT in teacher education, and Černochová, Jeřábek, and Vaňková offer a paper dealing with use of a DIYLab to understand a learning process.

A discussion on the effectiveness of using haptic simulators in higher education for dental students and other health-care disciplines is presented by from Cox, Quinn, San Diego, Patel, Gawali, and Woolford, who describe how innovations in teaching and learning strategies can improve their effectiveness. Okabe, Umezawa, and Yamaguchi then offer discussion of a backward learning support system that uses ontology to suggest prerequisites for understanding an item of which students may not have knowledge.

The last paper in this section, from Fluck and Hillier, examines the growing number of emerging eExam systems that allow students to demonstrate academic achievement using computers in schools and universities.

Computer Science Education and Its Future Focus and Development

The papers in this section are focused on research into the learning and teaching of computing, computer science, or informatics as a specialist subject in the curriculum. Different terms are used in different countries and contexts for this specialist subject but they all incorporate the study and design of computational systems. This focus separates these papers from the use of computer-based technologies for teaching and learning across a range of curriculum subjects, which is covered in the previous two sections.

Recently, concern was expressed in many countries about the position and nature of computer science in the curriculum, predominantly because a lack of computer science education has led to a dearth of computer scientists, which is a threat to economic well-being. In the first paper, which introduced a symposium incorporating eight papers focusing on curriculum issues, Webb et al. summarize the current situation of curriculum change and discuss the issues and challenges facing computer science education in schools. Micheuz's paper examines the situation in Austria as a specific example of how a country has responded to challenges of computer science in the school curriculum. Several subsequent papers consider issues for future curriculum design: Two papers (Haque; Przybylla and Romeike) consider curriculum needs in relation to industry and social needs, while another two papers focus on the changing curriculum at university level, with an analysis of change in an Australian university (Tatnall and Burgess) and an investigation of the changing capabilities of undergraduates (Strong et al.). The next five papers examine the issue of encouraging students into computer science and pedagogical approaches for retaining their interest (Brinda et al.; McInerney et al.; Shelton; Saito; Weigend).

The following three papers report on investigations of learners' and teachers' knowledge and beliefs in relation to computer science. Specifically, Hildebrandt reports on teachers' self-efficacy, while Pancratz and Diethelm focus on understanding of computer science concepts by learners, and Grillenberger and Romeike report more specifically on understanding of data management by both teachers and learners.

The remaining papers focus on learning programming, which has always been one of the most challenging aspects of learning computer science. These papers start with research in early years and primary education (Kalas and Benton; Keane; Tohyama). The next group of papers deal with learning programming and software engineering at university level (Higgins et al.; Holvikivi and Hjort; Matsuzawa et al.; Kramer et al.).

The Dublin Declaration

Finally the book presents "The Dublin Declaration," which is a distillation of evidence, identifying key aspects of innovation, development, successes, concerns, and interests in relation of ICT and education, but also showing where less success than expected has been achieved. It aims to offer recommendations and to support researchers, policymakers, and practitioners.

December 2017

Arthur Tatnall
Mary Webb

Organization

Program Committee

Don Passey	Lancaster University, UK
Sindre Røsvik	Giske Commune, Norway
Sigrid Schubert	University of Siegen, Germany
Andrej Brodnik	University of Ljubjana, Slovenia
Mikko Ruohonen	University of Tampere, Finland
Javier Osorio	University of Las Palmas in Gran Canaria, Spain
Denise Leahy	Trinity College Dublin, Ireland
Michael Tighe	Irish Computer Society
Arthur Tatnall	Victoria University, Australia
Mary Webb	King's College London, UK
Christine Bescherer	University of Ludwigsburg, Germany

Organizing Committee

John Ward	Irish Computer Society, Ireland
Denise Leahy	ICS Skills, Trinity College Dublin, Ireland
Declan Brady	Irish Computer Society, Ireland
Jim Friars	ICS Skills, Ireland
Tom O'Sullivan	Irish Computer Society, Ireland
Mary Cleary	ICS Skills, Ireland

The IFIP TC3 Dublin Declaration

Introduction

Every four years, the International Federation for Information Processing (IFIP) Technical Committee on Education (TC3) holds a World Conference on Computers in Education (WCCE). This significant event brings together researchers, policy makers and practitioners from across the world, to share the most recent research findings, policy concerns and focus, and examples of practitioners' interventions and needs. This event provides an important platform, both for gaining a view of the current situation and its contexts with regard to how digital technologies are being used across education (in primary, secondary, vocational, further, higher and adult education), and as a springboard for viewing possible futures based on the most up-to-date perspectives from research, policy and practice disciplines. This year, to support researchers, policy makers and practitioners, a Dublin Declaration has been created; a distillation of evidence, identifying key aspects of innovation, development, successes, concerns and interests, but also showing where less success has been achieved. Consequently, it offers recommendations for researchers, policy makers, developers and practitioners.

This Dublin Declaration is an important source for all those concerned with the development, deployment and uses of educational technologies. For researchers, the Dublin Declaration provides a view across current studies while also identifying gaps in our knowledge base. For policy makers, the Dublin Declaration shows the current focus of national and international concerns but also highlights those developments that are important for the future acquisition of digital capabilities and long-term skills. For developers, the Dublin Declaration highlights those innovations that are breaking new ground but also points to areas where gaps are evident. For practitioners, the Dublin Declaration provides examples of successful and effective practice while also offering ways to consider and develop new practices and pedagogies.

We hope that this Dublin Declaration will help with your endeavours, no matter what disciplinary area you are concerned with, and that you will look to take up the challenges presented here, in order to most effectively support the prospects of our learners, across the lifespan, and across society.

Don Passey
Chair of the IFIP TC3 WCCE2017 International Programme Committee

IFIP TC3 Dublin Declaration

Tomorrow's Learning: Involving Everyone

Background

The IFIP WCCE 2017, organised by TC3 and hosted by the Irish Computer Society (ICS), took place in Dublin from the 3rd to 6th July 2017, with a doctoral consortium held on 2nd July 2017.

The identification of key themes and trends from previous WCCEs led to the production of a series of recommendations, actions and visions. In 2005, the Stellenbosch Declaration called for actions to support digital solidarity, learners and lifelong learning, teachers and decision-making strategies, networking, and research. In 2009, the Bento Gonçalves Declaration called for actions to support the learner and teacher through curriculum initiatives, to develop research, learning environments, professionalism, and collaborative communities. In 2013, the Torun Vision set out two key challenges for the future. The first was to move from consuming to innovating; to creating, conceptualising and producing using programming and computer science (CS), as well as using information and communication technology (ICT) applications. The second was to deploy digital technologies to better support different interactions with different stakeholders, according to technologies selected and used (such as those with online or haptic features), accommodating institutional diversities, gender, cultural, native language, cognitive and social backgrounds.

This Dublin Declaration from the IFIP WCCE 2017 is informed by the many presentations, discussions and interactions during the Conference from across the entire group of delegates. These researchers, policy-makers, educators, and ICT practitioners in education, from five continents, met and worked together in Dublin, Ireland.

Chairs of all sessions were asked to provide summaries, stating up to three key ideas for the future that were raised in their sessions (keynote presentations, paper presentations, symposia, and discussion sessions). Following the Conference, members of the International Programme Committee (IPC) collated these summary points. Key themes were drawn out, and contents were analysed and distilled within those themes. Draft versions were further shared with members of the IPC, with chairs of Conference sessions, and with all members of the four working groups of TC3. The resultant final version, this Declaration, provides an informed view from the width of conference delegates as to how they perceive the focus for necessary future action in this field of technologies supporting learning and education for all.

The Current and the Future

Participants in the Conference shared the belief that in terms of computing, computer education and uses of technologies for teaching and learning we are, in 2017, at a pivotal point of change. It is clear that international, national and local computer and educational technology strategies, policies and curricula are shifting. Earlier and ongoing outcomes from the activities of important initiatives such as the European Computer Driving Licence (ECDL) have clearly contributed to this current state of play with regard to user practices and uses of ICT. The current status of computer access and uses across countries and the identification of key underlying development needs are clearly shown from the monitoring of international and national comparison data. For example, from the Programme for International Student Assessment (PISA) results run by the Organisation for Economic Cooperation and Development (OECD) and presented in the Conference; and from the International Association for the Evaluation of Educational Achievement's (IEA's) International Computer and Information Literacy Study (ICILS) focusing on computer and information literacy presented in previous IFIP TC3 conferences. Given the wide evidence base from a wealth of research studies and the outcomes presented throughout the Conference, learners of all ages and levels can benefit from, and should be enabled to develop opportunities that such technologies offer, not only for their individual futures but also for the future of our wider communities and society as a whole. However, young people need to have sufficient opportunities to be creators and not just consumers of ICT. The theme of the Conference was Tomorrow's Learning: Involving Everyone, which reflected a focal objective - to seek ways to assure the inclusiveness of technologies to support education, teaching and learning for all social groups. From the variety of opportunities presented, it is critical that teaching about computing does not replace the use of ICT to enhance learning across the curriculum, as ways in which ICT impacts on society and other aspects of digital literacy and digital agency (such as how to manage one's online presence) are fundamental knowledge for the current and the future. The balance between computing and ICT to enhance learning across the curriculum must be fully considered and accommodated. Importantly also, the balance between educational activities that involve non-computer use as well as computer use is an issue that needs wider consideration, as we move towards increased digital ubiquity in this digital era.

During the Conference, a large range of relevant contributions presented examples of practice of major importance and relevance, showing how improvement of education can be achieved through effective uses of technologies. Reviewing the entirety of evidence presented, we strongly recommend that stakeholders and decision-makers in education consider and invest in areas that Conference topics highlighted (detailed further in sections following), all of deep importance to the improvement of education through a consistent support of ICT. Following evidence supported by keynote presentations from policy perspectives, it is recommended that national investment is needed at a level of 7% of Gross Domestic Product (GDP) for education, compared to the current 5.2% as the OECD average. In addition, it was commonly agreed that for any strategy or policy in the educational arena to succeed, we must bring together contributions of researchers, policymakers and practitioners.

Computer Science Education

This was recognised widely as an area of growing and upmost importance. As we increasingly depend on well-educated professionals and digitally literate citizens, able to use computing and ICT in a broad set of circumstances and able to adapt in a flexible manner to a continuously changing technological environment, there are clearly implications for the social and economic sectors. Concerns were raised in this area; that we need far more research on aspects of inclusive curriculum, pedagogies and attitudes to computing, the need for more and well-trained computer science teachers, as well as the need for more professional educational support. In terms of economic drivers, there is need for any society to promote active producers rather than a society of passive consumers of technology, to create a wide set of computer scientists to sustain a competitive edge, and to have computer science-enabled professionals in all industries to support innovation. From a social point of view, computer science awareness provides opportunities to lead, create and innovate within society; and from a cultural perspective, it can be a powerful driver of cultural change. However, concerns have to be considered also; there is a trend towards starting computer science in the curriculum at a younger age, and this needs to be adequately supported by new programming environments that remove obstacles to learning, such as complex syntax. There is a need to look carefully at the conceptual basis of these approaches in order to develop important concepts for young learners through, for example, building procedures within Scratch (a widely-used programming environment for children) or through robotics (humanoid or handmade), as notions of procedural abstraction need to be integrated within curricular content, accommodating educational research in this field.

Our recommendations are:

- For an entitlement for young people to be educated in computing, incorporating computer science and computational thinking as the underlying academic discipline, as well as digital literacy - all young people have a right to become creators and not only consumers of ICT for their future.
- To enable more research into inclusive curriculum, pedagogies and attitudes to computing.
- To create more and well-trained computer science teachers.
- For more teacher professional educational support in integrating technology into lesson plans, and teaching across the curriculum, developing teachers as researchers in appropriate selection, design, implementation, reflection and dissemination of practice.
- To clarify use of terminology in this field, to ensure there is clear understanding whatever and wherever the audience is. Terms such as informatics, ICT, digitalisation, computers, etc., are often used indistinctly, although they are not interchangeable. A first pedagogical step should be to agree a common frame of terminology to avoid ambiguity or overlapping between different concepts.

Developing Countries

The gap between developing and developed countries in the use of ICT in education has not closed sufficiently to allow students from different parts of the globe to have the same opportunities to develop digital skills, competences and agency. The problem is becoming wider in some respects, because different groups of populations inside developing countries can have quite imbalanced access to technology. The differences between rural and city areas and, within the latter, between inner city and the rest, means that an appropriate development of specific technology learning according to economic capacity of the different groups must be adequately considered.

Our recommendations are:

- To focus on new pedagogical opportunities offered by mobile learning applications and their adoption in the education field.
- To consider infrastructure challenges neither as a matter of funding nor as a technocratic approach; school administrators and parents should be included in developing creative support and maintenance, as part of a wider holistic approach to development.
- There should be co-operation with countries with a high degree of ICT development in education, to share their experience in IT usage/skills in the educational domain.
- Approaches implemented when using digital technologies to enhance learning in multicultural environments into developing countries should be considered for wider potential adoption, but with full consideration given to contextual differences and implications arising for adoption.

Inclusiveness and Student Engagement

Evidence shows that not enough didactic ICT-based resources have been developed for those with disabilities. This huge void should be more actively covered, enabling all to directly contribute to wider social welfare. Reducing the gender gap also constitutes an important concern for wider social development; there is a need to develop innovative and imaginative ways to attract more girls into computing. Technologies, in their varied applications, can show themselves as a powerful means to facilitate skills through activities that could be initially thought of as highly complex and demanding. In this way, innovative technologies should be used to facilitate more inclusive learning, reducing the gender gap and promoting student engagement.

Our recommendations are:

- To encourage schools to implement problems and ideas from real life and from students' out-of-school interests, activities and hobbies, to allow children to enjoy solving them in a challenging way, even in their free time.

- To focus curriculum design on the needs of all learners and not to over-emphasise the needs of those who will enter the computing profession; the key ideas and concepts of computer science should be made accessible to all students.
- To develop digital stories into the curriculum as a tool to engage young learners in active uses of ICT from early ages.
- To develop emotional intelligence of our students, as this is often a missing component of all virtual learning environments and other digital resources. The goal is to pay closer attention to implementing this aspect into pedagogies that involve educational software.
- To develop strategies to encourage the use of handheld devices in education to boost computer literacy.
- To commission research to understand why the gender gap is being reduced, according to some recent research studies.

Teacher Education and Continuing Professional Development

Experiences of how teaching staff in all educational sectors are currently teaching computing, and using and teaching ICT, emphasise the need to foster greater involvement of schoolteachers in the use of ICT as part of their regular teaching activities. Teachers should be aware that ICT can be more than a mere tool for superficial engagement of learners; they can aid the development of deeper engagement and thinking. This can be achieved by starting from a requirement to develop ICT-based resources themselves, rather than having them provided or modelled. Such uses will need to be adequately balanced with uses of ICT as pedagogical tools across the curriculum. There is a critical need to call the attention of policymakers as well as teacher educators and teachers to engage positively with the design and development of computing curricula in this changing world. Introducing ICT effectively into teaching and learning is often challenging because change will be necessary. It is, therefore, essential that all stakeholders are engaged in agreeing change - parents, governors, teaching staff and local and regional bodies as appropriate. In developing appropriate practices, where educators in ICT need to work with educational technology companies, practice-based research shows examples of how some companies have supported projects to meet educational agendas. Involving teachers in using ICT purposefully may be developed through communities of teachers within schools and in wider communities, where they can engage in well-organised practice-based research, sharing their results and aiming at a wider analysis of the evidence rather than being isolated in the classroom. Multimodal web publication can be an effective way of sharing evidence in a form that teachers are willing to access.

Our recommendations are:

- To develop educators who can teach computational thinking rather than just teaching programming from standard lesson plans and textbooks.
- To build further capacity in digitally-literate teachers in every discipline.

- To crucially provide professional development for teachers, which should be problem-based and adopt project-based approaches supported by and supplemented with communities of practice, as these provide enormous potential for effective professional development.
- To ensure that all stakeholders are engaged in developments that lead to change through ICT, even at the stage of discussing the evidence.
- To recognise the importance of learning analytics as potential instruments to improve learning processes, but considering the need for such data to provide useful and important feedback to improve educators' work.
- To spread more widely the proof of successful interventions in this domain, taking the context of evidence fully into account when considering relevance for different situations.
- To identify recognised instructional practices in online teacher education to provide effective and accessible professional development, expanding educators' knowledge for teaching with emerging technologies.
- To promote ways of developing communities of research-active teachers to develop and disseminate their own evidence of the impact of ICT on teaching and learning.
- To identify blended learning (online and face-to-face) as professional development opportunities for engaging teachers in practical experiences for teaching with technologies.

Game-Based Learning and Gamification

Games, available in a widening variety of formats and types, all used with different but relevant didactical approaches, promise to be important instructional tools. While this field is still at an embryonic stage, consequently, further theoretical discussions are needed to ensure a common use and understanding of the terminology and scope of these tools. Game-based learning is not just centred on the game and its immediate outcomes, but the challenge is to relate these to other instructional activities to achieve wider and longer-term learning objectives.

Our recommendations are:

- To promote further research to set the basis of a comprehensive framework to support game-based teaching and learning at all levels of education.
- To train pre-service and in-service teachers in the use of game-based learning approaches.

e-Evaluation

To see computers used effectively in education, it is necessary to develop fair, reliable and resilient computer-based assessment methods. Assessment methods must go far beyond imitating paper-based assessment, and prioritise the pedagogical affordances of computers over administrative convenience. The use of computers in timed, supervised assessments offers the chance to transform curricula in the light of computational thinking.

Our recommendations are:

- To consider stealth assessment as an approach to formative (rather than summative) assessment that is seamless - woven deep into the fabric of the activity such as a game and not taking away the 'fun of learning'.
- To examine how the assessment approach from research can be taken into mainstream learning.
- To study the rapid rise in e-Examinations, for authentic assessment that matches modern workplace practices and many student learning experiences.

In Conclusion

For any of the topics above to be taken forward, they need to be afforded with greater levels of international cooperation and collaboration between researchers and practitioners, through appropriate research processes, from design to dissemination. In addition, research approaches in this field should continue to integrate and combine the expertise of education, psychology, sociology, computer science and economics to provide robust, well-rounded, critical perspectives to ensure the best outcomes to drive the future of education forward. High-quality interdisciplinary research is needed to establish a strong and informative evidence base before adopting large-scale implementation and investments in educational technology initiatives. An evidence base needs to assess the impact and integration of technology in the classroom through a synergy between quantitative and qualitative methods, where studies are framed in appropriate theoretical terms, with consistency between theoretical position, design, methodology, data collection and analysis. Conceptions of research, policy and practice should be revisited in this field. Teachers need to be considered to be producers of knowledge. Maintaining the variety of uses for learners of all ages, identifying outcomes that relate to contexts, and measuring impacts where purpose and future developments are fully considered, are all essential elements that need to be integrated into contemporary and future research, policy, teacher education, teaching and learning practices in this field.

October 2017

The IPC of IFIP WCCE 2017, acknowledging the significant contributions of presenters and chairs of the Conference, and members of the working groups of TC3.

Contents

Futures of Technology for Learning and Education

Changing Rationales for Computers in Education: From Liberation to Involvement

Steve Kennewell(✉)

Cardiff Metropolitan University, Cardiff, UK
skennewell@cardiffmet.ac.uk

Abstract. This paper examines the themes for two World Conferences on Computers in Education to characterize and theorize the shift in pedagogical rationale from 'liberating the learner' (the 1995 theme) to 'involving everyone' (the 2017 theme). The WCCE 1995 contributors' responses to the theme of liberation are analyzed in terms of how the affordances of digital technology for learning are orchestrated by teachers, students and the technology itself. The pedagogical effects of developments in the use of technology in education since 1995 are considered using four key examples, and WCCE 2017 contributors' responses to the theme of involvement are discussed in the context of these effects. The paper concludes that the shift from 'liberation' to 'involvement' represents a progression in expectations concerning how technology can aid learning, but that involvement requires that the learner should develop an intention to learn and an ability to orchestrate resources which teachers should help them to acquire.

Keywords: Rationale · Liberation · Involvement · Affordance Orchestration

1 Introduction

The use of digital technology to enhance learning has a 50-year history, and it is right that our current exploits should build on what has gone before. However, not only has the power of the technology changed considerably over the years, but the pedagogical rationale for its use has also shifted - albeit more subtly. These changes have implications for our research strategies and for the theories which underpin the application of technology to teaching and learning. As an example of this, I want to start by recalling WCCE 1995, whose theme was 'Liberating the Learner'. I am going to examine the meaning of this idea in general terms, then analyse how it was interpreted in 1995. I will next consider what we have learned about learner liberation through the use of digital technology during the intervening 22 years. Finally, I will discuss how the WCCE 2017 theme of 'Involving everyone' can be enriched by this reflection.

Liberty can take the form of freedom **from** prohibitions or restrictions, or of freedom **to** act as desired. Proposing (greater) liberty for the learner therefore raises question of what constraints are being relaxed, what actions are being allowed or facilitated in contexts where learning is expected, and what advantages these changes provide for the learner.

A. Tatnall and M. Webb (Eds.): WCCE 2017, IFIP AICT 515, pp. 3–12, 2017.
https://doi.org/10.1007/978-3-319-74310-3_1

The purpose of educational systems – primary schools, secondary schools of various types, and higher education institutions - is to organise a number of factors in order to facilitate learning more systematically than would occur in natural settings. To achieve this, such systems provide direct teaching and study resources; they also try to coordinate less visible influences such as support from parents and others including peers. But there are several factors which may influence whether and how learning actually takes place. These include the location, timing, pace and style of teaching, together with the resources available, organisational rules and the curriculum adopted by teachers. Effective management of these factors is key to successful learning, and any attempt to 'liberate the learner' may not achieve the desired outcomes if it merely shifts the balance of control of activity from the expert teacher to the novice student. Students may not know enough about their learning to manage it effectively by themselves. It follows that if digital technology is to improve education, it must help students to manage their learning; this has implications for our current aspiration for 'involving everyone'.

2 Framework for Analysis

In order to analyse this development in rationale from a pedagogical perspective, it will be necessary to adopt a framework which is sensitive to the detailed decisions and actions taken by teachers and learners when using ICT and other media as aids to learning. The terms *affordance* and *constraint* have been used widely to analyse how factors in the environment influence activity (see, for instance, [19, 31]). Although they have been interpreted in various ways in the literature, there is enough similarity in the meanings to avoid the need for precise definition here. They are valuable tools for the analysis of educational activity, particularly where students carry out actions in pursuing certain goals which are generally set by the teacher. Learners have options concerning their actions in pursuit of these goals, and make decisions based on the affordances and constraints presented to them by the learning environment. Whilst some of the features of the activity setting will be fixed, many others can be manipulated, and the term *orchestration* has also been used widely over recent years to characterize the manipulation of the environment for learning [24].

At a general level, "orchestration refers to how a teacher manages, in real time, multi-layered activities in a multi-constraints context" [12]. More precisely, it concerns the purposeful arrangement of affordances and constraints for students' actions during a task in order to bring about learning from their actions [19]. It is not only the teacher who can orchestrate activity; learners themselves can manage their environment to some extent. Orchestration can range from teacher intervention during collaborative activity using tablets in a primary school mathematics lesson [24] to students seeking help from teaching assistants in a university Physics class [12].

Five key elements comprise the orchestration of learning: design/planning, regulation/management, adaptation/flexibility/intervention and awareness/assessment [24]. In a formal setting, whether in a classroom or online, a teacher will typically:

- Design a task and plan the resources to be available to students
- Discuss the concepts and techniques relevant to the task
- Give procedural instructions
- Explain outcome expectations
- Monitor student activity and intervene with individuals or groups: adding or changing resources, instructions or expectations; answering and asking questions; providing prompts and explanations
- Evaluate outcomes, assess learning and provide feedback.

Students may also manipulate the affordances and constraints to help achieve the task goal, particularly by using peers to help explain ideas, clarify instructions and locate resources. This may inhibit the intended learning, however – for example if one student just copies the work of another or focuses merely on completing the task in the simplest manner [20].

An orchestration perspective provides a means of analysing the role of digital technology in learning and how it changes with increasing maturity and technological advance. In characterising how learners' actions are facilitated (the 'freedom to' aspect) together with how their actions are restricted (the 'freedom from' aspect), it offers a more sophisticated framework for studying the way in which learning is managed than the simple idea of balance of control.

3 Liberating the Learner

The contributions to WCCE 1995 demonstrated a number of themes concerning the nature of digital technology and its effect on the balance of control of learning. The Working Group papers suggested empowerment of the individual student to learn outside the teacher's sphere of influence [29], and the emergence of new contexts for learning: home and other locations outside school [7]. Individual papers provided a variety of perspectives on how this might be achieved.

Several were concerned with the design of intelligent tutoring systems which combine expert systems, artificial intelligence engines and models of individual student behaviour to manage learner activity in an online task (for example [2]). Whilst this certainly had the potential to liberate the teacher, and to enable a small number of staff to manage a large number of students in many locations, the orchestration was only shifted as far as the computer system which essentially acted a surrogate teacher. Indeed, the design and planning stages still required an expert human teacher, and whilst the system may have been able to build up an extensive database concerning the knowledge and learning approaches of a large number of individual students, the adaptation and flexibility required for effective intervention proved much harder to achieve.

Other software environments were designed instead to facilitate learner control supported by structure for their activities (for example [11]). Although the orchestration within these environments was fully programmed in advance and hence the affordances and constraints could not generally be adapted by the teacher, they did allow more learner orchestration than most traditional classroom tasks. Furthermore, when they were used in a classroom, the teacher could carry out most of the elements of orchestration including dynamic intervention. Some software was designed to act as the learner's partner in an activity, providing the equivalent of peer orchestration as what was described as a "social machine" [13] or "social learning system" [10]. In other cases, the software took the role of a tool in a construction task (for example [33]) or searching large databases [16]; these applications required learner orchestration on a different level, requiring creativity, planning and a critical approach.

Although there was frequent reference to student-centred learning, only one contribution referred to a personal learning environment [18]. This was facilitated by each student having a notebook computer to be used in school and home. There was no mention at all of learning management systems, although one contributor [23] did give a foretaste of things to come in describing how the World Wide Web (still in its infancy in 1995) was used to provide material for students and allow them to communicate asynchronously with tutors.

4 Discussion

In 1995 there was clearly a desire to use digital technology to help give students more influence over learning situations. The theme of 'liberating the learner' was interpreted quite cautiously, but the idea that the teachers' control could and would diminish in the digital environment ran right through the contributions analyzed. Consequently most papers were concerned with how this more student-centered scenario might be implemented in terms of technological design. The focus on orchestration in the analysis has brought out a variety of ways in which the management of learning might be shared amongst different participants: teachers, students and the technology itself. The key issue for implementing technological assistance in any setting is not what the balance of control should be, but what contribution each of the participants can best make to the processes involved in orchestration. It did not seem in 1995 that technology was at the stage of making a large, active contribution to either design/planning, monitoring/intervention or assessment/feedback, and for most contributors it remained a tool and resource for the human agents involved.

Control over the course of learning activity involves orchestration of relevant affordances and constraints; if teachers are to delegate at least some of this and technology is not (yet) ready to take it on, then students need to have some skills in orchestration. However, to many educationists orchestration represents "the empowerment of teachers as drivers of classroom activities" [12], and it is not clear what might persuade teachers to relinquish any of this power. The contributors to WCCE 1995 did not really address this issue. Whilst WG3.1 [29] envisaged that "the teacher becomes a learning guide or a mentor for the students, cooperating with pupils in a learning experience" only a small number of papers [15, 22, 28] explicitly considered changes in the teacher's role. Most seemed to assume that a move from direct teaching of students to authoring of materials was unproblematic, and that the key challenge for technology was to provide an adequate model of the learner in order to sequence their tasks and provide resources. In contrast, perhaps, was the promise of improved collaboration between students afforded by new communications technology, and there were examples of how to meet the challenge of orchestrating video conferencing [14] and text conferencing systems [4] so as to promote learning.

5 Developments Since 1995

Looking now from 2017, what progress have we made in the use of digital technology to 'liberate the learner'? Examples of developments since 1995 which have made a substantial impact on teaching and learning, include:

- Learning management systems: these can be accessed anytime, anywhere but despite the name, they do not actually orchestrate learning themselves, but rather provide a structure and features which support management of resources by teachers but impose significant constraints on learners [6]. Whilst these have been embedded widely in higher education institutions, their adoption in schools has been much less than was anticipated a few years ago.
- Interactive whiteboards: these also provide many features which can afford and constrain classroom activity, but have been largely used by teachers to facilitate their traditional approaches to orchestrating resources and are valued for their effects on motivating learners (see, for example, [20]). These devices have been very widely adopted in schools, but have had less influence in higher education.
- Web2 and Social media: structures such as blogs, wikis, news broadcasting and social networking have all been appropriated widely for educational purposes; they have affordances for interaction over distance and time, but pose considerable challenges for distributing the orchestration between teachers and students [3], and perhaps because of this they do not yet seem to have been adopted widely in educational institutions.
- Mobile learning and 1–1 classroom devices: again, they clearly offer affordances for action which is flexible in place and time, and also for individualised learning. The distribution of orchestration is again a challenge, and although in many institutions it is the norm for each student to have a computer in the classroom, their use in schools is often tightly controlled by the teacher and students are not allowed to use their own devices because of potential distractions [32].
- Gamification: this approach represents a particular mode of orchestration in which the activity setting takes the form of a game in some way. The constraints are managed by the computer according to the rules of the 'game' and the affordances for action are orchestrated largely by the learners. Perhaps for this reason, game-based learning is seen as particularly motivating for students [8]. As the active role of the teacher may be quite small, it is particularly suitable for use outside the classroom.

In each of these cases, it seems that the degree of adoption of the technology in different sectors is directly correlated with the fit between the form of orchestration supported by the technology and the traditional pedagogy of the teacher. In other words, ICT is used when it helps the teacher to do what they already do. Clearly, advances in didactics have not kept pace with advances in technology; does this mean that the call for 'liberating the learner' is even more valid than 22 years ago?

In many parts of the world, most young people are now 'digital residents' who live their lives online. They perhaps feel liberated in that they can find resources for learning whenever they want to, but this may be a naïve illusion. People leave traces when they search the internet, particularly if they have social media profiles, and can be 'found' at any time by individuals and organisations wishing to steer them towards particular options in their searches. These organisations may have commercial - or perhaps more salacious - interests rather than educational purposes. A simple call for 'liberation' no longer seems to represent our aspirations for the learner's relationship with education when the orchestration of their environment is so widely distributed. Merely freeing learners from constraints imposed by the teacher, curriculum etc. is unlikely to be fruitful when the affordances for action are so many and varied that orchestrating them become a massive challenge.

6 Tomorrow's Learning: 'Involving Everyone'

The current theme envisages that in future, technology will enable us to 'involve everyone' in learning. Is this an appropriate aspiration? Involvement seems to require more than just *access* to teaching and resources; it suggests that our aim for all should be *active participation* in learning.

A number of contributors to WCCE 2017 addressed these issues. Some identified the nature of the task as an important factor in motivating learning. The creation of a worthwhile product was seen as particularly significant [30, 34], particularly if this presented a challenge to learners [1], although such challenges must be seen as realistic targets by learners [25] and an alternative strategy involving finding, trying out and reflecting/discussing is also effective [32]. Digital technology can support game environments which engage learners actively with learning tasks within and beyond the classroom [1, 9] and increase students' interest in the learning process itself rather than just the grades achieved [1]. It can increase the 'learnability' of topics by positioning students positively in relation to difficult concepts [17]. Whilst a digital learning environment may be designed for active learning [34] or active participation [21], the affordances of the technology may not be sufficient on their own to sustain student engagement, and many learners need the support of the teacher or others, either in the classroom [25, 34] or online [21]. For learners accustomed to using technology on the move, physical activity with mobile devices outside the classroom also aids engagement in learning [32].

The idea of 'freedom' had not entirely disappeared; for some contributors, choice was seen as an important factor in involvement of learners. Being able to select a theme of personal interest to work on was motivating for students [30, 34], although there was some concern that students might only be motivated by themes in which they were personally interested [21]. Freedom to use heuristic methods in problem-solving was supported by digital environments [30], a situation which is reminiscent of the vision for LOGO classrooms in the 1980s which had largely disappeared in 1995 [27].

7 Discussion

The challenge of progressing from provision of access to teaching towards participation in learning can be informed by the analysis above. There is overwhelming evidence that digital technology motivates students to participate in activity; the difficulty comes in stimulating students to focus on learning from that activity. Teachers are generally adept at designing and preparing environments that offer affordances for all students in their charge, but we have noted that these environments are based largely on traditional pedagogy and may not exploit the full potential of the technology. The first stage in the development of active participation in learning involves being able to judge when digital technology can provide more or better affordances for *learning* rather than merely for task completion. But digital environments provide affordances for many other actions, and in order to avoid distractions, students must first adopt the teacher's intention, not just for task completion, but for achieving the intended learning outcomes.

The second stage is for students themselves to learn to orchestrate affordances and constraints for learning: this is the essence of 'intentional learning'. Effective learners do this already, but many students do not seek - or are prevented from using – prompts from peers, new resources, or even the digital tools which are familiar from everyday life. Digital technology can support this sharing of orchestration (see, for example, [28] which in 1995 was already dealing with this idea explicitly) but some learners will need support from teachers or other people [25].

8 Conclusion

The key to liberating learners is giving them ability to participate actively through orchestrating resources for learning, but I have argued that in order to ensure *involvement* in learning, learners must also have an *intention to learn* from their activity. Learners' intentions may not be the same as those of their teachers, however, and however liberated or involved learners are, the questions remains concerning what they are learning. Traditional responses to students' lack of focus on the intended learning involve imposing constraints such as rules for classroom behavior. In the digital environment, similar constraints such as blocking access to websites and banning mobile devices are likely to be unsuccessful and indeed counterproductive because of the students' abilities to overcome such constraints. A better route to improved learning may be for teachers to shift their efforts towards supporting all students in using their abilities to orchestrate the affordances of the digital environment in pursuit of the intended learning in ways observed, for example, in [5]. An aspiration of 'involvement' rather than 'liberation' for the learner offers teachers a positive role in the learning process rather than having to relinquish their power.

Having analyzed the changes in aspiration for technology's role in education over the past 22 years, it is tempting to speculate about what we might aspire to in 2039. Where technology is concerned, it is very risky to speculate on developments far into the future. In any case, technology's application to education depends very much on whether schooling in institutions remains the dominant approach for compulsory education. Furthermore, education is always largely controlled by people who experienced compulsory education at least 20 years previously, educational methods change little from one generation to the next. Will the current cohort of school students be the ones to bring about the paradigm shift afforded by ubiquitous digital technology? If so, in 22 years' time, we may well need to focus less on how to involve learners and more on **what** is learned and **who** controls learning. Perhaps then the theme for 2039 will be 'Liberating the Learner' – again!

References

1. Algamdi, J., Holland, C.: Game-play: effects of online gamified and game-based learning on dispositions, abilities and behaviours of primary learners. In: Tatnall, A., Webb, M. (eds.) WCCE 2017. IFIP AICT, vol. 515, pp. 55–63. Springer, Cham (2017)
2. Arruarte, A., Fernandez-Castro, I.: A two-phased development shell for learning environments: a design proposal. In: Tinsley, J.D., van Weert, T.J. (eds.) Proceedings of the Sixth IFIP World Conference on Computers in Education. Chapman & Hall, London (1995)
3. ASHE: Limits to student engagement. ASHE High. Educ. Rep. **40**(6), 75–87
4. Austin, R.: Quality learning through computer conferencing. In: Tinsley, J.D., van Weert, T.J. (eds.) Proceedings of the Sixth IFIP World Conference on Computers in Education. Chapman & Hall, London (1995)
5. Barnes, J., Kennewell, S.: Investigating teacher perceptions of teaching ICT in Wales. Educ. Inf. Technol. **22**(5), 2485–2497 (2017)
6. Bennett, S.: Learning Management Systems: A Review. AUT University, Auckland (2011)
7. Benzie, D.: IFIP working group 3.5: using computers to support young learners. In: Tinsley, J.D., van Weert, T.J. (eds.) Proceedings of the Sixth IFIP World Conference on Computers in Education. Chapman & Hall, London (1995)
8. Caponetto, I., Earp, J., Ott, M.: Proceedings of the European Conference on Games Based Learning, vol. 1, pp. 50–57 (2014)
9. Carvalho, A.A.: Konnecting: a mobile game to introduce freshmen to the evolution of communication. In: Paper Presented at World Conference on Computers in Education - Tomorrow's Learning: Involving Everyone, Dublin (2017)
10. Chan, T.W., Lai, J.A.: Contest-Kid: a competitive distributed social learning environment. In: Tinsley, J.D., van Weert, T.J. (eds.) Proceedings of the Sixth IFIP World Conference on Computers in Education. Chapman & Hall, London (1995)
11. Cumming, G., Zangari, M., Thomason, N.: Designing software for cognitive change: StatPlay and understanding statistics. In: Tinsley, J.D., van Weert, T.J. (eds.) Proceedings of the Sixth IFIP World Conference on Computers in Education. Chapman & Hall, London (1995)
12. Dillenbourg, P.: Design for classroom orchestration. Comput. Educ. **69**, 485–492 (2013)
13. Dowling, C.: The 'social' machine: the computer as a participant in social and cognitive interactions within the classroom. In: Tinsley, J.D., van Weert, T.J. (eds.) Proceedings of the Sixth IFIP World Conference on Computers in Education. Chapman & Hall, London (1995)
14. Evjemo, B., Eidsvik, A.K., Danielsen, T.: Cooperating school classes. In: Tinsley, J.D., van Weert, T.J. (eds.) Proceedings of the Sixth IFIP World Conference on Computers in Education. Chapman & Hall, London (1995)

15. Frath, P.: What context for liberated computer assisted language learning? In: Tinsley, J.D., van Weert, T.J. (eds.) Proceedings of the Sixth IFIP World Conference on Computers in Education. Chapman & Hall, London (1995)
16. Hammond, M.: Learning from experience: approaching the research of CD-ROM in schools. In: Tinsley, J.D., van Weert, T.J. (eds.) Proceedings of the Sixth IFIP World Conference on Computers in Education. Chapman & Hall, London (1995)
17. Jakab, C., Redman, C.: How interactives can change learnability of science concepts for young children – re-positioning them as learners 'who can and did'. In: Tatnall, A., Webb, M. (eds.) WCCE 2017. IFIP AICT, vol. 515, pp. 292–303. Springer, Cham (2017)
18. Jones, D.: The introduction of an information technology project: personal computing in the classroom. In: Tinsley, J.D., van Weert, T.J. (eds.) Proceedings of the Sixth IFIP World Conference on Computers in Education. Chapman & Hall, London (1995)
19. Kennewell, S.: Using affordances and constraints to evaluate the use of ICT in teaching and learning. J. Inf. Technol. Teach. Educ. **10**, 101–116 (2001)
20. Kennewell, S., Tanner, H., Jones, S., Beauchamp, G.: Analysing the use of interactive technology to implement interactive teaching. J. Comput. Assist. Learn. **24**(1), 61–73 (2008)
21. Kolbaek, D., Nortvig, A.-M.: An educational experience with online teaching – not a best practice. In: Tatnall, A., Webb, M. (eds.) WCCE 2017. IFIP AICT, vol. 515, pp. 304–313. Springer, Cham (2017)
22. McDougall, A., Cumming, G., Sussex, R.: Learner modelling by expert teachers: learner information space and the minimal learner model. In: Tinsley, J.D., van Weert, T.J. (eds.) Proceedings of the Sixth IFIP World Conference on Computers in Education. Chapman & Hall, London (1995)
23. Nott, M., Riddle, M., Pearce, J.: Enhancing traditional university science teaching using the World Wide Web. In: Tinsley, J.D., van Weert, T.J. (eds.) Proceedings of the Sixth IFIP World Conference on Computers in Education. Chapman & Hall, London (1995)
24. Prieto, L.P., Holenko-Dlab, M., Abdulwahed, M., Gutiérrez, I., Balid, W.: Orchestrating technology enhanced learning: a literature review and a conceptual framework. Int. J. Technol.-Enhanc. Learn. **3**(6), 583–598 (2011)
25. Saito, T.: Educational support on computing and informatics as means of empowering disadvantaged young people in developed countries. In: Tatnall, A., Webb, M. (eds.) WCCE 2017. IFIP AICT, vol. 515, pp. 515–524. Springer, Cham (2017)
26. Sharples, M.: Shared orchestration within and beyond the classroom. Comput. Educ. **69**, 504–506 (2013)
27. Tagg, C., Tagg, B., Oram, I.: Realizing a vision? In: Tinsley, J.D., van Weert, T.J. (eds.) Proceedings of the Sixth IFIP World Conference on Computers in Education. Chapman & Hall, London (1995)
28. Turner, J.: Involving the school teacher in liberating the learner from traditional school culture. In: Tinsley, J.D., van Weert, T.J. (eds.) Proceedings of the Sixth IFIP World Conference on Computers in Education. Chapman & Hall, London (1995)
29. van Weert, T.: IFIP working group 3.1: towards integration of computers into education. In: Tinsley, J.D., van Weert, T.J. (eds.) Proceedings of the Sixth IFIP World Conference on Computers in Education. Chapman & Hall, London (1995)
30. Wasif, N.: Creative coding with scratch: presentation of the pilot project in primary school. In: Paper Presented at World Conference on Computers in Education - Tomorrow's Learning: Involving Everyone, Dublin (2017)
31. Webb, M.: Affordances of ICT in science learning: implications for an integrated pedagogy. Int. J. Sci. Educ. **27**(6), 705–735 (2005)

32. Weigend, M.: Smartwalk: computer science on the schoolyard. In: Tatnall, A., Webb, M. (eds.) WCCE 2017. IFIP AICT, vol. 515, pp. 525–535. Springer, Cham (2017)
33. Wells, C.: Hypermedia authoring in the classroom: but what is required to make it really creative? In: Tinsley, J.D., van Weert, T.J. (eds.) Proceedings of the Sixth IFIP World Conference on Computers in Education. Chapman & Hall, London (1995)
34. Williams, L.: Involving everyone: using the "literacy from scratch" project to develop the computing and presentation skills of FE students with learning difficulties and disabilities (LLDD students), aged 18 to 24 years, and of their learning assistants. In: Paper Presented at World Conference on Computers in Education - Tomorrow's Learning: Involving Everyone, Dublin (2017)

Shaping Future Digital Citizens in Aotearoa/New Zealand Schools: Vision and Challenges

Nicki Dabner(✉)

University of Canterbury E-Learning Lab, Canterbury, New Zealand
nicki.dabner@canterbury.ac.nz

Abstract. The New Zealand Ministry of Education promotes the use of digital technologies in schools to support future-focused learning and to achieve the vision for New Zealand young people, as stated in the national school curriculum document, to become confident, connected, actively involved, lifelong learners. This vision statement, extended in meaning since its inception in 2007 to further encompass the development of digital citizens, has influenced the strategic direction for educational developments in New Zealand and is supported by a range of Ministry of Education initiatives. However, a number of challenges have arisen that impact the ability for New Zealand educators to fully implement this vision in schools. This short paper presents a review of literature that illustrates the vision for young citizens in New Zealand, and describes some current challenges faced by New Zealand educators as they aim to realize this vision in complex digitally enhanced environments.

Keywords: Digital citizen · Vision · Future-focussed education Initiatives · Challenges

1 Introduction

This short paper addresses two contemporary themes identified as focus areas for WCCE 2017: strategy and policy in education contexts and settings, and shaping the future for 'digital citizens'. These themes are currently being explored by the author within an interpretive case study investigating how educators within one Aotearoa/New Zealand school endeavours to foster the development of their students as future 'digital citizens'. The following focus questions were addressed within the broader literature review informing this study: what was the proposed vision for the development of digital citizens within the Aotearoa/New Zealand education system, and what challenges appear to impact the realisation of this vision in school settings. This paper presents a brief overview of literature illustrating the vision and challenges associated with the shaping of future 'digital citizens' in Aotearoa/New Zealand schools.

A. Tatnall and M. Webb (Eds.): WCCE 2017, IFIP AICT 515, pp. 13–18, 2017.
https://doi.org/10.1007/978-3-319-74310-3_2

2 The Vision within the New Zealand Education System

The New Zealand Ministry of Education published a discussion document in 2015 that illustrated a proposed vision for New Zealand education in 2025. This vision exemplified a "highly connected, interdependent education system that equips students with the skills for the future, fosters students' identity, language and culture, and prepares students to participate as successful citizens in the 21st century" [1]. The evolution of this vision and the use of digital technologies in schools in New Zealand has been progressive, but amplified with the introduction of the current national 'New Zealand Curriculum' [2] document in 2007, where notions of connectivity, future-focus, citizenship, globalisation and e-learning were embedded.

In 2012, a New Zealand research team analysed findings from ten years of research on practices and future thinking in education to identify emerging themes for future-oriented teaching and learning. It was intended this would inform the development of the Ministry's vision for a 21st century education system. In their subsequent report, 'Supporting Future-oriented Learning and Teaching: A New Zealand Perspective' [3], the authors used the term 'wicked problems' [4] to describe complex, value-laden issues that "span multiple domains; social, economic, political, environmental, legal and moral" and proposed that all levels of the educational ecosystem needed support to develop the capacities required for 'wicked problem-solving'. They further proposed that 21st century education must focus upon the development of learners' dispositions, capacities and competencies so they are able to "deal with new situations and environments, including those with a high degree of complexity, fluidity and uncertainty". They concluded with three key ideas to inform future policy development and strategies for 21st century learning in New Zealand: education for diversity supported by connectivity and connectedness, and coherence in the development of a shared vision for 21st century schooling.

In 2013, the Associate Minister of Education formed a reference group who examined 21st century learning principles in order to identify priorities that would transform teaching and learning in New Zealand, enabled by technologies that are becoming increasingly ubiquitous in society. The reference group proposed that equipping learners with 21st century skills and digital competencies would require significant change within the New Zealand education system and that a cohesive, coordinated, cross-sector and multi-stakeholder approach would be required to support this change. The subsequent 2015 Ministry document 'Towards Digital Fluency' [5] described a number of initiatives designed to "ensure all schools are equipped with state-of-the art infrastructure, teachers get the resources and support they needed to be digitally fluent, and every student benefits from the advantages of digital technologies for learning". Digital fluency and ensuring safe, secure online learning environments were identified as priorities in the document and a Ministry commitment made to enable digital access for all learners in New Zealand "regardless of location, learning needs or family background" [5].

The Ministry's commitment to the vision of young people as digital citizens continues today, with the Minister of Education announcing in 2016 that Digital Technology would be fully integrated into The New Zealand Curriculum document by

2018, the first change made to the curriculum since its publication in 2007. The Minister stated that this change would "ensure that we have an education system that prepares children and young people for a future where digital fluency will be critical for success."

3 Challenges to Achieving the Vision

Digital literacy must be addressed in schools to enable young people to become effective digital citizen. Student use of digital technologies has attracted the attention of researchers since digital technologies first became accessible in schools and homes. Researchers interested in this area have studied digital technology use by students in educational environments [6–8], home/informal environments [9] and across both environments [10]. Although the nature of many of these studies were initially regarded as oppositional (i.e. home versus school), they are increasingly becoming complimentary as the boundaries between technology use at home and school become less distinct [11, 12].

As opportunities for New Zealand students to use digital technologies inside and outside of the school environment increase, there has been an associated call for educators across the education sector in New Zealand to ensure students are equipped with the knowledge, skills and attitudes that enable them to engage effectively and safely in the digital realm within and beyond the school environment [13]. Digital citizenship provides a recognised framework to address these issues; however digital citizenship is not specified within the current New Zealand Curriculum document, nor mandatory for schools to address. Netsafe, an independent non-profit organisation in New Zealand supported by the Ministry of Education, and Ministry of Justice, assert that there has never been a greater need for schools and communities in New Zealand to work together in this area, as reliance on digital technologies escalates. In their 2016 'Digital Challenges and New Zealanders' Report [14], they proposed that creating safe online environments in education was becoming increasingly complex, as educators were "faced with the double challenge of integrating these technologies in a way that benefits education and maintains the safety of children and their data online". Posed as a 'big question' looking forward to 2016, Netsafe advocated that further developments for online safety measures needed to be multi-stakeholder collaborations and enterprises between industry, government, parents/whanau and schools, with a shift from "protective strategies towards those that promote healthy development of online behaviours". Netsafe also signalled important information for schools following the introduction of the Harmful Digital Communications Act [15], passed by the New Zealand Parliament in 2015. The introduction of this act is important for the Boards of Trustees, elected parents from the community who adopt the role of governors, managers and employers in New Zealand schools, as they are required by law to provide a safe physical and emotional environment for students and staff. If harmful communications are posted to an online service hosted by a school, the board may be held legally responsible. A school can be considered to be hosting if they manage an online environment where content is posted. This can include school website with comments sections, social media sites, blogs and apps that enable comments. These practices are becoming increasingly common in New Zealand primary schools. The act also provides avenues for individuals to report upon and organise the removal of harmful digital communications (e.g. material posted on websites and blogs, social media, emails and texts). School leaders are now able to contact Netsafe, with the permission of the individual, to report an issue. Criminal charges are now possible in serious instances for people over the age of fourteen, so students need to be very aware of potential implications if they are involved in incidents of cyberbullying or harassment of another individual. Netsafe also provides support to schools and parents to address cyberbullying.

The increased use of technologies in schools also presents challenges to teachers across at all levels of the educational arena [16], many of whom indicate they lack the knowledge, skills and understandings required to educate their students, and that they struggle to keep up with the impact of changes in the increasingly digital landscape [17]. A 2014 report published by Research New Zealand [18] indicated that the rate of technological change and professional development required in schools was challenging for staff, with only 14% of Principals indicating they believed all of their teachers had the skills to effectively manage the use of digital devices to support learning. These findings were endorsed in a 2014 New Zealand Council for Education Research [19] report. Findings revealed that although 70% of teachers indicated that their increased use of ICT to support learning was an achievement, 38% indicated students' learning was limited by their own knowledge and skills. In addition, 56% expressed concern about emergent safety issues and 55% were finding their working day had extended.

Challenges achieving the vision to develop 21st century digital citizens in schools also exist for those involved in initial teacher education in New Zealand, because they are also expected to prepare new teachers for digitally enhanced classrooms and increasingly collaborative teaching practices. Chai and Lim [20] acknowledged the complexity teacher educators face when proposing that pre-service teachers need to learn how to use digital technologies and manage the complexities of using them in classrooms, at the same time as developing beliefs, understandings, agency and a sense of teacher identify. Koehler and Mishra [21] added complexity by adding the need to develop TPACK; technological pedagogical and content knowledge, appropriate new pedagogical ideas, and refine their ability to apply these ideas. Instefjord and Munthe [22] offer pedagogical compatibility and social awareness to this complex list of requirements, plus the imperative to address this in an integrated manner. Add critical digital literacies and digital citizenship to this package and the complexity increases again.

4 Discussion and Conclusion

Although both the proposed and current vision for young people to become effective digital citizens in New Zealand education are laudable, cohesive strategies and continued resourcing is needed to address issues that may hinder the ability for this vision to be realised. Netsafe have brought digital citizenship to the forefront in education by producing a white paper in 2016 entitled 'From Literacy to Fluency to Citizenship:

Digital Citizenship in Education' [23]. They suggest that the proliferation of terms and abstract concepts used in education in New Zealand have impeded developments in this area and call for 'a consensus view' of the values, aims and knowledge underpinning these terms' so schools can move forwards with some common understanding and address this increasingly important area. Multiple opportunities for professional development must be available for teachers and resourcing provided for schools, to ensure their teachers are supported, and have the time to develop their skills, understandings and practices. Digital technologies and environments will continue to evolve and change is inevitable, thus resourcing will be an on-going requirement. Those involved in initial teacher education will need to ensure they are keeping pace with the changes in schools as they attempt to implement this vision for 21st century learning, and adjust programmes if required to encompass these changes. Staff in initial teacher education contexts may also require access to professional development and have time to be able to develop their own knowledge, skills and understandings [24]. This again has resourcing implications.

To conclude, the literature suggests that all members of the education sector in New Zealand will be required to become 'confident, connected, actively involved, lifelong learners' for the New Zealand vision for digital citizens to be fully realized. How this happens across the education sector provides fertile ground for research in New Zealand. This research will also be valuable in other countries, not least because of the high esteem in which the New Zealand curriculum is held.

Acknowledgements. The author would like to acknowledge the support provided by the university to enable the author to present this paper at the conference.

References

1. Ministry of Education.: New Zealand Education in 2025; Lifelong Learners in a Connected World (Draft). Ministry of Education, Wellington (2015). http://www.education.govt.nz/assets/Documents/Ministry/Initiatives/Lifelonglearners.pdf
2. Ministry of Education.: The New Zealand Curriculum. Ministry of Education, Wellington (2007). http://nzcurriculum.tki.org.nz/The-New-Zealand-Curriculum
3. Bolstad, R., Gilbert, J., McDowall, S., Bull, A., Boyd, S., Hipkins, R.: Supporting Future-oriented Learning and Teaching – A New Zealand Perspective. Report for the Ministry of Education. NZCER, Wellington (2012). https://www.educationcounts.govt.nz/publications/schooling/109306
4. Rittel, H., Webber, M.: Dilemmas in a general theory of planning. Policy Sci., **4**, 155–169 (1973). http://www.cc.gatech.edu/fac/ellendo/rittel/rittel-dilemma.pdf
5. Ministry of Education: towards digital fluency (2015). http://www.education.govt.nz/assets/Uploads/Towards-Digital-Fluency.pdf
6. Levy, R., Yamanda-Rice, D., March, J.: Digital literacies in the primary classroom. In: Hall, K., Cremin, T., Comber, B., Moll, L.C. (eds.) International Handbook of Research on Children's Literacy, Learning and Culture, First Edition, 333–343. Wiley (2013)
7. Otrel-Cass, K., Cowie, B., Khoo, E.: The SCIAnTICT project: technology-enhanced teaching and learning of primary science. SET Res. Inf. Teachers **3**, 26–31 (2015)

8. De Abreau, B.: Changing technology = empowering students through media literacy education. New Horiz. Educ. **58**(3), 26–33 (2010)
9. McPake, J., Plowman, L., Stephen, C.: Pre-school children creating and communicating with digital technologies in the home. Br. J. Educ. Technol. **44**(3), 421–431 (2015)
10. Jesson, R., Meredith, M., Rosedale, N.: Reconsidering home learning in the digital learning environment: the perspective of parents, students and teachers. SET Res. Inf. Teachers **3**, 35–42 (2015)
11. Bjørgen, A., Erstad, O.: The connected child: tracing digital literacy from school to leisure. Pedagogies Int. J. **10**(2), 113–127 (2015)
12. Plowman, L.: Rethinking context: digital technologies and children's everyday lives. Child. Geograph. **14**(2), 190–202 (2016)
13. The 21st century learning reference group: future-focussed learning in connected communities: a report by the 21st century learning reference group (2014)
14. Netsafe New Zealand: digital challenges and New Zealander: a focus upon the incident reports and queries made to Netsafe in 2015. Netsafe, Auckland (2016). https://www.netsafe.org.nz/safer-internet-day/documents/SID2016_DigitalChallengesReport2015.pdf
15. New Zealand parliamentary council office: harmful digital communications act 2015. http://www.legislation.govt.nz/act/public/2015/0063/latest/whole.html
16. Davis, N.E., Eickelmann, B., Zaka, P.: Restructuring of educational systems in the digital age from a co-evolutionary perspective. J. Comput. Assist. Learn. **29**(5), 438–450 (2013)
17. New Zealand Parliament Education and Science Select Committee: Inquiry into 21st Century Learning Environments and Digital Literacy (1.2a), Report of the Education and Science Committee (2012). https://www.parliament.nz/resource/0000243164
18. Research New Zealand: Digital Technologies in New Zealand Schools: A Report Prepared for the 2020 Communications Trust (2014). http://2020.org.nz/wp-content/uploads/2014/07/Digital-Technologies-in-School-2014-FINAL.pdf
19. Wylie, C., Bonne, L.: Primary and intermediate schools in 2013: main findings from the NZCER national survey. New Zealand Council for Educational Research, ISBN 978-1-927231-35-7 (2014)
20. Chai, C.S., Lim, C.P.: The internet and teacher education: traversing between the digitized world and schools. Internet High. Educ. **14**(1), 3–9 (2011)
21. Koehler, M.J., Mishra, P.: What is technological pedagogical content knowledge? Contemp. Issues Technol. Teacher Educ. **9**(1), 60–70 (2009)
22. Instefjord, E., Munthe, E.: Preparing pre-service teachers to integrate technology: an analysis of the emphasis on digital competence in teacher education curricula. Eur. J. Teacher Educ. **39**(1), 77–93 (2016)
23. Netsafe New Zealand.: from literacy to fluency to citizenship: digital citizenship in education. White paper. Netsafe, Auckland (2016). https://www.netsafe.org.nz/wp-content/uploads/2016/11/NETSAFE-WHITEPAPER-From-literacy-to-fluency-to-citizenship.pdf
24. Duncan-Howell, J.: Digital mismatch: expectations and realities of digital competency amongst pre-service education students. Aust. J. Educ. Technol. **28**(5), 827–840 (2012)

Digital Safety and Responsible Use Within a Primary School Ecosystems Community in Aotearoa/New Zealand

Nicki Dabner(✉)

E-Learning Lab, University of Canterbury, Canterbury, New Zealand
Nicki.dabner@canterbury.ac.nz

Abstract. With the New Zealand Ministry of Educations' emphasis upon e-Learning in educational settings, and the correlating increase in approaches to learning with digital technologies in New Zealand primary schools, primary school-aged students in New Zealand are increasingly using digital devices in school settings and at a progressively earlier age. As availability of digital devices outside of school also increases and the boundaries between usages blur, there is an imperative to prepare primary them to use digital devices safely and responsibly across multiple contexts, and for multiple purposes. Implementing a school-wide, cross-sector, multi-stakeholder approach has been proposed as the most effective way to prepare young people in this area. However, little is known about how such an approach is actualized in primary school settings, and the benefits and challenges associated with its adoption. Drawing upon ecological systems theory, this interpretive case study will examine how one New Zealand primary school addresses digital safety and responsible use within the school ecosystems community, how they engage with individuals, groups or organizations situated within other ecosystem communities, and the drivers, enablers, barriers and tensions they experience within these endeavours.

Keywords: Education · Digital devices · Digital safety and responsibility Ecologies · Case study

1 Introduction

Corresponding with the increased availability and use of digital technologies in many societies, there is increasing concern regarding the safety, behaviour, understandings and wellness of digital technology users who use these technologies to engage with digital content and participate within digital environments [1, 2]. The New Zealand Ministry of Education recognise both the pivotal role digital technologies have transforming teaching and learning in New Zealand schools [3] and the imperative for the education sector to ensure students are equipped to engage effectively and safely when using these technologies [4]. The term 'safety' is often used to describe things that afford security and protection from danger. Maurice et al. [5] define safety as "a state in which hazards and conditions leading to physical, psychological or material harm are controlled in order to preserve the health and well-being of individuals and the community" (p. 234). The notion of 'risk' is always associated with safety. Cibbora [6]

A. Tatnall and M. Webb (Eds.): WCCE 2017, IFIP AICT 515, pp. 19–23, 2017.
https://doi.org/10.1007/978-3-319-74310-3_3

describes risks as actions that included an element of uncertainty, that have a probability of occurrence and that could potentially have undesirable outcomes or consequences. Staksrud and Livingstone [7] classified three types of risks associated with children's participation in online activities using digital technologies (p. 368);

- Content risks: where children are the recipient of often mass-produced images and text (child as recipient);
- Contact risks: where children participate in adult- initiated online activities (child as participant); and
- Conduct risks: where children participate in peer to peer exchanges (child as actor).

Each of these risk categories have been identified in New Zealand, with associated issues such as cyberbullying [8–10], information disclosure [11, 12], overuse [13, 14] and unsafe use [15] now impacting primary school-aged students. All schools in New Zealand have a legal responsibility to ensure the safety of students during school hours. To minimise the risks associated with digital safety, schools may implement strategies to ensure the safety of students within the school environment, for example blocking access to websites and monitoring digital technology use by students. However, many of these strategies have little impact when the students leave the school grounds. Thus, the Ministry of Education identify digital fluency and ensuring safe online learning environments as priorities for New Zealand schools [16], proposing that equipping learners with 21st century skills and digital competencies requires a cohesive, coordinated, cross-sector and multi-stakeholder approach to change within the New Zealand education system. Key organisations with an interest in 'Internet Safety' in New Zealand [17–19] support this assertion, one stating that there has never been a greater need for schools and communities to work together as young people in New Zealand access the internet with increasing frequency via multiple access points, with a continuing trend towards mobile access.

Although one New Zealand school-based case study [20] has investigated the implementation of digital citizenship, a concept often associated with digital safety, within a secondary school setting, there are major gaps in research relating to primary school contexts and more notably, research investigating the ways teachers and schools work with parents/whānau and members of the wider educational community, who also reside within the educational ecosystem in New Zealand. The case study described in this thesis is intended to address this issue. The overarching question guiding this thesis is: How does a primary school approach digital safety and responsible use within their school ecosystems community? The following sub-questions will focus the investigation.

With regard to school leaders, teachers and school support staff:

(a) What perceptions do they have about digital safety and responsible use?
(b) How are digital devices used by students?
(c) How is risk constructed and managed?
(d) How is digital safety and responsible use encouraged?
(e) How do they work together, and with parents/whānau and members of the wider school community, to support digital safety and responsible use by their children?

Bronfenbrenner's 'Ecological Systems Theory' [21] and Davis' 'Arena with Change with Digital Technologies' [22, 23] will provide the theoretical frameworks for this study. Notions of 'space and place' [24] and 'networks', increasingly relevant to research involving digital technologies, will also be examined.

2 Methodology

Case Study methodologies as proposed by Stake [25] and Merriam [26] both resonate with me as a researcher as they closely align with my epistemological (social constructivist/social-cultural) orientation. They also provide best fit with the study as a naturalistic, interpretative inquiry. The case study will conducted in a primary school in the local region and undertaken over a one-year period. Purposive sampling will been used to identify potentially suitable schools for the study, the criteria being; age band coverage (spanning ages five-thirteen), high usage of digital technologies and collaborative teaching approaches, and evidence of a BYOD, a 'bring your own device', policy within the school. Although the unit of analysis will be the school and the parental community within this school, the interactions with external networks across other layers of the ecosystem will also be also considered. Ethical considerations will be identified and discussed with the school, and ethical clearance gained prior to the study commencing. Qualitative data will be collected utilising a range of appropriate data gathering techniques including interviews, observations and document review/analysis. Data analysis will be conducted recursively in association with data collection, and will involve forms of analysis that may include categorical aggregation, content analysis, analytical induction and direct interpretation. Strategies to enhance credibility and trustworthiness will include reflective commentary, triangulation (data/theory), member checks, and multiple observations conducted over the period of one year. Researcher positioning, and disclosure of bias will be declared and discussed to enhance data dependability. This research and the resulting thesis will draw upon my individual [27–31] and collective [32–35] experiences as a researcher of digital technologies, digital environments and online communities, many years of experience as an educator working in and with primary schools in New Zealand, and my enduring fascination and critical appraisal of the ways digital technologies and environments are impacting the way people live, learn and communicate in society. It is intended but not assured that the findings exemplify the myriad of ways digital safety and responsible use are being addressed across the educational ecosystem, thus potentially providing insights for the reader that could inform future policy directions in New Zealand and school practices beyond New Zealand. It is highly likely the findings will expose questions and issues that justify further examination in future studies. As such, this thesis will make a valuable contribution to research and literature in this field. Importantly, it also makes a valuable contribution to the development of this author as a quality researcher.

Acknowledgements. The author would like to acknowledge the encouragement provided by her Doctoral Supervisor to present this extended abstract at the consortium, as a valuable way to refine her thinking and the subsequent case study.

References

1. Ministry of United Nations Educational, Scientific, and Cultural Organization (UNESCO): Fostering digital citizenship through safe and responsible use of ICT: a review of current status in Asia and the pacific as of December 2014 (2015)
2. Ribble, M., Miller, T.N.: Educational leadership in an online world: connecting students to technology responsibly, safely, and ethically. J. Asynchron. Learn. Netw. **17**(1), 135–143 (2013)
3. Ministry of Education: New Zealand Education in 2025; Lifelong Learners in a Connected World (Draft). Ministry of Education, Wellington (2015)
4. The 21st century learning reference group: future-focussed learning in connected communities: a report by the 21st century learning reference group (2014)
5. https://www.educationcounts.govt.nz/publications/schooling/109306
6. Maurice, P., Lavoie, M., Laflamme, L., Svanström, L., Romer, C., Anderson, R.: Safety and safety promotion: definitions for operational developments. Inj. Control Saf. Promot. **8**(4), 237–240 (2001)
7. Cibbora, C.: Imbrication of representations: risk and digital technologies. J. Manag. Stud. **43**, 1339–1356 (2006)
8. Staksrud, E., Livingstone, S.: Children and online risk: powerless victims or resourceful participants? Inf. Commun. Soc. **12**(3), 364–378 (2009)
9. Von Marées, N., Petermann, F.: Cyberbullying: an increasing challenge for schools. School Psychol. Int. **3**(55), 467–476 (2012)
10. Monks, C., Robinson, S., Worlidge, P.: The emergence of cyberbullying: a survey of primary school pupils' perceptions and experiences. School Psychol. Int. **3**(55), 477–491 (2012)
11. Holfeld, B., Grabe, M.: Middle school students' perceptions of and responses to cyber bullying. J. Educ. Comput. Res. **46**(4), 395–413 (2012)
12. Davis, K., James, C.: Tweens' conceptions of privacy online: implications for educators. Learn. Media Technol. **38**(1), 4–25 (2013)
13. De Souza, Z., Dick, G.: Information disclosure on MySpace: the what, the why and the implications. Pastoral Care Educ. **26**(3), 143–157 (2008)
14. Seomun, G., Lee, J., Kim, E., Im, M., Kim, M., Park, S., Lee, Y.: Health effects of digital textbooks on school-age children: a grounded theory approach. West. J. Nurs. Res. **35**(9), 1184–1204 (2013)
15. Gutnick, A., Robb, M., Takeuchi, L., Kotler, J.: Always connected: the new digital media habits of young children. The Joan Ganz Cooney Centre at Sesame Workshop, New York (2011)
16. Valcke, M., De Wever, B., Van Keer, H., Schellens, T.: Long-term study of safe internet use of young children. Comput. Educ. **57**(1), 1292–1305 (2011)
17. Ministry of education: towards digital fluency (2015). http://www.education.govt.nz/assets/Uploads/Towards-Digital-Fluency.pdf
18. Netsafe New Zealand: From Literacy to Fluency to Citizenship: Digital Citizenship in Education. White paper. Netsafe, Auckland (2016). https://www.netsafe.org.nz/wp-content/uploads/2016/11/NETSAFE-WHITEPAPER-From-literacy-to-fluency-to-citizenship.pdf
19. National Library of New Zealand: Digital Citizenship in Schools (2016). http://schools.natlib.govt.nz/supporting-learners/digital-citizenship/digital-citizenship-schools#Defining-Digital-Citizenship

20. Research New Zealand: Digital Technologies in New Zealand Schools: A Report Prepared for the 2020 Communications Trust (2014). http://2020.org.nz/wp-content/uploads/2014/07/Digital-Technologies-in-School-2014-FINAL.pdf
21. Land, J.: A case study to investigate the implementation of a blended digital citizenship course within a New Zealand secondary school. Unpublished Thesis (2013)
22. Bronfenbrenner, U.: The Ecology of Human Development. Harvard University Press, Cambridge (1979)
23. Davis, N., Eickelmann, B., Zaka, P.: Restructuring of educational systems in the digital age from a co-evolutionary perspective. J. Comput. Assist. Learn. **29**(5), 438–450 (2013)
24. Davis, N.: How may teacher learning be promoted for educational renewal with IT? In: Voogt, J., Knezek, G. (eds.) International Handbook of Information Technology in Primary and Secondary Education, pp. 507–520. Elsevier, Amsterdam (2008)
25. Ciolfi, L.: Space and place in digital technology research: a theoretical overview. In: Price, S., Jewitt, C., Barry, B. (eds.) The Sage Handbook of Digital Technology Research. Sage Publications, London (2013)
26. Stake, R.: The Art of Case Study Research. SAGE Publications, Thousand Oaks (1995)
27. Merriam, S.: Qualitative Research and Case Study Applications in Education. Jossey-Bass, San Francisco (1998)
28. Dabner, N.: Weaving digital citizenship within pre-service teacher education: preparing graduate students for high-quality educational practices within modern learning environments and the virtual world. In: Society for Information Technology and Teacher Education International Conference (SITE), SITE Conference Proceedings, Las Vegas, NV, USA, 2–6 March 2015, no. 1, pp. 3115–3120 (2015)
29. Dabner, N.: An evaluative study of the use of e-portfolio's within a graduate teacher education qualification in New Zealand. In: Society of Information Technology in Teacher Education International Symposium (SITE), Christchurch, New Zealand, 28–29 April 2014 (2014)
30. Dabner, N.: 'Breaking ground' in the use of social media: a case study of a university earthquake response to inform educational design with Facebook. Internet High. Educ. **15**(1), 69–78 (2011)
31. Dabner, N: Design to support distance teacher education communities: a case study of a student-student e-mentoring initiative. In: 22nd Annual Society for Information Technology and Teacher Education (SITE) International Conference, SITE 2011, Nashville, TN, USA, 7–11 March 2011, no. 1, pp. 218–223 (2011). http://www.editlib.org/p/36262
32. Dabner, N.: GradNet: online communities providing support for beginning teachers during the provisional registration period in New Zealand. In: Proceedings of the 2006 Australian Teacher Education National Conference, Australian Teacher Education Association (ATEA) Conference on Making Teaching Public: Reforms in Teacher Education, Freemantle, Australia, 5–8 July 2006, pp. 67–74 (2006)
33. Mackey, J., Davis, N., Dabner, N.: Relevant, current and sustainable digital strategies to prepare future teachers to lead e-learning. In: 29th Annual Ascilite Conference, Wellington, New Zealand, 25–28 Nov 2012
34. Dabner, N., Davis, N., Zaka, P.: Authentic project-based design of professional development for teachers studying online and blended teaching. Contemp. Issues Technol. Teach. Educ. **12**(1), 71–114 (2012)
35. Dabner, N., Chowfin, A.: Project-based professional development: reflections in and on action implementing blended learning with primary school students. Comput. New Zealand Schools **23**(3), 248–261 (2011)

Determinants of Mobile Learning in Indigenous/Cultural Contexts: The Phenomenon in Canadian First Nations

Ben Akoh(✉)

Faculty of Education, University of Manitoba, Winnipeg, Canada
umakoh@myumanitoba.ca

Abstract. This goal of this qualitative study was to identify the determinants that assist post-secondary Indigenous learners in an isolated fly in-only community to adapt and orient themselves between Eurocentric and Indigenous ways of learning. Digital technology (specifically mobile devices) was used to produce documentation for their adaptation and orientation. The outcomes of the study produced determinants that informed learning with digital technology in the research context. Informants showed a deep understanding of the problem, they were well meaning, eager and responsive to the study. The problem was more complex and participant responses indicated that rethinking and restructuring of the goals and tentative solutions for successful learning were needed. The solutions cannot be simply more technology or more pedagogy. Future research is key, but those research efforts must enter the community with a truly open mind and without any pre-fixed solutions.

Keywords: Digital technology · Aboriginal · Manitoba · Pedagogy
Adult learning

1 Introduction

This qualitative study was to identify the determinants that assist post-secondary Indigenous learners in an isolated fly-in only community in Northern Manitoba to adapt and orient themselves between Indigenous and Eurocentric ways of learning. Digital technology, particularly mobile devices was used as a tool for producing documentation for how these learners adapted and oriented themselves. By understanding this negotiation and adaptation educators may be better positioned to understand key determinants for learning in Indigenous communities. They may also be able to facilitate technology mediated programming at the post-secondary level, especially in contexts where multiple worldviews are at play.

The ethnographic study produced a framework which highlighted a set of determinants that could: (a) guide policy makers, government agencies, school administrators, educators and students to better collaborate for negotiated learning and adaptations; (b) support these stakeholders to recognize that adaptations and orientations between cultures are required for Indigenous students to succeed, and (c) cause them to explore the affordances of digital technology for adaptations and orientations.

A. Tatnall and M. Webb (Eds.): WCCE 2017, IFIP AICT 515, pp. 24–34, 2017.
https://doi.org/10.1007/978-3-319-74310-3_4

Determinants as used in this study imply the presence of certain factors that produce expected outcomes that might have impact on a people and their community. The notion of determinants for societal benefit emanated from the public health sector. Irwin et al. noted that public health scientists in the 1940s observed that "social conditions decisively influence health" [10]. They further argued that "the sanitary campaigns of the nineteenth century and the work of the founders of modern public health reflected awareness of the relationship between people's social position, their living conditions, and their health outcomes" [10].

Since the 1940s there have been numerous agendas that tend to link other social determinants to health. The 1948 World Health Organization's constitution for instance had consistently linked agriculture, education and social welfare to social determinants of health. Research in examining the notion of determinants as an important concept in Indigenous Canadian education is captured in studies by Mignone and O'Neil [19] and by Mignone et al. [18].

Social capital as a determinant of health has both individual and ecological characteristics. Individual characteristics usually consist of education, income or gender. Ecological characteristics usually consist of the level of crime, level of pollution or the willingness for community members to help themselves. Access to information and knowledge that help individuals make informed decisions about their health are also important determinants of health. Digital technology, especially its use for learning have also been known to play an important role as a determinant of health.

The study was conducted in a rural, fly-in, Indigenous First Nations community located 940 km North of Winnipeg, Manitoba, in Canada. This community was accessible only by plane and winter ice roads. The remoteness of this community and its information and communications technology challenges made it a most appropriate research context for this study. The study was designed to explore the main research question, "What are the determinants that assist post-secondary Indigenous learners in a rural Manitoba community to adapt and orient between Eurocentric and Indigenous ways of learning?". Fourteen participants were involved in the ethnographic study.

Prior to colonization in the 1600s Indigenous people inhabited the land called Canada today. With the arrival of Europeans, they were colonized and their way of life was transformed. Their learning methods were undermined and they were stripped of their culture, land and identity. Terms such as systematic imperialism and "cultural genocide" have been used to describe these acts of colonization [4, 28]. The residential school system was a tool used to strip the Indigenous person of their identity. Indigenous people were no longer in control of their own education.

In 2004, after several years of negotiations, a post-secondary institution that would meet the educational needs of Indigenous learners in northern Manitoba was formed. The University College of the North, among many other approaches, was set up to undo some of the previous colonial wrongs and to provide "an inclusive range of credible, accessible and attainable post-secondary learning opportunities to Indigenous and northern residents" [22]. It did this through its eleven community centres spread across the northern parts of the province of Manitoba. This study was conducted in one of the eleven centres. The study participants were also adult students enrolled in a post-secondary program at the center.

At the university, traditional elders played an important role in shaping its direction and governance. Information and communications technology was used to connect the two main campuses to the eleven regional centres. Schools in the study community were known to historically register high attrition, low completion and participation rates.

2 Literature Review

Over the years, technology, policy and international development proponents have tried to address the social consciousness gaps missing from the crazed and rushed implementations of technology for poverty alleviation projects in Indigenous communities in developing countries. After several millions of dollars and pounds that resulted in little to no reforms, international financial institutions such as the World Bank and the IFC began asking serious but fundamental methodology questions: what went wrong, where, how, and why did these technology projects fail [12]?

Whereas some of these projects have somewhat contributed to improving certain economic, social, and cultural aspects of the Indigenous beneficiaries, there have been unintended consequences from their implementations. Most of which led to large-scale project failures. Beneficiaries completely lost faith and trust in the so-called technology for development and their implementers. Heeks [9] argued that only one-fifth of technology projects in industrialized countries succeeded at the time. They were even far less numbers in Indigenous communities in developing countries.

Educational technology requires more careful thought and planning than the quick brushstroke implementations of the past. Not many countries or groups can afford luxuries associated with trial and errors methods, especially Indigenous First Nations communities in Northern Manitoba where resources are scarce, cultural and geographical factors pose challenges and where funding to public schools is tight. A balance ought to be struck between the often small available funding and "innovation" in technology projects especially in Canadian post secondary institutions.

In this regard, the application of digital technology for education should distance itself from conjectural brush-strokes implementations that assume little recognition of the contextual and cultural specificities of their target communities [16]. The most obvious of these assumptions is that the cognitive requirements for negotiation and adaption to technology and its use in Indigenous contexts are not any different than those in other contexts. Technology implementations thereby result in the mismatch of policy, practice, and implementation between the context they were imported from and the one they were implemented.

But technology implementation can take on a different approach [1, 8, 17]. Approaches that negotiate between Indigenous methods and Eurocentric ones may be necessary. Such approaches see multiple cultures as different but equal. They are approaches that are founded on Indigenous principles, cultural methods, social capital, and pedagogical strategies.

Indigenous learning in Canada is varied and specific to an individual's learning milieu. It is "place-based and includes a variety of knowledge sources…[such as], the land [which] is the ultimate source of knowledge" [21]. Indigenous learning "cannot be separated from the larger social and cultural matrix from which it is defined". It is a process, and not an event, "spanning the four stages of the life cycle – child, youth, adult and Elder" [17]. Indigenous learning is holistic, connecting with the learner at the intellectual, spiritual, emotional and physical levels.

It is difficult to understand Indigenous learning perspectives using Eurocentric lens because "Indigenous knowledge does not fit the Eurocentric concept of culture, it is not a uniform concept among all Indigenous peoples; and it cannot be separated from its bearer or codified into a definition" [17]. It is for this reason that the study described in this paper focused on the Indigenous aspects of the learner. Technology was used in the study as a tool for the documentation of negotiations between Indigenous and Eurocentric learning. The term "Indigenous" is normally presented in lower case "i" but used in capital case "I" when it describes a noun or used along with the term "Eurocentric" in the same sentence.

This paper does not promise to promote digital technologies in an Indigenous community under the guise of development [29, 30]. Neither does it promise that digital technology could be the silver bullet for an emancipated Indigenous educational community. Certainly, it does not intend to replicate the failed development practices of the past. It focuses rather on how Indigenous learners negotiated learning and how they adapted between different worldviews. It then suggests how educators and researchers could frame pedagogy in an Indigenous culture-centric manner that respects and responds to the core needs of the Indigenous learner.

3 Study Design, Method/Methodology

The ethnographic study involved fourteen research participants consisting of two participant groups. The primary group consisted of eight participants who lived in the research community, had completed high school, were enrolled in a post-secondary program, could communicate in English and consented to participating in the study. Primary participants were directly involved in the research activities. The secondary group consisted of six participants who were either elders in the community or had provided technical, academic or administrative knowledge or support directly to the research community. Secondary participants were not directly involved in the study's activities but provided contextual information. All participants were identified using purposeful sampling method [7, 27].

Purposeful sampling allows an investigator to sample and select "*information-rich* purposeful cases for study in depth…from which one can learn a great deal about issues of central importance to the purpose of the inquiry… Studying information-rich case yields insights and in-depth understanding rather than empirical generalizations" [24]. Ethics approval to conduct the research was granted by the University of Manitoba Education/Nursing Research Ethics Board, and the University College of the North's Research Ethics Board.

Primary research participants utilized native applications on standard mobile devices such as the camera, video and voice recorders to create cultural digital artifacts from culture-centric community activities. These included: (a) participatory video (creating recordings of interviews with parents, family members, elders, community members, leaders; of community and farms/gardens); (b) picture/photo voice (images were used to create stories about their communities, family history and heritage); (c) personal connection story (participants created a paper map of their family tree, which they converted to digital form), and (d) personal reflections (production of critical reflection of learning practices and journey through self-questioning and assessment, used to create/update blogs and to create personal video logs). Digital artifacts were created in response to interview questions that participants asked their community members, relatives and elders. Some interview questions include: what stories can you tell about the community and traditions like trappings, hunting and gathering, the way of living, housing, medicine, parenting, food and learning?

These activities led to the production of digital artifacts that captured histories, family heritages, ancestry, and stories. Activities were conducted outside the classroom and within the community so that learning is consistent with Indigenous pedagogy. By undertaking the activities outside the classroom, participants were able to recognize their own cultural and Indigenous learning practices, and to use that as a base to connect with learning in the classroom.

A safe frame was essential for the study to be performed [20]. A safe frame is a set of principles, protocols, boundaries and understanding that gave participants agency, ownership, and control of the research activities and its products. The frame was defined by a series of policies and frameworks for conducting research in Indigenous communities. They consists of the *Ownership, Control, Access and Possession* framework [23], the *Tri-Council Policy Statement: Ethical Conduct for Research Involving Humans* [5], and the *Integrated Knowledge Translation* framework [6]. Principles were created by the participants themselves through several years of extensive relationship and confidence building between the research community and the researcher.

Upon completion of the research activities, digital artifacts were created. They were brought back into the classroom and primary participants reflected on and analyzed them. To help with their analysis, participants responded to the question, "What resonated with you most while conducting the research activities?". As a phenomenological study, their response helped to respond to the overarching research question, "What are the determinants that assist post-secondary Indigenous learners in a rural Manitoba community to adapt and orient between Eurocentric and Indigenous ways of learning?". Participants captured their reflection in blog posts, tweets, Wikipedia pages, and on notepads. By critically analyzing their activities, participants were able to:

(a) Produce documentation that reflected learning from a "familiar" Indigenous base of their culture to an "unfamiliar" Eurocentric learning context.
(b) Establish the requirements for understanding concepts in this new "unfamiliar" base in which they were expected to learn.
(c) Build the necessary bridges to transition from the familiar Indigenous cultural base to the unfamiliar Eurocentric cultural context.
(d) Make the cognitive shift from one to the other.

Primary participants were then interviewed using the following questions: (a) How valuable would educational technology, especially mobile technology contribute to your academic success and add value to your learning? (b) What individual stories emerge from your use of technology that you think contributes to or impedes your learning? (c) What factors motivate your use of educational technology such as mobile technology? (d) How could educational technology use improve engagement within your community?

Their responses formed the primary research data. They were recorded, anonymized, transcribed and checked for correctness.

Data analysis was performed to check for references to digital technologies such as mobiles devices, computers, electricity, cable infrastructure and the internet. It was also analyzed for references to culture, such as dances, story telling, community-based occupations, i.e. fishing, trapping, ceremonies, family gatherings and heritages. Emergent themes were further analyzed for sub-themes.

The Indirect Behavioural Measures method was used to identify cognitive movements from Indigenous learning to Eurocentric learning [25]. This method suggests that the researcher retrieves the required data based on inferences from participants' statements. This is different from directly interpreting their statements. Here, participants' attitude towards themselves could be inferred rather than as a measure of explicit behaviour. This approach is useful because some social cases may prevent research participants from speaking about themselves or providing data about their social behaviour. Sometimes participants may not be aware of the information required, may not have "insight into their behaviours", or may be tempted to "impression manage" the information they provide, thus affecting the quality of the data collected. Indirect Behavioural Methods "do not require an explicit response from participants, yet reveal reliable information about underlying cognitions" [25].

Upon analysis the study's findings produced broad themes in four areas:

(a) The technical, community, and cultural **disconnects** resulting from the application of digital technology for learning.
(b) The **socio-cultural challenges** associated with the implementation of digital technology for learning.
(c) The **unintended consequences** of digital technology that had negative impacts on the community.
(d) The **affordances** of digital technology for creating connections with content that enhanced learning.

4 Findings and Discussion

Digital technologies are a double-edge sword [14] capable of enabling or disrupting existing Indigenous practices. Simply because they produced positive outcomes in other contexts did not mean they could produce the same outcome in the research context. Their use was therefore carefully scrutinized so that they did not disenfranchise the research participants. Determinants are *italicized.*

The technical, community and cultural **disconnects** resulting from either the positive and/or negative impacts of digital technology on the community determined how community members related with themselves and how the participants leveraged digital technology for their learning. Specifically, the absence of a robust internet infrastructure created a technological "disconnect" that prevented the introduction of value added services such as tele-health or more advanced forms of learning with digital technology.

There had been past and renewed promises to build a northern wide fiber-optic infrastructure that would carry the traffic between northern Indigenous communities and from these communities to the south and then on to the global network [11]. Such infrastructure would be able to address some of the present challenges of learning with digital technologies.

Connecting the local with the global is an important determinant for economic development [13]. The availability of a community-wide fiber infrastructure is an essential determinant for learners to access and create Indigenous content, to transform from knowledge consumers to knowledge creators and to enable cognitive movements from one worldview to another to occur. However, the presence of a network alone is insufficient to deliver these sorts of value. More would have to be done to leverage the existence of digital technology for instance, for economic, social and cultural gains.

The presence of a collaborative platform that could leverage inherent Indigenous traditions of orality, collaboration and dialogue for solving problems and for developing the community is another important determinant. A collaborative platform could be extended to include all stakeholders that should have interest in the learning goals of the Indigenous community. Having the local government administration, provincial and federal government departments and the communities themselves become involved in dialogue for strengthening community development could be a significant determinant for sustainable service delivery in Indigenous communities. Value added services like tele-health and education could benefit from such platforms. If they exist, they should be strengthened so that better dialogue, collaboration and cooperation continues. If none exist, one should be created.

With respect to the value of such platform for Indigenous education, community members like parents should be invited to participate in the learning of their children. Specifically, they should be involved in Indigenous learning methods as a base for which other methods of learning including Eurocentric forms could be scaffolded.

The second thematic outcome focused on the **socio-cultural challenges** of digital technology implementation and its use for learning within the community. This outcome related to the confidence that community members had on digital technology's affordance. It also related to its affordance for fostering cognitive movements between worldviews.

Participants, who through some form of Indigenous culture-based reasoning were able to reflect on and to describe their skepticism of digital technology, were also able to reflect on digital technology's positive impact on their learning. They were able to decide whether or not it had an affordance to facilitate cognitive movement from one cultural space to another. *To necessitate its use, the presence of a safe frame was significant.* This frame ensured that some level of privacy of individual data and equity between cultures at play in the context and between actors involved in their learning should be present.

Another important sociocultural challenge to learning concerned the presence of trauma in the community. Trauma affected learning, and more so learning with digital technology. As a result, those who wanted to explore movements between cultures might have used digital technology created in one culture to implement learning in another culture without paying attention to its potential to produce harm. This kind of digital technology use seemed to produce trauma in the Indigenous community instead of positive affordances. It further hampered cognitive movements especially when learners feelings and emotions where not considered during the use of such technologies. Community members suffered various forms of traumatic experiences. In spite of these, they showed courage, resilience and they exhibited willingness to continue to learn. Even though trauma had resulted in the frequent deaths of community members, some by suicide, current traumatic circumstances reminded participants of the impact of past practices such as the residential school system, the role of such schools, and the lasting impressions they had made on them, their parents and grandparents.

Those who design and facilitate learning in Indigenous communities should remember that digital technology might be alien to the context of implementation. And as a result, could produce outcomes that may not be suitable to that context. They should also consider existing pedagogical strategies so that their learning methods holistically involves a recognition of the learners' history and includes consideration for their Indigenous culture as the base on which learning can be scaffolded and on which successful educational strategies can be developed. From this foundational base links to Eurocentric learning methods could be established. These are essential determinants for learning to take place in Indigenous communities.

The third outcome was concerned with the **unintended consequences** of educational technologies in the community. Individual and community related "connects" were established between digital technology and community members. Most of these connects were predicated on the recent upgrade of the local mobile infrastructure in the research community. Some unintended outcomes resulted from the use of digital technology and this upgrade. They seemed to enhance an existing undesirable bullying behaviour, by extending it to the online space. Cyberbullying emerged as a negative consequence of digital technology use in the community.

Even though it might be difficult to determine potential negative consequences of digital technology implementation such as cyberbullying, McLuhanistic methods for eliciting the impacts of digital technology [15] or the systemic order effects method [26] could enable educators to proactively elicit some unintended negative consequences and to prevent them before they happen. Cyberbullying should not be tolerated in any community, especially in an Indigenous learning context where suicide is rife.

As a double-edged sword, digital technology produced **affordances** that were somewhat positive and that could have positive impacts on learning on the study community. Besides producing more community-based training and awareness programs that leverage digital technology, pedagogical strategies that highlighted digital technology's positive affordances seemed to help shift learners' focus from the simpler social benefits of digital technology use to more profound uses. Digital technology seemed to help learners to transition from simply storytelling to storywork [2, 3]. Storywork are more advanced ways of using stories for learning. Learners explored digital technology's affordance to remember culture, to keep and maintain records and archives of community cultures and practices. This ability to utilize the "retentive" capacity of digital technology was useful for knowledge production and seemed to help community members to shift from consumers to producers of content.

The inherent ability of technology to create unsafe environments was contrasted with its ability as a tool for safety; one that could help learners communicate and interact safely and to safely share information, within the context of a safe frame. Its application here was done in a way that recognized, enhanced and did not undermine cultural practices for communication and interaction.

5 Conclusion

Digital technology was used as a tool to produce documentation for learning in an Indigenous context where learners were expected to learn and succeed using Eurocentric methods. Historically, learners in this context have been known to not succeed or drop out of school. Success here was often defined from a Eurocentric perspective. The Eurocentric methods of learning that have been associated with colonizing activities of the past have not helped. Even though recent approaches have led to the inclusion of Indigenous methods of learning in post-secondary education, there are still challenges in learners' understanding of expectations for success.

This study has shown that certain determinants are essential for learners to succeed in this context. Indigenous learners have shown that they would like to "feel good" about their learning. They have also indicated that they would like learning to take place in the confines of a safe frame, which is constructed on policies and frameworks that respect them and their tradition. They should be allowed as participants in the construction of this frame. They should be able to define the standards for equity and privacy between their culture and that of their educators. They should ultimately develop sufficient confidence in their educators for learning to the successful.

Within the confines of a safe frame, participants who felt good about their learning were more likely to engage, share and connect with others and to learn. Within this context, they were also able to create "new things", to innovate and to undertake learning that were previously not possible. Educators and learners should use digital technology to connect the past with the present, and to connect the present with the future such that it could help Indigenous learners to become more grounded in their culture. This grounding is essential as a scaffold for learning to take place in a foreign cultural context, i.e. Eurocentric contexts in which they are expected to succeed. In the face of current migratory patterns in which learners from other global contexts are introduced into and expected to succeed in Eurocentric learning contexts, the aforementioned determinants may be useful considerations.

More work is required to explicitly define the determinants for learning to take place in Indigenous communities. For instance, future research should explore the extent to which each determinant should be present for learners to succeed.

Acknowledgments. I am pleased to acknowledge the generous financial support of the Social Science and Humanities Research Council of Canada through the Manitoba Research Alliance grant: Partnering for Change – Community-based solutions to Aboriginal and inner-city poverty. I also appreciate my "community champion", and my doctoral advisory committee.

References

1. Aikenhead, G.S.: Toward a First Nations cross-cultural science and technology curriculum. Sci. Educ. **81**(2), 217–238 (1997)
2. Archibald, J.: Indigenous Storywork: Educating the Heart, Mind, Body, and Spirit. UBC Press, Vancouver (2008)
3. Atleo, M.R.: Understanding aboriginal learning ideology through storywork with elders. Alberta J. Educ. Res. **55**(4), 453–467 (2009)
4. Battiste, M.: Indigenous knowledge: foundations for first nations. Indig. Nations High. Educ. Consort., 12 (2005)
5. CIHR: Guide to Knowledge Translation Planning at CIHR: Integrated and End-of-Grant Approaches (2012)
6. CIHR: Integrated Knowledge Translation at CIHR: An Update. Participatory Research @ Lunch (2011)
7. Coyne, I.T.: Sampling in qualitative research. Purposeful and theoretical sampling; merging or clear boundaries? J. Adv. Nurs. **26**(3), 623–630 (1997)
8. Ezeife, A.N.: Using the environment in mathematics and science teaching: an African and aboriginal perspective. Int. Rev. Educ. **49**(3–4), 319–342 (2003)
9. Heeks, R.: Information systems and developing countries: failure, success, and local improvisations. Inf. Soc. **18**(2), 101–112 (2002)
10. Irwin, A., et al.: Social determinants of health, the United Nations Commission of. Int. Encycl. Public Heal. **1**, 64–69 (2008)
11. Taylor, J.: Indigenous company to bring high-speed internet to all of Manitoba's First Nations communities - Manitoba - CBC News. http://www.cbc.ca/news/canada/manitoba/manitoba-first-nations-technology-council-high-speed-internet-1.3699650
12. Laouris, Y., Laouri, R.: Can information and mobile technologies serve to close the economic, educational, digital, and social gaps and accelerate development? World Futures **64**, 254–275 (2008)
13. Mata, F.J., Pont, A.: ICT for Promoting Human Development and Protecting the Environment. IFIP Advances in Information and Communication Technology, pp. 1–245. Springer, Heidelberg (2016). https://doi.org/10.1007/978-3-319-44447-5
14. McGrail, E.: "It's a double-edged sword, this technology business": secondary English teachers' perspectives on a schoolwide laptop technology initiative. Teach. Coll. Rec. **108**(6), 1055–1079 (2006)
15. McLuhan, M.: Understanding Media: The Extensions of Man. MIT Press, Cambridge/London (1994)
16. McMahon, R., et al.: Putting the "last mile" first: re-framing broadband development in First Nations and Inuit communities (2010)
17. Michell, H., et al.: Learning Indigenous Science from Place (2008)
18. Mignone, J., et al.: Validation of a Culturally appropriate social capital framework to explore health conditions in Canadian First Nations communities. Int. Indig. Policy J. **2**(1), 1–19 (2011)
19. Mignone, J., O'Neil, J.: Social capital and youth suicide risk factors in First Nations communities. Can. J. Public Health **96**(Suppl. 1), S51–S54 (2005)
20. Miller, M.: Creating a safe frame for learning. J. Teach. Soc. Work **21**(3–4), 159–176 (2001)
21. Mitchell, H.: School science from the eyes of the woodlands cree: using the migawap… Can. J. Nativ. Stud. **32**(2) (2012)
22. MKO: University College of the North: A Vision for Our Future, Manitoba (2000)
23. OCAP/FNIGC: The First Nations Principles of OCAP. http://fnigc.ca/ocap.html

24. Patton, M.Q.: Purposeful sampling. Qual. Eval. Res. Methods **2**, 169–186 (1990)
25. Snowden, R.J., et al.: Indirect behavioral measures of cognition among sexual offenders. J. Sex Res. **48**(2–3), 192–217 (2011)
26. Souter, D., et al.: ICTs, the internet and sustainable development: towards a new paradigm. Int. Inst. Sustain. Dev., 39 (2010)
27. Suri, H.: Purposeful sampling in qualitative research synthesis. Qual. Res. J. **11**(2), 63–75 (2011)
28. TRC: Honouring the Truth, Reconciling for the Future: Summary of the Final Report of the Truth and Reconciliation Commission of Canada. Truth and Reconciliation Commission of Canada (2015)
29. Westhead, J.: Evans, Farm near Lake Naivasha, Kenya—Mobile for Development. http://www.gsma.com/mobilefordevelopment/evans
30. Westhead, J.: Jaipal, Remote Rural Community, India—Mobile for Development. http://www.gsma.com/mobilefordevelopment/jaipal

Adolescents' Internet Attitudes: A Study in an Experimental Greek Secondary School

Kleopatra Nikolopoulou(✉)

University of Athens, Athens, Greece
klnikolopoulou@ath.forthnet.gr

Abstract. This paper regards a validation study aiming to investigate secondary school pupils' internet attitudes. An 18-item questionnaire was administered to 260 adolescents (12–15 years old) of an experimental school, in Greece. Four factors were extracted: "affection", "perceived usefulness", "perceived control" and "behaviour". The factorial structure of the questionnaire was revealed. The majority of the pupils expressed strong perceptions towards the usefulness of the internet. Over 90% of the adolescents believe that the internet can allow them to do more interesting and imaginative work and that it helps them acquire relevant information. Gender and age were not significantly correlated to the factors. The frequency of internet use had positive correlations with the factor "Behaviour". "Perceived control" was statistically significant correlated with each of the factors "Affection" and "Perceived usefulness". The findings are discussed within the context of the safe introduction of digital tools ecosystems of this experimental school in Greece.

Keywords: Internet · Attitudes · Adolescents

1 Introduction and Research Background

In today's digital knowledge societies, internet literacy plays and will play an important role for all citizens to become information literate and lifelong learners. Today, pupils grow up in an environment where information technology and computers are used intensively. Adolescents have become one of the major groups using the internet for various purposes such as searching for information, communicating or playing games. In parallel, learners' perceptions and attitudes of the internet have been identified as important factors that affect learners' motivation, interest and performance in internet-based learning environments [1]. According to researchers [2], students' internet attitudes should be regarded as a component of internet literacy. Most of today's pupils are very comfortable with digital technology, while "digital citizenship" (the norms of behaviour with regard to technology use) regards several levels of responsibility for technology [3]. For example, pupils practise responsible use of technology and develop positive attitudes toward technology applications that support lifelong learning, collaboration and productivity. In the twenty-first century, citizens' attitudes toward using and learning the internet may determine the educational and economical development of a society. Students' internet attitudes may impact their future involvement in internet-related careers or activities.

A. Tatnall and M. Webb (Eds.): WCCE 2017, IFIP AICT 515, pp. 35–44, 2017.
https://doi.org/10.1007/978-3-319-74310-3_5

Assessing students' internet attitudes with validity and reliability is necessary for future internet related research. Tsai's et al. study [4] developed an internet attitude scale for high school pupils and identified the following four subscales: "perceived usefulness", "affection", "perceived control", and "behaviour". Perceived usefulness regards pupils' perceptions about the positive impacts of the internet on individuals and society, affection regards pupils' feeling and anxiety when using the internet, perceived control regards pupils' confidence about the independent control of the usage of the internet, and behaviour regards pupils' actual practice and frequency of using the internet.

Tsai and Lin [5] used the above mentioned scale in order to investigate Taiwanese adolescents' attitudes regarding the internet. They found that males expressed significantly more positive attitudes than did females on two aspects of the internet: perceived usefulness and perceived control. No significant gender differences were found in terms of the affection and behaviour aspects of using the internet. Tsai and Tsai [6] reported lack of significant gender differences in adolescents' frequency of internet usage.

This paper is a validation study aiming to investigate secondary school pupils' internet attitudes, in an experimental school in Greece. Investigating adolescents' attitudes regarding the internet is important as these are expected to influence their intentions, their practices (e.g., internet usage) and, in turn, their learning.

2 Objectives of the Study

The research objectives were:

1. To reveal the factorial structure of the internet attitude scale/questionnaire (see [4]) and the relationships among factors regarding pupils' internet attitudes.
2. To investigate the impact of pupils' individual characteristics (gender, age, frequency of internet use) on the "internet attitudes" factors.

3 Methodology

3.1 Context of the Experimental School and Sample

Before describing the sample, the context for the operation of experimental schools in Greece is briefly presented. According to the Greek Official Government newspaper [7], in experimental schools are tried new programmes of studies, new teaching tools, new textbooks and other educational materials, new teaching methods and ways of managing the school unit. Such pilot applications and methods are being designed by the Greek Ministry of Education, by Universities, as well as by DEPPS (education consultants) or by the same school units, with the aim to create fruitful conclusions with regard to the improvement of educational policy. Teachers working in experimental schools have increased qualifications (i.e., they hold postgraduate degrees and a PhD degree) so as to be able to conduct and evaluate new pilot methods, and to provide feedback for the improvement of the educational policy in Greek schools. Experimental schools are also linked to Universities and, as a consequence, these are the schools where University students carry out their teaching practice. Additionally, for the development of talents and inclinations of pupils, clubs are created and operate across the curriculum once or twice a week (approved by DEPPS): clubs relate to cognitive domains such as mathematics, science, language, literature and other fields such as art, sports, etc., in order to create nuclei of creativity and excellence that utilize the increased capacity of some pupils. Within the above described context, teachers and individual experimental schools are relatively autonomous (under the approval of DEPPS) in the way they organise the school's curriculum. Thus, any innovative practices (including ICT/digital practices) could come under the innovative educational practices. Teachers can also take initiatives such as to conduct research studies; their findings are expected to be useful for the educational community. The current study was undertaken after a teacher's initiative.

The sample consisted of 260 adolescent pupils of an experimental secondary/high school in Piraeus, in Greece. Demographic and individual characteristics of the sample (grade and age group, gender, frequency of internet use) are shown in Table 1. All pupils have access to a computer at home. The age of pupils ranged from 12 to 15 years old. Regarding frequency of internet usage, 53.8% of the pupils reported they make internet use "daily", while around 26.5% use the internet "2–4 times per week". There were no gender differences regarding the frequency of internet use. The questionnaire was administered at the beginning of the academic year 2016-2017. The responses were anonymous and the pupils were assured that there was not right or wrong answer.

Table 1. Demographic and individual characteristics of the sample (260 pupils)

Age group	*Gender*
12–13 years old (or year 7) (38.1%)	Male (51.2%)
13–14 years old (or year 8) (36.5%)	Female (48.8%)
14–15 years old (or year 9) (25.4%)	
Frequency of internet use at home	
Less than once per month (6.2%)	
Monthly (2–4 times per month) (13.5%)	
Weekly (2–4 times per week) (26.5%)	
Every day (daily) (53.8%)	

3.2 The Research Instrument

Data were collected by the use of a questionnaire, which consisted of two sections. Section A involved statements regarding pupils' demographic and individual characteristics (gender, year of study, age, access to a computer at home, frequency of computer use at home). Section B involved 18 statements/items aiming to investigate pupils' internet attitudes. All statements were taken from the study of Tsai et al. [4] who used the "Internet Attitudes Survey (IAS)" with Taiwan high school pupils. Their study separated the 18 items into four subscales/factors, as follows: their first group/factor involved five items (S14, S22, S26, S30, S32) related to "perceived usefulness", the second group/factor involved five items/statements (S5, S17, S21, S25, S29) related to "affection", the third group involved five items (S3, S15, S19, S23, S27) related to "perceived control", and the fourth group involved three items (S8, S16, S20) related to "behaviour". A detailed description of the four scales is presented below:

(1) *Perceived usefulness subscale*: measuring/assessing pupils' perceptions about the positive impacts of the internet on individuals and society. A sample item of this scale is "the internet makes a great contribution to human life".
(2) *Affection subscale*: measuring pupils' feeling and anxiety when using the internet. A sample item of this scale is "the internet makes me feel uncomfortable".
(3) *Perceived control subscale*: investigating pupils' confidence about the independent control of the usage of the internet. A sample item of this scale is "I can use the internet independently, without the assistance of others".
(4) *Behaviour subscale*: assessing pupils' perceived actual practice and frequency of using the internet. A sample item of this scale is "I spend much time on using the internet".

In Tsai's et al. study [4] the internal reliability indexes, alpha coefficients, were adequate for the first three subscales, 0.82, 0.71, and 0.68, and for the entire scale, 0.81. Alpha was relatively low (0.49) only for the fourth scale, regarding internet use behaviour.

In the questionnaire, the 18 items were presented in mixed order, and the pupils were asked to rate their beliefs on a 4-point Likert-type scale (1 = strongly disagree, 2 = disagree, 3 = agree, 4 = strongly agree). Seven items, S5, S17, S21, S25, S29, S15 and S8 were reversed from negative to positive wording.

3.3 Data Analysis

The statistical software SPSS version 20.0 (2011) was used for managing the data and conducting the statistical analyses (descriptive statistics, factor analysis, correlation analysis). Monte Carlo PCA for Parallel analysis [8] was used to conduct Parallel analysis.

4 Results

4.1 Descriptive Measures for Pupils' Views and Factorial Structure of the Questionnaire

To explore pupils' internet attitudes, a descriptive analysis was performed. Table 2 shows pupils' response rates (%) on the 18 items of the questionnaire (n = 260 pupils). The last column of the Table has added together the percentages of those who "agree" and "strongly agree". The majority of the pupils expressed strong perceptions regarding the usefulness of the internet. Indicatively, over 90% of the sample, believe that "the internet can allow me to do more interesting and imaginative work" (for S14: 93.1%), that "the internet helps me acquire relevant information I need" (for S30: 91.2%), while

Table 2. Pupils' response rates (%) on the 18 items of the questionnaire (n = 260 pupils)

	Strongly disagree	Disagree	Agree	Strongly agree	Agree and strongly agree
S14. The internet can allow me to do more interesting and imaginative work	3.5	3.5	33.5	59.6	93.1
S30. The internet helps me acquire relevant information I need	4.6	4.2	37.7	53.5	91.2
S26. The internet makes a great contribution to human life	5	14.2	40.8	40	80.8
S32. The internet makes society more advanced	7.3	11.9	44.2	36.5	80.7
S27. I can use the internet independently, without the assistance of others	6.2	15.4	33.5	45	78.5
S20. I spend much time on using the internet	8.1	14.6	38.1	39.2	77.3
S19. If I get problems using the internet, I can usually solve them one way or the other	6.9	15.8	48.8	28.5	77.3
S3. I could probably teach myself most of the things I need to know about the internet	7.7	18.8	40	33.5	73.5
S22. The internet enlarges my scope	5	21.5	45.8	27.7	73.5
S8. I only use the internet at school when told to^	13.1	16.5	39.2	31.2	70.4
S23. I do not need someone to tell me the best way to use the internet	9.6	23.5	30.8	36.2	67.0
S16. I use the internet regularly throughout school	19.2	33.8	28.8	18.1	46.9
S15. I need an experienced person nearby when I use the internet^	39.6	31.9	19.6	8.8	28.4
S29. When using the internet, I am not quite confident about what I am doing^	46.9	28.8	15	9.2	24.2
S25. I feel bored toward using the internet^	51.9	28.8	11.5	7.7	19.2
S17. If given the opportunity to use the internet I am afraid that I might damage it in some way^	57.3	24.2	10.4	8.1	18.5
S5. I hesitate to use the internet in case I look stupid^	64.2	18.8	10.4	6.5	16.9
S21. The internet makes me feel uncomfortable^	61.2	25	8.8	5	13.8

^items reversed (from negative to positive wording)

around 80% perceive as positive the impact of internet on individuals and society (items S26 and S32).

An exploratory factor analysis was performed, using Principal Axis Factoring method accompanied by the Oblimin Factor rotation method, in order to investigate the factorial validity of the 18 item questionnaire. KMO coefficient of sampling adequacy,

Table 3. Factor loadings per item (18 items)

	Factors			
	F1	F2	F3	F4
S21. The internet makes me feel uncomfortable	.817			
S17. If given the opportunity to use the internet I am afraid that I might damage it in some way	.815			
S5. I hesitate to use the internet in case I look stupid	.779			
S25. I feel bored toward using the internet	.731			
S29. When using the internet, I am not quite confident about what I am doing	.697			
S15. I need an experienced person nearby when I use the internet	.601			
S26. The internet makes a great contribution to human life		.805		
S22. The internet enlarges my scope		.733		
S30. The internet helps me acquire relevant information I need		.723		
S32. The internet makes society more advanced		.697		
S14. The internet can allow me to do more interesting and imaginative work		.539		
S19. If I get problems using the internet, I can usually solve them one way or the other			.695	
S27. I can use the internet independently, without the assistance of others			.669	
S23. I do not need someone to tell me the best way to use the internet			.639	
S3. I could probably teach myself most of the things I need to know about the internet			.627	
S8. I only use the internet at schools when told to				.716
S16. I use the internet regularly throughout school				.528
S20. I spend much time on using the internet				.525
Cronbach-a	0.847	0.761	0.661	0.332

All responses ranged from 1 (strongly disagree) to 4 (strongly agree).
Factor 1 (F1): "Affection", Factor 2 (F2): "Perceived usefulness", Factor 3 (F3): "Perceived control", Factor 4 (F4): "Behaviour".
Extraction Method: Principal Component Analysis. Rotation Method: Oblimin with Kaiser Normalization (a. Rotation converged in 8 iterations)

0.804, was satisfactory (data eigenvalues 4.25, 2.87, 1.46 and 1.34). The screen plot and the parallel analysis results support a four factor solution which was retained for interpretation. The first factor (F1) was labelled "Affection", the second factor (F2) was labelled "Perceived usefulness", the third factor (F3) was labelled "Perceived control" and the fourth factor (F4) was labelled "Behaviour". Table 3 displays the loadings and the Chronbach-a coefficient for internal consistency for each factor (F1 to F4). The first three factors show an acceptable internal consistency: Chronbach-a coefficient ranged from 0.661 to 0.847. Loadings with an absolute value greater than 0.5 appear in Table 3. The fourth factor labelled "*Behaviour*" was loaded by three items and had low reliability (Chronbach-a = 0.332). The "Perceived control" factor was statistically significant correlated with each of the factors "Affection" and "Perceived usefulness". Correlations were positive, as expected; small to mediocre significant correlation coefficients among factors ($p < 0.05$) were found (Table 4).

Table 4. Correlations among internet attitudes factors and the frequency of internet use

	Frequency of internet use	Affection	Perceived usefulness	Perceived control
Affection	.024			
Perceived usefulness	.097	.084		
Perceived control	.066	.151*	.274**	
Behavior	.286**	−.023	.061	.057

**Correlation is significant at the 0.01 level (2-tailed); *Correlation is significant at the 0.05 level (2-tailed)

4.2 Impact of Pupils' Individual Characteristics (Gender, Age, Frequency of Internet Use) on the "Internet Attitudes" Factors

In order to investigate the impact of specific individual characteristics (gender, age, frequency of internet use) on the "internet attitudes" factors extracted above (F1, F2, F3 and F4), an estimation of correlation coefficients was conducted (see Table 4). Table 4 displays the correlations among internet attitude factors and the frequency of internet use.

Positive correlations were found only between the frequency of internet use and the factor "Behaviour". A series of two-way analyses of variances were performed, each of which had as dependent variable the factors (Fl to F4) expressed by factor scores produced from factor analysis, and as independent variables the gender and the grade (i.e., pupils' age group) (see Table 5). There was no interaction effect between gender and grade. Additionally, no statistical significant correlations were found among pupils' grade (or age-group), gender and the factors (Table 5).

Table 5. "Internet attitudes" factor scores by gender and grade

	Grade (age group)						Gender			
	12–13		13–14		14–15		Boy		Girl	
	Mean	S.D.	Mean	S.D.	Mean	S.D.	Mean	S.D.	Mean	S.D.
Affection	.045	.839	.001	1.072	−.068	1.120	−.066	1.047	.069	.947
Perceived usefulness	−.020	.906	.073	1.039	−.076	1.083	.066	1.050	−.069	.944
Perceived control	.069	.909	−.069	1.012	−.004	1.115	−.015	1.067	.016	.928
Behaviour	−.365	.966	.300	1.013	.115	.863	.016	.995	−.017	1.008

Note: Values in the same row and sub-table not sharing the same subscript are significantly different at $p < .05$ in the two-sided test of equality for column means. Cells with no subscript are not included in the test. Tests assume equal variances (Tests are adjusted for all pairwise comparisons within a row of each innermost sub-table using the Bonferroni correction.).

5 Discussion and Conclusions

This was a validation study aiming to investigate secondary school pupils' internet attitudes, in an experimental school in Greece. This study adds to the body of empirical evidence regarding adolescents' internet attitudes. Investigating adolescents' internet attitudes is important as these are expected to influence their motivation and their practices. These, in turn, may impact on their learning.

With regard to the first objective (to reveal the factorial structure of the internet attitude scale/questionnaire and the relationships among factors regarding pupils' views), the analysis demonstrated that there were four factors in the 18-item questionnaire: "Affection" (Factor 1 or F1), "Perceived usefulness" (Factor 2 or F2), "Perceived control" (Factor 3 or F3) and "Behaviour" (Factor 4 or F4) (Table 3). This reveals the factorial structure of the questionnaire and indicates that literature-originated constructs of "internet attitudes" do not differ between adolescent populations of different countries (e.g., adolescents in Taiwan and in Greece). There was a very strong agreement with the factors proposed by Tsai et al. [4] - whose scale was used in this study. In particular, all factors included (were consisted of) the same identical items, with the exception of one item (S15: I need an experienced person nearby when I use the internet); this item, in Tsai's et al. study was included in the subscale/factor "perceived control", while in this study it loaded on the subscale "affection". As revealed in this study and as suggested by Tsai et al. [4], the factors "affection", "perceived usefulness" and "perceived control" should be distinct, when investigating pupils' attitudes towards the internet. The descriptive analysis revealed that there is a similarity of pupils' views-perceptions across cultures. Regarding pupils' views, the majority of them expressed strong perceptions towards the usefulness of the internet. Over 90% of the adolescents believe that the internet can allow them to do more interesting and imaginative work and that it helps them acquire relevant information they need. This finding can be linked to the context of the experimental school, which encourages innovative practices (e.g., integration of digital tools). Pupils' positive attitudes towards the internet may constitute a starting point to motivate them to carry out school work that integrates safely the internet. Regarding digital safety/security, Ribble [3] discussed nine areas of "digital citizenship" and provided strategies for teachers to employ and teach appropriate in-school behaviour: in the area 'education', a suggested strategy is to encourage pupils to come up with new and alternative uses of the internet and digital technologies.

With regard to the second objective, to investigate the impact of pupils' individual characteristics (gender, age, frequency of internet use) on the internet attitudes factors, it was found that: (a) there was no impact of pupils' grade (or age group) and gender on the internet attitudes factors, and (b) the frequency of internet use had positive correlations with the factor "Behaviour". Finding (a) above, is in some agreement with earlier studies which showed that gender differences were non-existent. Tsai and Lin [5] found that males expressed significantly more positive attitudes than did females on the subscales "perceived usefulness" and "perceived control", whereas no significant gender differences were found on the "affection" and "behaviour" subscales. Tsai and Tsai [6] reported lack of significant gender differences in adolescents' frequency of internet usage. Since the traditional gender gap in elementary and secondary school pupils seems to be narrowing [6, 9], it is suggested for gender differences to be investigated with regard to particular aspects of the internet, and also across generations. The finding that there was no impact of pupils' grade (or age group) on the internet attitudes factors was probably due to the small range of ages (i.e., 12 to 15 years old). Finding (b) above, was expected as the frequency of internet use is linked to the items of the factor "Behaviour" (e.g., items S16: "I use the internet regularly throughout school" and S20: "I spend much time on using the internet"). The fact that the frequency of internet use was not significant correlated to the other factors, makes stronger the argument/suggestion that the scales-factors "affection", "perceived usefulness" and "perceived control" should be distinct (discrete) when defining concepts related to internet views.

Limitations of this study include the narrow age-range of pupils and the lack of investigating other internet related variables (e.g., pupils' internet self-efficacy). In this study, the reliability coefficients (Cronbach's alpha) were adequate for the first three subscales (F1, F2 and F3 had 0.847, 0.761 and 0.661, respectively). This suggests that these internet attitude scales, which were developed by Tsai's et al. [4], are a reliable tool to investigate adolescents' internet attitudes across different countries and cultures (it allows for establishment of comparability with studies in different cultures). Since attitudes towards the internet are a multidimensional factor, it is considered as appropriate to describe adolescents' attitudes with respect to discrete dimensions (factors), such as those revealed by the questionnaire. It is suggested, this scale to be used with different adolescent and other target populations (e.g., young University students), in other countries, in order to reveal possible similarities and differences. New internet applications with new features, which cannot easily be foreseen, will appear in the future. Because of the rapidly changing digital technology, adolescents' internet attitudes need to be defined and measured throughout the time.

This small scale study was carried out in an experimental school in Greece. The policy of this school encourages teachers to undertake research initiatives, to disseminate the findings and to participate in the (self)-evaluation of the school unit. The findings of this study are expected to have implications for this school's "ecosystem".

According to Davis [10], information technology impacts multiple ecologies and it is also impacted by these ecologies. It is suggested for teachers to follow short in-service courses (e.g., organized by the information technology teacher-specialist) to be informed about safe internet uses under the umbrella of "digital citizenship" (this concept was defined and discussed by Ribble [3]). Teachers of various subjects need to be aware of pupils' positive views towards the internet, so as to motivate them to carry out innovative work within a safe environment. In this way, teachers' and pupils' practices may influence the school's context. Further research is planned to be conducted in this experimental school. It is suggested to investigate the relation between pupils' internet attitudes and their learning achievements. By adopting a robust methodology, the teacher-researcher (author of this paper) plans to investigate (a) appropriate and inappropriate uses of mobile technology by pupils, and (b) the ecosystem of this school with regard to information technology (e.g., teachers' technology use and practices in various subjects, as well as their perspectives).

Acknowledgments. The author would like to thank Prof. N. Davis for her suggestions on this paper.

References

1. Peng, H., Tsai, C.-C., Wu, Y.-T.: University students' self-efficacy and their attitudes toward the internet: the role of students' perceptions of the internet. Educ. Stud. **32**, 73–86 (2006)
2. Wu, Y.-T., Tsai, C.-C.: University students' internet attitudes and internet self-efficacy: a study at three universities in Taiwan. Cyber Psychol. Behav. **9**(4), 441–450 (2006)
3. Ribble, M.: Digital citizenship in schools. Second edition, ISTE (International Society for Technology in Education), 2nd chapter, pp. 15–44 (2011). https://www.iste.org/docs/excerpts/DIGCI2-excerpt.pdf
4. Tsai, C.-C., Lin, S., Tsai, M.-J.: Developing an internet attitude scale for high school students. Comput. Educ. **37**, 41–51 (2001)
5. Tsai, C.-C., Lin, C.-C.: Taiwanese adolescents' perceptions and attitudes regarding the internet: exploring gender differences. Adolescence **39**(156), 725–734 (2004)
6. Tsai, M.-J., Tsai, C.-C.: Junior high school students' internet usage and self-efficacy: a re-examination of the gender gap. Comput. Educ. **54**, 1182–1192 (2010)
7. Official Greek Government newspaper: context for experimental schools (2011, modified in 2015). (in Greek)
8. Watkins, M.W.: Monte Carlo PCA for parallel analysis (computer software). State College, PA, Ed & Psych Associates (2000)
9. Volman, M., van Eck, E., Heemskerk, I., Kuiper, E.: New technologies, new differences: Gender and ethnic differences in pupils' use of ICT in primary and secondary education. Comput. Educ. **44**(1), 35–55 (2005)
10. Davis, N.: Global interdisciplinary research into the diffusion of information technology innovations in education. In: McDougall, A., Murnane, J., Jones, A., Reynolds, N. (eds.) Researching IT in Education: Theory, Practice and Future Directions, pp. 142–149. Routledge, London (2010)

Health-Game Development in University – Lower Secondary School Collaboration

Jaana Holvikivi(✉) and Tuula Toivanen-Labiad

Metropolia University of Applied Sciences, Helsinki, Finland
{jaana.holvikivi, tuula.toivanen-labiad}@metropolia.fi

Abstract. This paper describes and analyses a case of multidimensional collaboration of in the development of an educational game. The parties included Metropolia University of Applied Sciences from Finland, Tokushima University from Japan, and a lower secondary school in Helsinki. The development team involved students from three different departments of Metropolia. The two-year project produced two successive prototypes of the game, which contained two hundred questions about health and well-being including oral health. School pupils tested the game several times and commented on its features. They gave critical comments relating to its design and visual properties, even though they were positive about the idea of learning health facts in an entertaining way. Even though the coordination of such a project with many parties involved is challenging, the actual design of the real content and functionalities of a serious game pose more challenges. Effective advance preparation and research on educational game designs and aims will be needed in the following phases of the work.

Keywords: e-Health · Health education · Serious games · Co-development

1 Introduction

Universities are increasingly employing multidisciplinary projects in order to insert understanding of real-life practices to the curriculum [1]. The Metropolia University of Applied Sciences that is located in the Helsinki area in Finland has adopted a concept called "innovation projects" to all its curricula, in which all third-year bachelor students are required to participate in a multidisciplinary product development project. The projects respond to product challenges from real world problems that have been presented by a company or an outside organization. The project teams are gathered from two or three different disciplines such as engineering, ICT, oral health, nursing, occupational health, media, or business studies. This paper describes one innovation theme that went beyond a single project to expand into several separate projects, as well as student final theses.

There has been a long-standing cooperation between the two universities involved, Tokushima University in Japan and Metropolia in Finland, which both have departments of Oral Health and Welfare. The cooperation activities included a two-year (2010–2012) project Evidence-Based Oral Health Promotion that developed a description of evidence-based oral health promotion for children, youth and the elderly. Health promotion competence profile in the degree programs in oral hygiene of both

A. Tatnall and M. Webb (Eds.): WCCE 2017, IFIP AICT 515, pp. 45–54, 2017.
https://doi.org/10.1007/978-3-319-74310-3_6

countries was expanded and strengthened to the evidence-based practice according to national and international recommendations. The shared knowledge, which was based on the collaboration, produced new tools for education. Another multi-disciplinary project was planned to continue the cooperation, with a wider perspective to the promotion of the health and well-being of adolescents, in particular. Due to different funding situations, each institution agreed to implement a project of its own. At Metropolia, degree programs in oral health care, public health nursing and information technology participated in this new project.

In this paper, we describe the course of the project and its results in terms of product and educational achievements. First, we explain how the project was embedded in the curriculum, and how collaboration with a lower secondary school evolved. We discuss the results based on feedback and interviews gathered by students, records of project meetings and intranet repository, and completed student work. Finally, we discuss the future of serious game development for health education in collaboration with many actors.

2 Background

National and international health policy guidelines address the promotion of health and well-being of different age groups in multidisciplinary collaboration, in networking and in cooperation among regional actors [2]. When the interest is the health promotion among children, the primary responsibility belongs to the family and the child. Nevertheless, this should take place in close collaboration with communal social and health care services, school teachers and nurses, and the school well-being group if such a group exists. In this project the focus was the health and well-being education of lower secondary school adolescents (14–16 years) in Finland and Japan. Official recommendations for the education include several components of health promotion, such as nutrition, physical activity, alcohol and drug use, injury prevention, oral health, prevention of communicable diseases, and promotion of sexual health.

Contemporary adolescents are often called digital natives referring to their fluency in using internet, mobile devices, and games. In this project, mobile technology was seen as a modern and efficient channel in getting young people to reflect on their health. Therefore, the market of health promotion applications in Finland was explored in the first phase of the project. No such mobile applications available in the promotion of health and well-being of adolescents where adolescents were the key actors when developing ones were detected. However, there were numerous web sites that provide information and guidance on well-being, such as the internet-based School Well-being Profile which was developed already in 2004, and which was well accepted in Finnish schools [3].

The promotion of the health and well-being of adolescents is presumably best achieved in the everyday environment, such as at school. Involving adolescents and giving them responsibility for their own health related issues seems to be the best way to recognize the need for support and help of networks and experts. In this project, a school in the metropolitan area, which provides primary and lower secondary education, was chosen as a partner. The collaboration between the school and the degree program in Oral Hygiene had started from the initiative of the school's well-being working group in the autumn of 2013. Based on the national school health survey results [4] the working group identified a need to improve the lifestyle and oral health of their pupils. The first step was to give an oral health educational session in the school, which was followed by an oral health fair the next year.

The main themes of the fair included avoidance of tobacco and alcohol use, promotion of oral self-care, prevention of oral infectious diseases, good nutrition and its impact on overall health, and aesthetic dental oral health. The methods included interactive discussions, demonstrations and a quiz. Learning materials included pictures, health indicators, and iPads, from which pupils could search for more evidence-based information. In total 150 pupils in the seventh grade participated in the activities of the fair.

2.1 Aims of the Project

The aim of the project that was called Umbrella was to involve adolescents as partners in developing mobile tools for the promotion of their health and well-being. Collaboration in the development of the tool was presumed to motivate young people based on reported experiences elsewhere [5]. They would feel ownership of the resulting product, and they would more willingly employ it later. The adolescents could actively take the responsibility for monitoring and promoting their own health and well-being. In addition, the purpose of the project was to motivate adolescents to self-care and improve their health literacy. The goal was active participation in developing a mobile application with close cooperation and support of peers, the school support network and experts.

The total time for development was planned for two years, consisting of two innovation project course cycles at the university. The innovation project usually lasts one semester, and includes 10 ECTS credits, which is equivalent of 270 h work. Each project course was implemented in its own department, but the development efforts were coordinated by instructors. Students in different teams met only once or twice during each course. The areas of oral health, clinical nursing, public health nursing, and information technology were involved. Moreover, in the partner school the health education teachers and the well-being working group were involved. The project followed Design-Based Research Model as its backbone [6].

2.2 Games in Education

Gamification and the use of educational games is currently increasing in primary schools despite it still being debated to some extent. There is no consensus on the usefulness of games in learning in general according to Kapp [7]. Kapp presented six carefully chosen meta-analysis studies that each examined between 7 and 105 studies that attempted to resolve the issue of effectiveness of games in education. The studies compared reported learning outcomes of game use to other methods, but the result was, not surprisingly, inconclusive. Overall, in more than half of the cases games were found somewhat beneficial. Nevertheless, meta-analyses tell little of individual cases as they could differ widely. Much depends on the type of game, how it is supported in the classroom, and what kind of learning it is designed to produce.

Dicheva et al. [8] conducted a literature survey on gamification in education, and found 34 empirical case studies, most published in 2013–14. According to their selection criteria, most research on gamification concerned higher education, as only two reports concerned the K12 education. Most cases (18) reported blended learning applications. The subject domain of the application of gamification was in most cases Computer Science or IT courses. They identified the following game mechanics: points, badges, levels, progress bars, leader boards, virtual currency, and avatars. As can be concluded from this list, the definition of gamification in the study was rather narrow. Games for building virtual worlds and other highly developed collaborative games were not necessarily included in the study. The majority of the papers that were examined reported encouraging results from the experiments, including significantly higher engagement of students in forums, projects and other learning activities, increased attendance, participation, and material downloads, positive effect on the quantity and quality of students' contributions, increased percentage of passing students and participation in voluntary activities and challenging assignments, and minimizing the gap between the lowest and the top graders. The papers also report that students considered gamified instances to be more motivating, interesting and easier to learn as compared to other courses.

Business games have been commonly included in the curricula of business studies and economics since the 1970s. However, the learning outcomes are somewhat controversial. In some cases, playing games could even lead to learning wrong behavioural patterns [9]. If the game design is based on extrinsic motivation such as collecting badges or points or winning other teams, such as reported in studies in Dicheva et al. [8], deeper meanings in the game world might be forgotten, and actual understanding of the phenomena does not increase as expected. In Harviainen et al.'s case, experienced business people were frustrated when playing business games where the winning strategy would not have been appropriate in real world [9]. On the other hand, simulation games that have been used in teaching vocational and professional skills, tend to result in more positive learning outcomes than traditional teaching [7].

The most recent meta-study by Hamari et al. in 2017 found education and health as the most common application areas for gamification studies [personal communication], which was the case also in their previous study in 2014 [10]. Obviously, there is a multitude of games and gamified applications offered for schools and young children. Moreover, virtual worlds and game environments such as Second Life, Minecraft and Sims are widely used in schools. Additionally, there is a great variety of games for science and mathematics, as well as language learning. Kevin Devlin and his company BrainQuake create mathematics learning video games such as Wuzzit Trouble, which is based on the idea that the game has to incorporate the logic of mathematics. The learning outcomes and results of game playing have been a subject of continuous scientific research. Overall, the group who played Wuzzit Trouble in an experiment showed a significant increase in number sense between the pre- and post-assessment, compared to the control group who did not [11]. Another mathematics game with similar principles called Semideus Schools was developed by a research team at

Tampere University of Technology (TUT). Its learning outcomes have been studied over the years, and also found to be positive [12].

Moreover, there is ample evidence that a constructivist approach where students participate in the design of the game and plan how to use it, yields very good results, especially in primary schools as reported by Kafai [5, 13]. Kafai has extensive experience in developing game design in school education, and the experiences of her teams have been successful in many kinds of schools, also where the pupils have been socioeconomically disadvantaged.

3 Research and Results

3.1 Development Process

Teachers in Oral Hygiene and ICT at Metropolia together with oral health professionals from the municipality originally planned the project based on benchmarking the application that had previously been developed by University of Tokushima. However, the focus immediately shifted from checking the dental status of individual pupils to educating pupils in taking care of their teeth and health. Collecting individual data from school children is strictly regulated by privacy protection, therefore the idea of follow-up of individuals was abandoned. The emphasis was placed on providing information in an easy to digest way and to let pupils experiment with their knowledge.

Oral hygienist students and public health and nursing students started working on the information content with 8th grade pupils as a target group. ICT students formed a team that started generating ideas for the game and writing a script for the game. Initially, all teams reported difficulties in orienting themselves as 13-year-old adolescents, and they were unsure whether they could reach the target group. How to design the game to look appropriate to the age-group was much discussed. However, as there was an agreement with the school, the possibility to test the appropriate level was anticipated. None of the students in these teams were familiar with an iterative and flexible development process that is common in game industry, which added to their anxiety. Altogether six ICT students joined the project at different times, 12 nursing students, and three oral hygienist students.

The first version of the game was designed to be tested in the annual oral health promotion fair in the school. The fair was being organized by another group of oral hygiene students for 8th grade pupils in the school gym and assembly hall. There were displays for pupils on tooth care that also offered samples such as toothpaste, which were provided by collaborating companies. The pupils participated in groups of seven, and they visited each display for 5 min where they were guided by oral hygienist students. One stand had four iPad tablets for testing the demo version of the game. After playing the game, the pupils were interviewed on their experience. A week later, the oral health students attended a health education lesson where they collected opinions of pupils through a feedback form, and conducted further interviews. Pupils were asked about the outlook of the game and its sound effects, functionality, structure, contents, as well as the formulation of the questions and their comprehension.

According to interview results, most pupils had a positive view of the game, but many felt that the content and questions were too demanding. When discussing the game they also raised wider questions such as what health actually means. The game inspired them to reflect on health issues which was an expected and successful outcome. On the other hand, some terms used in the game were unfamiliar, and therefore, students preferred to work with the game during health education lessons but they would not play in their leisure time. The visual implementation was too simple and not attractive enough. The pupils would have preferred more vivid colours, varied sound effects, and possibly 3D effects [14].

The next round of game development was based on the feedback from the school. New content was added and functionalities were improved. Some of the students continued in the same project but working on their final thesis project, whereas three groups of new students worked again on the health questions and information sources, improving the content of the game. The technical team also changed, and a graphical artist joined it. Unfortunately, there was a skill gap in the technical team and many aspects had to be reprogrammed. However, two successive prototypes were developed, which also could be tested in the following school fairs [15].

Some challenges in the setup of the project influenced the quality of results. The student teams in the three departments had vastly different schedules and they were working in different campus locations. Therefore, they met each other only a couple of times during completion of the project. The information was conveyed through instructors and a common intranet working space, where all intermediate deliverables were placed. The working space acted as an information repository also for successive student teams.

3.2 Results of Collaboration

The progress of the project was monitored in regular meetings of the instructor team, and regular collaborative discussions in video conferences with the Japanese partner. Students completed their assignments on schedule, and they analysed in their reports the success of their respective tasks. All that material is available on the project repository in the university intranet. Therefore, a continuous evaluation of the progress has been available for analysis.

The main results of the project were undoubtedly educational. Students had an opportunity to work with students from other professions, to work with a public school and its pupils, and to participate in a design project with stated aims. For most students, this was their only multidisciplinary experience during their studies. Moreover, the Finnish oral hygienist and nursing students got an opportunity to work in a multicultural setting and practice their language abilities, because all ICT students were immigrants who studied using English. Moreover, about one third of the school pupils had an immigrant background. Students produced material for the project as well as their course reports or final theses. They had an opportunity to see how their design was received by school children, which also helped them to understand customer opinions in their work.

The resulting application has a great amount of information on adolescent health through 200 questions, and the data presentation could further be tested and developed to be even more appropriate for the age group. The application works on a website where it can be tested, although it is still in need of technical fine-tuning. The game is a simple quiz-type of game with the possibility of choosing one of three difficulty levels. Players get points of each correct answer, which they have an option of sharing on Facebook [15]. This type of game allows knowledge testing, and as the correct answers can be expanded with an explanation, the player can also accumulate knowledge on individual topics. However, the learning effects were not tested yet, as the tool has only been used in usability testing situations (Fig. 1).

Fig. 1. Starting page of the game

The pupils of the school had been offered a glimpse into the game development process. In their answers to the opinion survey, they gave their opinions on game design and visual outlook, but unfortunately, the same pupils did not get an improved version which would have shown how their opinions influenced the design. Therefore, pupil involvement in the design could be thus far assessed as marginal from their point of view.

Somewhat similar efforts were conducted in other universities in Finland around the same time. The University of Applied Sciences in Kajaani developed a life planning game for 16 to 19 year olds called Game of My Life. The game was developed by information technology students specialized in game development together with health care students and the local support centre for mental health patients [16]. Health promotion indeed is to a strong trend in the serious game field.

4 Discussion

The resulting game still needs to be redesigned to look more professional in order to be fully translated into English and Japanese for the partner university. Many of the original game ideas were not implemented but they have potential for making the game more engaging. The surveyed pupils gave mainly positive assessments, even though it was observed in the classroom that they did not sustain interest for a long time. They also commented on the modesty of graphics, due to their experience of commercial products that are more polished (Fig. 2).

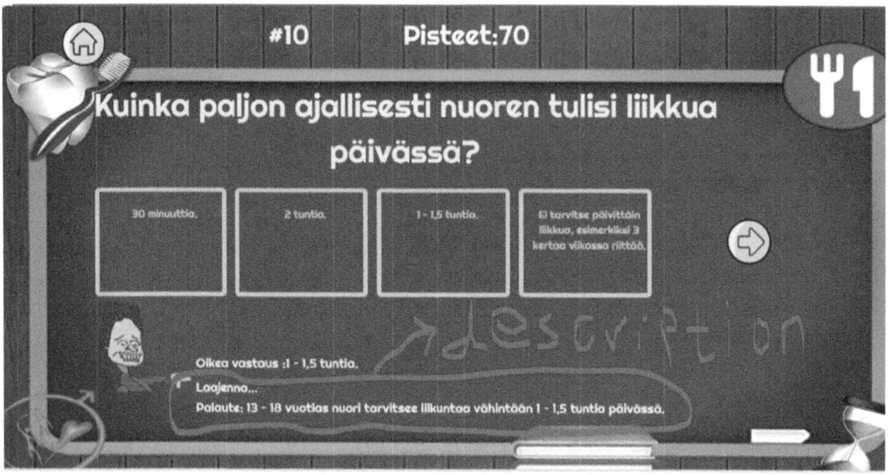

Fig. 2. A question page of the game

The ICT students certainly learnt how demanding game development in reality is. The cross-cultural aspect of the Finnish-Japanese collaboration remains to be tested. The preliminary application developed by the Japanese university was in the Japanese "cute" (kawaii) style, similar how public instructions are often displayed in Japan. The Finnish application had graphics that were developed in an international student team, which cannot be located to any cultural style. It would be an interesting step to see whether such a game can cross cultural barriers in terms of visuals, gaming logic or health education contents, particularly because of the large differences between primary education systems of the two countries.

Collaboration of many parties that were physically separated was a challenge. The varied course schedules and deadlines had to be negotiated in the project plan. In this case, teams could work quite independently as the tasks were not highly dependent on each other. Moreover, teacher collaboration faced challenges despite the efforts of all parties involved because of professional cultures in the participating departments were in many ways different. The busy schedules of instructors were another impediment that prevented close monitoring of student progress.

The team's lack of experience in serious game development became evident in the process. Unfortunately, there was hardly any research on the subject to be found, either, nor could any established models for this kind of development be detected. Game development for entertainment is done in an iterative manner, and after each round, the reception of the game is tested and the direction for next version is decided on feedback [17–19]. In the case of an educational game, the goals are wider than just entertainment:

the learning goals are more important than attractiveness [7]. Often there are no straightforward procedures for measuring learning except simply examinations. In this project, the idea of iteration was followed but the interview results from school pupils could not be utilized optimally, because the student development teams had little knowledge of educational goals. The design principles for simulation games that were developed in another Metropolia project could largely be applied in the case of a mobile game, as well. The simulation games were developed in multidisciplinary teams where the students of critical care acted simultaneously as subject experts and learners [18].

5 Conclusion

The mobile application was built in multidisciplinary collaboration between ICT students and oral and general health care students. The impact of the lower secondary school pupils in successive phases of the development was significant. The main goal of the game was to support health education and control of adolescent personal health knowledge. It was concluded that a mobile application of this kind is an appropriate tool in advancing health awareness, as well as oral health practices. Therefore, producing an international version would make sense, particularly in this setting where multicultural aspects are inherent.

Certainly, a multidisciplinary and cross-cultural project like this requires good planning and experience that the project team acquired through this work. Based on the current experience, the goals of the game can be set accurately both in terms of immersion and learning objectives. Participating students would need advance training in understanding the use of educational games and in adapting the iterative development in design. Also, an experimental language game project that was conducted around same time in Finland recommends an agile, iterative model for the development [19]. There will definitely be more similar projects in near future, and it is hoped that they can benefit from the experiences of these initial trials.

Acknowledgement. The study was partially supported by the European Regional Development Fund 6AIKA project EduDigi (code A72041).

References

1. Holvikivi, J., Lakkala, M., Muukkonen, H.: Introducing collaborative practices to undergraduate studies. In: Brinda, T., Mavengere, N., Haukijärvi, I., Lewin, C., Passey, D. (eds.) SaITE 2016. IAICT, vol. 493, pp. 47–55. Springer, Cham (2016). https://doi.org/10.1007/978-3-319-54687-2_5
2. Ministry of Social Affairs and Health: Quality Recommendation for Health Promotion. Publications of the Ministry of Social Affairs and Health 2009:8 (2009)
3. Lintonen, T., Konu, A.I.: The well-being profile - an internet tool for school health promotion. Promot. et Educ. **13**, 230 (2006)
4. School Health Promotion Study 2013. National Institute for Health and Welfare. Helsinki. http://www.thl.fi/fi_FI/web/fi/tilastot/vaestotutkimukset/kouluterveyskysely (2013). Available only in Finnish and Swedish

5. Kafai, Y.B.: Playing and making games for learning instructionist and constructionist perspectives for game studies. Games Cult. **1**, 36–40 (2006)
6. Wang, F., Hannafin, M.: Design based research and technology-enhanced learning environments. Educ. Technol. Res. Dev. **53**, 5–23 (2005)
7. Kapp, K.M.: The Gamification of Learning and Instruction: Game-Based Methods and Strategies for Training and Education. Pfeiffer, CA (2012)
8. Dicheva, D., Dichev, C., Agre, G., Angelova, G.: Gamification in education: a systematic mapping study. Educ. Technol. Soc. **18**, 75–88 (2015)
9. Harviainen, J.T., Lainema, T., Saarinen, E.: Player-reported impediments to game-based learning. Trans. Digit. Games Res. Assoc. **1**, 55–83 (2014)
10. Hamari, J., Koivisto, J., Sarsa, H.: Does gamification work? – A literature review of empirical studies on gamification. In: Proceeding of the 47th Annual Hawaii International Conference on System Sciences, Hawaii, USA (2014)
11. Pope, H., Mangram, C.: Wuzzit trouble: the influence of a digital math game on student number sense. Int. J. Serious Games. **2**(4) (2015)
12. Kiili, K., Devlin, K., Perttula, A., Tuomi, P., Lindstedt, A.: Using video games to combine learning and assessment in mathematics education. Int. J. Serious Games **2**(4) (2015)
13. Kafai, Y.B., Burke, Q.: Constructionist gaming: understanding the benefits of making games for learning. Educ. Psychol. **50**, 4 (2015)
14. Beck, E., Pyörre, M., Vihervuori, J.: Umbrella terveyspeli: uusi työväline nuorten suun terveysvalmennukseen. Metropolia AMK (2015). (In Finnish)
15. Tolessa, B.: Umbrella: A Web-Based Health Education Quiz Game for School Kids. Metropolia (2016)
16. Korhonen, T., Ravelin, T.: Monialaista tiimityöskentelyä hyötypelien parissa. Toolilainen **2016**(4), 32–33 (2016). (In Finnish)
17. Moogk, D.: Minimum viable product and the importance of experimentation in technology start-ups. Technol. Innov. Manage. Rev. **2**(3), 23–26 (2012)
18. Koivisto, J.-M.: Learning Clinical Reasoning through Game-Based Simulation: Design Principles for Simulation Games. University of Helsinki, Helsinki (2017)
19. Lappalainen, Y., Poikolainen, M., Trapp, H. (eds.): Tila haltuun! Suositukset virtuaalisen suomen opiskelun toteuttamiseen. University of Turku (2015). [In Finnish]

Game-Play: Effects of Online Gamified and Game-Based Learning on Dispositions, Abilities and Behaviours of Primary Learners

Jawaher Alghamdi(✉) and Charlotte Holland

Institute of Education, Dublin City University, Glasnevin, Dublin, Republic of Ireland
jawaher.alghamdi2@mail.dcu.ie,
charlotte.holland@dcu.ie

Abstract. This meta-level review of the literature set-out to examine the impacts of game-based/gamified learning on dispositions, cognitive abilities and behaviours of learners aged 6–12, and to identify the factors that contributed to these impacts. A total of seventeen relevant studies were identified that had been implemented across a range of disciplinary areas in the period under review (2005–2015). The results indicate that online gamified/games-based learning has been shown to increase the level of academic performance of learners, and improve cognitive competencies in problem-solving, multiplicative reasoning ability, self-efficacy and critical thinking. Learners' intrinsic motivation has been shown to have been enhanced through motivational factors (confidence, satisfaction and enjoyment) promoted within the online game design, and this had a direct effect on increasing engagement and improving academic achievement.

Keywords: Gamification · Gamified learning · Primary education

1 Introduction

The availability of new platforms and online technologies for the delivery of games has become an important factor in 21st century learning. According to Prensky [1], our education system needs to respond to the needs of our "digital natives" who, having grown up with the proliferation and permeation of technologies in their everyday lives, are said to be more technologically savvy and to process information (or learn) differently to previous generations. However, others such as Helsper and Eynon [2] contest the evidence base for such generalization that forms the basis of the concept of digital natives and instead have provided evidence that digital natives are perhaps better identified across a broader range of factors which move beyond the narrow generational concept, including the degree of immersion in the technology (i.e. breadth of online activities) and experience in using technology, as well as socio-demographic factors (gender dimensions and educational levels). Helsper and Eynon [2] further call for more evidenced based research exploring how younger and older generations learn through and engage with technology, so that our education system can respond appropriately to needs of our learners. In order to keep up with ever-changing

A. Tatnall and M. Webb (Eds.): WCCE 2017, IFIP AICT 515, pp. 55–63, 2017.
https://doi.org/10.1007/978-3-319-74310-3_7

information and communication technologies and to prosper within dynamic social, cultural and economic environments of the 21st century, learners need to develop and/or enhance skills such as critical thinking, teamwork, digital literacy, problem solving, collaboration and cooperation. According to Prensky [3] computer games provide a new way to motivate learners. Gaming is particularly important in supporting learners to interact, communicate and collaborate with each other, and thus can help facilitate types of learning required for 21st century living.

This review of the literature set-out to identify factors that impact on dispositions, behaviours and/or cognitive abilities of primary level learners' (6–12 years old), in game-based/gamified learning environments. For the purpose of this study, game-based learning refers to the use of stand-alone online games within learning contexts and the gamification of learning refers to features of gaming, such as competition and rewards systems, being used within online learning contexts.

2 Methodology

The electronic databases searched in this review were Science direct, IEEE (Institute of Electrical and Electronics Engineers) and Springer. The search terms included: "online game–based learning" "online digital game-based learning", "gamified learning" and "gamification", along with more specific terms such as "primary education" and "younger learner or children". The following search results were obtained: Science Direct (590 papers), IEEE (107 papers) and Springer (395 papers). Studies were selected with the following inclusion criteria; (1) have been published from 2005 to 2015, (2) have focused on primary education aged 6–12, (3) have been written in English language. It also should be noted that only those games employing an Internet or Wifi connection were considered 'online', and, consequently, papers presenting research on topics, such as digital based-learning without use of internet connection, were not included in this review.

Given the permeation of broadband/wifi and mobile technologies, this study took a particular focus on games being used for learning purposes that were accessible online through commonly used mobile devices with wifi connection (laptop and/or tablet technologies) and desktop computers with an Internet connection within classrooms or at home. Console games were thus excluded, as they are not *commonly* integrated within classrooms, as console games are often beyond budgetary constraints of many school systems – we do recognize that there are some notable exceptions to this such as Learning and Teaching Scotland's exploration and promotion of consoles in Scottish classrooms from 2006 onwards. Furthermore, there was emerging anecdotal evidence at the time of this review of games traditionally accessed via consoles being translated for use via PCs and/or mobile devices (the launch of Microsoft Educational Version of Minecraft in 2016 which is accessible by PC and Mobile phone is evidence of one such recent translation). Furthermore, this study was particularly interested in online games being used by the 6 to 12 year old age group. As such, the research terms used narrowed the search field to include games employing an Internet or Wifi connection for 6–12 year olds, while excluding console games. In total over 1000 papers were isolated using the initial search terms, and following a manual reading and review of each of these, only 17 studies were found to have met the criteria as outlined above for this meta-analysis, as explained below.

To enable the implementation of the selection criteria, and given the diversity of online games, two steps were taken in the selection process. First, during abstract screening, records reporting the same study were clustered together. Second, during full-text vetting, the references were reviewed, which resulted in the delivery of several papers relevant for the review but not covered in the databases. The literature review uncovered seventeen papers reporting on studies exploring the impact of online game-play. The questions that guided the review of each of the selected papers were as follows:

- What does this study reveal about dispositions, cognitive abilities and/or behaviours of learners within online game-based/gamified learning environments?
- What factors contribute to changes in learners' dispositions, cognitive abilities and/or behaviours within online game-based/gamified learning environments?

For the purpose of the review, Dispositions were understood as learners' attitudes or feelings towards engagement within the disciplinary area; Abilities were understood as development of learners' cognitive abilities within the disciplinary area; and, Behaviours were understood as the nature, types and degree of engagement in the disciplinary area within and beyond the classroom.

The findings from the selected papers were initially coded according to whether an increase, decrease or no change was recorded in the dispositions, abilities and/or behaviours of learners. The age-group, disciplinary area and size of study were also recorded. In addition, factors that contributed to changes in dispositions, abilities and/or behaviours of learners were noted. The outcomes from the coding process were then cross-tabulated to ascertain common outcomes and corresponding themes, and these were then presented within the frame of discussion under the headings of 'Dispositions', 'Abilities' and 'Behaviours' in game-based/gamified learning contexts.

3 Nature of Studies Under Review

Seventeen studies were identified that focused on online game-based learning/gamification across a range of disciplinary areas. Overall, the studies adopted research approaches that utilised solely quantitative or mixed methods, with solely qualitative approaches being less common. Furthermore, studies measuring cognitive abilities (academic achievement) tended to use pre-testing and post-testing of abilities, whereas the studies of behaviours and dispositions tended to use direct observation as their research tool of choice.

A variety of different online game-based learning contexts have been used; a cooperative educational online computer game [4], a collaborative educational online computer game [5–7], mini games [8, 9] and 3D online environments [10, 11], constructing games [20].

Mathematics and Science were the most common disciplinary areas for the studies under review. Five studies implemented online games in Mathematics course [4, 9, 14, 17] and another seven studies were in the disciplinary area of Science [6–8, 11–13, 15].

The remainder focused on other disciplinary areas, such as Geography [5, 10], English [5] and Literacy skills-Reading [18].

Most of the studies sought to explore the effect of engagement in online games on learners' dispositions. A number of studies explored the impact of engagement in online games on the learners' cognitive abilities such as problem solving, multiplicative reasoning ability and academic achievement. While a few studies examined the effect of engagement in online games on learners' behaviour, this review has found that only three studies have implemented gamification elements. Two of these studies integrate gamification elements within 3D virtual worlds [11, 20]. The study by Su and Cheng implemented gamification elements in a mobile learning environment [6].

4 Impact of Online Game-Based Learning/Gamification on Dispositions

Eleven studies focused on the effect of online games on learners' dispositions and attitudes [1, 4, 8, 10–13, 18, 20]. A variety of types of online gaming products, including 3D immersed games [10, 11] and mini games [8, 9] which support social interaction (cooperation, collaboration) and competition have been shown to positively enhanced primary learners' dispositions toward learning across a range of different disciplinary areas [8–11].

Game-based learning has been shown to promote an increase in positive attitudes towards disciplinary areas [4, 5, 12–14, 19] to make the learning experience more enjoyable [14] and to promote engagement beyond the classroom [19]. This can lead to learners exhibiting independent behaviours (becoming more self-directed, autonomous) and a positive shift in their interest towards the process of learning, as opposed to focusing on academic grades [10].

Game-based learning supports this through the inclusion of motivational gaming features such as fantasy and relevance [12], collaboration and team-based type activities [5], and appropriately designed aesthetic interfaces with attractive illustrations for example [5]. Immersive gaming environments that support 3D virtual engagement among multiple players were further shown by Tüzün et al. [10] to increase motivation through use of exploration, interaction, collaboration and through activation of player presence. The act of constructing games was also shown to increase positive attitudes and motivational levels [20], particularly if it involved experimentation and sharing of ideas – learners liked 'messing around with scripts' [20]. Ronimus et al. [18] found that the presence of reward systems had an initial significant positive effect on concentration levels. Su and Chengt [6] found that leaderboards, badges and missions increase learner engagement. Kuo [12] found that game and non–game learning environments should be more fun to motivate learners and keep them on task.

There were some cautionary notes about use of game-based learning in some of these studies. In a study by Ronimus et al. [18] when the novelty of using reward system within games wore off, the learners' engagement decreased. Furthermore, Ke and Grabowski [4] found that cooperative game-playing encouraged more positive dispositions than competitive game-playing towards the disciplinary area of maths. Also gaming environments without a sufficient degree of learning challenge – such as those involving just the gathering of information - can be perceived as boring as shown in a study by Tüzün et al. [10], thus decrease levels of motivation, engagement or interest in disciplinary area.

5 Impact of Online Game-Based Learning/Gamification on Cognitive Abilities

Ten of the studies specifically explored the impact of online games on learners' academic achievement [4–10, 12, 13, 15, 16] Some of these and other studies further examined the effect of online game-based/gamified learning on specific abilities such as problem-solving skills, multiplicative reasoning ability, self-efficacy [4–8, 10–13, 15, 16]. In terms of academic achievement, the results of these studies found game-based/gamified learning in general led to improvement in learners' academic achievement. This improvement comes from learners' enjoyment, involvement and satisfaction within the online gaming process [4–6, 8, 9, 13].

Overall these studies of online game-based learning/gamified learning have reported improvements in learners' cognitive abilities such as: problem-solving skills [9, 11, 15–17], factual knowledge [5], self-efficacy and confidence [6, 7, 15] and in learners' academic performance [4–8, 10, 12, 15, 16].

Online game-based learning/gamified learning has been shown to enable improvements in learning performance, knowledge and/or skills-sets through the use of the constructivist platforms and communication interfaces that promote collaboration, increase players enjoyment and/or value the ownership and personal expression [17]. In terms of academic achievement, Hwang et al. [8] found that competition and challenge of the online game resulted in an increase in learners' interest, with fuller involvement, concentration and enjoyment, and improved performance. In a study by Filsecker and Hickey [11] players interacting with each other through the 3D virtual space were shown to have a greater understanding of key concepts and increased interest in solving problems. Sung and Hwang [13] found that collaborative computer games enhances learners' confidence and self-efficacy.

Participants in a study of a mathematics educational game by Costu et al. [14] highlighted the need for enjoyment in educational games, but also cautioned about the need to keep a balance between entertainment and knowledge dimensions of game-based learning environments, recommending that the game be well-connected to the lesson learning outcomes. They further recommended that a competition-type use of the game would likely increase the level of engagement in the game.

A study exploring the potential of mobile gamified learning by Su and Cheng [6] highlighted the positive correlation between intrinsic motivation and learning achievement. In this case, the use of gamification features such as leaderboard, badges and mission resulted in an increase in learners' interest and satisfaction, and thus, positively impacted on their intrinsic motivation, which in turn is reflected in an increase in their academic performance.

A study by Vos et al. [20] concluded that game-makers demonstrated more cognitive competence (in deep learning strategies) than those who just played existing games. This indicates that the process of game creation is of more value from a cognitive perspective than that of game-playing.

A study into 3-D immersive learning environments by Tüzün et al. [10] showed significant learning gains among participants but highlighted the importance of the promotion of cooperative game play (with peer support) as opposed to competitive game-play (with no peer support). They concluded that co-operative game-play led to positive increases in both the participants' dispositions and academic performance, whereas competitive game-play only resulted in improved academic performance. A study by Ronimus et al. [18] on web-based game learning reported improvement in academic performance but cautioned that activities which are perceived by learners to have too high a degree of learning challenge can result in decreased interest in that activity.

A study of web-based geography game by Dourda et al. [5] showed considerable improvement in content knowledge and highlighted the need for cooperation with peers in achieving the learning outcomes. Dourda et al. [5] also found that teamwork, communication and collaboration inherent in game-playing enhance learners' satisfaction and enjoyment. A number of cognitive strategies were displayed, including abilities in skimming, scanning and translating web texts. Furthermore, it was noted that face-to-face compensation strategies (including gestures and facial expressions) were used in to overcome limitations in understanding the English language (their second-language) within the web-based content. A study by Garcia and Pacheco [17] further found that online game-based learning can improve understanding of key concepts and improve cognitive skills, through the use of collaborative elements in problem solving and by helping learners to build their own knowledge, and by providing direct contact with real problems.

In contrast, according to Kuo [12] learners' academic achievement can be improved by game and non-game learning environments. He found no significant difference for learning outcomes between online game-based learning and non–game based learning. The author concludes that design for both learning environment should be more fun to motivate learners.

6 Impact of Online Game-Based Learning/Gamification on Behaviours

Eight of the studies explore the impact of online games on learners' behaviour [5, 9–12, 17–19]. The results generally are positive with respect to learner behaviours. For instance, Kuo [12] found that learners visit online game environment after school time where no homework was required. Furthermore, the learners enjoy teamwork in the collaborative learning environment [5, 10]. Sandberg et al. [19] reported that learners spend more time within the online learning environment. Ronimus et al. [18] found the level of learning challenge increased playing time. Online games provided direct contact with real problems and provide better opportunities for promoting the participation by children [17]. On the other hand, Filsecker and Hickey [11] noted that gamification elements such as external rewards did not show any effect on learners' levels of engagement and playing time [18].

From a review of these studies, it is clear that online game-based learning/gamified learning can have positive impacts on learners' behavior, specifically in terms of increasing the level of engagement in learning activities within and beyond the classroom [5, 9, 10, 12, 17–19], but can also include features that negatively impact on engagement [11, 17].

The level of engagement of participants can be increased in online gaming through raising intrinsic motivation [8, 12], through inclusion of activities incorporating competition [14], through the inclusion of group work [5], and through self-directed activities that promote ownership and agency [5].

Participants in a study by Tüzün et al. [10] were so motivated by engagement in game-based learning that they had to be ejected on occasion from the computer room, and furthermore expressed the desire to play the game outside school time. In a study by Sandberg et al. [19], participants were motivated to engage in game-based learning in their own time by the use of smart-phone technologies platform. A study by Garcia and Pacheco [17] showed that the interactive platform provided direct contact with real problems and provides better opportunities for promoting participation of learners.

In a study by Hwang et al. [8], participants were found to be highly engaged in game-related activities that promoted intrinsic motivation. The level of intrinsic motivation was examined through flow-experiences. In the flow experience, participants fully engage with and are fully focused on the activity, and thus become intrinsically motivated to remain engaged in the activity (Csikszentmihalyi 1975, as cited by Hwang et al. [8]). The degree of learning challenge, control and enjoyment are core factors that can impact on the flow-experience, and thus, the levels of intrinsic motivation. In the study by Hwang et al. [8], the flow experience in the experimental group was shown to have significantly improved through the inclusion of 'instant interactions', 'explicit objectives' and 'dynamic challenges' within the game. A study by Ronimus et al. [18] showed high level of [learning] challenge increases playing time and concentration.

A study by Costu et al. [14] recommended the inclusion of competition features to increase levels of engagement by participants within game-based learning contexts.

In other studies, it was noted that the process of gaming promotes team-work and collaboration [5], and can result in increased desire to engage in learning at home [10].

Some studies have highlighted how particular features of online gaming/gamified learning environments can reduce levels of engagement. A study by Garcia and Pacheco [17] found that engagement can be negatively impacted by differing levels of abilities among group of participants (particularly when gaming occurs in the absence of supervision/outside of class-time). Moreover, Garcia and Pacheco [17] found that differing levels of computer skills resulted in participants preferring to collaborate face-to-face rather than within virtual contexts. Furthermore, a study by Ronimus et al. [18] found that while the presence of a reward can initially increase engagement, the effects of rewards as a motivating factor for engagement decreases over-time. Furthermore, this study found that shortcomings in the design of control, goal setting and feedback features in an online game may have contributed to lower participation levels within the online game. Finally, a study by Filsecker and Hickey [11] found no link between external rewards and disciplinary engagement.

7 Conclusion

This state-of-the-art review has examined the impacts of online game-based learning/gamified learning on learners' dispositions, cognitive abilities and behaviours, as well as the factors that have been found to contribute to changes in learners' dispositions, cognitive abilities and/or behaviours. The results demonstrate that online game-based learning/gamified learning has mainly positive effects on learners' dispositions, cognitive abilities and behaviours.

In the current review, the factors contributing to the successful implementation of game-based learning/gamified learning in enhancing young learners' dispositions include: motivational gaming features, social interaction (collaboration), immersive gaming environments, enjoyment elements, and some gamification elements (such as: feedback, leaderboards, and badges). Furthermore, the application of constructivist principles in game-design, inclusion of opportunities for social interaction (collaborative, cooperative) and integration of competitive features within game design have been shown to have positive impacts on learners' cognitive abilities and academic performance.

However, studies have also highlighted factors reducing levels of learners' engagement and motivation, and thus impact negatively on learners' dispositions, within games-based/gamified learning contexts. These include games with low levels of challenge and, conversely, games that promote competition between players, which have been shown to result in decreased levels of motivation, engagement or interest in disciplinary area; thus, impacting learners' dispositions. Interestingly, studies of games-based learning with too high a degree of challenge have also been shown to decrease learner interest and to negatively impact on their cognitive abilities and academic performance. Finally, game-designers need to be mindful that gamified reward system (whether attempting to motivate intrinsically or extrinsically) can positively, or negatively, impact on motivation levels of learners.

References

1. Prensky, M.: Digital natives, digital immigrants. Horizon **9**(5), 1–6 (2001)
2. Helsper, E., Eynon, R.: Digital natives: where is the evidence? Br. Educ. Res. J. **36**(3), 503–520 (2010)
3. Prensky, M.: Students as designers and creators of educational computer games: who else? Br. J. Educ. Technol. **39**(6), 1004–1019 (2008)
4. Ke, F., Grabowski, B.: Gameplaying for maths learning: cooperative or not? Br. J. Educ. Technol. **38**(2), 249–259 (2007)
5. Dourda, K., Bratitsis, T., Griva, E., Papadopoulou, P.: Content and language integrated learning through an online game in primary school: a case study. Electron. J. e-Learn. **12**(3), 243–258 (2014)
6. Su, C.H., Cheng, C.H.: A mobile gamification learning system for improving the learning motivation and achievements. J. Comput. Assist. Learn. **31**(3), 268–286 (2015)
7. Meluso, A., Zheng, M., Spires, H.A., Lester, J.: Enhancing 5th graders' science content knowledge and self-efficacy through game-based learning. Comput. Educ. **59**(2), 497–504 (2012)

8. Hwang, G.-J., Wu, P.-H., Chen, C.-C.: An online game approach for improving students' learning performance in web-based problem-solving activities. Comput. Educ. **59**(4), 1246–1256 (2012)
9. Bakker, M., Van Den Heuvel-Panhuizen, M., Robitzsch, A.: Effects of playing mathematics computer games on primary school students' multiplicative reasoning ability. Contemp. Educ. Psychol. **40**, 55–71 (2015)
10. Tuzun, H., Yilmaz-Soylu, M., Karakus, T., Inal, Y., Kizilkaya, G.: The effects of computer games on primary school students' achievement and motivation in geography learning. Comput. Educ. **52**(1), 68–77 (2009)
11. Filsecker, M., Hickey, D.T.: A multilevel analysis of the effects of external rewards on elementary students' motivation, engagement and learning in an educational game. Comput. Educ. **75**, 136–148 (2014)
12. Kuo, M.-J.: How does an online game based learning environment promote students' intrinsic motivation for learning natural science and how does it affect their learning outcomes? In: Proceedings of the First IEEE International Workshop on Digital Game and Intelligent Toy Enhanced Learning, Taiwan, pp. 135–143. IEEE (2007)
13. Sung, H.-Y., Hwang, G.-J.: A collaborative game-based learning approach to improving students' learning performance in science courses. Comput. Educ. **63**, 43–51 (2013)
14. Costu, S., Aydin, S., Filiz, M.: Students' conceptions about browser-game-based learning in mathematics education: TTNetvitamin case. Procedia – Soc. Behav. Sci. **1**(1), 1848–1852 (2009)
15. Serin, O.: The effects of the computer-based instruction on the achievement and problem solving skills of the science and technology students. Turk. Online J. Educ. Technol. **10**(1), 183–201 (2011)
16. Chuang, T.-Y., Chen, W.-F.: Effect of computer-based video games on children: an experimental study. Educ. Technol. Soc. **12**(2), 1–10 (2009)
17. Garcia, I., Pacheco, C.: A constructivist computational platform to support mathematics education in elementary school. Comput. Educ. **66**, 25–39 (2013)
18. Ronimus, M., Kujala, J., Tolvanen, A., Lyytinen, H.: Children's engagement during digital game-based learning of reading: the effects of time, rewards, and challenge. Comput. Educ. **71**, 237–246 (2014)
19. Sandberg, J., Maris, M., De Geus, K.: Mobile English learning: an evidence-based study with fifth graders. Comput. Educ. **57**(1), 1334–1347 (2011)
20. Vos, N., Van Der Meijden, H., Denessen, E.: Effects of constructing versus playing an educational game on learner motivation and deep learning strategy use. Comput. Educ. **56**(1), 127–137 (2011)

For ARGument's Sake! The Pros and Cons of Alternate Reality Gaming in Higher Education

Katerina Economides(✉)

Dublin City University, DCU St. Patrick's Campus, Dublin, Ireland
katerina.economides2@mail.dcu.ie

Abstract. This paper explores the potential of Alternate Reality Games, a type of Game-Based Learning experience, within higher education. The discourse opens by explaining the essence of ARGs; it then moves to present the findings from research in this domain, highlighting key benefits and challenges in using ARGs in higher education.

Keywords: Alternate Reality Games · Higher education
Game-Based Learning

1 Introduction

The benefits of digital games for education have been investigated in depth for at least the last two decades, with a number of researchers and educators vindicating games of all kinds and elevating them as tools for learning [1–3]. Within the Game-Based Learning field, one game format in particular deserves special attention due to its immersiveness and originality: the Alternate Reality Game (ARG). This paper will discuss the potential of ARGs within higher education. The first part of the paper will provide a short description of the game type and present a few examples of educational or serious ARGs, i.e. ARGs that have not been designed predominantly for entertainment purposes [4]. The paper then moves to present the findings from research in this domain, highlighting key benefits and challenges in using ARGs in higher education.

2 Essence of Alternate Reality Gaming

To understand what an ARG is, it is important to clarify a few terms that sound very similar, but cannot be used interchangeably: Augmented Reality, Virtual Reality and Alternate Reality.

In Augmented Reality the physical reality appears to be extended, expanded or elevated via the use of technology. As Olbrish [5, pp. 73–74] puts it, in Augmented Reality Games (also abbreviated as ARGs) 'there is a technology overlay on reality that contributes to play'. One recent example would the popular location-based game *Pokémon Go*, where players can interact with virtual characters situated in real life

A. Tatnall and M. Webb (Eds.): WCCE 2017, IFIP AICT 515, pp. 64–69, 2017.
https://doi.org/10.1007/978-3-319-74310-3_8

environments, with the use of their smartphone. Virtual Reality, on the other hand, is not a mere overlay of technology on the physical reality, but a complete simulation of reality facilitated by electronic equipment, such as virtual reality headsets. According to Cobbet [6] 'the basic difference between virtual and augmented reality is that the former completely locks you into the world, while the latter puts stuff on top of it'.

An Alternate Reality Game (ARG) does not *have* to use augmented or virtual technologies, although some ARG creators may choose to use them as part of the game. As the term 'alternate' suggests, an ARG creates a *different version of reality*, with the use of fiction. It can be defined as an interactive narrative 'that plays out in real time, using real communications media to make it seem as though the story were really happening' [7, p. 19]. The entry point to an ARG is traditionally called 'rabbit hole', as it is usually cryptic and acts as a 'hook' that draws players into the story. Once they enter the 'rabbit hole', ARG players are involved in a series of challenges that are deployed both online and in the real world [8]. In these immersive quests the participants navigate through real and fictional websites and social media profiles, decode encrypted messages, solve mind-boggling puzzles, gather clues and interact with fictional characters via email, chat or SMS, in order to progress through the story and resolve a mystery or provide a solution to a problem. For example, in one of the first successful ARGs, *The Beast*, the creators hid clues in the promotional material of the sci-fi drama *A.I. Artificial Intellingence*. After trying to make sense of the clues by searching online, the players uncovered the mysterious death of *Evan Chan*, one of the fictional characters of the game. *The Beast*'s story unveiled via a number of fictional websites, videos, audio messages, clues and puzzles that the players had to solve to progress through the game.

Apart from the numerous ARGs within the entertainment realm that are out of the scope of this paper, a number of ARGs have been created within the last decade for education and training, as well as for humanitarian reasons: to raise awareness for current social issues, to encourage empathy and to promote positive change. Among others:

- *EVOKE*[1]: A ten-week ARG where the players have to come up with creative solutions to social problems, such as poverty and water crisis.
- *World Without Oil*[2]: A game that asks the players to imagine how the first 32 weeks of a global oil crisis would be.
- *Traces of Hope*[3]: a game by the British Red Cross about a Ugandan teen that was separated from his mother after their village was attacked.
- *Tower of Babel*: A game designed to motivate secondary level students to learn foreign languages [9].
- *Plunkett's Pages*: An ARG helping students between the ages 14–15 discover the story of Ireland's 1916 Easter Rising [10].
- *The Source*: An ARG developed to introduce to public school students (aged 13–18) sensitive topics, such as sexual health, sexual orientation and homophobia [11].

---

[1] http://www.urgentevoke.com/.

[2] http://writerguy.com/wwo/metahome.htm.

[3] http://blogs.redcross.org.uk/podcasts/2008/10/traces-of-hope/.

It is evident in the literature that serious efforts have been made to harvest the educational potential of ARGs at different age groups and various learning fields. Nonetheless, the pedagogical benefits of the ARG have not been fully explored yet in a higher education context. More specifically, ARGs have been implemented in higher education only within the last decade. In the following section, we will see the main ARG studies that have been deployed at tertiary level, which will trigger a discussion on the evident strengths and weaknesses of the game when it is utilized in higher education.

3 AR Gaming in Higher Education: A Discussion on Pros and Cons

ARGs have been implemented in third level education a small number of times, in order to achieve various learning goals, such as: To support student induction during orientation week [8, 12]; to introduce freshmen students to library resources and services [13]; to promote physical activity [14]; to develop rhetorical and digital literacies [15]; to teach new media literacies and storytelling strategies [16]; to facilitate Computer Science education [17].

3.1 The Strengths

One quickly notices the variety in disciplines and learning goals in the aforementioned list of ARG studies. The diversity of ARG research in higher education suggests that ARGs are a highly versatile game format, which can be customized to fit the learning objectives of different educational disciplines. By adjusting the storyline, alongside the aesthetic and pedagogic design, it appears that ARGs can meet a variety of learning goals: from developing transferable skills such as socialization [8] to teaching complex techniques and concepts [17]. Other reasons why some educators in the reviewed studies seem to choose the ARG format, instead of other game types, appear to be of a practical nature: low development costs and accessible technology [3, 12]. ARGs utilize existing and relatively affordable technology, and so do not require the high costs of commercial game development. Moreover, due to their immersive nature, ARGs present an opportunity to apply theoretical knowledge in 'real-life' contexts, as students play as themselves instead of assuming a fictional game character [3] and can apply their skills and knowledge to resolve real-world problems [17, 18]. In fact, a number of studies suggest that there is real educational benefit in students applying pre-learned skills to design their *own* ARGs. Researchers have adopted this approach for several reasons: to inspire pre-service teachers in using ARGs in science teaching [19]; to practice multimedia design [18]; to teach new media literacies and effective storytelling practices [16]; to promote complex problem-solving [20]; to facilitate learning of computer hardware, software and applications [21]. It is evident in the literature that educational approaches where students first learn and then apply the knowledge in their ARG design can be quite effective for learning [20].

ARGs are designed as collaborative experiences, which in theory holds potential for social learning within educational contexts. The literature suggests that ARGs can indeed foster student collaboration and teamwork: There is evidence that ARGs can help to create team spirit [17], and that during ARG experiences students support and encourage each other [12], and can recognize the benefits of working as part of a team [20]. Moreover, the ARG experience may also have positive effects on the relationship between students and instructors, as it can help the former build a connection and a bond with students [16].

The majority of ARG studies in higher education offer preliminary evidence that the game format can be effective in facilitating learning. Indicatively: By the end of Hakulinen's study, the participants had learned many Computer Science concepts through the ARG puzzles [17]. Johnston et al. [14] found that the ARG had a positive effect on the students' physical activity. Battles et al. [13] found that the players had increased knowledge about the university library after completing the ARG. Moreover, the game format appears to be a fun way to engage students with the learning material. The participants appear to enjoy, among others, the elements of play [21], the sense of fun and the feeling that they are part of something special [12], and, lastly, the element of mystery in the narrative [13].

3.2 The Weaknesses

Despite its many advantages, the ARG format does not come without challenges. In fact, a number of limitations have been identified in the literature. The researchers have encountered low participation levels due to the cryptic nature of the game format [8], gradual reduction of engagement levels [12], as well as bias against games, which would be perceived as a waste of time by a number of students [8]. It is worth noting, however, that the gradual decrease in engagement during the ARGs could be an indication that shorter interventions would better hold participants' attention, engagement levels [13].

In terms of student participation, it becomes apparent via the literature that educational ARGs may be more effective when they are incorporated in the university curriculum. ARGs are traditionally voluntary and cryptic experiences that do not advertise themselves as games. This ARG design principle is known among ARG designers as 'This Is Not A Game' or simply TINAG [22]. While this principle seems to have been successful in higher education in one of the reviewed studies [17], others express concerns on the suitability of the cryptic nature of ARGs, as it can result in low participation levels as students may simply not be able to find the route into the game [8]. The literature suggests that a game-type like the ARG, which requires high levels of motivation and dedication to progress, would work best when it forms part of the formal curriculum and assessment [23]. Moreover, ARGs implemented in a 'controlled' environment potentially make it easier for instructors to assess students' performance.

Concerns are also expressed among researchers in regards to the re-playability of the game type. The design and development of an ARG appears to be a challenging and time-consuming endeavour, and the fact that it is played in real-time makes it difficult for the creators to reproduce it [13]. In addition, despite the efforts put in ARG design, student participation cannot be taken for granted (in voluntary ARGs) and the overall success of the game cannot be guaranteed [8, 13, 17].

4 The Verdict

This paper presented the main advantages and disadvantages of Alternate Reality Gaming in higher education, as they emerge from published research studies in the field. The studies discussed offer preliminary evidence that ARGs carry various educational benefits for quality learning within higher education, but their success cannot be guaranteed. ARGs are highly customizable games that can be applied in various contexts and themes, but there are several limiting factors that educators must consider when implementing ARGs for learning. Despite the challenges, researchers still recognize the potential of pedagogical ARGs and encourage further research in the area [8, 16, 17]. Further studies by the author will help determine which techno-pedagogic designs can limit the weaknesses and harvest the strengths of ARGs, for more effective ARG interventions in higher education.

References

1. Bowman, R.F.: A pac-man theory of motivation: tactical implications for classroom instruction. Educ. Technol. **22**(9), 14–17 (1982)
2. Gee, J.P.: What Video Games Have to Teach Us About Learning and Literacy. Palgrave, New York City (2003)
3. Lee, T.: This is not a game: alternate reality gaming and its potential for learning. FutureLab (2006). http://archive.futurelab.org.uk/resources/publications-reports-articles/web-articles/Web-Article477
4. Michael, D.R., Chen, S.L.: Serious Games: Games That Educate, Train, and Inform. Muska & Lipman/Premier-Trade, New York (2005)
5. Olbrish P.K.: Immersive Learning. Designing for Authentic Practice. American Society for Training & Development (ASTD), USA (2013)
6. Cobbet R.: Virtual vs Augmented: Which Alternate Reality is for You? Techradar: The Home of Technology, 24 October (2015). http://www.techradar.com/news/gaming/virtual-vs-augmented-which-alternate-reality-is-for-you–1307470
7. Philips, A.: A Creator's Guide to Transmedia Storytelling: How to Captivate and Engage Audiences Across Multiple Platforms. McGraw Hill, New York City (2012)
8. Whitton, N., Jones, R., Wilson, S., Whitton, P.: Alternate reality games as learning environments for student induction. Interact. Learn. Environ. **22**(3), 243–252 (2014)
9. Connolly, T.M., Stansfield, M., Hainey, T.: An alternate reality game for language learning: ARGuing for multilingual motivation. Comput. Educ. **57**(1), 1389–1415 (2011)
10. Lynch, R., Mallon, B., Connolly, C.: Revisiting history: using alternate reality games to tell a century old tale. In: Proceedings of the European Conference on Games-Based Learning, vol. 1 (2014)
11. Bouris, A., Mancino, J., Jagoda, P., Hill, B.J., Gilliam, M.: Reinvigorating adolescent sexuality education through alternate reality games: the case of the source. Sex Educ. **16**, 353–367 (2015)
12. Piatt, K.: Using alternate reality games to support first year induction with ELGG. Campus-Wide Inf. Syst. **26**(4), 313–322 (2009)
13. Battles, J., Glenn, V., Shedd, L.: Rethinking the library game: creating an alternate reality with social media. J. Web Librariansh. **5**(2), 114–131 (2011)

14. Johnston, J.D., Massey, A.P., Marker-Hoffman, R.L.: Using an alternate reality game to increase physical activity and decrease obesity risk of college students, vol. 6(4), pp. 828–838 (2012)
15. Nelson, S.: Crossing battle lines: teaching multimodal literacies through alternate reality games. Kairos, **17**(3) (2013). http://kairos.technorhetoric.net/17.3/praxis/nelson-et-al/index.html
16. Chess, S., Booth, P.: Lessons down a rabbit hole: Alternate reality gaming in the classroom. New Media Soc. **16**(6), 1002–1017 (2014)
17. Hakulinen, L.: Gameful approaches for computer science education: from gamification to alternate reality games, Doctoral thesis. Aalto University (2015)
18. de Beer, K., Holmner, M.: The design of an alternate reality game as capstone course in a multimedia post-graduate degree. In: Proceedings of the IATUL Conferences (2013). http://docs.lib.purdue.edu/iatul/2013/papers/30/
19. Bellocchi, A.: Practical considerations for integrating alternate reality gaming into science education. Teach. Sci. J. Aust. Sci. Teach. Assoc. **58**(4), 43–46 (2012)
20. Dondlinger, M.J., Mcleod, J.K.: Solving real world problems with alternate reality gaming: student experiences in the global village playground capstone course design. Interdisc. J. Problem-Based Learn. **9**(2), 3 (2015)
21. Warren S., Wakefield J.S.: Simulations, games and virtual worlds as mindtools. In: Spector J.M., Lockee B.B., Smaldino S.E., Herring M.C. (eds) Learning, Problem Solving, and Mindtools. Essays in Honor of David Jonassen, pp. 66–87, Routledge, New York, London (2013)
22. Philips, A., Martin A.: Business Models. In: Martin, A., Thomson, B., Chatfield, T. (eds.) 2006 Alternate Reality Games White Paper. International Game Developers Association (2006)
23. Moseley, A., Whitton, N., Culver, J., Piatt, K.: Motivation in alternate reality gaming environments and implications for learning. In: Proceedings of the 3rd European Conference on Games Based Learning, pp. 279–286 (2009). https://lra.le.ac.uk/handle

Large Effect Size Studies of Computers in Schools: *Calculus for Kids* and *Science-ercise*

Andrew E. Fluck[1(✉)], Dev Ranmuthugala[1], C. K. H. Chin[1], Irene Penesis[1], Jacky Chong[1], and Yang Yang[2]

[1] University of Tasmania, Launceston, Australia
{andrew.fluck, c.chin}@utas.edu.au
[2] University of Tasmania, Hobart, Australia

Abstract. This report describes two computer-based interventions in Year 6 (age 11–12 years) classrooms. The interventions positioned sophisticated software alongside multimedia learning materials to teach topics from curriculum objectives many years ahead of these students' chronological ages. These were transformative interventions (Fluck, 2003), changing what and how students learn when using computers. Students solved real world problems using integral calculus (Calculus for Kids) and studied both special relativity and quantum mechanics (Science-ercise). Calculus for Kids was conducted with 478 students in 26 schools from five Australian states; and Science-ercise was conducted with 187 students in five Tasmanian schools. Student learning achievement was measured using calibrated items in a post-test, with the students able to use the sophisticated software during the test. The results showed a majority of students exhibited learning achievements 4–6 years above their chronological age when using suitable computer tools. The studies bring into question the correct way to calculate effect sizes for such high impact interventions. Relying on Glass et al. (1981), we estimate this transformative use of computers in education achieved an effect size >4.0, well above Hattie's (2007) hinge point of 0.4 for a significant innovation. This approach offers a pathway to shorten the time between knowledge generation and its incorporation in school curricula.

Keywords: Computers · Effect size · Calculus · Advanced physics
Primary schools

1 Introduction

School curricula can change at a very slow pace. They are controlled by communities, politicians, educators and others, rather than content experts, so naturally innovations take time to be adopted. In contrast, technology and science is advancing at a very rapid rate [1]. Disparities between the lived world of children embedded in artefacts from recent knowledge and the school curriculum can lead to tensions for them and their teachers. For example, 2005 saw the celebration of the centenary of Einstein's publication of special theory of relativity [2], but this important scientific idea is rarely found in primary school classrooms. One way to bring new knowledge into schools may be to use computers. However, computers are not having the desired impact in education.

A. Tatnall and M. Webb (Eds.): WCCE 2017, IFIP AICT 515, pp. 70–80, 2017.
https://doi.org/10.1007/978-3-319-74310-3_9

A recent OECD report [3] shows a weak inverse relationship between computer investments in schools and learning achievement measured by PISA tests. This makes for a wicked problem in education.

2 Literature

Perkins [4] provided the concept of 'person-plus' to embody the shared cognition of a learner assisted by their notebook. In our projects, we acknowledge this notebook could be a notebook computer, or any kind of specialised electronic assistive device. This 'person-plus' view supports arguments for open book assessment, because it is closer to real-world problem solving. The assistive device improves information retrieval and accuracy, and Perkins argues this leads to higher order cognitive functioning. By extension, a student using modern digital technology can solve problems that are far more complex than traditionally expected. This models human adoption of other mind tools such as language, numbering systems and so on. Moursund [5] extended this thinking to divide problems into those which are more readily solved by humans alone, by computers alone, and those which are best solved by humans working in combination with computers. Increasingly we face the latter, so it makes good sense to selectively school our children to work in this mode where it is useful and appropriate.

Such an approach runs counter to traditional educational practice. The aim of most educational innovations is to teach the content set in the standard curriculum for a class of students, in a better or more engaging way. If computers are to radically transform the curriculum, it appears to be necessary to use them to teach content which is suited to their use. New technology often makes old methods redundant, so to teach handwriting with a computer keyboard would be unlikely to succeed. If our projects aspired to deliver novel content to Year 6 (age 11) students, the criteria for success would have to be different from 'teaching better' or 'more engagement'. The statistic of 'effect size' is often Cohen's *d*, but can also be a *Z-score* or an *odds-ratio* [6]. Effect size is the accepted measure of educational impact (see Fig. 1). Hattie's [7] meta-study of different classroom interventions established an effect size of 0.4 as the 'hinge point' at which a significant impact could be determined.

Fluck's transformative use of computers in schools [10] was the focus for this study. The highest effect size for transformative ways of using computers in class reported by Puentedura [9] was 1.6, relating to 'redefinition' activities. It is already well known that, in the right circumstances, children can use computers to achieve results that many observers see as 'beyond their years'. Papert and others were demonstrating this with Logo in the late 70s and Scardamalia and Bereiter with CSILE in the late 80s and 90s. Research teams have frequently shown outstanding effects when using well-designed software in properly supported educational contexts. We undertook this research with the specific intent to seek high effect size learning transformation through computer use.

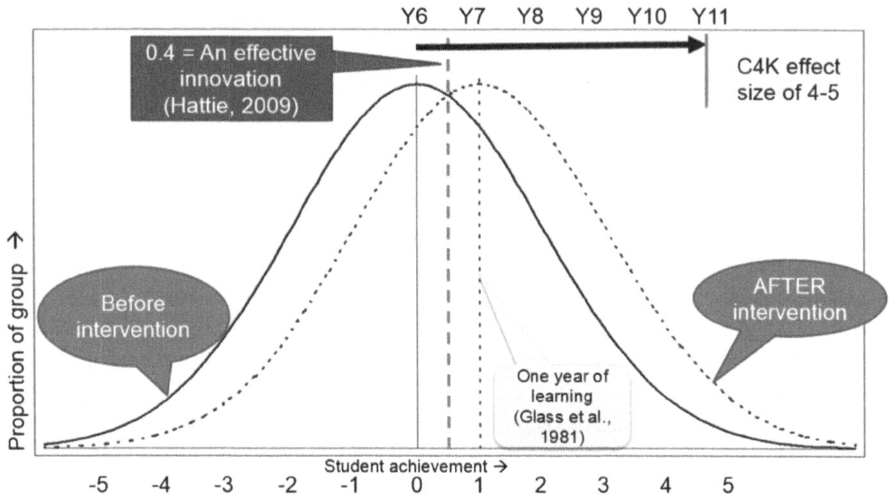

Fig. 1. Effect size of learning improvement (intervention or age) (after [8]). This also shows the impact of Calculus for Kids

3 Methodology

Our main conceptual tools were Rogers' [11] theory of innovation adoption, the non-template problem-solving method of Allen [12], a realistic mathematics education approach [13], and a methodology we are developing on the transformational use of ICT in school education which combines professional software tools with multimedia instructional materials.

In both projects described in this report, the basic design for the research was an intervention method using a cyclic approach, consisting of four stages: produce/modify learning materials, train the teachers, conduct intervention activity in schools, and assess results. The cycle was ongoing, ensuring continuous updating and modifications to meet changes and findings. We recruited schools for the projects from several Australian states, ensuring a wide range of ICSEA (Index of Community Socio-Educational Advantage) scores. The ICSEA is constructed so that the average score is 1000.

Local facilitators were chosen by each participating school and attended training sessions at the University of Tasmania. In subsequent years we brought previously-trained facilitators back for these sessions to provide feedback on their local implementation and induct new facilitators joining the project. This ensured new learning from each round was handed on to the next. This process was used each year to introduce the teaching techniques we developed to newly participating schools. Since we acquired perpetual licences for the software, schools could participate for up to three years. This gave us the opportunity to investigate the same process repeatedly used in the same school over several years to see if they obtained consistent results. For both projects, teachers received teaching materials and software, which will now be described.

The Australian Research Council funded the *Calculus for Kids* project. It taught Year 6 students to solve real world problems with integral calculus using computer algebra software. In the Australian curriculum, calculus is taught in Years 11 and 12 [14]. The teaching materials for *Calculus for Kids* comprised multimedia presentations (in PowerPoint); MAPLE workbook files with worked examples and practice questions; and PDF documents containing more demanding practice questions. The software was the computer algebra package MAPLE, installed on each student's computer workstation. The multimedia presentations included videos explaining concepts e.g. how algebra relates to more regular shapes and actions rarely met in real life, while calculus relates to more real, and less regular, shapes and actions. These explanatory materials gradually made way for operational skills training for the MAPLE program, and then showed how the principles and notation of integral calculus could be implemented by using the software. Topics included graphing functions, equations for parabolas, calculating definite integrals, areas between curves and of regions bounded by several curves using integrals. By the end of the twelfth lesson, students were able to solve real world problems using integral calculus by operating their computers. This learning achievement was assessed in the final thirteenth lesson through a post-test based upon the first year university engineering calculus examination, to which students responded using their computers running MAPLE. An example post-test item can be seen in Fig. 2.

A tent maker wants to know how much fabric is needed for the end section of her new design:

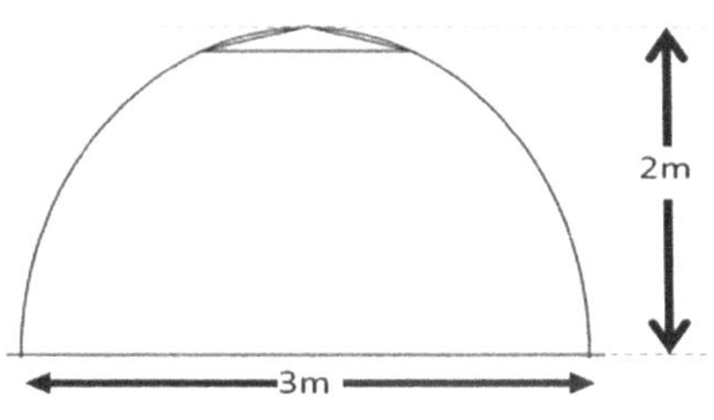

Find the equation to describe the parabolic shape (using $y = a(x - h)^2 + b$) and determine the amount of fabric for her.

Fig. 2. Post-test item from Calculus for Kids

The Ian Potter Foundation funded the *Science-ercise* project. The teaching materials were delivered as a similar set of multimedia presentations and a printed booklet for each student, together with some practical equipment such as constant velocity model cars and a parabola cannon. The software in this case comprised an Excel notebook file or its equivalent for iOS devices such as iPads. The file contained a worksheet for each of the six activities to simplify calculations. These activities included constant velocity motion, parabolic motion, double-slit optical interference fringes and the twins' paradox from special relativity. At the completion of the learning sequence, students undertook a short test to measure learning achievement assisted by their computers running the same software. For Science-ercise, the post-test items were modified from Tasmanian Certificate of Education Physics university entrance examinations (Year 11/12). See Fig. 3.

> Early in the morning, sunlight streams through an east facing kitchen window and projects an image of the window onto the western wall of the kitchen 2.5m away. The window is covered by a mesh security screen which has wires 1.3mm thick.
>
> Assuming sunlight has a mean wavelength of 560nm, what is the spacing of the fringes from a single wire projected onto the western wall?

Fig. 3. Post-test item from Science-ercise.

4 Results

Both the interventions in this study were designed to elicit learning outcomes from Year 6 students (11–12 years in age) comparable to those normally expected from much older students. The instruments used to validate this level of achievement were post-activity tests containing items from tests taken by such older students.

The classes selected for participation in these two projects were mixed-gender and mixed ability from a range of socio-economic backgrounds. *Calculus for Kids* was conducted in 26 schools from five states over seven years; and *Science-ercise* has involved 187 students in 5 Tasmanian schools over 13 months. Table 1 provides demographic data for the projects, establishing the representative nature of the sample populations.

Table 1. Demographic data for the interventions

	Calculus for Kids	Science-ercise
Male	263	81
Female	215	106
Total	478	187
Minimum ICSEA	873	890
Maximum ICSEA	1197	1032
Mean ICSEA (s.d.)	1041 (83.26)	994.82 (50.10)
Mean age on the day of the post-test (s.d.)	12.17 (0.98)	12.23 (0.21)
Minimum age	9.97	11.56
Maximum age	14.95	12.83

The key question was the extent to which participating students demonstrated high-level learning achievement in the post-tests. Normally at these levels (Year 11/12, first year degree courses), a pass mark is considered to be 50%, so the proportion of students attaining this level of achievement was the key determination to be made (see Table 2).

Table 2. Proportion of students achieving a pass mark

	Calculus for Kids	Science-ercise
Mean post-test score (s.d.)	67.55 (18.39)	48.13 (26.98)
Proportion of students with post-test scores >50% (s.d.)	82.6% (18%)	53.00% (26.9%)

The results show that a large proportion of students in the *Calculus for Kids* project achieved a pass mark on questions about practical uses of integral calculus. The Science-ercise project showed a bare majority of students achieved a pass mark. Anecdotally, we got the impression some schools in the latter project found the material more demanding and in some case were not able to finish the sequence of lessons.

Calculating an effect size for interventions such as these presents several methodological difficulties. Traditionally, effect size is calculated as Cohen's *d* based upon the difference in achievement obtained from the same or calibrated pre- and post-tests. In these projects, there were strong pedagogical reasons for omitting any pre-test. Firstly, the topics were outside the prescribed curriculum at these age levels, and therefore there was no reason to expect any knowledge of the topics whatsoever from the participating students. Secondly, the projects were constructed to generate enthusiasm and confidence for students tackling 'hard' concepts. This objective would have been compromised by starting the teaching sequence with a test highly likely to confound and disappoint most participants. As it was, the data show the students were drawn from populations with close to average ICSEA measures of social advantage, and the majority of participants achieved a post-test score pass mark.

The instruments used to measure learning achievement before and after the innovation are clearly crucial. Ideally, effect size is calculated by asking students to complete the same achievement assessment before and after the treatment/innovation. However, this is not always possible, desirable or feasible. Nor is it necessary. All that is required is that the measurements map onto a common scale. We chose to map the achievements of the students **onto an academic year level scale**. For the pre-test measures we used the national calibrated numeracy test results (NAPLAN). The post-test scores were mapped onto the calibrated first year engineering bachelor's course, and therefore to Year 13 on the common scale (university entrance occurs after Year 12). To calculate the effect size for *Calculus for Kids*, we initially found the correlation between pre-treatment academic year level (based on numeracy scores on standardised national tests) and the post-treatment year levels. This came to 0.56 with $p = 0.048$ which is statistically significant. Similar work was done with *Science-ercise.*

We used the conventional method for calculating the intervention effect size in the absence of a pre-test by mapping participants onto a common scale before and after the learning intervention (treatment) as shown in Fig. 4, and then calculating Cohen's *d*. This produced an effect size of 25.53 for *Calculus for Kids*, and 11.45 for *Science-ercise*. These are very high effect sizes.

In our second approach to determine effect sizes, we relied on Glass et al.'s [15] finding that normal learning progress is one standard deviation per year. Therefore, an intervention that produces learning achievements 5–6 years ahead of chronological age, equates to 5–6 standard deviations of progress, corresponding to an effect size of 6.17

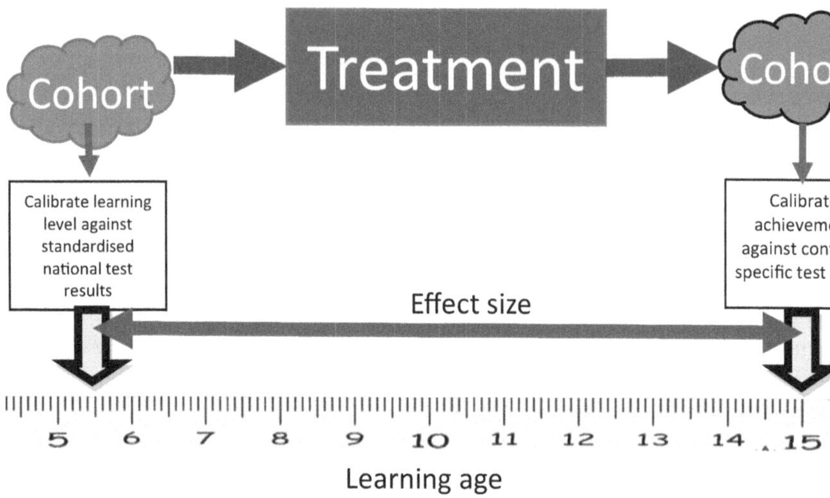

Fig. 4. Effect size from mapping to a learning age scale

in this case. This is well above Hattie's hinge point for a significant intervention. The *Calculus for Kids* intervention achieved an effect size greater than 4.0 [16]. Our *Science-ercise* project achieved similar success [17]. These effect sizes are over ten times the size of Hattie's hinge point for a significant intervention.

Looking further at effect sizes for non-traditional interventions, Wiliam [18] modified Glass's conjecture in 2004 by stating that learning achievement of "one third of a grade [was] equivalent to a standardized effect size of 0.21". Therefore, one academic year level would be equivalent to an effect size of 0.63. It seems this relationship declines with student age. Wiliam described this decline by saying "one year's growth in achievement typically ranges from around 0.25 to 0.4 standard deviations" and "for the NAEP tests, one year's growth is only about one fourth of a standard deviation". We adopted a conservative value of 0.3 SD per year of schooling. Even at 1.85, the effect size for the *Calculus for Kids* innovation is 4.6 times Hattie's hinge point of 0.4 (Table 3).

Table 3. Effect size measures for the two interventions.

	Calculus for Kids	Science-ercise
Mean pre-treatment academic year level (s.d.)	6.47 (0.32)	6.35 (0.05)
Mean post-test academic year level (s.d.)	12.64 (0.12)	11.45 (0.27)
Correlation (p)	0.56 (0.048)	0.60 (0.4)
Effect size:		
Cohen's d	25.53	26.26
Glass	6.17	5.10
Wiliam	1.85	1.53

5 Discussion

These projects have provided evidence that children as young as 10 can use computers to demonstrate higher order learning achievement when freed from contemporary curriculum and reporting constraints. The power of this evidence is increased by the geographical and social diversity of the participants, providing generalisation of the results and impetus for radical reform of learning. Policy makers require these practical demonstrations to inform the community and make political decisions about the content of schooling which are palatable and feasible.

It is important to discuss how best to calculate an effect size for these transformative uses of computers in school education. There are important issues of methodology to consider. We have been asked if our Year 6 students really understood integral calculus. Our response is they generally passed the university test designed to assess this specific learning achievement. A counter-argument is they had assistance, in the form of the computer software they used when solving the post-test problems. In return, we might argue the conventional students were allowed to use writing implements unavailable to our participants. It is evident we have no clear way to think about the impact of computers when transforming curriculum, but a clear imperative to do so given their pervasive use in professional and business life. In this paper we have applied three reasonable ways to calculate the effect size of the intervention. Even the lowest calculation provided a quantum almost four time the 'hinge point' for an effective innovation.

One way to view our work is to say the operational skills of operating MAPLE to solve definite integrals replaced the more complex operational skills conventionally taught in manipulating integral calculus formulae. Our participants needed to understand conventional mathematics notation, and demonstrated this by placing the correct values and symbols into the equations they constructed using the software. The computer did the work of actually crunching the numbers to evaluate the compiled expressions. To that extent, the students demonstrated the higher order learning achievement of solving real world problems using integral calculus. They were assisted by software able to undertake symbolic manipulation which freed them from the labour of lower order mechanical evaluation. We do not argue they showed higher cognitive function, just higher learning achievement.

We anticipate that project impact over time will be considerable. With younger students proven capable of higher order learning achievement through the sensitive use of computers, curriculum reform can bring current knowledge forward in schooling, leaving room and time for new ideas and socialisation. This will lead to a more advanced workforce capable of greater participation in the knowledge economy. The benefits will therefore be both economic and social.

It is important to note the important flow-on benefits of these projects. We have only demonstrated accelerated learning achievement of 4+ years with primary school students. However, similar processes could be put in place at other educational levels. For instance, first year undergraduates will be able to achieve learning outcomes at the Masters or even initial Ph.D. candidate level. Year 10 students will be empowered to demonstrate understanding from first year degree courses. We seek to engender this quantum leap in learning in areas where humans working with computers can perform better than either alone. Our work with Year 6 students can be a lever for future work at all educational levels.

6 Conclusion

These studies have provided in-principle demonstrations that children as young as ten years old can master advanced concepts through the use of sophisticated software. Participating students were drawn from a wide geographical range and a variety of socio-economic backgrounds, indicating the generality of the findings. However, the topics were strictly mathematical and scientific, so there is a need to widen the subject base to substantiate a general claim the curriculum should be re-thought. To broaden the subject base, we propose further research to build on this foundation.

A follow on study will explore curriculum redefinition as a way forward with important inspiration from the Europe-wide iTEC project that demonstrated higher order thinking in learning through envisioning classrooms of the future and established a bank of new teaching ideas [19].

Such a study will be foundational to a broader demonstration of curriculum transformation using computers. It will focus on the use of computational thinking throughout the curriculum, conceived as in Fig. 5.

As in the projects this report has described, we would continue to work with Year 6 students across Australia, using short effective interventions and specialist application software. While the project will provide starting point activities comprising six lessons for each of eight subjects, schools will participate in guided workshops that will generate specific plans appropriate for their own students. Key elements in each of the interventions will be:

- Short in duration (typically 5–7 lessons);
- Students to use a single computer software application for each intervention, generally free of cost to schools;
- Learning outcome will be a significant departure from the existing curriculum (4–6 years in advance of chronological age);

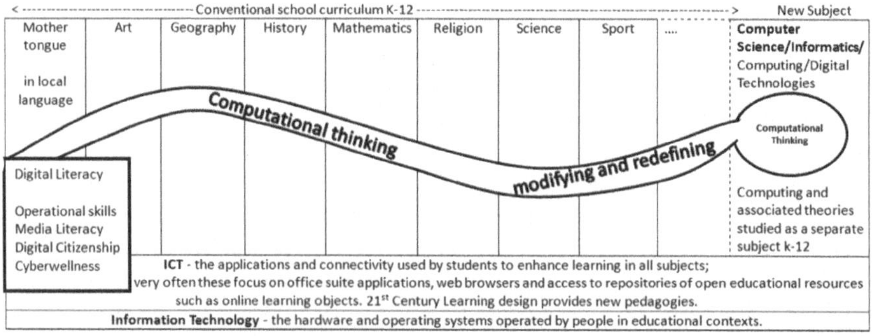

Fig. 5. Curriculum redefinition through computational thinking (after [20])

- A post-test of learning achievement accompanied by pre- and post-activity attitudinal surveys. For the latter we will modify the Attitudes toward mathematics inventory [21] to make it subject-generic and link with our previous work; also, the Mathematics and technology attitude scale [22, 23] will be similarly adapted.

This broader base, if successful, would provide strong evidence, through effect sizes of four or more, for curriculum redefinition. We can only hope this will be extended by inference from Year 6 to both older and younger students.

Acknowledgements. The authors would like to thank The Australian Research Council [under grant LP130101088], the University of Tasmania, the Ian Potter Foundation and Australian Scientific & Engineering Solutions Pty Ltd for financial assistance to support these studies.

References

1. Kurzweil, R.: Essay: The Law of Accelerating Returns (2001). http://www.kurzweilai.net/the-law-of-accelerating-returns
2. Einstein, A.: Zur Elektrodynamik bewegter Körper. Ann. Phys. **17**, 891 (1905). English translation On the Electrodynamics of Moving Bodies by Megh Nad Saha (1920)
3. OECD: how computers are related to students' performance, in students, computers and learning: making the connection. OECD Publishing, Paris (2015). http://dx.doi.org/10.1787/9789264239555-9-en
4. Perkins, D.N.: Person-plus: a distributed view of thinking and learning. In: Salomon, G. (ed.) Distributed Cognitions: Psychological and Educational Considerations, pp. 88–110. Cambridge University Press, Cambridge (1993)
5. Moursund, D.: Introduction to Information and Communication Technology in Education. University of Oregon, Eugene (2005). http://darkwing.uoregon.edu/~moursund/Books/ICT/ICTBook.pdf
6. Altman, D.G.: Practical Statistics for Medical Research. Chapman and Hall, London (1991)
7. Hattie, J.: Visible Learning: A Synthesis of Over 800 Meta-Analyses Relating to Achievement. Routledge, Abingdon (2009)
8. Coe, R.: It's the effect size, stupid: what effect size is and why it is important. Paper Presented at the Annual Conference of the British Educational Research Association. University of Exeter, England, 12–14 September (2002). http://www.leeds.ac.uk/educol/documents/00002182.htm
9. Puentedura, R.: SAMR: a brief Introduction (2015). http://hippasus.com/rrpweblog/archives/2015/10/SAMR_ABriefIntro.pdf
10. Fluck, A.: Integration or transformation? A cross-national study of ICT in school education. Ph.D. thesis, University of Tasmania (2003)
11. Rogers, E.M.: Diffusion of Innovations, 4th edn. The Free Press, New York (2010)
12. Allen, D.: Learning integral calculus through non-template problem solving. PRIMUS: Probl. Res. Issues Math. Undergrad. Stud. **11**(2), 147–160 (2001)
13. Gravemeijer, K., Doorman, M.: Context problems in realistic mathematics education: a calculus course as an example. Educ. Stud. Math. **39**, 111–129 (1999)
14. Australian Curriculum Assessment and Reporting Authority: The Australian Curriculum: Senior Secondary Mathematics – Information Sheet (2012). http://docs.acara.edu.au/resources/Senior_Secondary_Mathematics.pdf

15. Glass, G.V., McGaw, B., Smith, M.L.: Meta-Analysis in Social Research. Sage, London (1981)
16. Fluck, A.E., Ranmuthugala, D., Chin, C., Penesis, I., Chong, J.: Innovating with Calculus for Kids. In: Australian Council for Computers in Education 2016 Conference Refereed Proceedings, 29 September–2 October 2016, Brisbane, Australia, pp. 58–63 (2016)
17. Fluck, A.E., Ranmuthugala, D., Chin, C., Yang, Y.: Innovating with Science-ercise. In: Australian Council for Computers in Education 2016 Conference Refereed Proceedings, 29 September–2 October 2016, Brisbane, Australia, pp. 46–51 (2016)
18. Wiliam, D.: Standardized testing and school accountability. Educ. Psychol. **45**(92), 107–122 (2010)
19. Van Assche, F., Anido-Rifón, L., Griffiths, D., Lewin, C., McNicol, S. (eds.): Re-engineering the Uptake of ICT in Schools. Springer, Cham (2015). https://doi.org/10.1007/978-3-319-19366-3
20. Webb, M.E., Cox, M.J., Fluck, A., Angeli-Valanides, C., Malyn-Smith, J., Voogt, J.: Thematic Working Group 9: Curriculum - Advancing Understanding of the Roles of Computer Science/Informatics in the Curriculum in EDUsummIT 2015 Summary Report: Technology Advance Quality Learning for All, pp. 60–69 (2015)
21. Tapia, M., Marsh, G.E.: An instrument to measure mathematics attitudes. Acad. Exch. Q. **8**(2), 16–22 (2004)
22. Barkatsas, A.: A new scale for monitoring students' attitudes to learning mathematics with technology (MTAS). In: 28th Annual Conference of the Mathematics Education Research Group of Australasia (2004). http://www.merga.net.au/documents/RP92005.pdf
23. Pierce, R., Stacey, K., Barkatsas, A.: A scale for monitoring students' attitudes to learning mathematics with technology. Comput. Educ. **48**, 285–300 (2007)

The e-Fran Program: A Nation-Wide Initiative Supporting Research Projects to Foster Learning and Teaching Through Digital Technologies

Monique Grandbastien(✉)

LORIA, Université de Lorraine, Vandœuvre-lès-Nancy, France
monique.grandbastien@loria.fr

Abstract. This paper presents e-Fran, an on-going French initiative for linking academics from various disciplines and practitioners to design and test innovative ways of using digital technologies to improve learning outcomes. It is a research policy paper as first research results are not yet available. e-Fran is a nation-wide research program deployed in France from October 2016 over four years. The national context, the objectives, the project selection process and the funded projects are described as well as the follow-up actions.

Keywords: Digital plan for education · Research program
Research funding policy · Linking researchers and practitioners

1 National Context and Challenges

The technological revolution induced by digital technology is at the origin of major changes in our societies. The school must prepare students to integrate harmoniously into a society that has become digital. Bringing new ways of teaching and learning, digital technologies can also be an accelerator in educational success. Moreover the development of digital applications for education and training involve all the partners of education, including the players in the digital economy and, in particular, start-ups.

To face these major challenges, the French Ministry of National Education, Higher Education and Research [1] has adopted an ambitious strategy to make digital technology a factor in reducing inequalities. To improve the effectiveness of learning, to fight against dropping out, to develop the creativity of all and better prepare children to live and work as autonomous and responsible citizens in the society of tomorrow constitute the main axes of this ambition. Several initiatives brought this ambition into action, i.e. the public digital education service, whose mission is to organize and stimulate the provision of quality digital content and services to the entire educational community, the introduction of digital items in the curricula for all pupils aged from 6 to 16, the provision of many kinds of mobile devices, etc.

However, given the speed of changes, while deploying this policy, it is necessary to prepare the future. Indeed many questions remain unsolved, i.e. we encourage diversification of teaching practices using digital technology. Are all these practices

A. Tatnall and M. Webb (Eds.): WCCE 2017, IFIP AICT 515, pp. 81–86, 2017.
https://doi.org/10.1007/978-3-319-74310-3_10

successful? On the one end many papers report significant improvements [2, 3], but often they do not include very large scale evaluations over several years. On the other end, an OECD study [4] did not notice significant improvements among kids that were exposed to digital technologies, compared with kids that were less or not exposed. In this perspective, "improving education for the digital world" has been selected as a priority topic in the nationwide "Investments for the future" program [5]. This program supports innovative projects in several domains that are considered as key sectors for the future such as energy, ecology, health, etc., including research and education. It is directly piloted at the Prime Minister level and is running over a ten years period. In this framework, a program called e-Fran has been designed and the first call for projects launched in October 2015.

2 Main Innovative Characteristics of the e-Fran Program

As an investment for the future, the e-FRAN program aims to support innovative experiments, using digital technology, developed within primary, secondary and high schools, based on the identification of "educational territories of digital innovation". It aims at stimulating the creation of a shared culture around the challenges of education for the digital society and to support projects that mobilize a variety of partners (school education institutions, local authorities, companies, research laboratories, associations, other actors involved in education), in a multi-stakeholder approach.

The e-Fran program is managed by a public financial partner, La Caisse des dépôts [6]. The maximum available total funding was 30 M€ for projects running over 4 years and providing from their own an equivalent amount of money. It is the first large-scale education research program run in France, bringing together school leaders and teachers, research teams, businesses and local authorities.

Prof. J.-M. Monteil, the e-Fran program leader, explains his views [7] as follows: "One of the problems of the school is the important school failure due to the diversity of children which the learning environment had to cover. Today, apprenticeships are mainly organized around logic-mathematical and verbal abilities, while the intelligence is multimodal. Numerous digital technologies, allowing, for example a plurality of contexts, make access to information more likely for a large number of learners, through more varied treatment and presentation situations. This possibility of enriching learning contexts and environments can significantly increase the supply and pedagogical responses of teachers. It then responds to the diversity of learning behaviors, cognitive and social characteristics of pupils, thus promoting the expression of not yet expressed capabilities."[1]

It is a novel approach in the French National Education community, compared to previous initiatives [8] because it starts from the actors and includes them in the projects from the very beginning. The perspective is to qualify pedagogical practices and technological tools that support them by producing scientifically grounded results to create benchmarks for action and references that can be mobilized for teachers.

[1] Translated and adapted by the author.

Moreover it brings together people from the world of digital technology, scientists and educational practitioners who are too often working independently.

Furthermore, from a human resources view, it is expected that after 3 or 4 years of research at the heart of innovative educational practices, by a regular follow-up, a community of actors, researchers and digital industries and the commitment of 36–40 doctoral students in the framework of the projects will ensure scientific continuity and innovation.

Consequently, the specifications of the e-Fran call for proposals were particularly demanding: The proposals should federate around an innovative project, primary and secondary schools, local authorities, companies, research laboratories, associations, other actors in education, etc. They should be anchored in a delimited experimental territory enabling precise monitoring and evaluation, in particular on the results of pupils engaged in experiments, and ensuring a fast adoption of the results among practitioners. They should meet well-defined objectives, whether they approach digital technologies as a pedagogical resource, new competence to be acquired, social fact and research object. They should demonstrate a high potential for transforming practices that can be replicated in other places.

3 Results from the Selection Process

Despite these strong requirements, more than 100 proposals were submitted and 22 projects were accepted. An independent jury, who was particularly careful to ensure that all criteria were met at a very high level, evaluated the proposals. In line with the expected multi-partners consortium, the jury included one third of the members from the academic sector, another third from the education sector and the final third from the business sector. Table 1 gives a detailed overview of the diversity and the wealth that can be found in the selected projects.

Table 1. Main figures related to the e-Fran call for projects

Number of projects submitted (involving more than 1900 partners)	105
Number of projects selected (involving more than 450 partners)	22
Primary schools	158
Lower secondary schools	104
Higher secondary schools	48
Research laboratories	58
Teacher training institutes	10
Higher education institutions (i.e. universities)	25
Private companies	20
Local public bodies (i.e. town or regional councils)	24
Other bodies	12
Total investment (of which 20 M€ awarded by the e-Fran program)	**40 M€**

The projects started between October 2016 and January 2017 for a period of four years. The average funding of a project is € 1M supplemented by equivalent funding from partners.

For most projects, the research part includes funding for Ph.D. and post-doc students (over 3 years). So 42 Ph.D. students and 15 post-doc students or research associates are funded through the program, mostly in cognitive sciences, but also in education sciences, in computer science, in didactics, etc.), they are working in research units in close relation with schools and we consider this new research taskforce as a first achievement of the program. We provide hereafter some examples of accepted projects.

e-P3C: *How to address the diverse needs and strengths of students in the classroom, building on experimental psychology findings to develop a new Intelligent Tutoring System (ITS)? Proposed approach: This project aims at developing a new ITS offering each student different paths (gamified, abstract, context-based) to learn the same lesson. 40 teachers and inspectors (in charge of teacher training and evaluation) have been producing new teaching materials to build these different paths. An EdTech startup is developing the ITS. A large-scale randomized control design will include 8000 students from lower-secondary schools. Students in the treatment group will practice first mathematics and science with the ITS, whereas control group students will be taught either in a traditional way or using innovative non-digital teaching methods (Main à la Pâte). A huge amount of data will be collected through the ITS – together with paper-based pretests-posttests – to allow cognitive and social psychologists to assess and improve the impact of the ITS. Data analysis will also help to understand cognitive processes underlying learning, using students' logs.*

FLUENCE: *How to train pupils' fluency to support their reading and spelling? Proposed approach: This project aims to develop a Learning Management System offering specific devices to train fluency, adjust student practice to their needs (adaptive learning algorithm) and allow teachers to track individual progress (dashboard). These devices include a serious game "EVAsion" and an audiobook "Lectra", designed by three research teams (cognitive psychologists, neuroscientists, linguists) to help building prerequisite skills for fluency in reading in the short term. Later on, higher levels of fluency are expected to foster written comprehension and spelling. This project addresses both 6 y-o pupils to support their learning of reading, and 11 y-o weak readers as a remedial education strategy. The local Espé (teacher training centre) is a key partner of this project and both methods and findings from this research project will be shared with future teachers.*

SILVA NUMERICA: *How to foster practical learning in vocational studies (forestry field)? Proposed approach: This project targets vocational high schools offering the "forest-wood" training track. It aims to design a virtual and augmented reality platform: forestry professionals as well as high school teachers will work together to develop this virtual forest environment with features matching the national curriculum. Immersive learning is expected to improve students' skills and to foster interest and dedication to learning. An education research takes part in the project and will help design the platform in a way that is conducive to learning, as well as assess the impact of virtual reality on learning for each student.*

Some readers may object that the call for projects should have targeted a few major issues. This was not the case: the call was open to any theme as long as it was a research project on learning with digital technologies, involved a diversity of stakeholders (teachers, school management, tech and edtech companies, non-profit, local authorities, etc.). Priority was given to ambitious projects, no matter their focus. This may account for shortcomings in the diversity of selected projects, as important topics may not be addressed/others might be addressed in two or three different projects.

4 The e-Fran Program Follow-Up

A program follow-up has been set up in order to establish efficiency criteria and to ensure the success of these investments. In a rapidly evolving context, we have to foster networking and cross fertilization of projects as well as agile adaptation to further needs. Project leaders will meet on a regular basis.

A first big challenge is to give birth to a new generation of scientists used to work at the crossroads of high quality scientific research and close collaboration with practitioners. In that perspective summer schools will be organized among Ph.D. students funded by the program. These students belong to different labs, they work in different disciplines, but they share the same goal: better understanding the effects of digital technologies to enhance learning in a digital society and they bring complementary views which allow better results than isolated ones. Another facet of the same challenge is to give birth to a new generation of teachers, teacher trainers and other staff members who are convinced that there is no efficient innovation without close links with academic partners.

Another challenge is to associate partners who do not yet belong to the selected projects, in order to maximize the expected dissemination. A first direction is to associate new regions for covering all the country, for instance for early experimentations. Another direction is to associate private companies to allow them an early understanding of the kind of business they can develop to fulfil the educational sector's needs as they emerge from the projects.

5 Conclusion and Future Work

e-Fran is a large-scale initiative set up by the French state to finance innovative and promising investments for digital education in the country. It raises high expectations and should bring answers at the level of these expectations. Scientific findings will be published at the international level as usual. Processes and results have to be compared with initiatives from other countries in the same domain, i.e. IT curricula changes in UK [9]. However integrating the results into practices needs to take into account the cultural factors that play an important role in education. So the results have to be considered together with the innovative participatory processes adopted in the projects.

Acknowledgments. The author would like to thank J-M. Monteil for his inspiring documents, G. Leroux for her help in the figures of the program and all the members of the evaluation and piloting committees for fruitful discussions.

References

1. Ministère de l'Education, Plan numérique (2017). http://ecolenumerique.education.gouv.fr/plan-numerique-pour-l-education/
2. De Freitas, S.: Are games effective learning tools? A review of educational games. J. Educ. Technol. Soc. (2017, to appear)
3. Outhwaite, L.A., Gulliford, A., Pitchford, N.J.: Closing the gap: efficacy of a tablet intervention to support the development of early mathematical skills in UK primary school children. Comput. Educ. **108**, 43–58 (2017)
4. OECD, Students, Computers and Learning Making the Connection (2015). http://www.oecd.org/publications/students-computers-and-learning-9789264239555-en.htm
5. Commissariat Général à l'Investissement, Programme d'investissements d'avenir (2017). http://www.gouvernement.fr/investissements-d-avenir-cgi
6. Caisse des dépôts (2017). http://www.caissedesdepots.fr/espaces-de-formation-de-recherche-et-danimation-numeriques-e-fran
7. Monteil, J.-M.: Interview (2016). http://www.reseau-espe.fr/actualites/appel-projet-e-fran-interview-de-jean-marc-monteil
8. Baron, G.-L., Drot-Delange, B., Grandbastien, M., Tort, F.: Computer science education in French secondary schools: historical and didactical perspectives. ACM Trans. Comput. Educ. **14**(2), 27 (2014). Article 11
9. Sentance, S., et al.: Grand challenges for the UK: upskilling teachers to teach computer science within the secondary curriculum (2012). https://www.academia.edu/2456347/Grand_challenges_for_the_UK_Upskilling_teachers_to_teach_Computer_Science_within_the_Secondary_curriculum

Mobile Technologies Supporting Professional Learning Communities Within Pre-service Teacher STEM Education

Duncan Symons(✉), Christine Redman, and Jo Blannin

Melbourne Graduate School of Education, The University of Melbourne, Melbourne, Australia
Duncan.symons@unimelb.edu.au

Abstract. Over a three-year period, academics from the Melbourne Graduate School of Education, The University of Melbourne, have partnered with a range of academics to facilitate an elective subject for pre-service teachers (PSTs). These academics include staff from the Faculty of Science (The University of Melbourne), the Victorian Space Science Education Centre (VSSEC) and the Gene Technology Access Centre (GTAC) Together we have sought to develop and strengthen their teaching in the area of STEM (Science, Technology, Engineering and Mathematics) education. Students in this subject were supported to develop 21st century skills that enabled them to work effectively in Professional Learning Communities (PLCs). Pre-service teachers observed and responded to each other's teaching providing real time feedback using 'Padlet' (a readily available web based application). Following each lesson students used the resultant 'Padlet' data as a prompt to promote reflective discussion. We analyse excerpts of Pre-service teacher responses to an online survey as a means to gain some understanding of their perception of working in this way. Additionally, Padlet feedback was thematically analysed in an effort to understand how teacher candidates focussed their feedback and limitations of this approach to facilitating professional development. Through adoption of this tool, critical collaborative reflection was fostered.

Keywords: STEM education · Pre-service teachers · CSCL
Professional Learning Communities

1 Introduction

STEM education has been receiving increasing attention over recent years. It is seen to offer the potential to enhance development of various 'soft skills'; sometimes known as 21st century skills [1]. These skills include, but are not limited to, creativity, innovation, critical thinking, decision making, problem solving, metacognition, collaboration and communication.

STEM education is claimed to present a solution to preparing young people for jobs of the future. The Chief Scientist's Office of Australia reports that there is a growing demand for STEM qualified employees [2].

A. Tatnall and M. Webb (Eds.): WCCE 2017, IFIP AICT 515, pp. 87–96, 2017.
https://doi.org/10.1007/978-3-319-74310-3_11

Additionally, STEM education is seen as a potential approach to reversing high levels of disengagement with science and mathematics. Disengagement with these areas is reported to begin in primary school [3, 4].

With the promise of STEM education as a rationale, academics within the University of Melbourne's, Melbourne Graduate School of Education, working alongside academics and scientists from the Faculty of Science, the Gene Technology Access Centre (GTAC), the Victorian Space Science Education Centre (VSSEC) and the Melbourne Museum, have planned and facilitated an elective subject with pre-service teacher education students (PSTs) with an integrated approach to STEM education as a focus. The facilitation of the elective subject has been funded through the Reconceptualising Maths and Science Teacher Education Programs (ReMSTEP); an Australian Government program funded through the Office for Learning and Teaching (OLT).

Throughout the three years in which the elective subject has operated, academics working within the subject have been interested in helping students to develop Professional Learning Communities (PLCs) within their STEM planning and teaching. The context for the subject seemed ideally suited to the facilitation of PLCs given that teams of PSTs collaboratively teach each classroom of school children. A key component of the PLCs is an opportunity for students to observe each other teach and provide peer feedback. Whilst observing each other teach, PSTs utilised their mobile devices to record their observations on 'Padlet'; an online, virtual 'wall' that allows individuals to express their thoughts on a common topic easily and collaboratively. In this study, we have coded and analysed the feedback provided within the Padlets to gain an understanding of where and how PSTs directed their peer feedback when working in PLCs.

An additional source of data utilised within this study, were a series of three open ended online surveys. These surveys provided further insight into how PSTs viewed the process of engaging in PLCs and providing and receiving peer feedback.

We aim to address two research questions in this paper:

1. How do PSTs perceive peer observation and feedback, when utilising online mobile technologies?
2. How do PSTs focus their peer feedback when utilising online mobile technologies?

In the following sections, we will first provide some discussion of literature in the area of tertiary level peer learning and the use of online mobile technologies to facilitate Computer Supported Collaborative Learning (CSCL). Next, we will provide some discussion of the Context and Study Design. A discussion of the Results will then occur and lastly some Conclusions and Implications will be offered.

2 Literature Review

This literature review is divided into two Sub-sects. 2.1 and 2.2. Sub-section 2.2 provides background and discussion of literature supporting the first research question, whilst Sub-sect. 2.1 provides discussion of literature closely aligned with the second research question. Where possible the literature selected is based within a context of research in tertiary settings.

2.1 Peer Observation, Peer Learning and Professional Learning Communities

Whilst there is some variation in conceptions of what constitutes a PLC, Stoll et al. [5] state that "there appears to be broad international consensus that it (PLCs) suggests a group of people sharing and critically interrogating their practice in an ongoing, reflective, collaborative, inclusive, learning-oriented, growth-promoting way" [5]. The establishment and facilitation of a PLC can take many forms. However, a common component of PLCs is peer learning; regularly including peer observation and peer feedback. In the context of our study peer observation and feedback was central to the development of PLCs.

'Reciprocal peer learning' which includes 'peer observation', has been described as "mutually beneficial and involves the sharing of knowledge, ideas and experience between the participants. It can be described as a way of moving beyond independent to interdependent or mutual learning" [6].

Martin and Double [7] describe the benefits of this approach in staff professional development as follows:

1. improve and develop an understanding of personal approaches to curriculum delivery;
2. enhance and extend teaching techniques and styles of presentation through collaboration;
3. engage in and refine interpersonal skills through the exchange of insights relating to the review of a specific teaching performance;
4. expand personal skills of evaluation and self-appraisal;
5. to develop and refine curriculum planning skills in collaboration with a colleague; and
6. identify areas of subject understanding and teaching activity which have a particular merit or are in need of further development.

In the majority of literature exploring peer learning and peer observation there is agreement that feedback and observation should occur in a non-judgmental, objective and supportive manner [6–8].

Critiques of the approach however, contend that the goal of peer observation is easily subverted. Shortland [9], utilizes Derridean Deconstruction [10] to gain insight into how university documentation relating to the peer observation process can highlight issues of power imbalance between the observer and observees. Deconstruction is described by Chaffee [11] as "a way of rereading texts to uncover the silences in the history of philosophical and social thought and, as he (Derrida) acknowledges, to create silences of its own." Shortland [9] contends that the observer involuntarily, is placed in a more powerful position than the observee. Additionally, she argues that peer observation is used, at times, as a method of surveillance and used to ensure compliance by figures of authority or management. She states, "discussions revealed some staff members completing observation documentation simply to comply with the managerial requirements to do so, having not actually undertaken the observation process. A mechanism by teaching staff to highlight their perceived needs whilst minimizing their workload or an opportunity for resistance whilst not misbehaving?" [9].

With these critiques of peer observation in tertiary level education in mind, we aim to gain an understanding of PST perceptions of the process in our STEM education focused elective subject.

2.2 Mobile Technologies Enabling Computer Supported Collaborative Learning (CSCL)

Whilst there in an increasing volume of literature addressing the use of mobile devices, typically mobile/smart phones, tablets or in some cases lap tops, in teaching and learning contexts [12–14], little research exists specifically investigating the use of internet connected mobile devices to engage in collaborative, observational, feedback of peers within teacher preparation courses.

Symons et al. [15] describe Computer Supported Collaborative Learning (CSCL) as taking "place via the vehicle of technology (computers, tablets, mobile phones etc.) typically linked via an intranet or the internet". Dillenbourg [16] has explained previously, that in order for CSCL to occur, peers who are more or less at the same level, perform the same action, have a common goal, and work together.

The utilization of technology reported in this study, suggests an alignment with Dillenbourg's (1999) description of CSCL. PSTs, who are at the same level, performed the same action of engaging in the planning and teaching of STEM. They had the common goal of furthering the development of their practice and they did so in collaboration with each other and as such were 'working together'. Synergies between the conditions required for CSCL to occur and the collaborative, non-judgmental, shared support and accountability required of PLCs suggests that taking a CSCL based approach to the use of technology within PLCs is a natural and logical fit. We regard the use of mobile technologies reported in this study as an example of CSCL.

3 Context and Study Design

As a part of a STEM elective subject, which is undertaken in the final semester of their two year graduate Masters level degree, PSTs were required to teach a series of sequential lessons to primary school students taking an integrated STEM based approach. Across the three years in which the elective subject has taken place PSTs have worked with a number of schools in the inner suburbs of Melbourne, across an age range encompassing all of the primary years.

Before teaching within schools, PSTs have had opportunities to develop an ability to work effectively in PLCs through attendance at lectures and engaging in workshop activities designed to enable them to understand the different approaches that may be taken to establishing successful PLCs. For example, in addition to attending a lecture providing more general information about PLCs, PSTs also attended a lecture (from an international expert in the area) providing detailed information about Japanese Lesson Study [17]. They were then asked to draw links and synthesize the various materials.

Following, workshops and lectures, PSTs taught a sequential series of 4 weekly lessons to year 5/6 students (age 10–13). The data reported here is taken from a year in which the focus for teaching was on Bees and Bee adaptations. Specifically, PSTs were to facilitate a student inquiry investigating, why there has been a dramatic decrease in bee populations over recent years.

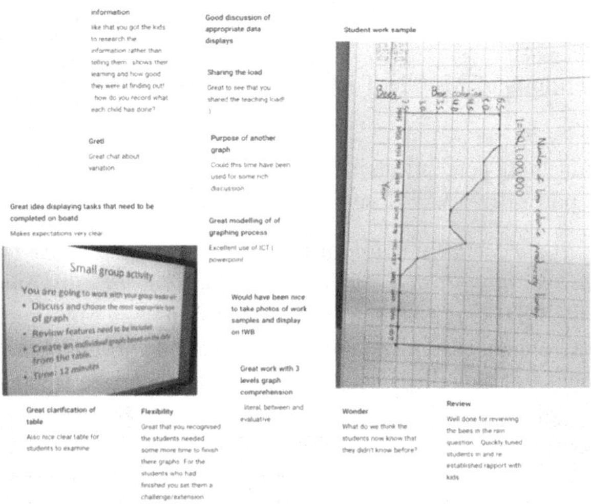

Fig. 1. Section of example Padlet

During the teaching of each of the four lessons a group would observe the teaching group and use their mobile devices to post short pieces of feedback related to the lesson that they were witnessing on 'Padlet'. At the conclusion of the lessons, each week, each of the Padlets would be displayed on a data projector and the group that had observed the teaching group would facilitate a discussion providing feedback about the teaching group's lesson. An example Padlet is provided in Fig. 1. In the example, we see the ability users have to upload multimedia, and provide real-time succinct feedback. Additionally, some understanding of the variety of feedback provided is available. Notably, some feedback focuses on mathematical understandings, whilst some is focused on pedagogical, technical and organizational matters.

Across the four weeks, each contribution, on each Padlet was coded and then aggregated in an effort to better understand on where the PSTs' feedback was focused. Codes allocated to contributions were, 'Science', 'Technology', 'Engineering', 'Mathematics', 'STEM' (indicating a contribution where concepts are integrated across the disciplines) and 'General Pedagogy'.

In addition, to data derived from Padlet we utilize qualitative data from 3, online, open ended, anonymous surveys to gain an understanding of how PSTs perceived their experience of working within a mobile technology supported PLC.

4 Results and Discussion

The results and discussion are divided into two sub-sections. Sub-section 4.1 provides a number of excerpts of responses to an online survey that was completed by PSTs within the elective. Analysis of these excerpts provides some indication of how PSTs perceived the technology supported peer observation process that was core to the subject. Sub-section 4.1 provides the results of aggregated student peer feedback taken from Padlet and some discussion of how these results suggest that PSTs focused their feedback.

4.1 PST Perceptions of Mobile Technology Supported Peer Observation Process

When asked about their perceptions of working within mobile technology supported PLCs and being part of the peer observation process, PSTs reported the following:

1. *I learnt how to successfully collaborate as a team and gained loads of exciting ideas and ways to support and encourage learning in my classroom.*
   In excerpt 1 the PST suggests that the process of engaging in a mobile technology supported PLC enhanced understandings of how best to collaborate. She emphasizes that she gained new ideas about creative approaches to teaching that she may not have had had access to if taking another approach to learning.
2. *I was really interested to see how others use the 5E framework and pedagogical tools in different ways. I am always really interested when people do things in ways I never thought of.*
   Excerpt 2 shows that the PSTs valued the opportunity to observe their peers interpreting, through teaching, the learning they had all engaged in, in University based workshops, in a classroom with 'actual' students. An implication here is that, whilst the PSTs have many opportunities to discuss and clarify their thinking in University workshops, the opportunity to actually see each other teach provides an insight that is not possible through discussion only.
3. *Mimicking the structure of how planning is done in schools I think this was a valuable team experience. Sharing of ideas made the unit more diverse and interesting.*
   The PST shares their view, in excerpt 3, that through planning and teaching within PLCs reinforced by technology supported peer observation, the process was a more authentic and faithful representation of what they believe will occur in their working life as a teacher.
4. *Great opportunity to teach a sequence of lessons to students and have feedback from peers and lecturers. Liked working collaboratively as everyone brought ideas to the table which were critically reviewed so on the whole lessons were at a high standard.*
   The PST reflects in excerpt 4, that the process of peer observation and feedback was a very positive experience. They share their view that the opportunity resulted in overall high quality lessons being planned and taught. It is interesting that the process of their teaching and planning being 'critically reviewed' was seen as a positive, where this could easily be perceived in a negative way.

5. *I feel far more confident in the teaching of STEM units. My knowledge background was strong and I was confident I knew the concepts very well. My experiences here have now given me the ability to know how to apply my knowledge and transfer the desired understandings to my students. Scaffolding their achievement of success criteria is achieved by designing appropriate activities and lessons that are hands on, engaging, student-led, and also, highly enjoyable and fun.*
   The PST, in excerpt 5, suggests that whilst their content knowledge in the various disciplines of STEM was strong, the process of engaging within the PLC and providing and receiving feedback through peer observation, strengthened their pedagogical content knowledge. This aligns with data collected, reported in the following sub section, suggesting that feedback was focused more on pedagogical approaches, than specific content in the STEM disciplines.
6. *It has been the most constructive process of science teaching I have experienced in the entire MTeach course. The feedback has been excellent over the course to allow us to refine and develop the lessons.*
   PSTs, prior to engaging in the STEM elective, had not had the opportunity to observe each other teach or provide and receive feedback from each other on their teaching. Comments from the PST in excerpt 6, indicate that this was a very useful component of the elective. PSTs have received feedback and critiques of their teaching throughout the course from University academic staff and mentor teachers, in addition to a range of anecdotal feedback. Excerpts, suggest that the PSTs at times, value the feedback from their peers as more meaningful than from individuals who they would consider to be assessing and judging them.

4.2 PST Focusses of Peer Feedback

Table 1 shows how PSTs focused their peer feedback within Padlet. It is clear that 'Engineering' and 'Technology' was not a focus of the teaching nor of feedback. This can largely be explained. As previously stated, in the year that this data was gathered the context for teaching was 'Bees and Bee Adaptations'. Whilst subsequent and previous years of the elective involved a greater focus on these disciplines, this context did not lend itself well to exploration and investigation with Engineering and Technology. Interestingly, the data shows that PSTs were by far and away most concerned with focusing their peer feedback on general pedagogical issues; providing 204 contributions with this as a focus. The next closest, Mathematics, received 66 contributions.

Table 1. Padlet derived feedback by PSTs by discipline

	Group A	Group B	Group C	Total
Engineering	0	0	0	0
General pedagogy	60	51	93	204
Mathematics	37	21	8	66
Science	19	11	25	55
STEM	6	1	5	12
Technology	0	2	0	2

It was of interest to observe that whilst only marginally, Mathematics was a greater focus of PST feedback than Science. Given, the Scientific nature of the context of this inquiry, we had anticipated that Science would be a greater focus during these discussions. Additionally, some researchers in the field of STEM education claim that Mathematics can often be overshadowed when working in a STEM context [18]. They suggest, that Science can be considered the 'dominant' discipline within the term. Data collected here, suggests that when working to develop and teach STEM based inquiry learning, Mathematics, if anything was of marginally greater an emphasis.

Table 2 provides insight into how PSTs' focus of feedback changed throughout the 4-week teaching sequence. Whilst, there were a greater number of overall Mathematics focused contributions compared to Science based contributions, no contributions were focused within the area of Mathematics in Week 1. We hypothesize that the scientific context of the teaching sequence was central to 'setting the scene' for the investigation. Further evidence for our hypothesis, relates to Science related feedback being in greatest evidence in the initial two weeks of the sequence.

Table 2. Focus of peer feedback from Padlet

	Week 1	Week 2	Week 3	Week 4
Engineering	0	0	0	0
General pedagogy	59	45	48	52
Mathematics	0	14	36	16
Science	13	19	6	17
STEM	3	1	3	5
Technology	0	0	0	2

5 Conclusions and Implications

Underpinning and supporting the peer observation process was a CSCL environment (Padlet) accessed through mobile technologies. A number of features were essential for mobile technologies to support PST feedback. These included, equality of contribution. All participants also had equal ability and agency to contribute through their personal device. PSTs had multiple opportunities to contribute. Unlike face to face feedback, they could build on and develop their feedback over the course of the lessons. They had the opportunity to edit and modify their own contributions making the process more fluid and dynamic. It is believed that the use of mobile technologies enhanced the metacognitive practices of the observers. In addition to having the ability to edit their own contributions, PSTs built on other PSTs contributions, allowing them to recognize aspects of the teaching process they may not otherwise have considered.

Critics of peer observation within PLCs have argued that the process is easily subverted. They suggest that it is easily manipulated by figures of authority, as an opportunity to ensure compliance and an opportunity to carry out surveillance [9].

Others suggest that staff are not qualified to judge their peers. There remains no definitive agreement about what constitutes the most successful teaching style or method, therefore any judgement or critique of peers, relies on the (peer) assessor's subjective view about what constitutes effective teaching practices [8].

We question how, when teaching at a school or tertiary level, even when a reflective approach to peer observation and feedback is utilized, can the power imbalance between observer and observee be reconciled?

We agree with Shortland [9], that the approach regularly taken to peer observation and feedback that occurs in professional teaching environments, usually only provides a small 'snapshot' of what has occurred throughout a sequence of teaching. Thus, it becomes difficult for an observer to know how the session relates to the rest of the program. With this constraint in mind, the quality and value of feedback is compromised.

Despite these reservations, we see mobile technology supported peer observation within PLCs as part of PST education and training as fundamentally different. Our PSTs are enrolled in their course with the purpose of preparing to become primary school teachers. Thus, they are positioned, upon enrolment in their course, as learners.

Survey data, collected as part of this study, indicates that rather than feeling surveilled or viewing the process as an exercise in compliance, PSTs embraced the process as an authentic learning opportunity. Relative, to the potential levels of disempowerment they experience when being observed by academic supervisors and mentor teachers, the process of observing and being observed by their fellow students is liberating, in that all participants in the process are striving to achieve the same goal; becoming the best teacher possible.

Unlike, examples provided in the literature [8, 9, 19], observers were able to view the entire teaching sequence (occurring over 4 weeks). Thus, PSTs were able to see how the sequence unfolded, avoiding issues associated with an observer having a disconnected understanding of how the teaching cohesively came together.

In addition, to gaining an understanding of how our PSTs perceived the process of technology supported peer observation within PLCs, we were interested in how our PSTs would focus the feedback that they posted in the CSCL environment (Padlet). It had been anticipated that the content focus of their feedback may predominantly lie in the area of science, as a result of literature suggesting that mathematics is often overshadowed within a STEM education context [18]. However, as reported, mathematics was of a slightly greater emphasis in PST contributions within the CSCL environment.

It had not been anticipated that the overwhelming majority of feedback would relate to observations and suggestions about general pedagogy. It may be that the PSTs felt more secure and confident offering feedback related to broader pedagogical issues. It is also possible that given that the teaching sequences were collaboratively planned amongst the PST cohort, there was a common understanding of the content being taught, therefore PSTs had less need to focus feedback on content areas. In the moment, pedagogical choices however are not necessarily shared understandings and therefore would compel observers to provide commentary or feedback.

Interestingly, no mathematics centred feedback occurred in the first week of data collection. We have argued that science has provided a context, or a tangible narrative, from which to 'steer' the STEM sequence of learning. Therefore, it is a major focus of feedback in the initial two weeks.

We suggest an implication for the planning of STEM sequences of learning, or for a general framework for STEM units; that science can be considered the 'host domain', from which engagement in the learning is launched.

Mathematics is later utilized within the STEM sequence of learning as a tool for the interrogation and analysis of data, helping to communicate understanding. Neither discipline need be overshadowed. Instead PSTs can be encouraged to achieve balance, utilizing science and mathematics in a purposeful, targeted and synergistic manner.

References

1. Griffin, P., McGaw, B., Care, E.: Assessment and Teaching of 21st Century Skills. Springer, Heidelberg (2012). https://doi.org/10.1007/978-94-007-2324-5
2. Prinsley, R., Baranyai, K.: STEM Skills in the Workforce: What Do Employers Want. Office of the Chief Scientist, Canberra (2015)
3. Sullivan, P., Tobias, S., McDonough, A.: Perhaps the decision of some students not to engage in learning mathematics in school is deliberate. Educ. Stud. Math. **62**, 81–99 (2006)
4. Martin, A.J., Anderson, J., Bobis, J., Way, J., Vellar, R.: Switching on and switching off in mathematics: an ecological study of future intent and disengagement among middle school students. J. Educ. Psychol. **104**, 1 (2012)
5. Stoll, L., Bolam, R., McMahon, A., Wallace, M., Thomas, S.: Professional learning communities: a review of the literature. J. Educ. Change **7**, 221–258 (2006)
6. Boud, D., Cohen, R., Sampson, J.: Peer Learning in Higher Education: Learning from and with Each Other. Routledge, Abingdon (2014)
7. Martin, G.A., Double, J.M.: Developing higher education teaching skills through peer observation and collaborative reflection. Innov. Educ. Train. Int. **35**, 161–170 (1998)
8. Cosh, J.: Peer observation: a reflective model. ELT J. **53**, 22–27 (1999)
9. Shortland, S.: Peer observation: a tool for staff development or compliance? J. Furth. High. Educ. **28**, 219–228 (2004)
10. Derrida, J.: Of Grammatology. JHU Press, Baltimore (2016)
11. Chaffee, D.: Structuralist and Post-structuralist Social Theory. Routledge, Abingdon (2009)
12. Ciampa, K.: Learning in a mobile age: an investigation of student motivation. J. Comput. Assist. Learn. **30**, 82–96 (2014)
13. Ekanayake, S.Y., Wishart, J.: Integrating mobile phones into teaching and learning: a case study of teacher training through professional development workshops. Br. J. Educ. Technol. **46**, 173–189 (2015)
14. Foulger, T.S., Waker, M.L., Burke, D., Hansen, R., Kim Williams, M., Slykhuis, D.A.: Innovators in teacher education: diffusing mobile technologies in teacher preparation curriculum. J. Digit. Learn. Teach. Educ. **30**, 21–29 (2013)
15. Symons, D., Pierce, R., Redman, C.: Exploring collaborative online problem solving as opportunity for primary students' development of positive mathematical identity. Australasian Association for Research in Education AARE, Melbourne (2016)
16. Dillenbourg, P.: What do you mean by collaborative learning? In: Dillenbourg, P. (ed.) Collaborative-Learning: Cognitive and Computational Approaches, pp. 1–19. Elsevier, Oxford (1999)
17. Iksan, Z.H., Nor, S.N.A.M., Mahmud, S.N., Zakaria, E.: Applying the principle of "lesson study" in teaching science. Asian Soc. Sci. **10**, 108 (2014)
18. English, L.D.: STEM: challenges and opportunities for mathematics education. In: Proceedings of the 39th Conference of the International Group for the Psychology of Mathematics Education, vol. 1, pp. 4–18. PME (2015)
19. Hammersley-Fletcher, L., Orsmond, P.: Evaluating our peers: is peer observation a meaningful process? Stud. High. Educ. **29**, 489–503 (2004)

Measuring Mobile Phone Dependence in Spanish and Greek High School Students Using a Short Scale: Validating Both Adaptations

Olatz Lopez-Fernandez[1(✉)] and Kleopatra Nikolopoulou[2]

[1] Department of Psychology, Nottingham Trent University, 50 Shakespeare Street, Nottingham NG1 4FQ, United Kingdom
olatz.lopez-fernandez@ntu.ac.uk, lopez.olatz@gmail.com

[2] University of Athens, Athens, Greece
klnikolopoulou@ath.forthnet.gr

Abstract. Mobile phones appear to have become one of the main entertainment features in adolescents' life, which has also been suggested to be potentially addictive. A shortened version of a scale used to detect this potential addiction, the Mobile Phone Problematic Use Scale (MPPUS-10; Foerster, Roser, Schoeni, & Röösli, 2015) has been extracted from the *Mobile Phone Problematic Use Scale for Adolescents* (MPPUSA; Lopez-Fernandez, Honrubia-Serrano, & Freixa-Blanxart, 2012). To validate this shortened scale, a cross-national study surveyed 1391 high school students in both Spain and Greece, assessing both socio-demographic variables and self- perceived mobile use dependency. The MPPUS-10 exhibited good factorial validity, good reliability, and similar mid scores in both countries. Results from sub-scale symptomatology showed consistency in elevated levels of craving, withdrawal, and loss of control related to mobile phone use in both countries. This study presents evidence of self-perceived mobile phone dependence in south-European high school students, but more research is needed.

Keywords: Mobile phone dependence · Smartphone dependence
Behavioural addiction · Cross-cultural study · High school students

1 Introduction

Interacting with mobile phones (such as smartphones) has now become embedded in the lifestyles of students from high schools across the world.

The International Telecommunication Union (ITU) [1] has reported that between 2007 and 2015, mobile-broadband subscriptions increased 12-fold globally. The ITU has recently ranked both Spain and Greece among the higher scoring European nations in the Information and Communication Technologies Development Index (IDI), with Spain ranking 31st (IDI = 7.92) and Greece 34th (IDI = 7.92) out of 40 global economies [1]. This Index is a benchmark for comparing the level of technological

A. Tatnall and M. Webb (Eds.): WCCE 2017, IFIP AICT 515, pp. 97–103, 2017.
https://doi.org/10.1007/978-3-319-74310-3_12

development in countries across the world. In the case of Spain and Greece, these two countries are reported to have among the highest domestic mobile minutes and message (SMS) economies (i.e., in 2014, the average domestic mobile minutes per subscription per month were 176 in Greece and 131 in Spain; the average SMSs sent per mobile subscription per month were 31 in Greece and 4 in Spain). In relation to mobile-broadband prices, for a pre-paid handset-based on a 500 MB monthly data allowance, again both countries are ranked in the first economies (Spain: n. 22 with 525 MB and Greece n. 61 with 600 MB). Finally, during 2015, mobile subscriptions per 100 habitants were 107.9 in Spain and 110.3 in Greece. These data exhibit how mobile phones are a widespread technology and highly used in both countries.

Nowadays, it is known mobile phone overuse can psychologically interfere with users' lives, potentially leading to negative health effects such as dependence-like [2, 3] and addiction symptoms [4]. Problematic Mobile Phone Use (PMPU) has been defined, partly, as a potential behavioural addiction through the use of mobile phones or smartphones. PMPU can cause issues for users when enacted as an excessive form of relationship maintenance, in banned and/or dangerous situations, and during addictive use [5]. These addictive symptoms can include cognitive salience, loss of control, mood modification, tolerance, withdrawal, conflict, and relapse [6]. To assess this potential addiction and its symptoms, the goal standard PMPU scale has been the *Mobile Phone Problem Use Scale* (MPPUS [2]), originally consisting of twenty-seven items, which has also been adapted to adolescents using twenty-six items (MPPUSA [7, 8]), and recently has been shortened to ten items also for adolescents (MPPUS-10 [9]). Furthermore, although a great part of the research into this potential addiction has a decade of psychometric research, with a number of validated PMPU scales, rarely are these scales exclusively tested within adolescent samples [10], and few times have they been discussed regarding their implications for this age group or secondary school education.

Basically, it has been argued that mobile phones predominantly affect adolescents in their social, affective, and behavioural spheres, impacting their relationship with parents and peers, and interfering with school and leisure activities [11]. However, to the best of the authors' knowledge, the field of mobile phone dependence has little research investigating its impact on high school students.

To date, there is a lack of research concerning the role of mobile phones in educational settings (such as high schools) and little is known about mobile phones in adolescents using a cross-cultural approach. Consequently, the objectives of this cross-national study were twofold. First, to compare the validations of a shortened screening tool to detect mobile phone dependence (the MPPUS-10) in Spanish and Greek, and second, to explore the perceived addictive symptoms in relation to mobile phones in adolescent high school students from both countries.

2 Method

2.1 Participants and Procedure

The study surveyed two convenience samples at high schools in both Barcelona (Spain: $n = 887$) and Athens (Greece: $n = 504$), at different snapshots of time (2012–2013 in

Spain and 2016 in Greece). The sample comprised of 1391 participants (Spain: 49.94% male; age range 12–18 years; Greece: 51.78% male; age range 12–18 years) sampled from high school students that voluntarily agreed to participate. Regarding the Spanish subsample, almost all students had their own mobile phone (79%); similarly, in the Greek subsample, all students possessed a mobile phone. The questionnaire was administered during class time, with the teacher present, and all responses were recorded anonymous.

2.2 Instruments

The survey was administered in each country with a paper-based format and comprised of two sections: (a) socio-demographics, (b) the Short Version of the MPPUSA [7, 8]: the MPPUS-10 [9]. The original version of the MPPUSA was English, as with the original MPPUS [2], previously validated in Spanish [7] and Greek iterations, which were translated using the translation-back translation method [12].

The MPPUS-10 [9] comprises of ten items rated on a Likert scale (ranging from 1 "Not true at all" to 10 "Extremely true"). The total score ranges between 10 and 100, with the highest score being the maximum presence of 'Mobile phone (dependence) problem use in adolescents' (see Table 1). The Greek version uses a Likert scale from 4 "Strongly agree" to 1 "Strongly disagree". The response rate of the MPPUS-10 in each country was 78.4% in Spain and 100% in Greece.

Table 1. MPPUS items by order in both versions: MPPUS-10 vs. MPPUSA, statements and its correspondent addictive symptom.

MPPUS-10	MPPUSA	Statement	Addictive symptom
1	2	I have used my mobile phone to make myself feel better when I was feeling down	Craving
2	8	When out of range for some time, I become preoccupied with the thought of missing a call	Withdrawal
3	17	If I don't have a mobile phone, my friends would find it hard to get in touch with me	Peer dependence
4	14	I feel anxious if I have not checked for messages or switched on my mobile phone for some time	Withdrawal
5	6	My friends and family complain about my use of the mobile phone	Loss of control
6	20	I find myself engaged on the mobile phone for longer periods of time than intended	Loss of control
7	22	I am often late for appointments because I'm engaged on the mobile phone when I shouldn't be	Negative life consequence
8	13	I find it difficult to switch off my mobile phone	Withdrawal
9	24	I have been told that I spend too much time on my mobile phone	Loss of control
10	7	I have received mobile phone bills I could not afford to pay	Negative life consequence

3 Results

The MPPUS-10 scores were in Spain (n = 887), M = 36.97, SD = 22.4 [range from 10–100]; while in Greece (n = 504), M = 20.75, SD = 4.64 [range from 10–40].

The item analysis of the scale per country is presented in Table 2 and Fig. 1.

Table 2. Item analysis of MPPUS-10 in Spanish and Greek adolescents

Item	Spanish adolescents n = 887		Greek adolescents n = 504		Spanish adolescents n = 887	Greek adolescents n = 504
	M	SD	M	SD	Factor and factor loading	Factor and factor loading
1	4.09	3.02	2.79	.94	F1: .69	F1: .47
2	4.07	2.94	2.47	.87	F1: .77	F1: .54
3	2.95	2.66	1.88	.88	F1: .84	F1: .53
4	2.69	2.66	1.3	.71	F2: −.41	F2: −.56
5	4.84	3.07	2.88	.91	F2: .45	F2: .61
6	3.28	2.82	2.18	.96	F1: .78	F1: .58
7	3.04	2.78	1.54	.77	F1: .87	F1: .62
8	3.72	2.94	2.23	.95	F1: .83	F1: 65
9	4.02	3.08	1.61	.86	F1: .73	F1: 44
10	4.26	3.07	1.87	.95	F1: .76	F1: .53

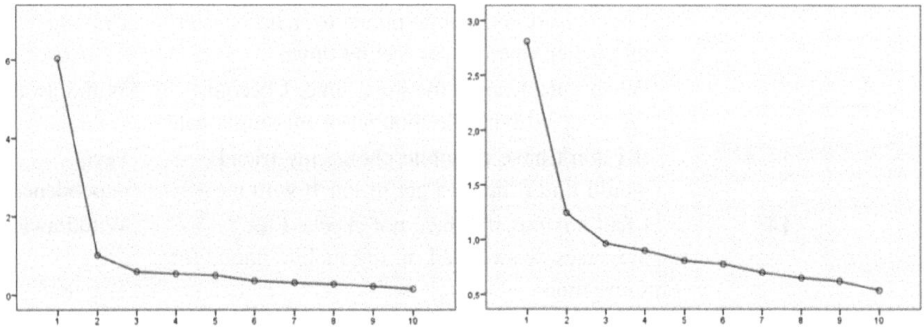

Fig. 1. Scree plots of MPPUS-10 in Spanish and Greek adolescents (X: eigenvalues, Y: components/factors)

There were slight differences between items regarding behaviors in both countries. The 10-item mobile phone dependence scale had good reliability according to Cronbach's alpha coefficients (α = .92 for Spain; α = .71 for Greece). The results obtained through an Exploratory Factor Analysis with Principal Component technique were similar in both countries (Spain: KMO = .93; Bartlett's test: $\chi^2(45) = 6055.98$; $p < .001$; Greece: KMO = .80; Bartlett's test: $\chi^2(45) = 626.5$; $p < .001$) and both yielded a two factor solution: explaining 70.42% of the total variance in Spain (Factor 1: 60.3% and Factor 2: 10.12%) and 40.5% of the total variance in Greece (Factor 1: 28.08% and Factor 2: 12.43%).

In relation to the association between sociodemographic and self-perceived mobile phone dependence in both countries, several relevant variables showed significant bivariate relationships. Gender was significantly associated with MPPUS-10 total score in Spain (but not Greece), with females being more prone to perceive themselves as dependent on using their phones ($t(884) = -2.05$, $Z = -3.124$, $p < .05$ [Men: $M = 35.46$, $SD = 23.39$, Women: $M = 38.53$, $SD = 21.27$]), contrasting to the Greek sample ($t(502) = -.024$, $Z = -.52$, $p = 0.981$).

In relation to the self-perceived addictive symptomatology of mobile phones, Spain high school students highlighted craving, withdrawal, loss of control and negative life consequences as primary symptoms, which again contrasted against Greek high school students, reporting relatively little craving, withdrawal, and loss of control symptoms.

4 Discussion

The first objective of this cross-national study was to compare the validation of a new shortened screening tool (the MPPUS-10) to detect self-perceived mobile phone dependence, in two adolescent samples studying at Spanish and Greek high schools. The second objective was to explore the reported addictive symptoms that adolescents, from both countries, perceived regarding their own mobile phone or smartphone usage.

Both MPPUS-10 versions showed good internal consistency across both temporal snapshots and geographical regions (i.e., 2012–2013 in Spain and 2016 in Greece), which is comparable to validations of the original shorter version (MPPUS-10, e.g., $\alpha = .85$ in Switzerland 2013 [9]) and original (longer) versions (the 27-item scale for adults (e.g. $\alpha = .93$ in Australia 2003 [2]) and 26-item scale for adolescents (e.g. $\alpha = .97$ in Spain 2012 [7], $\alpha = .95$ in United Kingdom 2010 [8])). However, the factorial structures were slightly different and not unidimensional, as expected from longer versions investigations [2, 7, 8]; this is likely due to the fact the MPPUS-10 was multifactorial (i.e., with five factors associated to symptoms: loss of control, withdrawal, negative life consequences, craving, and peer dependence [9]). However, in both our subsamples, the MPPUS-10 obtained a two-factor solution (F1: with almost all items, and F2: items related theoretically to withdrawal and loss of control, which could be argued to be craving and conflict addictive symptoms respectively). This could be due to the different snapshots of time, different countries, and cultures in which data was collected, among other potential confounds (e.g., socio-economic level, type of school, pedagogic approach).

In their study, Foerster et al. [9] did not find a threshold for differentiating between problematic and non-problematic adolescent mobile phone users. This supports the idea that problematic mobile phone use is on a continuum, with higher MPPUS-10 scores suggesting a higher likelihood of addictive mobile phone use in high school students. Therefore, based on these findings, little self-perceived dependence seems to exist, and when it does it appears to be more common in girls, but only in Spain [7].

Furthermore, when analyzing descriptive findings related to the addictive symptomatology, only craving, withdrawal and loss of control seem to be prevalent in both countries, with slight differences between cultures [7–9]. However, in our study 'peer dependence' does not appear to be a factor related to a potential mobile phone use addiction in adolescents. Finally, based on the overall descriptive score in both countries, the MPPUS-10 seems to show an average of 'mid-self-perceived' dependence in Spanish and Greek adolescents, attending to also that both countries are high ranked in mobile phone use [1].

Limitations of this cross-national study are the convenience samples used and collecting data in different academic years in both countries (although with the same methodology and instruments, and in same type of high school students). Moreover, future studies must transform the scores into a standardized procedure [13], for effective in-depth comparisons with each item, factor, and symptom, as well as the potential predictors, which have started to emerge in this preliminary and exploratory study.

Future research could also reinforce the validation of this short version for use in schools and educational settings (where adolescents develop their usual activities), in order to detect potential causes and consequences related to a certain degree of dependency on mobile phones (e.g., excessive attachments to others, excessive gaming [5]), or even perhaps a potential addiction to the range of mobile apps offered to adolescents (e.g., WhatsApp, Instagram, Facebook). Moreover, mobile phones are still commonly perceived as negative by high school teachers (who tend to be over 50 years old [14]). More research is needed regarding these professionals in educational settings, in order to collect their own perspectives on these issues. Nevertheless, mobile phones are now a potential tool for informal learning and leisure (as mobile phones, iPod and iPads are also used for improving learning outcomes [15]) and a prevalent communication tool that merits more research, especially in children from our contemporary societies.

Acknowledgments. The authors would like to thank to Niki Davis (Professor University of Canterbury, New Zealand) for contacting both researchers to do this paper and the World Conference on Computers in Education 2017. To the Chair of the IPC for IFIP WCCE 2017, Don Passey, for the opportunity to present it and the reviewers of this paper. Finally, to Professor Christopher Dawes and Lucy Justice (Research assistants at Nottingham Trent University) for proof-reading this paper.

References

1. International Telecommunication Union [ITU]: Measuring the Information Society Report 2016. ITU, Geneva (2016). https://www.itu.int/en/ITU-D/Statistics/Documents/publications/misr2016/MISR2016-w4.pdf. Accessed 07 Feb 2017
2. Bianchi, A., Phillips, J.G.: Psychological predictors of problem mobile phone use. CyberPsychol. Behav. **8**(1), 39–51 (2005)
3. Km, W., Park, B.-W., Lee, K.C.: Measuring smartphone dependence: a first step with emphasis on factor analytic evidence. Inf. – Int. Interdiscip. J. **14**, 3031–3047 (2011)

4. Kwon, M., Lee, J.-Y., Won, W.-Y., Park, J.-W., Min, J.-A., Hahn, C., Gu, X., Choi, J.-H., Kim, D.-J.: Development and validation of a smartphone addiction scale (SAS). PLoS One **8**(2), e56936 (2013). https://doi.org/10.1371/journal.pone.0056936
5. Billieux, J., Maurage, P., Lopez- Fernandez, O., Kuss, D.J., Griffiths, M.D.: Can disordered mobile phone use be considered a behavioral addiction? An update on current evidence and a comprehensive model for future research. Curr. Addict. Rep. **2**, 156–162 (2015)
6. Griffiths, M.: A "components" model of addiction within a biopsychosocial framework. J. Subst. Use **10**(4), 191–197 (2005)
7. Lopez-Fernandez, O., Honrubia-Serrano, M.L., Freixa-Blanxart, M.: Adaptación española del 'Mobile Phone Problematic Use Scale' para población adolescente. Adicciones **24**, 123–130 (2012)
8. Lopez-Fernandez, O., Honrubia-Serrano, M.L., Freixa-Blanxart, M., Gibson, W.: Prevalence of problematic mobile phone use in British adolescents. Cyberpsychol. Behav. Soc. Netw. **17**, 91–98 (2013)
9. Foerster, M., Roser, K., Schoeni, A., Röösli, M.: Problematic mobile phone use in adolescents: derivation of a short scale MPPUS-10. Int. J. Public Health **60**(2), 277–286 (2015)
10. Lopez-Fernandez, O.: Problematic internet and mobile phone use in adolescents in Barcelona and London. Doctoral thesis, University of Barcelona, Barcelona, Spain (2013). http://www.tdx.cat/handle/10803/126442. Accessed 11 Mar 2017
11. Choliz, M.: Mobile phone addiction: a point of issue. Addiction **105**, 373–374 (2010)
12. Brislin, E.W.: Back-translation for cross-cultural research. J. Cross-Cult. Psychol. **1**(3), 185–216 (1970)
13. Lopez-Fernandez, O., Losada-Lopez, J.L., Honrubia-Serrano, M.L.: A proposed method for the study of predictors for detecting excessive use of technology: problematic internet and mobile phone usage in adolescents. Aloma **33**(2), 49–58 (2015)
14. O'Bannon, B.W., Thomas, K.: Teacher perceptions of using mobile phones in the classroom: age matters! Comput. Educ. **74**, 15–25 (2014)
15. Martin, F., Ertzberger, J.: Here and now mobile learning: an experimental study on the use of mobile technology. Comput. Educ. **68**, 76–85 (2013)

Requirements for Mobile Learning in Vocational Training in the Field of Mechanical Engineering

Adrian Wilke(✉)

Department of Computer Science, Paderborn University, Paderborn, Germany
adrian.wilke@uni-paderborn.de

Abstract. Learning and working tasks in vocational education and training (VET) in the field of mechanical engineering comprise theoretical knowledge and practical activities, for instance, manufacturing a workpiece using a CNC turning machine. To clarify the requirements of these extensive tasks and the support by a mobile application, trainers of companies with training facilities were interviewed. The results of a qualitative content analysis with regard to application and task areas, communication patterns, learning materials, and expectations towards mobile learning are described in this article. Additionally, the resulting practical experiences and the expectations of trainers are included in an instructional design for the support of formal learning and working tasks in VET.

Keywords: Vocational training · Mechanical engineering · Mobile learning
Requirements analysis

1 Introduction: The Domain of VET and Mobile Learning

The dual system of vocational education and training (VET) in Germany takes place at two learning venues with training personnel of different specialization. In part-time vocational schools, the acquisition of theoretical knowledge is focused and supported by vocational teachers. In companies with training facilities, trainers give workplace-related instructions in practical contexts [1]. The tasks of trainers include the planning, execution, and reflection of teaching and learning processes. They have to develop qualification opportunities, while the demands are constantly changing, e.g. due to changing expectations of apprentices or media habits. In order to meet such challenges, teaching and learning methods have to be adapted [2].

Today's adaptions to teaching and learning methods are often related to e-learning systems. The utilization of the internet, technology, and digital media opens various possibilities to handle learning tasks in VET. For instance, there are the distribution of contents, visualizations, interactions among people and systems, different ways of structuring contents, assessments, and the support for reflection [3]. However, an education system has to meet the requirements of the respective underlying domain.

In contrast to office jobs, in-company training in the field of mechanical engineering and metal-working takes place at different areas of work, e.g. at shop floor locations and

A. Tatnall and M. Webb (Eds.): WCCE 2017, IFIP AICT 515, pp. 104–113, 2017.
https://doi.org/10.1007/978-3-319-74310-3_13

office areas. Therefore, mobile devices are more suitable for the assistance of e-learning systems than desktop computers [4]. Another argument for the integration of a mobile learning approach for VET is the learning behavior of the target group of apprentices in the field of metal-working. They prepare for examinations at home, in training companies, in vocational schools, and partially in buses and trains [5].

There have been several academic works combining VET in the dual system, mechanical engineering, and mobile learning. The project *Kompetenzwerkstatt* (literal translation: competence workshop) focuses on analyzing and describing work processes. In this context, the six categories of digital media for task-oriented learning mentioned above were worked out [3]. Another approach in engineering education is *competence snippets*. These are so-called knowledge floaters, short media-supported units of learning, accessible via QR-codes or NFC [6]. The project *KMU Smart Factory* focuses on manufacturing processes and awareness of the following types of contexts: locations, learning-objects, devices, cooperation, time, action, and users [7, 8]. The *Produktionslernsystem* (PLS, production learning system) uses visualizations of, inter alia, vertices and directed edges to document workflows in the car industry [4].

This article is part of the research project Mobile Learning in Smart Factories (MLS), which focuses initial VET in the field of mechanical engineering and learning and working tasks. To assist the main focus groups of apprentices and trainers, a mobile application for context-sensitive learning in training companies and related learning scenarios are under development [9]. Starting with an initial draft specification, the development of the project parts of software, learning scenarios, and conducted workshops proceeds in parallel to a refinement of the requirements (see Fig. 1).

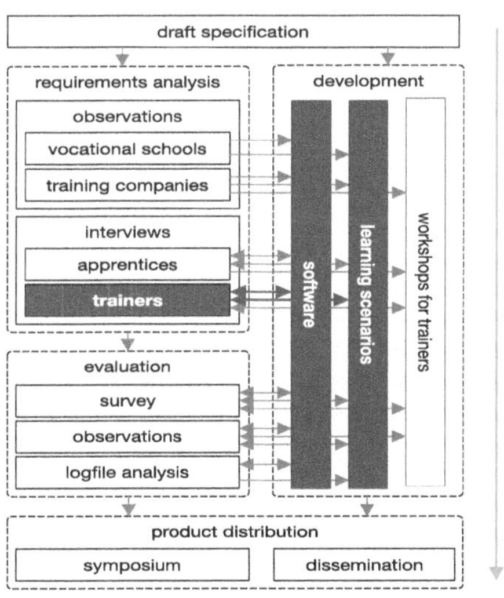

Fig. 1. Development process of the MLS project and focus of this article

In the first series of interviews, we asked apprentices for tasks and typical activities in their daily work, educational contents and materials in use, learning topics, and the usage of hardware and software in their learning environments. One result relating to learning activities in companies is the importance of practical tasks. The main activities of apprentices from the mechanical engineering sector (primarily in the training occupation of the metal cutting mechanic) are strongly related to action-oriented tasks in the context of work orders. At the beginning of work orders, trainers typically hand over mechanical drawings and instruct the apprentices to clarify necessary work procedures. Processing a work order takes place in six typical phases. Apprentices have to analyze the drawings, prepare a work plan for the production process, decide between alternatives within the production process, manufacture components, perform a quality control, and evaluate the results. The process consisting of these phases and the related learning materials can be supported by mobile devices and digital media to assist in issues of organization and self-regulated learning [5].

This basic research is part of the MLS requirements analysis. In our project, we interviewed trainers of companies with training facilities to refine the requirements and the development of the MLS software and learning scenarios. In this article, we focus on the investigation of the following research questions:

- Which fields of VET and mechanical engineering are suiting the targeted support with a mobile application from the trainer's point of view?
- Which tasks and activities of the current learning and working practice can be embedded in appropriate learning scenarios?
- How should possible technical features be implemented to assist in independent learning in VET?

2 Methods: Interviews and Qualitative Content Analysis

In this research, we conducted semi-structured interviews and carried out a qualitative content analysis of the transcribed interview contents. We visited five companies with mechanical engineering training facilities and interviewed nine trainers. (In four companies, respectively two trainers were interviewed.) The survey took place from May 2015 to May 2016. For the survey and analysis, we performed the following steps:

1. Preparation of the investigation by determining the research interests. These are everyday working practices in the apprenticeship, requirements for the support of VET by a mobile application, and related experiences of trainers.
2. Development of an interview guide with the following four main topics: requirements for mobile learning scenarios in vocational training (12 items), learning conditions and previous experiences of trainers (8 items), interests in technical systems (2 items), and expectations towards a developed system (2 items). For each of the 24 items, we prepared the following four types of questions: (a) Open-ended questions to introduce the area of interest, (b) a list of terms to check, if all relevant fields have been mentioned, (c) specific follow-up items to mention related fields of interest, and (d) optional control questions to keep up the flow of conversation.
3. We conducted semi-structured interviews using the developed interview guide. The conversations were audio recorded.

4. The audio records were transcribed with support of student assistants. To ensure consistency, a set of simple transcription rules [10] was applied.
5. We performed a qualitative content analysis. Therefore, we chose the method of theme analysis [11]. As an initial category system, the interview guide with 24 questions was used. In a first iteration of the analysis, we refined the categories to a final set of 30 categories. Afterwards, each transcript was independently coded by two people. In this step, the people marked text parts consisting of question-answer-pairs and assigned them to exactly one category. We chose this approach of coding instructions to maintain the contexts of the answers. Overall, 2,096 codings were assigned by two people. The coded segments were summarized per category.
6. We calculated the intercoder agreement [12] for each of the nine coded interview transcripts. This was done using the MAXQDA 12 software [13], the function "intercoder agreement", and the options "segment agreement" and "correlates 100%". The arithmetical mean of the nine resulting values of Cohen's Kappa is $\kappa = 0.9167$. This almost perfect agreement [14] is the result of pairing questions and answers and the following assignment of these pairs to exactly one of the predefined categories.

3 Results: Expertise of Trainers

To focus on the research questions, we describe the following topics: tasks and activities, communication among trainers and apprentices, task assignment, learning materials, and expectations of trainers towards mobile learning.

3.1 Tasks and Activities

With regard to the underlying ordinance [15], skills, knowledge, and competences in the industrial metal occupations should be imparted in a process-related way. This has to be done in three and a half years. To investigate, how these formal requirements are currently implemented in companies, we asked the trainers for types of tasks occurring in their training. The interviewees described the following tasks.

In addition to the practical characteristics of training facilities in contrast to schools, the training in companies differs from the diverse scope of tasks in vocational and mainstream schools. After some basic training in metal working, where filing and drilling are practiced, all tasks are production-oriented and embedded in the structure of a complete action. This is often represented as a sequence of the phases: inform, plan, decide, implement, control, and evaluate. Whereas the tasks, or rather work orders, follow the same structure, they are arranged by increasing complexity and differ in the machining processes used (e.g. milling or turning). Typically, workpieces are firstly produced on conventional lathes and milling machines and afterwards on Computer Numerical Control (CNC) machines. Work orders mainly are didactically prepared learning tasks. Starting with simple workpieces, the level of difficulty increases. This is put into practice by increasing the number of tolerances and refining their thresholds.

In other words, workpieces become more detailed. Another advanced task is the production of assemblies. Single components are produced and have to be assembled. Assemblies can be composed of components, which are produced using different machining processes. To complete such a task, milling and turning have to be mastered. In general, tasks are assigned in consideration of the individual learning progresses of apprentices. For high performing apprentices, tasks inspired by WorldSkills[1] competitions can be assigned.

The described tasks in different companies are similar to each other, as they are composed of connected sub-tasks, which are well-known as the model of a complete action, or rather, the programmed instruction [16, 17]. Each sub-task contains separate objectives, prerequisites, and activities. A major requirement for the assistance by an e-learning system is to match these properties and support overall solution- and learning processes. For instance, every working task includes the creation of a production sheet [18]. This depends on the analysis of a mechanical drawing, which can be enriched with 3D representations [5] and produces data, which should be reused at the manufacturing stage. Learners can reuse created and provided data in various contexts and use it for work planning [3]. Mobility becomes another requirement for the described tasks, as apprentices sometimes have to leave their workplace locations, e.g. to consult reference books [5]. In some instances, they plan the production process at the office and work on machines at the shop floor. In such cases, mobile devices can provide opportunities to connect learning *for* work and learning *at* work by applying generic knowledge to solve immediate work problems [19].

3.2 Communication and Task Assignment in the Apprenticeship

The use of mobile devices and technical systems offers various alternatives of interaction and collaboration. To gain an overview of the present communication patterns, we asked about communication among trainers and apprentices. The answers were often related to statements about the assignment of tasks and the use of mechanical drawings.

For all interviewed trainers, direct face-to-face communication is the most important channel for communication. On the one hand, this was explained due to the fact that trainers and apprentices are in immediate proximity during working hours. On the other hand, briefings for work orders take place on site, directly at the workspaces, right at machines. In this context, trainers frequently demonstrate work procedures on machines. Additionally, questions and discussions are also part of briefings. During the production, trainers inspect components and adjust the work progress, if it is necessary.

In addition to the importance of direct face-to-face communication, mechanical drawings are frequently mentioned. These are significant resources in the communication process and utilized for problem analysis and instructions. Additionally, order forms are considered important for the documentation.

As a result, regarding mobile learning in VET in the given domain and considering the trainers' view, the support of direct communication is not [sic] a required feature.

[1] WorldSkills: https://www.worldskills.org/.

Nevertheless, there can be advantages in supporting communication in the contexts of task assignment and feedback. For instance, apprentices have to document the execution of orders [15]. This has to be coordinated with trainers and is therefore a part of communication and the external evaluation by trainers. The documentation process can also become a part of the reflection process, e.g. in the form of an e-portfolio of finished tasks [3].

3.3 Learning Materials

Learning materials are an important factor in the apprenticeship. A crucial type of materials are mechanical drawings, which are used for the assignment, explanation, and discussion of tasks. Mechanical drawings are handed over and form the basis of verbal instructions. The drawings contain data about specifications such as dimensions, size tolerances, surfaces, and threads of workpieces and components of assemblies. In addition to the drawings, trainers give verbal instructions and clarify gaps in the following fields: the types of machining processes, machine tools to use, particularly important characteristics of tasks, guide times or deadlines, and the number of pieces to be manufactured. The most frequently used book is the Mechanical and Metal Trades Handbook [18], which is also permitted to be used in final examinations.

Even though the interviewed trainers are satisfied with the currently available learning materials, all interviewees stated that they would like to use additional materials. Regarding digital media and in contrast to print media, the adaptation of digital artifacts to the continuous, rapid modernization of production processes is more practicable. Additionally, digital representations have advantages of animated contents and mobility contrary to thick folders.

3.4 Expectations of Trainers Towards Mobile Learning

The expectations placed on an informatics system for VET address a broad range of aspects. Expectations, which are mentioned several times are the support of the training in general and the access to learning materials for apprentices. Expected advantages for trainers are a reduction of workload and a saving of time. These aspects would support the possibility of individual support of apprentices. Apprentices should benefit from the system for the duration of the entire apprenticeship. Altogether, the integration of a learning system has to achieve better work results.

A main advantage of digital media, which is mentioned by trainers, is visualization. The work with machines, which are not available locally, can be presented virtually, by using animations or videos. This is also the case for the understanding of internal parts of machines. Processes can be presented digitally, which avoids the need for disassembling machines. Additionally, data can be accessed nearby machines and other places of learning by the use of portable technical devices.

An important property of VET in training companies is independent learning. If a basic level of training is reached, apprentices should be able to work through tasks on their own. A digital learning system has to support them at the acquisition of related competences. This can be realized by providing relevant information for the solution of tasks, step-by-step instructions, assistance in self-assessment, or feedback of the current level of knowledge. A learning platform should be used complementary to existing procedures and solutions in VET.

For the function of trainers, the organization of tasks is important. On the one hand, this is assistance in the assignment of tasks. Depending on the current learning state and experiences of apprentices, trainers have to assign appropriate work orders in terms of complexity. On the other hand, the documentation of finished projects and treated contents is essential. For the evaluation of the learning progress of apprentices and the learning fields that have been covered, a digital system would be an added value.

4 Conclusion and Outlook: Mobile Learning in VET

We conclude this work with a summary of the main statements of trainers, which represent basic requirements for the investigated field, and present an approach for a mobile application to support VET and mechanical engineering.

4.1 Summary and Resulting Requirements

To recapitulate the interview results, we summarize the following aspects from the trainer's point of view:

- Regarding the support of trainers, a digital system should support the organization of task assignment and the documentation of work results.
- Tasks in VET and mechanical engineering are oriented to practical actions in production processes. They are often embedded in work orders, used in nearly the entire period of VET, and have a similar structure. Related sub-tasks contain their own objectives, prerequisites, and activities.
- Tasks should be processed by apprentices independently. Independent learning can be supported by step-by-step instructions, provision of materials matching the respective sub-tasks, and individual feedback. The most important learning materials are mechanical drawings and the Mechanical and Metal Trades Handbook [18].
- Direct face-to-face communication is an important factor, which has to be preserved. The underlying conditions in the visited companies are suitable, as contact persons in training facilities are reachable in the immediate vicinity.

These aspects, which were derived from the interviewed trainer's perspectives, represent basic requirements for the target group of trainers in the involved companies with regard to a mobile application in VET and the field of mechanical engineering.

In the following, we present a framework which aims to meet these requirements and which is currently being practically tested in eight training companies.

4.2 An Approach for a Mobile Application to Support Learning Tasks in VET and Mechanical Engineering

The current state of the instructional design for mobile learning in VET and mechanical engineering (see Fig. 2) is a refinement of the aspects of learning processes, learning

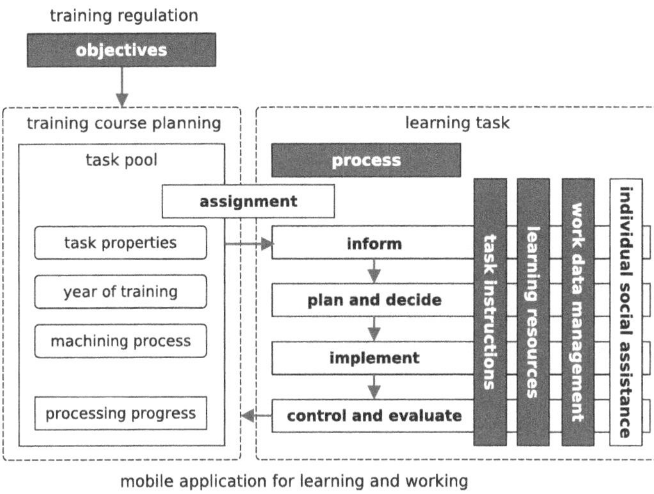

Fig. 2. Refined instructional design for independent learning tasks in vocational training and mechanical engineering embedded in a mobile application

materials, social assistance, and underlying conditions, such as teaching-learning-objectives [5]. Core of the MLS application is a domain-specific task pool, offering dedicated views for the roles of trainers and apprentices. Trainers are supported in the assignment of appropriate tasks by a filtering system, which is based on task properties (inter alia: year of training, conventional or CNC manufacturing, milling or turning, screw threads or slots). An integrated editor opens up the possibility to create new tasks or to customize existing tasks to meet company-specific requirements.

The system aims to support apprentices in completing tasks independently. Therefore, every learning task is segmented into a sequence of sub-tasks, which are typically related to the phases "inform", "plan and decide", "implement", and "control and evaluate". Sub-tasks are built on each other to meet the respective prerequisites and learning objectives. Visually, they are represented as a combination of the current state in the overall task, brief instructions, required information, related learning materials, and interactive elements (see Fig. 3). Learning materials and interactive elements are frequently reused in different phases to access previously created work data. High-quality learning materials have been integrated through a cooperation with a publishing house [18] and the respective metadata was indexed to realize a fast access. The most important theoretical contents are embedded directly into sub-task views, others can be accessed using a search engine. At the beginning of a task, apprentices have to analyze at least one mechanical drawing. Drawings are provided as vector graphics and interactive 3d representations. In the planning phase, apprentices have to prepare a digital production sheet. All entered data, notes, and learning materials can be reused afterwards during production, quality control and for reflection. The MLS application has been implemented as a web application to support the use of a broad diversity of mobile devices at different workplace locations and training companies.

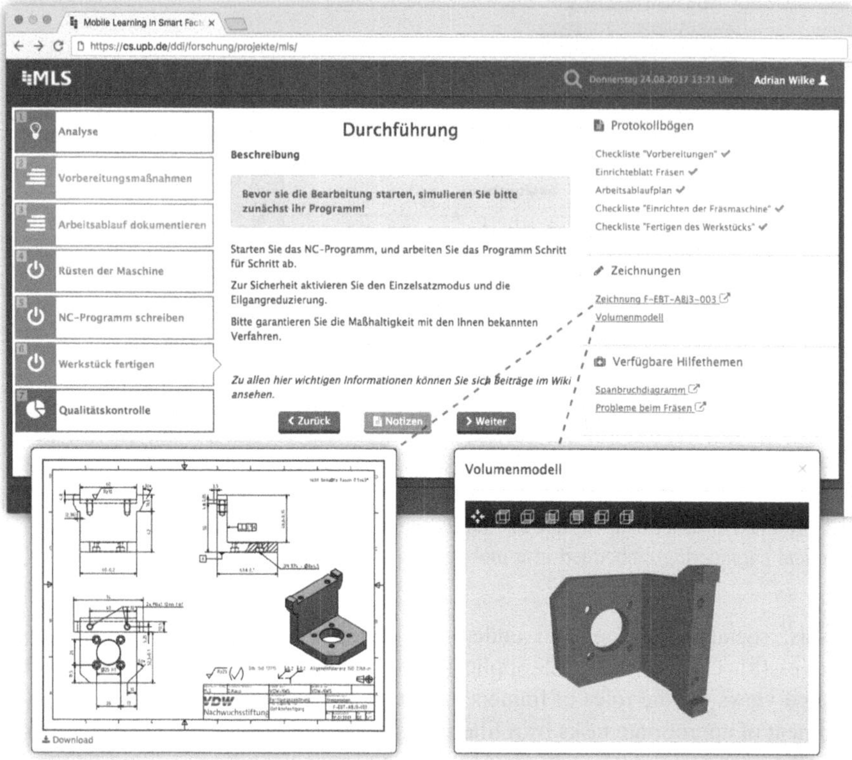

Fig. 3. Task view in MLS application, mechanical drawing, and interactive 3D representation

Acknowledgements. This work is part of the Mobile Learning in Smart Factories (MLS) project, which is funded by the German Federal Ministry of Education and Research (funding code: 01PD14009B) and implemented in cooperation with the non-profit company Nachwuchsstiftung Maschinenbau gGmbH.

References

1. Deissinger, T.: The German dual vocational education and training system as 'good practice'? Local Econ. **30**, 557–567 (2015)
2. Hensen, K.A., Hippach-Schneider, U.: Supporting teachers and trainers for successful reforms and quality of VET - Germany (2016)
3. Howe, F., Staden, C.: Work process oriented and multimedia-based learning in vocational education and training. In: Gessler, M., Freund, L. (eds.) Crossing Boundaries in Vocational Education and Training: Innovative Concepts for the 21st Century, pp. 25–32. Institut Technik und Bildung, Bremen (2015)
4. Engert, V.: Mobile Lernmöglichkeiten in der Automobilindustrie. In: de Witt, C., Reiners, A. (eds.) Mobile Learning, pp. 205–217. Springer, Wiesbaden (2013). https://doi.org/10.1007/978-3-531-19484-4_11

5. Wilke, A., Magenheim, J.: Requirements analysis for the design of workplace-integrated learning scenarios with mobile devices: mapping the territory for learning in industry 4.0. In: Proceedings of 2017 IEEE Global Engineering Education Conference, pp. 476–485. IEEE, Athens, Greece (2017). https://doi.org/10.1109/educon.2017.7942890
6. Jaschke, S.: Mobile learning applications for technical vocational and engineering education: the use of competence snippets in laboratory courses and industry 4.0. In: Proceedings of ICL2014, pp. 605–608. IEEE (2014)
7. Sonderegger, U., Merschroth, C., Zimmermann, M.: Mobile learning mit kontextbezogenen mobilen Diensten: Umsetzung in konkreten Szenarien und erste Erfahrungen. In: Rathmayer, S., Pongratz, H. (eds.) DeLFI 2015 Pre-Conference Workshops Proceedings, pp. 222–231, München (2015)
8. Sonderegger, U., Zimmermann, M., Weber, K., Becker, B.: Mobile learning mit kontextbezogenen mobilen Diensten in der "KMU Smart Factory": Szenarien und Lösungsansätze für Fertigungsprozesse. In: Rensing, C., Trahasch, S. (eds.) DeLFI 2014 Pre-Conference Workshops Proceedings, pp. 229–239. Freiburg (2014)
9. Wilke, A., Kowalewski, M., Magenheim, J., Margaritis, M.: Facing the upcoming challenges in vocational training with mobile learning. In: Brodnik, A., Lewin, C. (eds.) IFIP TC3 Working Conference "A New Culture of Learning: Computing and next Generations" Proceedings, pp. 405–406. Vilnius University, Lithuania (2015)
10. Dresing, T., Pehl, T., Schmieder, C.: Manual (on) transcription. transcription conventions, software guides and practical hints for qualitative researchers. Marburg (2015)
11. Mayring, P.: Qualitative content analysis: theoretical foundation, basic procedures and software solution (2014)
12. Lombard, M., Snyder-Duch, J., Bracken, C.C.: Content analysis in mass communication: assessment and reporting of intercoder reliability. Hum. Commun. Res. **28**, 587–604 (2002)
13. VERBI Software ed: MAXQDA 12 Reference Manual (2016)
14. Landis, J.R., Koch, G.G.: The measurement of observer agreement for categorical data. Biometrics **33**, 159 (1977)
15. Federal Institute for Vocational Education and Training: Ordinance on vocational education and training in the industrial mechanic (2007)
16. Deutsche Gesellschaft für Internationale Zusammenarbeit (GIZ) GmbH ed: Through Competence-Based to Employment-Oriented Education and Training (2013)
17. Bünning, F.: Approaches to Action Learning in Technical and Vocational Education and Training (TVET) (2007)
18. Heinzler, M., Fischer, U., Stephan, A., Paetzold, H., Kilgus, R., Näher, F., Gomeringer, R., Oesterle, S.: Mechanical and Metal Trades Handbook. Europa-Lehrmittel, Haan-Gruiten (2013)
19. Pimmer, C., Pachler, N.: Mobile learning in the workplace: unlocking the value of mobile technology for work-based education. In: Ally, M., Tsinakos, A. (eds.) Increasing Access through Mobile Learning, pp. 193–203. Vancouver (2014)

The Use of Tablets in Secondary Schools and Its Relationship with Computer Literacy

Kerstin Drossel(✉) and Birgit Eickelmann

Paderborn University, Paderborn, Germany
kdrossel@mail.upb.de

Abstract. The use of new technologies has become increasingly important in the light of the rapid technological progress made in what is commonly referred to as the digital age. Schools are now facing the challenge of imparting digital competencies to their students in order to ensure their participation in the society. In this context, mobile technologies do not seem to be used on a regular basis in schools. The present paper aims to identify the relationship between the frequency of tablet computer use and students' computer and information literacy (CIL), which currently constitutes a research gap. The data is gathered in a quasi-experimental design from an individual school in Germany. Drawing on data from tablet classes and control groups taught without tablet computers, the frequency of use and the students' level of CIL are examined. While results suggest that (1) students in tablet classes use tablets significantly more often, (2) the control group's level of CIL is higher than that of tablet class students, and (3) the theoretically established correlation between the use of tablet computers and CIL cannot be maintained, teachers indicate in interviews that there are indeed positive effects that go along with the use of tablet computers (4).

Keywords: Tablets · Computer literacy · CIL · New technologies School

1 Introduction

The use of new technologies and the acquisition of technology-related competencies have been widely considered relevant or even indispensable for the participation in a modern knowledge and information society, regarding both social and professional aspects [1–3]. The recent developments have led to an emergence of new challenges for schools and school systems, causing "the need for students to develop new forms of relevant skills like digital literacy or computer and information literacy" to be constantly growing [4]. The necessity to meet these challenges sees tablet computers as providing a variety of opportunities as mobile learning devices. International studies based on an increasing dissemination of tablet computers around the world have found tablet computers to have a positive effect at various levels of student learning, the latter serving as the ultimate point of reference here [5–10]. A meta-analysis of 23 tablet-related studies [11] revealed that a majority of research reports positive effects of tablet use on student learning outcomes, however, others indicate that tablet use may equally have no effect or even negative consequences. The authors conclude that

A. Tatnall and M. Webb (Eds.): WCCE 2017, IFIP AICT 515, pp. 114–124, 2017.
https://doi.org/10.1007/978-3-319-74310-3_14

"the fragmented nature of the current knowledge base, and the scarcity of rigorous studies, make it difficult to draw firm conclusions". In-depth investigations are advised (ibid.). While research on tablet computers for educational purposes is thus available, the frequency of use by school subjects as well as the relationship between the use of tablet computers and skills like digital literacy or computer and information literacy have so far not been a key research interest. This research gap is closed using data from the new, so-called TiGer project at a German upper secondary school, which in this respect provides current in-depth data from a unique control group design. The aim of the present contribution is to answer the question of how often students use tablet computers in class, what level of computer literacy they have and which role the tablet computers play with regards to the students' computer literacy.

Theoretical allocation of this research and the relationship between the use of new technologies and outcome variables is described in many theoretical models (e.g. [12, 13]). One elaborated and current model concerning Computer and Information Literacy (CIL) as an outcome is the ICILS 2013 framework [14]. The use of new technologies is a factor at the process level involving school and classroom factors. The other construct, namely CIL is modelled as an outcome. Contrarily to the established model of school quality and school effectiveness, the relationship between the use of ICT for learning and CIL is correlative.

2 Current State of Research

The current state of research will be presented in three sections: First of all, the use of new technologies at school with a focus on tablet computers is presented. In a second step, the students' computer literacy will be focused, before the current state of research regarding the relationship of computer use and CL will be addressed.

2.1 The Use of New Technologies at School

The fact that current research literature on mobile new technologies in education is still rather scarce reveals a first research gap that is addressed by the present contribution. In the following, new technologies in general will therefore be assessed with regards to the findings of previous research. It is particularly striking that in Germany, a traditional concept of media infrastructure using static computers in computer rooms is still common practice. The equipment infrastructure with regards to mobile devices, however, can be considered distinctly below average in comparison to Germany's neighboring countries participating in the study [15]. According to ICILS 2013, tablet computers were available to 6.5% of Grade 8 students in Germany only (ibid.). The equipment with tablet computers at German schools is therefore significantly below the EU average of 15.9%.

The international comparison further showed big differences in the use of computers at school. While 81% of students in Australia report using the computer at least once a week, only 31 percent of students in Germany report doing so [15]. Taking a closer look at the individual main subjects (including the test language (Language Arts: test language), mathematics and foreign languages (Language Arts: foreign)), it becomes evident that only three to four percent of students in Germany report a regular, i.e. at least weekly computer use in class. By international comparison, Germany therefore comes in last [15]. Data on the frequency of tablet use in different school subjects is therefore currently not available for Germany with only a few exemplary studies and pilot projects examining and evaluating tablet use in general and giving recommendations (cf. [16–18]).

2.2 Students and Their Computer Literacy

Studies around the world have investigated ICT-related competencies of students using different methods. Hakkarainen et al. [19] in Finland, for instance, used a design that relies on the students' self-reported competencies. Likewise, Osunwusi and Abifarin [20] base their comparative analyses on questionnaires administered to participants in Nigeria. For Chilean students, Claro et al. [21] used a performance-based assessment design – the ICTSfL test. The results merely show that the students' skills related to the use of ICT as consumers exceeded the skills of becoming producers using ICT (ibid.). Alternative designs in the qualitative domain include interviews of Indian students as conducted by Sampath Kumar et al. [22]. Results comprise rather specific findings based on the answers given by the interviewees. While the afore-mentioned studies tend to have a closer look at the data gathered, other studies from Australia have computed an overall ICT Literacy Scale using achievement tests, from which proficiency levels regarding computer literacy could be deduced (cf. [23–25]). These can then serve the purpose of being included in further analyses. While the Australian studies mentioned above display a scope limited to the Australian states and territories, international comparisons of the CIL students have at their disposal as shown by the IEA study of ICILS 2013 help to gain further insight into the competence levels of German students. According to ICILS 2013, Grade 8 students in Germany reach an average performance of 523 scale points[1], similar to the EU average (525 scale points) but significantly above the OECD average (516 scale points) and the international average of 500 scale points [15].

2.3 The Relationship Between the Use of New Technologies and CIL

Meta-analyses [26, 27] suggest there is a positive relationship between ICT use and student achievement in different subject areas. While ICT has been examined with respect to its influence on subject-related achievement such as mathematics and science, the use of new technologies and its relationship with computer literacy has thus far been investigated rather marginally. Only very recently, Rohatgi et al. [28] were able to show for data gathered in Norway that the use of ICT has an indirect impact on the CIL achievement of students, the intermediate construct being ICT self-efficacy. Sung et al. [29] in their meta-analysis have further found mobile devices to be more effective than desktop computers or laptops when it comes to students' learning

[1] Scale points are standardized to a mean of 500 points. Any deviations from this mean allow for a direct comparison between countries, i.e. 501 scale points and more are above-average, whereas 499 scale points and less are below-average.

performance. Focusing on direct effects again, the research interest of this contribution comprises both the teachers' and the students' use of the afore-mentioned technologies. As far as the teachers' use of computers is concerned, the international comparison shows a positive effect on CIL in Germany only, contrarily to Australia, Norway and the Czech Republic [30]. Regarding the school-related use of computers by students, the international comparison revealed consistently positive relations. Warschauer [31], for instance, was able to demonstrate that students attending notebook schools (including primary and secondary schools) learn to access, process and use information much better while also acquiring skills to integrate this information into written and multimedia presentations. Likewise, an Australian study conducted by the National Assessment Program ICT Literacy pointed out that the school-related use of computers shows a positive correlation with the students' ICT-literacy competencies [25]. The ICILS 2013 international comparison equally emphasized that the school-related computer use in most participating countries correlates positively with CIL. Only three countries, including Germany, showed a negative effect [32]. While some authors even seem to consider the literacy developed through the use of tablet computers to be a new, distinct literacy called tablet computer literacy (cf. [33]), the relationship between a school-related use of tablet computers and computer literacy has thus far not been addressed.

3 Research Questions

The following research questions can be deduced from the research desiderata described above:

I. How often do students use tablets in school? Is there a difference between students in tablet classes and the control group?
II. What level of computer literacy do students have at their disposal? Is there a difference between students in tablet classes and the control group?
III. Which role does the use of tablets play in this context? Is there a relationship between the use of tablets and computer literacy?
IV. To what extent do teachers experience a development regarding the tablet class students' computer literacy?

4 Methodology

4.1 Sample

In order to answer the research questions above, the present contribution uses the data provided by the TiGer project (*Tablets im Gymnasium evaluieren und reflektieren*). This project used scholarly guidance in the process of introducing tablet computers to Grade 7 students at an upper secondary school (*Gymnasium*) in the German federal state of North-Rhine Westphalia. From the beginning of the school year 2014/2015, tablet computers were used in Grade 7 classes. These mobile devices are owned by the students who could therefore also use them outside school. Two out of five parallel classes were fully equipped with tablet computers, while the remaining three classes continued without tablets, hence serving as control groups. The concomitant research involves an elaborate triangulation design of multiple perspectives. The focus of this contribution is placed on a quantitative student survey, gathering data both at the beginning of the school year when the students did not yet possess any tablet computers (Time of Measurement 1; ToM 1) and at the end of the 2014/15 school year, with tablet class students having worked with tablet computers while students from the control group have not (Time of Measurement 2; ToM 2). This quantitative data is subsequently complemented by qualitative teacher data, which was gathered in the form of open questionnaires.

4.2 Instruments and Methods

Composition of Longitudinal Section. In order to model the longitudinal section, all students who only participated at one time of measurement were excluded from the analyses. The original 119 participants were hence reduced to 105 students that constitute the sample. 43 of these were taught in tablet classes, whereas the remaining 62 attended parallel classes in which no tablet computers were used and that can hence serve as a control group.

Tablet use. The use of tablets was assessed in a subject-specific approach for all school subjects. In the following, the frequency of tablet use is reported for the main subjects of German, Mathematics and English. The five-tier response format ranged from *never* (1) to *every day* (5). At that, the use of tablet computers is regarded both subject-specifically and as a latent construct used for further analyses. The exploratory factor analysis of the subject-specific tablet use reveals that the three selected items show factor loadings on one factor with a very good reliability for both groups of students at both times of measurement.

Computer Literacy. For the purpose of assessing the students‘computer literacy, the National Educational Panel Study's (NEPS) computer literacy test for Grade 9 was used [34]. Due to the fact that a few tasks of the Grade 9 NEPS test were no longer up to date at the time of measurement – which can be attributed to the fast-paced development of new technologies – these tasks were replaced by corresponding items from the Grade 6 NEPS test. Example items can be found in Senkbeil et al. [35]. The paper-pencil test consisting of 36 tasks (including 30 simple multiple choice and 6 complex multiple choice items) depicts realistic problems embedded in a range of authentic situations using screenshots.

In order to estimate item and person parameters for computer literacy, a partial credit model was used and estimated in ConQuest [36]. In a first step, ability estimates were estimated as weighted maximum likelihood estimates (WLEs, [37]) with a metric of 500 and a SE of 100. As the same computer literacy tests were used at both times of measurement, the item parameters of ToM 1 are implemented to estimate the item difficulty of ToM 2. The results show for both times of measurement that the items exhibited good item fit. Moreover, the test showed a high reliability (.932/.865) and the different comprehension requirements foster a unidimensional construct. The correlation of the two WLEs amounts to .685 for the tablet classes and .678 for the control group. This suggests that the computer literacy construct remains relatively stable over time. In addition to measuring the students' competencies, open, qualitative questionnaires were handed out to the teachers teaching the tablet classes (N = 6). This complementary instrument results in a multi-perspective, triangulative design of the study, which is expected to contribute to the second research question of this paper.

5 Findings

5.1 Tablet Use

At the beginning of the school year (ToM 1), neither the students in tablet classes nor the students of the control group used tablet computers in their main subjects. The two groups therefore do not show significant differences (Table 1). It can hence be established that the starting situation is the same for all students. At ToM 2 – after one year – the results show that tablet class students use tablet computers at least once a week but not every day. No significant differences between the main subjects could be observed. According to expectation, the control group does not show any changes with respect to the first time of measurement – the use of tablet computers can still be considered an exception here. The differences between students from tablet classes and students from the control group were all found to be significant.

Table 1. Students' tablet use differentiated by tablet class and control group at ToM 1 and ToM 2

	ToM 1					ToM 2				
	Tablet classes		Control group		Sig	Tablet classes		Control group		Sig
	M[a]	SD	M[a]	SD	p	M[a]	SD	M[a]	SD	p
German	1.2	.61	1.2	.56	.839	4.3	.82	1.2	.51	.000
English	1.1	.55	1.3	.84	.289	4.5	.83	1.2	.70	.000
Math	1.1	.54	1.1	.53	.885	4.3	.97	1.1	.54	.000
Main subjects total	1.1	.54	1.2	.58	.512	4.5	.79	1.2	.51	.000

[a]1-never; 2-less than once a month; 3-at least once a month but not every week; 4-at least once a week but not every day; 5-every day

5.2 Computer Literacy

The computer literacy that students have at their disposal and the extent to which students from the tablet classes and from the control group show differences in their performance will be subsequently discussed. The average performance of the students taught in tablet classes before obtaining the devices is at 472 scale points, thereby displaying significantly lower scores than their fellow students from the control group (520 scale points) (Table 2). This result remains in force even after the introduction of tablet computers and repeated computer literacy measurement procedures after the

Table 2. Students' performance indexes (WLE) in computer literacy differentiated by tablet classes and control group at ToM 1 and ToM 2.

ToM 1					ToM 2				
Tablet classes		Control group		Sig	Tablet classes		Control group		Sig
M	SD	M	SD	p	M	SD	M	SD	p
472	102.5	520	94.2	.016	472	105.6	520	91.8	.015

school year. Both the control group and the tablet students attain – on average – the same competencies as they did at ToM 1, resulting in the fact that tablet students show a significantly lower average level of achievement regarding computer literacy yet again.

5.3 Relationship Between Computer Use and Computer Literacy – Students Achievement

As explained by means of the theoretical framework model, a correlation between the use of tablet computers and computer literacy can be assumed (Table 3). At ToM 1, this correlation is not significant for the tablet classes (at .207 with p = .225), but proves to be significant for the control group (at .364 with p = .007). The second time of measurement shows a substantially smaller correlation that is not significant in either case (−.011 for tablet classes; .183 for the control group).

Table 3. Correlations between the use of tablet computers and computer literacy differentiated by tablet classes and control group at ToM 1 and ToM 2

ToM 1				ToM 2			
Tablet classes		Control group		Tablet classes		Control group	
r	p	r	p	r	p	r	p
.207	.225	.364	.007	−.011	.945	.183	.157

5.4 Relationship Between Computer Use and Computer Literacy – Teacher's Perspective

In contrary to the findings from this performance test, the teachers' impressions as reflected by the qualitative data gathered from an open questionnaire do point to an improvement in the students' CIL. One teacher, for instance, found that "the students use the tablet more like a tool while the 'play instinct' decreases constantly. The exhausting of all of the tablets' functions is impressive. Information research, the preparing of presentations, drafting of e-mails and saving documents in clouds has become a routine for most [students]. The targeted use of apps also becomes more and more reflected." (Mrs Schmidt, 35 years old, teacher of Arts and Spanish). This reflects the experience of all six teachers, especially with regards to the more confident and reflected use of the new technologies. Individual teachers, however, also point to "alarming" cases, where "unconfident girls" are still showing difficulties in using basic applications after 1.5 years of using the tablet computers.

6 Discussion and Outlook

First of all, the analyses have shown that according to expectation, the tablets were used on a regular basis in the main subjects after their introduction. At that, students in tablet classes use tablet computers on an at least weekly basis, while the frequency of tablet use in the parallel classes without tablets did not change over time and still corresponds essentially to the category of "never". Hence, it is not surprising that students in tablet classes use tablets in class significantly more often than the students in the control group. This result primarily emphasizes the importance of material resources available to students that constitutes a prerequisite for the implementation of new technologies.

With regards to the second research question, it can be stated that the average computer literacy – as tested with the TILT test – was substantially lower among tablet students than among students from the control group both prior to and after the introduction of tablet computers. While the tablet students' level of CIL amounts to 472 scale points (i.e. below average), the control group's CIL is above-average (520 scale points). It further becomes evident that no improvement could be detected in either group as far as the students' performance is concerned. These findings were not to be expected, however, they do appear rather plausible when taking a closer look at the instrument with which computer literacy was tested – and its theoretical conception. In contrary to the findings from this performance test, the teachers' impressions as reflected by the qualitative data gathered from an open questionnaire do point to an improvement in the students' CIL. According to preliminary findings (teacher, student, and principal perceptions), the software applications used there did not correspond to those that were put to use by the tablet classes. For instance, students did not send e-mails with their tablets but communicated via specially-designed communication applications. Further differences were found with respect to the process components of the theoretical framework model of computer literacy. The way in which tablet students manage information, for example, is completely different from the way it is operationalized in the TILT test. The students used the tablets' cameras to digitalize and save documents – a competency that is not assessed by the instrument. It is, however, worth noting that for the German-speaking world, there is currently no valid and openly accessible instrument available to account for these diverse potential applications that are unique to tablet computers. With the development in this area being rather fast-paced – both with respect to software applications and hardware – the designing of a suitable and valid instrument does constitute a big challenge. A further possible explanation for the persisting difference in CIL could lie in the fact that students from the control group acquired their skills outside of the classroom. This remains to be verified and could constitute the focus of further analyses.

A third result of this contribution reveals that the assumed correlation between the use of tablet computers and computer literacy as depicted by the theoretical framework model [14] cannot be maintained. The same is true if these results are compared to multiple research findings that have asserted a direct relationship between the two constructs [19–22]. At first glance, this result therefore seems unexpected, while it does support the assumption that the TILT instrument could not measure the competencies as they were acquired by the students through the use of tablet computers.

From the teacher interviews (question 4), it becomes apparent that there are indeed positive effects that go along with the use of tablet computers (such as an increase in motivation, an improvement of organization and communication as well as a compensation for cancelled lessons). These, however, do not constitute the focus of this paper.

While the data of the study are not representative neither for Germany nor for the focused school form, it seems to be helpful to implement larger studies (e.g. large-scale assessments) in order to draw representative conclusions about the use of tablets.

References

1. Jordan, H., Hunter, E., Lee, I.C., Wighting, M., Derrick, M.G.: Tablet technology for educators. In: Proceedings of Global Learn 2016, pp. 94–100 (2016)
2. Katz, I.R., Macklin, A.S.: Information and communication technology (ICT) literacy: integration and assessment in higher education. J. Systemics, Cybern. Inf. **5**(4), 50–55 (2007)
3. Weinert, S., Artelt, C., Prenzel, M., Senkbeil, M., Ehmke, T., Carstensen, H.: Development of competencies across the life span. Zeitschrift für Erziehungswissenschaft. **14**(2), 67–86 (2011)
4. Lorenz, R., Eickelmann, B., Gerick, J.: What affects students' computer and information literacy around the world? – an analysis of school and teacher factors in high performing countries. In: Slykhuis, D., Marks, G. (eds.) Proceedings of Society for Information Technology & Teacher Education International Conference 2015. Association for the Advancement of Computing in Education (AACE), Chesapeake, VA (2015)
5. Li, S.C., Pow, J.W.C., Wong, E.M.L., Fung, A.C.W.: Empowering student learning through tablet PCs: a case study. Educ. Inf. Technol. **15**, 171–180 (2010)
6. Nguyen, H., Bilen, S., Devon, R., Wise, J.: Adopting tablet PCs in design education: student use of tablet PCs and lessons learned. In: Bastiaens, T., Carliner, S. (eds.) Proceedings of E-Learn: World Conference on E-Learning in Corporate, Government, Healthcare, and Higher Education 2007 Association for the Advancement of Computing in Education (AACE), Chesapeake, VA (2007)
7. Enriquez, A.G.: Enhancing student performance using tablet computers. Coll. Teach. **58**(3), 77–84 (2010)
8. Katzan, H.: Principles of tablet computing for educators. Contemp. Issues Educ. Res. **8**(1), 7–14 (2015)
9. Koile, K., Singer, D.A.: Development of a tablet-PC-based system to increase instructor-student classroom interactions and student learning. In: Berque, D., Prey, J., Reed, R. (eds.) The Impact of Tablet PCs and Pen-Based Technology in Education. Purdue University Press, West Lafayette, IN (2006)
10. Kontkanen, S., Dillon, P., Valtonen, T., Eronen, L., Koskela, H., Väisänen, P.: Students' experiences of learning with iPads in upper secondary school – a base for proto-TPACK. Educ. Inf. Technol. **22**, 1–28 (2016)

11. Haßler, B., Major, L., Hennessy, S.: Tablet use in schools: a critical review of the evidence for learning outcomes. J. Comput. Assist. Learn. **32**, 139–156 (2015)
12. Biagi, F., Loi, M.: Measuring ICT use and learning outcomes. evidence from recent econometric studies. Europ. J. Educ. **48**(1), 28–42 (2013)
13. Law, N., Pelgrum, W.J., Plomp, T.: Pedagogy and ICT use in schools around the world: findings from the IEA SITES 2006 study. CERC Studies in Comparative Education. Springer, Dordrecht (2008). https://doi.org/10.1007/978-1-4020-8928-2
14. Fraillon, J., Schulz, W., Ainley, J.: International computer and information literacy study: assessment framework. International Association for the Evaluation of Educational Achievement (IEA), Amsterdam (2013)
15. Fraillon, J., Ainley, J., Schulz, W., Friedman, T., Gebhardt, E.: Preparing for Life in a Digital Age: The IEA International Computer and Information Literacy Study International Report. Springer, Cham (2014). https://doi.org/10.1007/978-3-319-14222-7
16. Rellecke, D.: Digitaler Unterricht für alle. Das Internat Schloss Neubeuern ist Deutschlands erste papierlose Schule [Digital teaching and learning for all. The boarding school Schloss Neubeuern is Germany's first paperless school]. LA-Multimedia **8**(4), 10–12 (2011)
17. Spang, A.: Lernen mit iPad, App und Cloud im Musikunterricht. Neue Lernkultur am Beispiel der Kaiserin-Augusta-Schule in Köln [Learning with iPad, App and Cloud in Music classes. A new learning culture using the example of the Kaiserin-Augusta School in Cologne]. Computer + Unterricht. **25**(97), 26–27 (2015)
18. Welling, S., Stolpmann, B.E.: Mobile Computing in der Schule – Zentrale Herausforderungen am Beispiel eines Schulversuchs zur Einführung von Tablet-PCs [Mobile Computing at school – Central challenges using the example of a school experiment on the introduction of tablet computers]. Jahrbuch Medienpädagogik. **9**, 197–221 (2012)
19. Hakkarainen, K., Ilomäki, L., Lipponen, L., Muukkonen, H., Rahikainen, M., Tuominen, T., et al.: Students' skills and practices of using ICT: results of a national assessment in Finland. Comput. Educ. **34**, 103–117 (2000)
20. Osunwusi, A.O., Abifarin, M.S.: A comparative assessment of computer literacy of private and public secondary school students in Lagos State. Nigeria. Educ. Res. Rev. **8**(12), 881–889 (2013)
21. Claro, M., Preiss, D.D., San Martín, E., Jara, I., Hinostroza, J.E., Valenzuela, S., et al.: Assessment of 21st century ICT skills in Chile: test design and results from high school level students. Comput. Educ. **59**, 1042–1053 (2012)
22. Sampath Kumar, B.T., Basavaraja, M.T., Gagendra, R.: Computer literacy competencies among Indian students: the digital divide. Asian Educ. Develop. Stud. **3**(3), 267–281 (2014)
23. ACARA [Australian Curriculum, Assessment, and Reporting Authority]: National Assessment Program – ICT Literacy: Years 6 & 10 report 2011. ACARA, Sydney (2012)
24. MCEETYA [Ministerial Council for Education, Employment, Training and Youth Affairs]: National assessment program: ICT Literacy, Years 6 and 10. Report 2005. MCEETYA, Melbourne (2008)
25. MCEECDYA [Ministerial Council for Education, Early Childhood Development and Youth Affairs]: National Assessment Program. ICT literacy. Years 6 and 10. Report 2008. MCEECDYA, Carlton South (2010)
26. Li, Q., Ma, X.: A meta-analysis of the effects of computer technology on school students' mathematics learning. Educ. Psychol. Rev. **22**, 215–243 (2010)
27. Tamim, R.M., Bernard, R.M., Borokhovski, E., Abrami, P.C., Schmid, R.F.: What forty years of research says about the impact of technology on learning: a second-order meta-analysis and validation study. Rev. Educ. Res. **81**(1), 4–28 (2011)

28. Rohatgi, A., Scherer, R., Hatlevik, O.E.: The role of ICT self-efficacy for students' ICT use and their achievement in a computer and information literacy test. Comput. Educ. **102**, 103–116 (2016)
29. Sung, Y.-T., Chang, K.-E., Liu, T.-C.: The effects of integrating mobile devices with teaching and learning on students' learning performance: a meta-analysis and research synthesis. Comput. Educ. **94**, 252–275 (2016)
30. Gerick, J., Eickelmann, B., Bos, W.: School-level predictors for ICT Use in schools and students' computer and information literacy. Large-scale Assessments Educ. **5**(1), 1–13 (2017)
31. Warschauer, M.: Information literacy in the laptop classroom. Teach. Coll. Record. **109**(11), 2511–2540 (2007)
32. Eickelmann, B., Schaumburg, H., Drossel, K., Lorenz, R.: Schulische Nutzung von neuen Technologien in Deutschland im internationalen Vergleich [The use of new technologies in an international comparison]. In: Bos, W., Eickelmann, B., Gerick, J., Goldhammer, F., Schaumburg, H., Schwippert, K., Senkbeil, M., Schulz-Zander, R., Wendt, H. (eds.) ICILS 2013 – Computer- und informationsbezogene Kompetenzen von Schülerinnen und Schülern in der 8. Jahrgangsstufe im internationalen Vergleich. Waxmann, Münster (2014)
33. Hergüner, Ç.: Tablet computer literacy levels of the physical education and sports department students. Malays. Online J. Educ. Technol. **4**(2), 58–65 (2016)
34. Senkbeil, M., Ihme, J.M.: NEPS technical report for computer literacy – scaling results of starting cohort 4 in ninth grade (NEPS Working Paper No. 17). Otto-Friedrich-Universität/Nationales Bildungspanel, Bamberg (2012)
35. Senkbeil, M., Ihme, J.M., Wittwer, J.: The test of technological and information literacy (TILT) in the national educational panel study: development, empirical testing, and evidence for validity. J. Educ. Res. Online **5**, 139–161 (2013)
36. Wu, M.L., Adams, R.J., Wilson, M.R.: ConQuest: multi-aspect test software [Computer Program]. Australian Council for Educational Research, Camberwell (1997)
37. Warm, T.A.: Weighted likelihood estimation of ability in item response theory. Psychometrika **54**, 427–450 (1989)

Learners' Experiences in a Multicultural Remote Collaborative Learning Environment: A Case of ICT4D Course

Elizaphan Maina[1], Nicholas Mavengere[2(✉)], Francis Manzira[3], John Kihoro[4], and Mikko Ruohonen[2]

[1] Kenyatta University, Nairobi, Kenya
maina.elizaphan@ku.ac.ke
[2] University of Tampere, Tampere, Finland
Nicholas.Mavengere@staff.uta.fi, mikko.ruohonen@uta.fi
[3] University of Venda, Thohoyandou, South Africa
mfmanzira@gmail.com
[4] The Cooperative University of Kenya, Nairobi, Kenya
kihoro.jm@cuck.ac.ke

Abstract. Collaborative learning is advocated because of its pedagogical advantage, which allows knowledge construction through group discussions among learners. In a collaborative learning environment, there will be many learners with diverse cultures. The pedagogical advantages of collaborative learning include learners from different cultural orientation sharing unique learning experiences. The purpose of this study is to investigate learners' experiences in a multicultural remote collaborative learning environment among three countries, South Africa, Kenya and Finland. An Informational and Communication Technology for Development (ICT4D) course was offered to 51 online students from three Universities in the countries mentioned. The course was group-work focused and groups were comprised of students from different Universities. A questionnaire was designed and distributed online to these students. The objective of the questionnaire was to assess students' experiences in a remote collaborative, tools used and knowledge sharing in the course. Research findings indicated that students utilized well synchronous and asynchronous communication technologies but also faced challenges like time differences and unequal contribution and participation in groups. However, team work of the students was excellent owing to the fact that 17 students managed to achieve the goal of the virtual learning for ICT4D course through remote collaborative learning.

Keywords: Collaborative learning · Multicultural · Learners' experiences Universities · ICT4D

1 Introduction

Online collaboration learning is based on constructivist view of learning which requires learners and instructors to work together when solving problems, completing tasks, or creating products [1]. Creating online learning communities rich in collaborative

A. Tatnall and M. Webb (Eds.): WCCE 2017, IFIP AICT 515, pp. 125–133, 2017.
https://doi.org/10.1007/978-3-319-74310-3_15

learning tasks has been pointed out as of major benefit to adults who can share work related experiences around the globe [2]. In the past, collaborative learning has been restricted to the classroom environment because of the logistical difficulties in distance learning environment [3]. However, with the introduction of internet technologies in Learning Management Systems (LMSs) such as Wiki Spaces, workshops and forums for collaborative work, new opportunities for student collaboration in an online environment have been created [4]. In Computer Supported Collaborative learning different communication tools both video based and text based can be used to provide a platform for the group members to discuss adequately and express their ideas in the desirable form. Text based communication like chats, emails, blogs and forums are widely used to discuss group task in an online collaborative learning environment as they are widely available in most LMSs [5]. However, without other visual communication tools such as Skype, learners may miss facial expressions which are useful to monitor the partner understands of the concept in a remote collaborative learning environment. Therefore, if learners are joining groups in different locations, all types of collaborative tools should be availed.

According to [6] there are seven qualities of learning which are interactive, interrelated, and interdependent with each other. These qualities include:

1. Active: Learners' role in learning process is active; they are engaged in mindful processing of information and they are responsible for the result.
2. Constructive: Learners construct new knowledge on the basis of their previous knowledge.
3. Collaborative: Learners work together in building new knowledge in co-operation with each other and exploiting each other's skills.
4. Intentional: Learners try actively and willingly to achieve a cognitive objective.
5. Contextual: Learning tasks are situated in a meaningful real world tasks or they are introduced through case-based or problem-based real life examples.
6. Transfer: Learners are able to transfer learning from the situations and contexts, where learning has taken place and use their knowledge in other situations.
7. Reflective: Learners articulate what they have learned and reflect on the processes and decisions entailed by the process.

Some of these qualities do assess the collaborative learning aspect while others assess the quality of transfer of knowledge to individual learner. This paper utilizes these qualities of learning to assess the learners' perceived learning qualities on a remote collaborative learning environment.

Collaborative learning is of value in that it enables knowledge sharing and this increases the more diverse the collaborating group. Collaborative learning is even more important in today's environment characterized by factors, such as globalization. In addition, problem solving, for example in industries, is usually multi-disciplinary and thus making collaboration a necessity. There are efforts which need to be done, such as understanding students as users of the learning management systems [7, 8]. Recent studies show that online collaborative learning enhances knowledge construction and promotes learner centered learning pedagogy [9, 10]. In multicultural collaborative learning environment, there is a possibility diversity in cultural background can bring different ways of reasoning, cooperation skills and social relationship between group members [11]. These differences might influence the quality of collaborative learning and the perceived challenges on a remote collaborative learning environment. Cultural differences among team members should not be under estimated because they can cause conflicts, misunderstanding and poor performance. In addition this, [12] identified the following five typical challenges that are associated with multicultural teams: (i) Managing cultural diversity, differences and conflicts, (ii) Handling geographic distances, dispersion and despair, (iii) Dealing with coordination and control aspects (iv) Maintaining communication richness and (v) Developing and maintaining teamness. However, few empirical studies have analyzed student's experiences on remote collaboration in a multicultural learning environment [13]. In view of this, this study discusses the learners' experiences in learning ICT4D course which was offered online through remote collaboration to students from three different countries.

The Objectives were:

1. To investigate students' experiences on remote collaboration
2. To identify student preferred remote collaborative learning tools
3. To identify challenges and opportunities for offering an online course through remote collaborative environment
4. To identify students' perceptions on the quality of learning experienced through remote collaboration

2 Research Methodology

University of Tampere hosted an ICT4D online course in autumn 2016. The course was done in collaboration with University of Venda in South Africa and Kenyatta University in Kenya. The course was team-work focused and students from different universities were put in groups. Most of the course tasks about 80% were group tasks, so students had to collaborate remotely with students from other universities and submit course tasks.

2.1 Research Design

A descriptive survey using three Institutions of Higher Learning (IHL) in three countries was adopted. This research design was applied to investigate students' experience in remote collaborative learning environment. A descriptive survey was adopted as it could examine the situation the way it was and provide quantitative information that can be summarized through statistical analysis, thus providing the basis to answer our research objectives [14]. An online questionnaire was administered using a web-based tool (Google doc) to a group of students who registered ICT4D Course online in the three Universities. This approach was preferred because students are geographically dispersed; it enabled a faster collection of responses and the ease of exporting the data to Statistical Package for Social Sciences (SPSS) for analysis.

2.2 Sample and Sampling Procedures

A purposive sampling was done where the researchers requested students to voluntary register for ICT4D course in three Universities from three different countries. From the target institution the researchers requested the participants to register for the course online within a specific period of time and provide emails to the course co-coordinators. A total of 48 students registered but only 17 students managed to finish the course. Learning materials were availed through Moodle and all participants were required to enroll into Moodle in order to access learning materials.

2.3 Research Instruments

Data was collected through a questionnaire that consisted of items to capture student's demographic data, students' experiences in remote collaboration on ICT4D course, students' challenges in remote collaboration and students' perspective on the quality of learning experienced in a remote collaborative learning environment. To ensure validity, content related evidence was adopted and expert analysis was done to review the format and relevance of the items to the research objectives.

2.4 Data Collection and Analysis

The web based questionnaire was distributed through email invitations to the participants at the end of the course. The invitation email contained the purpose of the study and a link to the URL where the questionnaire was located. A total of 17 responded which was 100% for those who finished the course: The collected data was exported to SPSS and coded as per the research objectives. For quantitative data a descriptive analysis was carried out, such as frequencies and percentages on: demographic data, students' experiences in remote collaboration on ICT4D course. For qualitative data narratives based on themes for the students' challenges in remote collaboration and students' perspective on the quality of learning experienced in a remote collaborative learning environment was adopted.

3 Results

In this section, we present our results using descriptive statistics for quantitative data and narratives based on themes for the qualitative data.

3.1 Learner Demographic and Characteristics Information

The study findings on demographic and characteristics information are presented on Table 1. As shown in Table 1 the majority of the learners were doing masters.

Table 1. Frequencies on the demographic Information (N = 17)

Level of study	Frequency	%
Bachelor	5	29.4%
Master	8	47.1%
PhD	3	17.6%
Other	1	5.9%

3.2 Students Experiences on the Remote Collaborative Course Environment

In additional to demographic information, students' experiences on collaborative learning were captured using a 5-point Likert scale from *not at all (1) to totally (5)*, as shown in Table 2.

Table 2. Frequencies on Students experiences on the collaborative course Environment based on 5-point Likert scale

Students experiences	Frequencies				
	1	2	3	4	5
The course environment enabled me to easily contact other participants	1	4	5	4	3
I did not feel lonely in the course environment	0	2	3	9	3
The course environment enabled me to get a good impression of other participants	0	3	7	3	3
The course environment allowed spontaneous informal conversations	3	4	4	3	3
The course environment helped us to develop into a well performing team	3	3	4	1	6
The course environment enabled us to develop good work relationships with other participants	3	2	4	4	4
The course environment enabled me to identify myself with the other participants	0	6	2	6	3
I felt comfortable with the course environment	1	2	4	7	3
The course environment allowed for non-task-related conversations	4	3	3	6	1
The course environment enabled me to make close friendship with my team mates or other participants	4	3	6	2	2
How much do you value team/group work in your online learning experience	0	4	2	7	4

Results indicated that most participants were able to link to one another and interact socially.

3.3 Tools and Methods Used for Remote Collaboration

Apart from the tools which were availed in Moodle for group work, students were able to interact remotely through Skype, email, whatsapp, Facebook and edit documents remotely using Google drive and Google doc. Table 3 summarizes the remote collaborative tools and how the students utilized them.

Table 3. Remote collaborative tools used

Collaborative tool	Purpose
Google drive	To store data
Google Doc/slide	Report and presentation for group assignment, online editing shared documents
Skype	To discuss and write together
email	To contact and discuss group work
Whatsapp	To get connected and discuss group work
Facebook	To get connected and discuss group work

3.4 Challenges Encountered in Remote Collaboration

During the remote collaboration participants encountered a number of challenges such as un-equal participation, time difference, lack of face to face interaction, lack of prompt feedback and internet connectivity. Table 4 illustrates some cited examples for the challenges from students' perspective.

Table 4. Students' challenges in remote collaboration

Challenges	Cited example
Un-equal participation	• *Our group (group 5) has not really formed a group for working together. I have contributed in both assignments but some group members have not really contributed so much which is in my opinion ok as long everything contributes at least something. In the first assignment one of us took voluntary lead on the assignment and in the second one I took the lead in editing contributions. However, in the second assignment only me and one other person contributed so the remote group work has not worked* • *Some people just faded out from the group - they didnt participate and finally they left our Skype group. In addition, some people do not participate during the whole group task - they only participate during the last days and I feel that this is unfair for the others. So in my opinion, the group work is not working that well and I wish the amount of group work in this course would be smaller. I also have personal reasons for this opinion, because I think group work is not the best way for me to learn things*
Time difference	• *Everyone is in different time zone so it becomes an issue sometimes if instant feedback is required* • *It is hard to get everyone online at the same time so sometimes you have to wait to hear back from others. Also everyone has their own schedules so when one is ready some of the others have not yet even started. But it has worked out surprisingly easily*
Lack of face to face interaction	• *It is hard to get some of group members to do their part of the job, when you don't see face to face. Someone say that yes they will participate, but in the end, they haven't done anything. Someone doesn't even respond to your e-mail. Google docs is a good tool because there you can see who has written which part*
Lack of prompt feedback	• *Lack of communication, and late response* • *group members not answering to emails - group members sending personal emails instead informing the whole group - personal emails with requests such as "I have no time to contribute to assignment but please add my name to it" - group members not participating to assignments*
Internet connectivity	• *Wifi problems from my side so accessing the information on time was a challenge*

3.5 Students' Perceptions' on Remote Collaboration for Learning ICT4D Course

During the group work students were required to actively participate, construct knowledge together, conceptualize concepts and transfer knowledge to one another. In view of this, students were requested to identify among seven qualities of learning, which quality of learning they experienced during the remote collaborative learning. As shown in Table 5, Students perceived that all the qualities were realized with the aspect of collaboration been rated highly (70.6%).

Table 5. Frequencies and percentages (%) on Students' perceptions' on remote collaboration

Quality of learning	Frequency	%
Active	10	58.8
Constructive	10	58.8
Collaborative	12	70.6
Intentional	8	47.1
Conversational	10	58.8
Contextualized	7	41.2
Reflective	8	47.1
Transfer	11	64.7
None of the above	2	11.8

4 Discussion

The composition of the virtual team involved 52 participants from 3 countries where 4 were instructors, namely Kenya (2 instructors, 10 students), Finland (1 team leader, 27 students) and South Africa (1 instructor, 11 students). This formed a multicultural team which [12], defined as a task oriented group consisting of people of different nationalities and cultures. They were positioned in individual, geographically distant countries with participation in the learning process being virtual.

Collaborative learning experience in the ICT4D course had other dimensions besides academic aspect as demonstrated in Table 2, for example, social and knowledge sharing [16]. The social aspect of online learning has been emphasized as important to reduce loneliness in past research [17]. Loneliness in online learning is one of the reasons of high dropout rate. Therefore, group-work is one way of reducing loneliness by encouraging interaction in the groups. Knowledge sharing was a big component of this collaborative learning experience because of the diverse cultural background of the students. For example one student commented:

> *"it's a wonderful learning platform that allow for interactions of people even when they are far from each other"*

Regarding to remote communication as illustrated in Table 3 students were able to utilize both asynchronous and synchronous communication tools to share ideas and collaborate remotely. There were also challenges that were witnessed during the collaboration experience as demonstrated in Table 4. For example, in some groups not all the students participated well and contributed to the academic tasks. This made the workload much heavy on the other participants thus making it unequal distribution of the tasks but at the end, all the students in the group had the same grade. Another challenge was limited internet access for some students, which limited their contribution and hindered synchronous group communication. Despite these challenges, students appreciated the remote collaborative learning environment as it enabled them to realize some of the qualities of learning as illustrated in Table 5.

5 Conclusion and Future Work

The Remote collaborative learning for ICT4D Course allowed the students to develop shared culture that played a role in relationship building as groups virtually. Team work of the students was excellent owing to the fact that 17 students with the assistance of instructors managed to achieve the goal of the virtual learning for ICT4D course through remote collaboration. This was a step towards building and maintaining personal relationships of the participants virtually whilst ensuring that individuals developed commitment which enabled working towards achieving a common goal.

Collaborative learning opens up new avenues in the students' learning experience. It enables students' to learn about other cultures and thus broaden the understanding of different cultures. The experience in this course, with students from Kenya, South Africa and Finland offered such possibility. This collaborative learning experience is more challenging that the typical classroom learning experience. The challenges are worthy it in that it helps develop both academic and personal attributes of students. Understanding these challenges would help instructors to develop mechanisms which can address them and make remote collaborative learning more effective, appealing and satisfactory to students.

References

1. Maina, E.M., Wagacha, P.W., Oboko, R.: A model for improving online collaborative learning through machine learning. Model. Improv. Optim. Online Blended Learn. High. Educ. 204–219 (2014)
2. Bonk, C.J., Dennen, V.: Teaching on the web: with a little help from my pedagogical friends. J. Comput. High. Educ. **11**(1), 3–28 (1999)
3. Kimball, L.: Managing distance learning—new challenges for faculty. In: Hazemi, R., Hailes, S., Wilbur, S. (eds.) The Digital University: Reinventing the Academy. Springer, London (1998). https://doi.org/10.1007/978-1-4471-0625-8_3
4. Gitonga, R., Muuro, M., Nzuki, D.: Students experiences of using Wiki spaces to support collaborative learning in a blended classroom: a case of Kenyatta and KCA universities in Kenya. In: IST-Africa Conference Proceedings, pp. 1–10 (2014)
5. Muuro, E., Wagacha, P., Oboko, R., Kihoro, J.M.: Students' perceived challenges in an online collaborative learning environment: a case of higher learning institutions in Nairobi, Kenya. Int. Rev. Res. Open Distance Learn. **15** (2014)

6. Ruokamo, H., Pohjolainen, S.: Pedagogical principles for evaluation of hypermedia-based learning environments in mathematics. J. Univers. Comput. Sci. **4**(3), 292–307 (1998)
7. Mavengere, N., Ruohonen, M.: ICT4D 2.0 studies in virtual environment: context and user needs to foster learning process. In: IST-Africa Week Conference, pp. 1–8 (2016)
8. Leidner, D.E., Jarvenpaa, S.L.: The use of information technology to enhance management school education: a theoretical view. MIS Q. 265–291 (1995)
9. Muuro, M.E., Oboko, R.O., Wagacha, P.W.: Evaluation of intelligent grouping based on learners' collaboration competence level in online collaborative learning environment. Int. Rev. Res. Open Distrib. Learn. **17**(2) (2016)
10. Maina, E.M., Wagacha, P.W., Oboko, R.: Enhancing active learning pedagogy through online collaborative learning. Handb. Res. Act. Learn. Flip. Classr. Model Digit. Age 232 (2015)
11. Baker, T., Clark, J.: Cooperative learning–a double-edged sword: a cooperative learning model for use with diverse student groups. Intercult. Educ. **21**(3), 257–268 (2010)
12. Marquardt, M.J., Horvath, L.: Global Teams: How Top Multinationals Span Boundaries and Cultures with High-Speed Teamwork. Nicholas Brealey Publishing, Boston (2001)
13. Zhu, C.: Online collaborative learning: Cultural differences in student satisfaction and performance/Kulturelle Unterschiede in der Zufriedenheit mit und den Lernertr{ä}gen aus online-gest{ü}tztem kollaborativem Lernen bei Studierenden. J. Educ. Res. online **3**(1), 12 (2011)
14. Fraenkel, J.R., Wallen, N.E., Hyun, H.H.: How to Design and Evaluate Research in Education. McGraw-Hill Higher Education, New York (2012)
15. Frey, L.R., Gouran, D., Poole, M.S.: The Handbook of Group Communication Theory and Research. Sage, Newcastle upon Tyne (1999)
16. Illeris, K.: How We Learn: Learning and Non-learning in School and Beyond. Routledge, Abingdon (2007)
17. Kreijns, K., Kirschner, P.A., Jochems, W., Van Buuren, H.: Measuring perceived sociability of computer-supported collaborative learning environments. Comput. Educ. **49**(2), 176–192 (2007)

Collaborative Postgraduate Studies in Higher Education: A Case Study of South Africa

Francis Mungofa Manzira and Willard Munyoka(✉)

University of Venda, P Bag X5050, Thohoyandou 0945, South Africa
{francis.manzira, willard.munyoka}@univen.ac.za

Abstract. This research aimed to investigate the delivery of postgraduate study through incorporation of Google Applications and Skype technologies as collaborative tools. Participants were a cohort of full time working employees from a South African cohort of collaborating universities enrolled in the Post-Graduate Diploma in Higher Education course, located in Limpopo and Western Cape provinces. The data was collected through interviews from participants on Skype and Google technologies that include Google drive, Gmail, Google docs, Google spreadsheet, and Google chat. Data was analysed through ethnographic content analysis and conversational analysis. Based on the findings, it was evident that Google applications and Skype technologies support collaborative learning. The study results show that these technologies have an important role in future delivery of academic post graduate programmes in institutions of Higher Learning amongst working employees. This study recommends use of these technologies in scenarios involving multiple institutions across the world. Cloud computing has a pivotal role in enabling online collaborative learning activities and it enhances effective skills development in cases where students cannot afford to attend courses on full time basis due to work commitments or geographical location.

Keywords: Google apps · Collaborative applications · Cloud computing

1 Introduction

Computer supported collaborative work systems plays a significant role in enhancing productivity in different work environments and strengthens the effectiveness of teamwork. Advances in Information and Communication Technologies have led to a significant change in the coordination of activities from across a wide array of industries. Technologies that are currently on the market affect cooperation and coordination in teams working on a given task. Application of then new technologies continues to enable new ways of working in the business environment.

Several research works in Computer Supported Collaborative Work (CSCW) point out that application and use of technology affects coordination and there is a need for social organisation of cooperative work which if not properly handled may lead to problems, [13, 14, 39]. The advances in Information and Communication Technologies coupled with reduced bandwidth costs have enabled transmission of real time data to any remote site across the world that will be connected on the network, [3, 16, 17].

A. Tatnall and M. Webb (Eds.): WCCE 2017, IFIP AICT 515, pp. 134–148, 2017.
https://doi.org/10.1007/978-3-319-74310-3_16

CSCW are not only to be used for collaborative work purposes but they play a significant role in knowledge construction and also collaborative learning which is mainly facilitated through interconnectivity amongst participants involved. In addition, the new technological options available on the market also propel new types of knowledge management interactions that are based on micro-activities, [1, 9, 15–17]. The main rationale of this study was to investigate the gap closure of newly available Google technologies on collaborative delivery of a post graduate academic programme to students engaged as full time employees but are geographically dispersed. It was also the researchers' interest stemming from lack of empirical studies on the specific use of Google Educational Applications as a collaborative tool, in Higher Education, [19, 28, 30] argued in their research that there is still much to be investigated concerning the use of Google Educational Applications, which is often viewed as a much marginalised collaborative tool. As such it was of interest to have the study carried over a twelve months period. The students enrolled for the Post-Graduate Diploma in Higher Education course were full time employees at a University in Limpopo province, and three Universities in the Western Cape Province. There were six facilitators working with the students for administrative and course delivery purposes. They formed part of the Google drive administrators who had the responsibility of group administration tasks. As such all the information exchanged and shared was confined to only participants enrolled for the programme and had Gmail accounts. Students were using the Google applications in their communication, collaboration, information sharing and problem solving on group tasks allocated by the facilitators during the study. In addition, Skype and institutional emails were also being used to ensure effective delivery of intended message to the participants.

The study aimed to address the following research questions:

1. Can Google applications and Skype enhance collaboration among full time employees to advance higher qualification studies?
2. How effective are Google applications and Skype technologies in higher education academic collaboration?

2 Literature Review

2.1 Array of Collaborative Software Features

The commonly used software applications in collaborative activities include and are not limited to Eclipse (suite), eXo Platform, Google Apps, IBM Lotus Domino, InLoox, Microsoft SharePoint, Quick Base, Tiki Wiki CMS Groupware. They have a broad range of features which can be used by organisations in making decisions on which particular product to choose in addressing a problem at hand. Some of the most sought after features to consider for technology adoption include the following capabilities: Wikis, Web publishing, Calendaring software, Workflow system, Document Management, Discussion, Blogs, Surveys, Time Tracking, Charting, Bookmarking, Tagging, Rating and Comments Social software, Office suite.

These multiple features of software products have contributed towards increase in the use of collaborative software as they present tangible and intangible benefits to organisations. They determine activities that each product can support or not as various activities executed in a collaborative environment. Information sharing, communication and coordination are three main categories of why people engages in real time or asynchronous collaboration although other activities such knowledge creation, archiving or storage occurs simultaneously, [4, 9, 11, 16, 17, 22]. [32] focused on a case study on rapid adoption of data conferencing in a large corporation where minimum technical support was provided with no management mandate. More than 60% of the software below possesses at least ten of the eighteen features listed, which could reflect that the other products were specifically designed for all the collaborative activities of information sharing and communication collaboration. Costs and the nature of organisations operations can be among reasons of why such technologies cannot be adopted in some environments. [8] identified three important features of interaction that are central to successful collaboration as namely: intimacy among participants, rich supply of external resources, such as computers, and histories of joint activity of those interacting. These are key elements to the technologies for successful adoption and implementation by organisations for commercial or non-commercial purposes.

2.2 Google Applications for Work

Google Apps has become one of the most powerful communication and collaboration tools used in personal and business environments across the globe. It can be accessed via the web, so everyone can connect with everyone else, regardless of geographic location. Google apps are considered to be secure as access is only granted to people registered with the Google domain through username and password for login purposes, [27]. The apps are flexible, easy to use and web based as there are no installation or maintenance costs involved in the process, [29, 30]. In addition, because of the reduction costs of internet services couple with improved infrastructure and bandwidth, people can easily access the services at affordable costs. As cloud computing matures, several organisations are offering Software as a Service (SaaS) platform where a wide range of cloud based applications that can be used by businesses, governments, non-profit making organisations and individuals, [6, 23, 38]. Table 1 shows four categories into which Google's apps can be classified, namely communication, storage, collaboration and administration. Various applications in each of the categories makes it one of the most preferred in academic environment and as a free edition, it helps organisations with inadequate resources to significantly reduce installation, maintenance and licensing costs, [12]. According to [35], the emphasised the need by participants involved to uniformly adopt the same technology across for tasks at hand. Cloud computing provides Google with such a powerful advantage since a browser with internet connectivity are required thus rendering it free from operating systems platforms. The storage in Google cloud is provided free of charge to the users and security is guaranteed as the services can be accessed using a user name and password. Data security is guaranteed as it cannot be accessed by any person other than the account holder.

Table 1. Google applications

Usage	Google Apps	Characteristics
Communication	Gmail	Google Apps offer 25 GB of storage per user. It also offers powerful spam filtering and a 99.9% uptime SLA. All these are hosted by Google and there is no cost and no advertisements for students, faculty or staff
	Google Calendar	Helps teachers and faculties to organize their time. Anyone can easily schedule lessons and meetings. Multiple calendars can be overlaid to see when people are available - a great way to manage staff schedules (can send invitations and manage RSVPs)
	Hangouts	This is a communication platform developed by Google which includes instant messaging, video chat, SMS and VOIP features. Hangouts allow conversations between two or more users. The service can be accessed online through the Gmail or Google+ websites
	Google+*	It is a social network designed for business. Google+ makes it faster and easier to share and collaborate with your customers and team members
Storage	Drive	Provides a storage place for up-to-date versions of files from anywhere. Educators can share individual files or whole folders
Collaboration	Docs	Google Docs brings your documents to life with smart editing and styling tools to help you easily format text and paragraphs. You can choose from thousands of fonts, add links, images, drawings, and tables. These are provided free of charge. With Google Docs, anyone can create rich documents with images, tables, equations, drawings, links and more. Gather input and manage feedback with social commenting
	Sheets	Google Sheets can keep and share lists, track projects, analyse data and track results with the spreadsheet editor. There are some very useful tools like advanced formulas, embedded charts, filters and pivot tables to help get new perspectives on data
	Slides	Helps in the creation of slides with presentation editor, which supports features like embedded videos, animations and dynamic slide transitions. The presentations can be published on the web so anyone can view them, or they can be shared privately
Administrative	Sites	Sites are shared workspaces for classes and faculties. The students can build their own project sites without the need to write in code. It is as easy as writing a document. There are many pre-designed templates. In addition, Google Site provides a system and site-level security controls
	Vault	Google vault is an added archiving and e-discovery feature to Google Apps for Education. It is optional and adds archiving, e-discovery and information governance capabilities. With vault, anyone can define retention policies, place legal holds on users as needed, and can run reports on user activity and actions in the archive
	Admin	This enables management of Google Apps for your organization. The administrator can easily add users, manage devices and configure security and settings so your data stays safe. Administration shouldn't need a manual

2.3 Cloud Computing in Higher Education

The changing technologies on the market have resulted in the need to adjust interaction and collaboration amongst participants working in geographically dispersed environments. The paradigm of cloud computing has created the enabling environment which has resulted in people being globally connected through the cloud, for instance use of emails such as Gmail, Yahoo, Office365 or Hotmail [19, 27]. Continuous grown and improvement of cloud technology has led to widespread adoption of cloud services in different institutional activities. In addition, considered as benefits of such adoption identified by [4–6, 18, 36, 37], as: Increasing interoperability between disjoint technologies between and within institutions, Driving down the capital and total costs of IT in higher education, facilitating the transparent matching of IT demand, costs, and funding, it offer users and organizations convenient access to computing without having to understand the intricacies of exactly how processing is performed within the cloud, achievement of large-scale efficiencies without sacrificing performance. In addition, cloud computing has become a key component for online education as has been witnessed by the increase growth of massive online courses (MOOCs) coupled with affordability of hand held devices, data and widespread support to increase information and communication technology skills among the general public by governments of respective countries across the world, [20, 30, 36].

Technologies identified in Table 1 are also enabling elimination of geographical barriers thereby leading to widespread adoption in public and private institutions of Higher learning across the world. Some technologies are platform independent, with major changes being effected that are in responsive to the changing operating environment. It thus contributes towards enhancing productivity of the institutions among students and employees. Cloud computing service providers are offering higher education institutions, the opportunity to substitute their existing data centres, servers, applications and replacing the traditional campus machines with data and information in the cloud, [6, 19, 20].

3 Research Design

In this study, the Google Applications identified in Table 1 were introduced as collaborative platform to support group work from the inception of the course. In addition, there quarterly blocks for one week period in which participants would converge with the facilitators to wrap up on the assigned activities and present progress of assigned tasks. For the purpose of this study, there were twenty-four participants involved together with six facilitators. However, there was no need for classes on how to use the Google Applications although majority of the participants were not familiar with them. They had knowledge of internet technology, with other already using Gmail accounts for personal communication. They were later joined to the Google drive by the facilitators who acted as Administrators of the group. All the participants had access to the Google drive but only through the condition of having a Gmail account and linked to Google drive by the Administrators which enhanced security of activities that were being executed. As show below in Fig. 1, after login, the participant will choose the

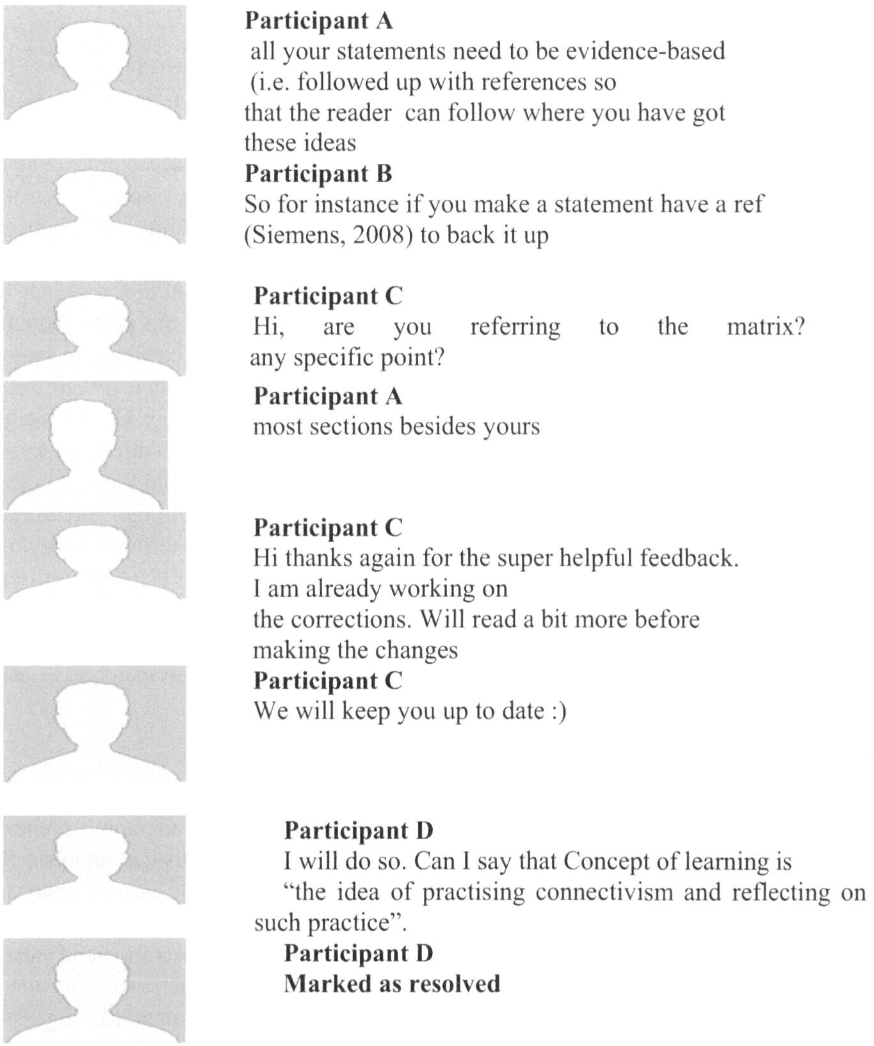

Fig. 1. Google chat conversational text

option of Google drive from the left panel that has been enlarged. The drive was the repository on the cloud where all data will be accessed. The Facilitator created additional folder for repository of various research materials to be used by the participants in process of research paper writing and execution of individual tasks related to the post-graduate diploma in higher education programme. In addition to the Google applications, Skype and personal institutional electronic mails were used to ensure that communication process was effective. Skype was mainly used for video conferencing by the participants when the need for meetings arose or in case one of the participants had an urgent matter that may require the facilitator to demonstrate practically or any of the participants to be engaged.

3.1 Method

The research adopted action research since the participants were actively involved in the programme over a twelve months period. "Action research aims to contribute both to the practical concerns of people in an immediate problematic situation and to the goals of social science by joint collaboration within a mutually acceptable ethical framework" [33]. According to [24, 25, 30], the strength of action research is in its focus on generating solutions to practical problems. It has the ability to empower practitioners through enabling engagement with research aspect and the subsequent development or implementation activities. [20, 25] maintains that Action research is participative and collaborative which is enable the participants of the post-graduate studies who had a common purpose, to solve group assignments, contribute in paper writing, evaluation of individual activities and projects. The participants involved were draw from a wider experience in the process of collaboration through Google technologies and Skype. Meetings were contacted at stipulated intervals through Skype which enable even conferencing calling. Minutes of the meetings would then be noted for reference purposes by the participants. Data was collected through structured interview. The interview allows obtaining of concrete, rich data through applying investigational perspective that was supported from research works of [7]. Standardised open ended questions were asked from participants with tape recording of the interview and notes taking simultaneously. The open-endedness allows the participants to contribute as much detailed information as they can and enables the researcher to ask probing questions as a means of follow-up [10].

3.2 Data Analysis

Having adopted action research, the inquiry therefore follows ethnographic content analysis as proposed by [2]. Rather than focusing entirely on statistical analysis of frequencies of identified themes in the content analysis, ethnographic content analysis involves a "reflexive analysis of the documents," and website conversations, [5]. Furthermore, this approach is used for studying reflexions of products in social interactions, and to comprehend the analysis of group participants in relationship to other group members in the online Google collaborative learning environment. [2] suggests that ethnographic content analysis is the most suitable data analysis technique when the objective of the results of the research are "commenting and narrative description" (p. 67), and for this reason the researchers decided to use this analysis technique to realize the aim of this research.

Content analysis emphasises the identification of different groups and sub-groups of content on studied concepts; and this can be achieved through either manual or automatized codification of online conversations, commenting, documents, interviews, or any other written information. Member checking was used to ensure validity of the results through sending the recorded responses to ensure validity and trustworthiness of the qualitative research results. Participants had the opportunity to review the accuracy of their statements that were recorded before the results were finalized. It is a process that ensure quality control of the results since errors are eliminated before final publishing of the results, [7, 31].

The researchers used thematic analysis, and the identification of sub-themes in the online Google collaborations amongst the participating students and facilitators; guided by a set of formulated research questions (serving the purpose of major guiding themes) as proposed by [2]. Additionally, the study implemented the five key-processes of content analysis proposed by Krippendorf [21]:

i. *Defining the analysis unit* – the word, paragraphs from the conversations, interviews, phrases, etc.
ii. *Sampling* – selection of the study units, which are representative for the research (in our case, this involves the Google drive collaborative learning platform).
iii. *Reduction* – reduction of the complexity of the content of the data analysed; guided by key research questions to achieve codification of key words and phrases.
iv. *Deduction* – contextual phenomena are analysed to identify the context of the research results (themes have already been guided and established along key research questions.
v. *Narration/Discussion* – the results are reported using narrative conventions to reach conclusion.

The next section outlines result findings for this research.

4 Results

Analysis of data collected from participants revealed that participants did benefit from use of Google Applications for the tasks that had been assigned. Given the fact that they were geographically apart, they managed to communicate, share and create knowledge in the process.

4.1 Real Time Collaboration

As the participants were geographically apart, it was not feasible that every time a meeting had to be done, people should meet. This concur with [24] who argued that online face-to-face discussions are invaluable in collaborative tasks and decision-making processes schedule where there are time, space and distance constraints. The respondents below agreed that Google applications provided them with the opportunity to work in a real-time environment as you can be able to simultaneously work on a document. Participants could easily see who was working on what section because when another participant makes an edit, their change will automatically appear on your screen when you are viewing the file, with their name next to their cursor so that you can see who is typing.

QUESTION 1 – What were the benefits of using Google drive for the assigned tasks allocated to you?

R1 "Google drive - collaborative work, working together in "real time", chat and comment features for feedback, can all work on one document at the same time, sharing of articles/books".

R2 "Google Drive has more affordances as there are many tools in the suite which can be used for co-writing, giving and receiving feedback, making changes to documents, either synchronously or asynchronously".

R3 "You can edit a file at the same time with other colleagues regardless of distance, only internet connection is required.

For instance, we managed to prepare a power point presentation for our next block session and trimmed to the right size since we were virtually together during the preparation".

R4 "When you are working on a document concurrently with other in the same space, you can chat with the participants viewing the document so that you don't have to email back and forth while you work. Anyone viewing the document and signed in to a Google Account will be included in the chat".

4.2 Video Conferencing

Participants needed to meet in the virtual environment for issues pertaining to meetings, allocation of tasks and provision of feedback. This was facilitated through using Skype which has a broad range of features, including instant messaging, free voice and video conferencing, its ability to use peer to peer. The use of quality videos fosters collaborative design, teamwork coordination, interactive discussions, and sharing of knowledge as participants feel involved in the activities. The responses below led to the conclusion that Skype is a convenient mode of communication where distance appears to be a barrier and time constraints. Besides being used for conferencing, [24] identified that Skype can be used to conduct interviews or focus groups in real time via the instant messaging feature, which allows multiple users to participate simultaneously by typing their comments in a common virtual room. Thus, it is a useful data collection tool for textual, audio and visual data.

QUESTION 2 – How convenient was Skype for the conferencing in your meetings and other tasks?

R1 "Skype provides opportunities to interact in real time seeing the person's face or just talking so that ideas can be clarified, people can interact in groups across geographical distances. It also has asynchronous affordances in the form of written messages offered through instant messaging service".

R2 "Skype allows for communication to occur in real time. We managed as a group to create repositories of data in Google drive for our tasks and the paper which the developed focusing on connectivism. The feedback process is more dynamic and colleagues assisted each other on a continuous basis either through voice calling with video or instant messaging services".

R3 "This is a very good group interactive video chat application with immense benefits that if was possible to deliver my course to students without being in class, I would have opted for such. In our case the group video chat enabled us to see and chat with each other on a single screen at the same time. It is possible that in the event of strong bandwidth, this tool can be used to address groups in large scale projects".

R4 "The immediacy of being able to share information, thoughts and knowledge. Real time discussions can be held with several people even though they are not in the same location. So, the geographical barrier is removed. Also, non-real-time communication is possible by reading replies and responses at a later stage. Also, time is no longer an issue as one can communicate and work 24/7.

I also think that if the group vibe is positive, the motivation and group dynamics can be greatly enhanced by the "social" part of using social media. So, it allows for personal interaction, which can be used to sustain and motivate the work ethics".

4.3 Technology Experience and Future Plans

New experiences with technology will develop learning capabilities and rethink on future course of action on how tasks can be reorganised. Participants expressed greatest enthusiasm after first encounter with Google and Skype technologies. It is of great importance that participants mind-set had been refocused especially on how to harness technology in their future endeavours within the career and work places.

QUESTION 3 – After your experiences with Google technologies and Skype, are you prepared to incorporate them in your future work projects in higher education?

R1 "Definitely yes: I find Google Drive to be most useful for the actual writing and giving and receiving more extensive feedback. The fact that people can write simultaneously across geographically distant contexts is a great affordance for collaborative work. It was interesting that we managed to work on a group conference paper as team through these technologies, I couldn't imagine it, great".

R2 "I have been using them socially but after this experience of formal setting, I do plan to incorporate it in the next collaborative tasks, be it on a local research or international research projects as the concept of collaboration cannot be isolated from the from the ever-growing Information and communications technologies that are the backbone".

R3 "I find Google Drive to be most useful for the actual writing and giving and receiving more extensive feedback process during conference paper production. The fact that people can write simultaneously across geographically distant contexts is a great affordance for collaborative work. Because these tools increase communication, generally the effective component of online learning is heightened and people become more vested and involved in task execution. These technologies also provide opportunities for formal interaction in a professional environment and for more personalised communication".

R4 "*As we continue to develop new Master degree programmes in our faculty, I believe this will be the best tool to interact with post graduate students pursuing research work, as the students can utilise Google Drive to deposit work in progress and completed tasks, I addition these applications enables virtual power point presentations. Due to increasing demand in the industry and wide adoption of technologies, this can assist the institution to capture a market of our own for employees in full time employment. Although face to face meetings cannot be completely eliminated, travelling, accommodation costs and lost time are drastically reduced".*

4.4 Apps Challenges

The reality of the applications in any workspace is that they require internet connectivity. Unlike global positioning systems they do not operate with satellite technologies.

Poor internet connectivity is a major setback in successful collaboration with the apps. From the responses recorded, it is evident that South Africa as a developing country, it still has challenges in terms of providing low cost mobile networks data and strength of the signals. [16] explained that video chat requires real-time communication and if the application over utilizes the link, it causes unfairness to other traffic and if it under-utilizes the link, it may cause low quality of video chat. Thus, with mobile devices, the uplink-downlink connection in 3G is asymmetric as the bandwidth is greatly determined by network signal strength in a given geographic area. For instance, it is stronger in urban areas and as you radiate to the outer peripherals it becomes weaker.

QUESTION 4 – What were the main challenges associated with using Google Apps and Skype you encountered in you activities?

R1 "When using mobile networks for internet connectivity on mobile devices such as iPad, smart phones and laptops, the bandwidth provided by mobile network service providers is sometime slow.

Cost of data bundles is a bit high since you are using voice integrated with a camera which demand high data volumes on mobile networks".

R2 "*Connectivity and associated cost of data transfer is always an issue .With a slow internet connection (mobile or land line) it's almost impossible to use this form of media interaction. Also data remains expensive; especially on mobile apps... this greatly limits the applicability. Especially something like Google docs or presentation can be very data intensive".*

R3 "Google Drive - sometimes is a bit slow when working on a presentation live. In this instance it was a new system to get to learn which was time consuming and challenging for a non-technologically minded person! With Skype it's not always easy to get a good video due to internet connection".

R4 "I did not encounter major challenges besides failure to connect with other colleagues who internet connectivity problems in some instances. Our institutional systems are quite stable and significant investments have been made in technological infrastructure".

4.5 Conversational Analysis

The conversation in Fig. 1 shows a brief exchange of messages by the participants when they were working on a group conference paper. Minutes of activities that were involved in the process are outlined in the below section. According to [34], conversational analysis (CA) aims to *'describe, analyze, and understand talk as a basic and constitutive feature of human social life'.* Conversation is the main way in which people gather or collaborate, exchange information, negotiate and maintain social relations [29]. [37] research findings analysis of data related to interactions in on line revealed that on line chat exhibits features of turn-taking, repair and adjacency pairs as important concepts in CA. These principles are deemed to be effective in the situation of online chat whereas a variation from what we would expect to find in face-to-face conversation can be noted. The extract in Fig. 1 shows synchronous communication between participants during the period of introducing connectivism as part of group tasks that were involved. Participants were regularly exchanging messages that would contribute towards executing the assigned task.

Discussion topic: Introducing Connectivism

Minutes of a meeting coordinated at Facilitator's office through Skype video conferencing

This section shows the minutes of a meeting that was conducted through Skype conferencing by the participants and facilitator who were geographically located at the universities in two provinces respectively. The meetings held lasted for a period of forty minutes minimum and one hour maximum. Tasks were organised and allocated according to the participant's background that was decided through input of what each participant considered being stronger in. Execution of the tasks would then precede through Google Applications after the allocation of tasks during the meetings.

Present: Participant A, Participant B, Participant D, Participant E, Participant F, (Skype), Facilitator.

Introduction to connectivism - ***Participant A***
Literature review on social media - few slides - ***Participant D***
Methodology - auto ethnography - Participant F
Comments on Google drive - ***Facilitator*** *will look at the role of the facilitator. Social interaction - looks at various aspects of connectivism and look for when it happened. Google chats, Actual presentation.*
What's App conversations - ***Participant B***
Emails, Looking at nodes of connectivism
- maybe c-map
Findings - ***Participant C***
The role of the facilitator - how much did the facilitator adhere to the role of a connectivist facilitator? What are the pros and cons of using connectivist ways of learning?
Creating the knowledge using the basis of a theory
How did we use connectivist knowledge?
Participant B & E *thought that they spent a lot of thinking time - hours and hours - social interaction is intertwined with academic aspects. Personality dynamics are more important here - you tend to say more things than if you were sitting around the table, We need to analyse why certain group members were connected and worked together and why others did not participate. What were the effects on both the connected and disconnected members and what was the impact on the learning process and the product?*

5 Conclusion and Future Work

It is possible that cloud computing enhances any form of online education although this research was focusing on full time employees who were attending block sessions of the course in specified times of the year and complementing other course related activities using cloud computing. Cloud computing tools enables dynamic group work approach and presents the opportunity for motivation and self-responsibility of students. They enable sharing and working on documents simultaneously irrespective of the geographical location of students, internet is the backbone technology required amongst the connecting parties involved in the learning process. It is important to note that Google applications as part of Computer-Supported Collaborative Work Systems are not just useful for the purposes of collaborative work. They are more critical on collaborative learning. A tremendous shift towards cloud computing is enabling institutions of higher learning to reduce expenditure on information and communication technologies and capitalize on the low-cost maturing technology available on the market. This article presents the potential of integrating two concepts, namely those of a virtual interactive room and a web-based collaborative work application in order to enhance knowledge construction and removing the barriers of distance encountered by working class, [14, 20, 26]. From responses obtained during the study, we can conclude that cloud computing through use of Google Applications and Skype technologies effectively facilitated collaboration amongst the participants who were involved in the study. Although they were operating from a distant, there was an achievement in executing the give tasks, knowledge sharing, building, communication and coordination. However, this study recommends use of these technologies in scenarios involving multiple institutions across the world.

References

1. Ackerman, M.S., Dachterai, J., Pipek, V., Volker, V.: Sharing knowledge and expertise: the CSCW view of knowledge management. Comput. Support. Coop. Work (CSCW) **22**(4–6), 531–573 (2013)
2. Altheide, L.D.: Reflections: ethnographic content analysis. Qual. Sociol. **10**, 65–77 (1987)
3. Bayerl, P.S., Lauche, K.: Technology effects in distributed team coordination—high-interdependency tasks in offshore oil production. Comput. Support. Coop. Work (CSCW) **19**(2), 139–173 (2010)
4. Bin, Y., Xinying, R.: Construction of 'cloud services' ring system in higher education. Software Guide Educational Technology, pp. 93–95 (2011)
5. Butnaru, I.G.: The method of ethnographic and content analysis in determining development factors of economic and managerial tourism performance. Procedia Econ. Finan. **20**, 104–111 (2015)
6. Cloud 101: Developing a cloud computing strategy for higher education (2012). White paper, https://www.cisco.com/c/dam/en/us/solutions/collateral/collaboration/cloud-collaboration/cloud_101_higher_education_wp.pdf. Accessed 20 Jan 2017
7. Creswell, J.W.: Qualitative Inquiry and Research Design: Choosing Among Five Approaches, 2nd edn. Sage, Thousand Oaks (2007)
8. Crook, C.: Children as computer users: the case of collaborative learning. Comput. Educ. **30**, 237–247 (1998)
9. Eseryel, D., Ganesan, R., Edmonds, S.G.: Review of computer-supported collaborative work systems. Educ. Technol. Soc. **5**(2) (2002). ISSN 1436-4522
10. Gall, D., Meredith, G., Joyce, P., Borg, R.W.: Educational Research: An Introduction, 7th edn. A & B Publications, Boston (2003)
11. Ganesan, R., Edmonds, G.S., Spector, J.M.: The changing nature of instructional design for networked learning. In: Steeples, C., Jones, C. (eds.) Networked Learning: Perspectives and Issues. CSCW, pp. 93–109. Springer, London (2002). https://doi.org/10.1007/978-1-4471-0181-9_6
12. Google Inc.: Google Apps for Education (2012). http://www.google.com/apps/edu. Accessed 10 Jan 2017

13. Harper, R.R., Hughes, A.J., Shapiro, Z.D.: Working in harmony: an examination of computer technology in air traffic control. In: EC-CSCW 1989, Proceedings of the 1st European Conference on Computer-Supported Cooperative Work, Sloug, UK, 13–15 September 1989, pp. 73–87. ACM, New York (1989)
14. Heath, C., Luff, P.: Collaboration and control: crisis management and multimedia technology in London underground control rooms. Comput. Support. Coop. Work **1**(1), 69–94 (1992)
15. Hernandez-Serrano, J., Choi, I., Jonassen, H.D.: Integrating constructivism and learning technologies. In: Spector, J.M., Anderson, T.M. (eds.) Integrated and Holistic Perspectives on Learning, Instruction and Technology, pp. 103–128. Springer, Dordrecht (2000). https://doi.org/10.1007/0-306-47584-7_7
16. Jana, S., Pande, A., Chan, A.J., Mohapatra, P.: Mobile video chat: issues and challenges. IEEE Commun. Mag. **51**(6), 144–151 (2013)
17. Jian, L.: On computer-supported collaborative learning under the support of cloud computing. J. Jixi Univ. **11**, 5–6 (2011)
18. Jonathan, G., Poltrock, S.: Computer supported cooperative work. In: Soegaard, M., Dam, R. F. (eds.) The Encyclopedia of Human-Computer Interaction. The Interaction Design Foundation, Aarhus (2014). https://www.interaction-design.org/encyclopedia/cscw_computer_ supported_cooperative_work.html. Accessed 12 Feb 2017
19. Katz, R., Goldstein, P., Yanosky, R.: Cloud computing in higher education. Educause (2009). http://net.educause.edu/section_params/conf/CCW10/highered.pdf. Accessed 15 Jan 2017
20. Koshy, E., Koshy, V., Waterman, H.: Action Research in Healthcare. Sage, Thousand Oaks (2010)
21. Krippendorff, K.: Reliability in content analysis: some common misconceptions and recommendations. Hum. Commun. Res. **30**(3), 411–433 (2004)
22. Luna, W., Sequera, J.L.C.: Collaboration in the cloud for online learning environments: an experience applied to laboratories. Creat. Educ. **6**(13), 1435 (2015)
23. Mathew, S.: Implementation of cloud computing in education-a revolution. Int. J. Comput. Theory Eng. **4**(3), 473–475 (2012)
24. Mavengere, N., Ruohonen, M.: ICT4D 2.0 studies in virtual environment: context and user needs to foster learning process. In: IST-Africa Week Conference 2016, pp. 1–8 (2016)
25. Meyer, J.: Using qualitative methods in health related action research. BMJ **320**, 178–181 (2000)
26. Moylan, A.C., Derr, S.A., Lindhorst, T.: Increasingly mobile: how new technologies can enhance qualitative research. Qual. Soc. Work **14**(1), 36–47 (2015). https://doi.org/10.1177/1473325013516988
27. Muuro, E.M., Wagacha, P.W., Oboko, R., Kihoro, J.: Students' perceived challenges in an online collaborative learning environment: a case of higher learning institutions in Nairobi, Kenya. Int. Rev. Res. Open Distance Learn. **15**, 132–161 (2014)
28. Nevin, R.: Supporting 21st century learning through Google Apps. Teacher Libr. **37**(2), 35 (2009)
29. Okuhara, M., Shiozaki, T., Suzuki, T.: Security architecture for cloud computing. Fujitsu Sci. Tech. J. **46**(4), 397–402 (2010)
30. Paliktzoglou, V., Stylianou, T., Suhonen, J.: Google educational apps as a collaborative learning tool among computer science learners. In: Assessing the Role of Mobile Technologies and Distance Learning in Higher Education, p. 272 (2014)
31. Paltridge, B.: Discourse Analysis: An Introduction. Continuum, London (2006)
32. Poltrock, S., Mark, G.: Groupware adoption in a distributed organization: transporting and transforming technology through social worlds. Inf. Organ. **14**, 297–327 (2004)

33. Rapoport, N.R.: Three dilemmas in action research. Hum. Relat. **23**(6), 499–513 (1970)
34. Scheid, E.J., Minato, L.H., de Oliveira, S.B., Charão, A.S.: Cloud computing with Google Apps for education: an experience report. J. Appl. Comput. Res. **2**(2), 60–67 (2012)
35. Sidnell, J.: Conversation Analysis: An Introduction. Wiley-Blackwell, Chichester (2010)
36. Van der Schyff, K., Kraussy, E.M.K.: Higher education cloud computing in South Africa: towards understanding trust and adoption issues. SACJ **55**, 40–55 (2014)
37. Wigdor, D., Shen, C., Forlines, C., Balakrishnan, R.: Table-centric interactive spaces for real-time collaboration. In: Proceedings of the Working Conference on Advanced Visual Interfaces, pp. 103–107 (2006). https://www.dgp.toronto.edu/~ravin/papers/avi2006_tabletopinteraction.pdf. Accessed 13 May 2017
38. Zaferanieh, E.: Conversation analysis of online chat. In: The First Conference on Language Learning & Teaching: An Interdisciplinary Approach, 30–31 October, pp. 1–9. Department of English, Mashhad Branch, Islamic Azad University (2012)
39. Zuboff, S.: In the Age of the Smart Machine: The Future of Work and Power. Basic Books, New York (1988)

Scaling a Model of Teacher Professional Learning – Harnessing MOOCS to Recreate Deep Learning Conversations

Deirdre Butler[1(✉)], Margaret Leahy[1], Michael Hallissy[2], and Mark Brown[3]

[1] Institute of Education, Dublin City University, Dublin, Ireland
deirdre.butler@dcu.ie
[2] H2 Learning, Dublin, Ireland
[3] National Institute for Digital Learning, Dublin City University, Dublin, Ireland

Abstract. This paper describes the most recent phase of an innovative model of teacher professional learning that has evolved over a decade (2006 to 2016). Building on the experiences of implementing this face-to-face model, the paper reports on the most recent phase which attempts to harness the emergence of a 4th wave of online learning. The initiative involves the design and development of a Massive Open Online Course (MOOC) that potentially enables the massive scaling up of access to this already validated model of teacher professional learning designed to shift teachers' pedagogical orientations through school focussed, job embedded teacher professional learning. The importance of maintaining key elements, threshold concepts and signature pedagogies in the design of MOOCs for teacher professional learning are discussed. The paper also explores some of the challenges and potential opportunities different MOOC delivery models offer for sustaining the types of collaboration, rich dialogue and ongoing reflection observed in earlier phases of the project.

Keywords: Teacher education · 21st century skills · Online learning MOOCs

1 Introduction

There is growing consensus among education leaders and researchers that both teaching and learning need to change to help students develop the skills they need to succeed in the 21st century (e.g. Ananiadou and Claro 2009). Stated goals for the development of "21st century skills" include critical thinking and problem-solving, communication, collaboration, self-regulation, information management and the ability to use digital technology effectively and reflectively (e.g. ETA 2010; OECD 2005; Binkley et al. 2012) have become commonplace in many countries. Despite this, teachers rarely have access to specific guidance or sufficient support on how to develop these skills in the classroom. Faced with this reality, the challenge is how to design professional learning experiences for teachers that enable them, in turn, to design learning activities so that their students can develop the dispositions, skills and competencies that are required to live and thrive in this complex, globally connected world

A. Tatnall and M. Webb (Eds.): WCCE 2017, IFIP AICT 515, pp. 149–160, 2017.
https://doi.org/10.1007/978-3-319-74310-3_17

of the 21st century. Against this backdrop, this paper describes an innovative model of teacher professional learning that has evolved over a decade (2006 to 2016). It begins by describing the professional learning model for teachers which was designed and developed in a single secondary school (Phase 1) before being expanded district wide (Phase 2). The impact of this job-embedded progamme is outlined indicating the shift in pedagogical orientation and the resulting student learning. It then explores how this face-to-face model of professional learning can be successfully reconfigured in an online environment to help scale up the initiative while also being mindful of the importance of maintaining key elements, threshold concepts and signature pedagogies in the design and development of the scalable model.

1.1 Background and Context: Teacher Professional Learning Framework

Originating in Microsoft's 'Innovative Schools Programme' (ISP), the focus of phase 1 was to design a framework for the teacher professional learning in an Irish secondary school to integrate digital technologies into teaching and learning. This approach was considered particularly important in Ireland because rigid state standards and a traditional exam-based system of education at secondary level constrain teachers' ability to change their instructional practices. It leaves them with little time or flexibility to introduce new ideas or practices.

In developing a framework for teacher professional learning, the lead authors (Butler and Leahy) realised the need not only to work closely with teachers and school management but also the necessity to concentrate on the teachers' beliefs and values as the starting point. This was based on research evidence that teachers' pedagogical orientations are a dominant factor in how they choose to use (or not) new technology in their classroom (e.g.; Law and Chow 2008; Shear et al. 2011). It follows from this line of research that professional learning programmes are most effective when:

(i) they are embedded into teachers' professional lives and communities within the school (National Foundation for the Improvement of Education 1996),
(ii) are focused explicitly on local goals for student learning (e.g. Darling-Hammond 1993), and
(iii) grounded in collective discussions of classroom practice (Warren Little 2003).

Previous experience in developing a model of professional learning had also led to the realisation that to change classroom practice, teachers need to ask questions about their existing classroom practices (Butler 2004). To this end, key features of the professional learning programme were that it was directly related to the teachers' stated needs and experiences, anchored in the meaningful context of their own classroom practices *and* teachers were challenged to question their practice. The Learning Activity/Student Work (LASW) framework developed by Stanford Research Institute, as part of the ISP (Shear et al. 2009), was the catalyst which enabled the teachers to design learning activities in which they embedded 21st century learning principles, develop the meta-language used to describe such learning environments and reflect on their teaching and the assignments they set their students (Butler and Leahy 2009, 2011). Finally, the programme was directly linked to a university postgraduate accreditation process.

Building on the success of Phase 1, the initiative was expanded to district level in Phase 2 to work with targeted group of teachers as peer coaches to support innovative and emerging new pedagogies and technologies to facilitate student learning and the development of 21st century skills. Management also requested that formal accreditation would continue to be a feature of the programme. In response, the Digital Learning Peer Coaching (DLPC) programme was developed (c.f. Butler and Leahy 2015).

1.2 Impact of the Professional Learning Framework

Across Phase 1 and 2, teachers, school leaders and management initially tended to view digital technologies as tools to support traditional practice. However, through participation in the programme, their understanding shifted and they began to perceive new technologies as tools that facilitate more progressive classroom practices and the development of their students' 21st century skills (Butler and Leahy 2015) This was evident by the emergence of the following trends in classroom practices:

- Student-centred learning
- Project based learning rather than discrete lesson plans
- Students working collaboratively in groups rather than individual learning
- Focus on learning not on subject "content"
- Awareness of/designing lessons with opportunities for students to develop 21st century skills
- Increase in teacher confidence to use a greater range of pedagogical strategies/ digital technologies
- Collaboration across and between subject departments/ripple effect

The shift in pedagogical orientation along with increased use of digital technologies in learning and teaching had a positive impact on student learning, resulting in learners:

- taking control of their own learning
- having greater ownership of the learning activities
- demonstrating more engagement/participation
- increased collaboration
- being active rather than passive in their learning
- taking on new leadership roles

1.3 Problems of Scalability

Although the developments and findings outlined above were encouraging, the issue of scalability has become increasingly problematic. Policy decisions in relation to the development of a range of "21st century skills" (NCCA 2009) as well as the ability and the need to use digital technology effectively and reflectively in schools in Ireland, has led to ongoing demands to extend this model of professional learning. In particular, the launch of the Digital Strategy (DES 2015) in Ireland identified "a need to ensure that

ALL teachers are equipped with the knowledge, skills and confidence to integrate ICT into their practice" (p. 7). As a way of addressing the issue of scalability, the possibility of using an innovative MOOC format was considered in the wider context of the emergence of a 4th wave of online learning (Picciano 2014) which builds on the principles and foundations of blended learning.

2 Scaling the Model of Professional Learning: MOOC Related Literature

The research literature to date suggests that MOOCs have been most successful for those learners who already hold an undergraduate college degree or higher (e.g. Ebben and Murphy 2014). While MOOC completion rates are low, prior level of schooling is a predictor of achievement in MOOCs (Greene et al. 2015); thus suggesting that teachers completing a MOOC for professional learning might be more likely to complete it than other participants (Hodges et al. 2016). In fact, Lauillard (2016) considers the use of a MOOC as a medium for the continuing professional learning of teachers as "a perfect fit" (p. 7).

2.1 Why a MOOC?

Although there are issues around completion and accreditation, MOOCs are now recognised as a valid form of professional learning in a number of professions. For example, in Ireland the Law Society in 2014 was the first professional body to successfully implement a MOOC with over 2000 participants as part of a formal professional learning programme. Since then, MOOCs have demonstrated their potential to attract large numbers of learners, particularly highly qualified professionals to participate in free education programmes (Laurillard 2016).

MOOCs can be defined as "typically involving structured and sequenced teacher-led activities (e.g. videos, readings, problem-sets) coupled with online assessments and usually some venue for student interactions such as a discussion forum" (Greene et al. 2015 p. 927). This typical and dominant form of MOOC is usually described as an xMOOC (Downes 2012). In contrast, MOOCs which emphasise connecting with learners through blogs and forums rather than on structured resources are referred to as cMOOCs (McGreal et al. 2013 in Jobe et al. 2014). They are designed so that learners can learn "through practice (construction and responding to feedback), discussion (comments and conversations) and production (negotiating an output for evaluation by others), making it a complex and valuable learning process" (Laurillard 2016; p. 16). The challenge in the tradition of a cMOOC is therefore to design learning experiences that support large numbers of teachers to engage in a model of co-learning, which as stated by Avalos (2011), involves:

> *networking and interchanges among schools and situations and is strengthened in formalised experiences such as courses and workshops that introduce peer coaching or support collaboration and joint projects...the lesson learned is that teachers naturally talk to each other, and that such talk can take on an educational purpose (cited in Laurillard* 2016*; p. 3).*

However, the challenge is how do you design and enable opportunities for large numbers of teachers to talk purposefully to one another online?

2.2 Can We Recreate Deep Learning Conversations Live Online?

Much of the study of interaction in online and distance education contexts has to date primarily focused on asynchronous communication, such as forums (written discussions) (e.g. Blanchette 2011). This research has found that asynchronous is valuable for considered discussion, where people have time to reflect and then respond. There is relatively little research conducted on synchronous oral discussions (Park and Bonk 2007). Therefore, the question if deep discussions can be facilitated using synchronous online learning tools is still an emerging area in the literature. What we do know is that, all too often, such live sessions have been found to be overly teacher directed (Hallissy 2014) and lacking meaningful interaction between the tutor and learners and between learners.

Recent technological advancements can support many activities which have the capability to enhance discussion including document sharing, editing LiveChat, and online polls. Nevertheless, we are still unsure if or how these tools can most effectively facilitate deep discussion and/or if there is a need for additional technologies to enable us to 'recreate' the live classroom space online. What we do know is that *interaction* is essential to meaningful online learning (Abrami et al. 2011, p. 1246). Such interaction is defined by Bannan-Ritland (2002) as a

> *two-way communication among two or more people within a learning context, with the purposes either task/instructional completion or social relationship-building, that includes a means for teacher and learner to receive feedback and for adaptation to occur based upon information and activities with which the participants are engaged (p. 6).*

There is also need to be mindful, "that frequency does not equal quality" (Hirumi 2002; p. 156 citing Northrup 2001) and as noted by Garrison and Cleveland-Innes (2005) "interaction does not necessarily translate into critical discourse and the integration of ideas into meaningful constructs" (p. 144). Issues such as the leadership role of the tutor, their pedagogical beliefs and disposition must also be taken into account.

Laurillard (2002) and Garrison and Cleveland-Innes (2005) place a high value on the leadership role of the tutor in "triggering" discussion and structuring the interaction to sustain interactions. While the affordances of synchronous online learning tools do matter, knowledge of how to construct and lead discussion using these tools is paramount towards promoting meaningful interaction. The critical factor is that the interaction promoted is a dialogue i.e. a two-way exchange, where learners are provided with feedback in order to take action (Laurillard 2002). It is through this type of iterative process that learners are believed to deepen their knowledge. Such interactions rely heavily on the skill and competence of the tutor to design quality discussions (Blanchette 2011) that allow tutor and learner to interact in a deep and iterative way.

The pedagogical beliefs of the tutor are also important. Being conversant with the online learning tools technology and comfortable in leading discussion does not ensure that deep discussion will be engaged in by all participants. Brookfield and Preskill (2005) suggest that if the tutor's pedagogical beliefs support the design and implementation of social constructivist learning theories then learners are more likely to engage in deep discussion 'live' online. Thus, from this perspective, discussion moves the power away from the tutor to create a more democratic model of learning where the learners take ownership for their learning. Through engaging in this type of discussion, participants stay focused on the topic, offer evidence to support their point of view (or explain the basis for that view), recall and summarise some of the multiple viewpoints that have been shared, attempt to identify connections between contributions already made and show how the discussion has changed their thinking or added to their knowledge. In short, they are able to contribute to the creation of new knowledge. In order to design and maintain such critical discussions with their learners Brookfield and Preskill (2005) identified nine dispositions that tutors need to develop, so they and their learners can engage in deep knowledge construction. Therefore, the tutor has a critical role to play in structuring and "scaffolding" the types of interactions that take place online (e.g. Rovai 2004).

Yet, the learner too has a key role to play in such settings as they need to take responsibility for their own learning and engage constructively with the tutor and their peers (Anderson and Garrison 1998). Learners can sometimes become frustrated with discussion viewing it as a waste of their time (Brookfield and Preskill 2005). While other learners may be considered "lurkers" (Salmon 2000) having "low" or "no visibility" (Beaudoin 2002, in Gulati 2004) resulting in 'silence' online, particularly in synchronous discussions when students are not actively participating.

Thus, tutors need to be aware that student silence may be an indication of other feelings such as a lack of confidence or trust to share a view or an opinion. It is at times like this that tutors need to consider how they can create a democratic classroom where everyone is encouraged to participate and where it is acceptable to remain silent. This type of democratic participation is encapsulated in a teacher education context in the Fully Online Learning Community Model (FOLC) described by Blayone et al. (2017) that builds on the Community of Inquiry (COI) model, which underpins contemporary approaches to the design of distance education, including MOOCs. This model also underscores the importance of teacher presence and rich and meaningful interactions as the basis of deep learning.

In summary, the literature on synchronous online learning suggests that the role of the tutor in designing and enabling meaningful interactions and discussion is essential. It also suggests that their pedagogical beliefs and their technical knowledge of the online technologies are key to ensuring deep discussions. However, there is limited evidence that synchronous online learning tools on their own without skilful facilitation and intervention by tutors can recreate welcome and safe places for learners to engage in open deliberation.

3 Design and Development of the 21CLD MOOC

To address the identified gap in the literature regarding synchronous online learning, and the potential of MOOCs as a means of scaling the model of teacher professional learning, funding was secured from Microsoft to design an online course. Working with a partner in the sector (H2 Learning), the intention was to develop a MOOC that would challenge and enable teachers to examine and change their own classroom practices, as they relate to innovative uses of digital technologies to support their own and their students' learning and the development of 21st century skills.

In keeping with Phase 1 and 2, a central feature underpinning the MOOC design was the tenet that it is teachers' understanding of 21st century skill requirements that influences the ways in which they use ICT (e.g. Shear et al. 2011). As previously established, when teachers' pedagogical orientations are underpinned by understandings of 21st century learning, they take on a more facilitative role, provide student-centered guidance and feedback, and engage more frequently in exploratory and team-building activities with students. Findings in Phase 1 and 2 were that the change in teachers' pedagogical orientation and the emergence of a culture of self-evaluation was directly attributed to the use of the Learning Activity/Student Work (LASW) framework and the deep discussions they engaged in around their classroom practice. To this end, rooted in the LASW Framework, (now called 21st Century Learning Design (21CLD), an eight-module, self-directed course was designed and developed over a nine month duration as a core component of the MOOC design. The modules explore what learning looks like in the 21st century and how innovative teaching practices can support student learning to develop the key 21st skills of collaboration, knowledge construction, self-regulation, problem-solving and innovation, skilled communication, and the use of ICT for learning. As well as defining, explaining and illustrating each of the skills, an integral part of each module is an 'in action' video in which teachers from across the world showcase how they have embedded a specific skill in their classroom. Each of thirteen teachers from countries such as Finland, Canada, South Africa and Australia have designed extended learning units for their students which focus on the development of 21st century skills while also embedding the use of a range of digital technologies. Feedback, mentoring and support was provided by the design team (Butler, Leahy & H2) on these learning units and the teachers were provided with hand-held cameras to capture the development of the learning process. Working with this footage, the design team then constructed a comprehensive "in action" video for each of the key 21st century skills.

As mentioned previously, Laurillard (2016) speaks of the need to design opportunities for more collaborative and constructivist engagement with teachers to promote "co-learning" (p. 3). To this end, we have embedded focused questions related to the design of learning activities into each MOOC module. However, to promote meaningful co-learning, we are aware of the need to challenge and support teachers as they engage in critical discussions around their understandings and classroom experiences of 21CLD in action. We know from Phase 1 and 2 that such discussions shifted teachers' pedagogical orientation and are a key element of the job embedded professional learning model which are readily supported through face-to-face interactions. Drawing on the literature outlined earlier in this paper, the challenge now is to embed these critical discussions in a MOOC environment. This challenge raises a number of further questions. What type of design is required in order to promote critically reflective dialogue through asynchronous online discussion? To what extent will asynchronous discussion fora need to be moderated and supported by other means such as synchronous "live" sessions?

3.1 Designing Opportunities for Online Deep Learning Conversations

Currently, any teacher can access the MOOC assets developed in Phase 3 of the initiative for the eight modules of the 21CLD course on the Microsoft Educator Platform. Within five months of its launch in February 2016 over 10,500 have participated in the modules and it is still consistently in the top 10 courses on the Microsoft Educator Platform. However, the content has not, as yet, been designed or hosted on a MOOC platform which would lend towards a more blended model of professional learning.

The next phase of development is therefore to take these assets and to relocate them on an intentionally designed MOOC platform where we can build learner experiences to recreate the deep professional learning experiences observed in Phase 1 & Phase 2. To this end the University has recently made the decision to join the FutureLearn platform which in terms of its design was strongly influenced by Laurillard's Conversation Framework (2002). However, the challenge remains to design the social supports within the MOOC structure to sustain the collaboration, dialogue and ongoing reflection that is necessary for the changes in pedagogical orientation and classroom practices. In particular, we need to establish if the technology exists and, if so, how to successfully embed it in the teaching and learning experience to support the deep engagement we witnessed in Phase 1 and 2.

Cognisant of our experiences in Phase 1 and 2, we strove to design a MOOC that could reach large numbers while also providing opportunities for teachers to learn through practice, discussion and production (Laurillard 2016). In this sense, we wanted teachers both to try out ideas in their classrooms and report back on their experience. We wanted to promote critical reflection and discussion as well as providing opportunities for teachers to share ideas and resources. Incorporating these elements would, we believed, result in scaling the model of teacher professional learning we had developed to date that is contextualised and meaningfully rooted in classroom practice. We are critically aware that a community of practice needs to be built around a MOOC, as opposed to individuals just working through the content on their own. The challenge as we begin to design the next iteration of the 21CLD MOOC is to explore if we can recreate the collaborative nature of peer-coaching and develop the communities of practice that can sustain a culture of self-evaluation. Given that professional learning is most effective when it is grounded in collective discussions of classroom practice (Warren Little 2003) our major concern is how can we recreate in an online environment those deep learning conversations which centred on teachers' classroom practices that were central to teacher learning in Phase 1 & 2. Therefore, in the next iteration of the 21CLD MOOC we want to explore if the synchronous online learning tools are up to the job of facilitating deep deliberation, as defined by Brookfield and Preskill (2005). We know, from Phase 1 and 2, that such deep deliberation is an essential component of an effective professional learning model. Thus, the only variable we are changing from Phase 1 and 2 is the medium through which we engage in deep discussion, moving from face-to-face to online and we want to explore if and how synchronous online learning tools can support such interaction.

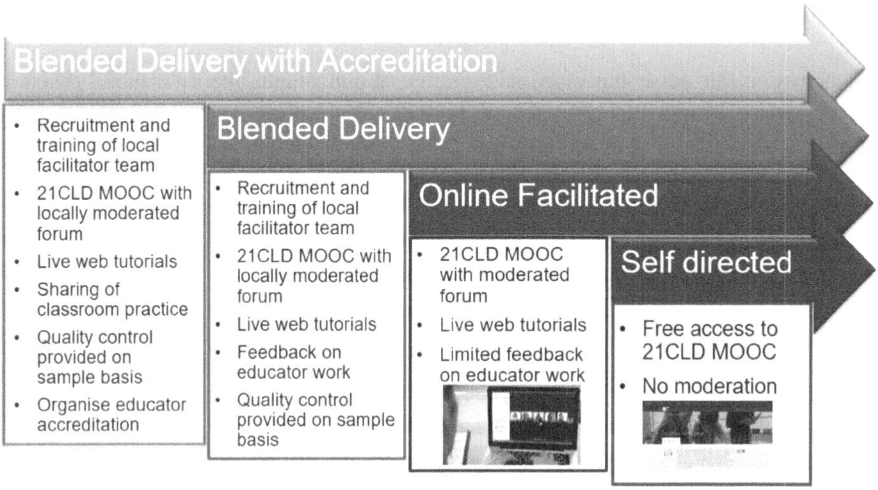

Fig. 1. Possible ways that the 21CLD MOOC can be developed

We are aware of the centrality of the role of the online tutor and the development of certain critical "dispositions" (Brookfield and Preskill 2005) so that participants will be able to engage in intense, debate and dialogue. In this case the disposition of deliberation appears particularly relevant as we want to provide teachers with an opportunity to engage in robust debate around their teaching practices, "to discuss issues as fully as possible by offering arguments and counterarguments that are supported by evidence, data, and logic and by holding strongly to these unless there are good reasons not to do so" (Brookfield and Preskill 2005, p. 13). This allows all to engage in robust debate where all views are valued. Deliberation has very much been to the fore in Phase 1& 2 with teachers engaged in robust discussion embedded in their classroom practices.

The literature also suggests that the facilitators' pedagogical beliefs and their technical knowledge of the online technologies are key to ensuring deep discussions. To this end for the initial pilot phase, the authors will be the facilitators using synchronous online learning tools to facilitate deep discussion with the 21CLD MOOC assets by working with a group of teachers in the southwest of Ireland recruited by the local teacher Education Centre. However, a basic assumption of this so-called 4th wave is that a one-size model of online professional learning will not fit all and that different strokes will be needed for different folks depending on the educational context (Picciano 2014). Consequently, in addition to this pilot we are continuing to explore other possible ways the 21CLD MOOC can be developed, as illustrated in Fig. 1.

A blended delivery model may be worthy of further development in our efforts to scale up the professional learning model, and to this end we have developed an accredited post-graduate certificate and diploma which is scheduled to begin in January 2018.

4 Conclusion

In conclusion, this paper has discussed a range of conceptual, theoretical and practical considerations around the potential of MOOCs for scaling up teacher professional learning. In addition, and in keeping with "the cMOOCs focus on community building, social interaction [and] peer review" (Jobe et al. 2014, p. 1581), we want participants to be able to work in peer groups, sharing experiences, ideas and expertise. This type of MOOC design also aligns with our job embedded approach that recognises the value of the experience and expertise that teachers can offer each other (Butler and Leahy 2015). Although with the support of Microsoft, the 21CLD resources are now available to a world-wide audience, we have still to develop ways that the school-embedded, job-focused model of teacher professional learning can be scaled effectively so that the teacher professional learning experience is contextualised and rooted in classroom practice. If the next stage is successful and we can recreate the deep discussions about learning online, our logical next step would include the identification of cohorts of teachers at local and regional levels that would be capable of supporting others. In this way, we would be recreating in an online environment the collaborative nature of peer coaching and developing communities of practices that would sustain a culture of self-evaluation similar to that which occurred in Phase1 and 2. We propose to trial this approach in Ireland in 2018 by working with the national network of teacher education centres.

References

Abrami, P.C., Bernard, R.M., Bures, E.M., Borokhovski, E., Tamim, R.M.: Interaction in distance education and online learning: using evidence and theory to improve practice. J. Comput. High. Educ. **23**, 82–103 (2011)

Ananiadou, K., Claro, M.: 21st century skills and competences for new millennium learners in OECD countries. Organization for Economic Cooperation and Development. EDU Working paper no. 41 (2009)

Anderson, T., Garrison, D.R.: Learning in a networked world: new roles and responsibilities. In: Gibson, C. (ed.) Learners in Higher Education, pp. 97–112. Atwood Publishing, Madison (1998)

Avalos, B.: Teacher professional development in teaching and teacher education over ten years. Teach. Teach. Educ. **27**, 10–20 (2011)

Bannan-Ritland, B.: Computer-mediated communication, eLearning and interactivity: a review of the research. Q, Rev. Distance Learn. **3**(2), 161–179 (2002)

Binkley, M., Erstad, O., Herman, J., Raizen, S., Ripley, M., Miller-Ricci, M., Rumble, M.: Defining twenty-first century skills. In: Griffin, P., McGaw, B., Care, E. (eds.) Assessment and Teaching of 21st Century Skills, pp. 17–66. Springer, Netherlands (2012). https://doi.org/10.1007/978-94-007-2324-5_2

Blanchette, J.: Participant interaction in asynchronous learning environments: evaluating interaction analysis methods. Linguisti. Educ. (2011). www.elsevier.com/locate/linged

Blayone, T., vanOostveen, R., Barber, W., DiGiuseppe, M., Childs, E.: Democratizing digital learning: theorizing the fully online learning community model. Int. J. Educ. Technol. High. Educ. **14**(13), 1–16 (2017)

Brookfield, S., Preskill, S.: Discussion as a Way of Teaching, vol. 2. Jossey-Bass, San Francisco (2005)

Butler, D.: Self-determined teacher learning in a digital context: fundamental change in thinking and practice. Unpublished Doctoral thesis, Dublin City University (2004)

Butler, D., Leahy, M.: Microsoft Innovative Schools Program Evaluation: Year Two Report – Ireland, in collaboration with Stanford Research Institute on behalf of Microsoft (2009)

Butler, D., Leahy, M.: Sharing classroom practices: a scalable, sustainable model of teacher professional development for learning in the 21st century. In: Proceedings of Society for Information Technology & Teacher Education International Conference 2011, pp. 1788–1794. AACE, Chesapeake (2011)

Butler, D., Leahy, M.: Moving towards innovation: the development of a sustainable framework for teacher professional learning. In: Shaping the Future: How Technology Can Lead to Educational Transformation (2015)

Darling-Hammond, L.: Reframing the school reform agenda: developing capacity for school transformation. Phi Delta Kappan **74**(12), 752–761 (1993)

DES: Digital Strategy for Schools - 2015–2020 (2015). https://www.education.ie/en/Publications/Policy-Reports/Digital-Strategy-for-Schools-2015-2020.pdf

Downes, S.: Massively open online courses are here to stay. Stephen's Web, 20 July 2012

Ebben, M., Murphy, J.S.: Unpacking MOOC scholarly discourse: a review of nascent MOOC scholarship. Learn. Media Technol. **39**(3), 328–345 (2014)

ETA (European Training Agency). Key Competences (2010)

Greene, J.A., Oswald, C.A., Pomerantz, J.: Predictors of retention and achievement in a massive open online course. Am. Educ. Res. J. **52**(5), 925–955 (2015)

Garrison, R.D., Cleveland-Innes, M.: Facilitating cognitive presence in online learning: interaction is not enough. Am. J. Distance Educ. **19**(3), 133–148 (2005)

Gulati, S.: Constructivism and emerging online learning pedagogy: a discussion for formal to acknowledge and promote the informal. In: Annual Conference of the Universities Association for Continuing Education - Regional Futures: Formal and Informal Learning Perspectives. Centre for Lifelong Learning. University of Glamorgan (2004)

Hallissy, M.: Building teacher professionalism in teaching-learning interactions between online tutors and learners during synchronous tutorials – a case study from Hibernia College. EdD, Institute of Education (2014). https://www.academia.edu/9427758/Building_teacher_professionalism_in_teaching-learning_interactions_between_online_tutors_and_learners_during_synchronous_tutorials_a_case_study_from_Hibernia_College

Hirumi, A.: A framework for analysing, designing, and sequencing planned elearning interactions. Q. Rev. Distance Learn. **3**(2), 141–160 (2002)

Hodges, C., Lowenthal, P., Grant, M.: Teacher professional development in the digital age: design considerations for MOOCs for teachers. In: Society for Information Technology & Teacher Education International Conference, pp. 2089–2096 (2016)

Jobe, W., Östlund, C., Svensson, L.: MOOCs for professional teacher development. In: Society for Information Technology & Teacher Education International Conference, 17 March 2014 in Jacksonville, Florida, USA, pp. 1580–1586. AACE (2014)

Laurillard, D.: Rethinking University Teaching: A Conversational Framework for the Effective Use of Learning Technologies, 2nd edn. Routledge Falmer, New York (2002)

Laurillard, D.: The educational problem that MOOCs could solve: professional development for teachers of disadvantaged students. Res. Learn. Technol. **24**(1), 29369 (2016). https://doi.org/10.3402/rlt.v24.29369

Law, N., Chow, A.: Pedagogical orientation in mathematics and science and the use of ICT. In: Law, N., Pelgrum, J., Plomp, T. (eds.) Pedagogy and ICT Use in Schools Around the World: Findings from the IEA SITES 2006 Study. The Comparative Education Research Centre, Hong Kong (2008)

McGreal, R., Kinuthia, W., Marshall, S., McNamara, T. (eds.): Open Educational Resources: Innovation, Research and Practice. Commonwealth of Learning and Athabasca University, Vancouver (2013)

NCCA (National Council for Curriculum and Assessment): Senior cycle key skills framework, Dublin (2009). https://www.curriculumonline.ie/getmedia/161b0ee4-706c-4a7a-9f5e-7c95669c629f/KS_Framework.pdf

National Foundation for the Improvement of Education: Teachers take charge of learning: transferring professional development for student success (1996). http://files.eric.ed.gov/fulltext/ED401251.pdf

Organisation for Economic Cooperation and Development (OECD): The definition and selection of key competencies. OECD, Paris (2005). http://www.oecd.org/document/17/0,3343,en_2649_39263238_2669073_1_1_1_1,00.html

Park, Y.J., Bonk, C.J.: Synchronous learning experiences: distance and residential learners' perspectives in a blended graduate course. J. Interact. Online Learn. **6**(3), 245–264 (2007)

Picciano, A.: A critical reflection of the current research in online and blended learning. ELM Magazine, Theme Issue, Issue 4/2014 (2014). http://www.elmmagazine.eu/articles/a-critical-reflection-of-the-current-research-in-online-and-blended-learning

Rovai, A.P.: A constructivist approach to online college learning. Internet High. Educ. **7**(2), 79–93 (2004)

Salmon, G.: E-moderating: The Key to Teaching and Learning Online. Kogan Pagan, London (2000)

Shear, L., Means, B., Gorges, T., Toyama, Y., Gallagher, L., Estrella, G., Lundh, P.: The Microsoft Innovative Schools Program Year 1 Evaluation Report. Microsoft, Seattle (2009)

Shear, L., Gallagher, L., Patel, D.: ITL Research: Evolving Educational Ecosystems. Microsoft, Redmond (2011)

Warren Little, J.: Inside teacher community: representations of classroom practice. Teach. Coll. Rec. **105**(6), 913–945 (2003)

Development of Web-Based Learning Scenarios in the Semantic Web – A Connection of Didactical Aspects and Ontological Structures

Sven Hofmann(✉)

Chair of Didactic of Computer Science, Technical University Dresden, Dresden, Germany
sven.hofmann@tu-dresden.de

Abstract. This paper investigates how teachers can be supported and guided in the planning of web-based learning scenarios. Using a graphical user-interface (GUI) the teachers should be able to choose existing learning-concepts and to realize them by web-based learning. Based on classical models of didactics a class-hierarchy of identifiers for learning-phases, learning-methods and learning-tools was developed, which is already in use by teachers in their practical work. After empirical studies this term set was transferred to scenarios of web-based learning. Didactical templates and patterns are derived. The developed term set and a competency model lead to a class-hierarchy, which is represented by an ontology for the semantic web. This ontological structure in combination with the GUI has to enable the saving, loading and sharing of learning scenarios based on web-standards. Using editors for creating the sets of meta-data and the ontology, this work offers first prototypical solutions. As part of an outlook on further research options for the mapping of the ontological structure into a learning platform are discussed. The aims of this investigation are first solutions to the largely automatic transfer of a planned learning scenario into a course structure of the chosen learning platform.

Keywords: Web-based learning · Didactical models · Ontology
Learning platform · Competency

1 Introduction

During their studies the students in teacher training learn much about didactical models, concepts and principals, which have evolved historically and which are used in Germany's schools. There are two separate parts of the didactics training – the general didactics and the specialist didactics in the two subjects of school having chosen by the students. Often they learn three different definitions of didactical terms for the same issue. These term settings are very different not only between the separate faculties of a particular university but rather between the universities of Germany. In addition the use of web-based learning scenarios required other notions and every content management system as part of a learning platform includes their own objects and structures.

A. Tatnall and M. Webb (Eds.): WCCE 2017, IFIP AICT 515, pp. 161–168, 2017.
https://doi.org/10.1007/978-3-319-74310-3_18

A guideline for teachers would be able to support the planning and realizations of web-based learning scenarios based on the didactical terms and transfer them into learning management systems. The frontend is a graphical user interface (GUI) which allows setting a sequence of learning-phases into a timeline in combination with learning methods and learning tools. The question was – how to represent the triples of phases, methods and tools for saving, reusing, editing and sharing on the web? The solution is an ontology, developed in the context of this work. Later it should be possible to export this ontological structure to different learning-platforms for creating a new e-learning scenario. So the teacher has the chance to plan and realize web-based learning scenarios using his own term setting without a deeper knowledge of the special object structure in the knowledge management system.

2 Didactical Models and Concepts

2.1 Classical Didactical Models

During their teacher training program the students get comprehensive knowledge about didactical models. They use them in the practical exercises and in their future professional work. Especially the model of educational-theoretical didactics by Klafki [1], the model of teaching-theoretical didactics by Heimann and Schulz [2] and also the model of curricular didactics by Mager, Möller and Meyer [3, 4] stand on the agenda of the didactical education. These classical models are based on a learning goal oriented approach and focus on input oriented teaching-learning scenarios.

Studies such as PISA [5] and PISA-E [6] showed among other findings the need for a standardization of education systems in the German states. They made clear, the educational process with rigid curriculum requirements is no longer appropriate in the international and federal-state context.

As a result a transition from input oriented teaching towards output orientation takes place. Educational standards for the control of the educational process got more into focus. The aim of these regulating standards is to make the different qualifications in the 16 German federal states comparable and replace the rigid curriculum guidelines by defined core competencies.

Learning scenarios based on an action theoretical principle with their phases start, work and transfer of the learning results become more important [7]. The teaching at German schools is increasingly determined by competency orientation and uses didactical scenarios which are focused on the development of self-organized thinking and acting based on different learning content [8]. The transformation from input oriented to output oriented teaching leads to a greater variety of methods. Didactic principles like problem orientation, redundancy and holism flow stronger into the planning and implementation of learning scenarios [9]. Teaching concepts like "web-based learning", "flipped classroom" bring more intensive use of digital media and support the communication between teachers and learners. This opens a new freedom of action in which the didactic aspects and the enrichment of the method repertoire are of primary importance.

2.2 Set of Didactical Terms

The realization of new learning concepts and the use of digital media caused the enlargement of the didactical term sets but also the magnification of their inconsistency. For the same issues different identifiers are in use. As an example of an identifier of the individual time sections in a learning scenario there are terms like "lesson phase", "learning section" and others in use. Here serious differences are to be seen not only between the universities but also between the individual faculties of the same university.

For the planning and realization of web-based learning scenarios platforms like Moodle or OPAL are available. These learning platforms contain a predefined quantity of course objects (e.g. internal pages, tests, tasks) being not conform to the didactical term set. This implies the necessity of unification of the term set in didactical context for their subsequent mapping in the object quantity of the learning platform.

In the first step a term set has been derived from classic didactical models and established teaching concepts. This set was evaluated with teachers of German schools in 2 stages. The first survey was carried out using a guide controlled interview. In this case a semi open card sorting gave as a result a first categorization of the didactical terms.

After completion of the cluster analysis and adaption of the term set a second survey by questionnaire took place with the same sample. This result was an increase of the scatter goodness from 48.1% after the first survey to 78.1% after the second.

Thus a largely standardized term set originated, which classifies the didactical terms for planning and realizing of web-based learning scenarios in a hierarchy of three classes *learning phase (p), learning method (m) and learning tool (t)* [11].

2.3 Templates and Patterns

The contemplation of possible combinations of learning methods (m) and learning tools (t) emerges frequently used (m, t)-pairs which represent typical teaching situations as a template and can be mapped in special course objects of the learning platforms.

The combination of each learning phase (p) with a (m, t)-template effects a (p, m, t)-triple describing a concrete teaching scenario. The sequencing of several (p, m, t)-Triples gives a complete learning scenario [11].

In practice proven learning-scenarios also consider didactical principles and institutional conditions [12]. Therefrom teaching concepts can be derived which are to be realized by web-based learning in learning platforms.

In view of the subsequent mapping of a scenario in the course structure on learning platforms the use of a standardized description language for the patterns makes sense. Solutions for the representation of standardized teaching scenarios by patterns using a special pattern language already exist. For example in context of the Pedagogical Patterns Project special patterns for the planning and execution of seminars [13] or of running a course [14] were developed. Fourteen didactical patterns to typical education scenarios in high schools were collected by Bergin supporting professors in their work [15]. All of these examples use their own special sets of didactical terms.

The special pattern language is largely unified. In these patterns language statements about *problem*, *requirements*, *context*, *solution* and *crosslinking* are included [16]. This pattern language should be transferred in the context of school education. Goodyear (2005) follows the idea to provide teachers with set of educational design ideas represented by design patterns. Examples for tasks like discuss, debate, summarize with different organizational forms and learning tools are released.

Using structured descriptions in pattern language these web-based learning scenarios based on an own term set which seems not completely compatible with the terms in didactics for German schools.

The developed graphical planning tool based on the evaluated set of didactical terms. For the following proven teaching concepts descriptions in pattern language are already prepared [11]:

- Concept of project work
- Concept of open learning
- Concept of problem-solving learning
- Concept of science oriented learning
- Concept of programmed instruction

The classification of the didactical term set in a formalized class hierarchy and the deriving of didactical templates and patterns form the base for a development environment, which supports the planning and realization of web-based learning scenarios and can be stored as an ontological structure in the net.

In the actual status a combination of all phases, methods and tools is possible. A compilation of suitable (p, m, t)-triples to prefabricated design patterns has to be implemented after a test phase with teachers.

2.4 Integration of a Competency Model

The research also focused on the inclusion of a competency model. Here a class hierarchy was derived, which contains in the first level the main classes of competencies – learning-competence, media-competence, social-competence and self-competence. These classes resulted from analyses of established competence models e.g. GERS [17] and selected curricula from Germany and Austria [18–20].

The competency model will be integrated in a further stage of the development environment. Here the user will be able to set a prescription for the degrees of competencies and their current degrees of the learners too.

A later version will provide a consulting function for teachers by accessing of this competence model. Depending on the differences between the prescriptive competence and the current degree – the learning needs - notes on particularly suitable templates will be given to the users. This consulting function has to be an adaptive system. So the teacher has the opportunity to bring his own experience into the system after the use of (p, m, t)-triples for the competence development in web-based learning scenarios [11].

3 Ontology

3.1 Representation of Didactical Term Sets

The available, largely formalized term set allows a structured development of web-based learning scenarios. The teachers will be guided by an environment which supports the data managing (saving, editing and sharing) of the scenario.

The developed planning tool should meet the following requirements:

- The learning scenario has to be planned and realized using the existing didactical term set.
- The result of the planning process is filed on the web and provides opportunities for reusing, editing, sharing, publishing and so on.
- The filing of the scenario complies with the standards for the web-based representation of learning processes (e.g. IMS-Learning Design, LOM - Learning Object Metadata) [11].

It became evident that an ontology meets these requirements for representation of learning scenarios. The exploration of existing ontologies, especially of their conceptual structure, shows particularly application areas in information retrieval, e-Commerce and knowledge management [21]. By mapping of web-based learning processes in an ontology a new area of use is opened.

Ontologies can be categorized by the level of generalization in top-level-ontology; domain-level-ontology and application-level-ontology ordered descending. The didactical term set is first placed in a context-independent top-level-ontology. This is to be considered as prototype and will change to a domain-level-ontology by developing a concrete learning scenario in the context of a specific teaching subject.

For mapping the didactical term set in an ontological structure the Web Ontology Language (OWL) is in use. This semantic markup language allows the implementation of the terms in a class hierarchy, the allocation of special attributes and the definition of relations between the classes. Ontologies formulated in OWL meet the following requirements on a technological level:

- The representation of ontologies on the web is possible.
- Interactions to other ontologies are supported.
- Special classes, relations and attributes are defined.
- The syntax is based on XML and confirms to W3C.
- The semantic representation of content corresponds to the standard [11].

Regarding the standardized representation of learning content ontologies, OWL also meets special requirements on the didactical level:

- The learning objects and their relations are described based on formalized languages.
- The semantic and elementary dependencies of the objects are formulated by ontology vocabulary.
- Logical compositions are defined by regulations.

In the present ontology for example it is possible to declare a phase in the class `LearningPhase` as successor of another. Thus a sequencing of the phases is possible and so a learning scenario is created. An object of the class `LearningMethod` is related to an object of the class `LearningTool` by the relation `has_to_use`.

The creation of ontology is supported by an editor. In this case the editor Protègè-2000 is in use. This is a frame based tool which is available as Open Source application and has a worldwide user-community. The development environment can be extended in the functionality by plugins [10] (Fig. 1).

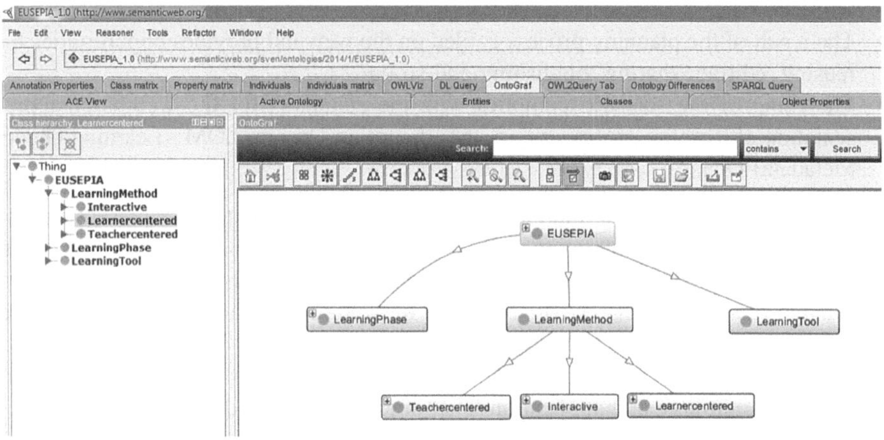

Fig. 1. Representation of ontology EUSEPIA in protègè

The ontology of the evaluated didactical term set forms the base of the surrounding development environment as a graphical user interface. It is set to the educational server of Saxony and can be use not only for the planning of the own learning scenarios but also for their sharing and further developing.

3.2 Graphical User Interface (GUI)

A graphical user interface (GUI) is placed on the ontology. The construct of GUI and ontology is named EUSEPIA (in German: "**E**ntwicklungs**u**mgebung zur **S**trukturierung von **E**-Learning-**P**rozessen **i**n der **A**usbildung", in English: Development Environment for structuring e-learning scenarios in education.) It allows the planning of learning scenarios by setting (p, m, t)-triples on a timeline. The client-server-structure manages the filing on the server sided ontology.

As part of a complex internship for students of media computer science first software solutions were created. The GUI and also functions for the managing of data exchange with the ontology are capable of work.

The client is a web application using different screens and supporting the teachers in their planning of learning scenarios intuitively. An implemented manager administers the scenarios and allows to publish the own scenarios and to make them available to other teachers. So a collaborative work between teachers is possible.

3.3 Summary, Current Status

The creation of EUSEPIA came out of the necessity to bridge the gap between the conceptual world of didactics and the objects in learning platforms. This will enable teachers to plan scenarios for web-based learning with their own didactical term set and to realize them without deeper knowledge about the internal structure of learning platforms.

A two-staged evaluated term set is the base which is in use in the teacher training of students and in the daily practical work of the teachers. The connecting element is an ontology, where the planned learning scenario is mapped in. This ontology was developed by the use of editors and oriented to the standards of software development. A GUI supports the user in their planning work. Actually this platform and first tools for saving, editing and sharing of scenarios are capable to test.

The client-server-architecture allows a completely web-based planning and the collaborative work with other teachers.

4 Outlook

After the further completing of the development environment the tool will be set on the education server in Saxony. The responsive layout has to be further developed.

The Saxon Universities and high schools cooperate on a common *Online Platform for Academic Learning (OPAL)*. Meanwhile this learning platform is available as parallel instance for the schools in Saxony. After the completion of the development work on EUSEPIA the creation of an interface to *OPAL-school* is planned. This will enable the integration of EUSEPIA as an authoring tool into the learning platform. So the teachers will be able to plan scenarios with the development environment and to generate an e-learning course largely automated.

It becomes clear that a lot of further development work is ready for realization. The project EUSEPIA has high potential for the establishing of web-based learning at schools by supporting teachers in their endeavour to serve a contemporary education by a meaningful use of digital media.

References

1. Klafki, W.: Die bildungstheoretische Didaktik im Rahmen kritisch-konstruktiver Erziehungswissenschaft. Oder: Zur Neufassung der Didaktischen Analyse. In: Gudjons, H., Winkel, R. (eds.) Didaktische Theorien. PB-Bücher Bergmann + Helbig, Hamburg, pp. 13–34 (2011)
2. Schulz, W.: Die lehrtheoretische Didaktik Oder: Didaktisches Handeln im Schulfeld. Modellskizze einer professionellen Tätigkeit. In: Gudjons, H., Winkel, R. (eds.) Didaktische Theorien. PB-Bücher Bergmann + Helbig, Hamburg, pp. 35–56 (2011)

3. Mager, R.F.: Lehrgang zur Formulierung von Lernzielen (2010). http://www.phsg.ch/Portaldata/1/Resources/bps_sek_i/zxtranet/ausbildungsunterlagen/Lehrgang_zur_Formulierung_von_Lernzielen.pdf. Accessed 3 Aug 2012
4. Möller, C.: Die curriculare Didaktik Oder: Der lernzielorientierte Ansatz. In: Gudjons, H., Winkel, R. (eds.) Didaktische Theorien. PB-Bücher Bergmann + Helbig, Hamburg, pp. 75–92 (2011)
5. OECD: The PISA 2003 assessment framework. Mathematics, reading, science and problem solving knowledge and skills. OECD, Paris (2003)
6. Baumert, J.: Pisa 2000 - die Länder der Bundesrepublik Deutschland im Vergleich. PISA-E. Leske + Budrich, Opladen (2002)
7. Zimmer, G.: Aufgabenorientierte Didaktik des E-Learning. Handbuch E-Learning, 4.Erg.-Lfg. (2003)
8. Baumgartner, P.: Taxonomie von Unterrichtsmethoden. Ein Plädoyer für didaktische Vielfalt. Waxmann, Münster (2011)
9. Sander, W.: Ein didaktischer Werkzeugkoffer: Tools für die Planung von Lernumgebungen (2009). http://studienseminar.rlp.de/fileadmin/user_upload/studienseminar.rlp.de/bb-nr/Praktika/Sander_Didaktische_Prinzipien.pdf. Accessed 19 Jan 2017
10. Gómez-Pérez, A., Fernández-López, M., Corcho, O.: Ontological Engineering. With Examples from the Areas of Knowledge Management, E-commerce and the Semantic Web. Advanced Information and Knowledge Processing. Springer, Heidelberg (2010). https://doi.org/10.1007/b97353
11. Hofmann, S.: E-Learning und ontologisch strukturierte Planung webbasierter Lehr-Lern-Szenarien. Entwicklung eines Leitfadens für Lehrende zur didaktisch-methodischen Umsetzung webbasierter Lehr-Lern-Szenarien im Kontext gymnasialen Unterrichts. Logos Berlin, Berlin (2015)
12. Jank, W., Meyer, H.: Didaktische Modelle. Cornelsen Scriptor, Frankfurt am Main (1994)
13. Fricke, A., Völter, M.: SEMINARS. A Pedagogical Pattern Language about teaching seminars effectively (2000). http://www.voelter.de/data/pub/tp/tp.pdf. Accessed 5 June 2014
14. Eckstein, J.: Learning to Teach and Learning to Learn. Running a Course (2000). http://www.pedagogicalpatterns.org/examples/LearningAndTeaching.pdf. Accessed 20 Jan 2017
15. Bergin, J.: Fourteen Pedagogical Patterns (2000). http://csis.pace.edu/~bergin/PedPat1.3.html. Accessed 20 Jan 2017
16. de Moura Filho, C.O., Derycke, A.: Pedagogical Patterns and Learning Design: When Two Worlds Cooperate (2005). http://dspace.ou.nl/bitstream/1820/474/9/09_DBU_review.pdf. Accessed 20 Jan 2017
17. Council of Europe: Common European framework of reference for languages. Learning, teaching, assessment. Press Syndicate of the University of Cambridge, Cambridge (2001)
18. Kerres, M.: Mediendidaktik. Konzeption und Entwicklung medien-gestützter Lernangebote. 3. Aufl. München: Oldenbourg, R. (2012)
19. Reisse, W.: Kompetenzorientierte Aufgabenentwicklung. Ein Lehrerhandbuch für die Sekundarstufen. Köln: Aulis-Verl. Deubner (2008)
20. Sächsisches Staatsministerium für Kultus: Lehrplan Gymnasium - Mathematik. Unter Mitarbeit von Sächsischen Bildungsinstitut. Hg. v. Sächsisches Staatsministerium für Kultus. Dresden (2013). http://www.schule.sachsen.de/lpdb/web/downloads/1530_lp_gy_mathematik_2013.pdf?v2. zuletzt aktualisiert am 30 July 2013
21. Meszaros, G., Doble, J.: A Pattern Language for Pattern Writing (2013). http://hillside.net/index.php/a-pattern-language-for-pattern-writing. Accessed 20 Jan 2017

Development of a Model to Assess the Digitally Mature Schools in Croatia

Gordana Jugo[1(✉)], Igor Balaban[2], Marijana Pezelj[1], and Nina Begicevic Redjep[3]

[1] Education Support Department, Croatian Academic and Research Network – CARNet, Zagreb, Croatia
{gordana.jugo,marijana.pezelj}@carnet.hr
[2] Department of Computing and Technology, Faculty of Organization and Informatics, University of Zagreb, Varazdin, Croatia
igor.balaban@foi.hr
[3] Department of Organization, Faculty of Organization and Informatics, University of Zagreb, Varazdin, Croatia
nina.begicevic@foi.hr

Abstract. This paper shows key steps in the development of a Model for Digitally Mature Schools in Croatia and reveals the results of assessment of digital maturity of schools in Croatia. In total, 151 primary and secondary schools were assessed against maturity levels using the instrument, and two different methods for gathering the data: self-evaluation and external evaluation. Notable differences were recorded between results of self-evaluation and external evaluation in favour of self-evaluation. Some of the factors that contributed to differences are lack of experience in conducting self-evaluation and additional training for external evaluators in opposition to written guidelines for conducting self-evaluation. The next step is to refine and upgrade the instrument based on comments and suggestions gathered during external evaluation and self-evaluation. Towards the end of the pilot project the final self-evaluation and external evaluation is planned to monitor schools' progress. In order to lower the differences between results of self-evaluation and external evaluation, besides upgraded instrument, school staff will be more intensively prepared for conducting self-evaluation.

Keywords: Digital maturity · Maturity framework · e-Schools
Self evaluation · External evaluation

1 Introduction

The concept of digital maturity of educational institutions is becoming increasingly important due to rapid development of ICT in education. The European Commission has also recognized the significance of digital maturity and offers support throughout its policies and programmes (see for example [1, 2]). This paper defines digitally mature schools as schools with a high level of ICT integration, and with a systematic approach towards using ICT in school management and educational processes. The usage of ICT in

A. Tatnall and M. Webb (Eds.): WCCE 2017, IFIP AICT 515, pp. 169–178, 2017.
https://doi.org/10.1007/978-3-319-74310-3_19

school no longer depends on individuals – it requires a systematic approach, planned and implemented by a school and relevant stakeholders such as the Ministry, etc. Therefore, it is mandatory to identify the areas and levels that define the digital maturity of a school in order to plan improvement in the integration and use of ICT (see for example [3].

The problem analysis of the Croatian education system from the perspective of ICT integration revealed several major constraints [4]:

1. Lack of a systematic approach to introducing information and communication technology into education and other processes in schools;
2. Lack of guidelines/a system of development of digitally mature schools;
3. Low level of use of the opportunities information and communication technology offers in the education system; and
4. Lack of an officially accepted framework and strategy for the development of digitally mature schools.

With respect to this, the e-Schools programme, co-financed from the Structural Funds of the European Union [5], was initiated in 2015 in order to support the development of digitally mature schools in Croatia. Its aim is to introduce ICT into the school system in Croatia in the period 2015–2022 in order to help primary and secondary schools to become digitally mature schools. The e-Schools programme consists of the pilot project, which started in 2015 and the major project, which will be implemented in the period 2019–2022, based on the results of the pilot project. The pilot project involves 151 primary and secondary schools, which accounts for about 10% of all the schools in Croatia. It is expected that an additional 700 schools will be included in the major project [5].

The main deliverables of this programme are the Framework for Digitally Mature Schools and the Instrument for Measuring the Digital Maturity of Schools, based on the framework. The results are used to plan activities for schools that would enable them to make progress regarding the level of digital maturity.

2 Structure of the Proposed Model

In order to support schools in the development of digital maturity, a model for digitally mature schools in Croatia was developed. The model consists of the following elements: a framework for digitally mature schools, an instrument for measuring the digital maturity of schools, the initial self-evaluation of schools, the initial external evaluation of schools, as well as the final self-evaluation and external evaluation of schools (see Fig. 1).

2.1 Framework for Digitally Mature Schools

The framework for digitally mature schools is a document that defines the areas, elements and levels of the digital maturity of schools. The methodological approach taken in the development of the framework was for the most part qualitative and included: (1) a comprehensive literature review on compatible frameworks and toolkits;

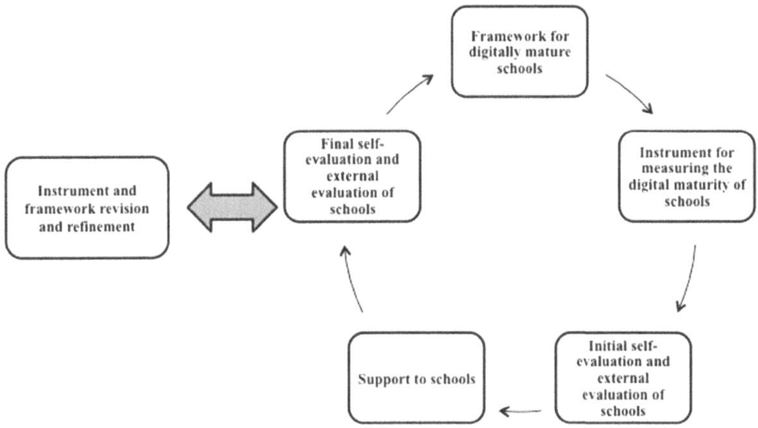

Fig. 1. Elements of the model for digitally mature schools

(2) a meta-analysis of selected frameworks and toolkits; and (3) testing and feedback through a series of expert consultation, workshops, focus groups and semi-structured interviews. A complete and in-depth procedure of framework development is available in [10]. Here we provide only a brief overview.

Two frameworks provide the basis for the development of the Croatian framework: The European framework for digitally mature organizations – DigCompOrg [1], and eLearning Roadmap [6]. The Croatian framework therefore consists of five key areas: (1) planning, management and leadership; (2) ICT in learning and teaching; (3) development of digital competences; (4) ICT culture; and (5) ICT infrastructure. Each key area is described by several indicators. In total, thirty-seven elements are defined across all key areas. For example, the elements used to describe key area (2) ICT in learning and teaching are: awareness, planning, use, digital content, evaluation of students, student experience; and Special educational needs.

In addition, five levels of maturity are also defined with respect to [7, 8]: basic, initial, e-enabled, e-confident and e-mature. It is important to stress that different maturity stages have been established for schools to plan their journey: where are they now and where they would like to be in the future. The different levels should not be read as 'judgmental', but as the stages of a maturation process.

Next, each of the elements is described in terms of the five different maturity levels. This resulted in a rubric that summarizes and graphically represents the areas, elements and levels of the digital maturity of schools. For further details on the framework, see [9, 10].

Based on the description of each element through the 5 different maturity stages, a general description for each maturity level can be given [10]:

Level 1: Basic. The school is not aware of the possibility of using ICT in learning and teaching or in its management processes. Therefore, the school does not take ICT into consideration in planning its growth and development. ICT is not used in learning and teaching. The educational staff (teachers) do not develop their digital competences. Online communication with the school is generally not possible. ICT infrastructure has not been provided yet and computers are used only in a few classrooms.

Level 2: Initial. There is awareness of the possibility of using ICT in learning and teaching and in school management processes, but it has not yet been implemented. A small number of teachers use ICT in learning and teaching. There is an awareness of the need to enhance the digital competences of teachers and students. However, a system for the professional development of digital competences still does not exist. The school is still inactive in the online environment and access to its own ICT resources is limited. The ICT infrastructure is generally undeveloped and computers with internet access are only available in a few classrooms.

Level 3: e-Enabled. The school is aware of the possibility of using ICT in all its activities, guides the development of its strategic documents and integration of ICT into these documents. ICT is used for working with students with special educational needs. The teachers advance their digital competences, develop digital content and have started introducing innovative teaching methods. The school participates in small ICT-focused projects. Access to different ICT resources is provided in most classrooms. Special attention is given to equipment maintenance and to controlling software licensing. The school is active online in terms of content presentation and communication.

Level 4: e-Confident. The school very clearly recognizes the advantages of ICT in its activities and integrates ICT into strategic documents, as well as into its everyday activities. The teachers use ICT for advanced teaching and assessment methods, as well as develop their own content and protect it by copyright. There is also a shared content repository which can be used by teachers and students. The continuous professional training of teachers for the purpose of acquiring digital competences is planned and performed. Students are encouraged to develop those competences. Access to different ICT resources is provided in most classrooms, and the procurement and maintenance of ICT resources is planned. The school is active with respect to ICT projects. The school is also very active online in terms of content presentation and communication. Software licensing is controlled and the security aspects of ICT resource use are taken into consideration.

Level 5: e-Mature. In strategic documents and school development plans, the school very clearly recognizes and requires the use of ICT in all its activities. Management practice relies on the integration and obtaining of data from all the school information systems. The approach to the development of digital competences of teachers and students is systematic, and professional training for the teachers and additional course activities for the students are available. The teachers use ICT for advanced teaching methods, for the development of new course content and the assessment of student accomplishments. Teachers and students regularly protect digital content by copyright. There is also a shared content repository available for use by teachers and students. Access to ICT resources from own devices is provided in all classrooms and other rooms in the school. The school independently plans and acquires ICT resources, which are available in nearly all classrooms and other rooms in the school. The entire school has a developed network infrastructure. An information security system has been developed and software licensing is systematically controlled and planned. The school is characterized by varied ICT project activities, cooperation between teachers and students, as well as between school and other stakeholders. This is achieved through the use of online communication tools and school e-services.

Although the Framework for Digitally Mature Schools was developed within the e-Schools pilot project, it can be applied in all Croatian schools. Schools can use the framework as a guide for planning and integrating ICT in teaching and learning, as well as in other processes. Policy makers and decision makers in the education system can use the framework to develop policies and initiatives leading to the successful integration of ICT into the education system.

The Framework for Digitally Mature Schools is the basis for the development of other elements of the model for digitally mature schools in Croatia.

3 Methodology

3.1 Instrument for Measurement of Digital Maturity of Schools

Since the main success criterion of the e-Schools programme is defined as an increased digital maturity of schools, it is necessary to accurately measure maturity at the beginning and at the end of the project in order to make a comparison between the initial and final level of digital maturity. For this purpose, an instrument for measuring the digital maturity of schools based on the framework has been developed.

The instrument for measuring the digital maturity of schools comprises an evaluation rubric consisting of 5 key areas and 37 elements described across 5 maturity stages and an accompanying questionnaire which main purpose is to offer a much simpler interface to the research participants than the rubric. During the pilot testing of the rubric, the research participants, in this case the school representatives, complained that filling the rubric was too complicated and therefore the questionnaire was developed to facilitate the data gathering from the research participants. The rubric is afterwards filled based on the answers of the school representatives from the questionnaire.

Once the rubric has been filled in based on the answers of the school representatives, the result algorithm calculates the maturity level for the school applying a taxicab geometry method. It shows the maturity level for each element, then a calculated level for all key areas, and in the end, the calculated digital maturity level of a school (see Fig. 2).

The instrument is accessible in cloud on a designated web server and will be used both in the self-evaluation and external evaluation of schools.

3.2 Initial Self-evaluation of Schools

An initial self-evaluation of schools is carried out in order to establish the baseline level of digital maturity before the project makes its impact. Another important reason is to educate principals and other school staff, and to raise awareness of digital maturity among the participating school staff members. The most important reason for self-evaluation in the e-Schools programme is its contribution to school improvement, to be achieved through reflection on their practice and identification of areas for action All 151 schools in the pilot project participated in the initial self-evaluation. School principals completed the questionnaire with help of other members of the school staff in June and July of 2016.

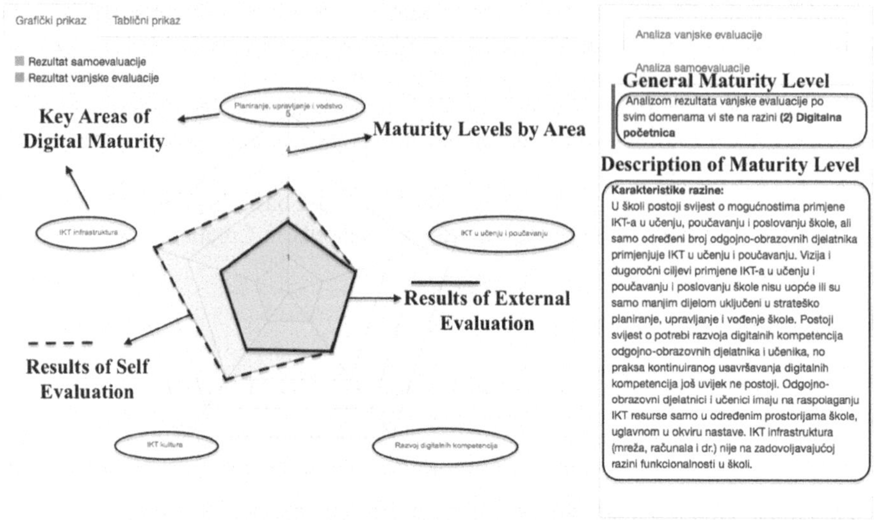

Fig. 2. Result display of instrument for measurement of digital maturity of schools – graph and text in respondents' native language (comparison between self-evaluation and external evaluation)

3.3 Initial External Evaluation of Schools

The external evaluation was carried out in the 151 schools participating in the pilot project in October 2016 by 23 external evaluators [10]. All external evaluators were trained in a workshop in order to ensure objective evaluation based on common criteria. The evaluators interviewed school principals and other members of school staff using the same instrument that was used in the self-evaluation. Evaluators also gathered some evidences supporting answers in the instrument, such as school curriculum and plans. Schools were asked to prepare the evidence to support their responses in advance. Additionally, the evaluators inspected the existing infrastructure and resources.

The validity of the questionnaire was assessed by calculating Cronbach's alpha to estimate the raters' consistency. All constructs exceeded the threshold of 0.60, which is considered to be adequate with respect to the very early stage of research and the context [11]. Therefore, the data could be analyzed with confidence.

4 Results

As is evident from Table 1, following the self-evaluation, 50% of the schools were found to be at the initial maturity level. A further 45% of the schools are e-enabled. Only 3% of the schools are e-confident, and only 1% are e-mature. There are no schools at the basic digital maturity level.

Table 1 also shows the distribution of digital maturity levels as calculated in the external evaluation of schools. According to the external evaluation, the majority of schools (82%) are at the initial level, and 18% of schools are at the e-enabled level.

Table 1. Results of self-evaluation and external evaluation of schools (N = 151)

Maturity levels/method	Basic	Initial	e-Enabled	e-Confident	e-Mature
Self- evaluation	0%	50%	45%	3%	1%
External evaluation	0%	82%	18%	0%	0%

Besides displaying the results for each school, the online system offers several other features. Namely, besides the in-depth analysis of the current level of digital maturity of a school, it is also possible to compare the results of self-evaluation and external evaluation. Additionally, each school is able to compare its performance against that of other schools, choosing between all schools, those from the same county, the same level, etc.

Moreover, based on the current maturity level of each element, the school receives a set of recommendations from the system on how to move to the next level. In other words, the schools receive information about the elements that require attention in order to be able to repair them.

Therefore, the instrument can be used as a tool to evaluate the school's digital maturity level, but it can also serve to identify areas for school improvement that will result in raising the school's level of digital maturity as well as its overall reputation and academic results.

5 Discussion

The results of self-evaluation showed higher levels of digital maturity in comparison with results of external evaluation as can be seen in Table 1. While self-evaluation resulted in 45% of e-enabled schools, external evaluation records only 18% of the e-enabled schools. Higher levels of digital maturity (e-confident and e-mature) were displayed by 4% of schools in the self-evaluation, as opposed to no schools in the external evaluation. The external evaluation recorded a majority of schools (82%) at the initial level, while the self-evaluation recorded 50% of schools at the initial level.

There are many factors that contributed to notable differences between the results of self-evaluation and external evaluation. First of all, the school staff participating in self-evaluation lack experience in conducting self-evaluation since most schools in Croatia are not included in any self-evaluation practice. Secondly, the concept of digital maturity in general is a new concept in the local context, and specifically some areas and elements of digital maturity are unfamiliar. For instance, there are no requirements for school principals related to their management and leadership competences and as a result most of them lack management and leadership competences. Thirdly, while the external evaluators were trained in a workshop for performing external evaluation, school staff were provided only with written guidelines on how to conduct self-evaluation. And finally, except for explanations for the most novel terms in the instrument, the respondents did not have any kind of support during the self-evaluation.

The next step is to refine and upgrade the instrument based on the comments and suggestions gathered during the external evaluation and self-evaluation. The main aim is to minimize the difference in the results between the self-evaluation and external evaluation due to the instrument itself.

Refinements and upgrades will be performed in two basic directions. The first direction involves modifying the online system hosting the instrument and the feedback based on user feedback. The introductory page has been completely re-written to introduce the evaluation procedure and its intention to the end-users in greater detail. Some questions/elements have been rewritten and better explained, taking into account the different backgrounds of the end-users. A dictionary of ICT terms has also been added and a hover option is available whereby the users can get an explanation by just hovering over the item. The radar chart showing the difference between self- and external evaluation has been added to the result display of instrument shown in Fig. 2. Additionally, with a detailed insight into the state of each of the 37 elements at the digital maturity level, the school also gets guidelines for improvement. The online system points to the elements that need to be improved to help the school plan its own improvement.

The second direction involves an introductory webinar which has been prepared for all end-users in order to better explain the process, the aims of the e-Schools programme and to motivate them for answering the questions in the instrument. The webinar participants will be able to ask and receive answers to all relevant questions. Participation in the webinar will raise the capacity of the school staff for conducting self-evaluation.

The final self-evaluation and final external evaluation of schools will be performed towards the end of the pilot project. The comparison between the results of the initial and final evaluation of the digital maturity of schools will hopefully show an increase in digital maturity, which is one of the main objectives and the main success criterion of the project. It will also show the effectiveness of measures taken to minimize the difference in the results between the self-evaluation and external evaluation.

In respect of the results obtained in the initial evaluation of schools, it is necessary to raise the level of digital maturity in Croatian schools by implementing a series of measures and activities. The measures and activities implemented within the pilot program address all the areas identified in the Framework for Digitally Mature Schools, including raising awareness of the importance and opportunities of using ICT in learning and teaching, ICT governance in, raising the level of digital competence of teachers, and modernizing the existing ICT infrastructure. The following resources and services have been provided: educational opportunities for teachers and school principals, document templates for the strategic planning of the introduction and use of ICT, digital educational contents, teaching scenarios, adequate ICT infrastructure, etc.

6 Conclusion

The main conclusion was that in spite of significant differences in the results between self-the evaluation and external evaluation, the identified general levels of digital maturity in Croatian schools are closer to the lower end of the 5-level scale, which indicates that it is necessary to raise the level of school maturity in Croatia by implementing a series of measures and activities within the school system. The final self-evaluation and external evaluation will be conducted towards the end of the pilot project with the aim of measuring the difference between the levels of digital maturity of schools at the beginning and at the end of the pilot project. It is hoped that the measures and activities implemented within the pilot program addressing all the areas identified in the Framework for Digitally Mature Schools will lead to increased levels of digital maturity. In case there is no significant increase in digital maturity, the Framework for Digitally Mature Schools, the instrument for measuring the digital maturity of schools and the project activities aimed at the development of digital maturity should be further explored, refined and revised.

The second important conclusion is that there is a notable difference between the results of the self-evaluation and external evaluation. This paper discusses the reasons for the difference identified by the researchers. A number of measures will be taken based on these reasons, with the aim of minimizing the difference in the results between self-evaluation and external evaluation. The comparison of the final results of self-evaluation and external evaluation will show whether the reasons were identified correctly and the measures implemented effectively. If a significant difference persists, the reasons and the measures will be additionally explored.

Acknowledgments. The authors would like to thank European Commission, Joint Research Centre, Institute for Prospective Technological Studies (IPTS), especially Yves Punie and Panagiotis Kampylis; and Professional Development Service for Teachers – PDST, especially Seán Gallagher, for their kind help and support in the development of a model for digitally mature schools in Croatia. The development of this paper was co-financed by the European Union from European structural and investment funds. The content of this paper is the sole responsibility of the authors.

References

1. Kampylis, P., Punie, Y., Devine, J.: Promoting Effective Digital-Age Learning - A European Framework for Digitally-Competent Educational Organisations. Publications Office of the European Union, Luxembourg (2015)
2. Up-scaling Creative Classrooms in Europe (SCALE CCR). http://is.jrc.ec.europa.eu/pages/EAP/SCALECCR.html. Accessed 16 Jan 2017
3. Assessing the e-Maturity of your School (Ae-MoYS). http://e-mature.ea.gr/. Accessed 16 Jan 2017
4. Kupres, D., et al.: Studija izvodljivosti pilot projekta e-Škole. Croatian Academic and Research Network – CARNet, Zagreb (2015)
5. Croatian Academic and Research Network – CARNet: e-Schools: Establishing a system for developing digitally mature schools (pilot project). Croatian Academic and Research Network – CARNet, Zagreb (2017)
6. The e-Learning Roadmap. http://www.ncte.ie/elearningplan/roadmap/. Accessed 25 July 2017
7. Love, D., McKean, G., Gathercoal, P.: Portfolios to webfolios and beyond: levels of maturation. Educause Q. **27**(2), 24–37 (2004)

8. Becta: Measuring e-maturity in the FE sector - Final report. Becta, Coventry (2008)
9. Begicevic Redjep, N., Balaban, I.: Okvir za digitalnu zrelost i procjena digitalne zrelosti škola u Hrvatskoj. In: Biljanovic, P. (ed.) MIPRO 2017 40th Jubilee International Convention Proceedings, pp. 717–722. Croatian Society for Information and Communication Technology, Electronics and Microelectronics - MIPRO. Rijeka (2017)
10. Begicevic Redjep, N., Balaban, I., Zugec, B., Klacmer Calopa, M., Divjak, B.: Framework for digitally mature schools. In: EDEN 2017 Annual Conference Book of Abstracts, p. 39. European Distance and E-Learning Network, Budapest (2017)
11. Loewenthal, K.M.: An Introduction to Psychological Tests and Scales, 2nd edn. Psychology Press, Hove (2004)

The "Secure Exam Environment": E-Testing with Students' Own Devices

Gabriele Frankl(✉), Peter Schartner, and Dietmar Jost

Alpen-Adria-Universität Klagenfurt, Klagenfurt, Austria
gabriele.frankl@auu.at

Abstract. In the 21st century, written exams continue to be the primary method of assessing factual knowledge. Conducting these exams online reduces the correction workload and offers advantages such as enhanced objectivity, assessment with the possibility to use software specific to the course and thus increased constructive alignment with teaching and learning processes. However, eExams are often conducted in spaces that are too small, since larger computer rooms are usually unavailable or not economically feasible. Hence, in June 2011, we implemented a system called Secure Exam Environment (SEE) that enables online testing in any lecture hall with electricity and LAN sockets using students' own devices while blocking access to unauthorized files or internet pages. Loan devices are offered to students that have no suitable device for the SEE. Assessment is conducted via Moodle and additional software (e.g. Eclipse, GeoGebra) can be used as well. The SEE also addresses important issues such as security, reliability, high availability, privacy, and flexibility. As of August 2017 we have conducted 1,241 such online exams with 46,342 students and are able to test up to 220 students concurrently. Furthermore, we offer students the possibility to choose their preferred time slot to sit an eExam within predefined weeks.

Keywords: Secure online testing · Secure Exam Environment
Security · Reliability · High availability · Privacy · Monitoring

1 Introduction

Grading is still an important and non-trivial part of modern university life, since it heavily influences student behaviour [1]. The assessment process "can be used as a means of channelling students' energies, and the feedback that it generates can provide students with an opportunity for reflection" [2]. Various approaches to assessment offer students the possibility to demonstrate their competences using a full range of examination modalities for different types of knowledge.

Student and teacher involvement in assessment, including digitally-enhanced assessment, is a crucial aspect of 21st century learning [3]. However, despite the large number of possible assessment strategies, the most common method in higher education is summative assessment, which evaluates factual knowledge with (mostly) standardized, semi-standardized and/or open-text questions, leading to a huge correction workload if conducted with paper-and-pencil exams. As a result, lecturers must

A. Tatnall and M. Webb (Eds.): WCCE 2017, IFIP AICT 515, pp. 179–188, 2017.
https://doi.org/10.1007/978-3-319-74310-3_20

allocate a large amount of time to assessing tests, a task that could be carried out more efficiently by automated systems.

Next to the noticeable time and money savings [4] due to automatic delivery, storage and the (semi-)automated correction of (semi-)standardized question types, along with the improved readability, structure and clarity of typed open-text answers, eExams offer various advantages and improvements for assessment. Online exams increase student engagement due to their relative novelty and provide greater flexibility if compared to traditional testing methods [4]. The greater efficiency of online exams provides students with instant grading and feedback [5]. Moreover, today's students are not used to extensive handwriting anymore [6], leading to hand pain and bad handwriting when taking paper-and-pencil exams. Furthermore, with eExams different handwriting styles do not influence the lecturer when grading. It is also easier, for example, to evaluate all the answers for a single question at once by switching between the different students' answers, thus enabling each question to be evaluated on its merits without being influenced by other answers provided by the student. Hence, online exams enhance objectivity in that they are not steeped in subjective construction processes. Additionally, eExams can be saved and shared between lecturers easily, offering the opportunity for (mobile) synchronous correction. Although the creation of online questions might require greater initial effort, the establishment of a question pool leads to a reduction in effort over time, thus guaranteeing the sustainability of online testing. Moreover, the digital format offers opportunities for statistical analysis of questions, improving the quality of questions over time. Finally, the shuffling of questions and answers decreases chances for cheating. Another and very promising advantage of online exams is the opportunity to include additional software and multimedia into the examination environment. Biggs and Tang [7] postulate that a well-founded lecture design includes assessment. Their concept of "constructive alignment" emphasizes the necessity of establishing coherence between all phases and elements of the learning process. Intended learning outcomes, teaching/learning activities, assessment tasks as well as grading should support one another [7, 8]. Although Biggs and Tang's [7] approach has received criticism, we are of the opinion that it is particularly useful in highlighting the power of assessment to shape students' experiences [9]. Thus, in order to ensure coherence, the software tools used for teaching and learning should be part of the examination process. This means that mathematical calculations and analysis, spreadsheets, literature essays etc., can be easily processed online using appropriate software. Being able to use specific software and multimedia in electronic exam environments facilitates the way to promising (hands-on) performance assessments too.

Despite all the positive aspects of eExams mentioned so far, we found a lack of technical solutions to conduct secure online exams for larger audiences. The problems we encountered were too small computer rooms as well as a lack of consideration of the security requirements which inevitably arise in the context of (electronic) exams: confidentiality, privacy, integrity, authenticity, and availability. The first four aspects are commonly addressed through cryptography (e.g. encryption of transmitted and stored data, and authentication of messages and users), whereas the last one is provided by redundancy and continuous monitoring of the IT system.

To overcome the existing shortcomings, we implemented the Secure Exam Environment (SEE).

2 The Secure Exam Environment (SEE)

The Alpen-Adria-Universität Klagenfurt (AAU) launched the Secure Exam Environment (SEE) for online testing in 2011 [10] with the aim of supporting large class sizes and modern teaching as well as testing strategies, while working within budgetary and organisational constraints. In particular, the SEE makes use of the students' existing technical resources, specifically their personal computers (laptops). The efficiency of allowing students to use their own devices is complemented by an effectiveness factor since they are presumably familiar with the hardware.

The SEE disables access to students' own files and data as well as to other internet sites. Loan devices are offered for those who do not own a laptop. As a result, institutional asset requirements as well as the associated maintenance costs are minimized. We are currently able to test up to 220 students simultaneously.

Furthermore, courses are becoming increasingly based on or supported by different software tools and programmes, for example a statistics programme or special mathematical software packages. Traditional testing methods do not allow testing related to the use and application of such software programmes; the SEE, on the other hand, offers this possibility which is consistent with pedagogical coherence [8].

The actual exams are presented as quizzes, a key component of the Moodle learning management system (LMS) utilised by the AAU.

2.1 How Do We Secure the SEE?

As with traditional exams, cheating is a major problem. On the one hand, the issue of impersonation must be addressed, on the other hand, access to (electronic) materials such as notes, books, (external) devices, or local or online resources which are not allowed during an exam must be prevented.

We discourage impersonation by requiring students to present a valid student ID card. In addition, we utilize the photo stored in each student's Moodle profile to verify that they are indeed using the correct login credentials. During the exam we compare the registration data with the (number of) students who started the exam in the Moodle course. Starting the exam from outside a lecture hall is not possible due to automated grouping of registered students in Moodle after registration, since solely the members of this grouping are able to open the exam (students leave this grouping by checking out with their student card after completing the exam). In addition, only devices with an IP address within the IP-range of the specific lecture hall are allowed to open the exam and the settings of the exam in Moodle only allow access via the Safe Exam Browser: students are only permitted to attempt the exam once, and the exam is available in the Moodle course only at the scheduled time and, once started, only for a certain period.

Preventing students from accessing materials which are not allowed during the exam is more complex. In contrast to other electronic exam environments (e.g. [11]), we avoid the use of special equipment and encourage students to use their own device.

However, accessing the Moodle server directly via a web browser running on the student's OS is an inefficient approach. In this case, blocking connections to Wikipedia or other online resources may be simple, but cheating by using materials stored on the local hard drive is rather easy. Since we do not want to force students to install additional software (such as lockdown modules) on their personal laptops, we have to use our own operating system (OS) in order to restrict the access to the local resources and programmes that are prohibited during the exam. We decided to boot this OS via the Preboot eXecution Environment (PXE) protocol over a local area network (LAN), since the handling of USB sticks or DVDs is very error-prone, time-consuming and inflexible, especially when additional software is needed, and the usage of WLANs is too insecure and interference-prone. Clearly, this requires that the client is able to boot via the network.

In order to support a very broad range of (private) laptops and prevent students from accessing local resources and programmes, our solution is designed as a minimal Linux system. At the moment, this OS is realized using Fedora and Knoppix, which enables us to boot Legacy or UEFI devices (both Apple and PC). In order to restrict the access to external resources, we implemented corresponding firewall rules. Since Moodle as an LMS not only provides exam features but also chatting capabilities and course related material, a solution was needed to prevent the access to such resources and activities during exams. Running an ordinary web browser in centOS – even when restricted with firewall rules – would not have completely solved the cheating problem. Fortunately, the Safe Exam Browser (SEB – [12]) is fully supported by Moodle-core. The SEB is much more secure than an ordinary browser, since it prevents students from opening other programmes or additional web browser windows during the exam and ignores certain key combinations or clicks. So by restricting the access to the exam page only, cheating by exploiting Moodle's features is not possible anymore. However, the SEB is only available for Windows XP, Windows 7 and MAC OS X. Therefore, we are forced to boot a minimized Windows 7 as a virtual machine on the minimized Linux system via VirtualBox [13] (see Fig. 1). Additionally, proprietary software which only runs on Windows systems is still widespread in the educational sector. On the one hand, the reliance on Windows 7 is a drawback in terms of performance, on the other hand, it adds flexibility regarding the management of the virtual machine image.

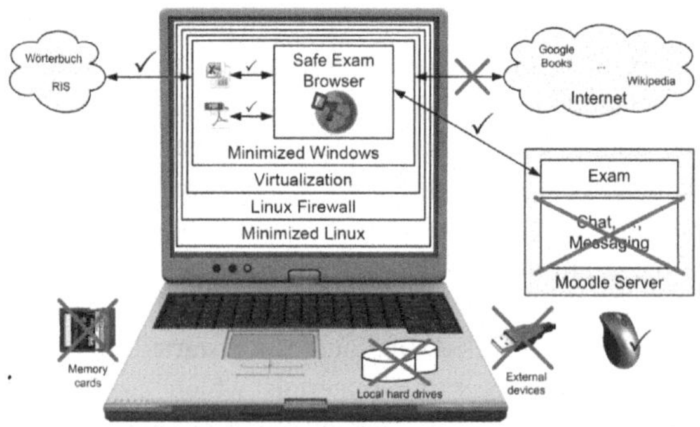

Fig. 1. The operating principle of the Secure Exam Environment (SEE)

Furthermore, hardware driver management is done completely in Linux, which is known for its broad hardware support especially for older hardware without the need to install specific drivers. The selection of the allowed programmes (beside the SEB) during the exam is set via a configuration file, which is retrieved from an Intranet Service. In the GUI of this service, administrators are able to configure the exam (e.g. only Calculator or Calculator and Excel or GeoGebra or Eclipse and PDFs allowed).

Starting an online exam using the SEE includes booting a minimized Linux from the LAN, then the minimized Linux automatically starts the Windows 7 virtual machine (VM), Window 7 automatically starts the SEB, the SEB automatically connects to the homepage of the AAU's learning management system Moodle, and finally users have to log in to Moodle and select the exam.

2.2 How Do We Ensure the SEE is Reliable?

Reliability for examiner and examinee is a critical issue and depends on the availability of (information) technology - e.g. computers and computer networking technologies - during the exam [4]. At the time of writing, the SEE depends on the online connection between the SEB and the Moodle Server. In case of network failure, none of the users can save current results or proceed to the next question. Thus, the temporary storage of the answers (during network failures) remains a problem. Fortunately, Moodle saves the last answer received and the progress of each examinee. Therefore, the examinee is allowed to continue the exam from the point where the error occurred after potential network problems are solved. In the worst case scenario, the last answer of the examinee is lost. Hardware failures of laptops are not a problem because all answers provided up to the failure would have been stored on the server and the student can simply continue his or her exam on one of our loan devices.

In the context of testing, archiving exams is another important aspect. According to Austrian legislation [14], documents related to written exams have to be archived for at least six months, whereas protocols of oral exams have to be archived for at least one year. Moodle, however, offers a practical solution as it automatically archives exams, which dramatically reduces the physical storage requirements and, as a positive environmental side-effect, the amount of paper needed (especially in the case of no-shows).

2.3 How Do We Maximize the Availability of the SEE?

The availability of the SEE can be affected by hardware failure, network drop outs or service outages.

In order to provide maximum availability of the network connection, we only support wired LAN connections at this point in time. Despite recent developments, WLAN remains too error prone and, additionally, a malicious user could perform a denial-of-service (DoS) attack on the WLAN access points quite easily and hence prevent all users from taking the exam. To achieve the DoS attack, a battery-powered pocket-sized WiFi jammer could be mounted close to or in the room where the eExams take place.

To ensure the maximum stability of the network system, the network department of our university provides high redundancy within the network-core, distribution-switches, firewalls and the border-router as well as load sharing with the Border Gateway Protocol (BGP) in a multihomed environment and redundant cables. The load is separated among different virtual networks. The equipment in use in the core and distribution layer are high-end-components. Furthermore, an uninterruptible power supply is guaranteed during eExams through a diesel generator.

In order to reach the high availability targets of our SEE, we started to monitor all hardware components and services involved in the eExam process. Drop outs of components or services or deviations from thresholds within defined time intervals result in alerts, allowing support staff to react to and resolve issues immediately, leading to crucial time-savings within the identification process of failures, a very high level of availability and continuous system optimization. Monitored components and services include availability of the SEE-servers (implemented with centOS) including CPU, storage as well as DHCP, NFS, TFTP and HTTP services; availability of the administration backend of the SEE including the corresponding HTTP service; availability of Moodle including HTTP-access, as well as end-to-end-tests in the lecture halls with minimal computers (Raspberry Pi); availability of the network (connection between SEE-server, clients and Moodle), and end-to-end performance tests within the network with probes (Raspberry Pi).

2.4 How Do We Protect the Privacy of Examinees?

The answers provided by the students as well as the grades they receive are private and must be protected as stipulated by the Austrian Data Protection Act [15]. Subsequently, we use encrypted and authenticated transmission lines between the SEB and the Moodle server (HTTPS) and the Moodle server uses login/password authentication for students and lecturers to ensure that access is only provided to authorized persons.

2.5 How Do We Support Flexibility for Examinees?

One service for students, which followed from the development of the SEE, are so called slotted eExams. For the execution of eExams with the SEE, we developed an online-process to register for an eExam some time before the test takes place as well as an online-registration process right before the exam in the lecture hall. Thus, exams, registration data as well as access rights are available online. These processes enabled us to offer several time-slots for an eExam within a week, from which students can freely choose when they want or are able to take an exam. Especially for students who are employed next to their studies, who need to foster children or relatives or whose mobility is restricted, this service is very helpful.

The decision as to whether an eExam is conducted in a traditional way on a fixed examination date or as an slotted eExam is made by the lecturer: slotted eExams can only work if a suitably large question pool is available, such that on different days randomly generated questions and/or exams are sufficiently dissimilar from each other.

3 Technical Obstacles and Challenges

One of the current restrictions of online exams is the required network connection. WLAN is still prone to failure, especially for larger groups of students. This results into another challenging aspect, namely that lecture halls require LAN and power sockets at least every second seat. Unfortunately, not all lecture halls fulfill these requirements and retrofitting is extremely expensive. The obstacle with the LAN sockets could be overcome with access points. However, using a device only with battery during exams is too risky.

A persistent challenge are new generations of students' laptops, requiring continuous adaptation of the SEE. For example, UEFI as a new interface between hardware and OS was rather complex. Moreover, some manufacturers started to disable the possibility of PXE-, resp. Net-Boots on their devices, forcing us to find workarounds. Furthermore, since a lot of new laptops come without Ethernet-sockets, we needed to integrate booting via adapters into the SEE.

4 Organizational Obstacles and Challenges

When it comes to eExams, organization is crucial: on the one hand, it is important for users to easily get through the process with the guarantee that everything will run smoothly, and, on the other hand, technological gaps need to be filled. Moreover, only a limited number of lecture halls is suitable for online exams for reasons mentioned above. Thus, lecturers have to book them early. Furthermore, it cannot be assumed that all students have a portable device. Loan devices must be ready for those students and in the case of technical problems or breakdowns of the students' own devices during the exam. The AAU currently has approximately 100 laptops serving as loan devices for students.

4.1 Organizational Challenges Before an Exam

Students can come to information days, where we change the boot-order of their devices to allow PXE-, resp. NetBoot. Thus, students get a briefing on how an eExam works before the actual exam preventing unnecessary stress.

Lecturers need support when executing online exams as well. In the preparation phase lecturers (in our case) can rely on the support of specially trained eTutors, who help with setting up a test or in choosing pedagogically suitable examination designs.

4.2 Organizational Challenges in the Lecture Hall

Right before the eExam, the registration equipment including computers and card readers, loan devices and LAN-cables as well as adapters have to be physically taken in the specific lecture hall. At the registration desk, students get a LAN-cable as well as a adapter and a loan device if needed and register for the eExam by scanning their student card with a card reader. Other possibilities for the technical identification of students like iris recognition, retina scanning or fingerprint identification would be available, but they would infringe privacy. Therefore, at the moment users are identified by comparing their face with the photo on their student card.

Technical support is provided for students before and throughout the examination. In case of a hardware failure, students get a preinstalled loan device and can continue the eExam immediately. Right after the exam it is a great challenge for the organizational staff to get back sound LAN-cables and loan devices. Students sometimes tend to remove the cables with not enough care, ending up damaging them.

4.3 Support After an eExam

Lecturers get support from the eLearning department after an online exam with the evaluating process or with a statistical analysis of questions.

5 Experiences with eExams at the AAU and Further Developments

In June 2011 we began offering online exams with the SEE. Table 1 shows the growth of eExams conducted with the SEE at the AAU over the last six years.

Table 1. The progression of eExams with the Secure Exam Environment (SEE), * in process

2011	2012	2013	2014	2015	2016	2017*	Total
288	2,717	7,475	7,082	8,954	10,391	9,435	46,342

5.1 (Dis-)Advantages for Students

In 2012 we surveyed students about the benefits of eExams as well as any obstacles, and technical problems encountered. We received 308 usable questionnaires from a total of 1,075 students. Results showed a positive attitude towards online exams across all four faculties of the AAU.

The majority of the students who took the survey claimed that the key benefits of online assessment include: rapid exam results, improved readability of free-text answers, improved structure and ability to revise answers, and noticeable time savings. Students also found eExams particularly interesting, convenient and in general better than paper-and-pencil exams. Some students did not see any difference compared with conventional testing methods. Students also appreciated the novelty associated with online testing, including its environmentally friendly nature (less paper and printing costs) and the fact that their hands got less tired than during a handwritten exam.

Still, students encountered quite few obstacles. Problems include the additional time that some students require for example to boot their device or to connect cables and difficulties with the structure of the exam or the types of questions. Some students also had troubles with typing and others were not familiar with the loan devices they were provided with. It is clear, however, that students reported more benefits than obstacles.

In addition to the survey, we noticed that students at our university usually do not make use of their right to personally contact the lecturer to ask for more valuable feedback on the exam results [2, 5]. This hurdle can be overcome with automated or individual feedback in eExams. The Moodle login-data shows that all students seize the chance to view feedback without the need for personal consultation instead. Moreover, eExams at the AAU are also used for self-testing to give students the opportunity to receive feedback on their performance (see also [5]).

5.2 (Dis-)Advantages for Lecturers

Lecturers commonly mention the automated evaluation of standardized questions and the convenience of avoiding hand-written exams as clear advantages of the SEE. Furthermore, questions can easily be created, stored, extended, organized, and reused for future exams, fostering sustainability and decreasing work load. Thus, the time savings can be devoted to new topics or in-depth discussion [5]. Since lecturers at the AAU can freely choose which type of exam to offer to their students, solely those lecturers who see more advantages than disadvantages in eExams use them.

5.3 Further Developments

Currently, we are only able to execute one eExam with specific settings, e.g. additional software, at the same time. Therefore, we are developing a boot environment which enables us to run eExams with various additional software simultaneously by recognizing the identity of the student and transmitting the proper exam environment, even in different lecture halls at the same time. Furthermore, the support of newer devices without LAN ports is in development. However, for the future it is planned to provide a WLAN access point. Finally, like every software solution, the SEE needs constant security and compatibility updates.

6 Conclusion

eExams extend the possibilities for assessment in terms of quality and efficiency. Better alignment in teaching, the opportunity to use additional software, reduced possibilities for cheating, and reduced effort for correcting exams are some of the many advantages. Nevertheless, they are only one of a variety of methods for assessing performance and giving students feedback on their learning progress.

However, bring your own device (BYOD) solutions are crucial for larger exams. Next to a broader use of existing methods for testing (online), such as pre-tests, self-assessment, peer-assessment or problem sets, to name a few, further research is needed to extend the flexibility of online assessment, for example, by finding solutions to utilize WLAN for secure eExams, and to optimize promising techniques such as adaptive testing.

References

1. Müller, F.H., Bayer, C.: Prüfungen: Vorbereitung - Durchführung - Bewertung. In: Hawelka, B., Hammerl, M., Gruber, H. (eds.) Förderung von Kompetenzen in der Hochschullehre, pp. 223–237. Asanger, Kröning (2007)
2. Marriott, P.: Students' evaluation of the use of online summative assessment on an undergraduate financial accounting module. Br. J. Educ. Technol. **40**(2), 237–254 (2009)
3. Gibson, D.C., Webb, M.E.: Data science in educational assessment. Educ. Inf. Technol. **20**(4), 697–713 (2015)
4. Hewson, C.: Can online course-based assessment methods be fair and equitable? Relationships between students' preferences and performance within online and offline assessments. J. Comput. Assist. Learn. **28**, 488–498 (2012)
5. Anakwe, B.: Comparison of student performance in paper-based versus computer-based testing. J. Educ. Bus. **84**(October), 13–18 (2008)
6. Fluck, A.: eExaminations Strategic Project Final Report for Academic Senate, University of Tasmania. Meeting 1/2011 (2011). Cited in Fluck, A., Hillier, M.: Innovative assessment with eExams. Paper Presented at the Australian Council for Computers in Education (ACCE) Conference, 29 September–2 October, Brisbane, Queensland (2016)
7. Biggs, J., Tang, C.: Teaching for Quality Learning at University. McGraw Hill, Berkshire (2011)
8. Müller, A., Schmidt, B.: Prüfungen als Lernchance: Sinn, Ziele und Formen von Hochschulprüfungen. Zeitschrift für Hochschulentwicklung, **4**(1), 23–45 (2009)
9. Sharpe, R., Oliver, M.: Designing courses for e-learning. In: Beetham, H., Sharpe, R. (eds.) Rethinking Pedagogy for a Digital Age. Designing and Delivering e-Learning. Routledge, London and New York (2007)
10. Frankl, G., Schartner, P., Zebeding, G.: The "Secure Exam Environment" for online testing at the Alpen-Adria-Universität Klagenfurt/Austria. In: World Conference on E-Learning in Corporate, Government, Healthcare, and Higher Education. Association for the Advancement of Computing in Education (AACE), Hawaii (2011)
11. SoftwareSecure. http://www.softwaresecure.com/. Accessed 16 Aug 2017
12. Safe Exam Browser (SEB). http://www.safeexambrowser.org/news_en.html. Accessed 16 Aug 2017
13. Virtual Box. http://ww.virtualbox.org. Accessed 16 Aug 2017
14. Bundeskanzleramt Österreich. http://www.ris.bka.gv.at/GeltendeFassung.wxe?Abfrage=Bundesnormen&Gesetzesnummer=20002128. Accessed 16 Aug 2017
15. Bundeskanzleramt Österreich. http://www.ris.bka.gv.at/GeltendeFassung.wxe?Abfrage=Bundesnormen&Gesetzesnummer=10001597. Accessed 16 Aug 2017

The Acceptance of Motion Detection Devices by the Elderly

Marcelo Brites-Pereira[1](✉), Maria João Almeida[2], and António J. Osório[1]

[1] University of Minho, Gualtar Campus, Braga, Portugal
marcelobritespereira@gmail.com
[2] University of Coimbra, Estádio Universitário, Stª Clara, Coimbra, Portugal

Abstract. Considering the importance of ageing well, the aim of this study is to understand how the elderly learn to use digital technologies of movement detection. With the study of motion detection devices, we intend to contribute to the development of knowledge regarding care and the occupational therapy needs of the elderly in the context of their quality of life.

Keywords: Elderly · Kinect · Nintendo Wii · Leap motion

1 Introduction

According to data revealed by the WHO, from 2001 to 2013 the number of elderly people per 100 young people grew from 102 to 136 [1].

The European Union has made considerable policy and financial efforts on research and action focused on active aging, launching initiatives and programs that have contributed to the development of social and health infrastructures and services, which help to respond nationally and regionally to some of the challenges of aging in today's society.

An example of these efforts is the Manifesto for European Friendship of the Elderly until 2020, launched in 2012 as part of the European Year for Active Aging and Solidarity between Generations. The manifesto has 10 proposals, of which Information and Communication Technology (ICT) learning and digital inclusion items should be highlighted. Faced with these facts, it is imperative that different modes of contact between the elderly and ICT are found, ways that promote physical activity and at the same time, allow real digital inclusion and social sharing. In fact, the practice of physical exercise decreases the risk of developing cardio-respiratory diseases, chronic-degenerative diseases, diabetes and dementia and increases better blood circulation, levels of social interaction, physical performance, happiness and prevents early death [2–5].

Therefore, affordable motion detection devices such as Kinect, Leap Motion or Nintendo Wii, can mediate physical activity appropriate for the needs of the elderly. Based on this notion, we considered it relevant to research and study, in detail, the characteristics of the process of using these technologies in activities that can be offered to the elderly population.

A. Tatnall and M. Webb (Eds.): WCCE 2017, IFIP AICT 515, pp. 189–195, 2017.
https://doi.org/10.1007/978-3-319-74310-3_21

2 Old, Elderly, or Senior?

There is a range of terminologies to characterize citizens over 65 years of age. For some experts, seniors, or senior citizens is the right terminology, whilst others prefer the term "seniors". The truth is that, according to de Oliveira the way we address the aged is irrelevant, since understanding and helping them is most important [6]. The author also states that "it is not worth using euphemisms to refer to the elderly." For him, the terminology 'old' may not be deprecatory, and can be considered affectionate when, for example the term, 'my old man' is used. However, the author acknowledges that the term 'old' has a derogatory sense in society and therefore assumes that, in a generic way, the socially accepted term is 'elderly' [6].

Therefore, elderly, according to the World Health Organization (WHO), is anyone that has reached the age of 65. However, the same organization reports that, in developing or underdeveloped countries, the term "elderly" could be referred to an individual aged 60 or less, since the average longevity in these countries is lower when compared with developed countries.

3 Physical Activity Using Motion Detection Devices

There are animal and human studies that suggest that physical activity, or its absence, has a strong influence on brain functions such as memory, cognition, learning, and the pathological counterpart of memory, such as cognitive decline in aging. These studies have increased the number of biological recognition mechanisms that attest the benefits of physical activity to brain health [5].

We know that about 30 years ago, the first studies regarding the interest of learning ICT by the elderly showed a negative reaction on the part of the participants. More recently, however, Dyck and Smither found a more positive reaction in the elderly over 55 [7].

Nowadays, it is known that the cause of the majority of the elderly that react negatively to the use of ICT is related to myths, like Wandke et al. who state that age does not constitute a barrier in learning [8].

Although memory does tend to lose its plasticity, the elderly tend to have a better memory of past events than working memory – also known as short-term memory - which may have an effect in learning about the use of new technologies. Therefore, based on this, it cannot be said that the elderly cannot learn, since many studies have shown that they can by stimulating short-term and long-term memory [9–11].

Using exergames with the elderly does not only imply brain functions, but also implies motivation and user acceptability. There are a number of theories that have been used to gauge technology acceptability. As an example, we have the self-efficacy theory, which demonstrates the power of believing that one can, the unified theory of acceptance and use of technology or the technology acceptance models, that are widely used among researchers to measure, anticipate and explain the user's actions [12–15].

Brox and Hernandez also exposed some strategies to persuade and motivate the elderly for change using exergames as a strategy for active healthy aging [16]. To motivate users, they also recommend "making an attractive and friendly user interface".

It is also important not to disturb the users while they are playing the games, but providing them with information in appropriate and opportune moments. Finally, the authors suggest using "social influence" to bring about behavior changes. Based on this, we would like to add the importance of playing exergames in a community setting, since studies suggest that people exercise more efficiently when this is done in the company of others [17].

Brox and Hernandez also state that "exergames have the potential to motivate the elderly to become more physically active, since it is perceived as fun to play" and believing in that, has led us to want to know more about the use of these devices among elderly. We also want to develop this research using 3 different devices to know more about the acceptability of these devices among the elderly and not discoloring social factors [16].

Given the advances in technology, Microsoft Kinect Xbox 360 has been developing new technology in which players can control the game without the need of hand controls, using only their own body, which is detected through their body temperature. This technology has been tested in institutionalized elderly people with some form of disability, since they may not be able to maintain and hold controllers due to the lack of muscular strength.

Leap Motion and Nintendo Wii with Wii Remote require mobility of the upper limbs, which does not exclude people with disabilities from physical activity. A study made by Chen et al. concluded that games have great potentials as a health promotion tool for the elderly with disabilities, since they stimulate social functions which are especially important for the elderly, because they can strengthen their general moods and decrease levels of depression and stress [18].

Playing also increases visual and fine motor abilities, as well as attention skills. Tests have showed that games have a positive influence in short-term memory and selective attention and motivation for the elderly [19–21]. However, there is a lack of studies focused on the acceptability and suitability of these technologies for the elderly.

4 Economic and Demography

Sedentarism, along with ageing, promotes the appearance of cardiorespiratory diseases, diabetes, neurodegenerative diseases and bone and muscle weakness, therefore quickening the aging process.

The adoption of the practice of physical activity by the elderly, often inactive and sedentary, improves their quality of life minimizing health costs and benefiting from greater longevity [22, 23].

Previous investigations have shown how technologies, like a computer, can help the elderly in socio-economic inclusion [24].

Our focus is not on the financial or economic problem, however it is important that countries are able to save money related to the care of the elderly as it is common that countries spend a great deal on care and treatment. Therefore, we focus on the prevention of aged related illnesses through education and physical exercise. Education is an act involving the integration and transformation of the individual, so through education, countries can save money and provide therapy against socio-economic "exclusion and obsolescence". For this reason, we will attempt to develop a research about how the elderly can use and learn how to use motion detection technologies [25] as our society today is getting older, faster, and as a result, there is a strong need to find a solution to keeping the elderly active and healthy.

One possible solution involves exercising with the aid of video games (exergames) which encourage the elderly "to remain active even when living in full-care environments. In this context, it is important to provide technology which is easy to set up in order to relieve nursing staff and reduce access barriers" [26]. By keeping the elderly active, it is also possible to provide an investment in prevention, social comfort and integration.

5 Problem and Objectives

According to Lees and Frank [4], a sedentary lifestyle is a problem that leads to premature death. Therefore, this project intends to investigate the use of motion detecting devices (Kinect, Leap Motion, Wii Remote) in the process of promoting physical activity for institutionalized elderly citizens (or in the context of active aging). In order to understand how to properly use such technologies, it is important to address this problem, as aging is a natural process that must be taken seriously. The dignity and quality of life of the elderly should be enhanced and enhanced with all the existing resources.

According to Cassola, et al. and Parra, there are still some limitations in digital motion detection technologies, which means that there is considerable room for improvement and research in this area [27, 28].

Thus, as a result of social and personal experience in different institutions, we found that sedentarism is, in some cases, an institutional problem, since the elderly, when institutionalized, become less active and in the short/medium term, more dependent on third parties for care and assistance not only in movement, but also in simple tasks such as feeding themselves. This sedentary lifestyle can, and should be changed. Greater autonomy for the elderly means a better quality of life, greater self-esteem and fewer depression related symptoms. Also, human and financial resources could be decreased as the number of bedridden individuals requiring more specialized care and attention would be reduced.

Therefore, there is a need to encourage the elderly population to participate in mediated physical exercise, taking into account their physical limitations, age and interaction. In order to better understand how to use the technologies of motion detection devices for the elderly to enjoy and benefit from active aging, bringing benefits in the treatment and prevention of possible degenerative diseases, we intend to:

- Research the acceptance of digital spaces by the elderly in day-care centers;
- Experiment with 3 motion-detecting devices in active aging activities;
- Analyze, through the observation and capture of video images, the mobility of the elderly in the interaction with the various devices for detecting movements;
- Analyze, through recorded interviews, the interest of the elderly population in ICT education.

6 Methodology

This investigation will start with a theoretical review of the literature, in order to understand and describe the state of the art in relation to elderly sedentarism. In second phase, there will be a practical intervention carried out through collaborative activities with institutions for the elderly for the implementation of the study.

To enable this interactivity, motion detection devices - Kinect, Wii Remote, Leap Motion – and exergames to enable physical activities in a creative and multidimensional way will be used.

Before beginning the practical session with the motion detecting devices, we will apply an OARS (Older Americans Resources and Services) questionnaire, which will permit the measurement of the degree of incapacity of every elderly person. The questionnaire allows the generation of functional assessment scales, divided by 5 large groups, using the Likert Scale score system. The final sum of the selected scores generates the accumulated functional disability score of each elderly person.

Each practical session will last 60 min in which every elderly individual will have 10 min for initial warm-up and, after that, 45–50 min of exercise during 12 weeks, three times per week, on alternate days, for 36 sessions.

The creation of videos in loco will constitute an innovation in the research method bringing benefits, and providing an important contribution to a visual anthropological investigation.

In addition, during the practice sessions, data will be recorded by direct observation and videotaped during the process of contacting the various digital motion detection devices.

For data analysis, we will use software Nvivo®, and the audio interviews will be transcribed. The notes taken during the direct observation will be crossed and the answers provided by the applied questionnaires will be statistically analyzed.

To preserve identity and privacy of those involved, the data will only be collected after the consent and authorization of the institution that will host the investigation and by the elderly directly involved in the research is provided.

At present, we are currently waiting for a favorable opinion from the Portuguese Commission for Ethics for Clinical Research (CEIC) and Portuguese National Commission for Data Protection (CNPD).

7 Expected Outcomes

From this analysis, we hope to learn how digital motion detection technologies and games can be readily accepted by the majority of the elderly in order to contribute positively to their active aging.

Acknowledgments. This research is being developed within the Ph.D. Program: Technology Enhanced Learning and Societal Challenges, funded by Fundação para a Ciência e Tecnologia, FCT I.P., Portugal, under contract PD/BD/128348/2017.

References

1. Ine, I.N.D.E.: População residente. In: Portugal com tendência para diminuição e envelhecimento (2014)
2. Bherer, L., Erickson, K.I., Liu-Ambrose, T.: A review of the effects of physical activity and exercise on cognitive and brain functions in older adults. J. Aging Res. **2013**, 8 (2013)
3. Hsiao, K., Rashvand, H.F.: Data modeling mobile augmented reality: integrated mind and body rehabilitation. Multimed. Tools Appl. **74**, 1–18 (2013)
4. Lees, S.J., Frank, W.: Sedentary death syndrome introduction: inactivity is an actual cause of death. AIDS **29**, 447–460 (2004)
5. Lista, I., Sorrentino, G.: Biological mechanisms of physical activity in preventing cognitive decline. Cell. Mol. Neurobiol. **30**, 493–503 (2010)
6. de Oliveira, J.H.B.: Psicologia do Envelhecimento e do Idoso (2005)
7. Dyck, J.L., Smither, J.A.-A.: Age differences in computer anxiety: the role of computer experience, gender and education. J. Educ. Comput. Res. **10**, 238–248 (1994)
8. Wandke, H., Sengpiel, M., Sönksen, M.: Myths about older people's use of information and communication technology. Gerontology **58**, 564–570 (2012)
9. (Mike) Moore, D.M., John, K., Burton, R.J.M.: Multiple-channel communication: the theoretical and research foundations of multimedia, pp. 979–1005 (1996)
10. Willis, S.: Methodological issues in behavioral intervention research with elderly. In: Bengtson., V., Schaie, K.W. (eds.) Handbook of Psychology of Aging, Academic Press, New York (2001)
11. Schmiedek, F., Lövdén, M., Lindenberger, U.: Hundred days of cognitive training enhance broad cognitive abilities in adulthood: findings from the cogito study. Front. Aging Neurosci. **2** (2010)
12. Nawaz, A., Skjæret, N., Helbostad, J.L., Vereijken, B., Boulton, E., Svanaes, D., Skjaeret, N., Helbostad, J.L., Vereijken, B., Boulton, E., Svanaes, D.: Usability and acceptability of balance exergames in older adults: a scoping review. Health Inf. J. **22**, 911–931 (2015)
13. Venkatesh, V., Morris, M.G., Gordon, B., Davis, F.D.: User acceptance of information technology: toward a unified view. MIS Q. **27**, 425–478 (2003)
14. Davis, F.D.: Perceived usefulness, perceived ease of use and user acceptance. MIS Q. **13**, 319–339 (1989)
15. Maddux, J.E.: Self-efficacy theory. In: Maddux, J.E. (ed.) Self-Efficacy, Adaptation, and Adjustment: Theory, Research, and Application, pp. 3–33. Springer, Boston (1995). https://doi.org/10.1007/978-1-4419-6868-5_1
16. Brox, E., Hernandez, J.E.G.: Exergames for elderly: social exergames to persuade seniors to increase physical activity. In: 2011 5th International Conference on Pervasive Computing Technologies for Healthcare (PervasiveHealth) and Workshops, pp. 546–549 (2011)
17. Mueller, F.F., O'Brien, S., Thorogood, A.: Jogging over a distance: supporting a «jogging together» experience although being apart. In: Chi Ea. pp. 1989–1994 (2007)
18. Chen, S.T., Huang, Y.G.L., Chiang, I.T.: Using somatosensory video games to promote quality of life for the elderly with disabilities. In: 2012 Proceedings 4th IEEE International Conference Digital Game Intelligent Toy Enhanced Learning Digitel, 2012, pp. 258–262 (2012)
19. Green, C.S., Bavelier, D.: Action video game modifies visual selective attention. **423**, 534–537 (2003)
20. Gamberini, L., Barresi, G., Majer, A., Scarpetta, F.: A game a day keeps the doctor away: a short review of computer games in mental healthcare. J. CyberTherapy Rehabil. **1**(2), 127–145 (2008). © Virtual Reality Medical Institute

21. Ijsselsteijn, W., Nap, H.H., de Kort, Y., Poels, K.: Digital game design for elderly users. In: Proceedings of the 2007 Conference on Future Play - Future Play 2007, p. 17. ACM Press, New York (2007)
22. Mazo, G.Z., Mota, J., Gonçalves, L.H.T., Matos, M.G., Carvalho, J.: Actividade física e qualidade de vida de mulheres idosas da cidade de Florianópolis, Brasil. Rev. Port. Ciências do Desporto. **8**, 414–423 (2008)
23. Mazo, G.Z., Mota, J.A.P. da S., Gonçalves, L.H.T.: Atividade física e qualidade de vida de mulheres idosas. RBCEH – Revista Brasileira de Ciências Do Envelhecimento Humano, Passo Fundo, 115–118 (2005)
24. Stewart, J., Bleumers, L., Looy, J., Van Mariën, I., All, A.: The potential of digital games for empowerment and social inclusion of groups at risk of social and economic exclusion: evidence and opportunity for policy European commission. Luxemburg (2013)
25. Zarifis, G.K., Gravani, M.: Challenging the 'European Area of Lifelong Learning': A Critical Response After a Decade of Ongoing Adjustments. Springer, Heidelberg (2012). https://doi.org/10.1007/978-94-007-7299-1
26. Gerling, K.M., Schulte, F.P., Masuch, M.: Designing and evaluating digital games for frail elderly persons. In: Proceedings of the 8th International Conference on Advances in Computer Entertainment Technology - ACE 2011, p. 1. ACM Press, New York (2011)
27. Cassola, F., Morgado, L., de Carvalho, F., Paredes, H., Fonseca, B.: Online-Gym: a 3D virtual gymnasium using kinect interaction. Procedia Technol. **13**, 130–138 (2014)
28. Parra, C.: Information Technology for active ageing: a review of theory and practice. Found. Trends® Human–Comput. Interact. **7**, 351–444 (2014)

Innovative Practices with Learning Technologies

The King Island Digital Stories (KIDS) Project: Telling Stories for Tomorrow's Learning

Jennifer Masters(✉)

Faculty of Education, University of Tasmania, Launceston, Australia
jennifer.masters@utas.edu.au

Abstract. The King Island Digital Stories (KIDS) project was an initiative to extend children's literacies through developing digital stories. The project was conducted over a ten-week term with 21 children in a Year 4/5 class. An ethnographic approach was used where the research team worked collaboratively in the classroom to scaffold individual children to represent their story ideas. The children were told that their stories needed to be about King Island and in their voice (first person) but otherwise, the stories could be about any aspect. The project was slow to start but a weekly sharing session helped the children to conceptualise and develop their stories. As the resources began to emerge, it was evident that the children were engaging effectively with the process of digital storytelling and developing their literacies, especially digital literacies. The resulting digital stories were diverse but collectively they communicated a tapestry of life on the island through the children's eyes.

Keywords: Digital storytelling · Literacies · Digital literacies
Sense of place

1 Introduction

The King Island Digital Stories (KIDS) project focused on King Island, an isolated island in the middle of Bass Strait, and the children who live there. The children at the local school benefit from living in a unique and pristine setting but are disadvantaged by their isolation and lack of connection with the wider world. The purpose of this project was to harness digital technologies in order to enable these children to represent their ideas and perspectives about their own place to share with a wider audience. Through this process the children learnt how to use technologies for communication and developed their literacies by preparing content for an audience as they articulated their understandings through the medium of digital storytelling.

2 Background

A 'digital story' is a short media production that is created with digital tools to present stories about life, place or personal perspectives. This genre of communication is linked to traditions of oral storytelling [1] and is readily accessible to ordinary people, in contrast with commercial or professional productions. Digital storytelling emerged in

A. Tatnall and M. Webb (Eds.): WCCE 2017, IFIP AICT 515, pp. 199–208, 2017.
https://doi.org/10.1007/978-3-319-74310-3_22

the 1990s [2] when suitable digital tools became available and affordable to the wider population and early adopters included educators, who were quick to connect with this medium as a way to engage children in learning. A significant benefit of using digital storytelling for teaching and learning is that it extends the concept of literacy. Sylvester and Greenidge [3] identified that digital storytelling promotes the development of 'emerging literacies' in addition to traditional literacies, that is, reading, writing, speaking and listening. Lankshear and Knobel [4] referred to these new literacies as 'digital literacies' and highlighted the plurality of the term. They proposed that the term encompassed a wide range of skills, techniques and approaches for using digital communication, including the capacity to adapt for new mediums as they emerge. Sylvester and Greenidge [3] suggested that digital storytelling could be used to extend children who found writing difficult. When presented with a less text-orientated form of communication, with audio and image, children were more motivated to create stories. Further, the process of 'polishing' their media production allowed these children to review and adjust until they were comfortable that their work was ready to share. Other researchers, for example, Blas et al. [5] highlighted that digital storytelling also allows for collective construction where children work together to produce a collaborative production. In this process children learn to construct narrative in a social way, through negotiation and reciprocal sense making.

Another powerful feature of digital storytelling is that it gives voice to people who don't often get to tell their stories. The stories might be about characters, journeys, locations or accomplishments but they are always told from a particular perspective and in the voice of the storyteller [2]. Emert [6] used digital storytelling to facilitate refugee children tell their stories and demonstrate their skills at storytelling in a tangible way. He asserted that "the opportunity to transform personal stories through visual media is particularly powerful for a population of learners whose life histories are marred by tragedy" (p. 401). Digital storytelling is also seen as an effective way to support Indigenous people to articulate their stories and promote their culture and a number of initiatives have been implemented with Australian Indigenous children. For example, the SWIRL program [7] was established in 1998 and is an ongoing project that connects pre-service teachers with remote communities to promote literacy and storytelling for young Indigenous children. Another project of this style is the Sharing Stories Digital Storytelling Program [8]. The Sharing Stories Foundation's charter is to protect and promote Aboriginal and Torres Strait Island cultures and languages and the Digital Storytelling Program provides workshops in Indigenous communities to facilitate young people to tell their stories. A common feature of this type of digital storytelling is the representation of place attachment, also known as "sense of place" [9]. This acknowledges that all stories are in a context and therefore they not only represent ideas and perspectives but are likely include a component of belonging and connection to the physical space.

The process of digital storytelling is highly personalised and therefore it is essential that the storyteller is empowered to build his or her own representation rather than being prescribed a formula for construction. This, however, doesn't mean that the teacher is redundant in the process. In fact, Ohler [10] suggested that the opposite is more likely, with the student needing careful guidance and advice throughout the process. In this circumstance, the teacher uses a process called *scaffolding* [11] to work with the storyteller to provide just-in-time support to use digital technologies to bring their story to fruition. In this study, the research team worked in this role to support children developing digital stories. This allowed the teachers in the classroom to watch how children could build their stories and how this in turn could support the development of digital literacies.

3 Method and Design

This research used an ethnographical approach in which the researcher was an active participant-observer [12]. This approach is often used when a project has a cultural focus and in this study it allowed the research team to participate in the project alongside teachers to provide support and expertise as the children work with digital technologies to create their stories.

The goals for the research project were to investigate how the children could:

- Work with digital technologies to create digital stories
- Develop their skills in digital literacies
- Enhance their communication skills through creating situated digital stories
- Create stories about sense of place and belonging

The research question for the study was:

How might digital stories about place be used to support children in a remote setting to develop literacies, digital literacies and communication?

The King Island Digital Stories (KIDS) project was funded through a Tasmanian Community Fund grant for $20,000 (AUD). This provided technological equipment such as tripods, cameras and software and enabled a project research officer to be employed to work with the children. The project was implemented in a Year 4/5 class at King Island District State High School. The class consisted of 21 children, 14 in Year 4 (age $\approx$ 10) and 7 in Year 5 (age $\approx$ 11). Two teachers taught the class as a team, with additional support staff at times. The project commenced at the end of Term 3 and the digital story production was implemented in the final term of the school year (Term 4). This provided approximately ten weeks for creating the digital stories.

While the term "digital storytelling" is often used in education as a blanket term for any sort of digital production, for example, retelling fairy tales or developing fantasy, this project aligned with a narrower, more traditional concept of digital storytelling described by Lambert from the StoryCenter [2]. In this context, a digital story tells a non-fiction narrative from a personal perspective. Further, while it is possible to use snips of video footage, a digital story is typically a collection of still images that is animated through transitions and includes a music soundtrack and an oral narration. The children in this study were told that their story needed to be real and in first person, with their 'voice'. It also needed a beginning, a middle and an end (so that it was a story) and it had to be about King Island. Their task was to develop a storyline and a script, collect images to illustrate their story, record their narration and decide on a music soundtrack and then put the digital story together using iMovie.

4 Findings

In the preparatory session at the end of Term 3, the children were asked to write a story about King Island using a 'story starter' card, depicting images such as local flora and fauna, history, pastimes or industries. They were told that their story should be realistic rather than fantasy and they should select an image that would remind them of something that happened to them, something they did or something that they were told about, as long as it was about King Island. The children were provided with a story sheet and were given 40 min to complete the task. These stories were used as a base writing assessment and revealed that the writing capacity of the children in the class varied considerably. While some children managed to fill two pages with a detailed story, others were struggling to write a sentence or two with considerable help from the teacher or a teacher aide.

The digital storytelling development commenced at the beginning of Term 4. The children were shown plenty of examples of digital storytelling. Some of these were sourced from online repositories, such as ABC Open (https://open.abc.net.au/) and the research team also made some example digital stories to model aspects such as focus on place, timing, voice and techniques, for example, transitions and green-screen methods. The children were given plenty of time to think about and talk about their digital story idea. A 'story circle' technique [2] was used to help children articulate their storyline. This process enabled individuals to flesh out their own story and it inspired others who were still struggling to develop their own story idea.

The students were each provided with a planning book to document their digital story. This book had room for brainstorming ideas, making lists of resources, writing a script, storyboarding the digital production and reflecting on the task. At the beginning of the term, the children worked on their digital story as part of their literacy sessions. These sessions were two mornings per week and the digital story was one of several tasks that the children could choose to work on. When they undertaking the digital story activity, the children could work independently or they could seek the help of the research team. Conversely, the two researchers would seek out individual children during this session to check on progress and encourage them to do more.

The researchers monitored each child's progress with a milestone checklist. After a few weeks in to the project, it was evident that while most children had spent time working on the digital story, not a lot of advancement had been made. The children had plenty of good ideas for stories and many had written a story plot but very few had started on the 'digital' component of the story. One sticking point seemed to be the sourcing of digital images. The children had iPads, a digital camera and a Go-Pro camera that they could borrow to capture images for the project. Further, most of them had access to a smart phone at home that they could use too. It seemed though that most of the images for the stories needed to be existing rather than created afresh and families didn't seem to have catalogued collections of images. The children had access to a USB stick to take home to collect images but these often came back with no images at all or only a few images, often of limited quality. Some of the children reported that they had a particular image that they wanted to use but it was on a device other than a computer and that they didn't know how to transfer it to a USB.

In order to overcome these impediments, it was decided to focus on a few of the more advanced stories to see if some completed digital stories might act as motivation for the other children. Two children, a boy and a girl, had managed to find a selection of photographs for their stories and so these two were used as pilot productions. The boy told a story was about rearing a baby kangaroo, while the girl told the story of her parent's wedding at Cape Wickham Lighthouse, the tallest lighthouse in Australia. These two stories were fast-tracked through production, with the boy volunteering to pioneer a green-screen narration. Although these first digital stories were only prototypes and rather hurried, they certainly had the desired effect. The two productions were shown to the class and the rest of the children were very impressed. There were many questions about the creation process and certainly a renewed interest in pushing ahead with the stories. Based on this outcome, it was decided that this strategy would be incorporated into the project. Rather than working through the stages systematically with all of the children in the class, two or three children were targeted for production at a time. This helped to 'spread the field' across the production steps, so some children might be still typing up their scripts, while others were preparing images, recording their narration, choosing music or compiling their digital stories in iMovie. The Monday literacy session became a regular sharing event where a few 'first cut' productions were shown to the rest of the class each week.

The advantages of this trickle strategy were multiple. Firstly, while the researchers still monitored the whole class for progress, they could dedicate blocks of time to work with a few children. This meant that a digital story could be constructed quite quickly and move from being a collection of media to a compiled video in a few hours. Not only did this provide fresh examples for children still working on their stories but it also meant that children who had completed the process could act as mentors for the other children. This was particularly beneficial for tentative children who were finding the process of recording 'talking head' footage with a green screen or even a simple voice recording quite intimidating. A further benefit was that there was less demand on the equipment at any given time. Further, children who completed their story earlier then had time to review and 'polish' their production before the end of term.

A disadvantage of this method, however, was that some children had to wait quite a few weeks before they got to work seriously on their production. This, conversely, could be seen as advantageous because it meant that children who were reluctant or procrastinating initially, had time to become interested in the project. Children who were at first not overly captivated in the process became more curious when they saw the success of their peers. The emerging examples were constant reminders of what could be achieved and then, if a child became desperate to complete their own story, they could usually be slotted in to the schedule quite quickly. While this delay may have potentially led to some children losing interest in their production, this was not the case in the study. The momentum built consistently over the term and by the week of the presentation all of the children had a story that they were keen to share.

It was interesting to note that this change in approach seemed to coincide with shift in the ownership of the stories [11]. In the initial stages, the digital story was one of several tasks that the children did during the literacy session. The children worked on the story because their teacher had listed it as a literacy task and/or the researchers suggested to a child that he or she should work on a component. As the project progressed, however, it was evident that all of the children in the class became more outcome focused and took on the responsibility of reaching milestones and completing stages. This, in turn, influenced how the project was implemented. Rather than just attending the literacy sessions, the researchers made themselves available to the children as much as possible, attending most days and working with individuals in a breakout room in tandem with other classroom activity. Instead of having to remind children to work on their story, it was more likely that a child would seek out the researchers, saying "I have this to do. Can you help me?"

Digital media production in the classroom is usually implemented with a documentation process where the children record their ideas and storyline with a storyboard [10]. This project followed this convention and, as identified previously, the children were provided with a bound storytelling book to document their progress. This book was useful in the initial stages when the children were recording ideas and writing a script but as soon as the production became visual, i.e., when the children started to select and collect images, the book seemed redundant. The images were collected and displayed on a computer or device, such as an ipad or ipod and the children browsed through them. When the child selected the images they wished to use, they were saved to the child's project folder. The most obvious next step was to drag the images into the timeline on iMovie and arrange them there. The idea of going back and storyboarding on paper didn't seem logical. Consequently, the children mostly didn't use the storyboarding chart provided in their project book.

Typically, digital media production in a classroom is completed as group work. There are several practical reasons for this. Firstly, it caps the number of productions that are completed. This means that the equipment is in less demand and the teacher has fewer projects to manage. It also gives children experience with collaborative creation where negotiation and cooperation are required. In this project, however, the digital stories were produced individually. To some extent, this was because project adopted the classic form of digital storytelling [2] where the storyteller provides a narrative from his or her own perspective. This direction in the project also related the focus on personal writing and literacy. Additionally, the funded project officer meant that children could receive personalised support. While this ratio would be a luxury in most classrooms, the project provided a rare opportunity to observe how an individual child can harness digital technology to express their own ideas with personalised scaffolding.

Whilst the children didn't create joint digital stories for the project they still engaged in plenty of social collaboration and this increased throughout the project. During the sharing sessions there was authentic and enthusiastic discussion about the productions. Often the discussion was about technical aspects but there was also conversation about story plots and creative features. One girl's story was about watching the fairy penguins return to the shore at dusk and her oral narration had impressive 'David Attenborough' tones. The other children picked this up immediately and copied the style in their chat about the production. This sense of play helped to highlight the very feature that made the story so effective.

There was also a strong social component to the digital production process. Although the researchers usually worked with individuals in a breakout area, it was not uncommon for other children to wander through, watch and contribute during this process. This was not discouraged and it soon became a valuable strategy for reflection and critical decision making. Further, as children completed their digital stories, they could in turn serve as valuable mentors for other who were still to undertake stages in production. So, even though the stories were not a group task, the children in the class experienced similar circumstances where negotiation and cooperation were needed. The difference in this case, however, was that each child was firmly the owner of their own story, and they would decide when advice or support from others would be applied.

The presentation of the digital stories to family and friends at the end of term was a natural focus for story production. Towards the end of term, activity became brisk as the finishing touches were put in place. The children created invitations that were posted to families and the teacher planned an afternoon tea that was prepared by the children before the presentation and then served after the event. The presentation was held in the school's auditorium and was extremely well attended. The sense of pride felt by the children, their families and the school was clearly apparent. A selection of the digital stories was also shown at the school's awards night later in the week. The children and their families were then asked for permission for the digital stories to be published on the project website. The website is available at www.kidsproject.net.au and is a lovely representation of the project journey and the children's understandings of sense of place.

5 Discussion

Being an active participant-observer in a study such as this provides a wonderful opportunity to reflect on teaching and learning using digital technologies. Some key reflections are presented here in light of the findings.

5.1 Task Progression

It is not easy to prescribe a lesson sequence for a project such as this. Instead, it is more realistic to have a good idea about the destination and then set off on the learning journey. In the beginning of the project a number of strategies were used to help the children conceptualise what they might tell a story about and this included outlining a basic scope, showing a wide range of examples and providing plenty of opportunities to talk about what they might create. It is actually difficult to do much more than this until the storyteller decides on the story and commits to the creation process. Then, once he or she has this ownership, it is relatively straight forward to support and encourage them. In this project, we needed to reach that 'tipping point' where some of the children are engaged with the task and forging ahead with their production. Once this happens, the other children see the process in action and are more likely to follow. Needless to say, this progression needs patience and takes time. While it is desirable to have a defined end point in sight, that is the presentation, it is essential that children are given extended time, weeks not days, in order to allow their stories to develop.

5.2 Sourcing Images

The realisation that children were having difficulties in bringing images from home came as quite a surprise. These children are growing up in the digital age and digital photographs are a common and frequent occurrence in their daily lives. It became evident though that while families take copious digital photographs of children, they are less likely to store and catalogue them. Many of the photos taken are for immediate consumption, either viewed directly on a smart phone, emailed to family and friends or posted on Facebook. Relatively few of these images are transferred to a computer to be stored for prosperity. Further, if families do have images on a computer or another storage device such as a USB then they are often difficult to find as they aren't catalogued or named systematically for searching. Additionally, when the children managed to find images that they wanted to use they often found it difficult to transfer them on to a USB. This could be because the format wasn't compatible (e.g. it could be on an iPod) or that they simply didn't know how to copy it to the drive. Further, quite a few of the images that were brought in were of dubious quality for digital story production. They were of low resolution, opportunistic rather than framed or in portrait rather than landscape orientation.

As the project progressed it became evident that quality images were going to mean the difference between good digital stories and a great digital stories. The children were encouraged to progressively accumulate a good collection of potential images to be stored in personalised folder. These included existing photos and also new photos taken for the project. The children were given tips on taking photos, such as using landscape orientation and considering the position of the sun. Some of the existing photos were cropped to change the orientation and framing. The researchers also developed an image bank of local pictures that could be used to supplement the children's image collections. This ensured that when the child selected images for their story they could afford to be discerning as they had plenty to choose from.

5.3 Documentation

As identified in the Findings section, the paper-based planning books provided for each child became peripheral during this study. This was interesting because most advice provided for teachers identifies that the storyboarding process is a critical component of digital storytelling [10]. It would have been possible to insist that the children used the book, even if the storyboard was contrived after the event, but it was decided that this was unnecessary, especially as most of the children seemed to retain a good grasp of their storyline from the display in the iMovie. This observation may indicate that learners in the digital age are truly moving away from paper and pencil planning. It may, however, have only worked in this case because of the individualised nature of this task. It was possible to do this with a single child but if the task had been a group effort where content negotiation was needed then a documented storyboard may have been a necessary step.

5.4 Managing Digital Storytelling in the Classroom

This project offered the luxury of having two experienced media developers to provide scaffolding for the children as they created digital stories. It isn't surprising, therefore, that the outcome of the project was a collection of imaginative and effective digital stories. One of the project classroom teachers was asked by other teachers if she could have implemented the storytelling activity without the project backing. She identified that she could see how effective it was but conceded that it would have been too difficult to implement without the support. This is completely understandable and explains one of the reasons why teachers who embark on digital media construction usually do opt for group productions. There are, however, some other strategies illustrated in this study that will help to facilitate sustainable digital media production in any classroom. In particular, the concept that it is possible for some children to move ahead with the process without have to ensure the whole class meets the same milestones in the same time is useful. This would mean that a teacher could work with a few students initially and then she or he would have experienced helpers to work with the remaining students. Another outcome of this study is that the children who participated in this project now have considerable skills in digital media production. Any work they do in future will be influenced by this experience and it is likely that they will be able to achieve similar outcomes without the careful scaffolding. Further, they will be able to work with other students who are novice learners in this area and their digital stories produced as part of this project will be tangible examples for other children.

5.5 Digital Storytelling and Literacy

This project started with asking the children to write a story using traditional paper-based methods, in a similar format to the national NAPLAN writing tests [13]. This material provided a useful starting point for the project and a benchmark for generic literacy standards. It wasn't appropriate, however, to simply compare this text against the scripts written for digital stories, in an attempt to look for some sort of progression. It was clearly evident that the definition of literacy needed to be far wider for this task and had to include multimodal aspects such as visual, oral, audio and information literacies, as well as digital literacies. The children in the classroom already had access to appropriate digital technologies including a few class computers and an iPad each. The additional technologies introduced with this project complemented the classroom resources and provided a good range of tools for digital storytelling purposes. Although most of the children hadn't attempted digital production before they were certainly ready to use these tools. They engaged willingly with the technical tasks such as writing scripts in Word, taking photographs with their iPads or the digital cameras provided, recording voiceovers with ipads or in the green screen studio and then using iMovie for video production. Perhaps the most important impact that the project had on the children's literacy wasn't learning the technical skills in isolation but experiencing the use of digital technologies driven by purpose. The digital story project provided a real context where the technology was used creatively to communicate their story about place to an authentic audience.

6 Conclusion

Digital storytelling incorporates 'old' literacies - writing, speaking, reading and listening - with 'new' literacies or digital literacies where learners use digital technologies as a medium to tell their stories. The King Island Digital Stories Project supported the children on King Island to engage with this process as they created stories about their 'place', a remote and beautiful island between mainland Australia and Tasmania. The Year 4/5 children not only learnt the technological skills for media production but they also learnt about harnessing technology for creative and communication purposes. It is anticipated that this experience will facilitate their engagement with literacies and help them to use technologies more effectively for tomorrow's learning.

Acknowledgments. The author would like to thank the Tasmanian Community Fund for funding the KIDS project.

References

1. Porter, B.: DigiTales: The Art of Telling Digital Stories. Bernajean Porter Consulting, Denver (2005)
2. Lambert, J.: Digital Storytelling: Capturing Lives, Creating Community, 4th edn. Routledge, New York (2013)
3. Sylvester, R., Greenidge, W.: Digital storytelling: extending the potential for struggling writers. Read. Teach. **63**(4), 284–295 (2009)
4. Lankshear, C., Knobel, M.: Digital Literacies: Concepts Policies and Practices. Peter Lang, New York (2008)
5. Di Blas, N., Paolini, P., Sabiescu, S.: Collective digital storytelling at school as a whole-class interaction. In: Proceedings of the 9th International Conference on Interaction Design and Children, pp. 11–19 (2010)
6. Emert, T.: Interactive digital storytelling with refugee children. Lang. Teach. **91**(6), 401–415 (2014)
7. Mahon, L.: Story writing in remote locations: authoring culturally appropriate literature with children. In: Yelland, N., Neal, G., Dakich, E. (eds.) Rethinking Education with ICT: New Directions for Effective Practices. Sense Publishers, Rotterdam (2008)
8. Sharing Stories Foundation: Sharing Stories (2014). http://sharingstories.org/
9. Avriel-Avni, N., Spektor-Levy, O., Zion, M., Rosalind-Levi, N.: Children's sense of place in desert towns: a phenomenographic enquiry. Int. Res. Geogr. Environ. Educ. **19**(3), 241–259 (2010)
10. Ohler, J.: Digital Storytelling in the Classroom: New Media Pathways to Literacy. Learning and Creativity. Corwin, Thousand Oaks (2013)
11. Masters, J.: Teachers Scaffolding Children Working with Computers: An Analysis of Strategies. VDM, Saarbrucken (2008)
12. Johnson, J., Avenarius, C., Weatherford, J.: The active participant-observer: applying social role analysis to participant observation. Field Meth. **182**, 111–134 (2006)
13. Australian Curriculum, Assessment and Reporting Authority (ACARA): NAPLAN (2016). https://www.nap.edu.au/naplan

Gender Difference in Handmade Robotics for Children

Paolo Tosato ✉ and Monica Banzato ✉

Department of Linguistics and Comparative Cultural Studies,
Ca' Foscari University, Venice, Italy
{ptosato, banzato}@unive.it

Abstract. There are several kits for sale in the educational market that aim to encourage children to interact with technology and programming through the use of enjoyable activities which incorporate tangible robots. However, less expensive "craft" alternatives are also available, including handmade robotics. This paper describes the development of *Rospino*, a robotics kit aimed at children aged from 9 to 11. The project is still being tested and is going through several design iterations based on feedback collected from teachers and children during the last year. The study presented in this paper is part of research still under development which aims to verify whether there are gender differences in self-efficacy and perceived engagement in handmade robotics activities. Despite the fact that some of the craft materials are not inherently attractive (e.g., rubber bands, bottle caps, pieces of wood, wires, etc. and could be labelled as "male stuff") and the low self-efficacy of the girls as measured in the pre-test, the results (among 133 primary school students) demonstrate that females have been involved at the same level as males in the activity.

Keywords: Handmade robotics · Gender difference · Computational thinking Self-efficacy · Perceived engagement

1 Introduction

The recent Italian Educational Reform introduces computational thinking into the schools, starting at the primary level [20]. The schools are preparing for the introduction of this new subject: (1) in-service teacher training on computational thinking and educational robotics activities; (2) the purchase of hardware and software needed to employ educational robotics in the classroom. At present, the schools are oriented towards solutions proposed by manufacturers of educational robotics [16] that offer increasingly interesting and attractive modular robotics kit to the world of education. However, there are other solutions less familiar to primary school teachers, such as handmade robotics with recycled materials. Based on constructionism theory, handmade robotics, which is, is considered one of the most fruitful approaches for learning and teaching technology [25, 27]. This evaluation concerns mainly high school students as there has been little use of Arduino in primary schools [19]. For this reason, we have designed an educational activity for primary schools, called *Rospino* [28], based on the Arduino platform [1]. This consists of a recycled materials kit accompanied by

A. Tatnall and M. Webb (Eds.): WCCE 2017, IFIP AICT 515, pp. 209–220, 2017.
https://doi.org/10.1007/978-3-319-74310-3_23

software that we have developed which is freely downloadable from the Web [28]. This proposed activity presents a challenge to primary schools because it offers a different approach than kits composed of manufactured building blocks, which have been described as "predefined plastic shapes, user manufactured plastic shapes, laser cut shapes and a combination of craft and LEGO" [29, 34]. These "tend to restrict design freedom as they provide a set of predefined physical shapes that could only be assembled in specific ways. Crafting using everyday objects as primitives shapes provides more freedom in creative exploration" [34]. A common feature of handmade robotics projects is the use of recycled materials chosen to see if they incentivise equally the involvement and participation of boys and girls in primary school (from 9 to 12 years old). This question is relevant if we consider that currently at the level of international research there is still little investigation of gender differences in relation to computational thinking and coding [12, 21, 33] and little is known of handmade robotics [9, 19]. Although there are no precise figures on the use of Arduino in schools, one review [14] of the Arduino platform, which was used in our proposal, revealed that females constitute less than 1% of users in high schools; though, the e-textile fab lab communities has recently attracted a significant number of female adolescents and women [13]. In addition, although there has been research on the cognitive aspects of the writing of coding and on the use of these platforms in order to acquire new skills, there is limited evidence about gender differences in attitudes, beliefs and perceptions, as compared to the level of involvement in educational activities as a whole [13, 19]. For this reason, the exploratory study presented in this paper aims to investigate differences in self-efficacy and learning engagement among students being taught handmade robotics. In particular, the research questions are: (1) are there gender differences in students' beliefs regarding self-efficacy after a *Rospino* robotics activity compared to before? (2) are there gender differences in learning involvement at the cognitive and perceptual levels during *Rospino* robotics activities?

The exploratory study was carried out on a total of 153 children in five primary schools in the northeast of Italy. It was presented as a relevant initiative, in education and pedagogy, to expand research studies in this sector. It was also intended to encourage interested schools, teachers and students to participate in handmade robotics educational activities. We present in Sect. 2 the characteristics of *Rospino* and the research conducted so far with teachers and children. Sections 3, 4, 5, 6, and 7 are devoted to presenting this research.

2 Rospino: Design Features

The *Rospino* project started with the aim of providing students an educational and economical kit of recycled materials (cardboard tablet, bottle caps, rubber bands, sticks and wooden cubes) to construct a basic robot, in order to stimulate their imagination and creativity. Throughout different development stages, *Rospino* has been enriched with other components that allow teachers and children to customize the robot movements: Arduino, breadboard, wires, batteries, servo motors and USB cable [28]. Together with these materials, software has been developed to simplify the robot programming [28]. Since this software has to be used by primary school children, it has been simplified as much as possible, following the principle established in the world of architecture which says "less is more".

2.1 Research and Development

The First Prototypes. All design decisions for Rospino are based on research and feedback from children and teachers, together with developmental psychologists and pedagogists. Over the past two years, the design of Rospino has had several iterations with the end-user. It has been tested in many public schools and in the laboratory.

Research with Teachers. From near the end of 2015 through early 2016, data was collected from 14 primary and middle school teachers; additional data was collected from 150 more primary and middle school teachers through 2016 and early 2017. Both groups of teachers were questioned about their perceptions, attitudes, beliefs and experiences of robotics in order to modify and improve the design of *Rospino*. These teachers were exposed to a *Rospino* prototype and took part in training sessions, semi-structured interviews, group discussions and questionnaires to help researchers improve *Rospino* software and kits. Teachers were generally enthusiastic about the use of handmade robotics for professional development and for educational activities in their classrooms, although they were novices in this subject (as many of them came from the humanities). However, they also made several suggestions to improve the original design of *Rospino*, including: (1) they asked to simplify the procedure to connect the robot-artefact with *Rospino* software; (2) since the construction of mechanical/electronic parts requires several steps and novice teachers of robotics find these difficult to remember, the employment of a video was indicated [4]; (3) finally, some teachers suggested that the use of *Rospino* kit might be an activity more "attractive" to boys than girls, while no such comment was made about the software.

Research with Children. Through 2015 and 2016, we held a number of sessions with non-selective groups of ten children each, aged from 9 to 10, from whom we collected the following feedback: (1) the parts required for the robot's construction should be easily manipulated and intuitively easy to connect; (2) the programming of the robot should be minimal as should the quantity of computer equipment needed; and (3) the recycled "decorative" material which is used to cover the robot skeleton should be designed and coloured more attractively. In these sessions, the children did not perceive or label the activities as boy things or girl things.

3 Present Research

From the experience gained so far, we concluded that although the *Rospino* kit might not be gender-neutral, no such opinion was offered about the *Rospino* software either by the children or their teachers. Therefore, we decided to try to determine whether the proposed handmade robotics is viable. To this end we took into account various studies which have been conducted to determine gender compatibility [5, 19, 34] in the educational field. We designed an educational workshop based on verbal, visual and computational storytelling activities [4] – employing group work and problem-based learning – in order to see whether gender differences emerged. To understand the impact of the educational robotics proposal, we conducted studies that were designed to answer the following research questions: (1) are there gender differences in students' beliefs regarding their self-efficacy after a *Rospino* robotics educational activity compared to before? (2) are there gender differences in learning involvement at the cognitive and perceptual levels during *Rospino* robotics activities? We conducted the study on a total of 153 children, from eight classes in five primary schools (see Sect. 5).

3.1 Gender Differences: Beliefs, Expectations and Perceptions

Our efforts to evaluate the effectiveness of the proposed handmade robotics (*Rospino*) and to determine gender differences in this regard follow from the goal of promoting educational interest in computational thinking. We were inspired in these endeavours by research milestones, such as Weiner's attribution theory [32], Bandura's self-efficacy theory [3]; Covington's self-worth perspective [10]; Atkinson's expectancy/value theory [2] and Eccles' achievement-related choices [11]. An acquaintance with these concepts helps one to see how students' choices are influenced. Among the many possible lines of inquiry, we decided to investigate expectancies for success and perceived engagement in a particular task. Expectancies for success are based on how much trust an individual attributes to his ability to succeed in a particular task, while perceived engagement is determined by the degree to which an individual perceives that task to be important, useful, and engaging in itself. Accordingly, we have carried out an initial survey aimed at investigating self-efficacy beliefs and the perceived engagement of children. As the relationship between gender, self-efficacy and perceived engagement in the field of educational robotics has not yet been sufficiently explored in primary schools, this work is intended as a contribution to filling that gap.

3.2 Self-efficacy and Gender

Expectations of success have their genesis in the concept of self-efficacy. Bandura [3] defines self-efficacy as "people's judgments of their capabilities to organize and execute courses of action required to attain designated types of performances". Research in this field has shown that students with high self-efficacy are able to persevere longer in their tasks, to demand more significant results from their research, to withstand the anxiety of schoolwork and achieve better results. It is important to note that there are no well-documented gender differences in STEM on self-efficacy.

3.3 Perceived Engagement and Gender

Self-efficacy is one of several factors that can affect the self-perception of students regarding their expectations of success. Childhood development from 9 to 12 is characterized by crucial physical, emotional, cognitive and social changes. At this stage, "girls [are] generally showing a decline in self-efficacy beliefs" [24]. To better under-stand this situation, we considered it essential to investigate aspects of perceptual and cognitive involvement in the learning of handmade robotics (User Engagement Scale [22]), together with the concept of self-efficacy [3]. In fact, it is necessary to explore the perceived engagement differences in cognitive capacity and problem-solving ability in girls and boys, and to combine this with affective variables, such as self-efficacy, which often are decisive for the selection of future studies and also are a primary source of gender differences with the passing of years. At this point, the relationship between self-efficacy and perceived engagement in relation to gender in the field of computational thinking has not yet been sufficiently explored.

3.4 Video Behavioural Observation

To further verify the students' experience of coding with Rospino, we decided to analyze videos of the operations the students performed during the workshop. The purpose was to examine what students learned in practice and what their difficulties were. The criteria used to evaluate the videos were based on the educational goals of the workshop: (1) knowing how to use the sequence structure; (2) been being able to distinguish a command by its attributes; (3) during the testing phase: been being able to distinguish between hardware problems and software problems.

4 Robotics in Primary Education

The international research literature on computing education continues to confirm a concerning under-representation of women in the IT sector [14, 30] and worrying results about gender impact [23]. In the recent past, computer use and activities related to ICT were seen as a field of "male domination" [7] and this perception continues today, despite slight improvements in gender balance [26]. Even though recent research [23] confirms the persistence of the gender gap, there is strong evidence to support the thesis that teaching educational robotics to students can have a positive effect on their subject choices [6]. Research indicates that the use of cross-disciplinary pedagogical classes which blend art, narration and technology advances the balance of gender participation [8, 29]. Rather than limiting themselves to a particular task-oriented application, girls displayed an interest in technology primarily as a teaching method for stimulating the development of creative and expressive skills. Having participated in this form of education, girls have a better chance of becoming students in STEM [15]. So far, the most interesting results for girls appear to be obtained with computational e-textile toolkits Arduino LilyPad [9] which employ soft materials and incorporate crafting techniques, such as sewing cloth, rather than employing motors and gears [5, 13]. However, other research which measured student engagement among ubiquitous computing platforms (such as, Scratch 2.0, Lego Mindstorms NXT, and Wearable Arduino LilyPad) found "that girls were emotionally engaged in robots as much as boys" [19]. In addition, the girls showed more interest in the robots than in Lilypad [19]. Avoiding historically feminine expressions and materials has led to encouraging results being achieved by other solutions, such as HandiMate (based on Arduino Nano) [34]. As regards self-efficacy, several studies have also found that girls' confidence levels increase with practice [19]. Nevertheless, despite increasing research in the field, there is little evidence to show that the students' perceptions, beliefs and attitudes are predictive of future choices [5]. Therefore, it is important to evaluate the consequences of programming computer systems with regard to students' attitudes and intentions to study programming in the future.

5 Methods

We conducted a small scale study to investigate possible differences in the impact of handmade robotics activities. Below are details of the participants, conditions and measures.

5.1 Participants

A total of 153 primary school students, comprising 87 males and 66 females, enrolled in this pilot study. The study was held during school hours. The students were aged from 9 to 11. The majority of the students had previous experience of software usage, but not of software development. Only three pupils had really tried to program, by participating in school robotics projects. Before proceeding with data analysis, incomplete questionnaires were eliminated. In addition, since the coding activity took place on different days, it sometimes happened that a student participated in only a part of the workshop, due to absence. In these cases, questionnaire answers were discarded. For this reason, only 133 students out of 153 were analyzed; this group comprised 75 males and 58 females, aged from 9 to 11.

5.2 Conditions

Educational activity was introduced for each class through the narration of a story, followed by a phase of drawing and construction of a robot, in which students plotted a few characters from the story and built one robot with *Rospino* kit. *Rospino* software was later presented to the children, after which they were left free to explore the development environment and to program certain movements of the robot. Finally, the students were invited to move the robot in a predetermined path, which they repeated in subsequent tests.

5.3 Measures

The questionnaires administered were: (a) pre- and post-test on the sense of self-efficacy; (b) post-test on cognitive and perceptual student involvement. These questionnaires were preceded by the compilation of data on gender and age, on the possession of a home computer, and on computing experience.

The self-efficacy, pre- and post-activity questionnaires administered to students employed the four-item Likert scale of five steps (ranging along an axis from (5) "completely agree" to (1) "completely disagree"). It investigated four aspects: (i) level of self-efficacy in learning activities and understanding of coding; (ii) expectation of doing well in activities one chooses to pursue; (iii) security of concluding one's chosen activities successfully; (iv) security of achieving excellent results from the activity of coding. The second questionnaire, which was administered after the workshop on robotics, was based on the User Engagement Scale. It employed the eight-item Likert scale of five steps, ranging from (1) “completely agree” to (5) “completely disagree”. This questionnaire was intended to measure the level of students’ engagement in their coding activity. The User Engagement Scale consists of a wide variety of questions, but for our sample formation and the context in which the activity took place, it was decided to limit the items to eight in order to investigate the following aspects: focused attention; novelty; involvement; aesthetics; perceived usability. These measurements were aimed at assessing the differences in effort perceived by boys and girls during the workshop.

6 Research Results

The results reported below are based on a non-probabilistic sample, as we were obliged to sample only that part of the population which was accessible in the circumstances. These can be characterized as ad hoc samples, drawn from those schools for which we were authorized to enter the classrooms and restricted by the availability of teachers to subject their students to research. For this reason, the validity of our sample is closely linked to the situation to which it refers and there is no guarantee of its validity in different circumstances.

6.1 Results Regarding Changes in Self-efficacy

Before analyzing the results, the reliability of the questionnaire was estimated by calculating Cronbach Alfa and obtaining an acceptable result ($\alpha = 0.70$); this data was confirmed by the inter-item correlation matrix (all values positive) and the corrected item-total correlation, which demonstrated good internal consistency among the questions. To verify whether the educational activities had produced an improvement in the sense of self-efficacy, a t-test for dependent samples was performed on data from 133 students; this revealed that the change (Pre: $M = 4.14$, $SD = 0.56$, range from 2.50 to 5.00; Post: $M = 4.25$, $SD = 0.57$, range from 2.25 to 5.00) was statistically significant ($t(132) = -2.06$, $p < 0.05$). Analyzing data split up by institution (see Table 1), it can be seen how the increase in self-efficacy was statistically significant only in two schools: School 2 (Pre: $M = 4.24$, $SD = 0.59$; Post: $M = 4.51$, $SD = 0.32$; $t(23) = -2.27$, $p < 0.05$) and School 4 (Pre: $M = 3.86$, $SD = 0.58$; Post: $M = 4.24$, $SD = 0.66$; $t(17) = -2.37$, $p < 0.05$).

Deeper analysis of these results, concerning School 2 and School 4 (see Table 2), put into evidence how the improvement of self-efficacy was statistically significant in female students, as highlighted performing both a t-test for dependent samples and a Wilcoxon test. More than this, it is interesting to underline that the level of self-efficacy in females was lower than males in the pre-test, while it is the same or higher in the post-test, and the same thing happens in other schools. This is very interesting if we consider that at this age (9–11) girls are more self-critical and less secure than boys.

Table 1. Self-efficacy per school

Institute		Mean	N	Std. deviation
School 1	Pre-test	4.2159	22	0.51925
	Post-test	4.2727	22	0.53956
School 2	**Pre-test**	**4.2396**	**24**	**0.58272**
	Post-test	**4.5104**	**24**	**0.31691**
School 3	Pre-test	4.2679	42	0.54491
	Post-test	4.2798	42	0.60031
School 4	**Pre-test**	**3.8611**	**18**	**0.58298**
	Post-test	**4.2361**	**18**	**0.65570**
School 5	Post-test	3.9722	27	0.53409
	Pre-test	3.9630	27	0.58303

Table 2. Self-efficacy per school and sex

Institute	Gender		Mean	N	Std. deviation
School 2	Male	Pre-test	4.3281	16	0.62396
		Post-test	4.5469	16	0.30576
	Female	**Pre-test**	**4.0625**	**8**	**0.47716**
		Post-test	**4.4375**	**8**	**0.34718**
School 4	Male	Pre-test	4.0208	12	0.60733
		Post-test	4.1875	12	0.76963
	Female	**Post-test**	**3.5417**	**6**	**0.40052**
		Pre-test	**4.3333**	**6**	**0.37639**

6.2 Results Regarding Perceived Engagement

After the workshop on coding a questionnaire consisting of nine items was administered to the children. This questionnaire was based on the User Engagement Scale [22] and was intended to measure the degree of student involvement in the activity of coding. The research collected data on the following aspects: focused attention, novelty, involvement, aesthetics, perceived usability.

Hypotheses. This study aims to determine whether there is a gender difference in the cognitive involvement of students in coding activities. If there are differences between the male and female populations, we should be able to reject the following assumption:

H0: the median of the population from which the sample of males is extracted is equal to the median of the population from which the sample of females is extracted: therefore, there is not a gender difference in cognitive student involvement.

Results. The class in which the experiment took place was drawn from primary schools; it was composed of 133 students aged between 9 and 11 years. From this group, two independent samples were created: one of 75 males and the other of 58 females.

Before analyzing the results, the reliability of the questionnaire was estimated by calculating Cronbach's alpha coefficient. The calculation of this index demonstrated a fair internal consistency of questions ($\alpha = 0.74$).

Since male data and female data are not distributed in a Gaussian way, instead of calculating a t-test, the Mann-Whitney statistical test was performed to analyze the results, reporting the following results: Mann-Whitney $U = 2043$ and relevant probability $p = 0.548$, which corresponds to Asymp. Sig. (2-tailed). Through these values it was possible to calculate the effect size $r_{equivalent}$, amounting to a value of 0.053, interpreted as a negligible effect size.

Data Analysis. Taking into consideration the results reported in the previous section, it is not unlikely that the observed data is the result of a true null hypothesis (H0 given in section "Hypotheses"): this is why we accept it.

The results suggest that most likely the male population ($n = 75$, median = 4.00, Q1 = 3.43, Q3 = 4.71) has a median score in the questionnaire concerning user engagement equal to that of the female population ($n = 58$, median = 4.14, Q1 = 3.43, Q3 = 4.57); therefore there is no empirical evidence of a gender difference ($U = 2043$, $z = -0.601$, $p > 0.05$, $r = 0.053$).

6.3 Analysis of Results of Video and Programs

The analysis of the data was intended to evaluate the achievement of the objectives described in Sect. 3: to detect the difficulties faced by the students during coding with *Rospino* software, and to collect information regarding students' involvement and their reactions when tackling obstacles. The results of the analysis follow: (1) more consecutive blocks "go ahead" (lack of optimization); (2) overload operation "turn right"/ "turn left", which is also associated with the operation "go ahead"; (3) lack of a strategy for the resolution of the problem (many trials and lack of planning). Moreover, videos put into evidence the students' main difficulty in robot assembly, that is to understand the differences among the three lines: input, power supply and ground. The issues listed above affected both males and females in the same way.

7 Discussion and Limitations of the Research

Based on the statistical results it could be stated that there are no differences between males and females. However, in our opinion, the interpretation of results should not be limited to the level of statistical results. We must take into account the psychological development that characterizes this age range and is different for males and females. In fact, adolescence for girls begins between 9 and 11 years, while for boys between 11 and 13 years [18]. Adolescence, more than the other stages of the life cycle, has been defined as a transition period characterized by profound and significant cognitive, affective, social, and physical changes which by challenging beliefs, attitudes, and thoughts affects the identity of teenagers and inevitably their security [31]. In adolescence, the maturation of analytical and introspective capabilities and the definition of one's own identity allow for a progressive reorganization. This process does not lack tensions and often includes complex issues that are still under exploration, especially in this increasingly digital society. Specifically at this stage of life, several studies of girls and boys of the same age, show that girls suffer a fall in self-efficacy [24] in the field of science compared to boys, and this gap increases as they grow older [17]. This data can also be seen in the self-efficacy pre-test results of our group of girls (see Table 2). However, we can notice that in the post-test the self-efficacy of girls has improved (in some cases it is equal to or greater than the boys). Therefore, in interpreting data, we must take into account the differences in development between males and females (mentioned above) and assume that girls have filtered and processed questions more critically and with a lower sense of security than their male colleagues (the pre-test confirms this hypothesis). Therefore in answering the research questions we can state that: though being more "self-critical" or "less secure" than boys, we can infer that girls show meaningful improvements in learning engagement and self-efficacy tests, equal to or better than boys. Therefore, our interpretation should be based not only on the statistical results but also on the psychological differences of males and females of adolescent age.

We can conclude, in this first phase, that the introduction of robotic craft activities has the potential to attract both girls and boys as active participants, despite the fact that they have used decisively non-material forms and expressions that historically have a more feminine orientation. These results were positive [5, 13], as the original feedback received from teachers, which had perceived robotics as primarily an activity for males, was contradicted by the children's self-reporting. In fact, we observed that after the initial indications given in the classroom, both males and females developed a sense of autonomy in the design and creation of their robots. The children assembled different materials with great dedication, making several hypothesis about what were the best building solutions. They paid careful attention to their artefacts' physical and aesthetic details, which resulted from their own creativity and from experimenting with their robots on the floor. They showed perseverance in physically improving their "creatures" (e.g., by looking for materials other than those proposed) and in using the software to program the paths of their robots on the floor (i.e., choosing the initial path of the robot and changing it according to the physical conditions it encountered). The children showed tenacity in achieving, through testing and retesting, their goal of making their robots do what they had predetermined. They felt that the activity was "very cool!", "an adult thing", "work for engineers".

The work has some limitations: we cannot exclude that previous experiences or implicit and explicit beliefs or gender stereotypes (transmitted by family, friends, or teachers) could have weighed on the thinking of the girls and boys. Although the workshop took place in curricular hours, the experiment was required to coexist with other school activities that required the children's attention and commitment. The novelty factor might also have influenced the degree of involvement of the children, as it emerged from the questionnaire.

For future work, we intend to strengthen this explorative study with longer periods of intervention and to enhance the pedagogical approach by employing cross-disciplinary studies. We will compare our proposal for handmade robotics with other educational robotics solutions, and we will deepen further exploration by qualitative research methods, in order to explore the children's expectations, attitudes, beliefs, and perceptions. To better understand the beliefs of children and the possible obstacles they encounter in their school career choices, we would like to explore the beliefs and stereotypes among other educational actors, such as teachers and parents, about school-based robotics activities.

Note: for reasons of national assessment of Italian university research, the authors must declare which sections each has written, in spite of the fact that work is entirely the result of continuous and intensive collaboration. Sections 1, 2, 3, 4 and 7 are by M. Banzato. Sections 5 and 6 are by P. Tosato. The authors would like to thank Matthew Hoffman for valuable comments.

References

1. Arduino. https://www.arduino.cc. Accessed 15 July 2017
2. Atkinson, J.W.: Motivational determinants of risk-taking behavior. Psychol. Rev. **64**(6p1), 359 (1957)
3. Bandura, A.: Social Foundation of Thought and Action. Englewood Cliffs, New Jersey (1986)
4. Banzato, M., Tosato, P.: An exploratory study of the impact of self-efficacy and learning engagement in coding learning activities in Italian middle school. Int. J. E-Learn. (IJEL). **16**(4), 349–369 (2017)
5. Beisser, S.R.: An examination of gender differences in elementary constructionist classrooms using lego/logo instruction. Comput. Schools **22**, 7–19 (2006)
6. Blank, D.S., Kumar, D.: Assessing the impact of using robots in education, or: how we learned to stop worrying and love the chaos. In: AAAI Spring Symposium: Educational Robotics and Beyond (2010)
7. Brosnan, M.J., Davidson, M.J.: Psychological gender issues in computing. Gend. Work Organ. **3**(1), 13–25 (1996)
8. Buchholz, B., et al.: Hands on, hands off. Mind Cult. Act. **21**(4), 278–297 (2014)
9. Buechley, L., Benjamin, M.H.: LilyPad in the wild: how hardware's long tail is supporting new engineering and design communities. In: Proceedings of the 8th ACM Conference on Designing Interactive Systems. ACM (2010)
10. Covington, M.V.: The motive for self-worth. Res. Motiv. Educ. **1**, 77–113 (1984)
11. Eccles, J.S.: Understanding women's educational and occupational choices. Psychol. Women Q. **18**(4), 585–609 (1994)
12. Grover, S., Pea, R.: Computational thinking in K–12 a review of the state of the field. Educ. Res. **42**(1), 38–43 (2013)
13. Kanjun, Q., et al.: A curriculum for teaching computer science through computational textiles. In: Proceedings of the 12th International Conference on Interaction Design and Children, pp. 20–27. ACM, New York (2013)
14. Klawe, M., et al.: Women in computing—take 2. Commun. ACM - Inspiring Women Comput. **52**(2), 68–76 (2009)
15. Larose, S., et al.: Trajectories of science self-efficacy beliefs during the college transition and academic and vocational adjustment in science and technology programs. Educ. Res. Eval. **12**, 373–393 (2006)
16. Lego Mindstorms. http://mindstorms.lego.com. Accessed 07 Aug 2017
17. Lent, R.W., et al.: Relation of self-efficacy expectations to academic achievement and persistence. J. Couns. Psychol. **31**(3), 356–362 (1984)

18. Lerner, R.M., Steinberg, L.: Handbook of Adolescent Psychology. JWS, Hoboken (2009)
19. Merkouris, A., Konstantinos, C.: Introducing computer programming to children through robotic and wearable devices. In: Proceedings of the Workshop in Primary and Secondary Computing Education. ACM (2015)
20. MIUR: Piano Nazionale Scuola Digitale. http://www.istruzione.it/scuola_digitale/allegati/Materiali/pnsd-layout-30.10-WEB.pdf. Accessed 08 Aug 2017
21. National Research Council: Report of a Workshop on the Pedagogical Aspects of Computational Thinking. National Academies Press (2011)
22. O'Brien, H.L., Toms, E.G.: The development and evaluation of a survey to measure user engagement. J. Am. Soc. Inf. Sci. Technol. **61**(1), 50–69 (2010)
23. OECD: The ABC of Gender Equality in Education. OECD Publishing, Pisa (2015)
24. Pajares, F., Schunk, D.H.: Self-beliefs and school success: self-efficacy, self-concept, and school achievement. Perception **11**, 239–266 (2001)
25. Papert, S.: Mindstorms. Basic Books, New York (1980)
26. Pechtelidis, Y., et al.: Between a rock and a hard place: women and computer technology. Gend. Educ. **27**(2), 164–182 (2015)
27. Piaget, J.: The Construction of Reality in the Child. Basic Books, New York (1954)
28. Rospino. http://www.projectschool.it. Accessed 03 July 2017
29. Rusk, N., et al.: New pathways into robotics: strategies for broadening participation. J. Sci. Educ. Technol. **17**(1), 59–69 (2008)
30. Schoolnet, E.: Computing our future. Technical report European Schoolnet (2014)
31. Urdan, T., Pajares, F.: Self-efficacy Beliefs of Adolescents. IAP, Charlotte (2006)
32. Weiner, B., et al.: Perceiving the causes of success and failure. L.E.A. (1987)
33. Wing, J.: Computational thinking. Commun. ACM **49**(3), 33–36 (2006)
34. Yoon, S.H., et al.: HandiMate: exploring a modular robotics kit for animating crafted toys. In: Proceedings of the IDC14, pp. 11–20. ACM (2015)

Assessment for Blended Learning Scenarios: A Decision Support Tool

Mary Webb(✉), Stylianos Hatzipanagos, Jonathan San Diego, Ehsan Khan, and Mateusz Goral

King's College London, London, UK
{mary.webb, s.hatzipanagos, jonathan.p.san_diego, eu.khan}@kcl.ac.uk

Abstract. This paper examines the process of designing assessment and how teachers in higher education, who are developing blended learning materials, can be supported to consider their approach to assessment and to select from the range of assessment opportunities that are becoming available. The paper presents the design and evaluation of an online decision support tool for assessment design, which was developed on a collaborative project across Indian and European universities. The tool was designed based on a shared framework of design and assessment principles which took account of the purpose of the assessment, knowledge and skills to be assessed and how and by whom the assessment was to be conducted. The tool was not intended to provide definitive advice but rather to support the decision-making process and professional development of teachers. This support would be provided during the use of the tool and as a summary at the end of the teacher's consultation with the tool. Overall, users were satisfied with the tool, as the data show, and were positive about using it in designing assessment. Recommendations that were made during the evaluation, for redeveloping the tool to make it more suitable for a wider audience are discussed.

Keywords: Assessment design · Online learning · Blended learning Assessment

1 Introduction

This paper examines the assessment design process and how it can be supported for teaching practitioners in higher education who are developing blended learning materials. Furthermore, the paper presents the design and evaluation of a decision support tool which was developed to support such needs. It is based on findings from the EQUAL Project [1] in which Indian and European universities worked in partnership to analyse needs of students and lecturers and common attributes across a partnership of universities and subject areas, develop design processes and implement electronic learning materials for use in a range of blended learning scenarios.

In order to support the development of these learning materials a series of face-to-face and online meetings between the partners on the EQUAL Project, including academics, students and learning technologists, explored theoretical

A. Tatnall and M. Webb (Eds.): WCCE 2017, IFIP AICT 515, pp. 221–230, 2017.
https://doi.org/10.1007/978-3-319-74310-3_24

concepts, ongoing design ideas and practical considerations. In this paper, we first present our analysis of the current state-of-the-art in assessment design and practice in relation to the needs of the project partners as well as significant theoretical and technological considerations. We then outline the design considerations identified as being essential for this project, followed by a presentation of the implementation of the tool. The results of our initial evaluation of the tool are then presented followed by conclusions and implications for future development among the partnership and for higher education more broadly.

2 Background and Literature Review

Terms such as formative assessment and summative assessment are now in common use in education but our experience suggests that these and related terms have varying meanings in different contexts and confusion remains; therefore establishing mutual understanding was a necessary first step in our project meetings. The term assessment itself is relatively unambiguous in that it refers to the checking of someone's knowledge, understanding, skills or capabilities. However, this same term is applied both to the process of checking and to the outcome of this process. Furthermore, in some educational circles, the term evaluation is used in place of assessment. On the EQUAL Project and in this paper we have used evaluation as a broader term relating to understanding the overall successes and failures of a course or programme rather than for assessing students.

Four perspectives on assessment have been identified as shown in the model presented in Table 1 [2]. This model distinguishes between a focus on the assessment process and on the results of the assessment. Furthermore, the model refers to "Assessment FOR learning" and "Assessment OF learning" [3]; terms which have been used in various educational circles in place of formative assessment and summative assessment respectively in order to emphasise the purpose of assessment and its relationship with learning. Referring to Table 1, Perspective 1 is about students learning from feedback discussions and information provided during an assessment process. Perspective 2, focuses on using results of assessment for adapting teaching and learning processes. The third perspective is about the extent to which students understand the assessment process and are able and willing to engage with it. This perspective reminds us that ensuring that our assessments are accurate reflections of students' achievements

Table 1. Four ways to think about assessment [2]

	PROCESS focus	RESULTS focus
Assessment FOR learning	*Perspective 1* Feedback discussions and information	*Perspective 2* Improvement decisions
Assessment OF learning	*Perspective 3* Degree of engagement with/understanding of process	*Perspective 4* Value judgements

is by no means straightforward. This need to understand what will be assessed and how the assessments will be conducted becomes particularly significant when students are learning not only from the materials and teaching sessions that lecturers provide, but from a broad range of online opportunities not necessarily recommended by the lecturers, including for example MOOCs. Perspectives 1, 2 and 3 are all key elements of formative assessment, which by definition supports students' learning and may be carried out by teachers, peers and/or students on themselves (self-assessment). Perspective 3 is important both for formative and summative assessment because in order to generate valid assessment information students need to understand the assessment process and engage with it. Perspective 4 is about making summative judgements for purposes of grading and accreditation. Clearly such judgements are important and necessary at transition points between elements of a programme of study and at the end. However, evidence suggests that students fail to attend to feedback comments when given grades [4] and hence overuse of summative judgements can be deleterious to students' learning.

When designing assessments, in addition to considering these four perspectives it is necessary to consider who/what is conducting and/or managing the assessment: student themselves, their peers, the teacher, a computer in an automated system. Self-assessment might be described as the gold standard of formative assessment. Students who are able to self-assess have the potential to become independent learners and to learn efficiently from the wide range of opportunities available including online materials and activities. The ability to self-assess is also necessary for self-regulated learning (SRL), a psychological construct which has been given much attention in recent years. SRL refers to an active, constructive process in which students intentionally set learning goals and then plan, monitor and regulate their cognitive, behavioural, emotional and motivational processes in the service of those goals in order to achieve optimal learning (Pintrich 2004). The evidence suggests that one of the best ways of developing students' ability to self-assess is through peer assessment [see for example 5].

The process of peer assessment involves students assessing each other's work against specified criteria and providing feedback to each other. For this to be a formative assessment process the feedback needs to focus on what the student has achieved and what they should do to improve their work, together with some ideas about how to go about this improvement [5]. In formative feedback, dialogue forms the mechanism by which the learner monitors, identifies and then is able to 'bridge' the gap in the learning process [see for example 6, 7]. Therefore, effective peer assessment processes become dialogic processes between students. Just as with self-assessment discussed above, a close relationship exists between good quality peer assessment processes and self-regulated learning. There is also a developing body of research in support of peer assessment as a summative assessment process. There is evidence that in some fields peer assessment is just as reliable as tutor assessment [8]. However, we believe that this does depend on the particular discipline and it is a practice that may meet resistance both by tutors and students. Specifically, in some of our partner universities there is a prevailing culture in which the expectation is for teachers to teach and provide feedback.

More generally, assessment practices in higher education have been changing and diversifying for some years. Currently new approaches are emerging based on developments in new technologies which are increasing the range of possibilities for assessments, including increasing opportunities for personalisation of assessments [9] and the capability for assessment to measure a broader range of knowledge and knowledge-in-action [10]. For example students can be assessed through simulations, e-portfolios and interactive games [11] rather than end of term exams and essays. The evidence is compelling that nature and form of assessment have a significant impact upon the student learning experience, approaches to learning, motivation, and retention rates [12].

In higher education, the nature of an institution often dictates how assessment practices have been developed. For example, open and distance learning environments have emphasized the necessity for formative assessment practices. Distance education in general has been proactive in formative assessment practices out of the need to find ways to provide systematic feedback and direction to students in the absence of the immediate contact and interaction that students have enjoyed with tutors in a campus setting [13]. However, in both types of environments, the impact of assessment on learning can be moderated by the use of appropriate assessment methods by teaching practitioners and practices have been supported/complemented by the use of computer assisted learning resources [14].

Computer-assisted assessment (most commonly in the form of automated quizzes or online objective tests) has been used by tutors in our partnership institutions. For instance, in a virtual learning environment (VLE) they may be used to monitor student understanding and progression. Text-based discussion fora (mainly asynchronous) has also been used for self and peer assessment purposes.

Online assessments require good Internet connections and discussions with some partner institutions revealed that infrastructure issues in India may render online assessments unfeasible in the short term. Therefore, consideration needed to be given to computer-based assessments that could be delivered off-line or within a local intranet. However, our expectations were that such technical problems would be resolved within a reasonable timescale and therefore institutions also need to look ahead to consider future options.

For assessment practices to be effective in relation to the four perspectives outlined above their place in the overall pedagogical design needs to be clear. Our view, in line with Black's [7] five-stage model of assessment in pedagogy is that assessment considerations and actions need to be integrated in all aspects of pedagogy so that there is a match between the aims and the specific learning outcomes, the activities to support the aims and the methods of assessment. In particular, in relation to designing online materials, design of assessment must be incorporated from the initial stages of the design process just as when a teacher is planning a lesson the learning outcomes, activities and assessments need to be designed to be closely aligned [7]. These decisions include the purposes of the assessment, consideration of whether the assessment is self, peer teacher or automated process as well as what knowledge and skills are to be assessed.

So, designing assessment may need a shared framework that would support our thinking and discussion in relation to specifying learning outcomes (LOs) and designing learning activities assessments. Bloom's taxonomy of educational objectives [15] was well known and respected by all our partner institutions. Bloom's technology was originally developed to facilitate sharing of test items between university faculties. More recently a revised version was developed [16] to take account of advances in cognitive psychology and other developments since the original taxonomy was published. In our view the revised Bloom's Taxonomy, while it does have some limitations, provides a useful framework for considering learning objectives and how to assess them.

Whereas Bloom's original taxonomy is arranged as a one-dimensional hierarchy with a built-in expectation of progression between levels, the revised framework is two-dimensional. There is still an indication of a hierarchy but it is acknowledged that categories overlap and the constraint of the "cumulative hierarchy" has been removed [17]. The taxonomy is generally represented as a table (see Table 2)

Table 2. The taxonomy table [16]

The cognitive process dimension						
The knowledge dimension	Remember	Understand	Apply	Analyse	Evaluate	Create
Factual knowledge						
Conceptual knowledge						
Procedural knowledge						
Metacognitive knowledge						

The intention is that any learning objective can be characterised in terms of both knowledge and cognitive processes and thus can be categorised into one of the cells in the table. Using the table to examine alignment between learning objectives, instructional activities and assessments is a key aim of the development of the taxonomy [17].

3 Design Considerations and Decisions

Our literature review and ongoing discussions of important theoretical and practical considerations presented above indicated that decision-making regarding assessments is complex. Nevertheless, we were moving towards a framework to support our thinking and development. The framework incorporated the considerations for designing learning outcomes together with the technical considerations and opportunities for implementing in online environments with specific reference to Moodle tools as Moodle was the platform in use across our partner institutions We could have presented the framework as a text-based report but that was less likely to be used by teachers in our institutions than a more focused and practical online tool. Such a tool could also be implemented as a simple checklist but that would be less helpful to teaching practitioners and teaching teams in thinking about consequences of their decisions. We expected that the tool might be useful beyond the project, although in the first instance the specific context of the project was the priority for this initiative. A tool to support such decision making must take a simple transparent approach and make users aware of limitations. The tool was not intended to provide definitive advice but rather to support the decision-making process and professional development of teachers within the partner institutions. This support should be provided during the use of the tool and as a summary at the end of the teacher's consultation with the tool.

The tool (accessible at: https://keats.kcl.ac.uk/course/view.php?id=34569) was designed to help the user in creating an assessment plan by asking a series of questions and highlighting the implications of their choices. The user begins with a Learning Outcome and proceeds by answering a series of questions concerning students, the context in which the assessment takes place, the nature of the knowledge and processes that are being assessed and the type of assessment including peer and self-assessment. With each question the tool also provides potential implications of the choices based on the theoretical and practical issues outlined earlier including the revised Bloom's taxonomy considering intended learning outcomes. Upon answering the questions the user is presented with some recommendations about methods of assessment they may want to consider, and some potential ways to implement it using an authoring software and to be made available in a virtual learning environment (e.g. Moodle as used in the EQUAL Project see Fig. 1).

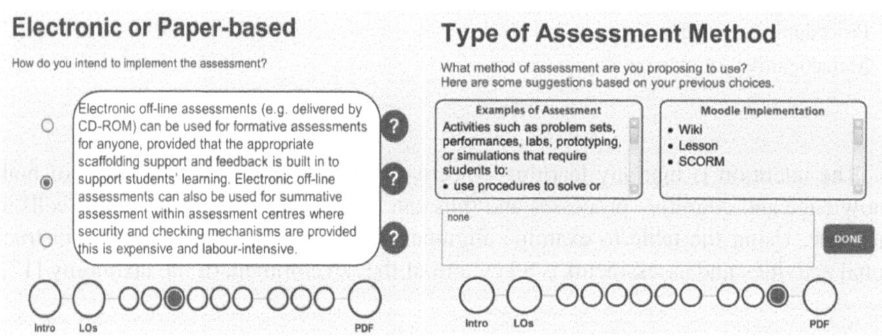

Fig. 1. Screenshots of assessment decision support tool (a) when the user is checking the implications of using "electronic off-line delivery" and (b) suggestions for assessments and ways of implementing after a user has input their series of answers.

The user can export all the recommendations and answers they gave into a PDF for reference.

4 Evaluation of the Decision Support Tool

The evaluation focused on: (1) examining how well the tool matched the expectations of the project members, and (2) gathering feedback to inform future updates. Data were gathered by a survey via SurveyMonkey and a focus group discussion in a workshop setup. Each of the partner institutions were asked questions concerning their expectations and experience of using the tool (using a combination of Likert scale type and open ended questions). Those who had used the tool to design assessment were additionally asked how they used it and were asked to provide links with examples. The workshop was part of a project meeting and all the partner institutions were represented. During the workshop the tool was demonstrated and then participants were invited to use the tool. The rationale for this approach was to also include participants that had not had a chance to try the tool beforehand. The discussion was captured as a series of statements on a flipchart visible to all participants.

The data collected both from the survey and the discussion were analysed. These comprised quantitative data from the survey and qualitative from the survey and the focus group discussion. The qualitative data were coded and themes were identified.

The tool workshop was attended by 16 members that participated in the focus group and in addition there were 7 participants' responses to the questionnaire. Responses indicated that the tool met users' expectations, typically "guiding the thought process preceding the creation of assessment situations". Focus group results also suggested a need to link the various LOs together as the following comment illustrates: "Tool appears linear. It makes it difficult to link various assessments together." This suggests respondents wanted a way to think about assessment for a module or programme as a whole. There were various suggestions on how to achieve that, such as: tying individual assessments to outcomes at the programme level, assessing a single LO in multiple ways, highlighting dependencies between LOs, etc.

It was also suggested that, apart from helping to situate the assessments in a wider context, the tool could also provide "more granular advice for certain assessment approaches". In other words, some participants wanted specific advice and suggestions on practical implementation, for example how to test mathematics concepts, critical reading, "practical projects and assessment of field work", etc. Both these comments and previous points about linearity are essentially about expanding the scope of the tool.

It was suggested that the tool was aimed at practitioners with a certain amount of knowledge and experience, rather than new lecturers, and it might be "more useful for people with some theoretical background (knowledge)". In the tool design, there is indeed an assumption that the user is familiar with certain concepts such as the distinction between formative and summative assessment, Bloom's taxonomy etc. A novice educator may not necessarily be familiar with all of the necessary background theory to use the tool effectively.

Currently the decision model used by the tool is quite straightforward in design. The final recommendation provided by the tool are influenced by the two final questions that the user is asked. Other questions are asked to help the user think about the various aspects of assessment, rather than to provide direct advice. The data suggested that the tool algorithm could be expanded to provide such advice in the form of "critical comments" and engage the user more in dialogue, for example by "warning that particular combinations [of choices] might not be optimal [for successful assessment design]". However, expanding this algorithm would make the tool more sophisticated at the expense of diminishing its well received simplicity, by increasing the complexity of design and implementation.

Finally, there were a few comments on the presentation and structure of the PDF output document, and minor suggestions for navigation improvements. During the workshop the tool did not work for some people who were using a particular type of browser, Internet Explorer, so testing across more browsers would be beneficial as well as regular updates on what browsers are supported.

5 Discussion

In this section, we discuss the potential value and feasibility of implementing the suggestions from our evaluation results. Firstly, in terms of target audience, user perception of the value of the tool, our data suggest that users thought that the current version of the tool was most useful to an experienced teaching practitioner who is familiar with educational theory; they further commented that "targeting people with lesser understanding of underlying educational theories might be more useful". This suggested that more needs to be done to introduce and explain different concepts used, not necessarily within the tool itself but perhaps by warning the user about the kind of (prerequisite) ideas they need to be familiar with before using the tool, and pointing them to sources they can use to learn about them.

Currently the tool can be used as a resource for those training other teachers in an academic development setting. The context of working collaboratively using the tool and learning from peers in a face-to-face setting seemed to be very effective in workshops we led using the tool, where the data were collected. This approach was consistent with the overall focus of the EQUAL Project which was to support the development of communities of practice [18] using blended learning wherever possible rather than entirely online learning. Learning design challenges for providing a stand-alone tool, which could be used for individual online learning, include ways of simulating the kind of situated learning where communities of practitioners converge in and around authentic practice, which is recognised to support effective professional learning [19, 20]. Bell and Morris [19] addressed these issues in the design of their online resources by providing a range of video clips of examples of practice taken from real contexts and with real practitioners. In the EQUAL Project we had already made a start on identifying examples of good practice across the project by developing a series of vignettes of assessment design practices and these might become the basis for a more comprehensive resource.

Consistent with the approach of Bell and Morris was a clear indication that the participants would like the tool to include more of the context in which assessment is developed. A few specific ideas that illustrated this were:

- relating individual LOs for sessions with overall module and programme LOs;
- highlighting dependencies between LOs;
- assessing one LO in different ways, etc.

On the other hand, more granular advice about implementation of assessment beyond existing guidance was also strongly suggested. There were also recommendations for including more critical feedback, such as highlighting to the user that their combination of choices was not optimal, identifying common prior conceptions, or providing suggestions for improvement based on best practice.

6 Conclusion

Overall users were satisfied with the tool, as the data show, and were positive about using it in designing assessment during the project. The fact that respondents predominantly focused on discussing enhancements and how the tool might evolve, rather than correcting or criticising its shortcomings, is a strong indication that the tool was well received. The survey results also suggest that the tool has achieved the purpose it was designed for. Furthermore, as sustainability of the project deliverables (to which the tool belongs) is a major concern of the participants, the suggestion the tool could be relevant and useful for educators beyond the project and become part of the project's legacy is a very positive reflection of its value.

In addition to the educational and design consideration discussed above all of the recommended changes would require a fundamental redesign of the underlying algorithm of the tool. Additionally, the software used to develop the tool was not designed to handle this order of complexity, so migrating to a different development environment such as JavaScript might be required. As such, a complete redevelopment might be the only way to incorporate design recommendations, the feasibility of which would have to be carefully evaluated.

References

1. E-QUAL Enhancing Quality, A.a.G.o.U.E.i.I. (2017). http://www.projectequal.net/equal/index.php
2. Webb, M.E., Gibson, D., Forkosh-Baruch, A.: Challenges for information technology supporting educational assessment. J. Comput. Assist. Learn. **29**(5), 451–462 (2013)
3. Assessment Reform Group, A. Assessment for Learning: 10 Principles (2002)
4. Butler, R.: Enhancing and undermining intrinsic motivation; the effects of task-involving and ego-involving evaluation on interest and performance. Br. J. Educ. Psychol. **58**, 1–14 (1988)
5. Black, P., et al.: Assessment for Learning: Putting it into Practice. Open University, Buckingham (2003)
6. Webb, M.E.: Beginning teacher education and collaborative formative e-assessment. Assess. Eval. High. Educ. **35**(5), 597–618 (2010)
7. Black, P.: Formative assessment – an optimistic but incomplete vision. Assess. Educ.: Princ. Policy Pract. **22**(1), 161–177 (2015)
8. Li, H., et al.: Peer assessment in the digital age: a meta-analysis comparing peer and teacher ratings. Assess. Eval. High. Educ. **41**(2), 245–264 (2016)
9. Yeh, S.S.: Understanding and addressing the achievement gap through individualized instruction and formative assessment. Assess. Educ.: Princ. Policy Pract. **17**(2), 169–182 (2010)
10. Clarke, J., Dede, C.: Assessment, technology, and change. J. Res. Teach. Educ. **42**(3), 309–328 (2010)
11. Gibson, D., Aldrich, C., Prensky, M.: Games and Simulations in Online Learning: Research and Development Frameworks. Information Science Publishing, Hershey (2007)
12. Ridgway, J., McCusker, S., Pead, D.: Literature Review of E-assessment. Futurelab (2004)
13. Hatzipanagos, S., Warburton, S.: Feedback as dialogue: exploring the links between formative assessment and social software in distance learning. Learn. Media Technol. **34**(1), 45–59 (2009)

14. Guri-Rosenblit, S.: 'Distance education'and 'e-learning': not the same thing. High. Educ. **49** (4), 467–493 (2005)
15. Bloom, B.S., et al.: Taxonomy of Educational Objectives, the Classification of Educational Goals - Handbook I: Cognitive Domain. McKay, New York (1956)
16. Anderson, L.W., Krathwohl, D.R., Bloom, B.S.: A Taxonomy for Learning, Teaching, and Assessing: A Revision of Bloom's Taxonomy of Educational Objectives. Longman, Harlow (2001)
17. Anderson, L.W.: Objectives, evaluation, and the improvement of education. Stud. Educ. Eval. **31**(2–3), 102–113 (2005)
18. Wenger, E.: Communities of Practice: Learning, Meaning, and Identity. Cambridge University Press, New York (1998)
19. Bell, A., Morris, G.: Engaging professional learning in online environments. Australas. J. Educ. Technol. **25**(5), 700–713 (2009)
20. Lave, J., Wenger, E.: Situated Learning: Legitimate Peripheral Participation. Cambridge University Press, Cambridge (1991)

Augmented Reality as a Tool for Authentic Learning of Clinical Skills in Early Years of Medical Training

Arkendu Sen[1(✉)], Calvin L. K. Chuen[1], Shiang Harn Liew[1], and Aye Chan Zay Hta[2]

[1] Jeffrey Cheah School of Medicine and Health Sciences, Monash University Malaysia, 47500 Bandar Sunway, Selangor, Malaysia
{arkendu.sen, liew.shiangharn}@monash.edu, ckleo8@student.monash.edu
[2] Department of Computing and Information Systems, Faculty of Science and Technology, Sunway University, Bandar Sunway, Selangor, Malaysia
aye.z@imail.sunway.edu.my

Abstract. To ensure adequate skill competencies, many medical schools with large student cohorts have introduced clinical skills practice in the early years. However, the range of clinical signs that can be simulated on a standardised patient (SP) – an actor, is limited while physical elicitation of clinical signs on authentic patients by numerous novice students or on themselves as peers, may be discomforting or unsafe. Augmented Reality (AR) has the affordance of incorporating the virtual to a real life clinical space unlike a fully virtual environment (virtual reality). AR of real-life clinical signs can allow simultaneous authentic learning and multiple clinical skills practice and addresses the concerns of discomfort of clinical skills practices of actual patients by novice medical students. A literature review on current instances of AR technology to aid authentic learning of clinical skills is discussed in light of these affordances. Alongside, our pilot work on developing an AR application - Clinical Augmented Reality Objects in Physical Examination (CAROPE), for the simulation of gastrointestinal signs is illustrated briefly. CAROPE has shown that mobile learning through AR of authentic clinical signs superimposed on specific areas of the body is achievable and accessible with current technology and has the potential in enhancing learning and facilitating clinical skills practice.

Keywords: Augmented reality · Early years · Medical education
Clinical skills · Authentic learning

1 Introduction

Traditionally, the early years of a medical school consist of building foundations in the basic medical sciences. With the evident benefits of early introduction of clinical skills to bridge the transition from theory to practice, many medical schools have since incorporated clinical skills training within the pre-clinical curriculum [1–3].

A. Tatnall and M. Webb (Eds.): WCCE 2017, IFIP AICT 515, pp. 231–242, 2017.
https://doi.org/10.1007/978-3-319-74310-3_25

Clinical skills taught in these early years classically consisted of basic generic clinical skills such as, rapport building in a doctor-patient relationship, history taking, counselling and physical examination [4]. Training sessions are conducted using standardised patients (SP) simulating a disease to create a safe learning environment for the students to practice on. An SP is a normal person, usually an actor, trained to act as a patient in a clinical skills session. In the case where a paid actor is not used, peers practice usually on each other and effectively act as SPs for one another.

In the scope of physical examination, there are limitations as to the variety of signs an SP can simulate. Maintenance of a bank of SPs with stable physical findings is time-consuming and costly [5, 6]. This requires previous identification and monitoring of SPs with similar physical findings [4]. In preference to experiencing the 'real thing', some students suggest incorporating videos or computer simulation into teaching [1].

Simulation-based learning with computer simulations and physical model is innovative but removes the patient-doctor human interaction element, resulting in little to no empathy skills training, which is crucial for the doctor-patient relationship.

Real patients, on the other hand, present several issues. The demand for these patients as subjects for physical examinations has far exceeded supply for even undergraduate clinical placements let alone pre-clinical students for real patient encounters [7] especially in countries like Malaysia with over 40 medical schools. Time constraints prevent optimal learning in the clinical setting [2, 4]; patient priorities take precedence where quality of teaching is inconsistent. Patients are often too sick and with acute conditions, at times with multiple problems causing distraction or distorted results during examination. Having yet developed professional empathetic attitudes towards these signs of interest, patients are at risk of feeling undignified as a novice's learning aid [8]; these patients may become conflicted and refuse their requests to learn.

Augmented reality (AR) holds promise in countering these limitations by augmenting clinical findings onto an SP or physical model in our shared space. AR technology, "A system that supplements the real world with virtual (computer-generated) objects that appear to coexist in the same space as the real world" has been an advent for industries for years and now made popular to the mainstream audience with the game Pokémon GO™. Recent advances enabled AR technology to be readily accessible on applications on smartphones and tablet devices via various AR software-development kits (SDK) such as Vuforia, Layar and ARtoolkit - many of which are open source and free-to-use.

This paper contributes to the current implementation of AR in teaching clinical skills at the early years (pre-clinically) of the medical curriculum by discussing a review of literature on AR technologies that have been developed for clinical skills education and their associated problems. The major contribution of this paper is to highlight a pilot project developed by the present authors to aid authentic learning of clinical skills in early years of medical education by simulating the clinical environment and how this review of literature has informed and guided this novel AR application development.

2 Methods

A literature survey was conducted to ascertain the current use of AR in the delivery of clinical skills education, their methods and associated challenges.

A search on databases DBLP, OvidMedline, CINAHL plus, Embase, Scopus, Web of Science, Google Scholar and ResearchGate were performed using the search terms ‘augmented reality’ OR ‘AR’ AND ‘clinical skills’ OR ‘physical examination’ OR ‘competencies’. Exclusion criteria included studies with projects beyond the early year curricula as the focus of the present paper was towards clinical skills training for pre-clinical students.

A detailed table of the review matrix has been included as an Appendix (Table 1).

3 Results

3.1 AR in Clinical Skills Education

Augmenting Sounds in Physical Examination. Early works by Mckenzie et al. [9] in 2004 demonstrated pre-recorded pathological heart and lung sounds that play through headphones when a stethoscope is placed over designated areas of auscultation on a mannequin, tracked by a sensor.

In a later work, pre-recorded fine crackles and real breath sounds were combined and played out through a modified electric-stethoscope [10]. To play the sounds over specified locations on chest auscultation, the SP cooperates to signal the correct timing of respiration clicking the controller when the student auscultates over that location.

Similar to the previous study, another study devised an innovative method of tracking where the stethoscope is placed, based on ECG signals to play augmented heart murmur sounds on the SPs correctly [11].

AR Mobile Learning. With readily available resources, AR developer kits and mobile devices, designing an AR application has become easily accessible and cost-effective for educators. In one project, Layar, as an AR developer platform, was utilized to develop a mobile AR heart murmur simulator for the Android system [12]. A shirt with imprinted AR tracking markers was worn and scanned to play heart murmurs through an electronic stethoscope and display visualization of the audio data in AR on the device.

Another project also opted for Layar, as their AR platform for its cost, support, simplicity and availability [13]. A range of equipment was tagged so students could scan the tags using their smartphones or tablet computers, pressing ‘buttons’ in AR that linked to various multimedia resources about the equipment for the students to explore.

Enhancing Engagement with a Mixed-Reality Environment. AR can be integrated into clinical simulations with existing physical models or modified ones to create a more immersive environment.

In one study [14], an AR headset, Google Glass, was used to incorporate video into a clinical simulation of acute asthma exacerbation for training of pre-licensure nursing students [14]. The video, pre-recorded with an SP, is played in their field of vision while they performed clinical skills onto a mannequin. Realism is markedly enhanced in creating an authentic environment for the students, increasing engagement with the mannequin as a patient, thus motivating problem-solving skills.

For an AR clinical simulation, Daher designed a unique interactive Physical-Virtual Head that is interactive to touch [15]. For visual effects, it uses projection of imagery onto the shell of a human head shape. Infrared cameras and lights track fingers that touch the shell and send graphic changes to the imagery projected. This creates a mixed-reality environment of a visually augmented patient within a shared physical space.

Incorporating AR Feedback. In a case study of the efficacy of real-time feedback [16], the study presents a novel pedagogy of clinical breast examination on a mannequin in AR. A video was streamed from a webcam input of the user's hands upon the augmented physical breast model, transformed into a virtual human. The virtual human was able to speak with pre-recorded human speech and was interactive to the learner's touch based on sensor data. Real-time feedback is visualized in AR with construction of touch maps of the pressure and coverage of the learner's palpation. A pattern-of-search map indicates the sequence of palpation during the examination.

Gap in Literature. The previous discussion highlights that though various specific AR applications for a particular skills training in one area (e.g. heart murmur or breast examination) exist, there is a need for one that acts as a common AR tool to aid clinical skills learning in all systems and which can simulate all the various signs on a SP or a patient superimposed on the exact location where such signs are manifested. Traditionally this is what early year preclinical students are taught, (in contrast to specialist training in clinical years) and for which the above AR application, as discussed may be applicable.

3.2 Clinical Augmented Reality Objects in Physical Examination (CAROPE)

This review of literature has led to incorporating some of the design process of AR applications to develop a clinical skills aid for clinical skills education in training early years' medical education.

The present authors have developed a pilot AR project, called Clinical Augmented Reality Objects in Physical Examination (CAROPE) that augments actual images of clinical signs superimposed on the skin. A simple design of readily available resources to demonstrate how physical signs can be presented visually with AR has been used.

Based on a standard clinical examination textbook [17], CAROPE began as a repository of signs associated with the gastrointestinal (GI) system. The GI system was chosen as a pilot due to its great variety of clinical signs encompassing various regions of the human body. One of the authors, a medical graduate familiar with the curriculum of the same university, selected the applicable signs.

The images of clinical signs available were collected from pictures available for non-commercial use from Open Educational Resources (OER) under Creative Commons licenses. Using photo-editing techniques for the present CAROPE development, these photos were enhanced and the transparency of the images was set. Following this, a 3D editing program was used to create 3D objects, applying these images as an overlay.

An AR application was elected based upon its simplicity and ease of use. Utilizing a common AR applications' image recognition technology, photographic image markers were used to launch the 3D objects within a mobile phone that were previously tagged. Once the marker is identified, the object appears on the screen of the mobile phone once the AR application is launched.

These markers are printed on stickers and adhered onto designated areas of the body to display these signs when scanned. Some are printed with information as to where and how it should be placed in relation to landmarks such as the umbilicus (belly button). For example, when the skin surrounding the umbilicus is augmented to display a bruise over it, the student can now describe it in detail during 'Inspection' and would be expected to perform 'Palpation' with care (Fig. 1).

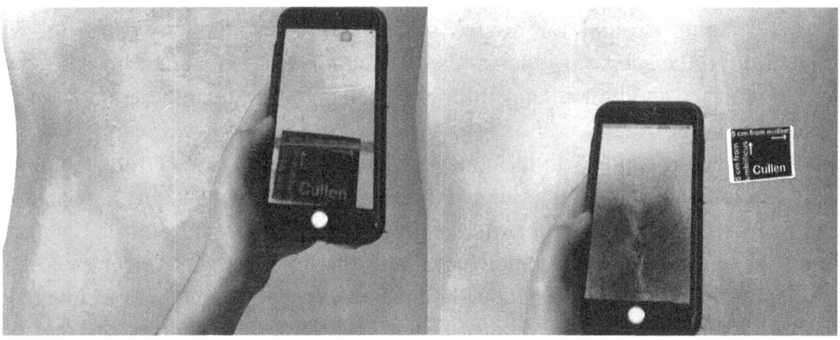

Fig. 1. Using CAROPE: Left: marker/trigger (black box) is scanned (red line). Right: Cullen's sign appears as an AR visual overlay on abdomen of a mannequin. (Color figure online)

To add a visual guide to 'Palpation' of the abdomen, the AR application is utilised to create a 'magic lens', similar to Blum et al.'s concept of a 'magic mirror' [18]. This serves to indicate to the user the precise location of underlying organ visually when the hand of the user is placed over it (Fig. 2). The mobile device camera acts as a 'magic lens'.

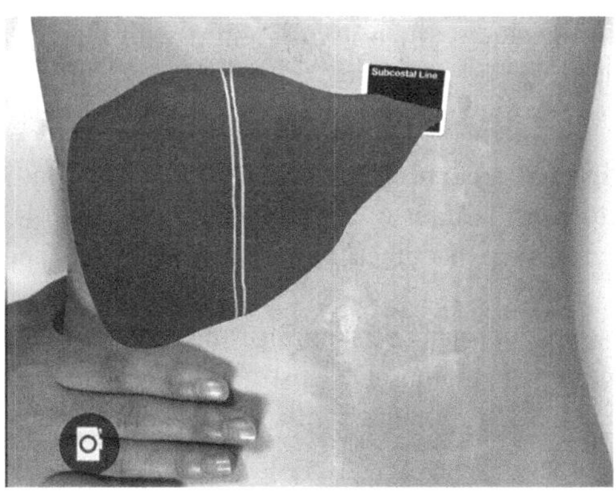

Fig. 2. A screenshot of the mobile device illustrating the magic lens concept to guide palpation of the liver on a mannequin

For its position to be precise, the coordinates and size of the 3D object are adjusted to match true-to-life measurements and proportions. Akin to body painting, the authors hope that this can facilitate mental visualisation of positions and locations of the underlying organs of the different regions of the abdomen.

4 Discussion

Blending of Realities. AR has been well documented for its application in medical education [19]. Its ability to blend the real and virtual could, especially for basic clinical skills, bridge the gap we see here between pre-clinical and clinical years by providing a training ground for novice students. As described by Vaughn, with a simple addition to the scenario - the sights and sounds of a real patient in AR, students felt more 'connected' with the mannequin [14]. This breaks down the boundaries of the disbelief simulations usually come with.

Students are motivated to think and learn actively in an AR setting. Unlike conventional teaching with the unanimated mannequins, students using AR can build interpersonal and communication skills as they learn empathy through the augmented encounters. By integrating augmented signs into the practice of physical examination, students can anticipate pathology they should be aware of and be able to identify and describe them accordingly. This contrasts with the current pedagogy of rote memorization within the pre-clinical years.

Supplementing Current Methods of Clinical Skills Training. On top of the benefit of peer physical examination in which students become more interested when the hands-on skill requires personal involvement, this can be further enhanced in AR as students can experience being their own learning subjects (SPs) by simulating signs onto each other.

In AR applications, such as in CAROPE, signs can be simulated without the need of disrobing and this can aid in the examination of sensitive areas such like the groin and genitals. However, it is true that discomfort may still exist for some students even when fully clothed. In the study which used a t-shirt with markers, the study reported that students felt quite exposed and uneasy wearing the shirt and being scanned by others [12].

Encouraging Self-directed Learning. As described in two studies, mobile learning enables the students to learn at their own convenience. It could be a form of distance education where the resource becomes more accessible and applicable in different contexts.

In Peyton's four-step approach of learning, medical curriculum concentrates on first two steps, 'Demonstration' and 'Deconstruction' of a skill by the clinical skills instructor [4]. By facilitating practice with AR, learners could find it easier to proceed to the next step of 'Comprehension' and followed by 'Performance'. Real-time feedback in the form of interactivity and live mapping of performance can be greatly enhanced with AR technology, resulting in improvement of the learner's performance comparable to an experienced clinician and the ability to perform independently [16].

Easily Accessible Resources. Like two studies, we found that integrating our educational content with AR technologies was a low-cost innovation due to the numerous available resources and the students' ability to navigate new technology easily. Students entering medical school presently have had experience using the Internet for both learning and social activity; these millennials have possessed advanced fluency in technology for most of their lives. Little training would be required for them to integrate most new applications of technology in their education.

In our project, we applied this into a readily-made AR platform - the application was designed for businesses and creatives to present 3D models in the real space with no pre-knowledge in programming. However, in order to effectively supplement live demonstration during classes, some training is necessary for clinical skills instructors [13] for its full integration.

Technical Limitations. Technical difficulties are a recurring theme in the application of AR technology. Frequently, scanning problems, Internet connectivity and compatibility are cited to be among the most common issues [13]. As for headsets, unfamiliarity with the device, short battery life and limited number of devices become limiting factors of their use [14].

When mobile learning is used, the learner is unable to use both hands to perform examination when holding a device to view the augmented form. When the mobile phone becomes the interface for AR, it lacks the immersive quality of an AR headset. In CAROPE, students need to close a displayed sign and scan again for the next marker. Mobile phone AR applications may be more accessible for the masses but may not provide the seamlessness required for realistic blending of realities.

As for our current work, the visualization of the sign is difficult to be seamlessly tracked when markers move or change in appearance. In our development of CAROPE, development of the project required experience in 3D modelling and photo editing software. As the objects are set in a definite size and position, not every augmented sign is accurately displayed for every body shape, size and skin appearance without adjustment within the application.

Further Works. It is suggested that with expansion to other clinical signs, the AR system could become an integral part of clinical skills education [10]. Further research is recommended to determine how AR can enhance simulation-based learning [14].

AR's potential in realistically augmenting SPs in clinical examinations needs to be evaluated [12]. To determine its true integration into the curriculum, measurement of independent usage by the students based on traffic of the application is possible.

In comparison to a fully virtual environment, it is argued that a mixed-reality interaction is important for an appreciable transfer of training with regards to patient interaction [9]. Further works are needed to compare augmented and virtual reality and each of their applicability to clinical skills pedagogy.

Limitations of Current Studies. Most studies are limited by small sample studies as AR has not been integrated in full-scale but is still under development.

5 Conclusion

Many medical schools have incorporated clinical skills in the early years of medical curriculum. With a limited range of clinical signs simulated by SPs and issues with real patients, AR can helpful in assisting the learning of clinical skills. Our literature review has reiterated how AR holds potential in creating a mixed-reality environment conducive for active learning [20] with a few studies that utilised AR in clinical examinations per se. To fill this gap, the authors have introduced CAROPE, a simple AR application easily accessible for use through current available resources, to aid clinical skills pedagogy by visualising signs and guidance to palpation.

With AR, CAROPE, especially through recreating some of the skin manifestations of clinical signs, can potentially be a helpful companion for preclinical curricula, rather than as a specialist training. This AR, unlike that in a fully virtual reality setting, simultaneously, along with clinical examination, engages leaners in a shared space allowing development of communication skills through human interaction to simulate an authentic clinical environment as happens in a clinical/hospital setting. Further work is necessary in its development and the evaluation of its role in clinical skills education.

Appendix

See Table 1.

Table 1. Studies of application of augmented reality technologies in clinical skills education

Paper, type of study and source	Design of the application	Method	Outcomes	Evaluation	Results	Recommendations	Sample
[9] Qualitative Scopus	Designed prototype to play augmented heart and lung sounds through headphones according to location of auscultation on mannequin	Prototype with mannequin as Augmented SP fitted with electromagnetic field generator and movable sensor connected to stethoscope head 3SPACE FASTRAK from POLHEMUS as tracker and tracked API from VRCO as the PC interface to obtain real time 6DoF updates of position)	–	Initial proof-of-concept evaluation by an EVMS doctor experienced in SPs and the training of auscultation	Positive	With refinement and expand fields of interest with abnormalities, system could become a useful and integral part of auscultation education	–
[10] Qualitative Ovid	Designed prototype to play lung sounds with pre-recorded fine crackles through a modified electronic-stethoscope	An electronic-stethoscope was modified to connect to the computer wirelessly. SP signaled timing of inspiration with wireless remote controller under exam suit	–	OSCE case for fourth year medical students	–	With refinement and expand fields of interest with abnormalities, system could become a useful and integral part of auscultation education	–
[11] Quantitative Scopus	Described a novel tracking method of placing symptoms at correctly identified auscultation areas based on recorded ECG signals to improve AR simulation	Pre-processing ECG signals, extracting and identifying relevant features with various algorithms to accurately distinguish four areas of heart auscultation	Accuracy of tracking	Five different classifiers, naive Bayes, Bayes network, k-nearest neighbor, multilayer perceptron and C4.5 decision tree were used for tracking assessment	Positive, accuracy of 95.1% and 87.1% on two different SPs	Improvement with real-time applications utilizing sequential beat classification leveraging intermittent movement of stethoscope. Need for Larger pilot study with diverse SPs recommended	2 male SPs

(continued)

Table 1. (*continued*)

Paper, type of study and source	Design of the application	Method	Outcomes	Evaluation	Results	Recommendations	Sample
[12] Mixed-methods Research Gate	A wearable clothing system to produce heart murmur simulation via mobile AR application scanning markers on the cloth	Layar AR system was used Android and Samsung tablets compatibility. The audio was played through an electronic stethoscope A visual annotation aid of the audio data was displayed on the device	Comparison with and without annotated AR visual aid, personal user experience on how easy to use	Survey	AR visual aid was preferred when murmur track was played. The AR system was found to be natural and easy to use. Stability of AR tracking was affected by Internet connection	Improvement by including different murmurs scenarios and suitability to be tested in medical examination. More extensive evaluation studies to measure educational outcomes in the AR system were required	15 medical students
[13] Mixed-methods DBLP	Presented an AR application on their smartphones or tablet devices with a range of multimedia resources about an equipment or skill for the students to explore	Layar AR system was used to build the application. The students scanned the marker-tagged equipment or skill and 'calls to action' buttons appear in AR to link to resources related to the clinical simulation scenario	User's personal perceptual experiences and derive meaning	Online evaluation questionnaire on Likert scale questions and open-ended questions, focus group session; analysis by NVivo 10 software	Marginally positive - comfortable with using technology quickly. Rated poorly int technical issues, scanning difficulty, device incompatibility and instructors not adept at integrating its use into teaching	Potential in geographically situated AR to support m-learning. Required continued development. Highly cost-effective for implementation within most schools	Surgical course (120 nursing students, 40 medical students, 5 instructors)
[14] Mixed-methods EMBASE	Designed a hybrid simulation to project a video into the students' field of vision during a simulation lab scenario	AR headset, Google Glass projected an acute asthma exacerbation scenario video previously recorded with an SP and streamed via YouTube	Performance, students' beliefs related to self-confidence and scenario design	Certified Healthcare Simulation Experts evaluate students' skills during simulation, Simulation Design Scale (SDS), Self-Confidence in Learning Scale (SCLS), open-ended questions	Positive. Adds to realism. Did not report performance scores	AR holds promise and enhances learning by improving realism and educational impact. When they practice, they learn more. Plans to expand case scenarios, adopt 3D imagery into the real environment	2 nursing program

(*continued*)

Table 1. *(continued)*

Paper, type of study and source	Design of the application	Method	Outcomes	Evaluation	Results	Recommendations	Sample
[15] Mixed-methods Scopus	Created a Physical-Virtual Patient (PVP) simulator that was interactive to touch and other body parameters	PVP was a semi-transparent shell with variable imagery projected onto its underside. Infrared cameras and infrared lights tracked fingers touch and sent cues to determine appropriate response verbally and non-verbally	Comparison between AR spatially and optically, its effect on user experience, its limitations, comparison to current simulators	–	–	Currently fine tuning experiments to measure outcomes	Nursing students
[16] Quantitative Web of Science	Incorporated real-time feedback of user performance in clinical breast examination in a mixed-reality environment	A webcam was streamed as a video of the user's hands upon the physical breast model, augmented into a virtual human. The virtual human articulated with pre-recorded human speech with a full range of facial expressions and gestures and was interactive to the learner's touch with sensor data. The performance of the learner was visualized in the video in real time as a touch map of pressure, coverage and pattern-of-search (sequence of palpation)	Study 1: Performance in students receiving compared to those not receiving feedback. Study 2: real time feedback in a mixed-reality environment reflects performance in the real world	Study 1: Coverage and percentage of breast palpated at correct pressure Study 2: Coverage and palpation pressure were rated using a structured checklist by a group of seven medical educators reviewing video of the performance	Positive	Significant educational benefit to performance of cognitive and psychomotor tasks. Further development on other physical examinations that involve palpation	Study medical students, interns and experienced doctors

References

1. Lam, T.P., Irwin, M., Chow, L.W., Chan, P.: Early introduction of clinical skills teaching in a medical curriculum–factors affecting students' learning. Med. Educ. **36**, 233–240 (2002)
2. Shuid, A.N., Yaman, M.N., Abd Kadir, R.A., Hussain, R.I., Othman, S.N., Nawi, A.M., Ugusman, A., Daud, F., Manap, R.A., Mohamed, I.N.: Effect of early clinical skills teaching on 3rd year medical students' learning: the student perspective. J. Taibah Univ. Med. Sci. **10**, 26–32 (2015)
3. Chinnah, T.I., de Bere, S.R., Collett, T.: Students' views on the impact of peer physical examination and palpation as a pedagogic tool for teaching and learning living human anatomy. Med. Teach. **33**, e27–e36 (2011)
4. Dhaliwal, U., Supe, A., Gupta, P., Singh, T.: Producing competent doctors - the art and science of teaching clinical skills. Indian Pediatr. **54**, 403–409 (2017)
5. Adamo, G.: Simulated and standardized patients in OSCEs: achievements and challenges 1992–2003. Med. Teach. **25**, 262–270 (2003)
6. Barman, A.: Critiques on the objective structured clinical examination. Ann. Acad. Med. Singap. **34**, 478–482 (2005)
7. Secomb, J.: A systematic review of peer teaching and learning in clinical education. J. Clin. Nurs. **17**, 703–716 (2008)
8. Barrows, H.S.: An overview of the uses of standardized patients for teaching and evaluating clinical skills. AAMC Acad. Med. **68**, 443–451 (1993). Discussion 451–443
9. McKenzie, F.D., Garcia, H.M., Castelino, R.J., Hubbard, T.W., Ullian, J.A., Gliva, G.A., Thomas, T.A., Skills, P.: Augmented standardized patients now virtually a reality, pp. 1–2 (2004)
10. Sun, B., McKenzie, F.D., Garcia, H.M., Hubbard, T.W., Ullian, J.A., Gliva, G.A.: Medical student evaluation using augmented standardized patients: new development and results. Stud. Health Technol. Inform. **125**, 454–456 (2007)
11. Kidane, N., Chemlal, S., Li, J., McKenzie, F.D., Hubbard, T.: Orientation invariant ECG-based stethoscope tracking for heart auscultation training on augmented standardized patients. Simul.: Trans. Soc. Model. Simul. Int. **89**(12), 1450–1458 (2013)
12. See, Z.S., Rengganaten, V., Billinghurst, M., Soo, S.: Mobile audible AR experience for medical learning murmurs simulation. In: SIGGRAPH ASIA 2016 Mobile Graphics and Interactive Applications on - SA 2016, p. 1 (2016)
13. Garrett, B., Jackson, C., Wilson, B.: Augmented reality m-learning to enhance nursing skills acquisition in the clinical skills laboratory. Interact. Technol. Smart Educ. **12**, 298–314 (2015)
14. Vaughn, J., Lister, M., Shaw, R.J.: Piloting augmented reality technology to enhance realism in clinical simulation. CIN: Comput. Inform. Nurs. **34**, 402–405 (2016)
15. Daher, S.: Optical see-through vs. spatial augmented reality simulators for medical applications. In: Proceedings - IEEE Virtual Reality, pp. 417–418 (2017)
16. Kotranza, A., Lind, D.S., Lok, B.: Real-time evaluation and visualization of learner performance in a mixed-reality environment for clinical breast examination. IEEE Trans. Visual Comput. Graph. **18**, 1101–1114 (2012)
17. Talley, N., O'Connor, S.: Clinical Examination. Elsevier, Chatswood (2015)
18. Blum, T., Kleeberger, V., Bichlmeier, C., Navab, N.: mirracle: an augmented reality magic mirror system for anatomy education. In: 2012 IEEE Virtual Reality, pp. 115–116. IEEE Computer Society, IEEE Xplore (2012)
19. Kamphuis, C., Barsom, E., Schijven, M., Christoph, N.: Augmented reality in medical education? Perspect. Med. Educ. **3**, 300–311 (2014)
20. Sen, A., Calvin, L.K.C., Aye, C.Z.H.: Towards smart learning environments: affordances and design architecture of augmented reality (AR) applications in medical education. In: Somani, A.K., et al. (eds.) Proceedings of 1st International Conference on SSIC 2017. Smart Innovation, Systems and Technologies, vol. 79, pp. 1–19. Springer Nature, Singapore (2018). https://doi.org/10.1007/978-981-10-5828-8

Evaluating Acceptance of a Haptic Learning Resource from Various Perspectives

Soonja Yeom[1(✉)], Andrew Fluck[2], and Arthur Sale[1]

[1] School of Engineering and ICT, University of Tasmania, Hobart, Australia
{Soonja.Yeom,Arthur.Sale}@utas.edu.au
[2] Faculty of Education, University of Tasmania, Launceston, Australia
Andrew.Fluck@utas.edu.au

Abstract. The Technology Acceptance Model (TAM) was the basis of this study to investigate students' acceptance of a haptic learning resource in anatomy education. Based on the two main elements, *perceived ease of use* and *perceived usefulness* of TAM, this study used additional elements such as gender, prior experiences with similar resources, learning preference modes, and enrolled undergraduate courses to investigate students' learning achievement and acceptance. No significant differences were found between genders or enrolled courses in the acceptance of the system in terms of 'ease of use' and 'usefulness' of the system. Students with previous experience with 3D were more favourable to a haptic device, this was statistically significant (p = .025) for "would use" and they also scored higher on the associated quiz (p = .050, Mann-Whitney U test).

Keywords: Learning resource · Haptic interface · Anatomy learning
Phantom Omni

1 Introduction

Learning resources are important for students to learn efficiently. This is even more so when students have different backgrounds such as prior experiences and varied reactions to the acceptance of technology. Gender, previous experience with 3D or haptic, and/or individual's preferred learning style may matter in the selection of learning resources.

As technology develops, various new learning resources become available to use. One such new resource was developed to give haptic feedback from virtual organs in human anatomy classes [1]. This relatively new resource may help various learners within a resource intensive subject area with somewhat limited opportunities for access to real anatomical specimens [2, 3].

What are the important factors influencing student acceptance of a novel resource? For example, how a learner reacts may vary according to their gender, preferred learning style, or previous experience with a similar type of resource. Students of different genders may accept different models and media differently. Various areas of experiments including olfactory and video media [4], the effect of multisensory of visual and tactile modality [5], gender differences in learning style preferences among

A. Tatnall and M. Webb (Eds.): WCCE 2017, IFIP AICT 515, pp. 243–250, 2017.
https://doi.org/10.1007/978-3-319-74310-3_26

undergraduate physiology students [6] and many more are related to the gender difference. It is hypothesised that kinaesthetic learners will accept the haptic learning resource more.

Multimodal deep learning has improved effects when compared with unimodal [7]. In order to understand the preferred sensory modality of students for learning anatomy, consenting students were administrated a printed form of version 7.2 of the VARK questionnaire. The VARK instrument is only one of many to measure learning styles or preferences [8] and Rohrer and Pashler [9] have questioned the value of learning styles. However, opportunities to assess kinaesthetic learning in higher education are rare, when the main research question here is to measure the level of acceptance of the haptic device as a tool. Therefore, this study provided an opportunity to investigate applicability for this age range with a haptic device.

Haptic sensory learning resources for dental learning or surgical training have been used [10, 11] with 79% of students benefiting from the study as kinaesthetic learners. This led us to investigate if the haptic sensory learning resource will have a similar effect in anatomy learning, at least for kinaesthetic learners.

2 Preferences for Accepting a Haptic Learning Resource

2.1 How the Study was Performed

The design research paradigm was adopted to assess acceptance of the haptic-anatomy system. The system has evolved as the user tests were done in a cyclic manner. Three different user tests were set up in similar settings with three different student cohorts from 2012 to 2013.

The Technology Acceptance Model (TAM) [15] was the basis for the acceptance questionnaire. TAM posits that usage of technology is influenced by perceived usefulness and ease of use [2, 13, 14].

Later variant branches came out of the original technology acceptance model from Davis [15] to the theory of reasoned action (TRA) and theory of planned behaviour (TPB) with many extensions or modifications in the technology acceptance field. Haptic enabling technology and TAM is another branch of TRA/TPB focusing more with haptic technology [16].

Ease of use and usefulness are the two important factors used to measure if the users will accept the system in this study which is based on TAM. TAM used a few questions to collect the data. These two main elements are used to measure the acceptance of technology of users. Each element of acceptance was measured based on ease of use and usefulness; then the acceptance was analysed with respect to other variables such as gender, prior experience, personal preferred learning styles, and their enrolled courses.

The questions used in the acceptance assessment survey were re-worded slightly between tests. Nevertheless, the essential questions were the same. A few additional questions were included in the survey as the system evolved. For example, 'were you performing well with the system?', 'did you get mentally stressed while using the system?', 'did you get physically stressed while using the system?', 'Would you use this system as an aid to learning when it is fully developed?', and 'Was the quiz useful as a check on understanding?' However, the focus to discuss here is how the system was accepted, based on student gender, preferred learning style, and their prior experiences with any similar sort of interface. The main questions to measure the users' acceptance were: 'was it easy to use the system?'; 'was the system useful?'; and 'would you recommend the system to the university to adopt?'.

The haptic-anatomy system was developed with the Phantom Omni [1]. A force-feedback pen was gripped by the user, who saw anatomical organs on a screen to learn to identify human internal organs and associated medical nomenclature [1, 12]. When any part of each organ was held and moved around, the user felt different haptic feedback depending on the hardness and texture of the organ. The three development versions were tested by three different user groups.

The user groups were from three different cohorts with 89 participants including 58 males and 31 females with average age of 20 years old as the system developed further at each cycle according to the design research paradigm [17]. The courses that the users were enrolled in were mainly Bachelor of Medicine/Bachelor of Surgery (MBBS), Bachelor of Education (Health and Physical Education and Outdoor Education), Bachelor of Exercise Science, and Bachelor of Human Movement. Bachelor of Computing students participated in user test 1.The first user test was done with 2nd year students, but the other two user tests were done with 1st year students. Hence our assumption was made that no pre-knowledge was present.

This study was approved by the Social Science Human Research Ethics Committee (HREC) Tasmania Network (reference H001743).

2.2 Different Elements Considered: Gender, Prior Experiences, and Acceptance

Gender differences were reported in the fields of education including medical related disciplines [18, 19], but hardly found in anatomy learning. In the area of this study, gender differences were insignificant with respect to questions regarding acceptance, unlike those studies [18, 19] which combined 'useful' and 'easy to use' for this learning resource (Fig. 1).

Acceptance of the interface was measured from the factors of usefulness, ease of use, and recommendation, which is an additional information provision on top of the normal elements of TAM. This is confirming information of its usefulness if they recommend the system be embedded in their curriculum at the university. A repeated measure ANOVA showed that there was no significant difference by gender, $F(1, 5) = .365$, $p = .572$, following the Greenhouse-Geisser correction, Epsilon = .068. However, there was a significant difference of haptic interface acceptance, $F(2, 10) = 8.14$, $p = .008$, following the Greenhouse-Geisser correction, Epsilon = .619. The interaction between acceptance of haptic interface and users showed that there was a significant difference, $F(2, 10) = 6.54$, $p = .015$, following the Greenhouse-Geisser correction Epsilon = .567.

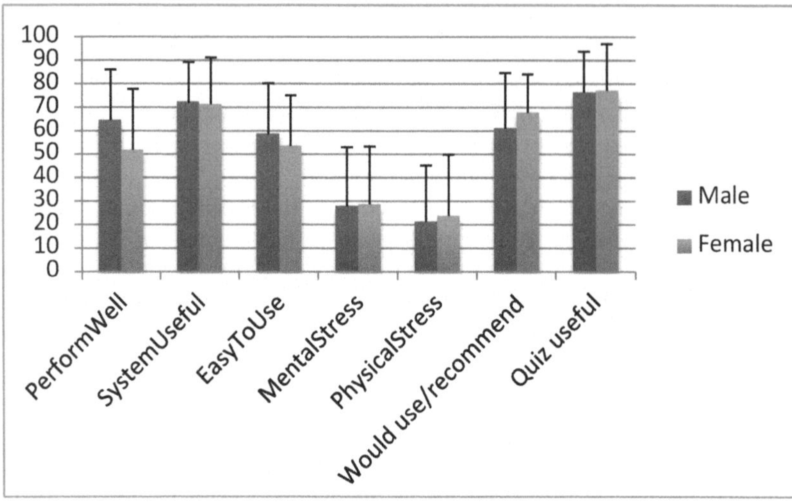

Fig. 1. Gender comparisons

2.3 Preferred Learning Style

A number of elements were used to find the factors for accepting a different type of learning resource. In order to find each individual's preferred learning style, the VARK (visual, aural, reading/writing, and kinaesthetic) learning style questionnaire version 7.2 was used [20, 21]. The analysis used the percentage of K element out of the four different learning styles, since the sample size was relatively small. However, the distribution of different learning styles was similar to the collected data on the VARK site.

Interpretation of the results was based on the four different learning styles and student acceptance of the haptic-anatomy system. Acceptance was calculated based on the responses from these survey items: (1) the system was useful, (2) the system was easy to use, and (3) I would recommend others to use it.

A repeated measure ANOVA showed that there was no significant difference (Fig. 2) among the mean of leaning styles, $F(3, 15) = 1.01$, $p = .414$ following the Greenhouse-Geisser correction, Epsilon = .169. Bonferroni-adjusted pairwise comparison demonstrated that the mean of acceptance related to the kinaesthetic learning style ($M = 64.44$, $SD = 6.13$) was significantly greater than the mean related to the visual learning style ($M = 55.28$, $SD = 8.83$). However, this result suggested that reading-learning style was not significantly different from kinaesthetic learning style, ($M = 63.61$, $SD = 4.1$). It also suggested that there was a significant difference between acceptance of students with kinaesthetic learning styles and those with auditory learning styles ($M = 70.83$, $SD = 3.10$).

A repeated measure ANOVA revealed that there was a significant difference between the means of acceptance of interface (usefulness, ease, and recommendation), $F(2, 10) = 20.88$, $p < .001$, following the Greenhouse-Geisser correction, Epsilon = .807. Bonferroni-adjusted pairwise comparison demonstrated that the mean of the

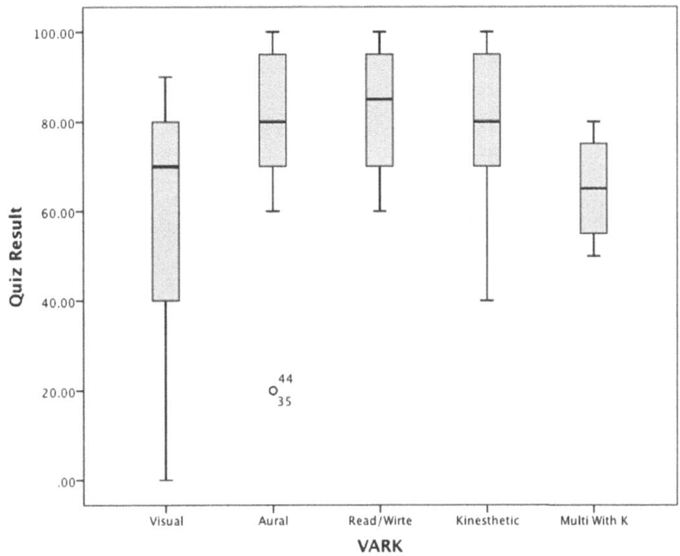

Fig. 2. Comparison of the quiz results from different groups of learning style

acceptance usefulness of interface (M = 75.88, SD = 2.60) was significantly greater than the ease of interface (M = 50, SD = 4.6), and recommendation of interface (M = 64.80, SD = 2.10).

2.4 Course Enrolled and Preference of Haptics

As users were enrolled in different courses (see Sect. 2.1), a question arose concerning their degrees. For example, Bachelor of Computing (BComp) students used the system more easily than others in different disciplines. User test 1 had 2nd year MBBS and BComp students, user test 2 had MBBS year 1, and user test 3 had MBBS year 1 and other health related courses such as health and physical education, etc. The analysis of variance showed significant main effects and no significant interaction after Greenhouse-Geisser adjustment to the degrees of course enrolled and the acceptance of haptic interface. There is a significant difference of the main effect of the acceptance of the haptic interface, $F(1, 18) = 20.49$, $p < .001$, following the Greenhouse-Geisser. A repeated measure ANOVA showed, however, that there was an insignificant difference among the mean of course enrolled, $F(2, 36) = 2.78$, $p = .075$, following the Greenhouse-Geisser. The interaction between current course enrolled and acceptance of haptic interface, showed that there was no significant difference, $F(2, 36) = .792$, $p = .461$.

The pattern of responses from three different user tests (Fig. 3) shows that the use of the system may have become harder as the versions advanced, but its usefulness was rated higher than the 'performed well' response. All of the three questions were rated higher by males than females with statistically insignificant differences in acceptance levels for all aspects.

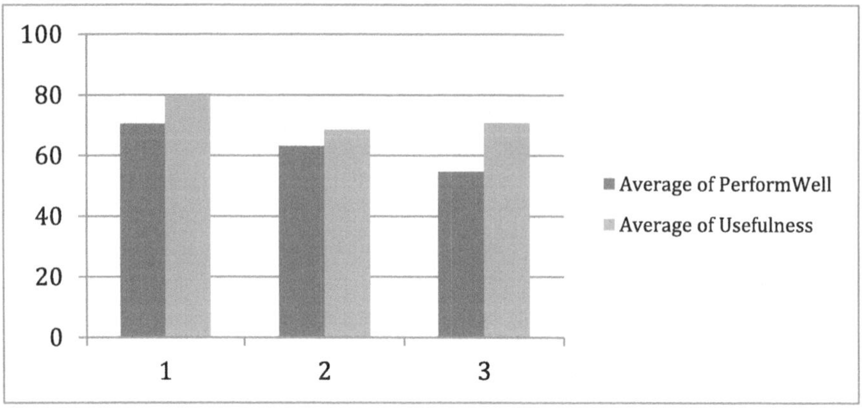

Fig. 3. Three user tests

2.5 Previous 3D Experience

Quite a number of students identified themselves as having prior experiences with 3D interfaces (n = 63) whereas very few users had used haptic interfaces before (n = 15). Users with prior experiences with 3D interfaces are more likely to assess the system positively (Fig. 4). The item, 'would you recommend' was significantly different as $p = 0.025$ from t-test between two groups with and without previous 3D interface experience. The post-activity quiz score was p = 0.050 with Mann-Whitney U test, showing another significant difference. Therefore, we could conclude previous experience with a 3D interface made users more likely to accept the haptic learning resource.

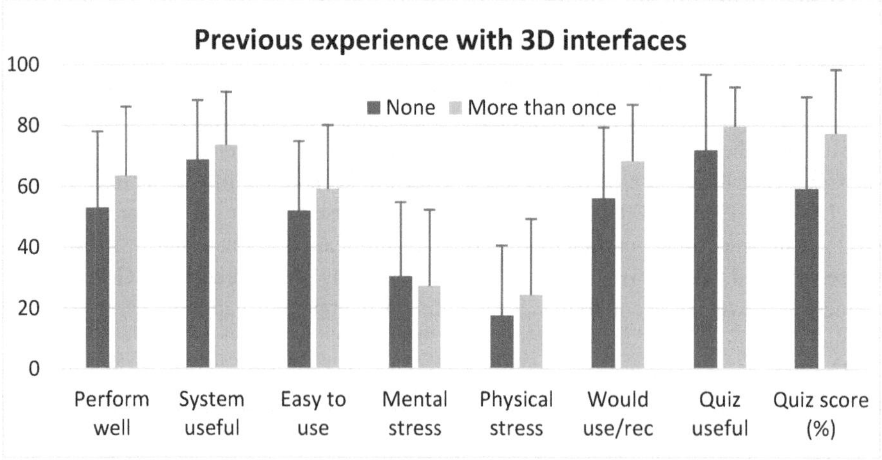

Fig. 4. Responses with/without prior 3D experiences

3 Conclusion and Future Direction

In such an important and difficult subject as anatomy, another type of resource will help students. The availability of different resources, including a haptic system, will assist students who are interested in learning differently.

No significant difference was found in different learning styles. This means, this system works for all different styles of learners, at the same time, it doesn't have any particular benefit to kinaesthetic learners.

However, the significant differences were found in 3D model users. They assessed the system as 'performed well'. Their quiz results were higher than for students without previous 3D experiences. When you have previous experiences with 3D systems, the more positive responses and the higher quiz results were found except the experienced ones found the system was more physically stressful. One thing we need to clarify was if the users were talking about the same level of 3D experiences. Most of them were talking about 3D images of games and other applications, unlike 3D models that can be manipulated as in the system here.

Gender differences were not found in this experiment, unlike most studies in the literature all. This could mean that the haptic system is gender neutral. However, the population for comparison was rather small (under 100 students).

In a future study, we hope to let students explore each anatomical object with their whole hand rather than just a single haptic touch point. This will be more natural for users, and will incorporate tactile (touch sensations) as well as force feedback. As the device develops rapidly, such new devices will add to the kinaesthetic learning experience of the haptic-anatomy system.

Acknowledgments. We thank the University of Tasmania for a Teaching Development Grant which enabled us to explore this new technology in class. Thanks also go to the teaching team and the students involved in the user tests.

References

1. Yeom, S., Choi-Lundberg, D., Fluck, A., Sale, A.: User acceptance of a haptic interface for learning anatomy. In: International Association for Development of the Information Society International conference on e-Learning (2013)
2. Chuttur, M.: Overview of the technology acceptance model: origins, developments and future directions. Sprouts Work. Pap. Inf. Syst. **9**(37), 9–37 (2009)
3. Craig, S., Tait, N., Boers, D., McAndrew, D.: Review of anatomy education in Australian and New Zealand medical schools. ANZ J. Surg. **80**(4), 212–216 (2010)
4. Murray, N., Qiao, Y., Lee, B., Muntean, G., Karunakar, A.: Age and gender influence on perceived olfactory and visual media synchronization. In: 2013 IEEE International Conference on Multimedia and Expo (ICME), pp. 1–6. IEEE (2013)
5. Alipour, M., Gorjian, B., Zafari, I.: The effects of songs on EFL learners' vocabulary recall and retention: the case of gender. Adv. Digit. Multimedia (ADMM) **1**(3), 140–143 (2012)
6. Padilla-Meléndez, A., Del Aguila-Obra, A., Garrido-Moreno, A.: Perceived playfulness, gender differences and technology acceptance model in a blended learning scenario. Comput. Educ. **63**, 306–317 (2013)

7. AlKhasawneh, E.: Using VARK to assess changes in learning preferences of nursing students at a public university in Jordan: implications for teaching. Nurse Educ. Today **33**(12), 1546–1549 (2013)
8. Coffield, F., Moseley, D., Hall, E., Ecclestone, K.: Learning Styles and Pedagogy in Post-16 Learning: A Systematic and Critical Review. Learning and Skills Research Centre, London (2004)
9. Rohrer, D., Pashler, H.: Learning styles: where's the evidence? Med. Educ. **46**, 634–635 (2012)
10. Esteban, G., Fernández, C., Conde, M.Á., García-Peñalvo, F.J.: Playing with SHULE: surgical haptic learning environment. In: Proceedings of the 2nd International Conference on Technological Ecosystems for Enhancing Multiculturality, pp. 247–253. ACM (2014)
11. Ullrich, S., Kuhlen, T.: Haptic palpation for medical simulation in virtual environments. IEEE Trans. Vis. Comput. Graph. **18**(4), 617–625 (2012)
12. Tercero, C.R., Najdovski, Z., Ikeda, S., Nahavandi, S., Fukuda, T.: Haptic feedback in endovascular tele-surgery simulation through vasculature phantom morphology changes. In: World Haptics Conference (WHC), pp. 359–364. IEEE (2013)
13. Marangunić, N., Granić, A.: Technology acceptance model: a literature review from 1986 to 2013. Univ. Access Inf. Soc. **14**, 81–95 (2015)
14. Zacharis, N.Z.: Predicting college students' acceptance of podcasting as a learning tool. Interact. Technol. Smart Educ. **9**(3), 171–183 (2012)
15. Davis, F.D., Bagozzi, R.P., Warshaw, P.R.: User acceptance of computer technology: a comparison of two theoretical models. Manage. Sci. **35**(8), 982–1003 (1989)
16. Oh, J., Yoon, S.-J.: Validation of haptic enabling technology acceptance model (HE-TAM): integration of IDT and TAM. Telematics Inf. **4**(31), 585–596 (2014)
17. Oh, E., Reeves, T.C.: The implications of the differences between design research and instructional systems design for educational technology researchers and practitioners. Educ. Media Int. **47**(4), 263–275 (2010)
18. Urval, R.P., Kamath, A., Ullal, S., Shenoy, A.K., Shenoy, N., Udupa, L.A.: Assessment of learning styles of undergraduate medical students using the VARK questionnaire and the influence of sex and academic performance. Adv. Physiol. Educ. **38**(3), 216–220 (2014)
19. Mohammadi, S., Mobarhan, M.G., Mohammadi, M., Ferns, G.A.: Age and gender as determinants of learning style among medical students (2015)
20. Fleming, N.D.: I'm different; not dumb. Modes of presentation (VARK) in the tertiary classroom. In: Research and Development in Higher Education, Proceedings of the 1995 Annual Conference of the Higher Education and Research Development Society of Australasia (HERDSA), HERDSA, pp. 308–313 (1995)
21. VARK Learn Limited. VARK: a guide to learning styles, and research and statistics (2016)

Modelling e-Learner Comprehension Within a Conversational Intelligent Tutoring System

Mike Holmes(✉), Annabel Latham, Keeley Crockett, and James D. O'Shea

Manchester Metropolitan University, Manchester, UK
m.holmes@mmu.ac.uk

Abstract. Conversational Intelligent Tutoring Systems (CITS) are agent based e-learning systems which deliver tutorial content through discussion, asking and answering questions, identifying gaps in knowledge and providing feedback in natural language. Personalisation and adaptation for CITS are current research focuses in the field. Classroom studies have shown that experienced human tutors automatically, through experience, estimate a learner's level of subject comprehension during interactions and modify lesson content, activities and pedagogy in response. This paper introduces Hendrix 2.0, a novel CITS capable of classifying e-learner comprehension in real-time from webcam images. Hendrix 2.0 integrates a novel image processing and machine learning algorithm, COMPASS, that rapidly detects a broad range of non-verbal behaviours, producing a time-series of comprehension estimates on a scale from −1.0 to +1.0. This paper reports an empirical study of comprehension classification accuracy, during which 51 students at Manchester Metropolitan University undertook conversational tutoring with Hendrix 2.0. The authors evaluate the accuracy of strong comprehension and strong non-comprehension classifications, during conversational questioning. The results show that the COMPASS comprehension classifier achieved normalised classification accuracy of 75%.

Keywords: Conversational Intelligent Tutoring Systems · Adaptive e-learning Comprehension assessment · Machine learning

1 Introduction

E-learning is changing the way in which students engage with learning materials. From video lectures to web-based content distribution and quizzes, the process of learning is shifting from human- to software-directed learning. Whilst much of the advancement in e-learning has focused on increasing the availability of information through digital technology, it has often neglected the important role that personalised tuition plays in supporting learning [1] and developing higher order skills.

Conversational Intelligent Tutoring Systems (CITS) [2] are a virtual assistant technology that place pedagogy at the heart of content delivery. CITS use natural language to discuss concepts with the learner, breaking down the tuition material into conversational interactions, asking and answering questions, identifying gaps in knowledge, and providing contextual feedback and corrective interventions. CITS have

A. Tatnall and M. Webb (Eds.): WCCE 2017, IFIP AICT 515, pp. 251–260, 2017.
https://doi.org/10.1007/978-3-319-74310-3_27

been shown to outperform self-directed learning and both digital and traditional book-based learning [3, 4]. To further improve the effectiveness of CITS tuition, research has turned to adaptive algorithms. Adaptive CITS personalise the learning experience for the student by, for example, changing content and pedagogy in response to learning style [5, 6] or emotional valence [7, 8].

Classroom studies [9–11] have shown that experienced human tutors can accurately estimate a learner's level of subject comprehension based on non-verbal behaviour. Non-verbal behaviour (NVB) is any non-verbalised communicative behaviour including gestures, facial expressions, facial actions, physiological, chemical and audible information. Cutting edge research [12] suggests it is possible to model comprehension automatically by computer analysis of non-verbal behaviour. Buckingham et al. [12] demonstrate that learner NVB can be used to model learner comprehension expressed during pre-recorded human to human interviews, conducted in a strictly controlled environment.

While the research [12, 13] indicates that learner comprehension levels could be used as a feedback mechanism for adaptation within a CITS, doing so in a live real-world environment presents a number of novel challenges:

1. Analysing live video in near real-time to track NVB in an uncontrolled environment (varying lighting, camera position),
2. Accurately modelling comprehension from NVB during conversation with a virtual tutor,
3. Producing accurate comprehension modelling without invasive body-attached sensors or prohibitively expensive specialised equipment.

In this paper the authors present an empirical study of comprehension classification integrated into a conversational intelligent tutoring system. The research aims to demonstrate that real-time classification of e-learner comprehension is a viable feedback mechanism for adaptation within a CITS. In a study conducted at Manchester Metropolitan University, 51 higher education students undertook a short course of tuition using a novel CITS, called Hendrix 2.0. Hendrix 2.0 has been designed to tutor computer programming at an undergraduate level. During the tutorial, Hendrix 2.0 automatically modelled learner comprehension in real-time using a novel machine learning based comprehension assessment and scoring system, now called COMPASS [14].

To evaluate the effectiveness of COMPASS real-time comprehension modelling within a CITS, the authors present classification accuracy results for binary 'strong comprehension' and 'strong non-comprehension' classifications. COMPASS achieved normalised classification accuracy of 75%. The results demonstrate that the comprehension modelling algorithm overcomes novel challenges, accurately modelling e-learner NVB during conversation with a virtual tutor, analysing NVB in near real-time in an uncontrolled classroom environment, and producing accurate comprehension classifications.

This paper is organised as follows: Sect. 2 presents an overview of related research and prior work on conversational intelligent tutoring systems (Sect. 2.1), interpretation of learner non-verbal behaviour (Sect. 2.2) and automatic comprehension classification (Sect. 2.3). Section 3 introduces Hendrix 2.0, a novel CITS, and describes the question-answer and comprehension classification processes. A study of COMPASS comprehension classification accuracy within Hendrix 2.0 is presented in Sect. 4, with results and discussion (Sect. 4.3). Section 5 presents the authors' conclusions and Sect. 6 presents the intended future work for this research project.

2 Related Work

2.1 Conversational Intelligent Tutoring Systems

Conversational Intelligent Tutoring Systems (CITS) [2] are a virtual assistant technology that place pedagogy at the heart of content delivery. CITS use natural language to discuss concepts with the learner, breaking down the tuition material into conversational interactions, asking and answering questions, identifying gaps in knowledge and providing contextual feedback and corrective interventions.

The Hendrix CITS [15] chats with a learner using written natural language, via a software interface. Hendrix is a goal-oriented conversational agent, designed to follow a scripted learning scaffold which is embedded within a graph of concepts. Hendrix is able to find connections between concepts in the graph and is then able to ask the learner questions, appraise the learner's knowledge and provide contextually relevant feedback. Hendrix asks the learner to demonstrate understanding by answering open questions. Hendrix can then appraise the correctness of the response by matching the learner's discursive response to a bank of pre-defined exemplar answer patterns. While Hendrix can interpret, match and search information in a sophisticated way, the pilot version of Hendrix is naïve to the learner.

The tutor's role in mediating the learning experience is personal, intimate, and uniquely crafted to the needs of the learner in question. Personalisation algorithms for CITS have become a focus of research in the field. Adaptive CITS use contextual personal information about the learner, their preferences, behaviour, emotions, or cognitive functions, to adapt the conversational tutorial content or system behaviour to meet the needs of the individual learner. Latham et al. [5, 6] demonstrated the effectiveness of adapting to learning style; others [7, 8, 16–18] have focused on the role of affect – or emotional valence – in mediating the tuition.

In this paper the authors introduce Hendrix 2.0, a novel CITS capable of modelling learner comprehension in real-time by observing learner non-verbal behaviour.

2.2 Interpreting the Non-verbal Behavior of Learners

Non-verbal behaviour (NVB) is any non-verbalised communicative behaviour, including movement, gesture, facial expression, sound, and chemical and physiological signals. Facial actions and expressions have been used to model learner emotional states such as boredom, confusion and frustration [7, 8, 18, 19].

Classroom studies [9–11] have shown that expert human tutors are able to recognise learner comprehension and non-comprehension states by observing the learner's non-verbal behaviour. By recognising and responding to comprehension indicative non-verbal behaviour, expert human tutors are able to prevent loss of motivation, feelings of hopelessness, frustration and boredom during complex learning, adapting tuition content and technique in response to non-comprehension impasse as it occurs. While affect cannot be dismissed as a useful feedback channel for an intelligent e-learning system, the flow of cognitive and affective states suggests that detectable affect may occur too late in the learning process to help prevent repeated impasse and loss of motivation. Hendrix 2.0 overcomes this problem by modelling learner comprehension in real-time, allowing the virtual tutor to identify and respond to points of impasse as they occur.

2.3 Comprehension Classification by Automata

FATHOM [12] is a comprehension classification system which analyses learner non-verbal behaviour to automatically classify comprehension during dyadic verbal interaction. The work demonstrates that video recordings of learners responding verbally to a human tutor can be computationally analysed to produce accurate classifications of learner comprehension levels during verbal student-tutor interactions.

Hendrix 2.0 integrates the real-time comprehension assessment and scoring system, COMPASS [14], to monitor learner comprehension during conversational tutoring. COMPASS is a novel artificial neural network (ANN) based classifier which can analyse live image stream data to survey observable learner non-verbal behaviour rapidly. COMPASS uses a combination of computer vision [20] and machine learning [21] techniques to produce a comprehension estimate for each one second of video footage. The system tracks 37 non-verbal behaviours, including head movement and rotation, eye gaze direction, blink rate, skin tone change and 5 meta-data variables, including gender and ethnicity. Observed behaviours for each one second of image stream data are summarised to produce a 42 variable cumulative behavioural feature vector (CBFV), a numeric vector representing the average behaviour of the learner over the one second time window. The CBFV is classified using a multilayer perceptron (MLP) network [21], outputting a single comprehension estimate on the scale -1.0 to $+1.0$, where -1.0 is non-comprehension and $+1.0$ is comprehension. Binary classification is achieved by applying a logistic threshold.

The COMPASS comprehension classifier was optimised and trained using pre-tagged recordings of students answering multiple choice questions [14]. Each recording was tagged as either comprehension or non-comprehension, depending on the correctness of the answer selected by the learner. The classifier achieved test normalised classification accuracy of 75.8%.

3 Hendrix 2.0

Hendrix 2.0 integrates two novel artificially intelligent systems: a novel conversational intelligent tutoring system, based on Hendrix 1.0 [15], and a novel comprehension classification and scoring system, called COMPASS [14].

Hendrix 2.0 interacts with the learner via a chat interface, as shown in Fig. 1. During interactions, Hendrix 2.0 uses COMPASS to model the learner's comprehension and produce a time-series of comprehension estimates and classifications (Fig. 1).

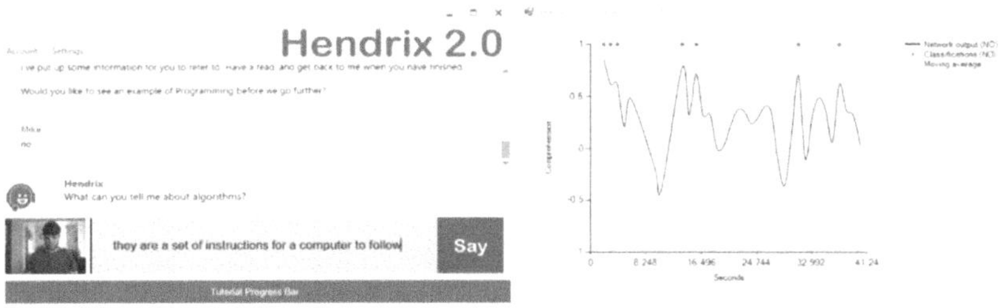

Fig. 1. Screenshot of Hendrix 2.0 chat interface (left) and real-time comprehension monitor (right)

Hendrix 2.0 structures conversational tutorial content by searching a graph of pre-defined subject knowledge which includes hierarchically structured concepts, definitions, examples, code samples, questions and more. During the conversation, Hendrix 2.0 will appraise the learner's understanding of the subject by asking the learner to explain concepts, answer questions or write basic programming code. Hendrix 2.0 can ask both simple questions requiring just a single word answer, for example 'true' or 'false', or complex questions requiring multiple words, phrases, mathematics or programming code.

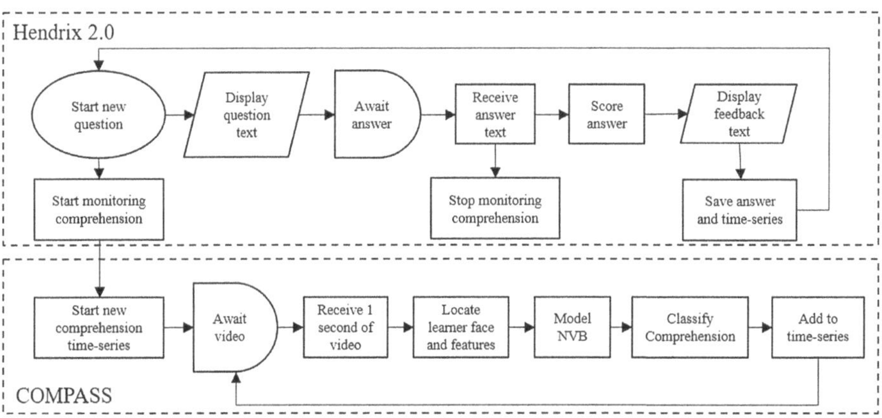

Fig. 2. Question, answer and comprehension monitoring process for Hendrix 2.0 with COMPASS integration

Figure 2 shows the process by which Hendrix 2.0 asks, scores and saves learner's answers. When a new question is loaded, Hendrix 2.0 simultaneously displays the question text and begins monitoring the learner's comprehension. COMPASS creates a new time-series and awaits video data to analyse. Hendrix 2.0 captures video footage from a front-facing webcam and passes it to COMPASS one second at a time. Each one second of video footage is analysed to produce a comprehension estimate, which is added to the time-series for the answer response period. Once an answer is submitted

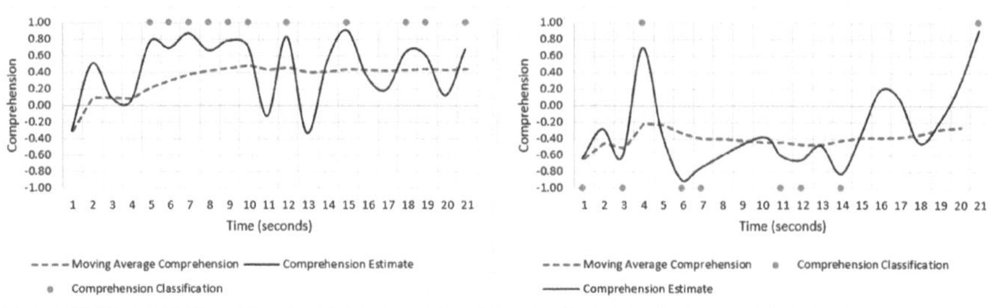

Fig. 3. COMPASS learner comprehension modelling for tutorial answers scoring 100% correct (left) and 0% correct (right)

by the learner, comprehension monitoring is stopped, the answer is automatically scored by Hendrix 2.0 and both the answer and the comprehension time-series are saved.

Figure 3 shows two exemplar comprehension time-series, generated during the study. The raw classifier output is shown as 'Comprehension', a continuous stream of values between −1.0 and 1.0 where −1.0 is strong non-comprehension and +1.0 is strong comprehension. 'Classification' dots show binary comprehension classification, using a threshold of ±0.6. A binary classification is made when the network output is either greater than or equal to 0.6 (*'strong comprehension'*), or when the network output is less than or equal to −0.6 (*'strong non-comprehension'*).

4 Study: Automatic Classification of e-Learner Comprehension During on-Screen Conversational Interactions

The aim of this experiment is to investigate whether COMPASS can be integrated into a conversational intelligent tutoring system, such as Hendrix 2.0, and whether the COMPASS comprehension classifier can accurately classify e-learner comprehension in real-time, from non-verbal behaviour, during conversational interactions.

4.1 Participants

The participant group consisted of 51 students from the Faculty of Science & Engineering at Manchester Metropolitan University. The gender demographics of the participant group were 80% male and 20% female. White European (or Caucasian) was the largest ethnic group, at just over 50%, with Asian (or British Asian) the second largest at 35%.

4.2 Method

In a study conducted at Manchester Metropolitan University, participants undertook a tutorial on computer programming using the Hendrix 2.0 CITS (Fig. 1). For each answer given by a learner, Hendrix 2.0 automatically assigned a score between 0 and 100%. During each answer period, Hendrix 2.0 programmatically passed a stream of web camera image data to the COMPASS [14] API for real-time comprehension classification (Fig. 2).

The 51 participants answered a total of 1,269 questions, answering on average 26 questions each. Across all answers, COMPASS classified 14,931 seconds non-verbal behaviour, and produced 7,027 binary comprehension classifications. The accuracy of comprehension classification is evaluated by calculating the true positive (predicted comprehension) and true negative (predicted non-comprehension) percentages for classifications made during answer periods scoring 50% or higher (observed comprehension) and periods scoring 25% or lower (observed non-comprehension).

4.3 Results and Discussion

Research [22] has found that in practical application culture, social norms, ethnicity, and gender all play an important role in mediating non-verbal behaviour. In line with the findings of Rothwell et al. [22], and the broader literature on cross-cultural non-verbal behaviour [23], separate classifiers may need to be trained for each demographic group to optimise performance. The results presented in this paper focus on the largest demographic subset of participants – white European males – who account for 58% of the data collected during the experiment.

For binary classification, true non-comprehension periods are defined as response periods for answers scoring 25% or lower. True comprehension periods are defined as response periods scoring 50% or higher.

Table 1. Classification accuracy for white males

Counts		Threshold	Classification accuracy (%)		
Answers	Classifications		Non-comp	Comp	Norm
532	3313	±0.6	54.09	68.74	60.64
	1926	±0.8	64.05	67.89	65.73

Table 1 shows the comprehension classifier accuracy for all white male response periods. At threshold ±0.6 3313 classifications are made during the 532 answer response periods, with a normalised classification accuracy of 60%. Increasing the threshold to ±0.8 reduces the number of classifications made by 40%, but increases normalised classification accuracy by 5%. While the results in Table 1 indicate that it is possible to detect comprehension and non-comprehension, classification accuracy is weak.

Table 2 shows comprehension classification broken down by question complexity. Classification accuracy at chance levels for simple questions may be explained by guessing. Simple questions require only a single word answer, such as 'true' or 'false', allowing a learner to guess the answer easily. Guessing behaviour results in 'strong

Table 2. Classification accuracy for white males by question difficulty

Question difficulty	Counts		Threshold	Classification accuracy (%)		
	Answers	Classifications		Non-comp	Comp	Norm
Simple	200	986	±0.6	35.48	52.90	42.49
		574	±0.8	36.56	50.79	42.86
Complex	332	2327	±0.6	62.91	74.54	68.33
		1352	±0.8	75.59	75.25	75.44

non-comprehension' behaviour becoming associated with a high answer score, reducing the evident accuracy of the classifier. Complex questions, which cannot be guessed easily require learners to formulate complex multi-part answers containing multiple keywords, phrases, mathematics or programming code, which can contain multiple conceptual elements. For complex questions the classifier achieves normalised classification accuracy of between 68% and 75%, similar to accuracy during training and testing of the classifier [14].

The results demonstrate that the COMPASS classifier can, with accuracy, detect and classify 'strong comprehension' and 'strong non-comprehension' indicative behaviours during conversational interactions with a conversational intelligent tutoring system, given the limitations highlighted. The results also highlight the consideration which should be given to the type of question being addressed to the learner, whether guessing behaviour is likely and whether the question challenges the learner sufficiently to evoke strong comprehension or non-comprehension behaviour.

5 Conclusions

In this paper the authors have presented a review of literature demonstrating the novelty of, and motivation for, the development of a method for real-time, automatic, modelling of e-learner comprehension by computational analysis of non-verbal behaviour. The authors have introduced a novel conversational intelligent tutoring system (CITS), named Hendrix 2.0, which is capable of modelling comprehension in real-time using a comprehension assessment and scoring system, named COMPASS. The authors have presented an experiment in which real learners undertake conversational tutoring using Hendrix 2.0, and their scoring tutorial answers and COMPASS comprehension time-series' are saved. The authors present results and discussion of classification accuracy and find that the COMPASS classifier can achieve 75% classification accuracy on 'complex' questions. The research presented here demonstrates that comprehension classification by computational analysis of learner non-verbal behaviour is a viable feedback mechanism for an adaptive conversational intelligent tutoring system, such as Hendrix 2.0. The results do highlight limitations and considerations: separate classifiers should be trained for each gender and ethnicity, and a separate classifier may also be needed for 'simple' questions, to identify and model behaviours associated with guessing.

6 Future Work

In future work the authors will investigate whether CITS adaptation based on '*strong non-comprehension*' classification improves a learner's tutorial and post-tutorial test score performances, when compared to a non-adaptive control group. To assess the effectiveness of the technology across all demographic subgroups of the participant cohort, training-set image data collection experiments should be repeated for each demographic subgroup. Data for each subgroup can be used to train and evaluate a demographic specific classifier.

References

1. Salmon, G.: Flying not flapping: a strategic framework for e-learning and pedagogical innovation in higher education institutions. ALT-J **13**, 201–218 (2005)
2. VanLehn, K.: The behavior of tutoring systems. Int. J. Artif. Intell. Educ. **16**, 227–265 (2006)
3. VanLehn, K., Graesser, A.C., Jackson, G.T., Jordan, P., Olney, A., Rosé, C.P.: When are tutorial dialogues more effective than reading? Cogn. Sci. **31**, 3–62 (2007)
4. VanLehn, K.: The relative effectiveness of human tutoring, intelligent tutoring systems, and other tutoring systems. Educ. Psychol. **46**, 197–221 (2011)
5. Latham, A., Crockett, K., McLean, D.: An adaptation algorithm for an intelligent natural language tutoring system. Comput. Educ. **71**, 97–110 (2014)
6. Latham, A., Crockett, K., McLean, D., Edmonds, B.: A conversational intelligent tutoring system to automatically predict learning styles. Comput. Educ. **59**, 95–109 (2012)
7. D'Mello, K.S., Craig, S.D., Gholson, B., Franklin, S., Picard, R., Graesser, A.C.: Integrating affect sensors in an intelligent tutoring system. In: Affective Interactions: The Computer in the Affective Loop Workshop at 2005 International Conference on Intelligent User Interfaces, pp. 7–13 (2005)
8. Lin, H.-C.K., Wu, C.-H., Hsueh, Y.-P.: The influence of using affective tutoring system in accounting remedial instruction on learning performance and usability. Comput. Hum. Behav. **41**, 514–522 (2014)
9. Alibali, M.W., Flevares, L.M., Goldin-Meadow, S.: Assessing knowledge conveyed in gesture: do teachers have the upper hand? J. Educ. Psychol. **89**, 183–193 (1997)
10. Machida, S.: Teacher accuracy in decoding nonverbal indicants of comprehension and noncomprehension in Anglo- and Mexican-American children. J. Educ. Psychol. **78**, 454–464 (1986)
11. Webb, J.M., Diana, E.M., Luft, P., Brooks, E.W., Brennan, E.L.: Influence of pedagogical expertise and feedback on assessing student comprehension from nonverbal behavior. J. Educ. Res. **91**, 89–97 (1997)
12. Buckingham, F.J., Crockett, K.A., Bandar, Z.A., O'Shea, J.D.: FATHOM: a neural network-based non-verbal human comprehension detection system for learning environments. In: 2014 IEEE Symposium on Computational Intelligence and Data Mining (CIDM), pp. 403–409. IEEE (2014)
13. Buckingham, F.J., Crockett, K.A., Bandar, Z.A., O'Shea, J.D., MacQueen, K.M., Chen, M.: Measuring human comprehension from nonverbal behaviour using artificial neural networks. In: The 2012 International Joint Conference on Neural Networks (IJCNN), pp. 1–8. IEEE (2012)

14. Holmes, M., Latham, A., Crockett, K., O'Shea, J.D.: Near real-time comprehension classification with artificial neural networks: decoding e-Learner non-verbal behaviour. IEEE Trans. Learn. Technol. **PP**(99), 1 (2016)
15. Holmes, M., Latham, A., Crockett, K., O'Shea, J.D., Lewin, C.: Hendrix: a conversational intelligent tutoring system for Java programming. Presented at the UK Workshop on Computational Intelligence, University of Exeter (2015)
16. Whitehill, J., Bartlett, M., Movellan, J.: Automatic facial expression recognition for intelligent tutoring systems. In: IEEE Computer Society Conference on Computer Vision and Pattern Recognition Workshops, CVPRW 2008, pp. 1–6. IEEE (2008)
17. Calvo, R.A., D'Mello, S.: Frontiers of affect-aware learning technologies. IEEE Intell. Syst. **27**, 86–89 (2012)
18. Bosch, N., D'Mello, S., Baker, R., Ocumpaugh, J., Shute, V., Ventura, M., Wang, L., Zhao, W.: Automatic detection of learning-centered affective states in the wild. Presented at the (2015)
19. Whitehill, J., Serpell, Z., Foster, A., Lin, Y.-C., Pearson, B., Bartlett, M., Movellan, J.: Towards an optimal affect-sensitive instructional system of cognitive skills. In: 2011 IEEE Computer Society Conference on Computer Vision and Pattern Recognition Workshops (CVPRW), pp. 20–25. IEEE (2011)
20. Viola, P., Jones, M.J.: Robust real-time face detection. Int. J. Comput. Vis. **57**, 137–154 (2004)
21. Haykin, S.: Neural Networks: A Comprehensive Foundation. Macmillan, Basingstoke (1994)
22. Rothwell, J., Bandar, Z., O'Shea, J., McLean, D.: Silent talker: a new computer-based system for the analysis of facial cues to deception. Appl. Cogn. Psychol. **20**, 757–777 (2006)
23. Bond, C.F., Omar, A., Mahmoud, A., Bonser, R.N.: Lie detection across cultures. J. Nonverbal Behav. **14**, 189–204 (1990)

The Value of Project Management Education for IT Professionals

Angela Lecomber[1] and Arthur Tatnall[2(✉)]

[1] See Differently Consulting and RMIT University, Melbourne, Australia
angela@seedifferently.com.au
[2] Victoria University, Melbourne, Australia
Arthur.Tatnall@vu.edu.au

Abstract. IT organisations and organisations with IT departments frequently procure project management training as part of their initiatives to improve business outcomes through professional education. This paper utilises the results of a research study that focused on the training of the project management methodology PRINCE2 in an organisation where IT was one of the departments. The longitudinal study over two and a half years reported on the adoption of the PRINCE2 project management methodology by sixteen employees following the successful completion of a PRINCE2 training course. Two different outcomes were observed: some individuals continued to develop their interest in PRINCE2 and looked for a stable network that will support their practice, even if they resigned from the organisation. The other outcome was that other individuals ceased using PRINCE2 for their projects if there was no imperative given by the organisation to use it and no example set by others in using it. The adoption outcomes from this study have implications as to the interventions that need to be implemented by organisations to derive the value from an investment in professional vocational education in project management for all relevant professionals.

Keywords: Project management training · IT professionals · PRINCE2 Professional vocational education · Actor-Network Theory

1 Introduction

In this paper we will argue that an important part of the education of IT professionals should relate to project management. Apart from the normal material relating to the disciplines of computing, IT professionals need to know about how IT systems can best be developed. They need to know how to go about designing a system, but also how to build and implement a system. They need to have a good knowledge of project management and this topic should be an important part of any professional education in IT. Many IT projects in recent years have resulted in failure [1] and so knowledge of the appropriate application of project management skills is vital for Information Systems professionals.

As project management evolves as a field of practice, companies are now realising that their entire business, including most of the routine activities, can be regarded as a

A. Tatnall and M. Webb (Eds.): WCCE 2017, IFIP AICT 515, pp. 261–268, 2017.
https://doi.org/10.1007/978-3-319-74310-3_28

series of projects. The Business Directory [2] defines a project as a: "Planned set of interrelated tasks to be executed over a fixed period and within certain cost and other limitations". Simply stated, we are managing our business by projects [3], and this is even more so in the development of information systems.

To improve the management of projects, project management methodologies are regularly employed with the aim of increasing project efficiency and effectiveness [4]. Public and private sector organisations invest significant resources into efforts, ranging from a review and tailoring of the current practices to the adoption or development of new project management methodologies [5].

Nonetheless, project professionals are trusted to deliver projects even if they are not accredited [6]. The Price Waterhouse Coopers [5] report stated that only 20% of professionals were certified in their organisation's preferred methodology. Why is this? Could this be due to the lack of connection between the theory of project management and its practice? There appears to be a gap between what education providers are offering and what is needed to deal with projects in today's work environment [7].

2 The Value of Professional Education in Project Management

The teaching and learning of project management have attracted the attention of many scholars within project management professional training [8]. This is especially true in the case of IT projects.

Since the Australian Computer Society (ACS) included IT Project Management in its Body of Knowledge for Computer Professionals [9, 10] most Australian universities now include one of more IT Project Management subjects in both undergraduate and postgraduate degrees. In most cases this involved practical work using software packages such as Microsoft Project to formalise these concepts. As well as IT project management education in universities, however, there is also substantial industry professional training in project management and it is this that this paper addresses.

In the 21st century, project management education and training is often still confined to the instructional approaches of the 20th century and focused on technical instrumentality [11–14]. That current approaches of educating and training project management professionals do not meet the need of modern enterprises is now well accepted [7]. In fact, Starkweather and Stevenson [15] found that there was no difference in project success rates between PMP (Project Management Professional) certified project managers and uncertified project managers. Both Starkweather and Stevenson [15] and Crawford [16] found that there was little or no empirical evidence that certified project managers making use of the popular methods of project management education are more successful than non-certified project managers.

Joslin and Muller [17] found that there was a positive relationship between the use of project management methodologies by project management practitioners and project success. Methodologies included both PMBoK[1] and PRINCE2 which are described as

[1] PMBoK is not a methodology but a Body of Knowledge.

project management 'best practices' by the respective 'owners' which are the Project Management Institute (PMI) and AXELOS[2] respectively.

Winter et al. [18] reported that practitioners found that mainstream methods and techniques could be a useful source of guidance for certain aspects, but they provided no guidance on 'how' to navigate the complexity of projects in the ever-changing flux of events.

At the heart of challenges faced by the discourse on project management education and training is the assumption that project management outcomes can successfully be predicted as a simple cause and effect relationship which imply a rigid utilisation of project management methodologies and a rigid control and measurement of outputs, and in effect an instrumental ideology [19].

Ojiako et al. [8] in their research on how engineering students perceive their learning experiences of project management found that the focus for learning should be on the student as a manager rather than a 'technician'. In such a role as manager, engineers would be expected to "grasp the complexity and fluidity associated with the range of interconnected social, technical, political, and economic factors that commonly matter within work packages and projects" [8: 57]. These findings are quite unsurprising. What is important is to introduce engineering students, and also IT students, to the complexities associated with projects. However there is a difficulty in achieving this due to the educational delivery of courses being narrowly compartmentalised and linked rigidly to learning outcomes [8].

3 PRINCE2 Project Management Methodology

PRojects IN Controlled Environments Version 2 (PRINCE2) is a methodology for managing projects and has grown to become a de facto 'standard' as a project management method in more than 150 countries worldwide [20, 21]. PRINCE2 is a methodology (as opposed to a body of knowledge such as PMBOK) that was developed for the UK Government to manage their IT projects and was based on soft-systems methodology [20–23]. The first version of PRINCE was published in 1989 [20, 21].

A multi-disciplinary research team from the Queensland University of Technology (QUT), financed by the former owners of the intellectual property of PRINCE2, the Office of Government and Commerce (OGC), undertook one of the first empirical studies into the impact of the PRINCE2 methodology on project performance [21]. The research study was entitled 'Creating Value in Project Management using PRINCE2' and also conducted parallel research on the impact of other unspecified (non-PRINCE2) contemporary project management methodologies.

The researchers interviewed PRINCE2 practitioners from a diverse range of industries (including Information and Communications Technology, Construction, and Transport) and across three major geographical regions (United Kingdom and Europe,

[2] AXELOS was set up in 2014 by as a joint venture between the UK Government and Capita with the aim of developing, managing and operating qualifications in best practice. It is used in methodologies formerly owned by the Office of Government Commerce.

United States and Australia) [21]. The researchers found that PRINCE2 was perceived as a very robust, comprehensive and pragmatic project management framework [21].

Problems and issues which impeded the adoption of PRINCE2 to projects were organisational and not methodological, and the dominant issue identified by participants was poor project sponsor/board performance and a reflection that organisations either do not know how, or do not possess the commitment to properly implement PRINCE2 [21]. This finding was supported by the research study reported in this paper.

Wells [4] explored the effectiveness in the workplace of project management methodologies including PRINCE2. Her research found that there was "a chasm between the intended strategic directions of the project management methodology and its actual contribution to projects, managers and their teams" [4]. According to Wells [4] the purported benefits are often not realised or can have unintended consequences at the project level and adversely affect project success.

Furthermore, Wells' [4] research on project management methodologies showed that the methodologies were useful for those that were at opposite ends of experience and accountability for projects:

- the inexperienced in project management, and
- those who were most senior in the organisation who were focused on the governance of projects.

In between these two ends of the spectrum, the "perceived benefits and advantages of using project management methodologies dramatically falls, to a minimum, corresponding to the middle ground of the range of perspectives" [4] the drop largely due to the drawbacks and limitations that the practitioners experienced in adopting the methodologies [4]. In other words, those who had some experience of project management considered the use of a project management methodology to be an overhead in their day to day work and did not use it. It was only useful for those who were inexperienced as it was a useful guide for them. It was also valuable for those who very experienced who were also senior managers as they were looking for ways to control projects and implement governance across the organisation by seeking a standard in delivering projects [4].

4 Research Study – Longitudinal Case Study

A research study was conducted by Lecomber [24] to understand how participants used and adopted the PRINCE2 methodology to workplace projects following a professional training course. The study, over two and a half years, used Case Study [25] as a method and consisted of both a questionnaire and focus group interviews. The research formulated qualitative answers to the main research question: 'How are practitioners influenced to apply project management 'best practice' (PRINCE2 in this study) in complex and dynamic environments?'

The study workplace consisted of a number of departments, one of which was an IT department. Two IT staff participated in the professional training program which consisted of sixteen staff drawn from the various departments across the organisation. Participants were questioned on what they thought of the training itself, how relevant it was to their own work and whether it would make a difference to their work in the future. The results showed that there were some participants who adopted as much of the PRINCE2 methodology as they were able for their work projects, and actively sought to improve their practice. Another group of participants had knowledge of the methodology but considered the overhead in using it far outweighed the benefit derived from using it.

To analyse these two different forms of adoption, Innovation Translation, informed by Actor-Network Theory (ANT) was used. ANT enables the researcher to think in terms of different translations (or adaptations) and to seek to identify the actors involved and the interactions that formed possible stable networks supporting those translations [26]. Innovation Translation has the advantage of being able to explain examples of partial adoption, and of situations where what is actually adopted differs from what was proposed [27]. This was particularly relevant for this study as it could be said that one group of participants made *only* a partial adoption.

ANT, also known as the sociology of translation [28, 29], was developed by science and technology scholars Callon and Latour, sociologist Law and others. It is a conceptual framework for exploring collective socio-technical processes and aims to follow the actors in a given network in the process of new network formation [29]. Innovation Translation, informed by ANT, argues that an innovation moves along as a chain of consequence by energy given to it by everyone in the chain whose actions shape the innovation to suit themselves [27].

Actors in this case include the trainer, trainee (learner), curriculum and the workplace. According to Blomquist et al. [11], a practice approach on project management requires the study of action, activities and actors within projects. There are actors at play even before Day 1 of the training course. These are AXELOS, the Examination Institute (APMG) and the Accredited Training Organisation (ATO). The ATO provides the training material and the trainer. The ATO obtains the PRINCE2 manual from a bookseller who procures this from AXELOS, whilst APMG dispatches the exam paper. The nature of the outcome of the training experience is a result of the interaction of the human actors (the trainer and the other participants) and non-human actors (training materials, timetable, exam papers, PRINCE2 manual and training venue). After the training, the participant project manager seeks then to adopt the innovation in the workplace. This research study seeks to understand both the interactions that occur during training as well as in the workplace after the training course with respect to the adoption of the PRINCE2 methodology.

Callon [28] defines four moments (stages) of Innovation Translation: problematisation, interessement, enrolment and mobilization. The four stages, if successful, lock the actors into the network and create a stable translation [30]. This research looked at adoption in the form of two different translations:

1. Some participants adopted as much of the PRINCE2 methodology as they were able for their projects and actively sought to improve practice. The study named this adoption as the Performing Translation (**PT**). Those who had adopted **PT** had a focus on continuous improvement in their practice. Those who adopt the **PT** are people who keep attempting to apply their learning and hence learn more. In addition, those who adopted the **PT** conducted their own research into 'best practice' outside of work hours.

2. The other group of participants who had knowledge of the methodology but considered the overhead in using it far outweighed the benefit derived from using it formed the Knowing Translation (**KT**). A **KT** sees nothing in the formal structures of PRINCE2 that is so valuable that they would sacrifice early delivery by going through procedures stated in the methodology. Those who had adopted the **KT** would only apply what they had learned to the workplace if they perceived adoption across the organisation.

In the case of **PT** participants, as their organisation did not have the supports such as strong leadership for using a methodology and a strong Project Management Office (PMO), some participants who adopted the **PT** eventually resigned from the organisation. In this research study, the PMO was weak and could not enforce the governance needed to support the use of PRINCE2.

Participants whose form of adoption was the Knowing Translation (**KT**) had knowledge of the Project Management methodology but considered the overhead in using it far outweighed the benefit derived. The lack of support from the top-down commencing with the Senior Leadership team and the original sponsor of the methodology had a strong influence on those who adopted the **KT**. A senior leadership team and sponsor must go beyond paying 'lip-service' to the methodology and actively comply with the methodology in terms of behaviours, responsibilities and expectations of their role on the project as sponsors and Project Board members.

5 Implications

The research results by Lecomber [24] thus identifying two adoption outcomes as a result of project management training could be used to assist organisations in their strategies to support embedding of learning outcomes following project management training. These results are congruent with the research conducted by the Sargeant et al. [21] study which showed that problems and issues which impeded the adoption of PRINCE2 to projects were organisational rather than methodological.

The value of professional vocational education and training in project management depended on what structures were in place in the organisation to support the adoption of the project management methodology.

These supports include:

- A strong Project Management Office (PMO)
- Senior leadership team that supports the use of the methodology
- Strong visible support by the sponsor of the methodology.

These issues have significant implications for the success of any project management training. It the training is not seen, by the participants, as relevant to their workplace and if appropriate organisational support is lacking then there is more likelihood that the training participants will become Knowing (KT) rather than Performing (PT).

6 Conclusion

IT professionals (and others) need to know how to go about designing a system, but also how to build and implement such a system and so should have a good knowledge of project management. For some, this is obtained in their university degree but for others it comes later, as a result of professional and vocational education. Given that in recent years many IT projects have resulted in failure, knowledge of the appropriate application of project management skills is a vital skill for all Information Systems professionals.

In this study, the emergence of two possible adoption outcomes has implications on how organisations derive value from their investment in professional project management education and training. As well as ensuring that the project management training is performed well, it is important that organisations commit to supports in place such as a strong PMO, senior leadership supporting the methodology and strong visible support from the sponsor if the organisation wishes to derive the value from the project management training otherwise the investment in training is a 'waste of money'. This is particularly important in the education of IT professionals.

References

1. Standish Group: CHAOS Report 2016: Outline. Standish Group, Boston (2016)
2. Business Directory: Project, February 2017. http://www.businessdictionary.com/definition/project.html
3. Kerzner, H.: Project Management Best Practices: Achieving Global Excellence. Wiley, New Jersey (2014)
4. Wells, H.: How effective are project management methodologies? An explorative evaluation of their benefits in practice. Proj. Manage. J. **43**(6), 43–58 (2012)
5. Price Waterhouse Coopers: Fourth Portfolio and Programme Management Survey (2014). http://www.pwc.com/gx/en/services/advisory/consulting/portfolio-programme-management/global-ppm-survey-2014.html Cited 2017
6. Konstantinou, E.: Professionalism in project management: redefining the role of the project practitioner. Proj. Manage. J. **46**(2), 21–35 (2015)
7. Ramazani, J., Jergeas, G.: Project managers and the journey from good to great: the benefits of investment in project management training and education. Int. J. Proj. Manage. **33**(1), 41–52 (2015)
8. Ojiako, U., et al.: Project management learning: a comparative study between engineering students' experiences in South Africa and the United Kingdom. Proj. Manage. J. **46**(4), 47–62 (2015)
9. Tatnall, A., Reyes, G.: Teaching IT project management to postgraduate business students: a practical approach. J. Inf. Technol. Educ. **4**, 153–166 (2005)
10. Burgess, S.: Curriculum Planning for Information Management, in Business Information Technology. Royal Melbourne Institute of Technology, Melbourne (1993)
11. Blomquist, T., et al.: Project-as-practice: in search of project management research that matters. Proj. Manage. J. **41**(1), 5–16 (2010)
12. Ojiako, U., et al.: The criticality of transferable skills development and virtual learning environments used in the teaching of project management. Proj. Manage. J. **42**(4), 76–86 (2011)

13. Skulmoski, G., Harman, F.: Information systems project manager soft competencies: a project-phase investigation. Proj. Manage. J. **41**(1), 61–77 (2010)
14. Thomas, J., Mengel, T.: Preparing project managers to deal with complexity – advanced project management education. Int. J. Proj. Manage. **26**(3), 304–315 (2008)
15. Starkweather, J.A., Stevenson, D.H.: PMP® certification as a core competency: necessary but not sufficient. Proj. Manage. J. **42**(1), 31–41 (2011)
16. Crawford, L.: Senior management perceptions for project management competence. Int. J. Proj. Manage. **23**, 7–16 (2005)
17. Joslin, R., Muller, R.: Relationships between a project management methodology and project success in different project governance contexts. Int. J. Proj. Manage. **33**, 1337–1392 (2015)
18. Winter, M., et al.: Directions for future research in project management: the main findings of a UK government funded research network. Int. J. Proj. Manage. **28**(8), 638–649 (2006)
19. Ojiako, U., et al.: Project management learning: key dimensions and saliency from student experience. Int. J. Proj. Manage. **32**(8), 1445–1458 (2014)
20. AXELOS: AXELOS Global Best Practice (2015). https://www.axelos.com/ Cited 2016
21. Sargeant, R., et al.: Creating value in project management using PRINCE2. Office of Government Commerce, London, UK (2010). http://eprints.qut.edu.au/52853/ Cited 2017
22. Checkland, P., Scholes, J.: Soft Systems Methodology in Action. Wiley, Chichester (1991)
23. Finegan, A.: Soft Systems Methodology: an Alternative Approach to Knowledge Elicitation in Complex and Poorly Defined Systems. RMIT Centre for Remote Sensing and Land Information (1994). http://www.csu.edu.au/ci/vol1/Andrew.Finegan/paper.html Accessed 15 Nov 1998
24. Lecomber, A.: Reshaping the project manager's project story: An adoption study of 'best practice' project management, in Information Systems. RMIT, Under examination (2017)
25. Yin, R.K.: Case Study Research, Design and Methods, 5th edn. Sage Publications, Thousand Oaks (2014)
26. Davey, W., Adamopoulos, A.: Grounded theory and actor-network theory: a case study. Int. J. Actor-Netw. Theory Technol. Innov. **8**(1), 27–33 (2016)
27. Tatnall, A.: Innovation translation as a research approach to theorising information systems implementation. Int. J. Network. Virtual Organ. **6**(1), 64–76 (2009)
28. Callon, M.: Some elements of a sociology of translation: domestication of the scallops and the fishermen of St Brieuc Bay. In: Law, J. (ed.) Power, Action and Belief. A New Sociology of Knowledge? pp. 196–229. Routledge and Kegan Paul, London (1986)
29. Latour, B.: Reassembling the Social: An Introduction to Actor-Network Theory. Oxford University Press, Oxford (2005)
30. Davey, W.: ANT, phenomenography and a research question in information systems. Int. J. Actor-Netw. Theory Technol. Innov. **6**(2), 1–9 (2014)

Learning Analytics for Formative Purposes

Bent B. Andresen(✉)

Danish School of Education, Aarhus University, Copenhagen NV, Denmark
bba@edu.au.dk

Abstract. This paper deals with teacher-driven learning analytics in primary and secondary education. First, it examines the transformation of the teachers' role in relation to learning analytics and provides evidence suggesting an approach where affinity groups of teachers, systematically analyse and gauge their efforts in relation to student's performance. Second, it presents results of research, currently in progress, concerning the implementation of teacher-driven learning analytics in educational settings (here in Danish schools). It focuses, among other things, on students' self-efficacy as a parameter to be analysed together with their academic performance. The notion of self-efficacy refers to students' beliefs about their capabilities to solve given tasks and problems and the paper provides evidence suggesting that perceived self-efficacy is an indisputably important factor to analyse.

Keywords: Learning analytics · 1:1 classrooms · Perceived self-efficacy Formative feedback

1 Introduction

The notion of *learning analytics* can be defined as the collection, analysis and reporting of data on students and their contexts for purposes of optimising learning and the environments in which it occurs [1]. This broad definition covers the majority of approaches to generating and analysing educational data that, of course, have various origins and scopes.

First, data on students' learning outcomes and wellbeing include larger sets of machine-readable data amenable to statistical analyses. Since it would not be practical to deal with these data manually, automated analysis is often conducted by external stakeholders. For example, this learning analytics is organised by school authorities at national, regional and municipal levels, national statistical agencies, data warehouses or international organizations (e.g. OECD, IEA and WHO).

The emergence of very large datasets in connection with the ongoing explosion in the availability of many different types of data is often called *big data*. A shift towards a culture of using big data to improve student learning is still in its infancy. However, the Danish stakeholders will be "reporting about the performance of the school system to the public" more frequently in the future and, intentionally, "the reporting framework could form the basis for the periodic publication of key national analytical reports" [2].

Typically, the publication of such results and reports takes too long to provide information about current students in time to fully serve teachers in primary and

A. Tatnall and M. Webb (Eds.): WCCE 2017, IFIP AICT 515, pp. 269–280, 2017.
https://doi.org/10.1007/978-3-319-74310-3_29

secondary education. For example, statistical analyses based on summative evaluations and dropout rates from last year or previous years do not really support current learning activities. From the teachers' point of view, the relevance of analytics based on exams, tests or surveys is lower when it regards previous students rather than students currently in the teachers' classrooms. For formative purposes, teachers need real-time analytics regarding effort, persistence and behaviour of present students' rather than of previous generations of students. To be proactive in their classrooms, teachers also need up-to-date analytics regarding current learning environments instead of previous environments.

Moreover, big data sets are often considered overwhelming by teachers and it is a challenge for them to make use of the patterns and trends [3]. For example, Danish teachers in primary and lower secondary education are encouraged by the Ministry of Education to make use of the results of national mandatory computer-based summative tests of all students. The tests are adaptive and items vary from student to student. Since many teachers have difficulties interpreting the tests' results and applying them into future learning plans, these results are seldom being used systematically for formative purposes [4]. In addition, teachers in youth education do not consider it fair to search and use this type of data on student performance in lower secondary education because learning requirements and activities are different at the upper secondary level [5].

Another example concerns sets of data on student wellbeing, which are currently generated at all public schools in Denmark. Student wellbeing is not defined or operationalised properly [6], but data on this issue are analysed under the auspices of the Ministry of Education for accountability reasons. Even though the Ministry arranges courses for school representatives in this field, the learning analytics are seldom used for formative purposes and the results of this type of assessment seldom influence teachers' planning of future teaching and learning activities [5].

The only exception from this general picture regards student's literacy, i.e. their ability to understand and process oral and written language [7]. In Denmark, most public schools employ reading advisors who support literacy development and the use of text-to-speech software [8].

To make proactive advising possible at scale, results of previous tests are used at the upper secondary schools in combination with current reading and writing tests. For example, contemporary data from language, reading and writing tests are analysed for proactive advising purposes.

As already mentioned, educational data have various origins. Besides big data, teachers can generate and analyse smaller sets of data on their own. This teacher-driven learning analytics implies a transformation of the teachers' role in relation to learning analytics, i.e. a shift from end-user to analyst of data. The latter role is the main topic of this paper that examines teacher-driven analytics of teaching and learning environments. The primary goal is to support teachers' decision making and the research question is: How can teachers generate and analyse data to help improve their practice and the learning outcomes for their students?

There is research evidence suggesting that analyses of equally weighted data from assessments of student's academic performance, teachers' observations and student surveys produce valid and reliable results that correlate with student performance [9]. To get the most reliable results, data from national tests or assessments of students' higher-order conceptual understanding are not sufficient. In other words, teachers have to focus on composite sets of data. To obtain the most valid, reliable and accurate analytical results, teacher-driven analytics should include learning outcomes, data from own observations in the learning environment and students' self-reported perceptions of teaching and the learning environment [10].

Student surveys are easy to administer in digital learning environments and a relatively inexpensive way to supplement other sets of data. To survey something as broad as the teachers' efforts and the learning environment requires breaking these issues down into various constructs that can be measured by simple questions [10]. For example, the students can be asked if they agree or disagree with statements like:

- "My teacher has several good ways to explain each topic that we cover in this class"
- "When I turn in my work, my teacher gives me useful feedback that helps me improve".

Responding to such questions, students provide information on specific aspects of teaching and the learning environment, so that teachers can improve their use of time, the application of information and communications technology (ICT) into the learning environments, the provision of feedback and their relationships with their students if needed.

There is research evidence suggesting that the students' responses demonstrate relative consistency, capture aspects of teaching and the learning environment that relate to desired learning outcomes and point to strengths and areas for improvement that the teachers value [9].

Teachers have to analyse data representing something indisputably important, including environmental facilitators and impediments [11]. Since summative assessments disengage some students, it is important to access students' learning behaviour for formative purposes [12]. In particular, it is important to access students' understanding of goal systems and outcome expectations [13].

Besides data on students' learning behaviour, teachers often focus on motivation that, among other things, depends on students' expectation and appreciation, i.e. their level of expectations before new learning activities and their level of appreciation during and after these activities [14]. Teachers can acquire knowledge in this field by analysing students' perceived self-efficacy. Perceived self-efficacy is a theoretical construct that relates to students' beliefs in their capabilities to solve given tasks and accomplish new tasks [15]. Items measuring these beliefs are closely related to students' perceptions of their capabilities to successfully undertake the actions required to complete different tasks [16]. An example question is [17]:

- "How confident do you feel about having to do the following mathematics task – calculating the gas mileage of a car?".

The extent to which students believe in their own ability to handle tasks effectively influences their behaviour in educational settings. Their confidence in being able to solve such tasks correlates strongly with their test achievements in the PISA studies [18]. Compared with other factors, it is the one factor that correlates best with students' achievement [19]. Consequently, perceived self-efficacy is a reliable non-cognitive indicator of students' performance [13, 20].

Students who do not believe in their ability to accomplish new tasks might not exert the effort needed to complete their tasks successfully. Often, students with low perceived self-efficacy do not appreciate self-directed learning [18]. For example, on average 30% of 16-year-old students feel helpless doing problem solving in mathematics and some of them have 'mathematics anxiety' that is associated with a lower score to the equivalent of almost one year of school work [18].

In sum, teachers should give high priority to analyse factors that influence students' perceived self-efficacy [21]. This paper presents results of research concerning the implementation of teacher-driven learning analytics in educational settings (here in Danish schools). In particular, it focuses on students' self-efficacy as a parameter to be analysed together with their academic performance.

2 Research Design

To explore teacher-driven learning analytics, we applied a mixed method research design where data was generated in several ways. Initially, we generated data about the implementation of teacher-driven analytics in public schools. More than 32,000 teachers were involved in the largest research- and development program in Denmark so far. More than 500 focus group interviews were conducted to generate data on pros and cons of teacher-driven analytics at public schools. In addition, digital questionnaires to teachers and students were used to generate information about benefits of the teacher-driven analytics.

Afterwards, we asked digitally innovative teachers regarding the application of ICT into 1:1 learning environments at upper secondary schools in the Danish Central Jutland Region. In 2015, 127 teachers responded (response rate 95%). In 2016, 64 teachers responded (response rate 81%). In 2017, 14 teachers from case schools participated (response rate 93%).

In addition, we conducted semi-structured focus group interviews at the participating schools with representatives of these teachers. Major themes were teachers' application of locally generated data and national indicators regarding student learning outcome, dropout rates and wellbeing.

Furthermore, we did a survey among students in youth education regarding learning experiences. In 2015, a total of 446 students from 25 classes at eight of the participating upper secondary schools answered questions about their teachers' efforts applying ICT into the learning environments (response rate 76%). In 2016, the respondents were 221 students from 12 classes at nine upper secondary schools (response rate 81%). In 2017, the respondents were 131 students from six classes at five upper secondary schools (response rate 86%).

3 Teacher-Driven Learning Analytics

The comprehensive Danish research and development project represents proof of concept regarding learning analytics serving teachers. Usually, teachers are meeting every two or three weeks in order to generate and analyse data on persistent impediments in learning environments. On these occasions, they also draw on relevant theories and research results [22]. In line with general recommendations, they concentrate on specific situations that they can improve rather than on more general learning conditions that are out of reach [23]. At first, they identify what they can and want to improve. Then, they systematically make sense of the educational data and take action based on the results of their analyses to prevent persistent learning difficulties and raise students' motivation. In other words, they make changes and gauge effects on the learning environment and student performance. For example a group of teachers would:

- Identify some educational factors that persistently create and sustain problematic situations
- Generate data on these factors
- Analyse and comprehend these data
- Identify some causes of the challenges
- Decide which factor(s) to change
- Plan how to implement this change
- Take action.

The regular teacher-driven analytics corresponds to systematically formative evaluation, which generally increases students' learning outcomes [24]. Our research provided evidence suggesting positive consequences of the data-driven approach because the groups of teachers act on their analysis, implementing important and necessary changes in the learning environments [22].

Since it takes time to systematically analyse facilitators and impediments in the learning environments, the available time sets a limit to the amount of data that teachers can generate and analyse. When schools, however, allocate additional time to teachers to build teams and analyse data closely related to students' learning, the results can be very successful.

When the teachers systematically increase their understanding of factors that create and sustain challenges in the learning environments, they develop their own analytical competencies and professional identity [22]. They also develop common pedagogical terminology and practice [25]. In particular, such practice fosters ongoing community dialogue regarding educational challenges and a shared understanding regarding student progression [26]. In addition, it fosters reflections concerning these challenges that guide improved teaching practices [27].

This, in turn, enhances teachers' professional wellbeing and strengthens their cooperation [22]. After 3½ years of teacher driven learning analytics, the teachers' collaboration increased to 573 on a scale with a set average value of 500 and their wellbeing increased to 525 on the same scale [28].

In Denmark, teacher development has traditionally been conceived and aimed at building the capacity of the individual teacher to enable him/her to perform better in the learning environment. There is, however, research evidence suggesting that teacher development is less effective than similar group solutions [29]. Teachers are more likely to use what they have learned when they engage in "job-embedded learning featuring teacher collaboration and use of coaches" [30]. Likewise, this collaborative approach improves students' learning [31]. In consequence, the better-performing countries in the world do not aim to have a few expert teachers at each school, but promote team-based solutions enabling teachers to claim ownership in shaping educational practice and to sustain improvement in the classrooms [29].

The Danish research and development project provides research evidence suggesting that teacher-driven learning analytics is feasible when organised as teamwork. Better than the individual teacher, teams of teachers master a data-driven approach, share knowledge about how students are learning and discuss other implications of data to support student learning [2]. This is in line with the theory of learning organisations, according to which teams of professionals build shared visions and engage in pro-active teams [32].

In the research literature, such teams are identified as *affinity groups* [33], *study groups* [34], *professional networks* [35] and *professional learning communities* [34]. Building affinity groups of teachers that meet regularly for the purposes of joint educational development enhance the collective capacity of teachers to create and pursue improved learning conditions for their students and it is considered one of the most successful methods of professional development [36].

4 Learning Analytics in 1:1 Environments

There is research evidence suggesting that teacher provided formative feedback influences the students' learning outcomes [37]. The provision of formative feedback helps teachers to acquire an overview of the progression of learning and to enhance students' learning outcomes and perceived self-efficacy. Danish teachers in youth education often use digital technology to assess students' understanding and performance (Table 1). The respondents entered a number between 1 (representing 'Not at all') and 9 (representing 'To a great extent'). On this scale, responses above "5" represent some or a higher degree of positive experience.

Table 1. Some results of teacher survey (2016).

The use of ICT influences your efforts to foster students' learning when …	Average response
Assessing students' understanding of the learning content	6.8
Engaging in formative assessments of students' performance	6.7

The confidence interval is rather small. With 95% probability, the true value is contained within a range that is the specified answer ±0.2. For example, when an average response is 6.8, the true value is between 6.6 and 7.0.

Denmark is the first country in the world to implement 1:1 classrooms at all public schools [38] and digital competencies of students are among the highest in the world [39]. In general, students are self-reliant in the digital learning environments with a 1:1 ratio between students and digital units connected to the Internet. Consequently, teachers can regularly use ICT to provide information and feedback. Besides oral feedback, written digital feedback contributes to students' perceived self-efficacy as well as their learning outcome (Table 2).

Table 2. Some results of student survey (2017)

Question	Your belief that you can solve your tasks well	Your outcome of school work
Oral feedback strengthens …	7.0	7.0
Written digital feedback strengthens …	6.4	6.6

The standard deviation of the responses is around 2. If an average response is 7.0, this means that the response of a number of students (approximately one sixth) is below 5. To develop and sustain an inclusive digital learning environment, teachers can thus identify and prevent impediments in the environment that disengage this particular group of students.

Teachers use online dialogues on a regular basis to positively influence the motivation of disengaged students. We did a survey in both 2015 and 2016 on the impact of this online dialogue between teachers and students on students' perceived self-efficacy (Table 3).

Table 3. Some results of teacher surveys

The use of ICT influences your efforts to foster students' learning when …	Average response 2015	Average response 2016
Providing an alternative explanation when students do not fully understand something	6.7	7.9
Answering awkward questions from students	6.6	7.3
Helping students to appreciate what they are learning	6.1	7.3
Strengthening students' beliefs that they can cope well with school work	6.1	7.0
Strengthening students' expectations in education	6.3	6.7
Motivating students who show little interest in schoolwork	5.6	6.8

The response distribution is stable over a short time. The questions with the highest response rates in 2015 also have the highest rates the year after (Tables 3 and 4). In general the responses were slightly higher in 2016, representing more positive learning experiences. This can be due to, among other things, the teachers' competence development, the use of ICT and the students' project work.

Whether and to what extent students expect to be able to cope with their educational tasks partially depends on requirements for their presentations and assignments. Therefore, teachers have to describe requirement and prose questions that are understandable for the students, so they become aware of what is expected in terms of assignments and presentations. Students' beliefs about their capabilities to solve given tasks highly depend on teacher clarity at these occasions [25]. Teachers often use ICT to provide information about students' assignments and the requirements in terms of digital products and/or oral presentations. In 1:1 environments, teachers have a wide repertoire of ways to do so, which students generally appreciate (Table 4).

Table 4. Some results of student surveys

When using ICT in education, to what extent does your teacher help you …	Average response 2015	Average response 2016
Understanding the requirements of your tasks (e.g. if you have misunderstood something)?	6.1	6.4
Obtaining assignments that you usually can solve?	6.0	6.4
Formulating good questions for your work?	6.0	6.3
Solving tasks that you have difficulty solving (e.g., by giving examples of solutions)?	6.0	6.3
Varying the ways you can achieve your goals (e.g. that you have access to materials in both text form and video)?	5.9	6.2

As already mentioned, students' learning outcome depends on how they assess their ability to meet the expectations set out at these occasions. Students who do not believe they can and will do well are less likely to be motivated for self-directed learning in terms of effort, persistence and behaviour than students who expect to succeed [40]. Whenever learning activities require reading and processing of texts, it generally reduces these beliefs and some students appreciate the use of multimodal learning materials including digital video that the teachers provide or the find on the Internet (Table 5).

Table 5. Some results of student survey (2017)

When using ICT in education, to what extent does your teacher help you …	Your belief that you can solve your tasks well	Your outcome of school work
Using materials that you find on the internet strengthens …	6.4	6.6
Individual student activities strengthen …	6.2	6.5
Using digital video clips strengthens …	6.0	6.2
Student collaboration on the internet strengthens …	6.0	5.9
Using digital texts strengthens …	5.6	5.7

Our surveys indicate that the teachers most often value the same activities as the students. This includes regular use of video-based or multimodal materials. According to teachers, video-based materials and student products strengthen students' outcome of school work and their perceived self-efficacy (Table 6).

As already mentioned, students' ability to understand and process oral and written content affects their development of other important competencies. With regard to regular use of text-based learning materials, there is quite a substantial difference in teachers' and students' responses. In the teachers' view, it does not really strengthen the students' belief in their own capacity. Many teachers consider literacy problems a learning barrier which inhibits students' perceived self-efficacy.

Table 6. Some results of teacher survey (2017)

Question	Belief in their own capacity
Submitting video-based student products strengthens students' …	7.4
Using video-based learning materials strengthens students'…	6.0
Using materials that the students find on the internet strengthens their …	5.9
Using digital texts strengthens students …	3.9

5 Discussion

When teachers provide formative feedback, it can enhance students' work in progress and belief in own abilities. Therefore, this kind of interaction influences not just their learning outcomes but also their perceived self-efficacy.

In general, it is a win-win situation when teachers evaluate and provide feedback to student drafts using ICT [25]. By assessing and commenting on student efforts, teachers gain an overview of the students' progress of learning and perceived self-efficacy. In particular, they can obtain and analyse real-time data on students' perceived self-efficacy and learning experiences, including their fulfilment of learning objectives and learning difficulties.

When teachers initiate new learning tasks, students can consider whether they will be able to solve these tasks successfully from the beginning. If the students believe that they are not able to solve the task successfully, they might expect some learning difficulties because self-efficacy correlates with learning outcome. Only indirectly, teachers experience perceived self-efficacy among students. Whenever teachers initiate new tasks, they thus have to find ways of obtaining information on this self-efficacy. For example, they can ask students to self-report their beliefs in their capabilities to accomplish their new task or series of tasks (Fig. 1).

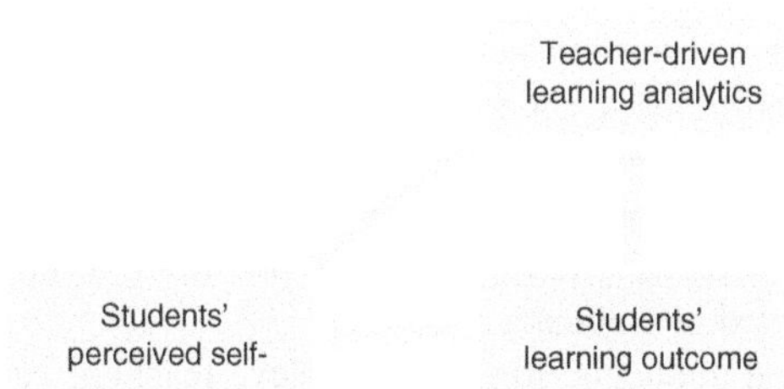

Fig. 1. Real-time learning analytics regarding student self-efficacy and performance

When teachers want to guide and support students, they can use digital technology to retrieve information about current perceived self-efficacy. By means of simple digital questionnaires, teachers can easily survey students' learning expectations and perceptions of their capabilities to successfully undertake the actions required to complete specific learning tasks. During learning activities, teachers can, among other things, use the results of these analyses to tailor their provision of feedback to the individual needs of the students.

Future studies can contribute to the development of digital standardised self-report questions regarding perceived self-efficacy that teachers can easily apply into 1:1 learning environments. For example, teachers can obtain and analyse real-time data including snapshots of perceived self-efficacy. These snapshots can be obtained at the beginning and during the students' learning activities. As already mentioned, they often represent the most reliable non-cognitive indicator of students' performance.

6 Conclusion

This paper provides evidence suggesting how teachers can generate and analyse data to help improve their practice and the learning outcomes for their students. The paper examines an approach adopted by some of the world's most improved school systems implementing team based learning analytics. In particular, it builds on research on the implementation of teacher-driven learning analytics in Danish primary and secondary education.

When affinity groups of teachers systematically increase their understanding of factors that create and sustain challenges in the learning environments, they at the same time develop their own analytical competencies and professional identity. This practice fosters an ongoing community dialogue regarding educational challenges in the 1:1 classroom and reflects these challenges to guide teaching practices. In addition, collaborative teacher-driven learning analytics foster the development of a shared understanding regarding student progression. This, in turn, enhances the teachers' professional well-being and cooperation.

The paper examines analyses of a theoretical construct: perceived self-efficacy that refers to students' perceptions of their capabilities to successfully undertake the actions required to complete specific learning tasks. This construct is considered the most reliable indicator of students' performance, i.e. the one that correlates best with students' learning outcomes. When students are asked to complete tasks in the 1:1 classrooms, their perceived self-efficacy correlates with their expectations of being able to do it. The greater self-efficacy, the greater the confidence that a task will go well and the less fear that it fails. In youth education, teachers often utilise online dialogue to strengthen students' perception of their ability to perform new learning tasks. When answering students' questions, guiding them and providing feedback to them, teachers also foster this perceived self-efficacy.

By identifying and reducing low self-efficacy, teachers can increase students' expectations regarding their learning outcomes. Using digital tools, teachers can obtain self-reported data regarding perceived self-efficacy. In particular, they can generate data on the students' beliefs whether they can solve their imminent tasks. Based on results of analyses of these data, teachers can then develop and sustain inclusive 1:1 learning environments.

Future studies can contribute to the development of digital standardised self-report questions regarding perceived self-efficacy, which teachers can easily apply into 1:1 learning environments.

References

1. Long, P., Siemens, G.: Penetrating the fog: analytics in learning and education. Educausereview (2011). https://er.educause.edu/~/media/files/article-downloads/erm1151.pdf
2. Nusche, D., et al.: OECD Reviews of School Resources: Denmark 2016. OECD Publishing, Paris (2016). https://doi.org/10.1787/9789264262430-en
3. Bill and Melinda Gates Foundation: Teachers know best. Making data work for teachers and students (2010). https://s3.amazonaws.com/edtech-production/reports/Gates-TeachersKnow Best-MakingDataWork.pdf
4. Bundsgaard, J., Puck, M.R.: Nationale test: Danske lærere og skolelederes brug, holdninger og viden. Aarhus Universitet, Aarhus (2016)
5. Andresen, B.B.: Pædagogisk indsatsteori – udvikling af ungdomsuddannelser. Inspirationsdokument 2 om indikatorinformeret praksis. Det Nationale Videncenter for e-læring, Aarhus (2016)
6. Meyer, G.: Lykkens kontrollanter. Jurist- og Økonomforbundets Forlag, København (2016)
7. Andresen, B.B.: Digital indsatsteori – lærerens syn på digitaliseringsindsatsen på ungdomsuddannelser. Anden rapport om følgeforskningen i tilknytning til eSkolerMidt-projektet. Det nationale Videncenter for e-læring, Aarhus (2016a)
8. Andresen, B.B.: Literacy, assistive technology and e-inclusion. J. Assist. Technol. **1**(1), 10–14 (2007)
9. Mihaly, K., et al.: A composite estimator of effective teaching. MET Project Research Paper. Bill & Melinda Gates Foundation (2013). http://k12education.gatesfoundation.org/wp-content/uploads/2015/12/MET_Composite_Estimator_of_Effective_Teaching_Research_Paper.pdf
10. Kane, T.J., et al.: Learning about teaching. Initial findings from the measures of effective teaching project. MET Project Research Paper. Bill & Melinda Gates Foundation (2010). http://k12education.gatesfoundation.org/wp-content/uploads/2015/12/Preliminary_Findings-Research_Paper.pdf
11. Gardner, H.: What do tests test? A commentary. Education World (2000). http://www.educationworld.com/a_issues/issues098.shtml
12. Webb, M., Ifenthaler, D.: Assessment as, for and of 21st-century learning using IT (2017, in press)
13. Bandura, A.: On the functional properties of perceived self-efficacy revisited. J. Manag. **38**(1), 9–44 (2012)
14. Pintrich, P.R., Schunk, D.H.: Motivation in Education. Theory, Research, and Applications. Prentice Hall, New Jersey (1996)
15. Bandura, A.: Guide for constructing self-efficacy scales. In: Urdan, T., Pajares, F. (eds.) Self-efficacy Beliefs of Adolescents, pp. 307–337. Information Age Publishing, Charlotte (2006)
16. OECD: PISA 2012 Results (2012). http://www.oecd.org/pisa/keyfindings/pisa-2012-results.htm
17. OECD: OECD program for international student assessment 2012. Student Questionnaire - Form A. OECD, Paris (2012)
18. OECD: Mathematics self-beliefs and participation in mathematics-related activities. In: OECD: Ready to Learn: Students' Engagement, Drive and Self-beliefs, vol. III. OECD, Paris (2013)
19. Bartimote-Aufflick, K., et al.: The study, evaluation, and improvement of university student self-efficacy. Stud. High. Educ. **41**, 1918–1942 (2016)
20. Dinther, M.V., Dochy, F., Segers, M.: Factors affecting students' self-efficacy in higher education. Educ. Res. Rev. **6**, 95–108 (2011)

21. Broadbent, J.: Academic success is about self-efficacy rather than frequency of use of the learning management system. Australas. J. Educ. Technol. **32**(4), 38–49 (2016)
22. Andresen, B.B.: Development of analytical competencies and professional identities through school-based learning in Denmark. Int. Rev. Educ., 1–18 (2015). http://link.springer.com/journal/11159
23. Sawyer, E., Dalzell, R.: Putting Analysis into Assessment: Undertaking Assessments of Need, 2nd edn. Jessica Kingsley Publishers, London (2011)
24. Hattie, J.: Visible Learning. Routledge, London (2009)
25. Andresen, B.B., Egelund, N., Nordahl, T.: LP-modellen – forskningsindsats og første resultater. Pædagogisk Psykologisk Tidsskrift **46**(6), 386–394 (2009)
26. Hattie, J.: Visible Learning for Teachers. Maximizing Impact on Learning. Routledge, Oxford (2012)
27. Vescio, V., Ross, D., Adams, A.: A review of research on the impact of professional learning communities on teaching practice and student learning. Teach. Teach. Educ. **24**(1), 80–91 (2008). http://www.k12.wa.us/Compensation/pubdocs/Vescio2008PLC-paper.pdf
28. Sunnevåg, A.-K.: LP: Danmarks største skoleutviklingsprojekt. In: Qvortrup, L. (ed.) Inklusionens historie og aktualitet, pp. 99–110. Dafolo, Frederikshavn (2014)
29. Fullan, M.: Choosing the wrong drivers for whole system reform. Centre for Strategic Education: Melbourne. Seminar Series Paper No. 204. East Melbourne VIC: Centre for Strategic Education (2011). http://edsource.org/wp-content/uploads/Fullan-Wrong-Drivers1.pdf
30. Duley, C.: A Guide for Increasing the Effectiveness of Professional Development in Schools and Districts. Vermont Department of Education, Vermont (2011)
31. Hattie, J.: What works best in education: the politics of collective expertise. Open ideas at Pearson. Pearson, London (2015). https://www.pearson.com/content/dam/corporate/global/pearson-dot-com/files/hattie/150526_ExpertiseWEB_V1.pdf
32. Senge, P., et al.: Schools That Learn. A Fifth Discipline Fieldbook for Educators, Parents, and Everyone Who Cares About Education. Doubleday/Currency, New York (2000)
33. O'Brien, M., et al.: How are the perceptions of learning networks shaped among school professionals and head teachers at an early stage in their introduction? Int. Rev. Educ. **54**(2), 211–242 (2008)
34. OECD: The professional development of teachers. In: Creating Effective Teaching and Learning Environments. First Results from TALIS, pp. 47–86. OECD, Paris (2009)
35. Hunzicker, J.: Characteristics of effective professional development: a checklist (2010). http://files.eric.ed.gov/fulltext/ED510366.pdf
36. Mourshed, M., Chijioke, C., Barber, M.: How the World's Most Improved School Systems Keep Getting Better. McKinsey, London (2010). www.mckinsey.com/~/media/mckinsey/dotcom/client_service/socialpct.20sector/pdfs/how-the-worlds-most-improved-school-systems-keep-getting-better_download-version_final.ashx
37. Black, P., Wiliam, D.: Inside the black box: raising standards through classroom assessment. Phi Delta Kappan **80**, 139–148 (1998)
38. Søby, M.: Synergies for better learning – where are we now? Nord. J. Dig. Lit. **8**(01–02), 3–11 (2013)
39. Bundsgaard, J., Pettersson, M., Puck, M.R.: Digitale kompetenser. Aarhus Universitetsforlag, Aarhus (2014)
40. Pintrich, P.R.: A motivational science perspective on the role of student motivation in learning and teaching contexts. J. Educ. Psychol. **95**(4), 667–686 (2003)

Feature Based Sentiment Analysis for Evaluating the Mobile Pedagogical Affordances of Apps

Muneera Bano[1(✉)], Didar Zowghi[1], and Matthew Kearney[2]

[1] Faculty of Engineering and Information Technology, University of Technology Sydney, Sydney, Australia
{Muneera.Bano,Didar.Zowghi}@uts.edu.au

[2] Faculty of Arts and Social Sciences, University of Technology Sydney, Sydney, Australia
Matthew.Kearney@uts.edu.au

Abstract. The launch of millions of apps has made it challenging for teachers to select the most suitable educational app to support students' learning. Several evaluation frameworks have been proposed in the research literature to assist teachers in selecting the right apps for their needs. This paper presents preliminary results of an innovative technique for evaluating educational mobile apps by analysing the feedback of past app users through the lens of a mobile pedagogical perspective. We have utilized a sentiment analysis tool to assess the opinions of the app users through the lens of the criteria offered by a rigorous mobile learning pedagogical framework highlighting the learners' experience of Personalization, Authenticity and Collaboration (iPAC). The investigation has provided initial confirmation of the powerful utility of the feature based sentiment analysis technique for evaluating the mobile pedagogical affordances of learning apps.

Keywords: Mobile learning · Sentiment analysis · m-learning pedagogies

1 Introduction

Over the last decade, a significant amount of research has been conducted to investigate the effectiveness of mobile learning apps in school education [1]. The number of apps has increased exponentially in the last decade and there are millions of educational apps available for educators and students. However, with overload of choice, and the increasing speed of technological development—much of which is driven by corporate markets rather than education [2], it has become challenging for teachers to efficiently select an app that best supports appropriate learning activity types and assessment strategies, and associated pedagogical preferences [3]. To add to these challenges, the majority of apps in repositories such as the iTunes Store are 'drill and practice' or 'instructive' in nature [4], underpinned by traditional behaviourist principles—essentially replicating traditional transmissionist approaches to learning [5–7]. As mobile apps develop and proliferate, the challenge for educators is to move beyond the hype and rhetoric [8] to focus on new mobile pedagogical opportunities with apps.

A. Tatnall and M. Webb (Eds.): WCCE 2017, IFIP AICT 515, pp. 281–291, 2017.
https://doi.org/10.1007/978-3-319-74310-3_30

App stores often provide the facility for user feedback (comments and ratings) in order to help teachers select apps, and for app developers to improve their designs. These customer ratings and reviews play a critical role in the mobile app market and directly influence app downloads. User feedback has already been used by practitioners and app developers as a source of information in activities such as selection of apps, customer satisfaction, versioning, and bug reports [9–11]. However, the main challenge is processing and synthesising this feedback into useful information. Considering review volumes, analysing every review manually is laborious and time consuming.

Sentiment analysis is an automated approach that aims to determine the polarity of sentiments and emotions within large textual datasets [12]. This approach is used to develop tools for calculating and monitoring the attitude and behaviour of app users from their feedback, comments and reviews in online social media and app review sites [10]. Sentiment analysis tools are a powerful utility in app ranking and selection; however, it has so far been underutilized in the education domain.

In this paper, we present the results of our preliminary investigation exploring the utility of a new technique for evaluating the pedagogical affordances of educational apps. The feedback and comments of app users are assessed for their alignment against evaluation criteria from a well-accepted, rigorous mobile pedagogical framework [13]. This framework focuses on three distinctive mobile pedagogies: personalization, authenticity, and collaboration. The objective of our research is to explore the utility of our novel technique incorporating sentiment analysis and informed by the m-learning pedagogical framework [13].

The main contributions of this research are: (1) Feature based sentiment analysis using the three mobile pedagogical constructs i.e. personalization, authenticity, and collaboration; and (2) initial confirmation of the usefulness of sentiment analysis for evaluating apps in education.

2 Background

2.1 Mobile Learning

Mobile learning (or m-learning) is described in numerous ways, but these descriptions all consider the nexus between working with mobile devices and the occurrence of learning: the process of learning mediated by a mobile device. Numerous characteristics of m-learning have been identified in the literature [14].

Over the last decade, a significant number of initiatives have been launched that aim to fully utilize and exploit mobile technologies and apps for educational purposes [15]. There is evidence that m-learning environments enhance students' performance [16, 17]. However, increase in the use of mobile devices does not imply their effective incorporation in educational policies and in practice, mobile devices are not effectively utilised in formal education [18, 19] for a variety of reasons [17, 20].

Various lists of recommended educational apps are available online [21, 22]. These lists are limited in what they provide because they don't guide the teachers and students about pedagogical understanding of how an app could be used to support teaching and learning. Therefore, they are not sufficiently practical to facilitate strong instructional planning and implementation [21]. This has resulted in a pressing need for an evaluation framework/rubric that facilitates the analysis of pedagogical affordances of educational apps.

2.2 A Pedagogical Framework for m-Learning: iPAC

Numerous frameworks have been proposed in the literature, ranging from complex multi-level models (e.g. [23]) to smaller frameworks that often omit important socio-cultural characteristics of learning or of pedagogy. Common themes include portability of m-learning devices and mobility of learners; interactivity; control and communication. The theoretical underpinning for the work described in this paper is a robust and validated mobile pedagogical framework [13]. Informed by sociocultural theory [24], it highlights three central and distinctive pedagogical features of m-learning: personalisation, authenticity and collaboration (or 'PAC'). The critical influence of context is signalled by the central location of 'time-space' at the core of the 'iPAC' framework, as depicted in Fig. 1.

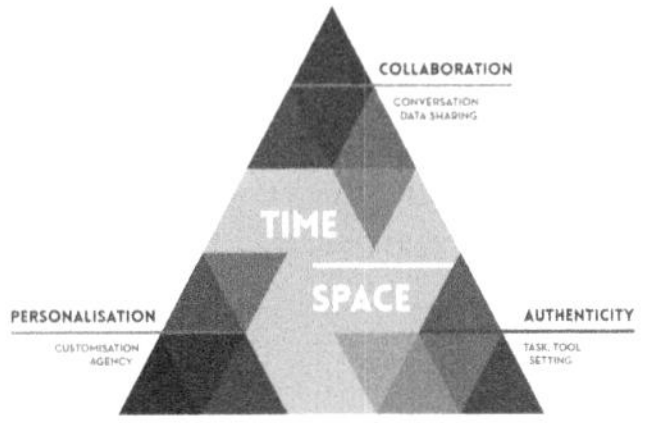

Fig. 1. The mobile pedagogical framework (iPAC) comprising three distinctive features of mobile learning experiences. Adapted from ([13], p. 8)

The personalisation construct consists of the sub-constructs of 'agency' and 'customisation'. High levels of personalisation would mean the learner is able to enjoy an enhanced degree of agency [25] and the flexibility to tailor both tools and activities, interacting with a strong sense of ownership of both the device and the learning process. The authenticity construct privileges opportunities for in-situ, participatory learning [26]. The sub-constructs of 'task', 'tool' and 'setting' focus on learners' involvement in rich, contextualised tasks, making use of tools in a realistic way, and driven by relevant real-life practices and processes [27]. The collaboration construct captures the conversational, networked features of m-learning. It consists of 'conversation' and 'data sharing' sub-constructs, as learners engage in negotiated meaning-making, forging connections and interactions with peers, experts and the environment [28]. This iPAC framework provides a useful lens to analyse mobile apps and how use of their features might leverage mobile pedagogies in a range of learning environments.

The iPAC framework has recently been used to inform research on m-learning in school education [29], teacher education [30, 35], indigenous education [31] and other areas of higher education [32]. For example, Viberg and Grönlund [33] used the framework to develop a survey instrument for eliciting students' attitudes toward mobile technology use in and for second and foreign language learning in higher education.

2.3 Feature Based Sentiment Analysis

Sentiment analysis is used to analyse human opinions, sentiments, judgements, reviews and behaviours about many aspects of life such as products, business, people, problems, subjects and their features [12]. Sentiment analysis aims to calculate the polarity of emotions in textual data by identifying the positivity or negativity of a statement. Sentiment analysis is one of the widely used evaluation techniques around the world, helping companies to improve their products based on customers' feedback. App stores provide users with facilities to submit their feedback and rank the apps with star ratings [10]. This data is used by the companies to monitor the app users' behaviours and sentiments.

Feature-based sentiment analysis is a specific type of sentiment analysis which aims to capture nuances about objects of interest. Different features of a product can generate different sentiments, for example a mobile phone can have a user-friendly interface but the battery life is very low. This scenario requires identifying relevant entities of interest, extracting these features from the data, and determining whether an opinion expressed on each feature is positive, negative or neutral.

3 Study Design

The investigation was carried out in the context of school-based mathematics and science education for two main reasons. Firstly, we are currently conducting a larger ongoing research project[1] about the effectiveness of mobile apps for science and mathematics in school education, driven by the strong 'political will' in many countries to improve maths and science learning and to build the capability of the workforce for future job markets. Secondly, there is currently a burgeoning interest in STEM education—see for example, the major recent reviews of m-learning research in both science [17] and mathematics [16] education. The investigation was quantitative in nature and addressed the key question: *What is the utility of feature based sentiment analysis for evaluating the mobile pedagogical affordances of educational apps?*

The steps in this investigation were as follows:

(1) We selected ten popular discipline-specific education apps (5 science and 5 mathematics) suitable for school students, as described in Table 1. The apps were chosen based on popularity in various forums and blogs.
(2) We used a commercial sentiment analysis tool, Appbot (https://appbot.co/), that extracts user reviews and ratings from the app stores and provides full utility of qualitative and quantitative analysis. Other similar sentiment analysis tools could

[1] https://www.uts.edu.au/future-students/education/about-education/news/optimising-mobile-intensive-pedagogies-arc-discovery.

provide the same functionality but we chose Appbot because it provides functions to search within reviews for specific words (i.e. feature extraction) and also allows filtering out relevant reviews that match particular concepts or words.

(3) We developed a word bank based on words in the literature associated with the three main constructs of the iPAC framework. Figure 2 shows sample words from these word banks.

(4) After using the word bank for feature extraction on all of the ten selected apps, we used Appbot to analyse the extracted reviews for the polarity of the sentiments. Data was collected covering reviews from the period of one year i.e. from January 2016 to January 2017 to limit the scope of our investigation.

Table 1. Selected apps for investigation (based on popularity in various forums and blogs)

	App	Store	Web link
Mathematics	Mathletics Student	iOS	http://au.mathletics.com/
	Myscript Calculator	iOS	http://www.myscript.com/calculator/
	GeoGebra	iOS	https://www.geogebra.org/
	MalMath	Google Play	http://www.malmath.com/
	Math: Mental Math Games	Google Play	https://play.google.com/store/apps/details?id=com.astepanov.mobile.mindmathtricks&hl=en
Science	Anatomy 4D	iOS	http://anatomy4d.daqri.com/
	Little Alchemy	Google Play	https://littlealchemy.com/
	NASA	Google Play	https://play.google.com/store/apps/details?id=gov.nasa&hl=en
	Skeptical Science	Google Play	https://www.skepticalscience.com/
	Star Walk	iOS	http://vitotechnology.com/star-walk.html

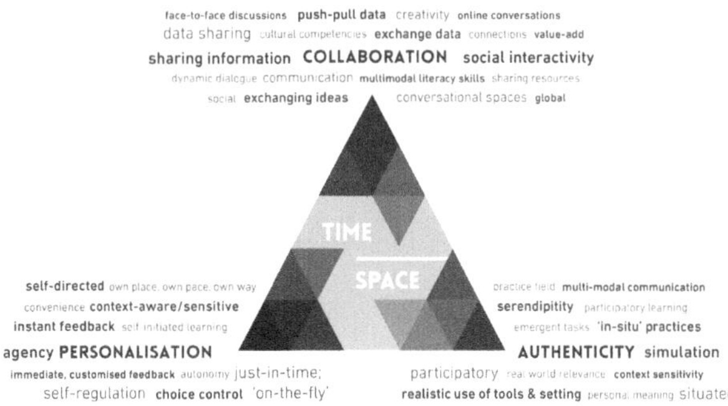

Fig. 2. Word clouds relating to the three constructs of the iPAC framework [13]

4 Results

Table 2 shows the total number of reviews, the percentage of positive sentiments, average of star ratings and the scores. These scores ranged from D− to A+ and are calculated based on the trends in the review sentiments, review volume, and star ratings as expressed by the app users.

In the domain of mathematics, MalMath and Myscript Calculator are on top of the list, whereas for science, Little Alchemy and NASA has received highest number of reviews. MalMath and Little Alchemy has received a significant number of reviews from the users and above 90% of these reviews contained positive sentiments. Next, we extracted the data based on the aforementioned word bank. Table 3 shows results for the number of reviews that matched the iPAC word bank. Table 4 shows the breakdown of the sentiments for the extracted reviews for the apps.

Table 2. Results from sentiment analysis of selected maths and science apps

		App	Review count	Positive sentiment	Avg review stars	Score
Maths	1	MalMath	10572	91.2%	4.5	A−
	2	Myscript Calculator	1488	89.3%	4.3	B
	3	Math: Mental Math Games	47	88.6%	4.4	C−
	4	GeoGebra	97	55.6%	3.1	D−
	5	Mathletics Student	122	21.2%	2.0	D−
Science	1	Little Alchemy	7929	92.3%	4.5	A
	2	NASA	4161	88.0%	4.4	A−
	3	Star Walk ™	584	94.1%	4.7	B−
	4	Skeptical Science	5	80.0%	4.0	D+
	5	Anatomy 4D	30	58.6%	3.3	D−

Table 3. Feature based sentiment analysis

Apps	Total reviews	Authenticity		Collaboration		Personlisation	
		Reviews	%	Reviews	%	Reviews	%
MalMath	10572	22	0.21	4	0.04	40	0.38
Mathletics	122	8	6.56	1	0.82	4	3.28
Geogebra	97	2	2.06	0	0.00	3	3.09
Math: Mental Math Games	664	4	0.60	1	0.15	6	0.90
Myscript Calculator	1488	19	1.28	3	0.20	31	2.08
Little Alchemy	7929	13	0.16	25	0.32	88	1.11
Skeptical Science	5	0	0.00	0	0.00	0	0.00
Anatomy 4D	30	1	3.33	0	0.00	1	3.33
NASA	4161	8	0.19	6	0.14	32	0.77
Star walk	584	12	2.05	3	0.51	22	3.77

Table 4. Breakdown of feature based sentiment analysis (P = positive, Nt = Neutral, Ng = Negative)

Apps	Authenticity			Collaboration			Personlisation		
	P	Nt	Ng	P	Nt	Ng	P	Nt	Ng
MalMath	22			4			37	1	2
Mathletics	1		7	1			1		3
Geogebra	1		1				2		1
Math: Mental Math Games	4					1	5	1	
Myscript Calculator	17	1	1		2	1	23	3	5
Little Alchemy	6	3	4	25			78	4	6
Skeptical Science									
Anatomy 4D	1						1		
NASA	5		3	4	1	1	29	1	2
Star walk	9		3	1		2	11		3

Overall, a nuanced picture of pedagogical affordances emerges for these ten sample apps. MalMath produced considerably more positive sentiments in *Personalisation* and *Authenticity*, however there weren't many reviews about the app relating to *Collaboration.* Myscript Calculator has generated positive sentiments for the *Personalisation* and *Authenticity* constructs, but have received only negative reviews for *Collaboration.* In the case of Little Alchemy, it generated significantly positive reviews for app features relating to *Personalisation* and some positive reviews in *Collaboration,* however received low volume of reviews with mixed sentiments in *Authenticity.* NASA received positive sentiments for *Personalisation* but not so favourable sentiments in *Collaboration* and *Authenticity* (Fig. 3).

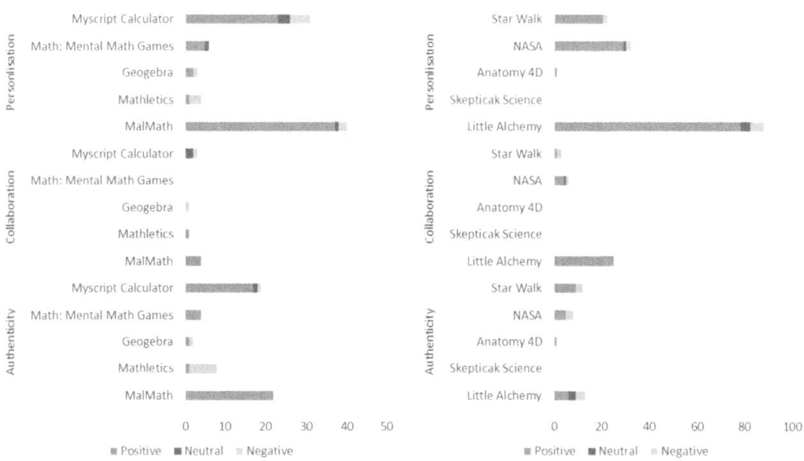

Fig. 3. Feature based sentiment analysis results. This provides the graphical representation of the feature based sentiment analysis results.

5 Discussion

The results provide evidence of what mobile pedagogical features of apps that users are choosing to comment on in their reviews, without any prompting from rubric or other more formal evaluation instruments. There was a trend in our results showing higher frequencies of positive sentiments relating to the *Personalisation* aspect of the selected apps. Past work has revealed that of the three iPAC constructs, *Personalisation* is the least exploited by teachers in their mobile learning task designs [29], with teachers evidently struggling to give opportunities for learners to control their learning (e.g. the pace of lessons and how m-learning tasks are undertaken). So, in some ways the result from the present study is surprising. However, assuming that our results comprised comments mostly from students and teachers, and given that our study only used recent app reviews (1 year), perhaps the 'struggle' discussed in [29] is the very reason that users 'noticed' these pedagogical affordances (relating to personalisation) i.e. app reviewers were mindful of their previous mobile learning experiences that quite likely lacked a sense of learner control. This claim is entirely speculative and future research will need to triangulate these findings. This triangulation can be performed in two ways: (1) with interviews and surveys of app users, (2) qualitative analysis of the text of the reviews and feedback from app stores and social media (e.g. Facebook or Twitter).

It is too early to draw conclusions about 'low volumes' of comments, other than users were not choosing to comment on such features. For example, just because users were evidently not frequently commenting on (or not 'noticing') app features relating to *Collaboration*, doesn't mean that these features are absent. Further research is needed to clarify the exact implications of low and high frequencies of sentiments. Informed by these results, we posit that sentiment analysis technique is a novel and effective augmentation of other more traditional app evaluation procedures. This type of innovative, two-tiered evaluation procedure will ultimately help educators (and app designers) to more accurately evaluate the pedagogical potential and value of education apps.

We also recognise the risk of deterministic views of emerging technologies [34] such as mobile apps, and we are certainly not advocating a 'one-size-fits-all' approach to selecting and using educational apps. There are many other factors (beyond pedagogical approaches) that contribute to the effective use of apps for learning, such as the teacher expertise, student characteristics and provision of technical support. However, there is value in teachers using procedures such as the one outlined in this paper to critically examine app features and their potential for leveraging transformational pedagogies [4] in and beyond the classroom.

6 Conclusion and Future Directions

In this paper, we have presented a preliminary investigation of exploring the utility of a new technique for evaluating the pedagogical affordances of educational apps. This technique uses feature based sentiment analysis approach to extract the feedback and comments of app users. We have used the results of sentiment analysis to assess their alignment against evaluation criteria from a rigorous mobile pedagogical framework (iPAC) [13]. The main objective of our research was to explore the utility our novel technique incorporating sentiment analysis and informed by the iPAC pedagogical framework. The preliminary results of our investigation have provided empirical evidence that using sentiment analysis is an effective way of incorporating the opinions of past users of educational mobile apps with use of the iPAC framework. These forms of feedback are very useful for the authors who developed the iPAC framework [13] in their ongoing studies of the usefulness and utility of this framework.

In relation to threats to validity, we concede that the precision of our results is impacted by the accuracy of the word bank and the limitations of the sentiment analysis tool (appbot), so the words may not have matched well against those words used in the reviews even though they may have been synonyms. We plan to extend our study to include deeper semantic analysis of the textual content of the reviews by using cutting edge Natural Language Processing technologies as well as newly emerged algorithms for opinion mining. Another future direction is the integration of the sentiment analysis technique with the recently developed rubric instrument[2] for app evaluation emerging from iPAC framework. It is recommended that teachers should ideally use this instrument after thoroughly exploring an app, and if possible, after using the app in their teaching. We plan to design a software tool that would seamlessly extract the sentiments of past users of an app to provide additional information about the app within this type of rubric instrument.

References

1. Sung, Y.-T., Chang, K.-E., Liu, T.-C.: The effects of integrating mobile devices with teaching and learning on students' learning performance: a meta-analysis and research synthesis. Comput. Educ. **94**, 252–275 (2016)
2. Traxler, J.: Current state of mobile learning. Mob. Learn.: Transform. Deliv. Educ. Train. **1**, 9–24 (2009)
3. Stevenson, M., et al.: Visualizing solutions: apps as cognitive stepping-stones in the learning process. Electron. J. e-Learn. **13**(5), 366–379 (2015)
4. Highfield, K., Goodwin, K.: Apps for mathematics learning: a review of 'educational' apps from the iTunes App Store. In: Mathematics Education: Yesterday, Today, and Tomorrow, pp. 378–385 (2013)
5. El-Hussein, M.O.M., Cronje, J.C.: Defining mobile learning in the higher education landscape. Educ. Technol. Soc. **13**(3), 12–21 (2010)
6. Goodwin, K.: Use of tablet technology in the classroom. NSW Department of Education and Communities (2012)
7. Murray, O.T., Olcese, N.R.: Teaching and learning with iPads, ready or not? TechTrends **55**(6), 42–48 (2011)
8. Peluso, D.C.: The fast-paced iPad revolution: can educators stay up to date and relevant about these ubiquitous devices? Br. J. Educ. Technol. **43**(4) (2012)

[2] http://www.mobilelearningtoolkit.com/app-rubric1.html.

9. Bano, M., Zowghi, D.: Users' voice and service selection: an empirical study. In: 2014 IEEE Fourth International Workshop on Empirical Requirements Engineering (EmpiRE). IEEE (2014)
10. Guzman, E., Maalej, W.: How do users like this feature? A fine grained sentiment analysis of app reviews. In: 2014 IEEE 22nd International Requirements Engineering Conference (RE). IEEE (2014)
11. Maalej, W., Nabil, H.: Bug report, feature request, or simply praise? On automatically classifying app reviews. In: 2015 IEEE 23rd International Requirements Engineering Conference (RE). IEEE (2015)
12. Pang, B., Lee, L.: Opinion mining and sentiment analysis. Found. Trends® Inf. Retr. **2**(1–2), 1–135 (2008)
13. Kearney, M., et al.: Viewing mobile learning from a pedagogical perspective. Res. Learn. Technol. **20** (2012)
14. Koole, M.L.: A model for framing mobile learning. Mob. Learn.: Transform. Deliv. Educ. Train. **1**(2), 25–47 (2009)
15. Wu, W.-H., et al.: Review of trends from mobile learning studies: a meta-analysis. Comput. Educ. **59**(2), 817–827 (2012)
16. Crompton, H., Burke, D.: Research trends in the use of mobile learning in mathematics. In: Blended Learning: Concepts, Methodologies, Tools, and Applications, pp. 2090–2104. IGI Global (2015)
17. Crompton, H., et al.: The use of mobile learning in science: a systematic review. J. Sci. Educ. Technol. **25**(2), 149–160 (2016)
18. Levin, T., Wadmany, R.: Teachers' views on factors affecting effective integration of information technology in the classroom: developmental scenery. J. Technol. Teach. Educ. **16**(2), 233 (2008)
19. Groff, J., Mouza, C.: A framework for addressing challenges to classroom technology use. AACe J. **16**(1), 21–46 (2008)
20. Goktas, Y., Yildirim, S., Yildirim, Z.: Main barriers and possible enablers of ICTs integration into pre-service teacher education programs. Educ. Technol. Soc. **12**(1), 193–204 (2009)
21. Cherner, T., Dix, J., Lee, C.: Cleaning up that mess: a framework for classifying educational apps. Contemp. Issues Technol. Teach. Educ. **14**(2), 158–193 (2014)
22. Lee, C.-Y., Cherner, T.S.: A comprehensive evaluation rubric for assessing instructional apps. J. Inf. Technol. Educ.: Res. **14**, 21–53 (2015)
23. Parsons, D., Ryu, H., Cranshaw, M.: A design requirements framework for mobile learning environments. JCP **2**(4), 1–8 (2007)
24. Wertsch, J.V.: Mind as Action (1998)
25. Pachler, N., Bachmair, B., Cook, J.: Mobile Learning: Structures, Agency, Practices. Springer Science & Business Media, New York (2009). https://doi.org/10.1007/978-1-4419-0585-7
26. Radinsky, J., et al.: Mutual benefit partnership: a curricular design for authenticity. J. Curric. Stud. **33**(4), 405–430 (2001)
27. Burden, K., Kearney, M.: Conceptualising authentic mobile learning. In: Churchill, D., Lu, J., Chiu, Thomas K.F., Fox, B. (eds.) Mobile Learning Design. LNET, pp. 27–42. Springer, Singapore (2016). https://doi.org/10.1007/978-981-10-0027-0_2
28. Wang, M., Shen, R.: Message design for mobile learning: learning theories, human cognition and design principles. Br. J. Edu. Technol. **43**(4), 561–575 (2012)
29. Kearney, M., Burden, K., Rai, T.: Investigating teachers' adoption of signature mobile pedagogies. Comput. Educ. **80**, 48–57 (2015)

30. Kearney, M., Maher, D.: Mobile learning in maths teacher education: using iPads to support pre-service teachers' professional development. Aust. Educ. Comput. **27**(3), 76–84 (2013)
31. Townsend, P.: Mobile devices for tertiary study-philosophy meets pragmatics for remote Aboriginal and Torres Strait Islander women. Aust. J. Indig. Educ. **44**(02), 139–149 (2015)
32. Kinash, S., Brand, J., Mathew, T.: Challenging mobile learning discourse through research: student perceptions of Blackboard Mobile Learn and iPads. Australas. J. Educ. Technol. **28** (4), 639–655 (2012)
33. Viberg, O., Grönlund, Å.: Cross-cultural analysis of users' attitudes toward the use of mobile devices in second and foreign language learning in higher education: a case from Sweden and China. Comput. Educ. **69**, 169–180 (2013)
34. Selwyn, N.: Looking beyond learning: notes towards the critical study of educational technology. J. Comput. Assist. Learn. **26**(1), 65–73 (2010)
35. Burden, K., Kearney, M.: Investigating and critiquing teacher educators' mobile learning practices. Interact. Technol. Smart Educ. **14**(2), 110–125 (2017)

How Interactives Can Change Learnability of Science Concepts for Young Children – Re-positioning Them as Learners 'Who Can and Did'

Cheryl Jakab(✉) and Christine Redman

Melbourne Graduate School of Education, The University of Melbourne, Melbourne, Australia
{cjakab, redmanc}@unimelb.edu.au

Abstract. This paper explores what young children can and will 'say and do' when positively positioned to think with scientific concepts using ICT interactives. The progress with meaning-making of three young children (7, 9 and 12 years old) when playing a game is tracked and analysed. How these children were positively positioned with the concepts and what this afforded them in the setting are outlined. Analysis of their 'sayings and doings', using affordances and positioning theory, details their progress in meaning-making with the offered chemistry concepts. What each child did with the three levels of thinking of chemistry (macro/sub-micro/symbolic), was tracked. Three chemical thinking storylines are described to highlight that exploring molecular and chemical symbolic thinking can lead young children to engage with more scientifically sophisticated thinking and is of interest to them. Many scientifically relevant questions were raised while 'playing' with the interactive. The game directed their attention to the chemistry concepts and led to meaning-making opportunities. This examination provides insights into how suitable interactives can offer, direct and help structure early 'knowing of' scientific concepts by positively positioning learners with the concepts. Implications for restructuring early learning opportunities with central concepts using ICT are proposed.

Keywords: Interactives · Early learning · Positive positioning
Science concepts

1 Introduction

Using 21st century ICT tools is changing possibilities in learning and teaching [1]. Many ideas that are difficult to explain using words alone become more readily interpreted and understandable when re-presented in diagrams, images, video and computer-generated imagery (CGI) combinations. They say a picture is worth a thousand words. What worth then, of today's interactives, simulations and visualizations? Making sense of many previously considered difficult concepts is made easier through today's multimodal offerings. Noss goes further in his research, showing available visualization and simulation tools afford [2] new 'learnabilities' and 'teachabilites' for all, for scientists, adults and children alike.

A. Tatnall and M. Webb (Eds.): WCCE 2017, IFIP AICT 515, pp. 292–303, 2017.
https://doi.org/10.1007/978-3-319-74310-3_31

The wealth of innovative interactive ICT resources available today includes many child-friendly educational interactive games, models, images and simulations.

The vast majority of the research into the use/s of ICT simulations and visualizations to support science learning have been conducted at secondary and tertiary levels [3]. The majority of the research focus is on "soft skills", that is, the uses of ICT as communication tools, for developing communities of learners, CoL [3] and for representing and modelling [4].

In science curriculum designs, young children are routinely introduced to chemistry through the sensory level of substances in their primary (elementary) schooling [5]. The particulate nature of matter or molecular thinking and chemical symbols are then included into chemistry in secondary schooling [6]. Thus the introduction to chemical science begins with macro-only activities involving exploration of physical and chemical changes, delaying the introduction of molecular and symbolic levels of chemical thinking until middle years or even late secondary years. It is argued this is due to the 'abstract' nature of the concepts [5, 6]. After decades of this approach, expressed in the literature are problems of conceptual load, 'difficulty' and lack of engagement with chemistry. These problems remain of great concern. The numerous difficulties learners experience with the three levels of chemical thinking (Fig. 1) have been well documented, over many decades.

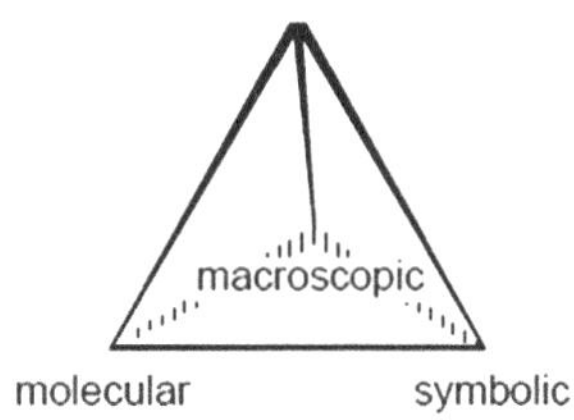

Fig. 1. Three levels of chemical thinking

As Skamp concludes in his review of the arguments, whether to teach particle ideas in primary science is still in debate.

The majority of research into ICT use in science learning is concentrated at secondary and tertiary levels. Using ICT can clearly support successful learning in science and other fields. We theorise that current visualisation tools can and will change developmental learning trajectories, that is, not only how we learn but what we can learn and when. Underpinning our research is the belief that the re-evaluation of how we view concepts, away from being accepted as abstract [7] in and of themselves, towards acknowledging that learning of any concept is contingent on the material and social supports that position a learner in a learning opportunity. We are interested in revisiting the early exploration of complex science concepts, the 'big ideas', with children today, using currently available multimedia and visualisation resources. We believe these could engage learners with new ways of seeing and doing and provide effective scientific-thinking learning opportunities that can better spark curiosity and motivation towards learning in sciences [8].

In this work, we explore a little described use of ICT in the 'new cultures of learning' for the initial offering of the three levels of chemical thinking to young children. The present study stems from a broader doctoral study conducted by author one and supervised by author 2 that was prompted by a long term interest in how science resources interact with and direct what children can know and do [9] and under what circumstances. Here we explore what happens when young children were offered particle of matter concepts in an interactive game that is specifically designed for young children to use [10]. We present the offering of concepts as re-positioning the learner with the concepts using Positioning Theory [11] to underpin the research design, conduct and analysis. Here we explore children making meaning with particle concepts, atoms and molecules, showing how they progress, when the conceptual tool [12] is made available for thinking with. What do young children do and say when positively (re-) positioned with ideas about particles of matter, one of the biggest 'big ideas' of science?

The major objectives of this paper are to:

- describe how material and social supports can be provided to positively (re-) position young children for initial 'knowing of' concepts of atoms and molecules using ICT; and
- highlight the engagement and scientific sophistication of young children's 'doings and sayings' when they are positively positioned with chemical concepts in suitable ICT interactives.

2 Methodology and Analysis

This paper is based on data collected in a broader doctoral study (HEAG 183/09 Ethics ID: 0828473) involving 24 self-selected volunteers, who were from one state primary school, located in central Victoria, Australia [13]. A sociocultural approach to the methodology was taken, acknowledging that the material and the social contexts that a child finds themselves in, constrains and enables particular learning trajectories. What learners are afforded, what they can and will do in meaning-making, is taken as contingent on circumstances. Sociocultural approaches add to the study of learning by seeing self-systems and social systems as mutually constitutive [14].

The methods of discursive psychology provided the answer to how to research meaning-making in social action [15]. Positioning Theory was employed to focus on the dynamic positions, acts and storylines enacted in the study interviews. Positioning Theory supports consideration and examination of how people take up positions and negotiate their identity in conversations and actions. The enactment of positions in a conversation is expressed in both speech acts and bodily actions. Positions emerged naturally in the research conversations between the interviewees and the interviewer while exploring the interactive Molecularium building games [10]. Storylines are extended interactions on a topic, that can often be revisited throughout an interview. Positions emerge in conversations and other social episodes, including conversational interviews. Storylines are returns to themes in sequences of acts/actions. Many storylines can be identified in any sequence of interactions. Using positioning theory encourages researchers to be aware, at all times, of the constant changes in positioning and (re-) positioning of the participants throughout interactions. In this paper, with its focus on chemical learning using ICT, the emergence of chemical storylines in the interview interactions are highlighted.

2.1 The Research Interviews

One-on-one conversational interviews were designed and conducted to explore the progress of individual children in using 'molecular thinking'.

The interviews were held in a neutral space familiar to the participants at a mutually agreed time. Each young participant was invited into being a knowing co-researcher, including choosing their study code name and having the research purpose explained.

The *double stimulus* conversational one-on-one interview form was designed for the doctoral research mentioned above and was audio and video recorded. The first *stimulus* invited the participants to interact with a wide range of representations of molecules and atoms. This began with establishing their existing everyday (intra-mental) knowledge by asking them 'What do you think of…?' when asked if they could read the word 'molecule' and then 'atom', They were then shown chemical images and formulae to discern if any were familiar from everyday life. The final step of this *stimulus* 1 step, which is the focus of the reporting in this paper, was designed to explore what they 'did and said' with the material assistance of 'playing' the interactive molecule 'Build' game on the Molecularium website [10]. (The *second stimulus of the* interview which is not reported on here, asked participants to use 'molecular thinking' to explain a macro level physical change, a commonly used starting point in early school chemistry.)

Every effort was made to maintain the research interview as an everyday conversation, applying positioning theory in the design and conduct of the interviews, as well as in the analysis of the interview conversations. This enabling interview involved ongoing and close attention by the interviewer to the child's doings and sayings in the context, with social supports aimed at keeping the experience as naturally conversational as possible, while maintaining focus on the researcher's project of chemistry meaning-making. Inter-mental activity was acknowledged as necessarily part of the interview process, with any natural teaching scaffolds forming part of the interactions. This interview design opens for research what the children could, will and do 'say and do' and under what circumstances [9, 16].

The three participants selected to report on in this paper demonstrated different levels of 'everyday' knowledge about atoms and molecules at the starting point of the study. The three also showed contrasting approaches to the interactive game. These three are referred to throughout by their self-selected code names, Mr. No-one, Zia and Robert. (We note here that the participant Mr. No-one was asked if Mr. N could be used instead, however he refused. We respect that decision here and use his chosen code name).

The youngest, seven year old Mr. No-one was still a beginning reader and could activate no prior knowledge of molecules or atoms when shown words and related images at the start of the interview; Nine year old Zia stated "small particles" when asked and Robert (11.9 years) had very high level everyday knowledge. Robert expressed great extant interest in/about the particulate nature of matter, giving an immediate accurate definition as a sentence ‘molecules are made up of atoms’.

The combined individual child-material support-social setting is the target research object. This is in contrast to research aimed at finding out what children currently know or can do relying solely on their own mental resources. This research targets what they can do with the ideas when positioned with material and social supports. The material support came in the form of a freely available interactive online molecule building game found at the Molecularium Kidsite Nanolab that is designed for use by young children The format of the game offers players opportunity to interact with numerous examples of chemical concepts at all three levels of chemical thinking, that is, the molecular, symbolic and macroscopic. The chemical conceptual categories of molecules and atoms, and their interrelationships, based on the proposition that ‘molecules are built from atoms’, are instantiated in the playing (Fig. 2).

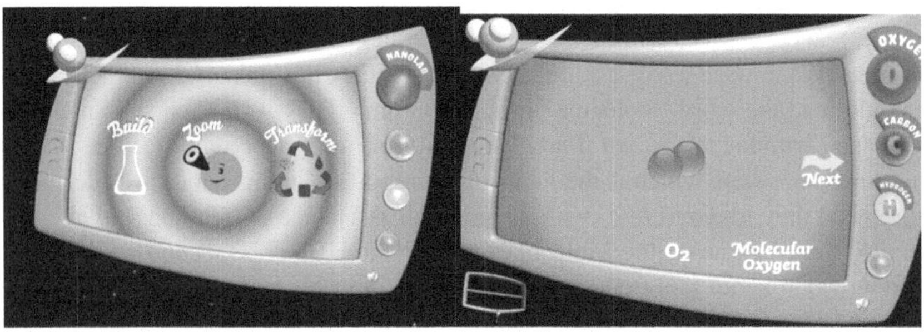

Fig. 2. Molecularium Kidsite Nanolab screen and example O_2

Using the Molecularium game players build a number of different molecules, offered in chemical symbol prompts, Players use three kinds of atoms, hydrogen, carbon and oxygen, to build molecules. This begins with O_2 and molecules get larger and larger, including methane and sugar $C_6H_{12}O_6$. After a successful ‘build’ of a molecule, macrolevel information about the substance built is provided by the game voice over. Thus, playing opens an initial experience for the ‘knowing of’ differentiated chemical concepts, that is, knowing about a range of substances at the molecular, symbolic and macro levels. The social other in this research is the interviewer, who scaffolded this experience by positively positioning the interviewee, in the setting. Interaction choices and turn taking maintain the conversation as natural and support concept learning in the conversation. The child’s own interests and projects were respected and supported while assisting a focus on chemical thinking throughout.

2.2 Analysis

The analysis, highlighting affordances and using positioning theory, isolated a number of chemical thinking storylines that were pursued in the conversations, as the participants interacted with the game with the social support of the more expert other [12]. The participant’s positioning and re-positioning shown in the ‘doings and sayings’ and their dispositions while playing with the interactive are the focus [6]. The interplay

Table 1. Summary of three students exploring the Molecularium

Molecule to build	Mr. No-one (7yo) (Very low starting knowledge)	Zia (9yo) (Typical medium starting knowledge)	Robert (11yo) (Very high starting knowledge)
O_2	Took control of mouse without hesitation, made several mistakes, retries – great willingness to explore as a game by trial and error. "This is fun"	"What do we have to do?" shared ideas openly in talk – read O_2 and reinterpreted as H_2O initially, aware of oxygen as word for a gas -the symbol unfamiliar	Immediate control of mouse and click on O saying out loud towards the computer (not to researcher social other) oxygen 'one atom'. Immediate 'reading' of subscript 2 as doubt, understood as a problem and rapid decoding with the game tool
H_2O	Still in control of mouse but makes several mistakes, retries and willingness to explore as a game – water named out loud as familiar. "I know ..."	"I know because ... so now I understand it" "that's what I drew" "I made water" "Water is two hydrogen and one oxygen" This is fun! Really, really weird – one more is hydrogen peroxide	Immediate build without support now subscript as known, next build H_2O_2 – symbol recognised as not seen before. "I Know..." Heard of hydrogen peroxide once the name was sounded by the game
CH_4 and other CHO's	Self talk-thinking out loud, "what could?" Effortful in any reading symbol, "What is that?" "Oh yes – gas"	What is hydrogen? "This is pretty easy!" Reading subscripts accurately	The space fill molecule rather than stick and ball basis of discussion "The sticks good when want to see how they are joined" "I like the way they move around to show the angles"
Sucrose	Did not get to this level	Counted numbers of carbons– discussed size of molecule	Opinions of benefits of space fill and ball & sticks in models

between the meaning-making with the tools at hand and the social supports that were needed moment-to-moment, identify the individual ways the participants progressed with the concepts in the game and the specific chemical storylines they focused on at various times.

A brief summary of the 'doings and saying' in molecule building activity for the three very different young co-researchers, Mr. No-one, Zia, Robert, is presented in Table 1. The analysis summary in Table 1 shows the approach to the game by Mr. No-one, Zia and Robert varied greatly.

3 Findings

Mr. No-one, the youngest of the three participants expressed no prior knowledge, was willing to use trial-and-error from the start, showing experience with such games. He took control of the mouse and made several mistakes. He was very willing to try and try again. In contrast, Zia asked for support with "What do *we* have to do?". The position Zia had taken is reflected in use of "we", showing she chose to share her problem of how to start. Robert, similar to Mr. No-one, was also ready to begin independently, willingly taking control of the computer mouse and starting to click on icons. Playing the game rapidly became their bodily focus, and in doing their clicks on H, C and O icons provided entry into thinking with and about particle concepts. Playing the game provided new words and images representing concepts. These new items of attention engaged their active interest 'in the doing' with the game.

The 'doings' showed the game aroused interest in, and competence with, the tasks of molecule building. The game directed the process in a step-by-step offering of more and more complex molecules to build. The immediate feedback from the game on success, or lack of success, encouraged each learner, in their own way, to focus efforts on the task of building the molecule shown as a chemical formula. Getting immediate feedback about whether they had pressed the right icon. A C (carbon), H (hydrogen) or O (oxygen) for atom kinds, the three participants each gained a number of experiences with examples. These incorporated the three levels of chemical thinking and introduced the meanings of chemical symbols as intended in chemistry. Re-positioning the participants with this interactive ICT game, along with suitable social scaffolding of their activity, provided individualised learning opportunity and appropriation of the offered concepts that are routinely accepted (in the much of the literature and curriculum designs) as too abstract for young children to use and learn. Each 'build' offered opportunity to 'read' (scientifically correct) chemical symbols. Incorrect clicks led to a 'start again' feedback, reinforcing that there is a right answer to the problem presented. The decoding of a number of instances of chemical formulae was linked in the game, through making clicks on icons, to a specific number of different kinds of atoms. Players thus *create* and observe accurate 3d images of molecules on the screen. Each molecule 'build' gave practice with three levels of thinking, with precise form and structure (as a space fill model that moved around to show it has shape), and at the same time the uses and properties of a macro world substance (e.g. water). The provision of verbal macro level information at the end of the 'build' connected the symbols and molecules to sensory level information. All three participants described here, kept their focus directed on building without any need for social prompting from the interviewer/researcher to do so. The game was of interest and motivated the participants to raise chemically sophisticated questions about atoms, molecules, their symbols and sensory level macro world substances. The following section describes some of the ways meaning-making progressed with the specific chemical thinking tool for these three positively positioned participants, each in their own way. The analysis summarised in Table 1 highlights that the game engaged all three in doing with the concepts offered by the game and in this setting.

Molecules with a small number of atoms (O_2, H_2O, CO_2, CH_4) were successfully built by all participants and larger sugar molecules by Zia and Robert (and the majority in the broader study). Mr. No-one and Zia were unwilling to say or 'taste the words' molecule and atom 'in the mouth' early on when asking questions, while Robert voiced the words readily.

Robert quickly progressed through all levels of the game, going on to extras including C_{60}. Zia began to say the words atom and molecule first quietly to herself and then more openly out loud after three builds. Mr. No-one in the same length of game playing time built only five molecules. All three showed they were equally engaged with the game, talking as they played by trial and error, and finally coming to be able to independently accurately decode the chemical signs. Each began to use the words molecule and atom and expressed great achievement when the game and ideas made sense for them.

3.1 Emerging Storylines

The participants' interactions with the game led to a wide range of scientifically relevant storylines emerging. Three storylines presented here highlight the entry positions and the effortful re-positionings these children experienced in using knowledge of particles concepts. The initial 'knowing of' the categories and kinds of these entities and the subsequent practice in using the metaphor of building molecules from atoms, directed participants to explore the scientific concepts and constrain their understanding towards the scientific. The selected samples of storylines below give some insights into the ways chemical meaning-making with the offered concepts progressed.

Storyline # 1 Reading chemical subscripts

At the first build, how to make the O_2 using clicks on buttons presented a problem for all participants. The 'O two' heard in the game voice over, was familiar. However, the numbers in the offered chemical formula, the two in O_2, which in chemistry stand for two of those atoms in the make up the molecule, were not immediately interpreted. When no number '2' was available as a button, all participants hesitated. The iconic nature of the sign meant the meaning of subscripts had not previously been considered as needing decoding by Mr. No-one, Zia or Robert (nor any participant in the broader study). The realization of a problem that an alternative to a 'two' was needed, gained a swift, appropriate response from Robert, (and others in the higher everyday knowledge group). Robert's swift resolution of his problem allowed his rapid progress, quickly moving through decoding further chemical formulae by applying the knowledge he gained when building O_2 and then H_2O. Mr. No-one showed he wanted to solve his problem by himself using trial and error, and did so, though slowly. Zia was least willing of the three to 'give it a go', needing encouragement by the social other to act. The prompt: 'what might the 2 be standing for?' led to a slow but correct action. All participants resolved the chemical subscripts problem during the playing and were conscious of having done so: as Zia actually stated when building methane "This is pretty easy!".

Storyline # 2 I know … H_2O
The whole sign, H_2O meant water for No-N, Zia and Robert, and indeed for all participants in the broader doctoral study. The chemical symbols were familiar from everyday life. The expression of 'I know' showed a connection between the symbols and the participants everyday life. Each expressed some interest in knowing more and raised questions about the symbols. The specific interpretive problem that the participants experienced with the chemical formulae signs early in the game indicated they were reading chemical symbols as iconic signs (e.g. H_2O = water) rather than reading them as intended in chemistry. The iconic signs recognized from everyday life, expressed as 'I know…' changed to be more scientifically meaningful chemical symbols that were open to decoding in playing with the interactive game. The game offered the opening to scientific information that chemical symbols represent atoms and molecules in a meaningful and knowable way.

Storyline # 3 This is … fun/interesting/easy
The three participants each expressed in words and their actions, engagement with the game, particularly their satisfaction with progress in the use of the signs. The molecular formulae, including O_2, H_2O, CH_4 were decoded. This provided practice in the idea that the letter represents a type of atom and the numbers the number of that atom in a molecule. This meaning and meaning-making experience was described positively as fun/interesting/easy/amazing. The representation of the built molecules as 3d objects on a screen was identified as new and very helpful to developing thinking about molecules. Robert expressed his own position of valuing, offering: "I like the way they move around to show the angles." By the third 'build' Zia's clicks on the screen buttons had become very fast, her decoding of the chemical symbols for molecules as clicks, was performed without doubt or hesitation. Indeed, in starting to build larger molecules containing H, C and O atoms she stated, in her self talk: "This is pretty easy!" while almost simultaneously asking out loud the scientifically relevant question: "What is hydrogen?". Mr. No-one was excited by successes. As a poor reader, but a willing learner in trial and error visual games, his progress was expressed in words as well as affect as "exciting".

4 Conclusions

The purpose of this project was to better understand how to position learners with contemporary technologies to open and support conceptual learning. This paper reports on what happened when young children were positively positioned with a digital game that is designed to introduce young children to scientific ideas of molecules and atoms and their chemical symbols. In the analysis the three young participants, each with a very different starting point knowledge, were motivated by a process of 'seeing what might be' that inspired them to move forward and explore the offered concepts with a sense of anticipation in the interactive molecule building game. While the three students are very different from each other, all three showed interest in the game's concepts, asked scientifically sophisticated questions about the chemical ideas offered and gained knowledge about these ideas in playing. They each stated at the end of their interview they would like to learn more about atoms and molecules and thought they should do so around eight years of age.

We take the main benefit of the game is that it offered the children all three levels of chemistry representation to use together as tools for their thinking. The participants raised scientifically appropriate questions and progressed with learning these three levels of chemical thinking, the macro world, sub micro-world and chemical symbolic. The game supported this by offering numerous examples of the chemical categories molecule and atom. Three specific kinds of atom - carbon, hydrogen and oxygen were shown as atomic chemical symbols (C, H, O) in molecules represented in chemical formulae (O_2, CO_2, H_2O, CH_4 etc.) and with 3d images of molecular structures that moved around in space. Alongside the molecular and symbolic level offerings was a commentary about the properties and uses of the substances on the macroscopic level (water, carbon dioxide, methane, sugar). Importantly, the analysis presented here shows the participants were highly engaged, as evidenced in their attention to the game, and in the interviewer's role declining as the game came with practice to provide all the learning supports needed. This research supports the notion that young children can be positively positioned to begin 'putting on molecular spectacles' [6] earlier than currently expressed in curriculum documents [5].

The Molecularium 'Build' game uses a metaphor of 'building' to show how atoms are the building blocks of molecules. The game players construct specified molecules with particular names and chemical formulae. That the participants were not building physically, molecules in actuality, was not a problem and was clearly obvious to all the study participants. Accepting the idea that representations create the world rather than reflect it the question arises, what other 'new' worlds might be available to young children through the use of ICT visualisations, beyond that of the particulate nature of matter that was afforded by playing with the Molecularium.

Implications. Our findings support the notion that re-positioning children with currently available ICT visualization tools, such as described here with The Molecularium site, can and will change the 'teachability' and 'learnability' of 'concepts' for learners. They can be positively positioned with suitable material and social supports. We call for the specific reconsideration of the current agreements about beginning chemistry curriculum designs, which currently only offer molecular and symbolic levels of thinking in secondary years. We propose that what young children can do and know, about the particulate nature of matter and other big ideas of science, needs to be revisited in light of what new multimedia and ICT representations, visualisations and simulations can offer to young children today.

In this research, knowledge offering of and meaning-making with the three levels of chemical thinking, was readily achieved with the well-designed interactive that provides multiple examples of categories and kinds of particles in an engaging game format that was designed for use of young children. The Nanolab Build game structures the experience of learning symbolic and molecular level signs and concepts, by stepping beginners and early novices through experiences with a range of examples in a game-like multimodal and interactive format. When thus positively positioned with the ideas of atoms and molecules and their chemical symbols, in words and images, the very idea can become available for young children to begin appropriating and making use of as tools for their thinking. That they can make use of the thinking tools in their meaning-making activity is shown in the scientifically appropriate questions asked while playing. Rather than the three levels of chemistry being thought of as too abstract for young children and particle ideas being the problem [5] chemical educators would do well to acknowledge that current visualisations are changing 'learnability' and can support more scientifically accurate and more sophisticated chemical thinking at a younger age than occurs in current practices. One of the benefits of an earlier introduction would be a decrease in conceptual load seen in senior secondary chemistry, by giving learners more time to appropriate the ideas and develop more habitual and expert uses of and with all three levels of chemical thinking.

When positively positioned with 'the idea' the ground is prepared, affording young children's learning experiences that constrain thinking towards more habitual use of scientifically sophisticated 'ways of seeing and doing'.

Acknowledgments. The authors would like to thank the child participants for their willingness to contribute to the research and the anonymous reviewers who contributed greatly to the refinement of the final version of this paper.

References

1. Noss, R.: Learning the unlearnable: teaching the unteachable. Dean's Lecture Series 2012. http://education.unimelb.edu.au/news_and_activities/events/deans_lecture_series/richard_noss
2. Gibson, J.J.: The Ecological Approach to Visual Perception. Houghton Mifflin, Boston (1979)
3. Smetana, L.K., Bell, R.L.: Computer simulations to support science instruction and learning: a critical review of the literature. Int. J. Sci. Educ. **34**(9), 1337–1370 (2012)
4. Wilkerson-Jerde, M.H., Gravel, B.E., Macrander, C.A.: Exploring shifts in middle school learners' modeling sctivity while generating drawings, animations, and computational simulations of molecular diffusion. J. Sci. Educ. Technol. **24**(2–3), 396–415 (2015)
5. Skamp, K.: Teaching chemistry in primary science: what does the research suggest? Teach. Sci. **57**(4), 37–43 (2011)
6. Kind, V.: Beyond appearances: students' misconceptions about basic chemical ideas, London (2004)
7. Turkle, S., Papert, S.: Epistemological Pluralism and the Revaluation of the Concrete. In: Harel, I., Papert, S. (eds.) Constructionism, pp. 161–192. Ablex Publishing Corporation, Norwood (1991)
8. Alexander, J.M., Johnson, K.E., Kelley, K.: Longitudinal analysis of the relations between opportunities to learn about science and the development of interests related to science. Sci. Educ. **96**(5), 763–786 (2012)
9. Siegal, M.: Marvelous Minds: The Discovery of What Children Know. Oxford University Press, Oxford (2008)
10. The Molecularium Project (2004). http://www.molecularium.com/kidsite.html
11. Howie, D.: Preparing for positive positioning. In: Harré, R., van Langenhove, L. (eds.) Positioning Theory, pp. 53–59. Blackwell, Oxford (1999)
12. Gauvain, M.: Cultural tools, social interaction and the development of thinking. Hum. Dev. **44**(2/3), 126–143 (2001)

13. Jakab, C.: Molecules as Tools: Discourse, Artefacts and Children's Meaning-Making About Particles of Matter. The University of Melbourne, Melbourne (2013)
14. Leach, J., Scott, P.: Designing and evaluating science teaching sequences: an approach drawing upon the concept of learning demand and a social constructivist perspective on learning. Stud. Sci. Educ. **38**, 115–142 (2002)
15. Harré, R., van Langenhove, L. (eds.): Positioning Theory: Moral Contexts of Intentional Action. Blackwell, Oxford (1999)
16. Jakab, C.: Talk about small: conversations with young children at play with molecule simulations. In: Redman, C. (ed.) Successful Science Education Practices: Exploring What, Why and How They Worked, pp. 71–92. NOVA Publishers, Hauppauge (2013)

An Educational Experience with Online Teaching – Not a Best Practice

Ditte Kolbæk[1(✉)] and Anne-Mette Nortvig[1,2]

[1] Aalborg University, A.C. Meyers Vænge 15, Copenhagen, Denmark
dk@learning.aau.dk, ame@pha.dk
[2] University College Absalon, Trekroner Forskerpark 4, 4000 Roskilde, Denmark

Abstract. Problem- and Project-Based Learning (PBL) is a widely used pedagogical method in higher education. Although PBL encourages self-directed learning and works with the students' own projects and problems, it also includes teacher presentations, discussions and group reflections, both on-campus and online. Therefore, the teacher's plans might be relevant to the students' projects, but that is not always the case. This study investigates how master's students interact with an online Problem-Based Learning design and examines how technology influences these interactions. The empirical data stem from lessons at an online master's course, and they were collected and analyzed using a netnographic approach. The study finds that concepts like self-directed learning and active involvement of everyone can have very different meanings from the teachers' and the students' points of view. If the students do not see the relevance immediately, they often leave the online sessions. Hence the title: This study describes an experience and provides a point of departure for further discussion, but it is not an example of best practices for online PBL.

Keywords: Problem-Based Learning · Human-computer science education

1 Introduction

This study explores a course in human-computer science education at Aalborg University. In all the classes, it is the teachers' intention to involve every student individually and in group participation, even though the students cannot meet face-to-face as they are geographically dispersed. The teachers' intentions were reified in the learning design, which included various technologies. However, once a learning design has been created and presented to the students, the teacher can never be sure that the students will respond to the design as intended. Kress and Selander [1] discuss this issue with the concepts of design *for* learning (the learning design that the teacher has created and shared with the students) and design *in* learning (the activities that actually take place when the learning design is in use). In this paper, we will look at the learning designs (i.e. designs for learning) that were created by the teachers, and at the students' reactions to these designs (as designs in learning).

The pedagogical foundation of Aalborg University is Problem- and Project-Based Learning (PBL) [2]. The idea behind this type of learning is that thinking begins in a

A. Tatnall and M. Webb (Eds.): WCCE 2017, IFIP AICT 515, pp. 304–313, 2017.
https://doi.org/10.1007/978-3-319-74310-3_32

forked-road situation, a dilemma with two or more alternatives [3]. Since different people think differently, it is preferable to think with others; consequently, the students are supposed to work in groups and to defend their projects during the exam (assessment) as a group. PBL is the pedagogical expression of the theory that learning is context-based and collaboratively constructed instead of individual and independent of context [4]. PBL requires that the students be curious. They must also be able to define problems and grasp theories that help them understand and examine these problems in order to come up with solutions, which they then evaluate and revise until they are satisfied with the result. Moreover, PBL requires teachers that be willing to give up their position of external boss or 'dictator' and take on instead the role of the leader of group activities [3]. This means that teachers present fewer lectures, exert less control over the content and assign fewer fixed literature lists than in more traditional pedagogical models. Instead, the teacher suggests content related to the aim of the course and the course description and supervises the students in all phases of the PBL [4]. As final assessment, the teacher leads the examination being the students' defense of their project report.

Some studies on PBL have found that it can be difficult for novice students to identify resources and to define the relevant problems [5], so facilitation or scaffolding of self-directed learning is key in PBL courses [6, 7]. Moreover, the teacher's facilitation and supervision are needed to scaffold complex conceptual tasks [8] when the PBL course takes place online, although technology can also be used to effectively scaffold the students' problem-solving [5].

This study is a keen reflection and a critical discussion of the teachers' dilemma of, on the one hand, providing efficient online lessons and scaffolds in order to help students understand important theories and find relevant resources, and, on the other hand, letting the students take responsibility for their own learning.

2 Methodology

This study utilizes online field-work in which participants' activities were observed by gathering data from the internet. We have used data logs obtained user logins for different internet sources to learn about computer-mediated communications between teachers and students, between students and technology, and among students. Hence, this participant-observational research may be classified as netnography [9, 14], a type of research in which the people under study interact and communicate via the internet. Generally, the role of the netnographic researcher is heavily influenced by the fact that the data are gathered online without contact with the subjects. On the one hand, the researcher experiences the same screens and online interactions as the informants, and on the other hand, the researcher has access to logged data that the participants normally do not have access to. In this study, however, we were familiar with the subjects, as they were students in courses that we taught. Consequently, we possessed – and were aware of – a double role, first as teachers (in September and October) and later as researchers (from November to January).

When the research area addresses an educational setting, some netnographic data can be collected from analytic data. Learning analytics is a relatively new field in educational research [10, 11], and although a common understanding of the concept is difficult to find among researchers, it is usually defined as 'the measurement, collection, analysis and reporting of data about learners and their contexts, for purposes of understanding and optimizing learning and the environments in which it occurs' [12]. The data thus consist of '[...] traces that learners leave behind' [13] in various educational settings, and these data can be used to understand and improve learning. Learning analytics often use big data, but researchers in the field also find that multifaceted data from mobile devices and from the physical world [10] may contribute to a picture of the way students respond to a learning design, interact and learn. Thus, in this study, our netnografic empirics consist of learning analytics data from two learning designs lasting eight hours in an online module with 70 university students.

3 Research Setting and Empirical Data

ILOO is a human-computer science-related master's program provided by the Department of Learning and Philosophy at Aalborg University. ILOO is the Danish acronym for IT, Learning and Organizational Change. Students and the teachers from two campuses, Aalborg and Copenhagen, attend the program. The students come from different backgrounds. Some have professional bachelor's degrees such as teaching; others hold bachelor's degrees in humanities or social science. The aim of this master study is to enable the students to work with learning, training and IT-related changes, including global perspectives in organizations. ILOO consists of 120 ECTS points (European Credit Transfer System) that should be completed within two years.

As mentioned, this study draws on two teaching sessions from autumn 2016. The course is obligatory, but attendance at the sessions is voluntary. Our data were created in two different sessions in the course 'Global Perspectives on Competence and Educational Development'. The two authors of this paper both taught two different sessions that lasted four hours each. The course lasted six weeks, that is, 24 h of teaching in total. Seventy-two students signed up for this course, but it took place during a period in which the students were encouraged to participate in internships in and outside Denmark. Therefore, the course was provided online, and the students attended from different countries and areas of Denmark. The learning designs and the data are presented below. The session 'Cultural Concepts in Global Perspectives' is presented first, followed by 'Citizenship in Online Settings'.

The lesson 'Cultural Concepts in Global Perspectives' was presented for the students on the Learning Management System of Moodle a few weeks before the course took place. Moodle provided a description and the aims of the four-hour lesson and showed the learning design (Table 1). On Moodle, the students could find two videos with two different cultural perspectives, the literature list and the three discussion fora, which were activated during the session. The students were supposed to read the literature before the session took place.

The teacher introduced the session in a video conference using a system called Adobe Connect. Thirty-six of the 72 students participated in the introduction to the session, which included a brief overview of the agenda and information about how to participate, such as pressing the 'raise your hand' button if you want to say something and utilizing the chat to make comments or ask questions. Then the teacher asked the students to work individually by watching the first video presentation of a cultural perspective. The video lasted 15 min and 20 s. The students identified a problem and suggested solutions in group sessions in Adobe Connect, and they described their findings in a written discussion forum in Moodle, which the other students could then comment on. The five groups drew conclusions from the discussion, which they then posted in Moodle. The teacher read the conclusions and summarized them in the videoconference. Then the students considered suitable methods for studying culture and added their suggestions in the discussion forum in Moodle. The second part of the lesson focused on five dimensions of culture, which were presented in a video that the students were supposed to watch during the lesson. Then the students were to provide examples of the five dimensions from their experience at the university or their workplace. Part three consisted of a summary of the four-hour lesson followed by feedback from the students to the teachers in the form of written comments in a Moodle discussion forum.

Table 1. Learning design for 'Cultural Concepts in Global Perspectives' (pauses are not indicated). The underscores indicate the websites that generated the data.

Time	Theme	Activity	Online space
Part I: 14.15 -14.30	Welcome and introduction	Listen.	Adobe Connect
14.30 – 14.50	'Culture in a post-cultural perspective'	Watch the presentation. Pause and take notes when needed.	<u>YouTube</u>
14.50 – 15.20	Exercise in a post-cultural perspective	Participate in a group discussion about the video. Post conclusions in Moodle.	Adobe Connect & <u>Moodle</u>
15.20 – 15.30	Summary	Listen and chat.	<u>Adobe Connect</u>
15.30 – 16.10	Exercise 2, Methods	1. Participate in a group discussion. 2. Individually reflect on the methods.	<u>Moodle</u>
Part II: 16.20 – 16.40	Cultural dimensions	Watch the presentation. Pause and take notes when needed.	<u>YouTube</u>
16.40 – 18.00	Three individual exercises	Write reflections; discuss cultural dimensions.	<u>Moodle</u>
Part III: 18.00 – 18.15	Summary	Listen and chat.	<u>Adobe Connect</u>

The learning design for the session ‘Citizenship in Online Settings’ was introduced in Adobe Connect by the teacher, who listed the content for the day and the students’ assigned activities. The first student task consisted of watching a video presentation on citizenship, which had been uploaded to YouTube. The students could watch it during the session but also before or after the session. For the second task, the students discussed questions about the video in Adobe Connect groups, and each student group created two questions for the others to discuss in writing in Moodle. The second part of the lesson focused on netnography as a method for investigating citizenship. After watching the second video presentation, which introduced the method of netnography, the students were to create a blog while pretending to be and see the world from the perspective of someone unlike themselves (such as a person with a chronic disease, a CEO, an old black man, a prince, an unemployed musician, a former beauty queen, etc.). Afterwards, they asked the bloggers questions in the role of an online researcher with a focus on citizenship. The teacher participated actively in all activities. At the end of the lesson, the students had time to sum up and evaluate the activities of the day in the Adobe Connect chat (Table 2).

Table 2. Learning design for citizenship in Online settings (pauses are not indicated). The underscores indicate the websites that generated the data.

Time	Theme	Activity	Online space
Part I: 14.15-14.30	Teacher presentation and introduction	Listen and find group.	Adobe Connect
14.30-15.15	Video presentation on citizenship	Watch the presentation. Pause and take notes when needed.	YouTube
15.15-15.45	‘Get a grip on citizenship	Participate in a group discussion about the video. Create two questions for the other groups.	Adobe Connect
16.00-16.30	‘Discuss and nuance the concept’	Discussion in Moodle: discuss the others’ questions in the group chat.	Moodle
Part II: 16.30-17.00	Video presentation of netnography	Watch the presentation. Pause and take notes when needed.	YouTube
17.00-18.00	‘To see the world from a specific point of view’	1. Create a blog on citizenship while playing a role. 2. Discuss methods for investigating citizenship online.	Moodle
Part III: 18.00-18.15	Conclusion and evaluation	Chat.	Adobe Connect

Next, we explored how the students engaged with our learning design in order to find the patterns in their activities and the relationship between our design for learning and the students' design in learning [1]. First, we tracked how many students were present in the online teaching space (Adobe Connect) at the beginning of the lessons (part I), in the middle (part II) and at the end (part III) in the early evening. Secondly, we used YouTube analytics to track how much our four videos were watched during the lessons and before/after. Thirdly, we counted the number of comments by current students in the four discussion fora on Moodle.

4 Analysis of the Data

In this project, we analyzed our own teaching designs in order to learn how the students reacted to our design *for* learning (the learning design that the teacher created and shared with the students). We also wanted to uncover the activities that actually take place when the learning design is enacted, i.e. the design *in* learning [1], Furthermore, we investigated how the technology supported or did not support full participation in the learning activities (Table 3).

Table 3. Overview of the collected data.

Data source	Topics in the lesson about cultural concepts in global perspectives				
	Lesson part I		Part II		III
Students in Adobe Connect	36		25		11
Video on YouTube watched during the lesson watched before or after the lesson	Number of views	Average % viewed	Number of views	Average % viewed	
	68 views	61%	53 views	60%	
	3 students	100%	5 students	80–100%	
Online discussion Adobe Connect, results in Moodle and number of student-produced comments	Student comments/students	Teacher comments/#teachers	Student comments/students	Teacher comments/#teachers	
	All 5 groups	0/2	21/8	1/2	
Students' feedback to teacher in Moodle					0
Data source	Topics in the lesson about citizenship				
	Lesson part I		Part II		III
Students in Adobe Connect	26		25		12
	32 views	39%	29 views	53%	
	1 student	100%	3 students	80-100%	
Online discussion Adobe Connect, results in Moodle and number of student-produced comments	Student comments/students	Teacher comments/#teachers	Student comments/students	Teacher comments/#teachers	
	25/9	15/2	40/10	11/1	
Students feedback to teacher in Moodle					17

Video conferences: lurking, listening and leaving

There were 36 students in the video conference (Adobe Connect) at the beginning of the lesson 'Cultural concepts in global perspectives'; that is half of the 72 students enrolled in the course. Only 25 students attended the second part of the lesson, and only 11 hung on for the third part. The lesson 'Citizenship' started with 26 students, which is a third of the students enrolled in the course. Twenty-five students stayed for the second part of the lesson, and only 12 remained to the end of the lesson. The number of students declines over time: from the beginning to the end of the lesson, and from the lesson in September (36 students started) to the lesson in October (26 students started). The design for learning included 72 students, but the design in learning meant that the number of actual participants declined, after starting with half of the population of 72 students. It is worth considering the impact of the technology, as it is surprising that the students left the session before the end, This caused them to miss an opportunity to learn from the teacher and from their fellow students, as intended in the learning design.

The students were familiar with both Moodle and Adobe Connect, as they had used both the semester before this study. Therefore, the reason for the lack of participation could not be a lack of knowledge regarding the technology.

However, fewer than half of the students entered the lesson in the video conference, and an increasing number of students dropped out during the lessons. Thus, we consider it essential to determine whether our learning designs at least engaged the few students who participated.

Video presentations: snooping and sneaking

Both lessons included two video presentations with important content. These videos were available before, during and after the course. Even when the learning design granted time for viewing the videos, far from all of the students took advantage of this opportunity. The first video in 'Cultural Concepts in Global Perspectives' had 68 views but the students had watched only 61% of the video. The second video in that lesson had 53 views, and the students only watched 50% of that video. The first video in 'Citizenship' had 32 views, but the students only watched 39% of the video. The second video in 'Citizenship' had 29 views, but the students only watched 53% of the video.

The design *for* learning included time for watching the full video, but to our surprise, we found that the design *in* learning showed that the students chose other activities. From the numbers, we construe that the students started to watch the videos, but after some minutes they stopped and maybe started over later on. Only a few students watched one or more of the videos in their entirety.

The technology provides easy access to content that teachers consider important, but students often fail to take advantage of this opportunity, even if they are familiar with the technology. The easy access to the video conference also makes it easy for the students to leave the online space without the teacher noticing it. First, the students can appear present in Adobe Connect when they stay signed in, but mentally they may not be present. The numbers show that some students participate less actively in the tasks, although they count as present in Adobe Connect. Second, the teacher cannot – even if she might have wished to do so – give students a disapproving glare as they leave the online learning space with a click.

Online discussions in Adobe Connect and/or Moodle: The few
In order to enhance engagement, learning and reflection, both lessons included online group discussions. Some group discussion took place in separate video conference rooms, and other discussions took place via posts in discussion forums in Moodle or via chat in Adobe Connect. In the lesson 'Cultural concepts in global perspectives', all five groups provided content for the exercise in part one without any teacher interaction, and eight students posted 21 comments on the individual exercise in part two, where the teacher posted only one comment. In the lesson 'Citizenship', nine students posted 25 comments in the first part of the lesson and the two teachers posted 15. In the second part of 'Citizenship', ten students posted 40 comments supported by eleven comments from the teachers. The design *for* learning invited all the students to participate actively in the reflections and discussions in order to support their learning and to enable them to construct reification of their learning in a social context. But the design *in* learning shows that very few of the students actually participated.

Evaluation of the session: Lack of engagement
Part III of the lesson included an online evaluation of the session. In the session 'Cultural concepts in global perspectives', the students were supposed to write their feedback in a Moodle Discussion forum within the last five minutes of the lesson. The last 11 students snuck out of Adobe Connect without posting any comments in Moodle. In the lesson 'Citizenship', 12 students provided 17 comments in the Adobe Connect chat forum, saying that the design was great and that time had flown during the lessons. This suggests that it was easier for the students to give feedback in an online environment where they and the teacher were present already. Likewise, it seems that it was harder for them to visit another website to provide feedback. The teacher's presence in the forum seems to support the students' engagement in the feedback, even though the students do not pay much attention to the feedback.

5 Discussion and Conclusion on the Research Question

How does an online learning design impact student engagement in problem-based learning?

The general tendency in this module is a lack of student participation. This tendency surprised and frustrated the teachers, who would like to find an explanation for the lack of student engagement. During September and October 2016, many students were busy with internships, which may have reduced their ability and/or motivation to participate in the sessions. Also, the course is a part of the PBL tradition [2, 15, 16] so the students worked on their own projects. The lack of engagement may be caused by the temptation to only participate in content that was directly applicable to their own PBL project.

Participation also declined over time – both over the four-hour sessions and during the six-week course. At the beginning of the lessons, 30 to 50% of the students participated, but only a sixth of the students remained at the end of the lessons. Furthermore, no students gave feedback as requested if they had to go to a new website to do so. Over the six-week course, student participation declined, perhaps because the project deadlines were approaching.

The pedagogy of PBL might suggest the interpretation that lessons are resources that the students pick and choose at their own convenience. Even when the teachers scaffolded the sessions, supervised the students and actively participated in the online discussions, the students' own projects seemed to define the relevance of each session for each student.

Moreover, the online learning environment seems to make students feel less obliged to participate, and they often failed to watch all of the teachers' presentations in the video presentations and instructions in the videoconference. The students also did not participate in the discussions and collaborative reflections that were supposed to be formulated in oral or written formats online. The online environment makes it easy for the students to sneak out without seeing teacher's disapproving look. Our PBL online designs for learning were designed to make it easy for the students to participate, and the designs offered many ways of interacting with the session content. But the learning designs also afforded many PBL reasons for different reactions to the teachers' learning design, many of which did not include participating in the collaborative online learning online. For us, the teachers, this was very frustrating; for the students, however, this might be a natural reaction to an online PBL and student self-directed learning.

The teachers had designed *for* learning and shared this design with the students, whereas the students had designed *in* learning by engaging in activities that related only to their own projects. In this study, the intersection between the design *for* and the design *in* learning was remarkably smaller than expected. Moreover, the teachers intended to provide technology that supported the students' learning, but this study shows that the students did not utilized the technology as planned in the teachers' learning design.

References

1. Kress, G., Selander, S.: Multimodal design, learning and cultures of recognition. Internet High. Educ. **15**(4), 265–268 (2012). https://doi.org/10.1016/j.iheduc.2011.12.003
2. Kolmos, A., Fink, F.K., Krogh, L.: The Aalborg PBL Model: Progress, Diversity and Challenges. Aalborg Universitetsforlag, Aalborg (2004)
3. Dewey, J.: The experimental theory of knowledge. Mind **15**(59), 293–307 (1906)
4. De Graaf, E., Kolmos, A.: Characteristics of problem-based learning. Int. J. Eng. Educ. **19**(5), 657–662 (2003)
5. Tawfik, A.A., Lilly, C.: Using a flipped classroom approach to support problem-based learning. Technol. Knowl. Learn. **20**(3), 299–315 (2015)
6. Barrows, H.: Problem-based learning in medicine and beyond: a brief overview. New Dir. Teach. Learn. **68**, 3–12 (1996)
7. Hmelo-Silver, C.E., Barrows, H.S.: Goals and strategies of a problem-based learning facilitator. Interdisc. J. Prob.-Based Learn. **1**(1), 4 (2006)
8. Saye, J.W., Brush, T.: Scaffolding critical reasoning about history and social issues in multimedia-supported learning environments. Educ. Technol. Res. Dev. **50**(3), 77–96 (2002)
9. Kozinets, R.V.: Netnography. Doing Ethnographic Research Online. Sage Publications, Thousand Oaks (2010)
10. Merceron, A., Blikstein, P., Siemens, G.: Learning analytics: from big data to meaningful data. J. Learn. Analytics **2**(3), 4–8 (2016)

11. Schwendimann, B.A., Rodriguez Triana, M.J., Prieto Santos, L.P., Shirvani Boroujeni, M., Holzer, A.C., Gillet, D., Dillenbourg, P.: Understanding learning at a glance: an overview of learning dashboard studies. In: International Learning Analytics and Knowledge, (EPFL-CONF-216917) (2016)
12. Vatrapu, R., Teplovs, C., Fujita, N., Bull, S., Long, P.: Towards visual analytics for teachers' dynamic diagnostic pedagogical decision-making. In: Proceedings of the 1st International Conference on Learning Analytics and Knowledge – LAK 2011, pp. 93–98 (2011)
13. Duval, E., Verbert, K.: Learning analytics. E-Learn. Educ. **8**(1), 1–5 (2012)
14. Hughes, J.: SAGE Internet Research Methods. SAGE Publication Ltd, London (2012)
15. Lajoie, S.P., Hmelo-Silver, C.E., Wiseman, J.G., Chan, L.K., Lu, J., Khurana, C., Kazemitabar, M.: Using online digital tools and video to support international problem-based learning. Interdisc. J. Prob.-Based Learn. **8**(2), 6 (2014)
16. Tambouris, E., Zotou, M., Tarabanis, K.: Towards designing cognitively-enriched project-oriented courses within a blended problem-based learning context. Educ. Inf. Technol. **19**(1), 61–86 (2014)

Peer Affective Factors in Peer Collaboration: Facebook-Based Collaborative Writing Activity Among Turkish High School EFL Learners

Hasan Selcuk(✉)

School of Education, Communication and Society, King's College London, London, UK
hasanselcuk35@hotmail.com

Abstract. This paper is about an investigation into student perceptions of peer affective factors during a Facebook-based collaborative writing activity among Turkish high school EFL learners. Two groups of three students, 16-year-old EFL learners at A2 level English proficiency (CEFR), undertook an online collaborative English short story writing exercise over seven weeks using Facebook. I gathered data from focus group discussions, online one-to-one chats and online discussion threads from both groups. Although small-scale, valuable insights were obtained into peer affective factors that emerged throughout the writing exercise, and were concerned with receiving/giving praise and motivational phrases, the use of informal language and humour in writing during the exercise as well as in relation to feeling comfortable with each other. The students claimed these factors greatly aided the development of their writing skills.

Keywords: Affective factors in online learning · Online collaborative writing Web-based foreign language learning

1 Introduction

A broad definition of collaborative writing, according to Storch, is "the co-authoring of a text by two or more writers" [23, p. 2]. With the rapid growth of Web 2.0 technologies, in recent years, research on classroom-based collaborative writing in an English as Foreign Language (EFL) context has shifted to online collaborative writing. Previous research on collaborative writing in an EFL context has commonly used wiki (Lund [16], Kessler [10], Miyazoe and Anderson [19], Lin and Yang [15], Chao and Lo [3], Li and Zhu [14]), weblog (Miyazoe and Anderson [19]), and Facebook group (Bani-Hani et al. [2]) as online tools. Previous research on online collaborative writing has also revealed that online tools (wiki, weblog and Facebook group) facilitated the collaborative writing process for EFL learners (Lund [16], Miyazoe and Anderson [19], Lin and Yang [15], Chao and Lo [3], Bani-Hani et al. [2]). Moreover, online collaborative writing showed progress in EFL learners' writing development (Kessler [10], Miyazoe and Anderson [19], Bani-Hani et al. [2]). Li and Zhu [14] also investigated peer interaction patterns in online collaborative writing. However, no research has been

A. Tatnall and M. Webb (Eds.): WCCE 2017, IFIP AICT 515, pp. 314–322, 2017.
https://doi.org/10.1007/978-3-319-74310-3_33

conducted on how EFL learners interpret peer affective factors in online collaborative writing. To fill this gap in research, I undertook exploratory research to investigate students' perceptions of peer affective factors through the medium of Facebook-based collaborative writing activity among Turkish high school EFL learners. In this paper, I aim to report on this exploration of Turkish high school EFL learners' perceptions of peer affective factors during such a writing activity. This paper consists of five sections. I first introduce the paper. The second section constitutes a review of literature pertinent to peer affective factors in peer collaboration. The third section provides a methodological framework. The fourth section presents the findings and discussion and the fifth section concludes the paper, and considers implications of the study.

2 Literature Review

In this study, the importance of peer affective factors was observed amongst the participants during the online short story writing activity. Before outlining previous studies on peer affective factors on peer collaboration, I first draw on Vygotsky's views on affective aspects of learning. He held that cognition and affect are indistinguishably interconnected to each other, as he exemplifies in his assertion:

> *When we approach the problem of the interrelation between thought and language and other aspects of mind, the first question that arises is that of intellect and affect. Their separation as subjects of study is a major weakness of traditional psychology, since it makes the thought process appear as an autonomous flow of 'thoughts thinking them-selves' segregated from the fullness of life, from personal needs and interests, the inclinations and impulses of the thinker* [26, p. 10].

Under the Vygotskian optic, Stahl [22] viewed cognition as a social process which enabled learners to build knowledge and solve problems through group interaction. Webster's Seventh Collegiate Dictionary [18, p. 15] defined 'affect' as (1): feeling, affection (2): the conscious subjective aspect of an emotion considered apart from bodily change." According to Shroader and Cahoy [21], affective domains comprise a learner's attitudes, emotions, interests, motivation, self-efficacy and values. Cooper [4], who has researched the role and place of empathy (which involves caring and emotions) with school teachers and their students, also emphasised the inextricable interconnection of cognition and affect contending that the two go hand in hand in learning. Cooper's work is relevant in that the groups in my study felt the need to elect a peer leader to take on a leadership and instructional role, indeed a caring role. On this point, Cooper writes that: "Affect is central to communication and the formation of relationships between people' [4, p. 5].

Previous studies on collaborative writing in an EFL context have mainly centred on cognitive and linguistic aspects of learning. In what follows, I identify certain affective aspects of learning through different types of peer collaboration, such as written/oral peer feedback. Although there have been no studies on collaborative writing in an EFL context focusing on peer affective factors in peer collaboration, there are a few studies of relevance on peer feedback in this context. This is particularly the case in relation to writing (e.g. Kurt and Atay [11], Yastibas and Yastibas [27], Lee [13]) and in speaking as well as oral peer feedback on collaborative presentation in the study of Nguyen [20].

The studies of Kurt and Atay [11] and Yastlibas and Yastibas [27] revealed that peer feedback had a facilitating effect on EFL learners' writing anxiety. Lee [13] showed that the use of praise during peer feedback in writing activities was low, because many EFL learners appear to lack confident about their English competence, and therefore shun using it. Nguyen [19] found that the use of spoken motivational phrases when working together in pairs for a task enabled the participants to create an emotionally supportive environment where they engaged with the task as well as building a rapport, feeling comfortable and increasing their self-confidence.

Other studies focused on the dimension of peer affective factors in collaborative learning contexts outside the field of EFL highlighted trust and respect among learners in pair/group work (e.g. Dale [6]) as well as the positive effects of friendship on collaborative learning (e.g. Kutnick et al. [12]; Vass [25]; Jones and Pellegrini [9]; Hartup [8]). Moreover, the findings of Anderson and Simpson's study [1] revealed that in online small group discussions the participants built a strong sense of community with more affective support than with online whole class discussions. I end this brief review with the powerful conclusion of Hartup [8, p. 1] from his study on the effect of friendship in collaborative learning, which was that 'friends provide one another cognitive and social scaffolding'.

3 Methodology

In this research, I aimed to explore Turkish high school EFL learners' perceptions on peer affective factors during a Facebook-based collaborative writing activity. The focus on this aspect of this research is reflected in the following research question: How Turkish high school EFL learners interpret peer affective factors during a Facebook-based collaborative writing activity?

I decided to use a qualitative approach, as I considered this to be consistent with the foci of the research. According to Merriam [17, p. 13] a qualitative approach concerns "understanding the meaning people have constructed, that is, how people make sense of the world and the experiences they have in the world".

As there was limited literature on investigating peer affective factors in peer collaboration in a context of EFL writing either in a classroom setting or online setting both in Turkey and the rest of the world, I decided to employ an exploratory study in FB group, which is an online social networking site. The study was designed as a Facebook-based collaborative writing activity. There are two underlying reasons why I chose to undertake my study through the FB group. First, the writing skills seem not to have received enough attention in English language lessons in many Turkish high schools. EFL teachers in these schools are compelled to follow the English Language Teaching (ELT) curriculum required by the Turkish Ministry of National Education [24] and have little time to spare for extended writing activities or for classroom research. This evident lack stimulated the idea of planning an online collaborative writing activity. Second, I was aware that Turkish teenagers are attracted to FB as a social networking site (SNS). As pointed out by Demirtas [7], most of the FB users in Turkey are between the age of 18 and 35. In addition to this, this author has reported that there are 18.1 million online social networking users who are 15 years old and above. Therefore, I decided to exercise my intervention in the aforementioned groups as I believed this would engage their interest.

As I designed this research as an exploratory study, I first undertook a pilot study prior to the main study. The pilot study had an impact on main study methodology in determining sample size, shaping the research question and framing the design of methods. Regarding the sample size, one of my colleagues working as a teacher of EFL in Turkey agreed to help me find participants after I had obtained official consent from the Provincial Directorate of National Education and the school's principal. I presented my pilot study to a class of 34 students, six participants volunteered to involve in the pilot study. Then, I asked them to form two groups of three and produce a short story in English with their group members in a FB group over four weeks. I decided to undertake the main study with a sample of two groups of three in total six participants. I found this sample size revealed rich insights and so decided to repeat the format for the main study. Conducting the pilot study helped me firm up a clear research question for guiding the main study. In the pilot study, I used three focus group discussions but I observed that some of the pilot study participants could not or did not want to express their opinions or feelings openly in front their friends. In fact, some of them chose to do so by sending private messages or chat requests through FB. Bearing this in mind, I decided to employ online one-to-one chats as well as focus group discussions for the main study. Furthermore, anticipating that participants' narratives might not be sufficient, I therefore planned to use the participants' online discussion boards in their FB groups for the main study to give further credibility to the data.

Concerning the main study, after obtaining official consent from the Provincial Directorate of National Education and the school's principal, another colleague of mine presented my research project to their classroom and a total of six Turkish high school EFL learners in two groups of three participated in the study voluntarily over seven weeks. These six EFL learners and participants of the main study, were 10th graders (16 years old, 4 females, 2 males) and their English level was considered as pre-intermediate, according to the CEFR (Council of Europe [5]), A2 level. For ethical considerations, these participants' real names were anonymised and pseudonyms were used instead. To draw distinction between two groups of participants, henceforth, I call the first group (Nila, Gonca & Deniz) group A, while the second (Ali, Attila & Selma) was named group B.

In the main study, participants in groups were asked to write a short story in English with their group members collaboratively in a FB group created only for the study. Participants were asked to undertake this writing activity outside of school hours online. During the writing activity, participants used their smartphones and/or laptops to produce their short story collaboratively. Participants were asked to meet once or twice a week in a Facebook group to produce their short story collaboratively within seven weeks. During the study, each group of participants arranged 10 meetings within seven weeks. My role as researcher in this study was as a facilitator throughout the writing activity. I decided to become a facilitator for the main study participants because as reported by some of the pilot study participants, they had difficulties in deciding on a particular topic for their short story as a group and they had spent nearly two sessions before all agreeing on what they wanted to write about. Moreover, from the pilot study I observed that until they understood what was required of them, they needed considerable facilitator input, although subsequently this need diminished substantially. In the light of this, I decided to provide a short story topic for the main study participants as this would save time in them getting started. I encouraged participants to work together with minimal facilitator support. I attended all 10 meetings in a FB group for both groups. I provided participants with a short story topic and gave some guidance for them to start their short story. At the beginning of the writing activity, both groups of participants felt a need to select a group leader among their group partners when the facilitator's guidance was, for the most part, withdrawn during the early stages. Concerning the election of a group leader, some participants reported that they felt a need to select someone who seemed to them confident and knowledgeable about how to chair a group discussion, was comfortable with making decisions about what to write in a session and who, in their estimation, had better English knowledge than the other group partners in the group.

At the beginning and in the middle of the writing task, the participants were mostly dependent on their group leaders' assistance and guidance. However, towards the end of the task, when group leaders gave more freedom to their group partners and as the latter's confidence developed, the role of group leaders began to diminish. In its place, individual teacher agency developed and group partners at this stage began to contribute collectively when completing the writing exercise.

In this study, I gathered data mainly from focus group discussions, online one-to-one chats and FB group discussion threads from both groups.

4 Findings and Discussion

One of the key findings of Lee's [13] study that was concerned with peer feedback in EFL writing indicated that many participants did not feel confident about praising their peers due to lack of experience and knowledge about how to give peer feedback. In contrast to what Lee found in her study, in my study, the group leaders gave frequent praise to their group partners. As explained by the group leaders, one of the main reasons why they used praise was to increase peer collaboration during the online short story writing exercises. According to the participants of this study who received praise from group leaders, they thought that this was motivational for them in relation to writing in English. In this research, the participants considered that peer affective factors were:

- Giving praise (e.g. well done! excellent! good work!) as group leaders;
- Receiving similar comments of praise from group leaders;
- Giving motivational phrases (e.g. you're doing well, don't give up, we're with you) as group leaders or a group partner;
- Receiving motivational phrases such as the above from group leaders or from a group partner(s);
- Feeling comfortable with each other when undertaking the writing exercise;
- Informal language use in group discussions including terms of endearment (such as darling, honey, and love) and the use of text speak and emoticons;
- Use of humour when undertaking individual writing tasks.

There follows an extract from a conversation of group A (Nila, Gonca & Deniz) to provide a context for the employment of informal language use in group discussion with terms of endearment.

Nila: Hello my darlings ♥♥♥ you there?
Gonca: Yes, my sweetheart. I'm here.
Nila: Where is Deniz?
Gonca: She'll be here in a minute. She sent me a text. She just came home from shopping with her mum.
Nila: Okay. Let's wait for her then.
Gonca: Let's listen to this song while waiting for Deniz. https://www.youtube.com/watch?v=KUmZp8pR1uc [Amy Winehouse- Rehab]
Deniz: Sorry being late. Here I'm my darlings. I love you ♥♥♥
Gonca: Love you ♥♥♥♥

Nguyen's [20] study, which examined peer collaboration in an EFL speaking task among six pairs, revealed that some motivational phrases (e.g. "don't worry!", "everything will be alright after all") used by the pair partners enabled them to support each other in sustaining task engagement, building a rapport, increasing self-confidence and feeling a sense of safety when undertaking the activity. In line with the findings of Nguyen, the participants in my study claimed that such motivational phrases increased their self- confidence about writing in English as the quotation below shows:

Ali: "At a boxing match, the audience usually say some words, such as 'keep on, you can do it, don't give up now' and especially in films, after hearing these words, boxers stand up and keep fighting with their opponents. This writing exercise for me was like a boxing match. Every time I felt weak when it comes to writing in English, Selma's [the group leader] motivating words helped me gain self-confidence and keep on writing [in English]" (focus group discussion, 2).

In this study, the participants also emphasized that they felt comfortable with each other when undertaking the writing exercise. The main reason why they said they felt this way was attributed to the developing friendships among the group partners. In the study of Kutnick, Blatchford and Baines [12], friendship among peers in a group work was found to be a foundation for building trust between group partners, the ability to communicate effectively and the capacity to resolve problems jointly with peers. One of the key findings of Dale's [6] study, albeit in the rather different context of L1 ninth-grade students, was that trust and respect among group partners in collaborative writing enabled students to feel comfortable with each other when discussing the emerging text. In my study, both groups built a comfortable and supportive environment where group partners felt relaxed with each other when undertaking their online short story writing exercise in groups as the following quotation shows:

Ali: "My group partners are my classmates and friends. I've known Attila since primary school. We're best friends. I've known Selma since the first grade in high school. Obviously, the fact that we know each other made me feel comfortable when doing this writing exercise, because I could tell them when I faced problems and sought help. They didn't judge me at all. Selma was a very good teacher and Attila was a good partner who supported me whenever I had difficulty writing in English. I think knowing each other is a sort of collaboration in this writing exercise" (focus group discussion 4).

Thus, in line with the findings of Dale, the outcomes of my study lend weight to the importance of the concept of peers feeling comfortable with each other during a collaborative writing process when a sense of friendship is present. Furthermore, in this study, as recounted by the participants, becoming comfortable with each other when undertaking the writing exercise enabled them to reduce the apprehension and the anxiety they felt initially towards writing in English as well as being able to share their writing-related problems. Studies by Kurt and Atay's [11] and Yastibas and Yastibas [27] on 'writing anxiety' in the field of EFL context have mostly focused on the use of peer feedback. In my study, it was found that anxiety was greatly reduced as the collaborative exercise got underway. The participants began to feel increasingly comfortable with each other after receiving motivational phrases (e.g. you're doing well, don't give up, we're with you) and praise (e.g. well done! excellent! good work!) from their team leaders. In addition, informal language, including terms of endearment (e.g. darling, honey and love) and 'text speak' with emoticons along with humour from their peers enabled them to work in a relaxed way when undertaking their individual writing. As explained by the participants, praise motivated them to continue their writing in English especially the giving and receiving of motivational phrases when one of their group partners had difficulties in pursuing a writing task. The findings from this study about reducing anxiety, feeling comfortable and using humour build on the findings of Kurt and Atay [11] and Yastibas and Yastibas [27].

Based on the participants' recounting, informal discussions in an online setting, Facebook enabled the participants to feel comfortable with each other when undertaking the writing exercise, and the use of informal language in group discussions (such as they would not normally use out of the Facebook setting) including terms of endearment, the use of texting language and emoticons, and the use of humour when undertaking individual writing tasks. This is I suggest because Facebook is an environment that they use regularly for their social interaction and that affords the support of a culture of emotional support and care and a feeling of being part of a community, supporting the findings of Anderson and Simpson [1]. Such a culture enabled the students to cope in a very mature way with disputes and concerns that were invariably part of the collaboration. The dimensions of peer collaboration, peer leadership and the associated affective factors lead me to pull together the various strands that created a powerful peer teaching and peer learning environment in this study where the small group unit has been central.

5 Conclusion

As reported by the participants, the peer affective factors comprised giving/receiving praise, giving/receiving motivational phrases, feeling comfortable with each other when undertaking the writing exercise, informal language use in group discussion and the use of humour when undertaking individual writing tasks. According to their comments, feeling comfortable with each other had a positive impact on their writing development, because it reduced apprehension about writing in English and made it easier for them to reveal their writing-related problems to their group partners. In addition, receiving praise from their group partners motivated them to write in English and motivational phrases as well as the use of terms of endearment from both group leaders and group partners, helped them increase their self-confidence in engaging in set tasks. Evidence from, for example, participant Ali's accounts shown below reveals the satisfaction and pride the participants felt regarding the outcomes of the collaborative writing exercises. They said that they had found the process enjoyable and their view, and one to which they were entitled to have as the key participants in this study, was that their knowledge of English as well as their ability to write more effectively had improved as a result. As Ali, for example, commented in the final focus group on his feelings of his personal and writing skills development.

> *"Above all, I had great fun during the writing exercise and noticed and learnt how the skill of writing could be developed and practised outside the classroom setting. I feel more confident in myself and my writing skills in English" (focus group discussion 4).*

I end this paper with what I consider to be a rather insightful quotation from a student who identifies what she perceives as a crucial gap in her experience as a learner, a gap that resonates with the initial motivation for my undertaking this research:

> *"I really hope that in the near future our teachers understand that students can learn from each other and give more group work exercises, not only in English lessons, but also on other courses" (Ali: focus group discussion, 4).*

There are very positive implications for teachers to consider, given restricted time, in incorporating some independent student collaborative writing both in and outside the classroom, for which some Turkish teachers have already expressed considerable enthusiasm as a way to enhance and extend their pedagogical repertoire and learning opportunities for the students.

Acknowledgements. The author would like to would like to express his deepest gratitude to his supervisors, Dr. Jane Jones and Dr. Mary Webb for their generosity, constant encouragement, and valuable advice.

References

1. Anderson, B., Simpson, M.: Group and class contexts for learning and support online: learning and affective support online in small group and class contexts. Int. Rev. Res. Open Distance Learn. **5**(3), 1–15 (2004)
2. Bani-Hani, N.A., Al-Sobh, M.A., Abu-Melhim, A.R.H.: Utilizing Facebook groups in teaching writing: jordanian EFL students' perceptions and attitudes. Int. J. Eng. Linguist. **4**(5), 27–34 (2014)
3. Chao, Y.-C.J., Lo, H.-C.: Students' perceptions of wiki-based collaborative writing for learners of English as a foreign language. Interact. Learn. Environ. **19**(4), 395–411 (2011)
4. Cooper, B.: In search of profound empathy in learning relationships: understanding the mathematics of moral learning environments. J. Moral Educ. **39**, 79–99 (2010)
5. Council of Europe: Common European framework of reference for languages: learning, teaching, assessment. Cambridge University Press, Cambridge (2001). http://www.coe.int/t/dg4/linguistic/Source/Framework_EN.pdf. Accessed 20 June 2017
6. Dale, H.: Collaborative writing interactions in one ninth-grade classroom. J. Educ. Res. **87**, 334–344 (1994)

7. Demirtas, M.: An analysis in purpose to the Facebook and Twitter users in Turkey. Br. J. Arts Soc. Sci. **9**(2), 116–125 (2012)
8. Hartup, W.W.: Cooperation, close relationships, and cognitive development. In: Bukowski, W.M., Newcomb, A.F., Hartup, W.W. (eds.) The Company They Keep: Friendship in Childhood and Adolescence, pp. 213–237. Cambridge University Press, New York (1996)
9. Jones, I., Pellegrini, A.D.: The effects of social relationship, writing media, and microgenetic development on first grade students' written narratives. Am. Educ. Res. J. **33**, 691–718 (1996)
10. Kessler, G.: Student initiated attention to form in wiki based collaborative writing. Language Learn. Technol. **13**(1), 79–95 (2009)
11. Kurt, G., Atay, D.: The effects of peer feedback on the writing of anxiety of prospective EFL teachers. J. Theory Pract. Educ. **3**, 12–23 (2007)
12. Kutnick, P., Blatchford, P., Baines, E.: Grouping of pupils in secondary school classrooms: possible links between pedagogy and learning. Soc. Psychol. Educ. **8**(4), 349–374 (2005)
13. Lee, S.C.N.: Written peer feedback by EFL students: praise, criticism and suggestion. J. Komaba Engl. Educ. **1**, 129–139 (2010)
14. Li, M., Zhu, W.: Patterns of computer-mediated interaction in small writing groups using wikis. Comput. Assist. Lang. Learn. **26**(1), 62–81 (2013)
15. Lin, W.C., Yang, S.C.: Exploring students' perceptions of integrating Wiki technology and peer feedback into English writing courses. Teach.: Pract. Crit. **10**(2), 88–103 (2011)
16. Lund, A.: Wikis: a collective approach to language production. ReCALL **20**(1), 35–54 (2008)
17. Merriam, S.B.: Qualitative Research: A Guide to Design and Implementation. Jossey-Bass, San Francisco (2009)
18. Merriam-Webster's Collegiate Dictionary, 5th edn. Merriam-Webster, Springfield (1970)
19. Miyazoe, T., Anderson, T.: Learning outcomes and students' perceptions of online writing: Simultaneous implementation of a forum, blog and wiki in an EFL blended learning setting. System **38**, 185–199 (2010)
20. Nguyen, M.H.: EFL students' reflections on peer scaffolding in making a collaborative oral presentation. Engl. Lang. Teach. **6**(4), 64–73 (2013)
21. Schroeder, R., Cahoy, E.S.: Valuing information literacy: affective learning and the ACRL standards. Portal: Librar. Acad. **10**(2), 127–146 (2010)
22. Stahl, G.: Group Cognition: Computer Support for Building Collaborative Knowledge. MIT Press, Cambridge (2006)
23. Storch, N.: Collaborative Writing in L2 Classrooms: New Perspectives on Language and Education. Multilingual Matters, Bristol (2013)
24. The Turkish Ministry of National Education: Secondary school (grade 9–12) English language teaching curriculum [Ortaoğretim kurumları İngilizce dersi oğretim programi] (2011). https://dyned33.files.wordpress.com/2011/09/ortac3b6c49fretim-ingilizce-dersi-hazc4b1rlc4b1k-9-12-sc4b1nc4b1flar-c3b6c49fretim-programlarc4b12.pdf. Accessed 29 July 2017
25. Vass, E.: Friendship and collaborative creative writing in the primary classroom. J. Comput. Assist. Learn. **18**(1), 102–110 (2002)
26. Vygotsky, L.S.: Thought and Language. MIT Press, Cambridge (1986)
27. Yastibas, G.C., Yastibas, A.E.: The effect of peer feedback on writing anxiety on Turkish EFL (English as a foreign language) students. Procedia- Soc. Behav. Sci. **199**, 530–538 (2015)

Primary School Students' Choices in Writing Opinion Essays: Using ICT Combined with Self-Regulated Strategies

Catarina Liane Araújo(✉), António José Osório, and Ana Paula Loução Martins

Research Centre in Education, Institute of Education, University of Minho, Braga, Portugal
catarinaliane@gmail.com, {ajosorio,apmartins}@ie.uminho.pt

Abstract. The process of learning how to write is a demanding, slow, and complex process. Primary school students often experience problems in writing and, therefore, teachers should provide scientifically validated strategies to empower their performance, such as Self-Regulated Strategy Development (SRSD). Reflecting on the changes in the social reality and students' personal interests, the inclusion of Information and Communication Technologies (ICT) in the educational context and practice in writing has also become exceedingly relevant. However, using ICT associated to other teaching methodologies is not always explored in the classroom. In a quasi-experimental study, 178 fourth grade students participated in an opinion essay writing intervention, during 12 weeks (90 min/week), using SRSD instruction model (n = 89) and an ICT variant of SRSD called SRSD + ICT model (n = 89). We analyzed the impact of these two interventions through the analysis of opinion texts produced, by handwriting, for students one week before and one week after the intervention according to the elements, quality, number of words and number of linking words. Both showed positive results in the students' writing skills, although the results from the SRSD + ICT model were better. These results reinforce the pertinence and usefulness of this model in the teaching-learning process of writing that should be discussed and tested in different contexts.

Keywords: Writing · Self-Regulated Strategy Development
Information and communication technology · Primary education
Evidence Based Practice

1 Introduction

Writing is a complex, slow and demanding activity that requires knowledge, training and the mobilization of multiple processes (e.g. Hayes Model of Writing [1]). In an increasingly demanding and competitive society, we consider that early teaching of writing opinion essays is fundamental in order to enable students to possess the necessary skills and tools to clearly express their point of view on what surrounds them.

A. Tatnall and M. Webb (Eds.): WCCE 2017, IFIP AICT 515, pp. 323–334, 2017.
https://doi.org/10.1007/978-3-319-74310-3_34

It is in primary education that teachers and students spend more time in teaching and learning the writing process and, according to curriculum goals and programs, it is expected that students will acquire important writing skills during this teaching stage. However, it is known that there are students who present problems in writing, which translates into the presence of inferior writing performances when compared with their peers (e.g. quality, extension) and misperceptions about their knowledge and self-efficacy in writing. Moreover, teachers also state they lack the knowledge to effect strategies necessary to deal with the difficulties these students experience.

Consequently, schools are not providing adequate answers to the level of writing [2, 3]. Therefore, it is necessary for teachers to be familiar with effective teaching and intervention practices supported by evidence from well-conducted research studies in order to help their students succeed. Self-Regulated Strategy Development (SRSD) is an example of this, recognized as an Evidence Based Practice (EBP), which is an explicit, flexible and robust instruction model with international scientific validity, and considered highly effective in writing [2]. Despite this, further research is still needed in order for students to become competent writers [4]. It is therefore fundamental to develop more powerful and explicit interventions with students with writing problems [5].

Another of our concerns is that we need to accept that today new challenges have been placed on teachers and students in the writing process as a consequence of technological expansion in society, which has increased the diversity and complexity of writing formats and media. Consequently, this sometimes results in a disconnection between writing activities both inside and outside the classroom [6]. Therefore, being able to write properly, according to the different contexts of communication and including the use of technologies, is becoming increasingly important for the academic, social and professional development of students [4], and continues to advocate conservative pedagogical practices, ignoring the new environments and formats of written communication [7].

In this sense, we propose an adaptation of the SRSD model that integrates the self-regulated use of ICT resources and methodologies, as well as other EBP in the classroom during the teaching-learning process of writing opinion texts, calling this: the SRSD + ICT Model.

Thus, the aim of this study is to verify the impact of the SRSD + ICT model in the opinion essay writing performance of 4th grade primary school students, and which we consider to have the potentials to improve students' writing performance, even when students are writing manually, helping them to understand and execute the writing process. We will also describe the elements that contributed to the construction of the SRSD + ICT model.

2 Background

The results of the last 35 years of research developed around the world show that the SRSD model has a confirmed positive effect on students' performance in writing and in promoting students' self-efficacy, attitudes and motivation for writing, including students with Learning Disabilities (LD) and Writing Problems (WP), which tends to be maintained and generalized [8, 9]. Nevertheless, the success of using the SRSD model with all students is not guaranteed, depending on who, with whom and how the intervention is applied. Thus, researchers in writing recognize the need for more research with the SRSD model that reflects the complexity of writing learning and student's diversity [4].

Nowadays, Information and Communication Technologies (ICT) are socially compelling and attractive resources for most students [10, 11]. Also, ICT consist of powerful, interactive and flexible tools for the teaching and conclusion of quality writing among students, with and without LD [12]. Thus, several authors advocate for learning spaces with planned practices, which include the use of multimedia and technology, which offer interesting, diversified, authentic and purposeful writing tasks [13].

Although research in the field has recognized the potential of ICT in education, it is known that the use of technological resources alone is not a more effective determinant of learning, since its effectiveness will always depend on other aspects (relevance, resources, motivation, predisposition to use, perceptions of effectiveness) [14].

3 The Present Study

In this context, given that the SRSD model has a flexible nature, it allows us to combine it with other EBPs and adapt practices to the needs of teachers and students.

Before start the intervention, the students involved in this study defined goals to be achieved by the end of the intervention: the main objective of improving the writing of opinion texts and a specific objective according to the category in which they presented the lowest performance in writing quality of the following: (a) theme and typology; (b) information coherence and adequacy; (c) structure and cohesion; (d) morphology and syntax; (e) vocabulary repertoire; (f) spelling in the pre test. An example of a specific goal defined by a student was "writing opinion pieces with fewer errors."

3.1 Interventions (SRSD and SRSD + ICT Intervention)

The instructions of the models were carried out in the classroom context by the same researcher, with verification of the procedures adopted by the class teachers using a context of preventive intervention [18]. We recognize that the intervention in the classroom is a limitation of the study, but this allows us to study the impact of these interventions in a less studied context and later to make it available to students in order to respond to their characteristics and needs.

After that, each group of students started the intervention SRSD or SRSD + ICT model, with the same instructor. We have applied all the principles, characteristics and stages of the SRSD model in conjunction with Revised Bloom's Taxonomy (remember, understanding, applying, analyzing, evaluating and creating) in both groups. Thus, the Revised Blooms' Taxonomy [15] allowed us to guide the teaching-learning process, in order to respect the complexity of the processes and sub processes involved and the maturation of students' cognition.

SRSD model

In the SRSD model, we followed its typical characteristics, procedures and steps. Initially, the following phases were used: (1) developed knowledge about linear writing and its contexts (e.g. What do you know about writing? What type of essays do you know?); (2) discussion about the characteristics typically present in quality opinion essays (e.g. What is a good essay?); (3) modeling the writing of linear texts (instructor explicitly shows how students can do the self-instructions stages, self-monitor their progress and feedback, undertake self-reinforcement with positive demonstrations or self-statements and reflect about how to use different writing strategies and techniques) and (4) memorization, through the use of mnemonics for all essays POW [8]: *P*ick my idea, *O*rganize my notes, *W*rite and say more (POW was adapted in Portuguese to PATO [10]) and the use of mnemonics Structure for opinion essays, adapted in Portuguese from TREE (Topic sentence - *Head*; Reasons - *Trunk* and Explain reasons and Ending - *Members*); (5) peer practices and (6) independence. The following Fig. 1 (see below) shows some students' activities using SRSD model (self-statements, drawing used to plan writing and PATO mnemonic).

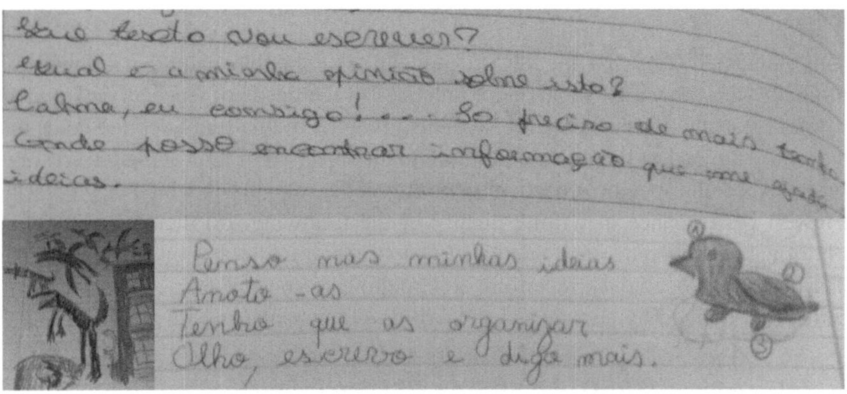

Fig. 1. Representation of SRSD model and some activities in classroom

This group did not use ICT during the intervention but used a variety of materials such as searching in books or publications on school placards, which ensured the approach contained aspects similar to those used in the SRSD model. Subsequently, after this study, the students and teachers of this group had the possibility of receiving the instructions with the SRSD + ICT model.

SRSD + ICT model

In the SRSD + ICT model, we initially used the following phases: (1) development of knowledge about linear writing and its contexts; (2) discussion about the characteristics typically present in quality opinion essays; (3) modeling the writing of linear texts and (4) memorization, through the use of mnemonics for all essays (PATO) and for opinions essays (Structure). Later, we proceeded with the following phases: (5) development of knowledge about multimodal writing; (6) discussion about the characteristics and contexts of multimodal writing, including the different writing formats (e.g. auditory, visual); (7) modeling the multimodal writing. In these phases, we also included the use of ICT tools in the process according to these steps: (a) the presentation of tools and some of the potentialities for writing; (b) discussion with students and (c) modeling the use of tools in text production. After that, we followed on with peer practices (8), where all students explored the use of research-based ICT tools (e.g. word processor, spell checker, mental maps, speech synthesizers and others) and reflected on how and when ICT could support their learning process of writing. In this way, all the students experimented with different tools and had the possibility to choose whether or not to use a certain tool during the writing process. Furthermore the students analyzed individual or group potential and identified the constraints of specific use of ICT in the writing process. The Fig. 2 (see below) shows the explicit approach of areas that contributed to the SRSD + ICT model for the teaching-learning process of writing opinion essays. The following Fig. 3 (see below) shows an example of mental maps created by students using SRSD + ICT model.

Finally, the students' independence in writing was stimulated and, together with the teacher, each student decided if and when to use ICT for their writing process, as well as using other forms of writing to help their writing process (e.g. auditory, visual). It should also be noted that the ICT resources of the students' families, including computers, tablets and mobile phones, were used and that the introduction of these technologies in the classroom for writing promoted more active and proactive dynamics among students.

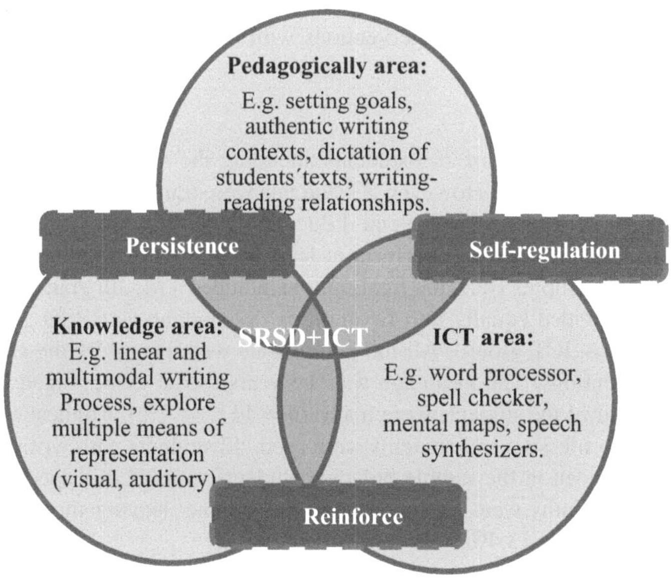

Fig. 2. Representation of explicit approach of areas that contributed to the SRSD + ICT model and same activities in classroom.

Fig. 3. Mental maps created by students during the opinion essay writing process using SRSD + ICT model, in Coogle

4 Methodology

This study used a quasi-experimental methodology to analyze the impact of two different interventions, SRSD + ICT and SRSD, in 178, 4th grade student's performance of writing opinion essays, divided equally into two groups, after 12 weeks of instruction (90 min/week) in Braga, Portugal. Variables such as gender, presence of socioeconomic support to families, presence of writing problems and presence of special educational needs were controlled. Also, the writing practices of students in the classroom, collected through observations, interviews and a questionnaire for teachers, were taken into account for the interpretation of the results. We also evaluated the fidelity and social validity of the interventions with students and teachers.

4.1 Participants

The initial sample consisted of 205 students attending the 4th grade of public school education in Braga, Portugal. However, 23 students were transferred, missed the pretest or corresponded to students in Special Education and Specific Curriculum. Also, another 10 students who did not perform at least two-thirds of the intervention were excluded from the sample. Thus, the final sample included 174, 4th grade students, and this sample was divided equally into two groups (87 students in SRSD group and 87 students in SRSD + ICT group). All the participants were taught by the same teacher during the interventions. The mean age was 9.5 years (SD = .578, ranged from 9–12) and more than half of the students were males (n = 111, 54.1%). Application protocols validated by full professors and students were used. 42 students with writing problems (20.5%) were included in the sample however students supported in special education and specific curriculums were excluded from the sample, leaving the rest who were integrated in the sample (3.4%).

4.2 Writing Measures and Procedures

Assessments tasks procedures. Students were asked to write an opinion essay one week before the start of the instructions (pretest) and one week after the instructions (posttest). For each text, a topic question about familiar subjects that guided the writing of the text was given (e.g. What is your favorite season of the year?; What is your favorite game?) and students then had 45 min to write their opinion essays.

Evaluation procedures for score performance in writing opinion essay. After collecting pre and posttest students' opinion essays samples their performance in writing opinion essays was evaluated according to the *structure*, *quality*, *number of words* and *number of linking words of written opinion essays* and using the following instruments described in Table 1.

Table 1. Instruments used for scoring performance

Variables measures	Instruments and scores
Elements	*Instrument used:* Elements score scale of opinion essays from Scardamalia and Bereiter [16]. One point per presence of: (1) topic sentence; (2) reasons; (3) arguments; (4) examples; (5) final sentence. The final structure score is a result of the sum of the points obtained. Repeated ideas are only counted once
Quality	*Instrument used:* Portuguese National Scale for the assessment of the Writing performance of 4th grade students [17]. Assign a score between 1(unsatisfactory) and 5 points (Excellent) in each next dimensions: (a) theme and typology; (b) information coherence and adequacy; (c) structure and cohesion; (d) morphology and syntax; (e) vocabulary repertoire; (f) spelling. The quality scores result of the average of the evaluated in each dimension previous presented
Number of words	The number of words was recorded on the computer using Microsoft Office and verified by the authors (e.g. 1 meaning 1 words writing)
Number of linking words	Linking words are words that serve to connect ideas in a sentence that can help writer to addicting (e.g. also), sequencing (e.g. first) illustrating (e.g. for example), comparing (e.g. similarly), qualifying (e.g. except), contrasting (e.g. alternatively), summary (e.g. in short), emphasizing (e.g. above all) or establish relations of cause and effect (e.g. because) in the essay. The number of linking words was counted manually. For each linking word different is assigned by 1

Analysis procedures. For data collection, analyses of descriptive statistics were performed through frequency measurements, central (mean) and dispersion (standard deviation), extreme (maximum and minimum) and quartile patterns using SPSS. Inferential statistics were used through the Student's t-Test for the comparison of means between independent sample and also analysis of variance for repeated measurements for determining and analyzing significant differences between elements, quality, number of words and number of linking words on the intervention (SRSD or SRSD + ICT).

5 Results and Discussion

As expected, according to the results obtained in previous studies, the positive results of the use of the SRSD model in writing performance [e.g. 4, 19, 20]. As for the SRSD + ICT model, given the combination of several EBP, self-regulation processes and models of educational technologies with positive evidence in the orientation of the learning process, we expect that it can contribute to the improvement of the writing performance of these students. Thus, the results of the writing performance of students' opinion essays are presented below in Table 2:

Table 2. Students' opinion essay writing performance between pretest and posttest in each intervention according to the elements of writing, quality of writing, number of words and number of linking words.

Writing style	Time	Interventions group	
		SRSD	SRSD + ICT
		M (SD) (n = 87)	M (SD) (n = 87)
Opinion essay			
Elements	Pre test	3.51(1.50)	3.53 (1.23)
	Post test	5.87 (2.23)	6.71 (1.86)
Quality	Pre test	3.02 (0.89)	2.96 (0.81)
	Post test	4.03 (0.63)	4.34 (0.55)
Number of words	Pre test	93.93 (31.51)	108.95 (33.38)
	Post test	90.19 (39.64)	114.14 (33.79)
Number of linking words	Pre test	2.64 (1.12)	2.97 (1.07)
	Post test	4.22 (2.26)	4.86 (1.78)

The results in Table 2 demonstrate that those students in the SRSD group presented a minor performance before the intervention in writing elements (with an average of at least three elements between topic sentences, reasons, contra reasons, examples or final sentence), number of words and number of linking words (less variety and quantity) than students in the SRSD + ICT group.

In contrast, the quality is lower than with students in the SRSD + ICT group. After the interventions, we observed significant improvements in elements, quality and number of linking words of opinion essays in both groups. The opinion essays were more structured (with the basic structure of this gender), were of better quality (Students progressed from unsatisfactory assessments to very good assessments) and were also more diversified using a greater number of linking words which allowed their writing to become more perceptible to readers, and helped in the organization and presentation of ideas and messages in the text to both the writer and the reader.

Regarding the number of words, used in the essays, these groups had opposite behaviours. In the SRSD group, there was an increase in the number of words while in the SRSD + ICT, there was a decrease, although both groups wrote better after their interventions. Therefore, we believe that the SRSD group extended their ideas more, while the SRSD + ICT group was more objective in their writing. These results are contrary to what was expected, since some investigations [e.g. 14] have shown an increase in the length of texts produced by students after intervention with this model. In this study, it was also possible to verify an improvement in the quality and structure of the texts produced by the students after the intervention, even with shorter texts. Possibly, these results are due to the fact that a guideline for the minimum number of words was used and students understood the essential elements of the text, thus reducing redundant or ancillary information, which brought the number of words written by the students closer. In contrast, students from the SRSD + ICT group, who benefited from the SRSD + ICT intervention, wrote longer texts after the intervention with a higher quality and structure, which seems to indicate the positive effects of this intervention for the development of the ideas produced in the text, translated in the extension of the same. From the above, it seems that the use of the SRSD + ICT model provided the students with the skills and knowledge that enabled them to improve the quality, structure and extension of texts produced. In any case, it should be noted that the results presented could be different with another group of students, and it is therefore important to develop further studies that use the SRSD + ICT model in other contexts in order to verify if the benefits evidenced at the extension level of the texts are retained or, if the results are different.

Analyzing the results obtained, according to the analysis of variance for repeated measurements, it can be verified that the variables of writing performance present a highly significant value ($p = 0.00$) in the results of the groups and in the explanation of the variance of the same, in the interception between the effect of the writing performance variables with the group ($p = 0.00$) or between the effect of the writing performance variables with the moment ($p = 0.00$). It should also be noted that the moments present a significant effect ($p \leq .05$) on the total variance of the results. Analyzing the result obtained in the *Mauchaly's sphericity test* it was verified, as expected, that the *sphericity* assumption is not met with the performance variables ($p = 0.00$) and between the performance variables in the moment writing ($p = 0.00$), so that the values corrected through the *Greenhouse-Geisser* were also analyzed, being the variables ($p = .335$) and the variables x moment ($p = 336$). Also, the differences found were attributed to the necessarily reduced size of this quasi-experimental design.

The results obtained in the simple linear model of repeated measures (2×2) between the SRSD + ICT and SRSD groups and the two moments of evaluation (pre-test and post-test) in the study variables (writing performance variables: structure, quality, extension and connectors) by analyzing the tests of inter-subject contrasts.

It was possible to verify, through the test of effects between subjects, that there is a differentiated effect of the intervention type (SRSD + ICT intervention and SRSD) presents a highly significant value ($F = 20.594$, $p = .000$), which is maintained by interception between the group × moment × performance variables in writing ($F = 2575.595$, $p = .000$). Thus, the results show that SRSD and SRDS + ICT interventions contributed to the improvement of these 4th grade students' writing performance of opinion essays, specifically in the elements of opinion essay, quality of writing and the use of linking words which was what we had expected.

The fact that the SRSD + ICT model obtained even more positive results than those previously observed with the SRSD model as an evidence-based practice, underlines the importance of discussing how ICT can contribute to supporting the learning of writing and the analyses of how the use of the SRSD model with ICT can be positive, reiterating the importance of the transversal use of the self-regulation process to the different learning approaches. The results also reinforce the positive effects of ICT in the writing process of students already previously evidenced by other authors and in other research contexts (e.g. [20–22]). Therefore, this highlights the role of this model with respect to the individual needs of students where all are included. It also reinforces the importance of integrating the use of ICT in a self-regulated way in students' writing skills [23, 24] and could be explained, given the set of authors who defend its benefits, by the social and cultural changes in the use of ICTs and the fascination of children with these tools. It was also verified that there existed a greater dispersion in the results obtained by the students, which proves that not all students react in the same way to the use of ICT in the SRSD model, aspects previously mentioned by Tavares and Barbeiro [23].

In that way, the reflexive and critical processes were privileged in the writing process by students and teachers. For example, with regards to the word processor, some students had already used it and considered it a positive tool in the organization of texts, while other students considered writing on the keyboard a waste of time because they were not used to this form of writing. Thus, the use of the SRSD + ICT model during the teaching-learning process seems to demonstrate positive effects on students' writing performance, and helps students to understand and deconstruct the writing process, even when they write without using ICT.

6 Conclusions and Implications

The SRSD + ICT and SRSD interventions also demonstrated an improvement in the results regarding the structure, quality and number of argumentative connectors of the text. However, the SRSD + ICT intervention had a more positive effect on these variables since there were initially no statistically significant differences between the SRSD + ICT and SRSD groups regarding the performance in the structure, quality and number of connectors used in the opinion text. However, after the interventions, the existence of statistically significant differences between these groups was observed. Thus, the fact that the SRSD + ICT model obtained even more positive results than those previously observed with the SRSD model, as an evidence-based practice, underlines the importance of discussing how ICT can contribute to supporting the learning of writing and analyzes how the use of the SRSD model with ICT can be positive, reiterating the importance of the use of self-regulation processes transversal to different learning aspects. It highlights the role of this model in respect to the individual needs of students, where all are included.

In syntheses, both interventions showed positive results in the students' writing although the SRSD + ICT model was better. These results highlight the importance of the use of ICT in a self-regulated and associated SRSD model in order to understand the writing process of opinion essays and also, reinforce the pertinence and usefulness of this model in the teaching-learning process of writing that should be discussed and tested in different contexts.

Acknowledgments. The authors are greatly appreciative of the grants and support received in relation to the work presented in this paper, which was carried out at the Research Centre in Education, University of Minho, and financed by the Technology and Science Foundation (FCT), Portugal, by way of a PhD Grant SFRH/BD/86175/2012 that Araújo, C. L. received. We would also like to thank all the students, teachers, parents and school directors who participated in this research and also to all the researchers who shared their knowledge and help with this team to design and implement the SRSD + ICT interventions.

References

1. Hayes, J.R.: Evidence from language bursts, revision, and transcription for translation and its relation to other writing processes. In: Fayol, M., Alamargot, D., Berninger, V.W. (eds.) Translation of Thought to Written Text While Composing, pp. 15–25. Psychology Press, Nova Iorque (2012)
2. Harris, K.R., Graham, S.: Self-regulated strategy development in writing: policy implications of an evidence-based practice. Policy Insights Behav. Brain Sci. **3**(1), 77–84 (2016). https://doi.org/10.1177/2372732215624216
3. McKeown, D., Brindle, M., Harris, K.R., Graham, S., Collins, A.A., Brown, M.: Illuminating growth and struggles using mixed methods: practice-based professional development and coaching for differentiating SRSD instruction in writing. Read. Writ. **29**, 1105–1140 (2016). https://doi.org/10.1007/s11145-016-9627-y
4. Harris, K.R., Graham, S.: "An adjective is a word hanging down from a noun": learning to write and students with learning disabilities. Ann. Dyslexia **63**(1), 65–79 (2013). https://doi.org/10.1007/s11881-011-0057-x
5. Graham, S., Harris, K.R.: Designing an effective writing program. In: Graham, S., MacArthur, C., Fitzgerald, J. (eds.) Best Practices in Writing Instruction, pp. 3–25. Guilford, New York (2013)
6. Vue, G., Hall, T.E., Robinson, K., Ganley, P., Elizalde, E., Graham, S.: Informing understanding of young students' writing challenges and opportunities: insights from the development of a digital writing tool that supports students with learning disabilities. Learn. Disabil. Q. **39**(2), 83–94 (2015). https://doi.org/10.1177/0731948715604571
7. MacArthur, C.A.: Reflections on research on writing and technology for struggling writers. Learn. Disabil. Res. Pract. **24**(2), 93–103 (2009)
8. Graham, S., Harris, K.R.: Writing Better: Effective Strategies for Teaching Students with Learning Difficulties. Paul H. Brookes, Baltimore (2005)
9. Graham, S., Harris, K.R.: Almost 30 years of writing research: making sense of it all with "The Wrath of Khan". Learn. Disabil. Res. Pract. **24**(2), 58–68 (2009)
10. Araújo: Dificuldades de Aprendizagem Específicas: Um estudo Quantitativo sobre o uso de Estratégias de Autorregulação numa Turma Inclusiva. Dissertação de Mestrado em Educação Especial na área de Especialização em Dificuldades de Aprendizagem Específicas, Universidade do Minho, Braga, Portugal (2011). http://hdl.handle.net/1822/19536. Accessed 31 Jan 2017
11. Cope, B., Kalantzis, M.: Multiliteracies: Literacy Learning and the Design of Social Futures. Macmillan, Melbourne (2000)
12. Kress, G.: Literacy in the New Media Age. Routledge, Londres (2003)
13. Beach, R., Friedrich, T.: Response to writing. In: MacArthur, C., Graham, S., Fritzgerald, J. (eds.) Handbook of Writing Research, pp. 248–262. Guildford Press, Nova York (2006)

14. Kellogg, R.T.: Training writing skills: a cognitive developmental perspective. J. Writ. Res. **1**(1), 1–26 (2008). https://doi.org/10.17239/jowr-2008.01.01.1
15. MacArthur, C.A., Schwartz, S.S., Graham, S.: A model for writing instruction: integrating word processing and strategy instruction into a process approach to writing. Learn. Disabil. Res. Pract. **6**, 230–236 (1991)
16. Bereiter, C., Scardamalia, M.: From convertation to composition: the role of instruction in a developmental process. Adv. Instr. Psychol. **2**, 1–64 (1982)
17. Portuguese National Scale for the assessment of the writing performance of 4th grade students. http://bi.iave.pt/exames/download/PF-Port41-F1-2015-CC.pdf?id=6105. Accessed 31 Jan 2017
18. Fuchs, D., Fuchs, L., Vaughn, S.: Response to Intervention: A Framework for Reading Educators. International Reading Association, Newark (2008)
19. Graham, S., Harris, K.R.: Students with learning disabilities and the process of writing: a meta-analysis of SRSD studies. In: Swanson, H.L., Harris, K.R., Graham, S. (eds.) Handbook of Learning Disabilities, pp. 323–344. Guilford Press, New York (2003)
20. Festas, I., Oliveira, A.L., Rebelo, J.A., Damiao, M.H., Harris, K., Graham, S.: Professional development in self-regulated strategy development: effects on the writing performance of eighth grade Portuguese students. Contemp. Educ. Psychol. **40**, 17–27 (2015). https://doi.org/10.1016/j.cedpsych.2014.05.004
21. Englert, C.S., Zhao, Y., Dunsmore, K., Callings, N.Y., Wolbers, K.: Scaffolding the writing of students with disabilities through procedural facilitation: using an internet based technology to improve performance. Learn. Disabil. Q. **30**(1), 9–29 (2007)
22. Jonassen, D.H.: Computadores, Ferramentas Cognitivas. Desenvolver o pensamento crítico nas escolas. Porto Editora, Porto (2007)
23. Tavares, C.F., Barbeiro, L.F.: As Implicações das TIC no Ensino da Língua. Ministério da Educação, Direcção-Geral de Inovação e de Desenvolvimento Curricular, Lisboa (2011)
24. Graham, S., McKeown, D., Kiuhara, S., Harris, K.R.: "Meta-analysis of writing instruction for students in elementary grades": correction to Graham et al. (2012). J. Educ. Psychol. **104**(4), 896 (2012). https://doi.org/10.1037/a0029939

Towards a Framework for Developing the Emotional Intelligence of Secondary School Students Through the Use of VLEs

Felix Donkor[1(✉)] and Rob Toplis[2]

[1] Woolwich Polytechnic School, London, UK
fdonkor@woolwichpoly.co.uk
[2] UCL Institute of Education, London, UK

Abstract. Although increasingly schools are using Virtual Learning Environments (VLEs) to teach students and society now understands the importance of Emotional Intelligence, the VLEs currently installed in schools can be said to be 'emotionally unintelligent' and do not help to inspire and encourage students to become emotionally self-aware, empathetic and responsible citizens. Meanwhile, designing a VLE that is emotionally intelligent and consequently responsive to students' emotional and academic needs remains a challenge for both developers and educators. By adopting a process of inductive reasoning, this study draws upon the perceptions of 150 students, 35 teachers and 5 learning support assistants (LSAs) from one secondary school in London (United Kingdom) as well as 2 VLE Content Developers, to propose a framework which, it is argued, can support teachers in helping their students to develop both Emotional Intelligence and academic abilities. Data collection methods used included semi-structured interviews, questionnaires as well as staff and students' focus groups. 5 approaches towards validation (context-based, theory-based, criterion-related, response and consequential) are used to enhance the credibility of findings. Primarily, this paper aims to stimulate thinking and consequently knowledge that will lead to the design of VLEs that emphasise and capture the emotional dynamics of classrooms and society.

Keywords: Emotional Intelligence · VLEs · Secondary schools
Education

1 Introduction

This paper seeks to address an emerging area of need, namely Emotional Intelligence in VLEs. Given the increasing use of VLEs and Information and Communication Technologies (ICTs) in classrooms, and the likelihood that such interfaces may well be limited in the qualities of interpersonal relations and group social dynamics compared to those that take place in face-to-face learning environments, the paper argues that increasing attention to aspects such as Emotional Intelligence is a worthy topic in VLE design and implementation. Consequently, the paper shares some insights about how to more effectively combine VLEs and face-to-face learning environments in order to gain the maximum benefits of both.

A. Tatnall and M. Webb (Eds.): WCCE 2017, IFIP AICT 515, pp. 335–345, 2017.
https://doi.org/10.1007/978-3-319-74310-3_35

Since the launch of microcomputers into schools in England in the 1980s, some researchers have observed that there has been continuous introduction of 'new' ICT initiatives into school education [1]. Some of these so-called new technologies like interactive whiteboards, digital recorders and voting systems, succeeded to an extent, in reconfiguring classroom practice in some schools [2]. However, it has been argued that in most instances 'money has been spent on ICT on the basis of faith or blind belief in its vocational (and sometimes pedagogical) value, rather than on any basis of evidence' (p. 28) [1]. One of the areas that the VLEs installed in schools fail to explicitly address is how they support or are used to support the development of students' Emotional Intelligence [3, 4]. Yet, we now accept that Emotional Intelligence is crucial for cognitive development and also for success in life, as it influences our motivation, resilience and ability to work effectively with others on learning tasks by helping us to keep in check those negative emotions that can distract the learning process [5].

In mathematics education within the secondary school structure of England's education system, for example, we continue to witness the widespread adoption and use of several ICT. It is not uncommon nowadays to see the use of laptops, PCs and tablets in classrooms. In effect, applications, programmes and websites such as the MathsWatch VLE, PiXL MathsAPP, 10 Quick Questions, Mymaths and Live maths amongst others have grown in popularity in mathematics classrooms. Whilst these resources, to a large extent, help in improving outcomes in mathematics for students and schools that have learned to harness their affordances, their very nature promote individualism amongst students. This is because, their use, in most cases, requires students to individually watch video clips and to complete associated tasks. Not much can be said about the power of these resources to encourage students to work collaboratively on tasks, supporting each other on the way and thereby engaging less able or less motivated students. Even the most able or very motivated students could potentially miss out on opportunities to gain deeper understanding about the topic being learnt or the ability to empathise with peers who may be struggling on the same tasks that they may be working on. The sense of isolation and lack of social support associated with such online learning can therefore make the learning process more challenging for students [6] and consequently lead to frustrating and uninspiring experiences for students [7]. More recently, VLEs such as Fronter and Blackboard devoted attention to tools such as whiteboards and shared tasks, intended to support collaboration. Sadly, they too failed to consider how to foster and sustain conditions that support social contexts. In effect, whilst schools may be succeeding in improving academic outcomes for most students, they may also be neglecting opportunities to help students avoid emotionally unintelligent behaviours such as bullying, sarcasm and narcissism, if they do not find new ways of motivating and encouraging students to work collaboratively within the secured learning environments they have installed. Therefore, it is both imperative and critical to study the roles that VLEs can play in helping to develop students' Emotional Intelligence [3].

2 Current Study

2.1 Context

This study aimed to build upon previous studies that examined the success factor of using VLEs to support Emotional Intelligence amongst secondary school students [3, 4], by identifying a framework that will support teachers and schools in the process. It considered the experiences and views of 35 teachers (10 of whom were key informants and had been purposefully selected because they had previously been identified by their departments as lead teachers with regards to the use of the school's VLE), 5 LSAs and 150 students between the ages of 11–16, all from one school in London. 2 VLE Content Developers were also consulted as part of the study. The perceptions of these participants formed the basis of the proposed framework (Fig. 1) for supporting the development of secondary school students' Emotional Intelligence through the use of VLEs. Hence, it may be argued that the proposed framework has been driven by pedagogy as opposed to technology [7, 8].

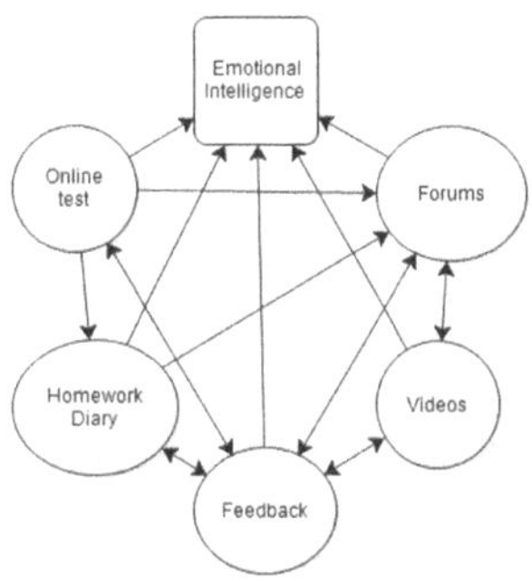

Fig. 1. Framework for developing secondary school students' Emotional Intelligence using VLEs

Due consideration was given to ethical issues throughout the study. For example, it was ensured that informed consent was obtained from the school's leadership and all participants, including anonymity and the right to withdraw at any stage.

2.2 Procedure

Ten individual semi-structured interviews were conducted with the 10 key informants during which the following key questions were asked:

1. What does the term Emotional Intelligence mean to you?
2. In what ways do you think the school's VLE should be used in order for it to help in developing students' Emotional Intelligence?
3. Which VLE tools did you trial?
4. In what ways (if any) do you think that the VLE tools trialled encouraged or supported:

(i) Reflection
(ii) Self-awareness/self-regulation
(iii) Empathy
(iv) Trust
(v) Motivation
(vi) Collaboration and relationship management

5. In what ways (if any) did the use of collaborative tools help in
   (i) Fostering trust/good relationships?
   (ii) Establishing a positive classroom ambience in subsequent lessons?
6. Please talk me through any particular observations you made whilst trialling the suggested tools.
7. Is there anything else you would like to ask or add?

Questions 1–5 were used as a guide to maintain the focus of the study. Question 6 was used to encourage critical reflection and to offer interviewees the opportunity to share their experiences and observations in relation to using the VLE tools. Question 7 was to give interviewees the opportunity to ask any other questions pertaining to the study and for them to share their thoughts.

As a requirement, interviewees were asked to trial the use of at least two of the following VLE tools about a month prior to the interview: forum, videos, test tools or tools for leaving feedback. To improve upon the internal validity of the data collection process, each teacher was provided with a pro forma that highlighted some of the Emotional Intelligence attributes that they were to look out for. For example, they were asked to note down observations in relation to how the use of forums, videos, online testing and feedback impacted on students' self-confidence, self-awareness, motivation to use the VLE, relationship with others online and in class, empathy and trust [3]. The interviewees were consequently given opportunities to talk about their observations during interviews. This included their perceptions of how the VLE tools encouraged reflection, self-awareness/self-regulation, empathy, trust, motivation for learning, collaboration and relationship management. They were also asked about how the use of collaborative tools helped in fostering good relationships and positive classroom ambience in subsequent lessons. Furthermore, answers to the following questions were elicited from 10 focus groups each comprising 5–7 students:

1. How does watching a topic-related video before/after lessons affect your emotions in the classroom?
2. How does topic related-videos provided before/after lessons affect the quality of classroom discussions?
3. Describe how the use of VLE tools such as forums, videos and tests impact on your:
   (i) Self confidence
   (ii) Ability to reflect on tasks
   (iii) Willingness to join in group discussions
4. How do you feel about the responses offered by your peers in online forums?
5. To what extent does the use of VLE forums and discussion encourage you to become empathetic towards others?
6. Describe ways in which the VLE may be used to foster good relationships.

The study also included staff focus groups at the initial stages to ensure that the concept of Emotional Intelligence is well understood by all staff involved. Staff and student questionnaires were used in the later stages of the study to support or dismiss findings from the interviews and focus group discussions. All questionnaires used in the study were anonymously administered using online survey tools.

2.3 Validating the Current Study

Admittedly, most attributes in educational and social research are not directly observable or measureable. Hence much controversy can be expected to exist about the findings of such studies. To help alleviate doubts about the validity of the approaches to this study as well as conclusions drawn from them, Table 1, adapted from the extant literature [9], was used as a guide to aid the critical examination of key aspects of the study. This ensured that due recognition was given to the validation process and also allowed for more robust conclusions to be drawn.

Table 1. Showing how validation was ensured in this study

Context-based validation	Are the aims of the research study consistent with its context? What are the constraints?
Theory-based validation	Are the methods chosen supported by the literature? Do all the tasks that are to be undertaken have sound theoretical basis? In other words, examine what the extant literature says about Emotional Intelligence in relation to VLEs and how the current study fits in. Compare findings with existing theory
Response validation	Use a sample that is representative. Ensure that questions used/asked are adequate and appropriate – **internal validity**. Also, make sure that all questionnaires are piloted. Follow-up on incomplete responses. Use exploratory interviews to examine respondents understanding of key terms in order to ensure that participants are approached from their perspective. By using a triangulation of methods examine the findings obtained from using different approaches to see if the different methods are giving the same responses. Also, ask some key informants to review draft case study report – **construct validity**
Criterion-related validation	Do not impose preconceived ideas by using a predefined framework with which to code the data obtained. Let other people (at least two) code the same data. Examine whether or not the same themes arise – if not, probe further - **construct validity**. This action should also help in ensuring that the research approaches and hence its findings are reliable
Consequential validation	Examine the impact of the different tasks on stakeholders. For example, examine the effect of introducing new characteristics to the VLE on students'/teachers' motivation to use the VLE. This may be achieved by for example, comparing the total login statistics prior to and after embedding into the VLE qualities that promote Emotional Intelligence. Where possible, directly observe activities within the VLE

3 Data Analysis

All interviews were transcribed by one of the researchers in order to enhance familiarity with the data and to ensure that interview transcripts were as accurate as possible. Interview transcripts were subsequently emailed to interviewees so that they could validate them by adding to or taking away from what had been recorded. This represented the most effective means of validating interview data and it ensured that the data used in the analysis represented exactly what the interviewees had intended. The revised interview transcripts were then imported into NVivo 10 software for analysis. The analysis included: identifying the words and ideas that interviewees frequently referred to, coding responses into predetermined categories [3], searching for patterns amongst the codes and building a logical chain of evidence. Focus group data were presented as summaries of each group's discussions as opposed to transcripts of the dialogue that took place. By comparing and contrasting the data obtained from the different focus groups, it was possible to assess if the themes that emerged from one group also emerged from the other groups. Hence, the validity of the strategy was enhanced although this approach also meant that key points raised could not always be traced to the person who made them for clarification. To facilitate analysis, the data collected were coded using the predetermined categories [3]. Staff responses to the questionnaires were initially analysed separately from the students' responses. The process involved grouping all answers to a question, reading through answers to open-ended questions to identify common themes and then comparing and contrasting such themes with those that had emerged from the interviews and focus groups.

4 Results and Discussion

4.1 Findings

The proposed framework (Fig. 1) is underpinned by the following findings that resulted from the data analysis of all the data collected in the study:

- VLE tools can be used to facilitate revision and peer-support
- Emotionally intelligent behaviour in class or in a VLE is underpinned by emotional and cognitive maturity
- The ability to give and accept feedback when working within a virtual environment facilitates the development of emotionally intelligent attributes
- Strategic use of VLE tools can promote collaborations and positive relationships, both online and during face to face classroom sessions
- Strategic use of VLE tools can promote self-esteem, self-confidence, self-awareness, self-regulation, motivation and empathy (SSSME)
- Teachers require time and support to successfully develop as well as use VLE tools to meet the needs of students

4.2 Explaining the Framework

The framework suggests five inter-related activities that need to underpin the practice of teachers if they are to help their students to develop Emotional Intelligence attributes. The arrows show how the variables are related and the extent to which they depend on each other. Double-ended arrows have been used to show interdependence between variables. It can be seen that there is an arrow pointing to Emotional Intelligence from each of the five variables. This highlights the primary proposal of the framework, developing the Emotional Intelligence of secondary school students through the use of VLEs requires the effective use of all the five variables in the model.

It is easily recognisable that the numbers of arrows pointing to the key variables vary. This emphasises two things: Firstly, it shows which other variables that a particular key variable depends on for successful use. Secondly, it gives an indication of the relative importance of a key variable to the framework. In other words, it is being proposed for example, that the use of forums and feedback represent the two most important key variables within the framework. Both are connected by four arrows (to the other key variables), indicating that they support or can be supported by the activities undertaken within the other key variables. What is being illustrated here is that a VLE forum, for example, can be used to provide guidance and support for students as part of the homework they will be required to do. Used this way, students are able to access support from peers and teachers as well as provide support and information to others. This study showed that using VLE forums in this way helps students to develop SSSME. The framework also suggests that a VLE forum should be used to provide a platform for students to support each other with online tests; to discuss issues raised in a video resource; and to provide positive feedback in relation to academic achievements as well as contributions to discussions. This study showed that, used this way, VLE forums allowed students to interact with one another in a friendly manner thereby encouraging them to work well with each other beyond the physical classroom environment. As a consequence, one teacher (anonymous questionnaire respondent) stated that students are encouraged to continue to build their relationships and are in a better position to positively support each other. Another colleague responded during the interview that VLE forums make it possible for students to relate to the opinions of other people 'whom they may not socially mix with in a normal classroom setting'. As a consequence, they suggested that students' ability to empathise and also to interact with such individuals is facilitated. It also emerged that because students know that their opinions are important and that 'everyone else is going to read them' they take time to form such opinions carefully and in the process become more self-aware.

Compared with the setting up of online tests, or the recording, editing and uploading of video resources, using forums and feedback within a VLE are two activities that do not require a lot of effort to set up. Yet they have enormous potential in terms of helping to support Emotional Intelligence development in secondary school students. This point of view found some congruence amongst all the teachers who were interviewed and it was apparent that these represented activities that participants more readily engaged in within the school's VLE. All ten teachers who were interviewed in the current research reported 'immediate' benefits in terms of providing support, starting a discussion, exploring a new topic or providing a platform for expressing opinions. Similar to the findings of this research, some earlier researchers have observed that introducing interactive elements such as VLE forums enables VLE users to communicate and engage interactively with each other [10]. Other research studies, though undertaken within the further education sector, also offer support for the use of forums and feedback in VLEs. For example, an earlier study has shown that opportunities to receive quick feedback from tutors and to use discussion forums represented the most useful VLE components for students [11]. Furthermore, that study reported that 83.33% of the 108 students who took part in a research considered forums as the most useful VLE component whilst 55.56% opted for learning through feedback [11].

Apart from its connections with the other key variables, the use of feedback in VLEs underpins the successful adoption of every key variable in the proposed framework. This is the reason for placing 'feedback' at the base of the diagram in Fig. 1. In other words, the point being projected is that the successful use of feedback in VLEs is the basis upon which the VLE tools proposed can be effectively used to develop students' Emotional Intelligence. For, positive performance feedback yields higher motivation and engagement whereas negative feedback has the propensity of reducing motivation and promoting frustration [12]. Moreover, there is some indication in the extant literature that suggests that the emotionally least skilled benefit not merely from receiving feedback on their Emotional Intelligence, but from receiving it in a way that mitigates their defensiveness and propels them toward constructive development [13].

The absence of a connection (arrow) between videos and online tests in the proposed framework does not suggest that videos cannot be used to support tests or vice versa. The connection is absent because it would be unrealistic to expect teachers to create video resources that related to every test that they put on the VLE. That said analysis of the fieldwork data showed that well-tailored video resources relating to tests, when put on a VLE, can lead to effective revision, successful learning and significant improvements in achievement for most students (see also [3]). This in effect can promote confidence and stir up positive emotions, as well as the motivation to try harder or contribute positively to subsequent classroom discussions [14]. However, the findings of the current study suggested that using VLEs in this way limits students' capacity to discover information for themselves and consequently can reduce their ability to become creative learners.

The primary purpose of the Homework diary within the framework is to ensure that everyone enters and uses the VLE. This is because in schools teachers are supposed to set homework regularly and students are expected to complete such homework. Adopting and enforcing the use of a Homework diary within a school's VLE, therefore, serves as a means of ensuring that teachers and students use the VLE and consequently, are exposed to its affordances as well as other useful resources within it.

4.3 What Are the Enablers and Inhibitors?

This study highlighted the fact that for a VLE to be used to support Emotional Intelligence it must first be embraced by its users. This in turn depends on the perceived ease of use of the VLE and how well the user interface supports educational contexts

[10, 15]. The staff questionnaire showed some congruence with this assertion as 86.2% of teachers and LSAs indicated that they were encouraged to use the VLE because of its perceived ease of use. Teachers and LSAs also reported that 'access to support' is a major factor that influences their decision to accept and use the VLE. The study brought to light that a poorly planned or presented VLE page – one which is difficult for learners to use – is as off-putting as a poorly presented web page or a poorly planned lesson.

It was also noted that the successful use of reflective journals represents another key enabler for using VLEs to support Emotional Intelligence. This is because an effective reflective journal enables users to recognise patterns in their work; to consider impacts on their emotions; to establish causal links; and to discriminate between the positive and negative effects of their emotions. With particular reference to the use of forums within the framework, this study showed that that the success of VLE forums depends on students' emotional and cognitive maturity, supervision and the subject matter. The current study found that that if students are using the forum because they are interested, then they will develop positive relationships. On the contrary, one of the key informants highlighted that 'forums can also lead to very negative relationships when students begin to choose between whom to respond to and whom to ignore'.

Similar to observations made by previous researchers [11], findings of the current study revealed that staff workloads; their familiarity with the use of the VLE; and the lack of time to experiment with VLE tools represented the main inhibitors to using the VLE tools proposed. It was apparent also, as with [1, 16], that user resistance is a crucial inhibitor that needs to be addressed if the proposed framework is to be successfully implemented across a department or school.

5 Conclusions

One of the key tenets of the Personal, Social, Health and Economic Education (PSHEE) curriculum in England is that it aims to inspire and encourage students to become kinder, confident, thoughtful and responsible citizens in the communities in which they live. Somehow, these qualities are not fully captured by the technologies that are used to support learning in schools. So, whilst teachers talk to students about the need to develop self-awareness, social awareness and relationship management skills, they unwittingly point the same students in the direction of individualism through the technologies that have been adopted. The current study proposes therefore, that whilst VLEs should be designed to fit around curriculum areas and must be used for teaching and learning, they should enable students to be reflective and to manage relationships. Such collaborative learning opportunities will without doubt, help students to collaborate with their peers on cognitive tasks, to value being part of a group, and also to appreciate the social and interpersonal aspects of learning [12]. The current study has shown that the benefit of helping students to develop their Emotional Intelligence abilities when they work within a VLE transcends that environment. This is because subsequent classroom discussions are likely to be reflective, collaborative and hence more productive. The classroom environment itself can thus be expected to exude calmness and emotional stability, thereby promoting trust, collegiality and the maximisation of students' potential. Indeed, VLEs have come to stay. Therefore, now that they are being used to teach students and schools do understand the importance of Emotional Intelligence, it is imperative and critical to study their efficacy and productivity [3]. The framework proposed in this study represents one way that teachers may use the 'emotionally unintelligent VLEs' currently installed in schools to help students to develop their Emotional Intelligence abilities. However, there may yet be other ways by which educators may manipulate the level of student engagement by intentionally selecting materials and integrating them into the learning process [17]. VLE designers may also have new ideas. It is hoped though that this paper helps to stimulate thinking in the areas discussed and thereby offer knowledge that will lead to the design of VLEs that emphasise and capture the emotional dynamics of classrooms and society.

References

1. Wellington, J.: Has ICT come of age? Recurring debates on the role of ICT in education, 1982–2004. Res. Sci. Technol. Educ. **23**(1), 25–39 (2005)
2. Crook, C., Cluley, R.: The teaching voice on the learning platform: seeking classroom climates within a virtual learning environment. Learn. Media Technol. **34**(3), 199–213 (2009)
3. Donkor, F.: Towards emotional intelligence behaviour within virtual learning environments: perceptions of secondary school teachers. Int. J. e-Learn. Secur. **4**(1), 359–365 (2014)
4. Donkor, F.: Using VLEs to support emotional intelligence: a secondary school perspective. In: Reynolds, N., Webb, M. (eds.) Proceedings of 10th IFIP World Conference on Computers in Education, Torun, Poland, 2–5 July, pp. 36-44 (2013)
5. Goleman, D.: Emotional Intelligence: Why it can Matter More than IQ. Bloomsbury Publishing PLC, London (1996)
6. Kim, C., Park, S.W., Cozart, J.: Affective and motivational factors of learning in online mathematics courses. Br. J. Edu. Technol. **45**(1), 171–185 (2012)
7. Hove, M.C., Corcoran, K.J.: Educational technologies: impact on learning and frustration. Teach. Psychol. **35**(2), 121–125 (2008)
8. Cooper, B., Brna, P.: Designing for interaction: creating and evaluating an empathic ambience in computer integrated learning environments. In: Dautenhahn, K., Bond, A., Canamero, L., Edmonds, B. (eds.) Socially Intelligent Agents – Creating Relationships with Computers and Robots, vol. 3, pp. 189–196. Springer, Boston (2006). https://doi.org/10.1007/0-306-47373-9_23
9. Selvaruby, P.S., O'Sullivan, B., Watts, D.M.: School-based assessment in Sri Lanka: ensuring valid processes for assessment-for-learning in physics. In: Coll, R.K., Taylor, N. (eds.) Education in Context: An International Perspective of the Influence of Context on Science Curriculum Development, Implementation and the Student-Experienced Curriculum, Sage, London (2008)
10. Liu, I.-F., Chen, M.C., Sun, Y.S., Wible, D., Kuo, C.-H.: Extending the TAM model to explore the factors that affect intention to use an online learning community. Comput. Educ. **54**(2), 600–610 (2010)
11. Limniou, M., Smith, M.: Teachers "and students" perspectives on teaching and learning through virtual learning environments. Eur. J. Eng. Educ. **35**(6), 645–653 (2010)

12. Mullins, D., Deiglmayer, A., Spada, A.: Shaping knowledge co-construction. In: Baker, M., Andriessen, J., Järvelä, S. (eds.) Affective Learning Together: Social and Emotional Dimensions of Collaborative Learning. Routledge, Abingdon (2013)
13. Sheldon, O.J., Dunning, D., Ames, D.R.: Emotionally unskilled, unaware, and uninterested in learning more: reactions to feedback about deficits in emotional intelligence. J. Appl. Psychol. **99**(1), 125–137 (2014)
14. Stiggins, R.: From formative assessment to assessment for learning: a path to success in standards-based schools. Phi Delta Kappan **87**(4), 324–328 (2005)
15. Mueller, D., Strohmeier, S.: Design characteristics of virtual learning environments: State of research. Comput. Educ. **57**(4), 2505–2516 (2011)
16. Shin, D.H., Biocca, F., Choo, H.: Exploring the user experience of three-dimensional virtual learning environments. Behav. Inf. Technol. **32**(2), 203–214 (2013)
17. Taylor, S.S., Statler, M.: Material matters: increasing emotional engagement in learning. J. Manag. Educ. **38**(4), 586–607 (2013)

Enhancing Learning in a Virtual Environment: Qualities of Learning in Different Learning Modes

Nicholas Mavengere(✉), Mikko Ruohonen, and Katriina Vartiainen

CIRCMI, Faculty of Natural Sciences, University of Tampere, Tampere, Finland
{nicholas.mavengere,mikko.j.ruohonen,
katriina.vartiainen}@uta.fi

Abstract. Virtual learning is increasingly common due to factors, such as technological advances and globalization. Research presented in this paper is based on a virtual ICT for Development-course that was offered three times by a Finnish university. The course participants were from Finland, Germany, South Africa and Kenya. During the three course implementations, three different learning modes – traditional teacher-focused learning, team-work focused learning and a blend of the two – were utilized. Our research goal was to better understand practices that enhance the learning process in a virtual environment. We collected data by three online questionnaires that were sent to the course participants by email after completing the course. In total, we received 61 responses. We discovered that the students' perceptions of the richness in qualities of learning were different in each course. This paper discusses this difference in line with the different learning modes used. These results encourage us to further research the link between learning modes and qualities of learning to (1) validate the findings with a larger sample, (2) compare them to previous studies in the field, and (3) to potentially propose generalizability of the findings.

Keywords: Virtual learning · Virtual course · Teacher-focused learning Team-work focused learning · Qualities of learning

1 Introduction

Efforts to improve the learning process are ever required. This is due to the increasing possibilities of offering learning, for example, learning using social media and learning management systems. Especially, the technological advances of online and distance learning open up new avenues to the learning process and its research [1]. Thus virtual learning is well appreciated in theory and practice [2]. In addition, the learning process should always be improved in line with advances in learning technologies. But negative effects should also be unearthed and efforts to reduce their effects should be done. This is important in trying to maximize the gains from virtual learning and reduce the negative effects.

A. Tatnall and M. Webb (Eds.): WCCE 2017, IFIP AICT 515, pp. 346–354, 2017.
https://doi.org/10.1007/978-3-319-74310-3_36

The background of this paper is in a virtual course that was offered at the University of Tampere in 2015–2016. The course was offered three times in total, during two academic years. We always tried to improve the learning process from the first experience which was traditional teacher-focused learning to the third experience which was team-work focused and the second experience which was the blend of the two, that is, the first and third course experience, and referred to as *blended* in this paper. This study is based on these experiences in an attempt to *understand practices that enhance the learning process in a virtual environment*. By enhancing the learning process we argue that qualities of learning should always be sought. Therefore, this study assesses the learning qualities in the three classes, namely, teacher-focused class no. 1, blended class no. 2 and team-work focused class no. 3. The qualities of learning are elaborated in the next section. Thus, the research question is: How can the learning process be enhanced to promote the qualities of learning in a virtual environment?

The next section elaborates the qualities of learning, which are used as a measure in enhancing the learning process. After that, the virtual course conducted in three classes (class no. 1, 2 and 3 noted above) is described. Then, the data collection methods are described and results are highlighted, followed by discussion and conclusion.

2 Qualities of Learning

Vuopala, Hyvönen and Järvelä suggested seven qualities of learning derived and extended from [4]. They argued that the qualities are interrelated, interdependent interactive. These qualities of learning are as listed below:

1. "*Active* - Learners' role in learning process is active; they are engaged in mindful processing of information and they are responsible for the result.
2. *Constructive* - Learners construct new knowledge on the basis of their previous knowledge.
3. *Collaborative* - Learners work together in building new knowledge in co-operation with each other and exploiting each other's skills.
4. *Intentional* - Learners try actively and willingly to achieve a cognitive objective.
5. *Contextual* - Learning tasks are situated in a meaningful real world tasks or they are introduced through case-based or problem-based real life examples.
6. *Transfer* - Learners are able to transfer learning from the situations and contexts, where learning has taken place and use their knowledge in other situations.
7. *Reflective* - Learners articulate what they have learned and reflect on the processes and decisions entailed by the process."

Additionally, we include the *conversational* quality of learning in our palette as an individual element, even though [3] viewed it as a part of the collaborative learning quality. The conversational quality is defined as "Learning is a social and dialogical process in which learners are able to utilize the knowledge of other members of the learning community during the knowledge building process" [3].

We used these qualities of learning as a measure to evaluate and improve the learning process. Thus, in this paper, they are understood as aspects that can enrich the learning process and experience of students.

3 The Virtual Learning Course

The University of Tampere offered a virtual course, entitled Development 2.0, that is, Information and Communications Technologies for Development 2.0. The course was done with three groups of students, referred to as class 1 (Autumn semester 2015), class 2 (Spring semester 2016) and class 3 (Autumn semester 2016) [5].

In class 1, the 32 participants were from Finland, Germany, and South Africa. In the end, 31 of them completed the course. In class 2, there were 32 participants from Finland, Germany, and South Africa. 27 completed the course. Finally, class 3 had 57 participants who were from Finland, Kenya and South Africa. Of them, 17 completed the course. The Fig. 1 shows the numbers of participants per class and teaching style.

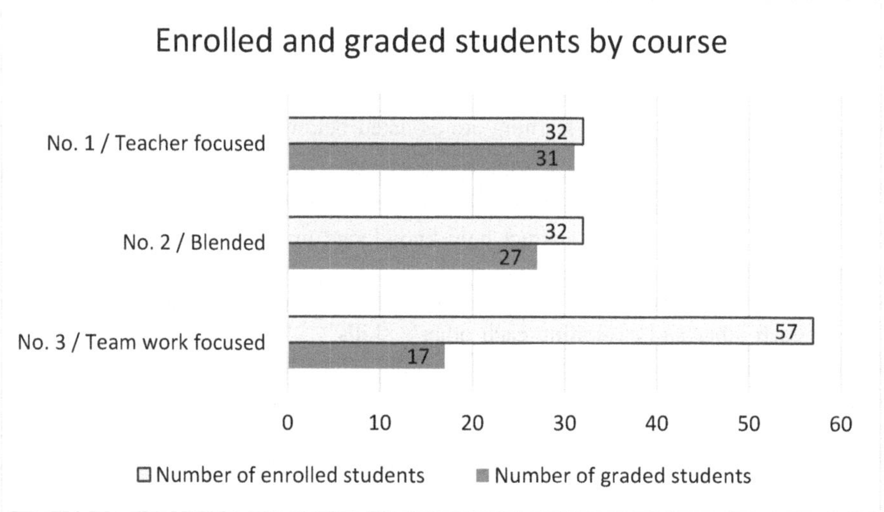

Fig. 1. Course participants

Three different but related teaching modes were used in the three classes namely teacher focused, blended and teamwork focused as shown in Fig. 1. In class one, teacher focused mode was such that the teacher uploads the learning material and the learners study and respond to the different tasks e.g. learning diaries and essays assessed by the teacher. Thus, the learning was mainly controlled and assessed by the teacher in class one. In class three, teamwork focused mode was such that the class tasks were mainly group work and the learners assessed each other's work [6]. For example, wiki construction tasks in which each group had a wiki page to develop and evaluate another group's page. Class two, referred to as blended, was the blend of class one and class three, that is, about half teamwork and also teacher focused tasks.

4 Data Collection Methods

The data was collected in three online questionnaires that were sent to the course participants by email after completing the course. The questionnaires focused on the overall virtual learning experience of the students, while general comments regarding the course contents were also collected.

In this paper, we particularly focus on a multiple choice question which evaluated whether the virtual learning environment was experienced to provide a platform for the different qualities of learning that were described earlier in the paper.

The number of responses to the question under investigation per questionnaire are listed in Table 1. In conjunction with the questionnaire findings, the grades of the courses are analyzed in the next section, results.

Table 1. The number of included and excluded responses

Questionnaire for	Number of included responses (n)	Number of excluded responses due to conflicting answers
Class 1	32	1
Class 2	16	1
Class 3	13	0

5 Results

The three classes had different average, minimum and maximum grades as shown in Fig. 2. There grades for the three classes are very close, no big difference noted. The teacher focused class 1 had the highest average grade (score 4.37) followed by team-work focused class 3 (4.00), and finally the blended, class 2, with the least average grade (3.35).

When comparing the virtual learning experience between the classes from the perspective of whether the virtual learning environment provided a platform for the different qualities of learning, the results show that the respondents from the three classes perceived the qualities of learning somewhat differently. Figure 3 portrays these findings: *Transfer* and *collaborative* learning were the most perceived qualities of learning in the class 2, while for class 1 and 3 *constructive* learning was perceived the most.

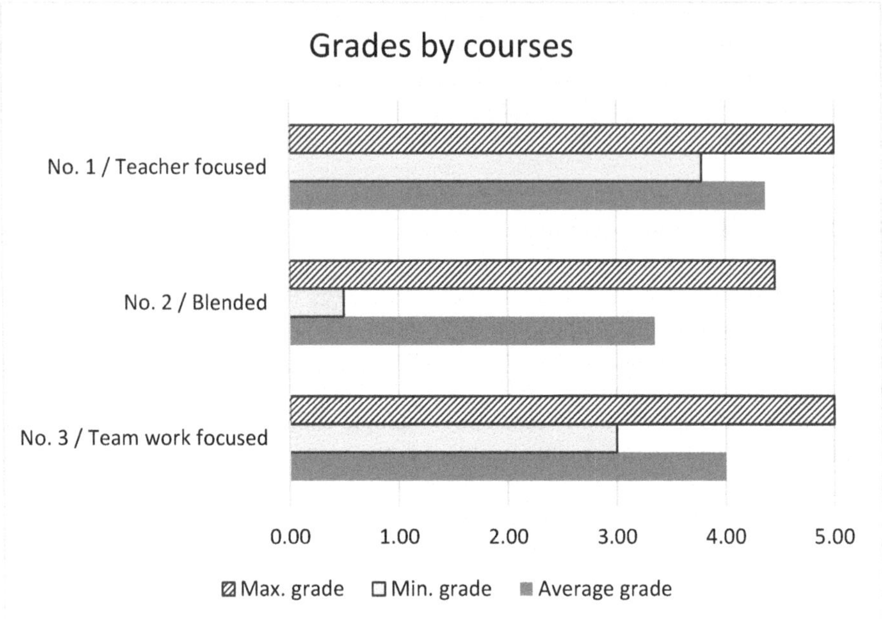

Fig. 2. Grades in the virtual course

It is interesting to note that almost all of the qualities of learning, that is, *active, constructive, collaborative, conversational*, and *transfer* learning, were perceived by 50% or more of the respondents for the classes 2 and 3. Only *contextualized* and *reflective* learning in class 2, and *intentional* and *contextualized* learning in class 3 received a score lower than 50%.

However, on the contrary, almost all the qualities of learning were perceived by fewer than 50% of respondents in class 1: Only *constructive* and *contextualized* learning received a score higher than 50%. This could be an indication that team work focused learning is perceived as offering a richer set of qualities of learning than teacher focused.

As we then investigated the relationship between the number of perceived qualities of learning and the average scores in the three classes, we found no straightforward positive relationship between a high average grade and a high number of perceived qualities. Please see Table 2 and Fig. 4.

This observation is interesting. However, drawing conclusions from it would require further research on other, potentially influencing factors around the course implementations and perceived qualities of learning. These factors could include issues such as the timing of the course within the academic year, the previous online learning experience or the number of years of academic studies of the students.

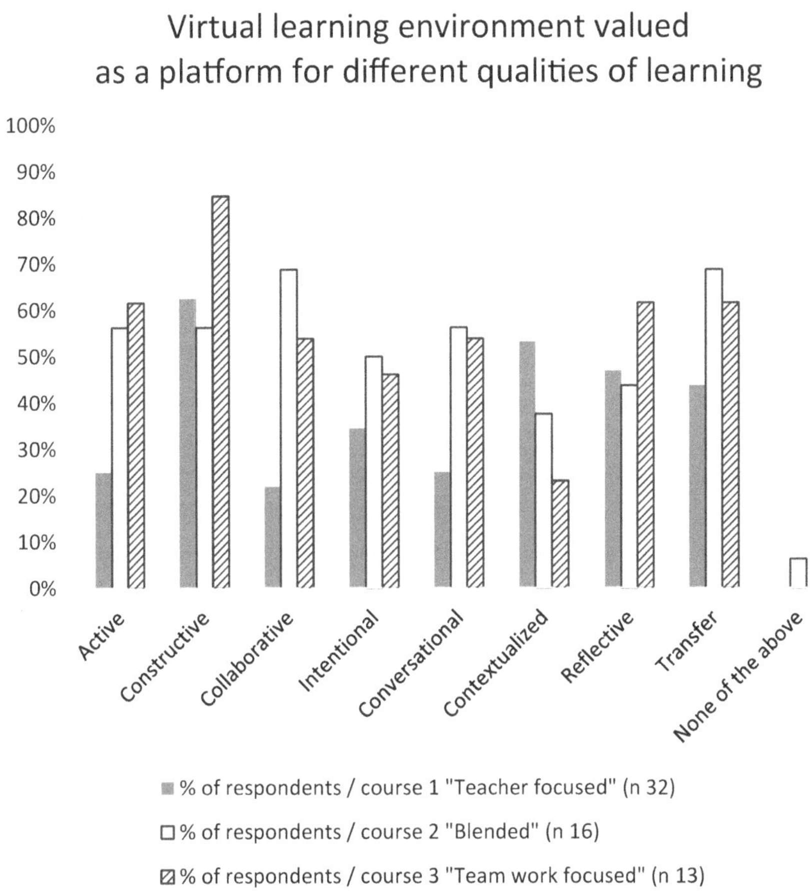

Fig. 3. Perceived qualities of learning in the three classes (class no. 1, 2 and 3)

Table 2. The number of perceived qualities of learning and average grades

Class	Number of perceived qualities of learning by 50% or more of the respondents	Average grade
Class 1	2	4.37
Class 2	6	3.35
Class 3	6	4.00

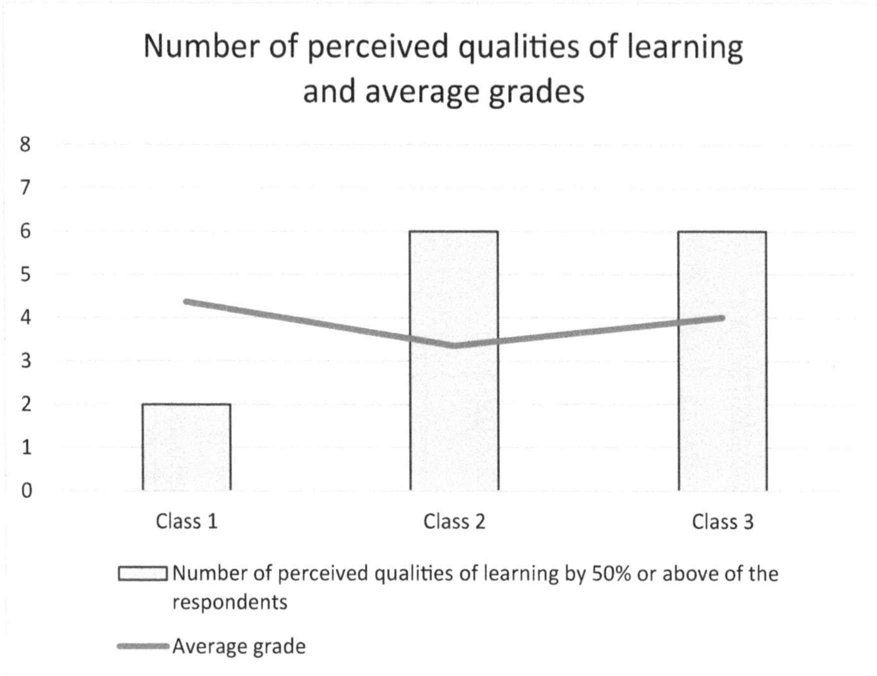

Fig. 4. The number of perceived qualities of learning and average grades

6 Discussion

The increase in learning technologies due to the advances in technology also means an ever increasing room for improvement in terms of the learning process. This study looks at three learning processes, namely, teacher focused, team-work focused and a blend of the two referred to as blended. The results show varying learners' accomplishments from these three learning processes. For instance, the teacher focused had the highest students' completion ratio, that is, 31 out of the 32 students completed the course, and also the highest average grade. The team focused course seemed more demanding for the students with 17 out of 57 students completing the course. However, the team-work focused class had the highest number of different perceived qualities of learning [2]. It should be noted also that the courses were organized in different times of a year, this could have influenced the number of students, well as, the number of students who completed the course. For example, the course offered close to holiday season like Christmas tended to have few students. This could also influence the results as a whole, such as, perception towards the learning qualities and the class performance.

Mavengere and Ruohonen noted that the community of inquiry (COI) theoretical framework, Fig. 5, emphasizes presence and interaction of cognitive, social and teaching elements. She further investigated the COI in a virtual learning environment and concluded that elements of cognitive, social and teaching presence were evident in online discussions. Thus, this is supporting our efforts of trying to improve interactions in virtual learning by introducing teams and group tasks. However, there are challenges in virtual learning, for instance, in a diverse class environment as in this research case, whereby students are from Finland, Kenya, Germany and South Africa. Our observation is that the noted advantages of team work in a virtual learning environment are more than the disadvantages.

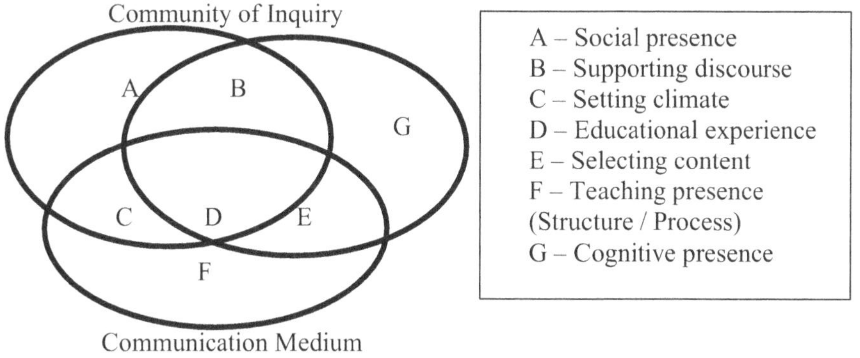

Fig. 5. Community of inquiry model [8]

Garrison, and Anderson noted that the term 'community of inquiry', Fig. 5, was first used by [10] to refer to a learning environment where "students listen to one another with respect, build on one another's ideas, challenge one another to supply reasons for otherwise unsupported opinions, assist each other in drawing inferences from what has been said, and seek to identify one another's assumptions" [10]. The teacher facilitates such a learning environment. This supports the notion made in this research that a richer set of qualities of learning exists, when moving towards teamwork orientation.

These results encourage us to further research the link between virtual learning modes and qualities of learning to validate the findings with a larger sample and interviews, compare results with other related studies in the field and gain further insights in improvements in the learning process.

7 Conclusion

Learning is integral in today's continuously changing environment. In addition, the global nature of the environment makes virtual learning attractive because of convenience, time and cost factors. This study highlights different learning processes in an attempt to promote virtual learning and maximize the benefits from the experience. Three learning processes, namely teacher focused, teamwork focused and a blend of the two in a virtual learning environment showed different results in terms of academic performance and learners' perception to the qualities of learning. Learning process should always be improved in line with the advances in learning technologies. But negative effects should also be unearthed and efforts to reduce their effects should be done.

References

1. Tobarra, L., Robles-Gómez, A., Salvador, R., Hernández, R., Caminero, A.C.: Analyzing the students' behavior and relevant topics in virtual learning communities. Comput. Hum. Behav. **31**, 659–669 (2014). http://dx.doi.org/10.1016/j.chb.2013.10.001
2. Vuopala, E., Hyvönen, P., Järvelä, S.: Interaction forms in successful collaborative learning in virtual learning environments. Act. Learn. High. Educ. **17**(1), 25–38 (2016). http://journals.sagepub.com/doi/abs/10.1177/1469787415616730
3. Ruokamo, H., Pohjolainen, S.: Pedagogical principles for evaluation of hypermedia-based learning environments in mathematics. J. Univ. Comput. Sci. **4**(3), 292–307 (1998)
4. Jonassen, D.H.: Supporting communities of learners with technology: a vision for integrating technology with learning in schools. Educ. Technol. **35**(4), 60–63 (1995)
5. Mavengere, N., Ruohonen, M.: ICT4D 2.0 studies in virtual environment: context and user needs to foster learning process. In: IST-Africa Week Conference 2016, pp. 1–8 (2016)
6. Kreijns, K., Kirschner, P.A., Jochems, W., Van Buuren, H.: Measuring perceived sociability of computer-supported collaborative learning environments. Comput. Educ. **49**(2), 176–192 (2007)
7. Lim, H.L.: Community of inquiry in an online undergraduate information technology course. J. Inf. Technol. Educ. **6**, 154–168 (2007)
8. Garrison, D., Anderson, T., Archer, W.: Critical inquiry in a text-based environment: computer conferencing in higher education. Internet High. Educ. **11**(2), 1–14 (2000)
9. Garrison, D., Anderson, T.: E-learning in the 21st Century. RoutledgeFalmer, London (2003)
10. Lipman, M.: Thinking in Education. Cambridge University Press, New York (1991)

Online Teacher Education: Transforming Teachers' Knowledge for Teaching with Digital Technologies

Margaret L. Niess(✉)

College of Education, Oregon State University, Corvallis, USA
niessm@oregonstate.edu

Abstract. This case study focuses teacher education toward the design of online learning educational environments to guide in-service teachers' development of technological pedagogical content knowledge (TPACK), the knowledge for effectively integrating technologies in their classroom instruction. This study describes a researcher-designed learning trajectory instructional approach that highlights key online instructional features that guide teachers in improving and refining their TPACK. In an online Masters' degree program, the research-based learning trajectory transforms teachers' knowledge for teaching mathematics with technologies by focusing on the development of their knowledge-of-practice through "systematic inquiry about teaching" with technology that considers "learners and learning, subject matter and curriculum, and schools and schooling" [6]. The multiple case, descriptive study provides a rich description of how the features of the learning trajectory influence nine K-12 teacher participants' thinking about their own thinking with the technology for learning mathematics and their thinking about their students' thinking and understanding when learning with multiple technologies. The study concludes by proposing that teacher educators consider incorporating such a researcher-designed learning trajectory instructional approach to interweave descriptive tasks with specific pedagogical strategies in order to enhance teachers' knowledge for teaching their content with technology – their TPACK.

Keywords: Communities-of-learners · In-service teachers · Learning trajectory Knowledge-of-practice · Online

1 Introduction

Tomorrow's learning must engage everyone, in particular the teachers who are now challenged to integrate more and more technologies as learning tools. With the rapid pace of new designs of more robust technologies as learning tools, teachers are at a disadvantage because they have not learned with these newer technologies. Instead, they must examine how these technologies support learning of the content as well as which pedagogical strategies effectively engage students in learning with the technologies. In other words, they must identify, orchestrate, and manage different strategies and learning tasks in their content areas to effectively support students in the 21st century critical learning skills. They must continue learning today in order to guide

A. Tatnall and M. Webb (Eds.): WCCE 2017, IFIP AICT 515, pp. 355–365, 2017.
https://doi.org/10.1007/978-3-319-74310-3_37

students in learning for tomorrow. Teacher educators are then challenged to respond to an important question: How can today's teachers engage in learning about the technologies and about teaching with the technologies while they are actively teaching in their classrooms?

Teachers' knowledge for teaching for tomorrow is far more than just an understanding of the subject matter content. It ultimately necessitates a robust pedagogical knowledge along with knowledge for teaching with the vast array of technological innovations. The task calls for a reformed view on teachers' knowledge: Technological Pedagogical Content Knowledge [1–3], otherwise referred to as TPACK [4]. TPACK, as shown in Fig. 1, describes a transformation of teachers' 20th century knowledge at the intersection of content knowledge, pedagogical knowledge and technological knowledge that ultimately supports teachers in strategic thinking of when, where, and how to guide students' learning with technologies.

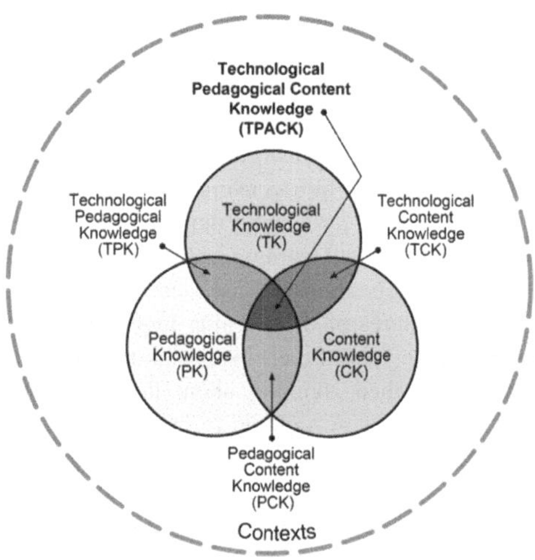

Fig. 1. Representation of Technological Pedagogical Content Knowledge (TPACK) as teachers' transformed knowledge. Reproduced by permission of the publisher, © 2012 by tpack.org

While the TPACK construct is recognized and supported by extensive research and scholarly work, teacher educators must design professional in-service learning experiences for transforming teachers' knowledge into a strong pedagogical understanding so they understand and are able to guide their students in collaborating and communicating as they engage in inquiry tasks using multiple technologies as learning tools. When determining appropriate instructional strategies for developing teachers' TPACK, Mishra and Koehler [2] warn:

> *There is no single technological solution that applies for every teacher, every course, or for every view of teaching. Quality teaching requires developing a nuanced understanding of the complex relationship, and using this understanding to develop appropriate, context-specific strategies and representations. (p. 1029)*

Thus, teacher professional development must guide teachers in relearning, rethinking, and redefining teaching and learning as they know and learned it. Basically, today's teachers must confront their current conceptions for integrating technologies as learning tools in their content areas [5] in order to develop the reformed and transformed TPACK understandings.

Among the educational settings for teachers' professional learning experiences, online instructional avenues now provide increased access for teachers who are actively teaching. Teacher educators must design effective online learning experiences for reframing teachers' knowledge. This situation must happen today as the new technologies are evolving at an increasing rate. What are the key features for an online learning trajectory to help teacher educators redesign teachers' learning experiences? What online learning trajectory effectively engages teachers in knowledge-building communities but also provides them with an understanding of the pedagogical challenges for establishing similar communities of learning with technologies in their classrooms? How can teachers gain classroom-based learning experiences where they apply their learning about teaching with technologies?

This case study relied on a researcher-conjectured and empirically supported learning trajectory to enhance in-service teachers' TPACK for teaching with technologies new to them as learning tools. The primary question for this study was: How might a TPACK learning trajectory support a blend of teachers' online communities-of-learners with practical teaching experiences so that they have the opportunity to apply their TPACK in ways that advance their knowledge toward a TPACK-of-practice?

2 Perspectives

Reframing in-service teachers' knowledge to reflect the ideas described by TPACK requires systematic inquiries about teaching, learning, subject matter and curriculum, and schooling much as described in Cochran-Smith and Lytle's conception of "knowledge-of-practice" as a "transformed and expanded view of what 'practice' means" (p. 276). This conception assumes that knowledge is "socially constructed by teachers who work together and also by teachers and students as they mingle their pervious experiences, their prior knowledge, their cultural and linguistic resources, and the textual resources and materials of the classroom" (p. 280). This conception of teacher learning necessitates incorporation as an inquiry community where reflection is a central component [5–7]. This vision is, therefore, referred to as a TPACK-of-practice.

Learning trajectories are "ordered network of experiences" where students move from "informal ideas, through successive refinements of representation, articulation, and reflection, towards increasingly complex concepts over time" [8]. The online teacher in-service learning trajectory in this study engages the teacher as the student in the instruction designed to move from informal ideas about teaching with technology through successive refinements toward a transformed knowledge for teaching with technology. Purposely, this experience models the instructional strategies for teaching with technologies.

In this study, a researcher-conjectured and empirically supported online learning trajectory [9] guided the instructional strategies using a social metacognitive constructivist instructional framework with essential tools and processes; these features propelled the content development for the online asynchronous, text-based learning professional development. The case study then examined the teachers' advancement in their TPACK-of-practice resulting from their experiences in the course that blended teachers' practical experiences with their online community interactions.

2.1 Tools

Two significant tools were incorporated in the asynchronous, text-based, online experiences – a community-of-learners and reflection. Previously, learners in online experiences typically have been required to make sense of new information in isolation with only asynchronous avenues for making connections with other learners and the instructor. Now, in through this learning trajectory, an essential tool was a community-of-learners, where the learners communicated and interacted in discussions about the presented tasks and ideas. The intent was to establish the social presence of the learning community such that it functioned as a knowledge-building community.

Multiple researchers have described the importance of a social presence, establishing community member participation and educational experiences that result in meaningful learning, open communication, and group cohesion [10–16]. Garrison and Cleveland-Innes [11] explained the importance of engaging learners in active roles in online environments to support them in building their understanding as they make sense of new information and ideas. A community-of-learners tool provides a dynamic integration of social, cognitive, and teaching presences found to be essential in higher order learning, where they also claim "the reflective and collaborative properties of asynchronous, text-based online learning are well adapted to deep approaches to learning (i.e., cognitive presence)" (p. 145).

The second essential tool in the online learning trajectory was identified as reflection. Critical reflection supported the cognitive presence throughout the online learning trajectory. Learners engaged in reflection were supported in multiple ways, such as preparing content reflective essays as well as reflective essays on the community-of-learners' engagement and providing peer reviews or other learners' work. Also, in this study, the teachers used a TPACK reflective tool for guiding their reflections on their progress with four TPACK components and their emerging TPACK development level [3, 9].

2.2 Processes

Another primary component of the online learning trajectory included essential processes when using the tools for learning. These processes engaged the social and cognitive presences in the social metacognitive constructivist framework: shared/individual knowledge development and inquiry. As the learners engaged in the community-of-learners' activities, they shared their understandings of how they interpreted the ideas. As the discussions evolved and their shared understandings became more robust, each learner's individual knowledge was enhanced. With the primary trajectory tools (community-of-learners and reflection) the teacher-participants moved between group and individual knowledge building where they created understanding that more clearly reflected a worldview with respect to the course content [17–19]. In other words, their individual knowledge expanded beyond that which they developed independently.

Another key process with the knowledge-building communities was the use of inquiry-based activities and tasks to support opportunities and experiences where the teacher-participants were engaged in negotiating their understanding of the content. The inquiry process engaged them in constructing their understandings, where they took ownership of their learning, starting with questions and explorations leading to the investigation of worthy questions, issues, problems or ideas. They asked questions, gathered and analyzed information, generated solutions, made decisions, and justified their conclusions. These actions interwove multiple technologies, instructional approaches, and content topics through multiple units. Throughout this process, the teacher-participants consistently engaged in thinking and reflecting about the dynamic interactions among content, pedagogy and technology that emerged as a result of the tasks in their online learning experiences [20, 21].

3 The Program

The Master's program in Mathematics Education focused on developing teachers' TPACK-of-practice for teaching mathematics with technologies. Four specific courses, as described in Fig. 2, focused on developing their TPACK-of-practice, first by focusing on framing their Technology Knowledge (TK) with Technological Pedagogical Knowledge (TPK), Technological Content Knowledge (TCK), and Pedagogical Content Knowledge (PCK) and second on having them apply this technological knowledge in their teaching practice. The culminating course (SED 594) engaged the in-service teachers in learning and reflecting about their teaching with technologies in multiple ways – academic technology coursework and practical teaching experiences where they implemented and reflected on their ideas and plans.

This fourth course, a blend of online discussions and practical teaching experiences, directed the participants' attention toward examining instructional strategies for teaching with technologies. They concurrently engaged in developing a Scoop portfolio [22], where they designed a five-day sequence of lessons, taught the lessons (reflecting daily and cumulatively on the instruction), and assessed their students' progress in meeting the objectives. The teacher-participants consistently engaged in two reflective thought processes: reflection-in-action and reflection-on-action [7] as they engaged in the practical experiences in this course. They videotaped two lessons where they analyzed and reflected on their instruction and student interaction in the lessons.

As they engaged in this practical experience, they used the online collaborative groups to discuss and explore different instructional strategies, tools, and processes for teaching with technologies. They cooperatively explored and examined reform-based instructional strategies – visible thinking, student discourse, grouping structures, and multiple representations for motivation and engagement. Towards the end of the course, the participants conducted peer reviews of others' Scoop portfolios to improve the communication of the events and thinking.

Perspective	**SED 520**	**SED 521**	**SED 522**
Framing Technology Knowledge (TK) with Technological Pedagogical Knowledge (TPK), Technological Content Knowledge (TCK), and Pedagogical Content Knowledge (PCK)	*Primary emphasis:* Pedagogical tools and processes for learning with technologies; learning through collaboration, reflection, inquiry, and shared/individual knowledge. *Secondary emphasis:* Multiple multimedia technologies and 21st century literacy in mathematics	*Primary emphasis:* Pedagogical tools and processes for learning with technologies: learning through collaboration, reflection, inquiry and shared/individual knowledge. *Secondary emphasis:* Digital image and video technologies for higher order thinking in mathematics.	*Primary emphasis:* Spreadsheets as algebraic reasoning tools. *Secondary emphasis:* Designing mathematics problems for solution with dynamic and dependable spreadsheets; designing curricular units that integrate the problems.
Applying technology knowledge in practice	**SED 594** *Primary emphasis:* Design, implement, analyze, and reflect on teaching a technology-infused five-day instruction in mathematics classroom. Present artifacts in electronic Scoop portfolio. *Secondary emphasis*: Instructional strategies, tools and processes for learning with technologies: explorations through collaboration, reflection, inquiry, and shared/individual knowledge development.		
TPACK-of-Practice	TPACK		

Fig. 2. Instructional model for developing teachers' TPACK-of-practice

4 The Study

This descriptive case study examined how the practical teaching experiences blended with teacher-participants' inquiries as a community-of-learners influenced their rethinking, relearning and redefining teaching of mathematics with multiple technologies. The course progression engaged them in inquiry about instructional strategies for teaching mathematics with technologies as they simultaneously engaged in systematic inquiry of teaching in their classrooms. The primary research question examined how and in what ways this Scoop inquiry (designing, teaching and analyzing a five-day unit with technology) and the community-of-learners' collaboration influenced the transformation of their TPACK-of-practice.

Nine (9) K-12 in-service teachers (8 females, 1 male; teaching elementary (2), middle school (3) and high school (4)) agreed to participate in the study as they examined their teaching of mathematics with technology in their classrooms. All had taught more than three years, most between 4 and 8.

4.1 Data Sources and Evidence

Individual teacher case binders for each teacher-participant [23] included the Scoop electronic portfolio, the online discussions from the community-of-learners' inquiries, and the final course reflective essays. Independent analysis of the case binders revealed patterns and themes in the discussions and reflections, capturing each teacher's progression and outcomes from the Scoop experiences and the community collaborations. Each analysis documented the teacher-participants' knowledge progression with evidence of their TPACK-of-practice and thinking framed with respect to four TPACK components [3] throughout the practical Scoop tasks and the online collaborative discussions: (1) overarching conceptions about the purposes for incorporating technology in teaching mathematics; (2) knowledge of students' understandings, thinking and learning in mathematics with technology; (3) knowledge of curriculum and curricular materials that integrate technology in learning and teaching mathematics; (4) knowledge of instructional strategies and representations for teaching and learning mathematics with technologies. Collectively, each participant's TPACK-of-practice was described and confirmed. The completed case binders clarified the nine descriptive case analyses while also validating the cross case themes from the Scoop portfolios, online discussions, and the final essays considering this primary research question: What is the impact of the teachers' experiences in the online course that blends the teachers' practical experiences with their online community discussions (orchestrated by the researcher-conjectured learning trajectory) on their TPACK-of-practice?

5 Results

Analysis of the nine K-12 mathematics teachers' blended online experiences revealed the development in their TPACK-of-practice. The teacher-participants' experiences and reflections in their practices and discussions described how their TPACK knowledge was influenced. Two representative cases (using pseudonyms) as Teacher 1 (Ms. A) and Teacher 2 (Ms. B) describe the patterns and the diversity of classroom situations. The Scoop blended course influenced the teachers' developing knowledge for teaching mathematics with technologies as revealed by their classroom artifacts, expressions and reflections. This presentation summarizes the transformations in their TPACK-of-practice throughout these experiences.

5.1 Teacher: Ms. A

Through the blended Scoop experiences and online discussions, Ms. A was motivated to implement and examine instructional strategies that were new and different for her typical instruction – working with graphing calculators and using small group work. Her primary instructional mode had consistently been teacher-centered but the Scoop teaching provided an opportunity to test more student-centered instructional strategies. Through her video analyses, she observed that having students working in groups provided opportunities for the students to share ideas; she noted how these opportunities enhanced the students' engagement and learning. "Through the video analysis and my own reflections, I felt I did witness students using discourse." The variety of opportunities for reflections throughout the blended online course led her to conclude that she wanted to move to more student-centered strategies and she wanted technology to be part of that effort as noted in this comment:

> *The strategies of grouping, problem solving, questioning, and student discourse all allow the learning environment to be centered on students who are actively engaged... I want to use more technology centered activities...Technology must be integrated using instructional strategies; on its own, it is not an instructional strategy.*

The combination of the online discourse with other teacher-participants as they investigated and discussed the various instructional strategies encouraged Ms. A to try these different instructional strategies as she also implemented technology in her instruction. The entire process resulted in recognition and acceptance of the importance of student-centered strategies and group work. Trying new ideas through this blended course was also seen in the case of Ms. B who wanted to go beyond the technologies to enhance her knowledge beyond those she had previously used with her students.

5.2 Teacher 2: Ms. B

Ms. B used the Scoop blended course to integrate multiple technologies for teaching mathematics – technologies that supported communication, collaboration, and inquiry around the mathematical ideas. As she said, "Prior to this year, I have not had much experience with student-centered, hands-on, technology-rich, discovery learning strategies." So in this experience, she added multiple data collection probes to engage students in gathering real data for generating exponential, logarithmic and logistic functions. She recognized that integrating real time data collection with spreadsheets and Google Docs for analysis provided her with an opportunity to conduct a deeper analysis of her instruction as she incorporated multiple different instructional strategies as to what she normally did in her primarily direct instruction classroom strategies. Ms. B was particularly interested in strategies that involved whole group and small group discussions, inquiry learning and real-world applications while taking advantage of the basic features of the multiple technologies. In the videos, she saw how the students "were engaged in discovery learning, brainstorming, technology-enriched lessons, discussion, collaboration, and other strategies." She viewed how they interacted, shared ideas, and provided their understandings of the ideas. This recognition underscored for her the importance of "being a guide rather than the sole provider of information" as she had more typically done. Her community-of-learners' discussions supported the implementation of these multiple strategies for more student-directed instruction. In particular she noted that when engaged in discourse, the students were more confident and comfortable communicating their ideas to the class or their small groups. "When they get stuck on a problem, they talk it out and only turn to me for help if they cannot come to a common agreement." Through this process, she recognized that she "learned that they can do more student-centered activities with the right amount of support." She closed with a promise for her future planning: "I will remember this as I plan other lessons."

5.3 Cross Case Analysis

These two cases described the major influence of the Scoop blended course through the teachers' classroom actions as they integrated technologies as mathematics learning tools. The research question for this study focused on identifying how and what in this blended course provided access to understanding the teachers' TPACK-of-practice. In all nine cases, the teachers recognized the value of incorporating student-centered instruction, an instructional strategy that dominated their online discussions but had not previously dominated their classroom instruction. The Scoop portfolios provided clear descriptions of the classrooms, with pictures of the classrooms and students in action along with presentations and analysis of varying levels of student work. The reflections prior to, during, and following each lesson revealed multiple opportunities for the teachers to think about and learn from their technology-infused lessons. The online discussions became sounding boards for ideas, helping the teachers to think through the ideas, encouraging them to experiment with multiple technologies and instructional strategies as they taught the mathematics they had previously taught in different ways – thus examining their TPACK-of-practice. The cross case analysis for all of the teachers revealed three themes from the blended Scoop process.

1. Throughout the Scoop classroom activities, the teachers were engaged in action research. They examined and discussed various instructional strategies with their online colleagues while they considered how those instructional strategies added to their teaching, supporting student learning. They identified more student-centered discourse and grouping strategies as keys to teaching with technologies, where they guided or facilitated students in higher order thinking with the technologies.
2. Throughout the Scoop blended course, the teachers' reflections consistently caused them to review, rethink, and rephrase their conceptions, connecting their instructional actions with students' successful learning experiences – in essence transforming their knowledge for teaching mathematics with technologies. These reflective actions helped them "think about how to apply the knowledge they received in their experiences for making changes in their instruction" [24].

3. The multiple artifacts gathered through the design and implementation of their instruction with technologies in the Scoop classroom experiences provided the primary support system for their thinking and online discussions. This third theme highlights the importance and value of having access to multiple artifacts as objects to think with [25] as they engaged in the reflective processes.

6 Significance and Implications

As teacher education programs expand to incorporate and take advantage of online learning contexts, teacher educators need to understand how teachers incorporate their thinking about teaching mathematics with technologies into their classroom practice – their TPACK-of-practice. The online learning trajectory used in all four of the courses in the Masters program engaged in-service teachers in knowledge-building communities, guiding them in reframing their knowledge for designing student-centered, problem-based learning with the integration of technologies. The culminating course, the Scoop blended course, revealed specific benefits of such a blending for a teacher education course. Blending the Scoop electronic portfolios (where teachers individually examined their teaching with technologies) with an online community-of-learners collaboration and inquiry about instructional strategies resulted in teachers' enhanced thinking about teaching with technologies. They engaged in (1) action research as they taught with technologies and (2) reflective thinking about their teaching with the technologies where they concurrently (3) used multiple artifacts as objects to think with while developing knowledge for teaching mathematics with technologies. While this study identified one method for incorporating online learning to guide teachers' development of their TPACK-of-practice, teacher educators need to continue the search for additional ways to guide and support teachers as they teach with technologies, as new and more robust technologies become available for learning tools. The challenge is to incorporate more social metacognitive constructivist features in the online environments to better reflect the more collaborative nature of today's teachers as they continue to build their knowledge for teaching.

References

1. Angeli, C., Valanides, N.: Pre-service teachers as ICT designers: an instructional design model based on an expanded view of pedagogical content knowledge. J. Comput.-Assist. Learn. **21**(4), 292–302 (2005)
2. Mishra, P., Koehler, M.J.: Technological pedagogical content knowledge: a framework for teacher knowledge. Teachers Coll. Rec. **108**, 1017–1054 (2006)
3. Niess, M.L.: Preparing teachers to teach science and mathematics with technology: developing a technology pedagogical content knowledge. Teach. Teach. Educ. **21**, 509–523 (2005)
4. Thompson, A.D., Mishra, P.: Breaking news: TPCK becomes TPACK! J. Comput. Teach. Educ. **24**(2), 38–64 (2007)

5. Loughran, J.: Effective reflective practice: in search of meaning in learning about teaching. J. Teach. Educ. **53**, 33–43 (2002)
6. Cochran-Smith, M., Lytle, S.L.: Beyond certainty: taking an inquiry stance on practice. In: Liberman, A., Miller, L. (eds.) Teachers Caught in the Action: Professional Development That Matters. Teachers College Press, New York (2001)
7. Schön, D.A.: The Reflective Practitioner: How Professionals Think in Action. Basic Books, New York (1983)
8. Confrey, J., Maloney, A.: The construction, refinement, and early validation of the equipartitioning learning trajectory. In: Proceedings of the 9th International Conference of the Learning Sciences, vol. 1, pp. 968–975 (2010)
9. Niess, M.L.: Central component descriptors for levels of technological pedagogical content knowledge. J. Educ. Comput. Res. **48**(2), 173–198 (2013)
10. Garrison, D.R., Anderson, T., Archer, W.: Critical inquiry in a text-based environment: Computer conferencing in higher education. Internet High. Educ. **2**(2–3), 87–105 (1999)
11. Garrison, D.R., Cleveland-Innes, M.: Facilitating cognitive presence in online learning: interaction is not enough. Am. J. Distance Educ. **19**(3), 133–148 (2005)
12. Hill, J., Song, L., West, R.: Social learning theory and web-based learning environments: a review of research and discussion of implications. Am. J. Distance Educ. **23**(2), 88–103 (2009)
13. Kinsel, E., Cleveland-Innes, M., Garrison, D.R.: Student Role Adjustment in Online Environments: From the Mouths of Online Babes. uwex.edu, pp. 1–5 (2005)
14. Rourke, L., Anderson, T., Garrison, D.R., Archer, W.: Assessing social presence in asynchronous, text-based computer conferencing. J. Distance Educ. **14**(3), 51–70 (1999)
15. Sung, E., Mayer, R.E.: Five facets of social presence in online distance education. Comput. Hum. Behav. **28**(5), 1738–1747 (2012)
16. Swan, K., Shih, L.F., Hiltz, S.R.: Assessment and collaboration in online learning (2006). https://scholar.google.com/scholar?hl=en&q=Swan%2C+Shen%2C+%26+Hiltz%2C+2006&btnG=&as_sdt=1%2C38&as_sdtp=
17. Dunlap, J., Lowenthal, P.: The power of presence: our quest for the right mix of social presence in online courses. In: Mizell, A.P., Pina, A.A. (eds.) Real Life Distance Education: Case Studies in Practice. Information Age Publishing, Charlotte (2014)
18. Rienties, B., Tempelaar, D.T., Lygo-baker, S.: Redesigning teaching presence in order to enhance cognitive presence, a longitudinal analysis. In: Akyol, Z., Garrison, D. (eds.) Educational Commmunities of Inquiry: Theoretical Framework, Research and Practice, pp. 109–132. IGI Global, Hershey, PA (2013)
19. Swan, K.: Virtual interaction: design factors affecting student satisfaction and perceived leaning in asychronous online courses. Distance Educ. **22**(2), 306–331 (2001)
20. Roberts, B.: Interaction, reflection and learning at a distance. Open Learn. **17**(1), 39–55 (2002)
21. Wheatley, G.H.: The role of reflection in mathematics learning. Educ. Stud. Math. **23**(5), 529–541 (1992)
22. Borko, H., Stecher, B., Kuffner, K.: Using artifacts to characterize reform-oriented instruction: the scoop notebook and rating guide. (Technical report 707). National Center for Research on Evaluation, Standards, and Student Testing, Los Angeles, CA (ERIC Document Reproduction Service No. ED495853) (2007)
23. Meyers, J.D., Chappell, A., Elder, M., Geist, A., Schwidder, L.: Re-integrating the research record. Comput. Sci. Eng. **5**(3), 44–50 (2003)
24. Dieker, L.A., Monda-Amaya, L.E.: Reflective teaching: a process for analyzing journals of preservice educators. Teach. Educ. Spec. Educ. **18**, 240–252 (1995)
25. Papert, S.: You can't think about thinking without thinking about thinking about something. Contemp. Issues Technol. Teach. Educ. **5**(3/4), 366–367 (2005)

Understanding the Best Way to Embed ICT in Teacher Education

Amber McLeod(✉) and Kelly Carabott

Monash University, Clayton, VIC 3800, Australia
amber.mcleod@monash.edu

Abstract. Every Australian school teacher is required to include instruction in information and communication technology (ICT) in their teaching. Thus, ICT in education, including technological, pedagogical and content knowledge (TPACK), needs to be taught to every pre-service teacher (PST). A drop in the digital competence of high school students suggests many PSTs may not be reaching the levels of ICT competence envisaged to deliver the Australian Curriculum. Universities are grappling with the most effective way to address this. This paper focuses on the effectiveness of embedding ICT in education units in two different ways. Qualitative data was collected from PSTs from units in which ICT was actively embedded: in one, ICT was embedded as a content delivery tool only; in the other, PSTs were additionally required to create a digital learning object as part of the assessment task employing experiential learning. Findings indicate that when PSTs are required to create using digital technologies they gain a deeper understanding of TPACK and have greater intention to use ICT in their future classrooms.

Keywords: Computers and society · Initial teacher education
Information and communication · Technology · Experiential learning

1 Introduction

Although included in the Australian Curriculum [1], many students leave school without achieving the minimum level of digital competence deemed acceptable [2]. This suggests that digital technologies are not always taught effectively. Therefore, the ways PSTs are taught ICT requires examination.

In Australia, education degrees can gain accreditation by stating that ICT is embedded within their units. It is unclear, however, whether current methods of embedding are effective. In this paper, we explore two different methods of embedding ICT in education units to show the effectiveness of each approach.

2 Context

ICT is taught to Australian school students in two ways [1]. First, there is a dedicated technologies learning area made up of two strands: design and technologies and digital technologies. Second, the focus of this paper, ICT is a general capability, to be

A. Tatnall and M. Webb (Eds.): WCCE 2017, IFIP AICT 515, pp. 366–375, 2017.
https://doi.org/10.1007/978-3-319-74310-3_38

embedded across disciplines which all teachers are expected to incorporate in their lessons. In addition, the Australian Professional Standards for Teachers [3] mentions ICT explicitly in three standards and has implications for the others:

Standard 1. Know students and how they learn.
Standard 2. Know the content and how to teach it.
2.6 ICT: Implement teaching strategies for using ICT to expand curriculum learning opportunities for students.
Standard 3. Plan for and implement effective teaching and learning.
3.4 Select and use resources: Demonstrate knowledge of a range of resources, including ICT, that engage students in their learning.
Standard 4. Create and maintain supportive and safe learning environments.
4.5 Use ICT safely, responsibly, and ethically.
Standard 5. Assess, provide feedback and report on student learning.
Standard 6. Engage in professional learning.
Standard 7. Engage professionally with colleagues, parents/carers and the community [3].

The most recent results of the Australian National Assessment Program indicate that the percentage of Year 10 students reaching proficiency level for digital technologies is concerningly low (52%), and show a statistically significant drop in digital competence across all cohorts of students [2]. These results indicate that teachers are ill equipped to teach ICT to the level required; and that students entering university cannot be assumed to have a proficient level of digital competence, in other words, digital competence should be addressed in education degrees.

The idea of the 'digital native' [4] persists in universities, evidenced by the push to move education into online environments, but while technology is embedded in young people's lives, their skills are not uniform and they use a limited range of established technologies [5, 6]. It is unsurprising then, that PSTs are not reaching the level of digital competence expected [7, 8]; education degrees should ensure this.

The TPACK model [9], an essential part of ICT, suggests that teachers need an understanding of Content Knowledge (CK), Pedagogical Knowledge (PK) and Technological Knowledge (TK) in order to effectively incorporate technology. It appears that many education degrees do not explicitly address ICT [10, 11]. While some degrees include a technology unit [12, 13], they may not adequately prepare PSTs for the complexities involved in integrating ICT in lessons [14]. Many universities embed ICT with varying degrees of effectiveness [11] and methods units often have almost no technology [12]. If education degrees are not designed to have a strong influence on how PSTs use technology graduate teachers may be unable to deliver the digital technology components of the curriculum as envisaged.

Where ICT is embedded, the digital competence, interest and time constraints of each academic influence the extent. PSTs suggested little was done to help them understand how ICT could facilitate their own teaching or teaching of their subject in their education degrees and 9% did not believe their lecturers embedded ICT at all; only 26% believing their education lecturers modelled ICT well [15, 16]. Successfully incorporating ICT into education degrees requires PSTs to not only understand why ICT could be used to support learning and teaching across the curriculum, but to also *experience* this (17). However, many teacher educators lack this knowledge and experience themselves (17). Current embedding practices, which range from a transmission lecture approach (didactic) to a combination of transmission and hands on (constructive) learning, fall short of the results expected of a more experiential approach. This research explores how such an approach could more effectively incorporate ICT, including TPACK, into education units.

Kolb's experiential learning cycle involves forming abstract concepts, testing them in new situations, a concrete experience, and observation and reflection, which is then used to form further abstract concepts [18]. Experiential learning allows students to apply the knowledge or conceptual understanding gained to real world problems. When the relevance of the experience is revealed, motivation, self-direction and organisation are increased allowing students to more effectively integrate new material with prior knowledge [19]. Students are able to learn at their own pace or level, allowing differentiated learning [20] which is particularly important in digital competence as PSTs arrive at university with varying levels of digital competence.

In this paper, which seeks to add to the data on the most effective method, we compare traditional and experiential learning methods of embedding ICT.

3 Methodology

This study was conducted using qualitative methods: focus groups and written reflections to compare two different methods of embedding ICT including TPACK knowledge in university units. The research questions that guided the study were:

1. Is there evidence of improved confidence with ICT (TK)?
2. Is there evidence of increased understanding of the pedagogical implications of using ICT (PK)?
3. Is there evidence of increased understanding of the ICT requirements for teachers (CK)?
4. Is there evidence of an increased likelihood of PSTs using digital technology in the future?

3.1 Participants

Data collected in 2016–17, as described in Table 1, was thematically analysed.

Table 1. Description of cohorts and data collection.

	Cohort 1	Cohort 2	Cohort 3
Pedagogical approach	ICT in lectures and tutorials only	ICT embedded in lectures, tutorials and assessment	
Participants	7 1st yr PSTs undergraduate	28 4th yr PSTs undergraduate	36 1st yr PSTs postgraduate
Unit description	**Learning in a university context**	**Practical education**	**Arts, design & health education**
ICT used for unit	Prezi, PowerPoint, Moodle, Zaption, Zeetings, Kahoot, Poll everywhere, Padlet, easel.ly, Quizlet live, Monash library, Google Scholar, Flipquiz	Kahoot, Powtoon, Emaze, PowerPoint Moodle, YouTube, Aurasma, iPads, Sock puppets, Geocaching, Pokemon Go	Socrative, Quizalize, PowerPoint, YouTube, Prezi, websites, Socrative, Quizalize, Audacity, Sphero, Ollie, coding applications, Google docs, Padlet
ICT content discussed	The importance of digital competence at university and in education	Digital competence, SAMR, TPACK, binary code	ICT curriculum, digital competence, experiential learning, maker spaces
ICT required for assessment		50% of grade. Groups create & present digital resource. A few instructional videos were provided, but digital platforms not specified because of transient nature of digital technology, selecting and learning to use ICT individually was an intended part of skills development	
Data collection and analysis	Focus groups recorded and transcribed	PSTs wrote a personal reflection	

4 Results and Discussion

The data and discussion of the data will be presented together in this section.

4.1 Is There Evidence of Improved Confidence with ICT (TK)?

Cohort 1: A surprising majority of Cohort 1, who had completed school within the last two years, indicated that they did not have a lot of experience using digital technologies at school. Also, while they had been encouraged to use digital technology at university, exposed to a number of new digital technologies in this particular unit and now felt more confident with those programs and platforms, they did not feel that their ICT skills had been increased through participation in the unit. Rather, they had gained a better understanding of the digital technologies they liked and did not like. An exception was increased confidence in using digital technologies such as Google Scholar or the Library Website to research their assignments. PSTs did suggest that being shown and given the opportunity to play with programs in this unit made them more likely to use them in the future, as opposed to other units where:

> *Some of my [lecturers] just said, 'Oh this is a good website you can use it' but they haven't shown us at all, I don't remember any of them (Cohort 1).*

One PST, who rated her ICT skills as 2/10, suggested that she would only use a program if she was forced to for an assessment, as she had for a YouTube assignment.

Cohorts 2 and 3: While a number of PSTs found that their ICT skills were improved through the assignment, others who had perhaps overestimated their ability, realised that digital technologies were not as simple as many had thought, with a number of comments on the time and work involved in the assignment. For example:

> *Creating this digital resource has given me an insight into the effort, time and technological knowledge that is needed to develop such a resource (Cohort 3).*

It seems that PSTs who only used ICT in class were presented with the option of engaging in an essentially passive way. This resulted in little change in their technological knowledge and competence. However, when required to actively engage with ICT for their assessment, PSTs extended their abilities, increasing digital competence. Students noted that participation in the experiential learning cycle as part of their assessment proved to be challenging, but ultimately rewarding.

4.2 Is There Evidence of Increased Understanding of the Pedagogical Implications of Using ICT (PK)?

Cohort 1: When asked their opinions of the ICT they had used in the unit and if they would use them in their own teaching, there was surprisingly little enthusiasm. PSTs indicated that they could not see the "academic" value of using the programs, except as games or gimmicks to motivate students. The PSTs acknowledged that the colours, music, and fun layout of the programs encouraged them to engage with the content in a way that pen and paper would not. Anonymity, allowing students to be wrong without embarrassment, being able to work at your own pace, and instant feedback were cited as benefits to using many of the programs. PSTs were critical of other aspects, such as timers, which may stress students. This shows they were beginning to develop a pedagogical understanding of how ICT may influence learning.

Interestingly, PSTs had difficulty imagining using the programs in other settings. While they could all appreciate the use of the programs for the final years of school, few thought they would be appropriate for younger children, believing that the programs were not structured enough, giving students the opportunity to misbehave in class; that use of the programs required a level of thinking which primary students would not be capable of; and that it is more important for young students to develop "practical skills" such as reading books or writing. Typical comments included:

> *Padlet generates deep thought you wouldn't find in primary school – you don't need in-depth in primary school.*

In addition, there was concern that even at the upper levels of high school, there was too much emphasis on technology and other skills were being neglected, as illustrated in this comment about a final year school student:

I knew a friend that was always on laptops ...she suffered because she couldn't write fast enough ... Using technology should be [limited] because having other skills like handwriting are important (Cohort 1).

PSTs recognised tasks at the substitution level of the SAMR model even though they had not been introduced to the model. They suggested that using programs such as Word to do their assignments was no different to using pen and paper.

Cohorts 2 and 3: PSTs suggested that creating a digital object as an assessment task helped them understand the problems their own students may face, for example:

Working on our resource gave me a student's perspective. Although I have been a student for the last four years, this felt like the first time I compared my own feelings to what student thoughts might be (Cohort 2).

A number of PSTs noted that the opportunity to put theory into practice helped them understand the theory in more depth, it had also changed their attitudes about using digital technology in the classroom as they realised the learning opportunities digital technologies allow if used well, with particular reference to the SAMR model, Bloom's taxonomy and practical or experiential learning pedagogy. They gained a better understanding of how digital technologies could transform education.

While I am confident in using ICT, I don't automatically include it in my lessons – in fact in the past I have struggled to find interesting and relevant ways in which to do so. I have been reluctant to use ICT just for 'the sake of it'. Being exposed to the SAMR model and having an opportunity to put it into practice has helped me significantly in understanding how ICT may be used effectively in the classroom... Previously I had not realised how ICT may assist in encouraging students to a deeper level of thinking, I had seen it purely as a superficial engagement tool (Cohort 2).

The contrast in comments about the pedagogical value of digital technology in the classroom between those PSTs who did not use digital technology in their assessment with those that did, is striking. Cohort 1 had difficulty viewing digital technology as anything more than a substitutional level tool to be used to motivate higher level students. Cohorts 2 and 3, after being placed in the position of learners themselves, realised the level of thinking and engagement required in order to create a digital object was deeper than expected. In addition, as they were required to evaluate the level of their resource on the SAMR scale, the advantages and possibilities of digital technology in education became easier to imagine.

4.3 Is There Evidence of Increased Understanding of the ICT Requirements for Teachers (CK)?

Cohort 1: The majority of PSTs felt surprised at the amount of digital technology used in the education degree and indicated that they were worried about using digital technologies at schools. In this, their first year of the education degree:

It's been drummed into us; it's going to be a really big thing at school (Cohort 1).

As the majority of PSTs had not had significant experience with digital technology at school themselves, many suggested they would "wait and see" which technologies schools were using and then learn those, rather than forming their own ideas.

Three students were surprised at the educational technology tools available, as they had not been exposed to them in their own education, and suggested that perhaps teachers were unaware of what was available, for example:

> *I found it shocking that it's not... made available to teachers or advertised. I would assume a lot of teachers wouldn't know about that. It isn't broadcast.*

Cohorts 2 and 3: Cohort 2 related the assignment to the teacher standards – although no specific standard was suggested. While many related the assignment to the standards specifically mentioning ICT, a number indicated that this assignment had developed in them a better understanding of the Teacher Standards, for example:

> *I had not realised how frequently ICT was included in the AITSL standards. This emphasis on ICT reminds me of the significance of using such technology in the classroom, as well as how it may be used – as a resource to teach content knowledge or discipline-specific skills, or to teach the importance of safe ICT use (Cohort 2, Standard 1.2: Understand how student learn).*

> *I was thinking about the elements of redefinition that our task encompassed, it actually brought to mind the idea that ICT could be used as a platform for involving parents and carers in the educative experience of my students (Cohort 2, Standard 3.7: Engage parents/carers in the educative process).*

Cohort 3 reflected upon whether creating a digital presentation had helped them engage more deeply with the unit content, which had a focus on the ICT general capability. Through examination of the PSTs digital storyboards and their reflections, it became evident that the assessment task had increased understanding of how digital technology is integrated throughout the curriculum. PSTs showed a more explicit understanding of the links between curriculum and the use of digital technology to support student outcomes.

While Cohort 1 were aware that digital technologies were important in schools, they were unsure of what they would be required to know or do, suggesting instead that they intended to take their cues from more experienced teachers, perpetuating the existing use of digital technology at school. Cohorts 2 and 3 were much more aware of the digital technology requirements and could see valid pedagogical reasons for their inclusion in the teacher standards and the Australian Curriculum.

4.4 Is There Evidence of an Increased Likelihood of PSTs Using Digital Technology in the Future?

Cohort 1: While Cohort 1 were not as enthusiastic as expected about the technology used in the unit, after a hands on experience with a program they were impressed by, they indicated a willingness to use it in their own teaching, for example:

> *I feel more comfortable integrating it into a classroom now that I've used it personally and learned from them rather than had you just thrown them at me Week 1 Semester 1 and said "use these" (Cohort 1).*

Cohorts 2 and 3: Reflections indicated that almost all PSTs felt better prepared to use digital technologies in their own classroom, with many excited at the idea.

> *I will continue to use the SAMR model in conjunction with my students' needs and interests, and the curriculum to assess and guide my decisions in the type of ICT I use in the classroom (Cohort 2).*
> *This task has taught me a variety of knowledge and skills which I see myself implementing in my own future classroom... I was quite nervous being creative about my lessons, especially whist on placements where I found most teachers taught through textbooks. Once developing a deeper understanding, I gained confidence in myself and my ability to create lessons that are practical yet engaging for students (Cohort 2).*

All cohorts appeared to understand that they will be required to use ICT in their teaching, however, those cohorts who had created a digital object as part of their assessment seemed more eager to incorporate digital technologies in their lessons. After being learners themselves, students had a deeper appreciation of the pedagogical, technological and content learning involved in creating their objects.

4.5 Other Findings

Although beyond the expectations of this study, there was evidence that some students in Cohort 2 were moving towards a tentative understanding of the TPACK model as illustrated by comments such as the following:

> *By co-creating a digital timeline about the events of WW2, I learnt an incredible amount about this period in history. In spite of the fact that I am a ... history buff, and... quite well read on the topic. As such, my eyes have been well and truly opened to the learning potential that exists when students are asked to create their own digital resources. Further, I believe that the creativity and freedom involved must have a positive impact on student engagement. As a teacher, if I were to ask my students to create a digital educational resource addressing a particular curriculum history in-depth study, I would be confident that they would be engaged in the task and effectively learning not only content knowledge, but practical history skills (such as research methodology, critical thinking and analysis) and ICT skills (such as responsible use of ICT, resource-checking and understanding how to imbed files in a document or presentation).*

As Cohort 2 were students in their fourth and final year of an undergraduate education degree, their pedagogical and content knowledge would have been considerably more advanced than the other two cohorts, both in first year.

5 Limitations and Challenges

This study compared cohorts from the first year and final year of their degrees. As such, pedagogical understandings and content knowledge or professional expectations may well have been significantly different. In addition, participants were not separated by age or degree (postgraduates or undergraduate) and so increased technological ability which may have developed beyond high school level through work or other study was not taken into consideration. The authors stress that this is an initial investigation into the efficacy of different methods of embedding which will be extended to include a wide cross section of PSTs.

A challenge was that the effectiveness of embedding ICT in tutorials relied heavily on the students' willingness to engage in the tutorial.

6 Conclusion

The complexity of ICT integration in an Australian teacher education program is highlighted in this study where responsibility to design units that optimize PST readiness for the workplace is emphasized. While the most effective method of embedding digital content in education units is not yet clear, the importance of using considered pedagogical practice when educating PSTs to exploit technology appropriately in their teaching is. The findings suggest that when experiential learning using digital technology for assessment is used in addition to active embedding, PSTs are more likely to understand ICT (and TPACK). A greater intention to use digital technology in education was developed and PSTs began to see beyond its superficial ICT, enabling them to engage in a deeper, experiential evaluation of ICT for learning.

While opportunities to participate in digital tasks were modelled and presented to all cohorts through delivery of content in tutorials and lectures, we believe there are two reasons why Cohorts 2 and 3 appeared to gain a greater understanding of the role of digital technology in education than Cohort 1. First, the assessment task was compulsory for their university qualification. The value of participation in assessment tasks was therefore much higher than in tutorial activities, leading to motivation to engage, problem solve, and use self-directed learning to produce an artefact of high quality. While not all PSTs participated in the tutorial tasks, all Cohort 2 and 3 PSTs participated in the assessment. Second, participation in experiential learning, where time is available to experiment, reflect and form new ideas, may lead to a deeper understanding than participation in a 50-minute tutorial activity. PSTs were required to put themselves in their learner's shoes, step outside their comfort zone to create, reflect and problem-solve using digital technology as the basis.

The findings from this study are relevant for those involved in both module design and development of assessment criteria, as well as stakeholders in all levels of education. Further investigation into the most effective ways to embed ICT to gain a more nuanced understanding of the complexities involved include a focus on assessment tasks, including a wider range of education units, which aspects of ICT and TPACK are being covered, and the ICT knowledge of academics.

References

1. Australian Curriculum, Assessment and Reporting Authority: General Capabilities (2016)
2. National Assessment Program: 2014 NAP ICTL public report (2014)
3. Australian Institute for teaching and School Leadership. National professional standards for teachers: ICT statements for graduate standards (2014)
4. Prensky, M.: Digital natives, digital immigrants. Horizon **9**(5), 1–6 (2001)
5. Jones, C., Ramanau, R., Cross, S., Healing, G.: Net generation or digital natives: is there a distinct new generation entering university? Comput. Educ. **54**(3), 722–732 (2010)

6. Margaryan, A., Littlejohn, A., Vojt, G.: Are digital natives a myth or reality? university students' use of digital technologies. Comput. Educ. **56**(2), 429–440 (2011)
7. Sánchez, J., Salinas, A., Contreras, D., Meyer, E.: Does the new digital generation of learners exist? a qualitative study. Br. J. Educ. Technol. **42**(4), 543–556 (2011)
8. Duncan-Howell, J.: Digital mismatch: expectations and realities of digital competency amongst pre-service education students. Australas. J. Educ. Technol. **28**(5), 827–840 (2012)
9. Mishra, P., Koehler, M.: Technological pedagogical content knowledge: a framework for teacher knowledge. Teach. Coll. Rec. **108**(6), 1017–1054 (2006)
10. Banas, J.R., York, C.S.: Authentic learning exercises as a means to influence preservice teachers' technology integration self-efficacy and intentions to integrate technology. Australas. J. Educ. Technol. **30**(6), 728–746 (2014)
11. Murray, M.C., Pérez, J.: Unraveling the digital literacy paradox: how higher education fails at the fourth literacy (2014)
12. Brown, D., Warschauer, M.: From the university to the elementary classroom: students' experiences in learning to integrate technology in instruction. J. Technol. Teach. Educ. **14**(3), 599–621 (2006)
13. Hsu, P.S., Sharma, P.: A systemic plan of technology integration. Educ. Technol. Soc. **9**(4), 173–184 (2006)
14. Lawless, K.A., Pellegrino, J.W.: Professional development in integrating technology into teaching and learning: knowns, unknowns, and ways to pursue better questions and answers. Rev. Educ. Res. **77**(4), 575–614 (2007)
15. Black, G. Smith, K.: Hot topic: ICT in pre-service teacher training: strategic ICT advisory service (2009)
16. Lei, J.: Digital natives as preservice teachers: what technology preparation is needed? J. Comput. Teach. Educ. **25**(3), 87–97 (2009)
17. Tondeur, J., Roblin, N.P., Van Braak, J., Fisser, P., Voogt, J.: Technological pedagogical content knowledge in teacher education: in search of a new curriculum. Educ. Stud. **39**(2), 239–243 (2013)
18. Kolb, D.A.: Experiential Learning Experience as A Source of Learning and Development. Prentice Hall, Upper Saddle River (1984)
19. Weinberg, A., Basile, C., Albright, L.: The effect of an experiential learning program on middle school students' motivation toward mathematics and science. Res. Middle Level Educ. **35**(3), 1–12 (2011)
20. Beard, C.M., Wilson, J.P.: Experiential Learning: A Best Practice Handbook for Educators and Trainers. Kogan Page Publishers, London (2006)

DIYLab as a Way for Student Teachers to Understand a Learning Process

Miroslava Černochová, Tomáš Jeřábek(✉), and Petra Vaňková

Faculty of Education, Charles University, Prague, Czech Republic
{miroslava.cernochova,tomas.jerabek, petra.vankova}@pedf.cuni.cz

Abstract. The authors introduce their experiences gained in the EU project *Do It Yourself in Education: Expanding digital literacy to foster student agency and collaborative learning* (DIYLAB). The project was aimed to design an educational procedure based on DIY philosophy with a student-centred and heuristic approach to learning focused on digital literacy development and later to verify it in teaching practice in primary and secondary schools and HEIs in Finland, Spain and the Czech Republic. In the Czech Republic the project DIYLAB was realized as a teaching approach in initial teacher education with Bachelor and MA degrees for ICT, Biology, Primary Education and Art Education student teachers. DIYLab activities represented occasions for student teachers to bring interesting problems related to their study programmes and also their after-school interests. An integral part of DIYLab activities was problem visualisation using digital technology; visual, film, animation, etc. served as a basis for assessing both pupils' digital competence and their problem-solving capability. The DIYLab have influenced student teachers' pedagogical thinking of how to develop pupils' digital literacy and to assess digital literacy development as a process and not as a digital artefact. Following the project, the DIYLab approach is being included in future Bachelor and MA level initial teacher education with the aim to teach student teachers (1) to design DIY activities for digital literacy development supported inter-disciplinary relations in school education, and (2) to use digital technology to oversee and assess learning as a process.

Keywords: Digital literacy · DIY · DIYLab activity
Visualisation of learning process · Student teacher

1 Introduction

Since 2006, ICT has been included in the curriculum as compulsory for primary, lower and upper secondary education in the Czech Republic with the aim of developing digital literacy and the use of ICT skills so that pupils are enabled to use standard ICT technology. In schools there is, however, a tendency for ICT lessons to focus on outcomes which can be produced by basic formats using a typical office suite (for example, using a word processor, spreadsheet and presentation program) and on the ability to search and to process information (primarily via the Internet).

A. Tatnall and M. Webb (Eds.): WCCE 2017, IFIP AICT 515, pp. 376–386, 2017.
https://doi.org/10.1007/978-3-319-74310-3_39

Some pupils and HEI students manifest their discontentment against how digital technology is used in schools. They show teachers they are more experienced in using digital technology than their teachers. The 2006 ICT curriculum is a thing of the past. It does not sufficiently reflect new and advanced technology and the need to implement innovative teaching approaches in digital literacy development which emphasises the educational potential for new ways and strategies of learning, not just user skills.

Thus the Czech government approved in 2014 the Strategy of Digital Education [9] that would contribute, among other things (1) to create conditions for the development of the digital literacy and computational thinking of pupils, and (2) to create conditions for the development of the digital literacy and teachers' computational thinking.

The DIYLab, being grounded in DIY (do-it-yourself) philosophy, is an example of an innovative approach to education which worked in schools and enabled the development of digital literacy. Pupils at all levels were at first cautious but attracted to the idea and motivated to learn. Teachers were empowered by coming to understand another strategy to enable students' learning.

2 The DIY Concept

The concept of DIY is not totally new. It can be found when speaking of the development, for example, of amateur radio as a hobby. The DIY movement has developed and spread step by step into different branches (technical education, Art, science, etc.). It has common features: it brings together enthusiastic people (who have the same aim and interest) to solve in a creative way interesting problems in their field and mutually to share "manuals" on how to proceed or how "you can do it yourself".

Globally, there is a generation of DIY enthusiasts and supporters who join in various communities or networks. There is nothing that could limit activities of this generation of creative and thoughtful people; if they need to know something to be able to realise their DIY ideas they learn from one another. The DIY generation very often uses ICT for their creative initiatives. The DIY generation visualises stories to document the process explaining how problems were solved to be shared as tutorials by others. Freedom to make and to create using ICT is perceived as freedom of access, in the choice of tools and technology, and a release from reliance on specific software and hardware tools; it is using a variety of resources, making copies and sharing outcomes and methods.

3 Implementation of DIY into Education

To apply DIY in schools means enabling pupils to bring into school interesting ideas from the extra-curricular environment and to create conditions for their exploration; to put them within a school curriculum and to (re)arrange circumstances for collaboration and sharing experiences, in a similar way to that in which scientists and experts might work. Through such processes pupils can use their knowledge and skills from different subjects and interests so they can keep discovering new things and interdisciplinary contexts and connections [10]. In such activities pupils organise themselves, their procedures and processes; principles of autonomous learning are thus being put into practice.

According to Kafai and Peppler [5], it is possible to incorporate DIY activities into programming, designing models, constructing robots, creating manuals (tutorials) on how to do or how to learn something (for example, how to count using an abacus). Thus, DIY can potentially contribute to further mastery in the use of digital technology and consequently improve digital literacy. DIY in school contexts corresponds with the concept of learning as "the natural, unstoppable process of acquiring knowledge and mastery" and being aware that "the vast majority of the learning in your life doesn't happen when you're a kid in school" [6, p. 22].

This article focuses on DIYLab activities implemented through the project DIYLab in teacher education at the Faculty of Education but also includes an example from a school since one of the participant teachers was also a student teacher at the Faculty.

First, it was necessary to map ideas of student teachers and teacher educators *if, why and how* to bring topics from outside students' activities into their study programme. The student teachers were expected to integrate their own interesting problem related to their life or hobbies, but unfortunately the majority of them did not come with any own initiative waiting for a task formulated by their teachers. It emerged that student teachers who participated in DIYLab had not been used to bringing their extra-curricular interests, hobbies, or expertise into university study. After that, it was necessary to specify a framework and key features of the DIY activities which were consequently realised by student teachers.

4 A Model of DIYLab Activity

Imperative in the practice of DIYLab is that all who apply the DIY idea in their activities endeavour **to share with the outside world how they proceeded and how they solved a problem**. They develop tutorials which visually (using movie, animation, etc.) document the process, explaining how problems were solved and what was learned. This means of transmitting to others how to proceed may be perceived as an author's self-reflection of his/her learning. Story-telling - a narrative assemblage - is a very important attribute of the DIY creation process [4, p. 300]. The publishing of a procedure or a manual on how to create or produce something or how something was made can help others to produce something similar; it can help others to learn new methods or to create something completely new and original. The concept of DIY aligns with young people's experiences who point out that in schools "we miss so much of the richness of real learning, which relies on failure, trial and error, getting to know people, and reaching for things you didn't think were possible" [6, p. 75].

4.1 Key Features of DIYLab Activities

A model of DIYLab activities was based on DIY philosophy which is a student-centred, heuristic approach to learning and problem-solving and which implies six pedagogical principles for approaches to learning (Table 1). A key aim of DIY activities beyond solving a problem is to provide a manual on how to solve the problem. This "handbook" is then published in a form which can be shared with others – the best and easy to understand way is in a visible form (e.g., video, animation).

Table 1. Six pedagogical principles for a design of DIYLab activities

Feature of DIYlab activity	Idea	Authors, resources
(1) To support collaborative learning	Members of DIY communities collaborate mutually	
(2) To have the characteristics of inquiry-based teaching and learning methods	DIY communities dedicate their time to original problems which have not been solved and which are different to traditional school tasks	
(3) To support transdisciplinary knowledge	To enable pupils to bring into school interesting ideas from the extra-curricular environment and to create conditions for their exploration. If pupils have an interesting problem to be solved, they do not worry about which school subject it relates to	Sancho-Gil et al. [10]
(4) To contribute to autonomous/self-regulated learning	Documenting how to proceed for others may be perceived as an author's self-reflection of his/her learning. DIY communities enjoy to find a solution "Building new tools and paths to help all of us learn"	Jocson [4, p. 300], Kamenetz et al. [6, p. 20]
(5) To contribute to digital literacy improvement	"DIY youth voluntarily spend a lot of time in intense learning, they tackle highly technical practices, including film editing, robotics, and writing novels among a host of other activities across various DIY networks." To develop *photo-visual digital thinking skill* as a component of digital literacy	Kafai and Peppler [5], Eshet-Alkalai [3, p. 3219], Eshet-Alkalai [11, p. 93]
(6) To be connected with the curriculum	School curriculum/study program for HEI students	

The requirement to visualise a learning process about "how the problem can be solved" as a message for others follows several reasons. Firstly, visual tools are normally understood as comprehensible regardless of which languages we speak. Secondly, we are all, student teachers included, increasingly surrounded by visual stories (e.g. YouTube, animated instructions for passengers how to behave during a flight). The skills required to use digital technology for visualisation fully correspond to a concept of digital literacy defined by Eshet-Alkalai [11, p. 93]: "digital literacy involves more than the mere ability to use software or operate a digital device; it includes a large variety of complex cognitive, motor, sociological, and emotional skills, which users need in order to function effectively in digital environments." Eshet-Alkalai's conceptual model of digital literacy consists of five digital literacy thinking skills, including the "*photo-visual digital thinking skill*: Modern graphic based digital environments require scholars to employ cognitive skills of "using vision to think" in order to create photo-visual communication with the environment. This unique form of digital thinking skill helps users to intuitively "read" and understand instructions and messages that are presented in a visual-graphical form, as in user interfaces and in children's computer games" [3, p. 3219].

5 Specification of a Research Field

The implementation of the DIYLab project in teacher education was an opportunity to focus on the development of pedagogical thinking in student teachers; primarily to enrich by using an innovative didactical approach to digital literacy development, and to understand better the learning process.

The project DIYLab was expected to answer questions such as *how much* student teachers are capable of visualising their learning, *which type of visual description* (narration) student teachers would produce or *how difficult* it is for them to visualise their learning process. The student teachers had not been used to considering why and how to visualise the learning process. They had studied learning theory in aspects of pedagogy and psychology. Therefore, it was expected that they would find visualising their learning processes challenging because they had never undertaken such a pedagogical task. During their HEI study, they mainly do self-reflections from didactic situations, teaching processes or learning only in oral or written forms, but not in a visual manner.

5.1 Research Methodology

Participatory Action Research - PAR ([1, 7, 8]) was the research methodology adopted since it allowed active engagement, intervention and the opportunity for participant observation. The approach was also consonant with the democratic values implicit in the above-stated DIY philosophy. The impact of DIY approach on teacher education was studied using qualitative research methods (focus groups, questionnaire surveys, interviews, observations and analyses of student teachers' DIY outcomes). Teacher educators evaluated not only the *originality* of student teachers' DIYLab activity procedures, but also how much these DIY activities corresponded to *the six pedagogical principles* (see Fig. 1) and to what extent student teachers managed *to visualise a process* and their ways of thinking and learning.

5.2 Characteristics of Student Teachers Participated in DIYLab Activities

From January 2015 to January 2016, at the Faculty of Education, 192 part-time and full-time student teachers (aged at least 20 years) and eight teacher educators from four departments (IT and Technical Education, Art Education, Biology and Environmental

Studies, and Primary Education) were introduced to the DIY philosophy within compulsory courses focused on pedagogy, ICT education, computing education, biology, educational technology, multimedia etc.

6 Analysis of Some DIYLab Activities Performed by Student Teachers

The student teachers worked on 16 themes for DIYLab activities and produced within one semestre 81 digital outcomes of different quality and content: *Multimedia project* (6 DIY digital objects/11 students), *Design of Android applications* (4/11), *Little dances with Scratch* (4/12), *Collection of examples of problems which human cannot solve without using computer* (6/28), *Contemporary trends in WWW pages development* (5/9), *Teaching learning object development* (4/12), *Wiki of teaching activities* (1/8), *Educational robotics project* (6/16), *Anatomy and morphology of plants* (5/20), *Biological and geological technology - field trips* (2/3), *How I'm becoming a teacher* (17/23), *Animated stories* (11/13), and *Teaching with tablets* (10/26). Some of them were published on the HUB (hub.diylab.eu).

6.1 Ways in Which the DIYLab Activities Met the Defined Requirements

(1) **Collaborative learning**

The collaborative approach to DIYLab activities was the most irregular one, and was dependent on each particular process and students. For the part-time student teachers who live and work in different places of the Czech Republic and only meet during classes at the Faculty of Education collaboration and co-operation with their co-scholars are more fitting and appropriate than for full-time students. Some DIYLab activities were extremely specialised and tasks had to be solved individually.

(2) **Inquiry-based teaching and learning**

DIYLab activities were not for student teachers routine tasks usually assigned in seminars. In some cases, the student teachers faced technological problems (see *Building android apps* or the specific solution for *Installing a camera in a birdhouse* for the subject Multimedia Systems), in another cases they faced more theoretical didactic problems (see *Collection of examples of problems which human cannot solve without using computer*).

(3) **Trans-disciplinary knowledge**

Almost all of DIYLab activities had trans-disciplinary overlap. In some cases, the trans-disciplinary co-operation became obvious only thanks to the DIYLab project and had an impact in forming a student teachers' professional competence of self-reflection (e.g. *How I'm becoming a teacher*). Nearly thirty per cent (28.5%) of ICT student teachers stated that in their DIYLab activity they did not use knowledge from other subjects; if there was any required knowledge from other subjects, it was mostly from physics, mathematics, English, geography, medicine or cinematography or computer science, and rarely from biology, chemistry or art. Nevertheless, they appreciated the opportunity to collaborate with students of other study specialisations very much, and due to such collaboration from their point of view they learned a great deal.

(4) **Autonomous/Self-regulated learning**

The dimensions of independent learning and self-regulation underpin the whole process and were actively promoted, taking due account of the diversity of the students and their willingness to learn by new means. The student teachers appreciated the DIYLab approach to learning from two perspectives: they learned (a) another approach to solve an issue, and (b) how to properly lay out their work, to visualise and organise tasks in order to find solutions.

(5) **Digital literacy improvement/Digital competence**

In carrying out the DIYLab activities the student teachers worked with quite a narrow range of hardware and software which was largely determined by the technical equipment available at the Faculty of Education or in the resources available through their respective Bachelor's and Master's degree studies. Most of the student teachers involved in DIYLab activities were ICT students. In general, in the case of ICT student teachers it was virtually impossible to determine any improvement or progress in their digital literacy. Based on the outputs, the students were mostly using video, presentation and text editors. For ICT student teachers, the majority of DIY activities were only an opportunity (sometimes a routine) to apply their digital literacy skills to solving problems, while for Art or Biology Education student teachers DIY activities distinctively contributed to improvement of their skills in using digital technology. As a result of involvement in DIYLab they learned to create animations etc. DIY activities with ICT student teachers increased their didactic thinking about the role and possibilities of digital technology in education; besides that, they assisted their Art Education peers to be able to do animations or Biology student teachers to design a technological solution and to install a camera in a birdhouse.

(6) **Connection to study programmes/Curriculum**

The student teachers did their DIYLab activities during one semester as a part of their final work with the aim of gaining credits and grades. Each DIYLab outcome consisted of two main parts: (i) a product as a solution of the problem (e.g., SW application, a set of 3D tools, models, database, mechanical drawing, electric circuit, robot), and (ii) a digital object (e.g. video, movie, animation) which visualises a process demonstrating how student teachers were progressing, how they learned a problem and how they managed to resolve a DIYLab activity.

Figure 1 shows the results of a questionnaire survey focused on how teacher educators evaluated their DIYLab activities connecting the six pedagogical principles. From this evaluation the following average values for each item are derived: contribution to autonomous/self-regulated learning (4.8), digital competence improvement (4.4), connection with the curriculum (4.3), support to trans-disciplinary knowledge (3.9), inquiry-based teaching and learning (3.6), and support for collaborative learning (3.1).

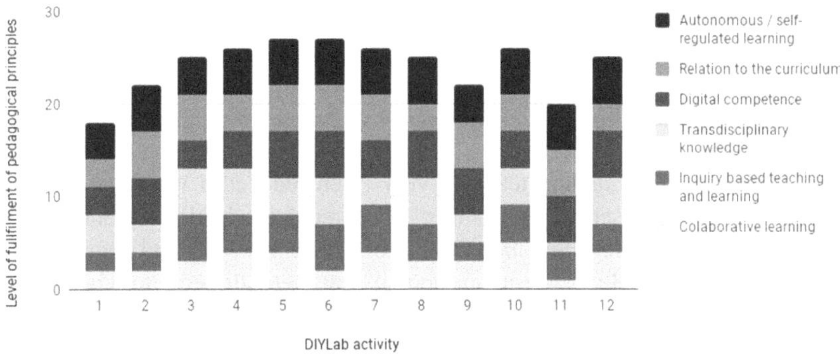

Fig. 1. Teacher educator's evaluation of their DIYLab activities using a scale 0–5 with 0-being no accomplishment and 5-being maximal accomplishment. (Source: [2])

The majority of problems solved in DIYLab were not characteristic of inquiry-based problems. Teacher educators invested a lot of time facilitating student teachers to develop a DIYLab idea. For the teacher educators it was not always easy to motivate their students to bring their own projects. Students seemed to be afraid to step into new territory. The main motivation to carry out their DIY activities for some student teachers lay in getting credits, not in solving problems. In part-time study, there was not much time for defining and understanding a problem for inquiry-based teaching and inter-disciplinary links. Potentially, this is an advantage since it may have contributed to increased online collaboration between students and an increase in collaborative learning. There were several factors (teacher educator, student, solved problem, study specialisation, motivation, experiences, etc.) that influenced a way how particular pedagogical principles were accomplished in each individual DIYLab activity (Fig. 1).

6.2 Examples of DIYLab Activities Carried Out by Bc Degree Student Teachers

The student teachers on ICT Bachelor Studies' courses counted on their teachers to assign them a topic. Despite some of them work in computer companies or specialise in some aspect of computing, they rarely came up with their own proposals. When they had some ideas for topics for DIYLab activities these were related to their hobbies (e.g. diving, gardening, theatre). Some of them were surprised that they had to do something linking knowledge and experiences from different branches or disciplines.

For example, there was a student who was interested in scuba diving and who proposed a project, *Diver's LogBook* (see http://hub.diylab.eu/2016/01/27/divers-logbook/). Another student is part of a theatre group, Kašpárek and Jitřenka, and she decided to initiate a project entitled, *Database Development – database of theatre ensembles* (http://hub.diylab.eu/2016/01/27/database-development-database-of-theatre-ensembles/). Bc. student teachers of Biology who studied the life of birds in a nesting box directed their activities to a project, *Bird House* (http://hub.diylab.eu/2016/01/27/bird-house/). In courses focused on digital technology, one ICT student looked for a solution as to *How to create an animated popup message in Adobe After Effects.*

Bachelor student teachers weren't used to thinking about *what* and *how* they had learned, much less *how* to visualise their own learning process. They didn't consider thinking about learning and reflection on DIYLab activity to be "professional". Unlike Art Education students, the ICT student teachers are advanced in digital technology, but they lack knowledge and skills to observe and to visually display and present processes. Bachelor ICT student teachers very often reduced a visualisation of their DIYLab procedure to a set of screenshots. They recognised DIYLab only from the technological point of view and the extent to which software and hardware were applied. Generally, for Bc. student teachers it was very difficult to visualise their learning in DIY activities. They were not particularly interested in the pedagogical concept of learning and how to visualise its process because in Bc. study programmes the main focus is on acquiring knowledge from particular branches (Biology, ICT, Art, etc.), rather than understanding the learning process involved.

6.3 Examples of DIY Activities Carried Out by MA Degree Student Teachers

The MA degree student teachers did their DIYLab activities predominantly within didactic subjects or courses making limited use of technology. The majority of them were part-time students who work in schools as unqualified teachers of ICT or Informatics subjects, and so most of them tried to apply the DIYLab idea in their teaching with their pupils.

MA student teachers thought about and mediated the topics and the purpose of DIYLab activities more deeply than Bachelor-level students mainly due to the fact that they realised their DIYLab activities primarily in courses focused on didactics' aspects and contexts. MA student teachers elaborated some general themes proposed by their teacher educators.

The requirement to record and visualise a learning process did not surprise MA student teachers. They understand how important it is to visualise a learning process from a pedagogical point of view. Data taken from such visualisation can help teachers to understand better the learning outcomes of their pupils. However, they had no experience in the process of visualisation. Similarly to the Bachelor-level students, they very often reduced a visualisation of DIYLab procedure to a set of screenshots. A few of them did an animation of their way of thinking about the DIYLab activity. (e.g., *Problems which a human cannot solve without using a computer – tomography*). Some of them did a tutorial (*An animated story about a small wizard*, https://www.youtube.com/watch?v=QA1skX4GiBI). Some of them developed a methodical guide how to work with pupils (*DIY_Little Dances in Scratch – Start to move_CZ*, http://hub.diylab.eu/2016/01/11/little-dances-in-scratch-start-to-move/diy_little-dances-in-scratch-start-to-move_cz/), some did a comic strip.

6.4 Examples of DIY Activities Carried Out by Pupils and Completed in Lessons Managed by ICT Student Teachers on School Practice

Some part-time ICT student teachers decided to apply DIYLab to their class teaching in schools where their pupils did similar DIY activities. All these experiences from schools demonstrate a great enthusiasm and motivation to learn and to solve problems related to after-school activities and through which they develop their digital literacy.

For example a girl (aged 15) enjoys recording and editing digital sounds in her free time. She designed a DIYLab activity as a sound story-telling of a boy who would like to meet his girlfriend (https://www.youtube.com/watch?v=a8TzZCAzxKo). She describes how she produced the story-telling as a movie in which she explains what she did, how she collected sounds and which software applications were used in her work (https://www.youtube.com/watch?v=jbSID9_B72k).

7 Conclusions

Although the EU project has now ended, the Faculty of Education will continue DIYLab activities as a compulsory assignment and an integrated component on courses for Bachelor degree ICT study and for full-time and part-time student teacher of MA degree ICT study. Great attention will be given to (i) ways how to motivate student teachers to choose appropriate topics from their after-school interests and hobbies and to design DIY activities for inquiry-based learning, (ii) methodological approaches as to how to visualise a process of learning in Informatics, Computing or ICT subjects; diaries, scenarios, process-folios or log books used in Art Education or in technical or technological oriented branches will be used as an inspiration for such an approach in ICT teacher education, and (iii) how to support a close interdisciplinary collaboration among student teachers and teacher educators.

The challenge for the Czech context is to change the culture from teacher-dependency to students as independent, autonomous learners in the classroom. Creativity in content, methods and pedagogy are absolute requirements to achieve this goal. The DIYlab project showed differences and limits in the culture of approaches to creativity from a pedagogical point of view: If we compare the DIY learning in educational practice in Prague with approaches to creative learning in Barcelona, which is a popular place for international creative artists and DIY communities, in the Czech context the DIYLab will need much longer to break free from the bureaucratic concept of teaching and the assessment of learning outcomes.

The value of the evaluative criteria in framing the DIY process and the parameters used enabled analysis and could support the design and thinking by teachers considering using the DIY method.

References

1. Bergold, J., Thomas, S.: Participatory research methods: a methodological approach in motion [110 paragraphs]. Sozialforschung/Forum Qual. Soc. Res. **13**(1), Article id: 30 (2012)
2. Černochová, M., et al.: D4.6 General Report: The DIY Labs in Action, March 2016
3. Eshet-Alkalai, Y.: Real-time thinking in the digital era. In: Khosrow-Pour, M. (ed.) Encyclopedia of Information Science and Technology, 2nd edn., pp. 3219–3223. Information Resources Management Association, USA (2009). https://doi.org/10.4018/978-1-60566-026-4.ch514

4. Jocson, K.M.: Youth media as narrative assemblage: examining new literacies at an urban high school. Pedagogies Int. J. **7**(4), 298–316 (2012)
5. Kafai, Y., Peppler, K.: Youth, technology, and DIY: developing participatory competencies in creative media production. In: Gadsden, V.L., Wortham, S., Lukose, R. (eds.) Youth Cultures, Language and Literacy. Review of Research in Education, vol. 34 (2011)
6. Kamenetz, A., et al.: Learning Freedom and the Web. Mozilla Festival (2010). http://learningfreedomandtheweb.org/Mozilla_LFW.pdf
7. Kemmis, S.: Exploring the relevance of critical theory for action research: emancipatory action research in the footsteps of Jürgen Habermas. In: Reason, P., Bradbury, H. (eds.) Handbook of Action Research: Participative Inquiry and Practice, pp. 91–102. Sage, London (2001)
8. Kemmis, S., McTaggart, R.: Participatory action research: communicative action and the public sphere. In: Denzin, N.K., Lincoln, Y.S. (eds.) Handbook of Qualitative Research, 3rd edn, pp. 559–603. Sage, Thousand Oaks (2005)
9. MoEYS: Strategie digitálního vzdělávání (2014). http://www.msmt.cz/uploads/DigiStrategie.pdf
10. Sancho-Gil, J.M., Hernández-Hernández, F., Fendler, R.: Envisioning DIY learning in primary and secondary schools. In: Seminar.net - International Journal of Media, Technology and Lifelong Learning. vol. 11, no. 1 (2015)
11. Eshet-Alkalai, Y.: Digital literacy: a conceptual framework for survival skills in the digital era. J. Educ. Multimed. Hypermedia **13**(1), 93–106 (2004)

Innovations in Teaching and Learning Strategies to Improve the Effectiveness of Using Haptic Simulators in Higher Education for Dental Students and Other Health Care Disciplines

Margaret J. Cox, Barry F. Quinn, Jonathan P. San Diego, Jesal Patel, Kiran Gawali, and Mark Woolford(✉)

Dental Institute, King's College London, University of London, London, UK
Mj.cox@kcl.ac.uk, mark.woolford@kcl.ac.uk

Abstract. This paper briefly reviews the teaching and assessment strategies developed over ten years of trials with over 1200 undergraduate students to make effective use of virtual haptic simulators in higher education disciplines such as dentistry and nursing. In the last five years (2012–17) these strategies have evolved to include a range of technology enhanced learning resources (TEL) in a blended learning setting to assess the performance progression of students' learning cavity preparation skills. Every students' performance outcomes were retrieved from the hapTEL simulator log files for each task including the percentage of caries, healthy tissue and pulp removed. The use of a blend of video recorded short lectures followed by face to face teaching, pair working, haptic, visual images and sound feedback, and individual student assessment record keeping showed an improved reliability in performance of the work-stations and a consistently higher rate of student's log files records compared with previous years. Records of students' performance collected over two years showed that the HapTEL system enabled students to perform better at cavity preparation after practising over two sessions.

Keywords: Higher education · Dental education · Haptic simulators
Technology enhanced learning · Clinical skills · Curriculum innovation
Assessment techniques · Healthcare professions · Blended learning

1 Background

Haptics means the sense of touch and involves the science of incorporating this and the interaction with the external environment through touch. As a tool for teaching and learning it is one example of Technology Enhanced Learning (TEL) which is particularly useful for the teaching of skills involving touch control and hand-eye coordination in the different healthcare disciplines in higher education (HE) [1–3]. The growth of computer technology and increasing use of TEL in all sectors of education

A. Tatnall and M. Webb (Eds.): WCCE 2017, IFIP AICT 515, pp. 387–397, 2017.
https://doi.org/10.1007/978-3-319-74310-3_40

have led to changes in the delivery of courses which can transform the way that some schools, colleges and universities support teaching and learning [4, 5].

There have been many previous studies reporting on the various benefits of using haptic simulators in dental and medical education which support curriculum innovation and development in university teaching and learning [6–8]. Furthermore, previous longitudinal studies into the impact of the use of the hapTEL simulator on students' learning have shown that students taught in Year 1 of the Dental undergraduate programme using only the hapTEL simulator achieved similar accuracy compared with those taught traditionally when assessed at the end of the course sessions [9]. Measurements of the effects of using haptics on students' psychometric skills, which are important skills for health care professionals, also showed improvements over time from using the hapTEL simulators (ibid.). Other studies have also shown that different haptic simulators can enhance students' learning of clinical skills in different curriculum settings [10] and have a positive impact on their skills development over time [11]. This body of evidence has led to growing expectations that traditional learning and teaching systems will need to adapt and change in universities in order to keep up with students' expectations and benefit from the opportunities which TEL can offer to teaching and learning [5, 12].

However, in spite of this growing body of evidence, haptic and other technologies are often not easily adapted into the HE curriculum because of insufficient understanding of how they can best be integrated into courses and individual sessions. Entwistle [13], in 1987, identified a range of institutional, epistemological and pedagogical influences of the quality of learning achieved from an analysis of a wide range of research studies into the impact of innovative teaching on HE students' learning shown in Fig. 1. By using this model, Entwistle, Nisbet and Bromage [14] demonstrated how this conceptual framework can be used to identify the important influences on using an innovation and its impact on students' learning experiences and to map the data collected from a range of methods to various aspects likely to influence the quality of learning achieved within the conceptual model.

We can see from this framework that any contribution to students' learning of haptic simulators or traditional phantom head simulators or any innovation in HE will depend amongst other influences upon the students' perceptions of the teaching-learning environment, how the course content is selected, organized, presented and assessed, how the teaching-learning environment is designed and implemented and so on.

Previous studies of the haptic system discussed above have focused on the impact on students' learning and attitudes and the integration into the curriculum [2, 8, 9]; the focus of this paper therefore is on how the teaching and learning environment has been designed and revised from when the systems were first used in 2008 to the present day, and what teaching strategies and assessment techniques have produced the most consistent improvement and measures of students' learning progression.

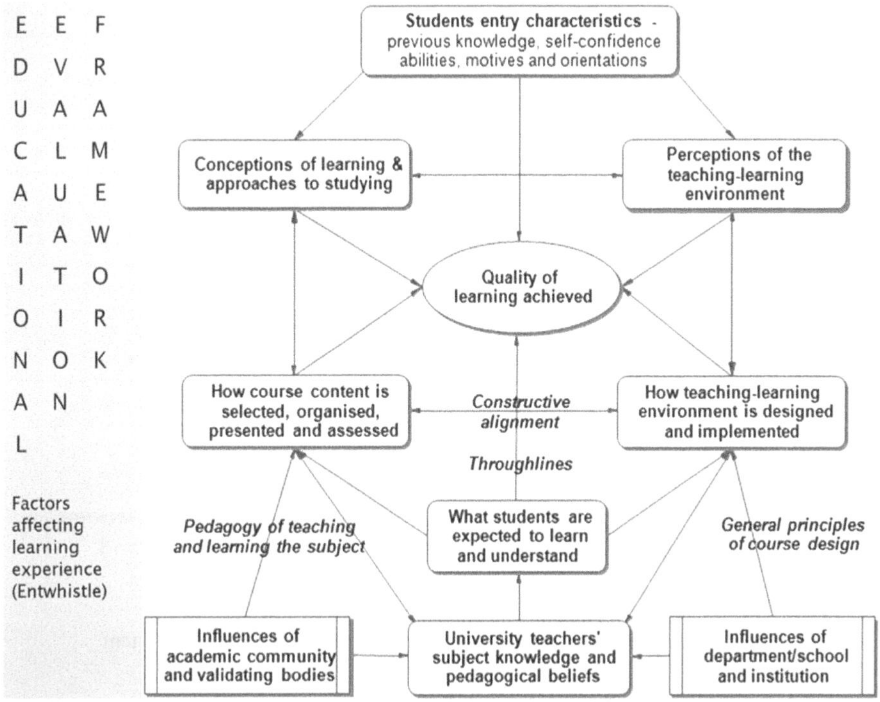

Fig. 1. A model of the teaching-learning process in higher education. (Entwistle [13])

2 Introduction to the Study

In order to address the range of factors identified by Entwistle [13] the approach taken by the hapTEL project for the development of the system is shown in Fig. 2 involving an iterative development process between the technological development, curriculum innovation and integration and educational evaluation. This framework represents the links between the three elements of a robust strategy for developing and evaluating a Virtual Simulator or any other innovation in education.

3 Development of the hapTEL Virtual Simulator

The virtual hapTEL simulator, shown in Fig. 3 below, was developed iteratively from 2007. Following a series of upgrades and modifications resulting from extensive student and teacher evaluations, twelve curriculum systems were installed in the hapTEL teaching laboratory in September 2008. Further minor improvements were made consequent to each year's undergraduate student use. The haptic work-station consists of a haptically-enabled modified dental drill (or in the case of teaching injections to nursing students, a syringe) providing realistic force-feedback to the operator/learner during use within the virtual clinical environment. For the dental students, this

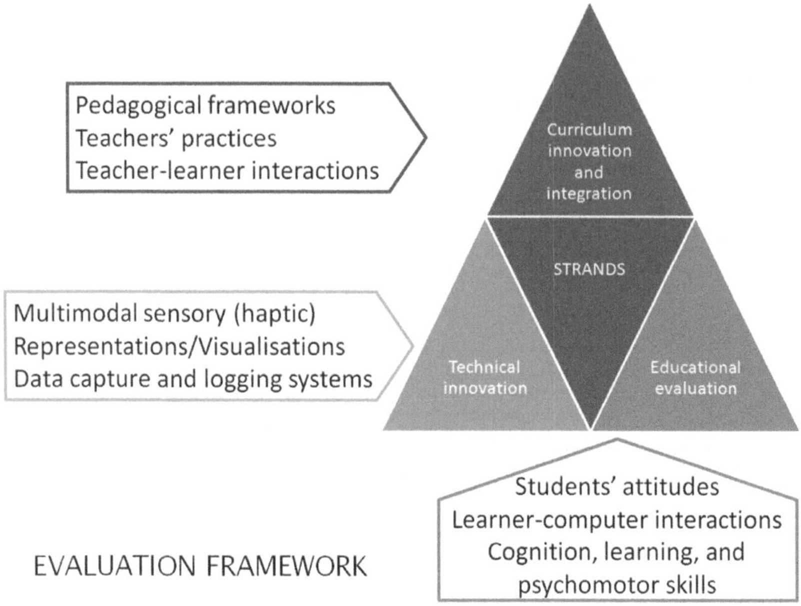

Fig. 2. Development and evaluation framework for the hapTEL system

environment, which includes a set of teeth in a jaw and the dental drill, is displayed on a 3D dual-screen system viewed by the operator using 3D glasses (Fig. 3). A camera which tracks the movement of the student's head provides colocation of the image with the student's position so that the student can move his or her head around the mouth to get the best view as in real life. The virtual hand-piece (shown on the screen) is operated by the student holding the real drill. The speed of the drill can be pre-selected by the student and the power is controlled using the foot pedal.

Learners can select from a choice of scenarios and complexities which generally involve a decayed cavity lesion requiring excavation. The system is set up to log raw data of each attempt and feeds back information such as the amount (%) of decay, enamel, dentine and pulp removed at the end of the attempt. Users can replay their attempts on the screen to assess and learn from their performance.

The priorities regarding the design of the curriculum version were to develop a system which:

- was as close in design as possible to the 77 traditional phantom head dental chairs which the students would also be using;
- would have a large enough display so that pairs of students and supervising tutors could see the simulated mouth on which the student was working;
- would be cheap enough to enable the project to have 12 identical functioning systems from the start of the student trials;
- would be robust enough to require minimum maintenance;
- could be used by students working in pairs as 'dentist' and 'dental nurse';

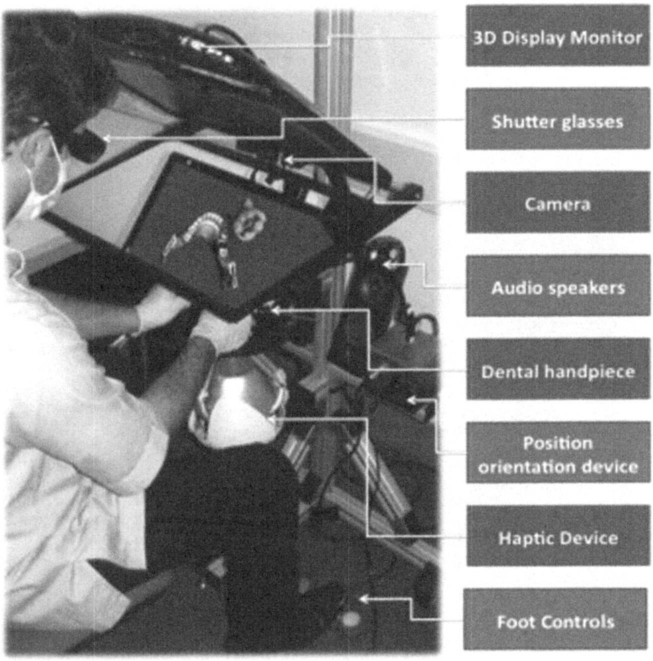

Fig. 3. hapTEL curriculum dental simulator

- would store all the actions of the students including video playback so the students, researchers and tutors could monitor and review the students' work;
- would store all the achievement scores of the students such as percentage of decayed tissue removed, healthy tissue remaining and whether or not the pulp had been exposed.

4 Evolvement of the Teaching and Learning Setting and Workshop Activities

From the incorporation of the curriculum version of the hapTEL system into the undergraduate dental curriculum in October 2008, the teaching and learning settings have changed as a consequence of yearly evaluations of the range of issues previously identified by Entwistle [13] and previous project results reported in Sect. 1 (e.g. see Shahriari-Rad [9]). Figure 4 below shows the tutor demonstrating to the pair of students how to use the work-stations which was part of the teaching approach for every year of the study. However, many other aspects of the blended learning environment have changed to prevent the malfunctions of the system and to improve the confidence of the students to take charge of the learning activity.

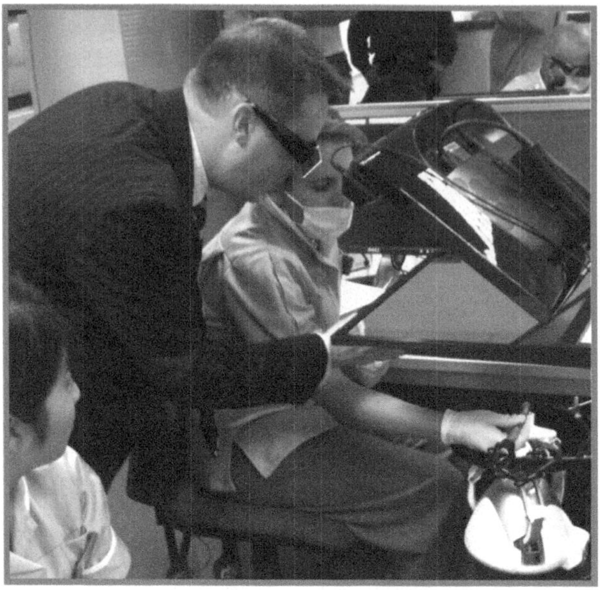

Fig. 4. Tutor instructing students in the hapTEL virtual laboratory

Table 1 below shows the teaching and learning settings and strategies used in the hapTEL laboratory over the last nine years showing how the organisation and assessment procedures have changed as a result of yearly evaluations and staff and student feedback. During the first four years of the project there were 12 complete machines available for use by 24 students per session in parallel with the rest of the year's cohort (98 students) working in the traditional 'Phantom Head' Laboratory. This enabled a direct comparison to be made between the hapTEL and traditional students' learning experiences, the results of which are discussed in Sect. 1 above. During this period the hapTEL machines were still under development and were technically unreliable at times requiring the presence and support of a skilled cybernetic technician. As one can see from this table the number of staff required to support the student sessions has reduced from five during 2008–11 to only 2–3 since 2012. This has been possible by providing more training to the students on how to use the machines and by pre-empting possible hiccups through the previous years' experiences which have been addressed in the introductory videos.

In comparison with the traditional laboratory setting in which 70+ students would be working on Phantom Head dental work-stations with only three tutors and two to three technicians present, the support staff for only 12–14 students in the hapTEL lab is greater. However, in the traditional lab most of the tutor feedback is after a tooth operation has been completed whereas in the hapTEL lab, the system itself provides dynamic immediate feedback on the procedures themselves to every student and additionally the log files of their performances at the end of every operation.

Table 1. Teaching and learning setting and blended learning strategies (2008–2017)

Year	Teaching and learning setting and blended learning strategies
2008–11	1 – hour introductory lecture followed by 24 students working in pairs on the 12 machines in the hapTEL laboratory for 1.5 h supervised and assisted by a senior clinician, 3 assistant tutors and 1 technician. 3 sessions (4.5 h) in total. Log file records stored of every student action and task achievement. (see [9], for more details)
2012–14	Introduction to the workshop session by a non-specialist lecturer followed by 12 students working in pairs on the 6 machines in the hapTEL laboratory for 1.5 h supervised and assisted part of the time by a senior clinician, assistant tutor and TEL support person. 2 sessions (2 h) in total. Log file records stored of every student action and task achievement
2014–16	Introduction to the workshop session by a pre-recorded video of Dental specialist lecturer and face-to-face non-specialist lecturer followed by 12 students working in pairs on the 6 machines supervised and assisted part of the time by a senior clinician, assistant tutor and TEL support person. 2 sessions (1.5 and 1 h respectively). Log file records stored of each student's action and task achievement. Students' individual photos of their log files submitted for assessment by academics
2017	Same as for 2014–16 but student log-files recorded by the student on individual assessment sheets during the actual sessions and then submitted for assessment

Following the completion of the research phase of the hapTEL project (2007–11), the machines were then integrated into a revised dental curriculum to take account of the results from the earlier attitude study by Green [15] which had shown that students perceived there to be a greater value in using the hapTEL simulators **before** using the 'phantom head' in order to prepare them for the more complex clinical tasks which the latter required.

During 2012–14, although the hapTEL sessions were now included yearly in the first year of the Dental Undergraduate curriculum (BDS-Year1), the sequence of activities in each first session for a tutor group of students (N = 10/12) was a 20 min introduction given by a lecturer but not always a dental clinician, followed by a 5 min demonstration on one of the machines, followed by students working in pairs (one as the dentist operating the hand-piece and performing the cavity preparation: and the partner operating as the dental nurse controlling the instrument selection, speed of drill etc.). They would then change places for the second half of the session.

While working on the virtual dental work-stations the students are always required to wear their personal protective clothing (PPE) to familiarise themselves with wearing aprons, gloves and masks in all clinical settings. Additionally, they wore 'shutter' glasses which enable them to see the image in 3-D; and a camera (located below the screen) tracking their head movements around the haptic jaw moves the image to match their viewing position. The 'show records' option enables the students to see the log files on the screen of the results of their cavity preparation. An example of one student's results for Cavity 2 (a floating tooth with a small carious lesion) is shown in Fig. 5 below.

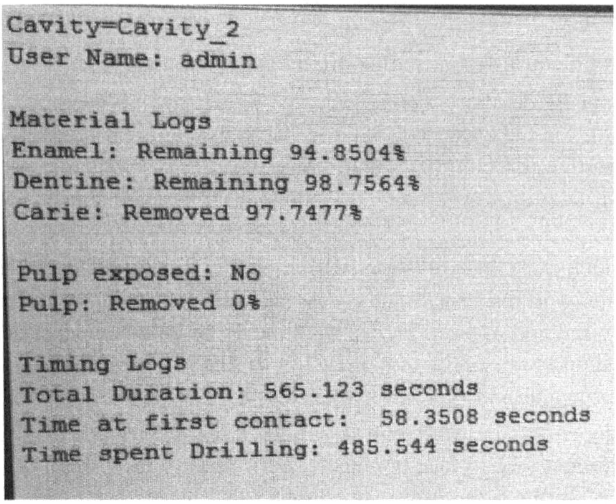

Fig. 5. Student iPhone photo of his log files result for Cavity 2

The log files, displayed in Fig. 5, show that the student succeeded in preserving 94.8504% of healthy enamel and 98.7564% of dentine while removing 98.7564% of the caries without exposing the pulp, which is a very good result.

During the sessions held in 2014–16 (see Table 1), once the option to end the drilling procedure had been chosen by the student taking the part of the dentist, then there was no further opportunity to remove more healthy tissue to improve his/her task results. This sometimes resulted in students forgetting to photograph every attempt. Furthermore, not all the students remembered to take photos of their results before swapping over with their partner in spite of repeated reminders. Table 2 below shows the results for a sample of 10 students (out of 121) for the task called Cavity 3 which requires the students to remove as much caries as possible for a tooth located in a lower jaw.

The results in Table 2 show that seven out of ten students exposed the pulp which is to be avoided if possible when working on real patients. However, all ten students managed to remove over 83% of the caries while retaining over 91% of healthy enamel and 96% of dentine which is a good result for Year 1 novice students' first attempts. These detailed individual results are not possible in the traditional Phantom Head Laboratory because the students' performances are only assessed by the end results as observed by the tutor. There is no computed result.

In order to improve the students' understanding of the clinical skills and concepts they were aiming to learn, from the previous years' results (up to 2014) we decided to make further changes to the teaching strategies and students' learning activities as follows:

- For the introduction to Session 1, we prepared a series of short videos of a Senior Dental Consultant explaining to all the students the reasons for the activity, the procedures they should follow, how to wear their PPE, work in pairs and how to operate the hapTEL system.

Table 2. Sample of 10 students' log file results for Cavity 3 (tooth in lower jaw) in 2016

Cavity 3							
% of healthy enamel remaining	% of healthy dentine remaining	% of caries removed	Pulpal exposure	% of pulp removed	Time at first contact - secs.	Time spent drilling - secs.	Total duration - secs.
93.00%	99.00%	98.00%	Yes	0.50%	17.50	277.96	313.02
91.88%	97.77%	94.30%	Yes	0.02%	14.11	99.03	117.71
97.03%	96.99%	91.58%	Yes	0.30%	17.81	131.81	159.76
98.34%	96.79%	82.44%	Yes	0.72%	218.11	430.44	671.30
96.56%	99.57%	96.77%	No	0.00%	91.48	485.24	581.60
97.91%	98.92%	83.69%	Yes	0.61%	146.53	52.19	270.52
96.53%	97.30%	89.61%	Yes	0.87%	9.03	203.28	218.39
97.87%	99.75%	94.09%	No	0.00%	11.48	170.26	198.90
96.24%	96.71%	94.44%	Yes	0.39%	26.88	102.86	137.29
96.29%	99.81%	96.42%	No	0.00%	31.73	163.89	202.88

- In addition to demonstrating to the student group in each session, how to start up and operate the hapTEL work-station, a senior TEL expert demonstrated how to trouble shoot the work-stations to remedy regular minor problems (e.g. the system freezing, shutter glasses switching off, drill needing recalibrating) which improved the students' confidence and satisfaction when using the system.
- In order to obtain 100% of the log-file results, this year (February and March, 2017) all students have been issued with an assessment sheet at the beginning of every session on which they have to record every attempt made on every task (cavity) similar to those shown in Table 2. These achievement sheets are then collected at the end of every session and submitted for data entry to the Dental Institute's academic centre.

Table 2 above is one example of many student records to show the detailed feedback which the system can provide to each and every student. Evidence of improvement to their learning has been reported in previous papers as discussed in Sect. 1. What we have found in this study is that when students are provided with these individual results at the beginning of the second session, they are keen to use them as a starting position for improving their skills and performance further. There is no traditional or other haptic system currently available which provides this important tool for effective formative assessment in dental education.

5 Discussion and Conclusions

The previous research evidence reviewed in this paper in Sect. 1, including the analysis of ten years of over 800 students results [9, 16] have shown that the use of haptic simulators do enhance students' learning when used in an *appropriate educational setting*. The hapTEL system provides a dynamic real time feedback to the learner which has been shown by many previous studies into formative assessment that this enhances students' understanding [17, 18]. The study of the various educational settings reported in this paper shows that using haptic simulator enable students to work repeatedly on dental procedures consequently refining and improving their skills with little additional costs such as purchasing plastic teeth.

As discussed above, because the hapTEL system has no incorporated structured lesson plans or goals the additional blended activities have been evaluated throughout the sessions every year over the last 10 years through student feedback, the results of the log-files, the frequency of the systems crashing, the attendance rate for the students, and the speed at which the students can progress through the tasks. It is often assumed by other HE Dental Schools as discussed earlier that the most effective pedagogical approach to using haptic work stations (and other simulators) is to provide all the structured activities and student instructions within the system itself. However, we have found that by providing specific educational objectives through the videos before they start using the systems and by providing the individual assessment sheets and tutorial real-time guidance, the students have been more focused on achieving good outcomes as shown in the example results above and the 100% returns of their log-files.

In conclusion, the evidence presented in this paper shows that the benefits of using virtual reality simulators for dental and other healthcare programmes may significantly advantage students in their learning and in the longer term improve the treatment of patients. It also shows that it is not necessary to have a complete range of features in order for students to benefit from its use. The hapTEL system is much less diverse than the traditional Phantom Head system yet the evidence of 10 years of results from over 1200 students has shown that using it still enhances the learning of the students over just two sessions. What this paper argues is that the educational settings in which these simulated activities occur needs careful planning and timing with additional materials and goals to maximize the educational impact of the experience.

References

1. Walsh, L.J.: Use of simulated learning environments in dentistry and oral health curricula. In: Walsh, L.J. (ed.) SLE in Dentistry and Oral Health: Final Report. Health Workforce Australia (2010)
2. San Diego, J., Cox, M.J., Quinn, B.F.A., Newton, J.T., Banerjee, A., Woolford, M.: Researching haptics in higher education: the complexity of developing haptics virtual learning systems and evaluating its impact on students' learning. Comput. Educ. **59**, 156–166 (2012)
3. Wang, D., Zhao, S., Li, T., Zhang, Y., Wang, X.: Preliminary evaluation of a virtual reality dental simulation system on drilling operation. Biomed. Mater. Eng. **26**(Suppl. 1), S747–S756 (2015)
4. Cox, M.J., Niederhauser, D.S., Sakamoto, T., McDougall, A.N., Castillo, N., Røsvik, S.: Researching IT in education. J. Comput. Assist. Learn. **29**(5), 474–486 (2013)
5. Laurillard, D.: Rethinking University Teaching: A Conversational Framework for the Effective Use of Learning Technologies. Routledge, London (2013)

6. Manogue, M., Mcloughlin, J., Christersson, C., Delap, E., Lindh, C., Schoonheim-Klein, M., Plasschaert, A.: Curriculum structure, content, learning and assessment in european undergraduate dental education. Eur. J. Dent. Educ. **15**(3), 133–141 (2011)
7. Schoonheim-Klein, M., Wesselink, P.R., Vervoorn, J.M.: A community of learners in the evidence-based dental clinic. Eur. J. Dent. Educ. **16**(1), 174–179 (2012). https://doi.org/10.1111/j.1600-0579.2011.00693
8. Hindmarsh, J., Hyland, L., Banerjee, A.: Work to make simulation work: 'Realism', instructional correction and the body in training. Discourse Stud. **16**(2), 247–269 (2014)
9. Shahriari-Rad, A.: Enhancement of clinical skills assessment using haptic technology. Ph.D. thesis. King's College London. University of London (2014)
10. Cox, M.J., Quinn, B., Vervoon, M., Wesselink, P.: Evidence from the dental education communities: review of the field. J. Dent. Res. **94**(B) (2015)
11. Cox, M.J., San Diego, J.P., Quinn. B.F.: Clinical skills learning with touch technology. CyberTherapy Rehabil. 164 (2012)
12. Beetham, H., Sharpe, R.: Rethinking Pedagogy for a Digital Age. Taylor & Francis Publications, Milton Park (2013)
13. Entwistle, N.: A model of the teaching-learning process. In: Richardson, J.T.E., Eysenck, M., Piper, D. (eds.) Student Learning: Research in Education and Cognitive Psychology, pp. 13–28. Society for Research into Higher Education, Milton Keynes England, Philadelphia (1987). Open University Press
14. Entwistle, N.J., Nisbet, J.B., Bromage, A.: Teaching-learning environments and student learning in electronic engineering. In: Verschaffel, L., De Corte, E., Kanselaar, G., Valcke, M. (eds.) (2005)
15. Green, T.-A.: Students' Perceptions of Two Different Simulators. Ph.D. thesis. King's College London (2014)
16. Shariari-Rad, A., Cox, M.J., Woolford, M.: Clinical skills acquisition: rethinking assessment using a virtual haptic simulator. Technol. Knowl. Learn. **22**(2), 185–197 (2017). https://doi.org/10.1007/s10758-017-9308-1
17. Black, P., Wiliam, D.: Assessment and classroom learning. Assess. Educ.: Princ. Policy Pract. **5**(1), 7–74 (1998)
18. Eaton, K., Reynolds, P., Grayden, S., Wilson, N.: A vision of dental education in the third millenium. Br. Dent. J. **205**(5), 261–271 (2008)

Ontology-Based Backward Learning Support System

Masao Okabe[1], Masashi Umezawa[2(✉)], and Takahira Yamaguchi[3]

[1] Department of Management and Communication, Faculty of Life Design, Tohoku Institute of Technology, Sendai, Japan
okabemasao@tohtech.ac.jp
[2] SoftUmeYa, LLC., Tokyo, Japan
ume@softumeya.com
[3] Department of Administration Engineering, Faculty of Science and Technology, Keio University, Tokyo, Japan
yamaguti@ae.keio.ac.jp

Abstract. One of the main goals of introductory courses of a university is to make freshmen well prepared for subsequent intermediate courses. But nowadays it becomes difficult because academic skills of freshmen differ very much. To resolve this problem, this paper proposes an ontology-based backward learning support system called EduGraph. If a student cannot understand some learning item, EduGraph, based on its ontology, suggests him or her prerequisites for understanding the item, and he or she can learn them using EduGraph. For the student, to understand the incomprehensible item can be a short-term goal because prerequisites for it are suggested, and he or she is expected to keep intrinsically motivated to understand the item. EduGraph can also support a student to organize what he or she learns into his or her integrated knowledge, because its ontology is based on a well-designed upper ontology for learning and can organize learning items properly. Actual applications to several introductory courses from 2015 suggest that EduGraph is effective.

Keywords: Ontology · Concept map · Backward learning
Intrinsic motivation

1 Introduction

More than half of students go on to higher education in Japan. That means that academic skills of freshmen vary very much and unfortunately some of them do not have academic skills necessary for learning at a university. One of the main objectives of introductory courses for freshmen is, hence, to make students with different academic skills well prepared for subsequent intermediate courses. But, under the actual environment where one teacher has to teach a large number of students in a large classroom, this is hardly achieved. To resolve this problem, this paper proposes an ontology-based backward learning support system called EduGraph.

A. Tatnall and M. Webb (Eds.): WCCE 2017, IFIP AICT 515, pp. 398–408, 2017.
https://doi.org/10.1007/978-3-319-74310-3_41

The structure of this paper is as follows. Section 2 reviews related works. Sections 3 and 4 present the proposal. Section 5 describes tentative evaluation. Finally, Sect. 6 summarizes the proposal and points out some future works.

2 Related Works

2.1 Motivation and Short-Term Goal

Motivation is a key factor for successful learning. There are two kinds of motivation, intrinsic motivation and extrinsic motivation. According to Ryan and Deci [1], intrinsic motivation is defined as the doing activity for its inherent satisfactions rather than for some separable consequence, and extrinsic motivation is a construct that pertains whenever an activity is done in order to attain some separable outcome. Ideally, intrinsic motivation is more important, but there is no general way to make all students motivated intrinsically because intrinsic motivation exists in the nexus between a student and a task [1]. Therefore, to make a student intrinsically motivated, setting a task or a goal appropriate to the student is important. Stipek suggests that an appropriate level of challenge can be achieved by adjusting goal for students with varying skill levels and also that to avoid discouragement on a long-term task, it is better to set short-term goals [2].

2.2 Backward Design and Backward Learning

Backward design is an instructional design method developed by Wiggins and McTighe [3]. Its point is "the end in mind first". Teachers tend to focus on lessons and textbooks without a clear image of desired results. In backward design, desired results are determined first, before teaching method or lessons are considered. Its advantage seems obvious since the objectives of a course are to get desired results.

This "the end in mind first" policy is now being applied also to instructions themselves. For example, "Backwards Learning Organizer" [4] is a template with which students clarify their goals first. Although the basic principle "the end in mind first" is the same, the meaning in backward learning as instructions is substantially different from the one in backward design. It seems mainly to help students clarify their short-term goals and intends to keep students intrinsically motivated. In some domains, there are several "the end in mind first" instructional practices. For example, in the domain of proof problems at high-school mathematics, Sasaki [5] shows that a proof by backward inference is more understandable to students than one by forward inference. Sasaki claims that a proof by backward inference fits students' thought processes better than one by forward inference. In this case, "the ends in mind first" is a short-term goal and also help student intrinsically motivated.

2.3 Concept Map and Ontology

A concept map is a graph with nodes that are concepts to be learnt and with links among them. It was developed by Novak [6] in 1972, based on the learning psychology by Ausubel [7]. That is, it supports meaningful learning, and not mere rote learning, by helping a learner organize his or her cognitive structure to encourage a deep level of integrated knowledge [8]. Integration of knowledge is important, but it is also true that a concept map has limitations for this purpose. That is, there are many concept maps, but there is no integrated concept map.

An ontology is defined as "an explicit specification of a conceptualization" [9]. More intuitively saying, similar to a concept map, an ontology at least represents concepts and relations among them in some domain, and it is often represented by a graph with concepts as its nodes and with links between them. Compared to a concept map, an ontology is more general-purpose, but if an ontology is applied to learning, it can be very similar to a concept map. Actually, there are many proposals of learning methodologies or learning support systems using ontologies, including [10–12]. In the domain of history, Muroya et al. [13] propose self-exploratory learning based on a learner's interest, using Linked Open Data (hereafter, LOD), which is a kind of ontology. In this LOD, nodes are historical events, places where events occurred, persons who engaged in events, and so on, and these nodes are linked each other. Following links of an event, based on his or her own interest, a learner can get deep understanding of the event. This is very similar to what a concept map intends to do. In addition, this LOD may make a learner intrinsically motivated to understand the event, which is a short-term goal.

An ontology has a similar problem as a concept map. There are many ontologies in many domains, which are often overlapped. But, they are not integrated and, even worse, they are sometimes inconsistent. To resolve this problem, several upper ontologies are developed [14–18]. An upper ontology is a top-level domain-neutral ontology to be a basis of more specific domain ontologies. If domain ontologies are developed based on the same upper ontology, they are expected to be consistent each other and to be integrated based on the upper ontology. Unfortunately, there is still no consensus on what an upper ontology should be used. But, apparently, BFO [14] is the most widely used upper ontology. It was originally developed as a basis of biomedical ontologies, but now it intends to be a basis of most of ontologies, not limited to biomedical ones, and aims to promote consistency in description of scientific data and then to promote interoperability of scientific data in electric format among computers [19].

3 EduGraph

EduGraph is a simple ontology-based learning support system, which supports backward learning, giving a short-term goal for each student, and motivating him or her intrinsically. It can be used by a teacher in a classroom in a usual manner and also by students themselves outside a classroom.

EduGraph mainly consists of two parts. One is a slide part and the other is an ontology part. In the slide part, a teacher can easily create slides in Markdown [20], a simple markup language, and upload them on the Web. Both a teacher and students use them via a browser just same as usual slides. Slides for one class usually contain several learning items, each of which are normally explained by one to at most several slides and can be a short-term goal. A teacher can construct slides for one class, combining sets of slides for several learning items in any order.

In the ontology part, EduGraph ontology structures all learning items as its nodes with several types of relationships among them. Each node has a link to slides that explain the learning item. The structure of EduGraph ontology is simple and can be represented fully by a graph. A teacher can easily expand EduGraph ontology using Neo4j [21], a graph database. Using the ontology part, for any learning item, a student can easily access slides that explain it, by tapping or clicking the corresponding node of EduGraph ontology by a smartphone or a PC (Fig. 1).

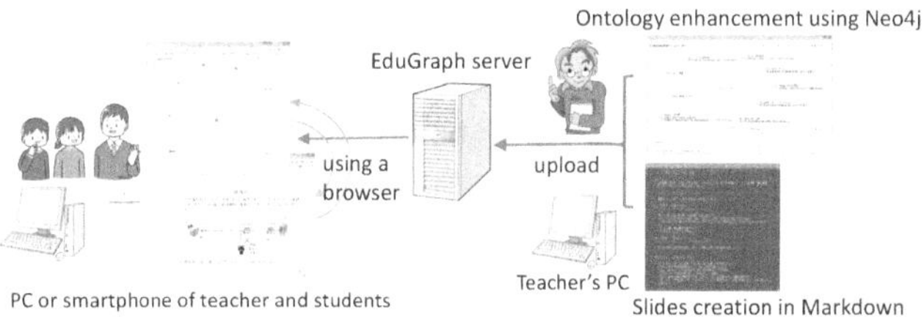

Fig. 1. Overview of EduGraph

4 EduGraph Ontology

4.1 Relationship Type

EduGraph ontology is a key component of EduGraph and has two important roles. One is to navigate a student to backward learning if he or she still has difficulty in understanding what he or she has learnt, and the other is to help a student incorporate what he or she has learnt into his or her integrated knowledge. For these purposes, EduGraph ontology currently has four types of relationships as shown at Table 1. All of them are very popular relationship types, except that EduGraph uses general terms for students who are not familiar with ontologies. For example, Edugarph uses "part", rather than "is_part_of". But, "part" of EduGraph is extended from usual "is_part_of". "Is_part_of" is usually applied to physical things such as "a piston is_part_of an engine". From the point of learning, this means that, to understand an engine, it is necessary to understand a piston. From this point, "part" of EduGraph is extended and can be applied to any learning item, not limited to one about a physical thing. If learning item A is "part" of learning item B, it means that, to understand learning item B, it is necessary to understand learning item A, that is, learning item A is a prerequisite for learning item B. If a student does not understand learning item B, even with slides that explain it, he or she goes back to learning item A and learn it. For this learner, learning item B is a short-term goal, and he or she can understand it, with backward learning of learning item A.

For the purpose of getting integrated knowledge, all the relationship types, including "part", are used. But, to support integration of any learning items, EduGraph ontology needs to be based on a well-designed upper ontology.

Table 1. Relationship types of EduGraph ontology

Relationship type	Notation	Meaning
Subclass	A - subclass → B	B is a subclass of A
Example	A - example → B	B is an example (instance) of A
Part	A - part → B	B is part of A
Related item	A - related item → B	B is related to A

4.2 Upper Ontology of EduGraph Ontology

Originally, EduGraph ontology was planned to be developed based on BFO. But, BFO was not suitable for an upper ontology of EduGraph ontology. Firstly, objectives are different. The objectives of BFO are interoperability of scientific data in electric format among computers, but the objectives of EduGraph ontology are to navigate a learner. Secondly, domains are different. BFO now intends to be a domain-neutral upper ontology. But, BFO seems to be slightly influenced by its origin as a basis of biomedical ontologies. From the point of learning, there are a lot of so-called abstract concepts to be learnt, but BFO only has a class called "Generically dependent continuant" (see Fig. 2) for them, probably because they are not important to biomedical ontologies.

Therefore, EduGraph ontology has its own upper ontology. It is somewhat different from BFO because of the reasons above. Basic structure of the upper ontology of EduGraph ontology, in contrast to BFO, is as follows.

Identification of Learning Item. To design an ontology, identification is a big issue. For example, it is not easy to decide how to treat Beethoven Symphony No. 5. In some situation, Beethoven Symphony No. 5 may mean its score, and in another situation, it may mean its performance. Hence, usually, from an ontological point of view, Beethoven Symphony No. 5 as a score and as a performance should be distinguished from each other. BFO is a high-level upper ontology and does not influenced directly by this issue but takes this position. From the point of learning, in most cases, a learner learns all aspects of Beethoven Symphony No. 5, including its score and its performance. Hence, EduGraph ontology has one node for Beethoven Symphony No. 5 as one learning item, instead of having different nodes as a score and as a performance.

Universals and Particulars. One of the top-level dichotomies is universals and particulars. BFO does not have this top level dichotomy and only categorizes universals. Particulars are out of the scope of BFO, because BFO is to provide universals that can classify particulars for its objectives. EduGraph ontology does not have this top level dichotomy either and mainly structures universals because usually a learning item is a general thing, that is, a universal. But, sometimes, a particular may be a learning item, or even if it is not a learning item, it may be important if the particular as an example helps a learner understand a general thing (a universal). In that case, EduGraph ontology classifies the particulars under the universal as its instances.

Structure. EduGraph has the same top-level dichotomy as BFO, except that EduGraph uses general terms "Static thing" and "Dynamic thing", instead of "Continuant" and "Occurent", which BFO uses. BFO has three direct subclasses of "Continuant" called "Independent continuant", "Generically dependent continuant", and "Specifically dependent continuant", as shown in Fig. 2. Generally speaking, "Independent continuant" is a class of entities that exist independently, whether tangible or not, and "Dependent continuant" is a class of entities that exist dependent on another entity. BFO distinguishes "Generically dependent continuant" from "Specifically dependent continuant". The latter is a class of entities that exist dependent on another entity which cannot be changed, and its typical subclass is "Quality". On the other hand, the former is a class of entities which exist dependent on another entity, which can migrate one entity to another, and its typical subclass is "Information", which BFO itself does not have. Intuitively saying, a so-called abstract concept has many representations, and each representation is a specifically dependent continuant and this abstract concept is a generically dependent continuant. An abstract concept and its representations are strictly distinguished in BFO. But, from the point of learning, it is rarely necessary to distinguish between them, because, generally speaking, what should be learnt is not a representation but its meaning. Hence, in EduGraph ontology, "Specifically dependent continuant" and "Generically dependent continuant" are merged to just "Dependent thing" and the difference between a representation and its semantics is ignored. Thus, in EduGraph ontology, "Static thing" has two direct subclasses called "Independent thing" and "Dependent thing", as shown in Fig. 3.

BFO has two direct subclasses of "Independent continuant" called "Material entity" and "Immaterial entity". The interesting thing is that "Immaterial entity" includes only boundary, region and site (space) and that a so-called abstract concept is not an immaterial entity. This is partially because, philosophically, BFO stands on realism and not conceptualism, and partially because BFO classifies an abstract concept as a generically dependent continuant. Boundary, region and site are important in biology, but from the point of learning, compared to many abstract concepts to be learnt, boundary, region and site are not important. Therefore, in EduGraph ontology, "Independent thing" has two direct subclasses called "Tangible thing" and "Intangible thing", and "Tangible thing" is almost the same as "Material entity" in BFO, but "Intangible thing" is much broader than "Immaterial entity" in BFO and includes abstract concepts, or some portion of "Generically dependent continuant" in BFO.

Treatment of Role. From an ontological point of view, it is important to decide what subclasses of an entity are appropriate. For example, usually, man and woman are subclasses of person, but lawyer and teacher are not subclasses of person, because if a person is a lawyer at some time, he or she may cease to be a lawyer and may become a teacher at another time. Lawyer and teacher are usually treated as roles that person can have or that depend on person. Hence, BFO has class "Role" as a subclass of "Specifically dependent continuant". Then, a question may arise as to whether man and woman are really subclasses of person or just roles that person can have. But, from the point of learning, it is not important to distinguish roles from subclasses. To learn more details of a learning item, it often happens that some portion of the learning item is learnt more, and both classifications are important. So, in EduGraph ontology, both man and woman, and lawyer and teacher are subclasses of person. But to distinguish between them, a subclass relationship can have a name. Since man and woman are subclasses of person from the point of gender, these subclass relationships are named “by gender”, and since lawyer and teacher are subclasses from the point of profession, these subclass relationships are named “by profession”. There are several more simplifications and modifications, and in consequence, class hierarchy of the upper ontology of EduGraph ontology becomes as shown in Fig. 3.

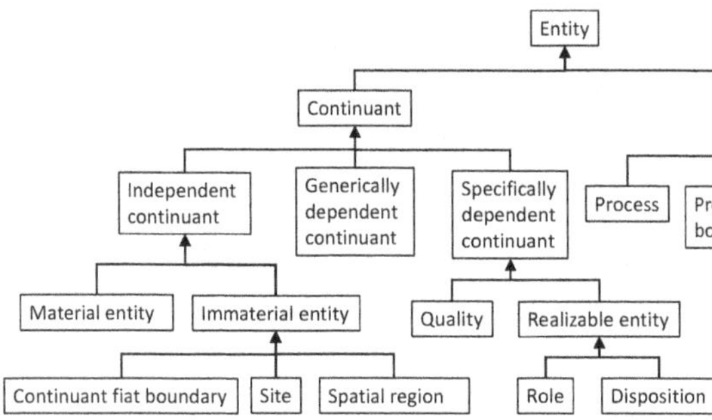

Fig. 2. Upper part of BFO

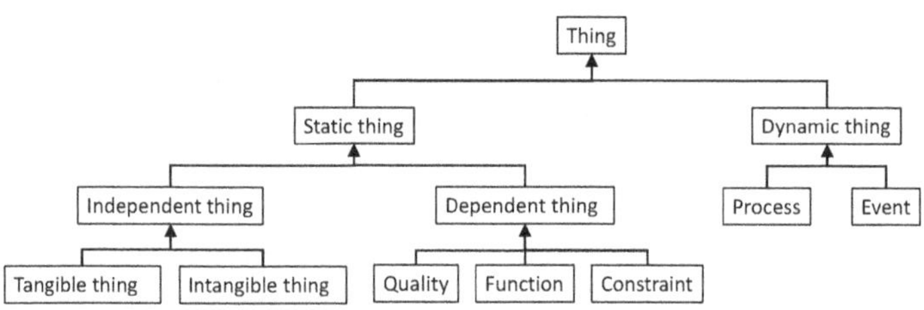

Fig. 3. Upper ontology of EduGraph ontology

5 Tentative Evaluation Through Actual Applications

5.1 Application to “Introduction to Information Technology” in 2015

From 2015, at a university that one of the authors works for, EduGraph is actually used in some of introductory courses. “Introduction to Information Technology” is one of the courses that EduGraph were first used in 2015.

Course Explanation. It is an introductory course for freshmen, and covers basics on information technology, all of which are necessary to understand subsequent courses on information technology. In Japan, some high schools provide a similar course and some not. Hence, students’ backgrounds for this course differ, but its goal is the same.

How EduGraph Was Applied. The contents of this course are fairly standardized and the contents in 2015 and in 2014 are almost the same, except that the slides in 2015 were prepared in Markdown, not in PowerPoint as in 2014, and that the contents in 2015 were structured by EduGraph ontology.

The course was taught at a classroom equipped with a computer for each student. At the first class, all slides for the course structured by EduGraph ontology were provided to all students. For each class, students were requested to self-study the slides using EduGraph before the class and after the class. When they did not understand a learning item, they did backward learning, navigated by EduGraph ontology. Students were also requested to submit a minute paper of their self-studies. In a classroom, a teacher used the slides as ordinal slides, but more time was spent to explain items on which students raised questions and in which students expressed a special interest at the minute papers. Figure 4 is some screen shots of EduGraph and shows the relation between EduGraph ontology and slides.

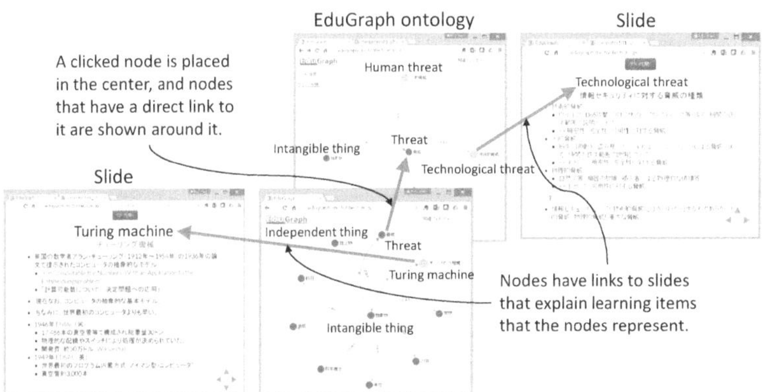

Fig. 4. Some screen shots of EduGraph

Results. Figure 5 is a histogram of the exam scores in 2014 and in 2015. Since most of the questions of the exams are 4 answer choice questions, scores less than or equal to 25 means that they did not learn at all. Regrettably, about 10% are such students both in 2014 and also in 2015. Except them, the portion of poor students (scores between 26 and 50) becomes less than 40% in 2015, compared to more than 50% in 2014. The portion of good students (scores more than 75) increased significantly in 2015, compared to in 2014. Table 2 shows some overall statistics of the exam scores in 2014 and in 2015. The average score in 2015 is 7 points higher than that in 2014 ($p = 0.021$). Since this comparison is not based on a properly designed experiment, it cannot be concluded that this improvement is achieved mainly by EduGraph, and is significant, even with $p = 0.021$. But still, the result suggests that EduGraph is effective. Unfortunately, it also suggests that EduGraph is not successful for motivating students who will not study. For more details please refer to our previous paper [22].

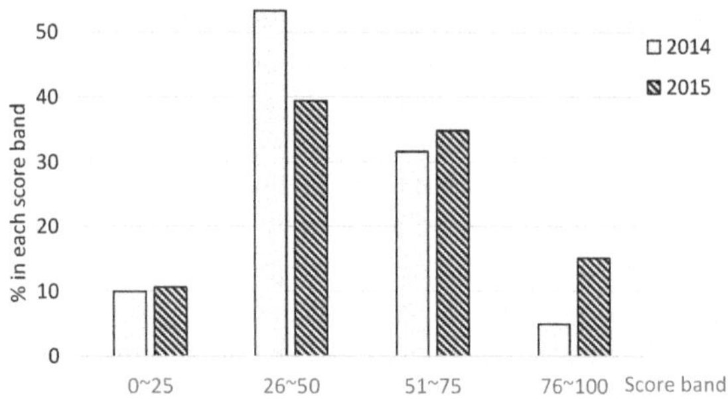

Fig. 5. Histogram of exam scores in 2014 and in 2015

Table 2. Some statistics of exam scores in 2014 and in 2015

	2014	2015	Difference (2015–2014)	Note
Number of students	60	66	6	
Mean	44.4	51.4	7.0	$t = 2.03$, $P(T > t) = 0.021$
Standard deviation	18.1	20.2	2.1	$f = 1.25$, $P(F > f) = 0.194$

5.2 Other Applications and Discussion

Currently, several introductory courses use EduGraph, including "Introduction to Information Technology" in 2016. The authors feel that EduGraph gradually becomes more effective as experiences and know-how on using EduGraph are accumulated. However, the portion of students who will not learn hardly decreases, although students somewhat motivated learn more with EduGraph. In addition, even excluding these students, it is not clear why students learn more with EduGraph. Hopefully, EduGraph may generate intrinsic motivation. But, in the courses that use EduGraph, teachers encourage students to learn by themselves outside a classroom, using EduGraph. This may generate extrinsic motivation.

If EduGraph is successful for generating intrinsic motivation by showing a short-term goal and learning items to be learnt backward, it is not clear how far it is effective. For example, suppose that a student does not understand learning item A, and that he or she learns learning item B that is necessary to understand learning item A. But unfortunately, if he or she does not understand learning item B either, he or she has to learn learning item C and so on. It is not clear what depth of this recursiveness can keep his or her intrinsic motivation to understand learning item A.

6 Summary and Future Works

This paper has proposed EduGraph, an ontology-based backward learning support system, which intends to respond to the difficult situation that students with different academic skills need to achieve the same goal.

Similar to preparing slides in PowerPoint, a teacher can prepare slides using EduGraph. In a classroom, a teacher can use them as ordinal slides, and, outside a classroom, students can use them by their own smartphones or PCs. EduGraph ontology, based on a well-designed upper ontology, structures all learning items on slides. Navigated by EduGraph ontology, each student sets his or her own short-term goal and learn it backward, motivated intrinsically.

Our experiences from 2015 suggest that EduGraph is effective. We will continue to achieve good results, applying EduGraph to more introductory courses, and will also make an objective experiment that evaluates how much and in what way EduGraph is effective.

Acknowledgments. A part of this research is supported by the Japan Society for the Promotion of Science KAKENHI Grant Number 15K12423.

References

1. Ryan, R.M., Deci, E.L.: Intrinsic and extrinsic motivations: classic definitions and new directions. Contemp. Educ. Psychol. **25**(1), 54–67 (2000)
2. Stipek, D.: Motivation to Learn from Theory to Practice, 3rd edn. Allyn & Bacon, Boston (1998)
3. Wiggins, G.P., McTighe, J.: Understanding by Design. ASCD, Alexandria (2005)
4. Backwards Learning Organizer. http://www.thoughtfulclassroom.com/tools/PDFs/Backwards_Learning_Organizer.pdf. Accessed 21 Jan 2017
5. Sasaki, T.: An examination of studies based on backward reasoning in high school mathematics. Bull. Tokyo Univ. Grad. Sch. Soc. Welfare **5**(2), 103–108 (2015). (in Japanese)
6. Novak, J.D., Alberto, J.C.: The theory underlying concept maps and how to construct and use them, Technical report IHMC CmapTools 2006-01 Rev 01-2008 (2008)
7. Ausubel, D.P.: Educational Psychology: A Cognitive View. Holt, Rinehart and Winston, New York (1968)
8. Chu, K.-K., Lee, C.-I., Tsai, R.-S.: Ontology technology to assist learners' navigation in the concept map learning system. Expert Syst. Appl. **38**(9), 11293–11299 (2011)
9. Gruber, T.R.: A translation approach to portable ontology specifications. Knowl. Acquis. **5** (2), 199–220 (1993)
10. Snae, C., Brueckner, M.: Ontology-driven e-learning system based on roles and activities for Thai learning environment. Interdisc. J. Knowl. Learn. Objects **3**, 1–17 (2007)
11. Gaeta, M., Orciuoli, F., Ritrovate, P.: Advanced ontology management system for personalized e-learning. Knowl.-Based Syst. **22**, 292–301 (2009)
12. Baker, E.L.: Ontology-based educational design: seeing is believing, Resource Paper 13, National Center for Research, Graduate School of Education, University of California, Los Angeles (2012)
13. Muroya, D., Hayashi, Y., Seta, K.: LOD-based support for self-exploratory learning in history. The Japanese Society for Artificial Intelligence, SIG-ALST-B504-04, pp. 17–21 (2016). (in Japanese)
14. Smith, B.: Basic Formal Ontology 2.0 Specifications and User's Guide. https://github.com/BFO-ontology/BFO/raw/master/docs/bfo2-reference/BFO2-Reference.pdf. Accessed 10 Jan 2017

15. DOLCE: a Descriptive Ontology for Linguistic and Cognitive Engineering. http://www.loa.istc.cnr.it/old/DOLCE.html. Accessed 15 Jan 2017
16. Suggested Upper Merged Ontology (SUMO). http://www.adampease.org/OP/. Accessed 15 Jan 2017
17. Sowa, J.F.: Top-Level Categories. http://www.jfsowa.com/ontology/toplevel.htm. Accessed 21 Jan 2017
18. Mizoguchi, R.: YAMATO: Yet Another More Advanced Top-level Ontology. http://download.hozo.jp/onto_library/YAMATO101216.pdf. Accessed 10 Jan 2017
19. Apr, R., Smith, B., Spear, A.D.: Building Ontologies with Basic Formal Ontology. The MIT Press, Cambridge (2015)
20. Markdown Here. http://markdown-here.com/. Accessed 10 Jan 2017
21. Neo4j. http://neo4j.com/. Accessed 10 Jan 2017
22. Okabe, M.: Ontology-navigated tutoring system for flipped-mastery model. In: Proceedings of The ICALT 2016: 18th International Conference on Advanced Learning Technologies, vol. 18, no. 10, pp. 1814–1820 (2016)

eExams: Strength in Diversity

Andrew Fluck[1](✉) and Mathew Hillier[2]

[1] University of Tasmania, Launceston, Australia
Andrew.Fluck@utas.edu.au
[2] Monash University, Melbourne, Australia
Mathew.Hillier@monash.edu

Abstract. This study examined the growing number of emerging eExam systems that allow students to demonstrate academic achievement using computers in schools and universities. Using a mixed-methods case study approach, the research gathered data from a desk audit, followed by field observations and interviews in selected countries. Thematic investigation of the data revealed commonalities and differences in the eExam systems. The findings show the main systems under development are divided into two groups. The first are alternative booting systems that make an entire, identical operating system and application suite available to each candidate. The second comprises a variety of secure web-browser solutions. Both approaches permit the use of software applications, but it is not yet clear whether this affordance can transform curricula. It is clear there is tension between administrative convenience that saves staff time, and the transformational potential of computers in education that would alter what students learn as well as how they learn. This tension is epitomised by the different proportions of undergraduate examinations conducted using computers, ranging from 1% to 40% in some institutions. What was also clear from the data were the intentions of some countries and institutions to raise this to 100% in a five year span.

Keywords: eExam system · Administrative convenience
Pedagogical affordances · Software applications

1 Introduction

An eExam (e-exam) is a "timed, supervised, summative assessment conducted using each candidate's own computer running a standardised operating system" [1]. This distinguishes them from online assessments, learning platform-based assessment environments or web-based tests.

Several authors have used the 'eExam' terminology. Held referred to examinations conducted through a learning management system as eExaminations or eExams in 2011 [2]. In 2012, Breke studied eExams in calculus at university level in Norway but focused on the MyMathLab application rather than a dedicated and common operating system [3]. More recently, the Rector's decision at Jyväskylä University referred to electronic exams as eExams [4]. Perhaps the earliest mention in the sense of the Wikipedia definition was by Hesketh in 2010 [5] when lodging code in Launchpad:

A. Tatnall and M. Webb (Eds.): WCCE 2017, IFIP AICT 515, pp. 409–417, 2017.
https://doi.org/10.1007/978-3-319-74310-3_42

"eExam aims to create a restricted Ubuntu environment in which students may perform exams on their own laptops".

These examples begin to show the global proliferation of eExams and similar ways in which computers are being used by candidates in high stakes assessments. This paper reports eExam developments in a number of countries. The paper shows how a desk audit of the literature identified a range of national contexts for study. This was followed up by field observations and interviews with eExam management teams to gather more specific data. A thematic analysis of this material is then presented, with a synthesis of findings into a table of key indicators/features/attributes. A discussion of the findings draws out important implications for the future.

2 Literature

eExams have been reported in several countries. Nigerian universities are collectively using various eExam approaches for selecting and assessing undergraduates [6]. John Dermo carried out a broad survey of student eAssessment perceptions in the University of Bradford, England [7]. eExams in Turku, Finland were described by Kuikka et al. [8] in the context of 'aquariums' – rooms covered by security video cameras in which students take assessment on computer without personal supervision. Bussières, Métras and Leclerc reported use of the commercial software 'ExamSoft', in pharmacy courses in Canada [9]. Forty-two American states require the use of ExamSoft by those who wish to take the bar (law) exam on a computer [10]. Examsoft supports choice answers and a simplified word processor for longer (non-automatically marked) responses, and is suitable for paper-replacement assessments where candidates can choose between keyboard and pen. A similar, but open source product is TCExam (tcexam.org) as used in the University of Innsbruck [11].

In Australia, the authors are involved in a nation-wide project called *Transforming exams: a scalable examination platform for BYOD invigilated assessment* [12]. The increasingly large enrolments in tertiary classes and the reduction in public funding in most 'western' nations means that educational institutions are no longer able to keep up with the demand for computer provision. This is true for campus-based computer lab where the ratio of university-supplied lab computers per student is dropping while demand for ICT continues to grow. This has engendered a strategic shift towards the use of bring-your-own-device (in this case, laptops) in many higher education institutions in more developed countries. Institutional policies and IT services are increasingly supporting BYOD for students within the pre-tertiary education sector as well. Consequently, it seems most likely that BYO laptop based approaches will be the only viable way forward for large-scale examinations. We therefore focus the majority of our analysis on solutions that adopt a BYOD approach to equipment provision.

eExams are considered to have several important advantages. On a cognitive level, e-exams promote effective learning by facilitating the testing a range of skills, knowledge, and understanding [13]. These pedagogical advantages stand in contrast to the administrative advantages reported for eExams, such as providing instant feedback to students and reducing load on staff [*ibid.*]. Other advantages of eExam systems include ease of use, low cost to operate, and ability to improve the quality of student feedback [14]. E-exams also offer several benefits over paper-based examinations as these systems allow multimedia elements including video, virtual views, scenarios, software tools and simulations [15]. Supporters see them enabling a broad pedagogical landscape for the assessment of 21st Century capabilities. In this regard, post-paper assessments become possible – assessments that cannot be delivered in the conventional paper-based context because they incorporate multi-media or require creative use of computer software applications. Such post-paper assessments may also influence curriculum, moving teaching towards the 'redefinition' end of the SAMR framework [16]. This will provide an impetus for educators to incorporate creative computer use into instruction, increasing the level of student cognition in Bloom's taxonomy [17].

Dawson provided an interesting alternative view to these reasons for adopting eExams [18]. He considered five threats to exam security, including injecting prepared text into the system, or copying the question paper and software using a 'cold boot' attack that could achieve the same outcome. For institutions where exam questions are confidential for reuse, the latter raised some concerns (although the cold boot attack did require cooling computer memory to temperatures below zero Celsius). Other institutions publish exam papers through their libraries, so the attack was not significant. In addition, the copying of software or electronic exam files could be instrumental to hacking into the security of the system. Security reliant on obfuscation was rejected as far back as 1851 [19], which is no less valid today in the world of computers. Sindre and Vegendla [20] took a more holistic approach to eExam security, using attack-defence trees to argue they are no less secure than paper-based exams. Further they argued that for e-exams to be acceptable they only need to be 'not worse' than paper based exams. Indeed eExams do offer additional affordances, as outlined earlier with respect pedagogical flexibility when compared to paper-based exams. A computer-based exam is also more reflective of knowledge production, use and problem solving in contemporary work and society.

3 Method and Approach

This study examined the design approaches taken by a variety of publically funded eExam projects and commercial competitors. The procedure comprised a desk audit, followed by observational visits and interviews with staff actively implementing eExams in schools and universities. The objective is to ascertain design characteristics that might foster success in the academic ecology of these educational environments over the broadest possible range. Success for an eExam system is very widely defined within this study, conveying sufficient desirable characteristics for the system to be chosen alongside, or in preference to, pen-on-paper examinations. These characteristics often include resilience, reliability, capability to handle many questioning styles etc. The functionality of an eExam system needs to be considered in a holistic fashion, looking beyond the context of the candidate providing responses to questions. Thus, the way assessors compose questions is an important consideration, as is how answer scripts are reticulated to markers, and marks consolidated with other assessment components into the institutional repository of student achievements.

The desk audit considered a range of eExam system reports from around the world, many of which have been cited in the previous section. From this audit, the following characteristics and concerns were distilled (see Table 1). These were then listed as issues for further investigation. This issues list acted as an up-front frame for observational visits, and as prompts when conducting field interviews.

Table 1. Focus areas for investigation in field work

Issue for investigation	Example questions
Attitudes of staff	Are exam composers, invigilators and markers supportive of the system?
Attitudes of students	Are most candidates in favour of the system? Are alternatives available for those that want to opt out?
Ease of use	What skill levels do candidates require above and beyond those expected for normal study?
Equity	Can any candidate access different resources to respond to assessment stimuli?
Technical reliability	Are the chances of a technical failure resulting in lost answers similar to pen-on-paper methods?
Comparison with hand-writing	Do eExam candidates achieve at different levels to handwriting candidates?
Method of invigilation	Is an official required in person?
Off-campus use	Can the system be deployed off-campus?
Harmony with existing exam infrastructure	Are cables deployed for networking or electrical power, causing trip hazards for invigilators?

Following the desk audit, visits to a number of universities and school examination boards were arranged. Where possible, an observation of an eExam was conducted, and interviews held with responsible staff in settings they chose, to gather more information about design considerations using the questions from Table 1. Where necessary, funnelling was used to probe specific issues and identify areas considered important by respondents. These interviews were transcribed into a standard template, and respondents provided an opportunity to correct the text. Key themes and elements from the field observations and interviews were extracted from the observations and interview records using the three-step Interpretative Phenomenological Analysis process [21]. First, the observations and interview statements were grouped into clusters. Second, these clusters were condensed into themes, and finally the themes were tabulated as key features for the different systems.

4 Findings

Data were collected from both school and university contexts. This paper presents a sub-set of the data that were chosen to represent a range of different national contexts, and a comparison of school and university sectors within a single country. The four systems illustrate the tension between BYOD and institutional hardware provision.

Table 2 illustrates the similarities and differences for just four of the eExam systems investigated. The table provides some minimum technical details about each system, alongside more overarching detail on the extent of use, place of origin and support for post-paper assessments.

Table 2. Key features of some eExam systems

	eExam v.6	Secure Exam Environment (SEE)	Abitti	eXam
Equipment	BYOD	BYOD and loan laptops	Institutional or BYOD: teacher laptop	Institutional or BYOD
Location	Any	On campus	Any	On campus
Access initiation	Boot from USB	Boot from Ethernet	Boot from USB	Any web-browser
Marking (lecturer/automatic)	Mostly lecturer	Both	Both	Mostly lecturer
Schools or universities?	Both	University	Schools nationwide	Universities
Software	Modified Ubuntu, Office suite, browser, Moodle, and selected applications	CentOS, Virtual PC, WindowsXP,, Secure Exam Browser, LMS e.g. Moodle	DigabiOS (Debian 8 Linux); Firefox	REST; AngularJS & Toastr-libraries; KEditor; MathJax
Local penetration (institution)	<1%	~40%	100% by end of 2019	10%
Global penetration	10 universities, and 1 professional accreditation authority	1 university	All high schools in Finland	Most universities in Finland
Institution and city of origin	Monash University, Melbourne	Alpen-Adria, Klagenfurt	Finnish Matriculation Board, Helsinki	CSC - IT center for science Ltd, Espoo
Country of origin	Australia	Austria	Finland	Finland
Within-exam access to software tools	Yes	Yes	Yes	No
Availability	Open source	Private – collaboration sought	Open source	Private – may become open source
Autosave period	2 min	?	Per character	?

This table can be read in conjunction with a table of Digital Exams in Scandinavian countries [22], which lists many internal and commercial eExam systems. Increasingly, educational organisations are tending to encourage the use of bring your own device (BYOD) eExam systems because this is the only financially viable way of providing every candidate with a reasonably modern computer. Although computer laboratories are used by some eExam systems, these cannot provide sufficient candidate seats when scaled to the full deployment of exams in relatively short times. In addition, computer laboratories may have been designed to facilitate collaboration, whereas examinations generally require candidates to be isolated from one another.

A clear security difference emerges between systems that boot from USB or Ethernet, and those that boot from the internal hard drive of the client computer. The former are more prevalent with scalable BYOD platforms, while the latter are restricted to institutional equipment. All approaches attempt to provide institutional control over the assessment context for the duration of the examination, to ensure integrity.

The affordances of the four systems illustrate another difference. Most of them facilitate selected response questions (multiple-choice, fill in the blank, True/False, matching). Others are browser-based, so can only offer a simplified word processor without the rich toolset candidates are accustomed to using. Finally, three of the four systems allow candidates to use sophisticated software tools beyond these two affordances, which makes possible the posing of creative questions requiring higher order thinking and complex constructed responses. However, the Abitti system only allows a screenshot from the software tool to be submitted, where the eExam system and SEE permit candidates to return digital artefacts and data files. Examples could include a formatted report containing charts and tables, an engineering schematic within a computer aided design (CAD) file, a spreadsheet file containing formulae or a working computer program written using Python.

These advanced affordances can lead to more authentic assessment that mirrors real world creative problem solving, within the constraints of a fair, time-bound examination. This rich pedagogical landscape offers a mechanism for eExams to influence curriculum transformation, but is in sharp contrast to the administrative convenience of other systems supporting restricted question types. Most of the interviewees saw little impact on curriculum, indicative of the long road ahead before this tension is resolved.

Finally, the penetration levels of the systems vary from less than 1% to 100% (by 2020). The explanation appears to be in the strategic thinking on the part of institutions and leadership within each national context. Where a strong direction to proceed with eExams at the national level has been set, a high level of penetration of eExams can be achieved over a small number of years. Otherwise, external threats from the environment (such as ‘contract cheating’) may be the only alternative impetus that can achieve transformational change in a similar timescale.

5 Discussion

Within this diversity was a lack of consistency in the relationship between schools and universities. Finland had strong but separate eExam systems in schools and universities. From a student perspective, a consistent approach to high-stakes assessment might be considered less stressful.

The findings show a movement to BYOD solutions, probably because these are economic for the institution, and scalable to a large number of students for cohort-wide examinations. Similarly, eExam implementations with higher penetration can be used at any location. All three of the externally booted solutions used a version of the Linux operating system, but there were diverse 'flavours'. These all supported the use of software tools, whereas the browser-based solution did not. The trend was towards open-source software may be associated with greater security confidence or local appetite towards fostering homegrown innovation rather than limiting adoption to 'off-the-self' solutions. The autosave period was a useful way of assessing the reliability of the systems but in many cases, this could be configured to taste and may also be linked to the risk appetite of system owners.

One of the most striking findings of this study was the diversity of approaches to eExams. We understand that such diversity can be expected from the outset of such an innovation, but as with telephones and computers, a convergence will emerge in the future. Beneficial characteristics will be adopted more widely, and designers will integrate these into their products.

Table provides some inspiration for successor systems which may be expected to prioritise the more favoured affordances discovered in this data. Within-exam software tool access may become more widely available, and autosave periods are likely to come down. International offerings of open-source material will need to be poly- or multi-lingual. A wider menu of question types can be expected, which also embrace data-file submissions from the creative use of in-assessment software tools.

6 Conclusion

Change can often be stressful. The initial investigation showed many concerns about the introduction of eExams (Table 1), and a diversity of technological approaches under development (Table 2). With so many diverse approaches to eExam system development, there appears to a need to facilitate greater collaboration amongst eExam system developments and users. This would foster the sharing of productive features and strategies to enhance security, reliability and assessment capabilities.

Missing from the data gathered were the views of laptop computer makers and assessment policy officials. Computer makers appear to be crucial to eExam system developers because their future roadmaps can permit or hinder particular technical approaches. For instance, the secure exam environment from Austria requires an Ethernet port on each candidate computer. However, recent equipment put on sale from Apple has only a single USB-C port. Windows 10 incorporates a secure boot feature, which makes it difficult for general users to follow a standard procedure to boot from an alternative operating system. Manufacturers are tending to ring-fence their software ecosystems, partially to protect financial interest, but also to improve equipment reliability for customers. Similarly further work is needed to assess the strategies used when implementing eExams. Providing contextual support and training for teachers and administrators may enable them to move beyond replication and augmentation towards better utilising the power of technology in educationally transformative ways.

Assessment policy officials are sponsoring trials of eExam systems in many institutions. The driving forces of eExam adoption are currently unclear or are masked by competing priorities. Many interviewees considered the administrative convenience of their eExam systems, as well as the technological affordances. The administrative benefits were digital reticulation of questions and answer scripts, and in many cases, the marker time saved by automatic assessment. Technological affordances were seen as potentially transformative of curricula, but there was scant evidence of this happening in practice. Further study of the impact of eExam adoption on assessment and curriculum design is urgently required.

Acknowledgments. The authors would like to thank the Australian Government Office of Learning and Teaching for financial support.

References

1. Wikipedia: eExam. The Free Encyclopedia (2017). https://en.wikipedia.org/w/index.php?title=EExam&oldid=761439215. Accessed 23 Dec 2016, 6 Feb 2017
2. Held, P.: Implementing e-learning and e-examination in European universities: factors of success. In: Proceedings of International Conference on the Future of Education, pp. 116–120. Simonelli Editore University Press, Florence (2011). http://conference.pixel-online.net/edu_future/common/download/Paper_pdf/ELE06-Held.pdf
3. Brekke, M.: Early testing of eExams in calculus at University level. In: Paper presented at NVU Conference 2012 Norway (2012). https://catalogue.pearsoned.co.uk/assets/hip/gb/uploads/Research%20Paper%20on%20MyMathLab%20by%20Morten%20Brekke%20-%20presented%20at%20NVU%20Conference%202012%20Norway.pdf
4. University of Jyväskylä: general guidelines for electronic exams: rector's decision of 13 January 2016 (to supplement section 40 of the degree regulations of the University of Jyväskylä) (2016). https://opiskelu.jyu.fi/en/instructions/topics/general-guidelines-for-electronic-exams
5. Hesketh, J.: eExam: code development in Launchpad (2010). https://launchpad.net/eexam
6. Adebayo, O., Abdulhamid, S.M.: E-exams system for Nigerian universities with emphasis on security and result integrity. Int. J. Comput. Internet Manag. **18**, 1–12 (2010)
7. Dermo, J.: E-assessment and the student learning experience: a survey of student perceptions of e-assessment. Br. J. Educ. Technol. **40**, 203–214 (2009)
8. Kuikka, M., Kitola, M., Laakso, M.-L.: Challenges when introducing electronic exam. Res. Learn. Technol. 22, 22817 (2014). http://dx.doi.org/10.3402/rlt.v22.22817
9. Bussières, J., Métras, M., Leclerc, G.: Use of Moodle, ExamSoft, and Twitter in a first-year pharmacy course. Am. J. Pharm. Educ. **76**(5), Article 94 (2012)
10. Donovan, D.: Wake forest law grad sues ExamSoft over bar exam debacle. North Carolina Lawyers Weekly, 18 Aug 2014
11. University of Innsbruck: Prüfungsraum (exam room). https://community.uibk.ac.at/web/ecampus/eexams/prufungssraum
12. Fluck, A., Hillier, M.: Innovative assessment with eExams. In: Australian Council for Computers in Education Conference, Brisbane, 29 September–2 October (2016)
13. Jamil, M., Tariq, R.H., Shami, P.A.: Computer-based vs paper-based examination: perceptions of university teachers. Turk. Online J. Educ. Technol. **11**(4), 371–381 (2012)

14. Snodgrass, S.J., Ashby, S.E., Rivett, D.A., Russell, T.: Implementation of an electronic objective structured clinical exam for assessing practical skills in preprofessional physiotherapy and occupational therapy programs: examiner and course coordinator perspectives. Australas. J. Educ. Technol. **30**, 152–166 (2014)
15. Hillier, M., Fluck, A.: Arguing again for e-Exams for high examinations. In: Proceedings of the 30th Australasian Society for Computers in Learning in Tertiary Education, 1–4 December. Macquarie University, Sydney, Australia (2013)
16. Puentedura, R.R.: SAMR: moving from enhancement to transformation (2013). http://www.hippasus.com/rrpweblog/archives/2013/05/29/SAMREnhancementToTransformation.pdf
17. Krathwohl, D.R.: A revision of Bloom's taxonomy: an overview. Theor. Pract. **41**(4), 212–218 (2002)
18. Dawson, P.: Five ways to hack and cheat with bring-your-own-device electronic examinations. Br. J. Educ. Technol. **47**, 592–600 (2016). https://doi.org/10.1111/bjet.12246
19. Hobbs, A.C.: Security through obscurity. Article in Wikipedia (1851). https://en.wikipedia.org/wiki/Security_through_obscurity
20. Sindre, G., Vegendla, A.: E-exams versus paper exams: a comparative analysis of cheating-related security threats and countermeasures. In: Presented at the Norwegian Information Security Conference (NISK) (2015). https://www.researchgate.net/publication/299498076
21. Smith, J., Osborn, M.: Interpretive phenomenological analysis. In: Smith, J.A. (ed.) Qualitative psychology (2nd edition): A practical guide to research methods, pp. 51–80. Sage, London (2008)
22. Hörnblad, P., Brenner, M.: Digital exam. SUNET Incubator project, NORDUnet (2016). https://portal.nordu.net/display/Inkubator/Digital+Tentamen

Computer Science Education and Its Future Focus and Development

Computer Science in the School Curriculum: Issues and Challenges

Mary Webb[1(✉)], Tim Bell[2], Niki Davis[2], Yaacov J. Katz[3], Nicholas Reynolds[4], Dianne P. Chambers[4], Maciej M. Sysło[5], Andrew Fluck[6], Margaret Cox[1], Charoula Angeli[7], Joyce Malyn-Smith[8], Joke Voogt[9], Jason Zagami[10], Peter Micheuz[11], Yousra Chtouki[12], and Nataša Mori[13]

[1] King's College London, London, UK
{mary.webb,mj.cox}@kcl.ac.uk
[2] University of Canterbury, Christchurch, New Zealand
{tim.bell,Niki.Davis}@canterbury.ac.nz
[3] Michlala - Jerusalem Academic College, Bar-Ilan University, Ramat Gan, Israel
yaacov.katz@biu.ac.il
[4] University of Melbourne, Melbourne, Australia
{nreyn,d.chambers}@unimelb.edu.au
[5] UMK Toruń, University of Wrocław, Wrocław, Poland
syslo@mat.umk.pl
[6] University of Tasmania, Hobart, Australia
andrew.fluck@utas.edu.au
[7] University of Cyprus, Nicosia, Cyprus
cangeli@ucy.ac.cy
[8] Education Development Center, Waltham, USA
jmsmith@edc.org
[9] University of Amsterdam, Amsterdam, Netherlands
J.M.Voogt@uva.nl
[10] Griffith University, Nathan, Australia
j.zagami@griffith.edu.au
[11] Alpen-Adria-University of Klagenfurt, Klagenfurt, Austria
peter.micheuz@aau.at
[12] Al Akhawayn University in Ifrane, Ifrane, Morocco
Y.Chtouki@aui.ma
[13] University of Ljubljana, Ljubljana, Slovenia
natasa.mori@fri.uni-lj.si

Abstract. This paper is based on analysis and discussion undertaken over several years by researchers, policymakers and practitioners from a range of countries which vary in their approaches to the curriculum for Computer Science. The discussions, undertaken predominantly within the International Federation of Information Processing (IFIP) and EDUsummIT communities were motivated by a need to examine the rationale, issues and challenges following some concerns across the globe about the position and nature of Computer Science in the school curriculum. We summarise our findings and focus specifically on challenges for the computer science education community in

A. Tatnall and M. Webb (Eds.): WCCE 2017, IFIP AICT 515, pp. 421–431, 2017.
https://doi.org/10.1007/978-3-319-74310-3_43

communicating, clarifying needs and promoting curriculum change in order to encourage Computer Science in the curriculum both theoretically and practically.

Keywords: Computer science · Curriculum rationale
International perspectives · Informatics

1 Introduction

This paper introduced the symposium: "From Curriculum Visions To Computer Science And Computational Thinking In The Curriculum In Practice" [1] at the World Conference on Computers in Education. The paper is based on an analysis and discussion of the rationale, issues and challenges for Computer Science in the school curriculum (K-12) that was initiated by the Curriculum Task Force of the International Federation of Information Processing[1] (IFIP) and continued at EDUsummIT 2015[2] as well as by IFIP meetings and conferences. We summarise and focus specifically on challenges for the computer science education community in communicating, clarifying needs and promoting curriculum change in order to encourage the realisation of the roles of Computer Science in the curriculum both theoretically and practically. The discussions have involved experts from many different countries and the analysis has focused in particular on a comparison across seven countries: Australia, Cyprus, Israel, New Zealand, Poland, UK and USA. The situation of the curriculum for Computer Science varies between these countries. In some, e.g. Cyprus, Poland and Israel, Computer Science has existed as a curriculum subject for many years. For others the curriculum for Computer Science has recently been substantially revised after a period of neglect followed by calls for reform [2–4]. Even in those countries where Computer Science in the curriculum has a long history, there are differences in approach and in the importance of various factors that affect curriculum design and implementation. Thus our discussion, based on this range of experiences led to a rich range of issues and considerations and a set of questions, some of which we were able to address and others remain as challenges.

When discussing the curriculum for Computer Science, the need to identify an acceptable working definition for Computer Science as a curriculum subject was a key consideration. Some popular definitions [5] are:

1. It seeks to answer the following questions: What is information? What is computation? How does computation expand what we know? How does computation limit what we can know? [6].

[1] IFIP is the leading multinational, apolitical organisation in Information and Communication Technologies and Sciences; IFIP was originally set up under the auspices of UNESCO and continues to have a formal consultative status within UNESCO.

[2] EDUsummIT is a global community of researchers, policy-makers and educators committed to supporting the effective integration of Information Technology (IT) in education by promoting active dissemination and use of research.

2. The study of computers and algorithmic processes, including their principles, their hardware and software designs, their implementation, and their impact on society [7].
3. The scientific and practical approach to computation and its applications and the systematic study of the feasibility, structure, expression, and mechanization of the methodical procedures (or algorithms) that underlie the acquisition, representation, processing, storage, communication of, and access to information (Wikipedia 2017).

In addition, definitions based on areas of knowledge can be found through widely adopted curricula, such as the ACM/IEEE Computer Science curriculum for undergraduates [8].

We favoured the Wikipedia definition as reflecting more recent consensus and current practice, so we will use that definition throughout this paper. The Wikipedia definition captures the key idea that the function of any physical computing device can be abstracted to applying algorithms to data, and hence this definition captures the key elements of the technical side of computing.

In our exploration of the definition of Computer Science as a curriculum subject we also recognised that the name given for the curriculum subject varies across different countries. For example, Informatics, as a curriculum subject, is slightly broader than Computer Science, but is the term used widely across Europe to refer to this discipline. The Joint Informatics Europe & ACM Europe Working Group on Informatics Education use the term Informatics to "cover the entire set of scientific concepts that make information technology possible" [2, p. 9]. We also recognise the importance of other aspects of computing and computer use such as digital literacy, which may be linked into a curriculum grounded in the academic discipline of Computer Science. In this paper we have focused only on the underlying scientific discipline in order to examine its importance and we have used the term Computer Science in order to restrict the definition.

In this paper we first summarise the challenges and solutions identified at EDUsummIT 2015. Then we explain: the rationales for incorporating Computer Science in the curriculum; arguments regarding the position of Computer Science in the curriculum; the nature of curriculum design and the specific major challenges for designing and implementing a Computer Science curriculum.

2 Key Challenges and Issues

Table 1 summarises the issues and solutions identified at EDUsummIT 2015 for advancing understanding of the roles of Computer Science in the curriculum. While the order of challenges shown in Table 1 represents a logical progression for considering curriculum rationale and design, the order of priority and difficulty will vary across contexts. Furthermore there are interrelationships between the issues identified in Table 1 as discussed in subsequent sections.

Table 1. Challenges and solutions for advancing understanding of the roles of computer science in the curriculum [adopted from 9, p. 64]

Challenge	Solution/recommendation to P, E, I, R
Key: Policy maker (P), Educator (E), Industry partners (I), Researcher (R)	
1. Lack of clear understanding (outside the field of Computer Science) of Computer Science as an academic discipline	(a) Adopt a globally agreed statement of Computer Science as a discipline in its own right (P, I, R, E) (b) Articulate the nature, importance and relevance of Computer Science to society and education (P, I, R & E)
2. A need for Computer Science as a distinct subject in school curricula is controversial and poorly understood	Disseminate and communicate a clear rationale to different stakeholders about the need to have Computer Science as a distinct subject in school curricula (P, I, R & E)
3. Computational thinking, a core component of Computer Science, is considered to be important in 21st century skills, but due to its complexity, it is difficult to implement in schools	Promote computational thinking through the means of a Computer Science curriculum, which aims at making computational thinking commonplace (P, R & E)
4. The development of Computer Science school curricula is impeded by insufficient empirical evidence of student learning to support content definition and sequencing	Design Computer Science curricula based on a content analysis, and continue to research students' learning difficulties as well as the effects of different pedagogical approaches. (E & R)
5. Previous ICT curricula deliveries poorly prepared students for Computer Science in further/higher education or professional employment	Facilitate better smart partnerships between education systems and industry/professional associations. (E & I)
6. Integrating Computer Science across other subjects in school curricula has been ineffective	Identify clear learning outcomes, assessments and standards for Computer Science. (E, I, P & R)
7. Teachers' professional development in a newly introduced Computer Science subject is a challenge in quality and quantity for many countries	(a) Encourage more Computer Science graduates to become teachers. (P, I & E) (b) Add Computer Science specialisation to pre-service training for primary teachers. (P & I) (c) Make Computer Science professional learning a requirement for periodic teacher re-accreditation/licensing. (P) (d) Schools need resources to free teachers to undertake the professional learning and preparation for a new Computer Science subject. (P)
8. Identifying and allocating the additional resources for teaching Computer Science is a challenge	(a) Some of Computer Science can be taught without computers. But computers can enhance the learning experience. (P, E, I & R) (b) Teacher training needs to provide skills in using the available resources in the most efficient way. (E) (c) Identify, and if not available, commission teaching support materials in mother-tongue language especially for younger students (P, E, I)

3 Rationales for Computer Science in the Curriculum

Arguments for the inclusion of Computer Science in the curriculum are compelling, as evidenced by many countries adopting it as a mandatory part of their curriculum. The reasons were summarised at EDUSummIT 2015 as economic, social and cultural [5, 9]. The economic rationale rests not only on the need for a country to produce computer scientists to sustain a competitive edge in a world driven by technology but also on the need for Computer Science-enabled professionals in all industries to support innovation and development. The social rationale emphasises the value in society of a diverse range of active creators and producers rather than just passive consumers of technology. Such capability provides people with power to lead, create and innovate within society. The cultural rationale rests on enabling people to be drivers of cultural change rather than having change imposed by technological developments. Alongside these three rationales, we frame the inclusion of Computer Science in school curricula with respect to two further dimensions for evaluating its contribution [5]:

1. the beneficial context: the individual learner; society; humanity and the ecology upon which we all depend; and the wider universe.
2. the timescale for the benefits of the learning to be experienced: immediately; the lifetime of the individual learner; years within transformation of a social system; the expected duration of humanity or the lifetime of the universe.

Furthermore we claim that Computer Science is necessary for education because of its increasing importance for knowledge generation in a range of important areas of human endeavour. Computer Science is heralding new developments in many areas of science and technology and data science in particular, which links machine learning with programming skills. Moreover it is providing new methods for knowledge discovery [see for example 10].

Immediate broad educational benefits for students in learning Computer Science include potential benefits for thinking and problem solving. There is a long history of research into the benefits of learning programming for developing general thinking and problem solving skills [see for example 11]. The issue remains controversial and the debate has been enlivened recently by the revised focus on computational thinking [12, 13] which we argued is best developed through Computer Science including programming since (1) programming makes an excellent vehicle for students to explore the concepts in a concrete way and (2) implementing the concepts in a program provides a means for students to check their thinking. As their expertise in computational thinking develops, students would be expected to use their skills and build their understanding of applications of computational thinking via a range of examples across different subjects.

In summary the arguments outlined here present a strong case for the importance of Computer Science in the curriculum for 21st-century learning. Its importance for individual learners, in particular, leads to our recommendation that learning Computer Science is an entitlement for all school students and recent curriculum development takes this approach [14].

4 The Position of Computer Science in the Curriculum

Following on from the clarification above of Computer Science as an academic discipline and therefore the basis for a curriculum subject for schools, is the debate about how the curriculum should be organised. In most countries, at least at secondary level, the curriculum is subject-based. The major arguments for positioning Computer Science as a distinct subject in the K-12 curriculum were articulated at EDUSummIT 2015 as: (1) its importance as a disciplinary area as explained above; (2) the evidence that integrated approaches to curriculum delivery have failed to prepare students for higher education and (3) the importance of computational thinking, which we argued is best developed through Computer Science, including programming, and then built upon in other curriculum areas. Computational thinking involves developing ways of analysing and solving problems, designing systems and understanding human behaviour that draws upon concepts fundamental to Computer Science. Furthermore, while computational thinking is beneficial in many curriculum areas, and doesn't require programming at all, representing a solution to a problem as a program provides a way of evaluating the solution thus providing students with feedback and ways to proceed. Therefore we argued that computational thinking should be implemented through Computer Science learning including programming.

The challenges created by the limited empirical evidence for development of understanding and skills in Computer Science relate to the structure and organisation of the curriculum together with pedagogical considerations. Curricula design may be guided by epistemological considerations and other constraints [15, 16] and later informed by empirical evidence. Therefore, in spite of the limited empirical evidence on which to base curricular design, many Computer Science curricula exist and many countries have recently re-designed Computer Science curricula. An analysis of developments in five countries as well as a review and content analysis of curriculum reports [14] suggested key issues to consider when designing Computer Science curricula. First there is a consensus across various curriculum reports [2, 3, 17] about the key concepts and techniques of the discipline. However there is as yet no consensus about the importance of more general intellectual practices such as persistence in working through problems and tolerance for ambiguity as well as the importance of collaborative learning and social competence developed through group work. Furthermore an emerging consensus regarding the best starting age for Computer Science being young, about five to seven years old, came from a comparison of curriculum development in three out of the five countries examined: Poland, UK, Australia. The importance of a young age for starting to learn Computer Science was also an outcome from the panel discussion at IFIP TC3 Conference in Vilnius, 2015 [14]. The availability of programming environments and other software designed to support younger learners in learning programming was identified as one of the key factors that have supported this early development of Computer Science learning [18]. Arguments for starting Computer Science at an early age include: (1) learning programming is difficult but a consensus is emerging that learning some of the techniques, approaches and thinking involved in programming at a younger age enables more students to become successful in programming and (2) developing student self-efficacy in programming and Computer Science at an earlier age may reduce the gender gap [14, 18].

There are arguments that Computer Science might be taught from pre-school age but there is also a need for caution and further research into pedagogical issues [19]. While it is possible for pre-schoolers to engage with pre-programming systems and concepts from Computer Science, the real foundational material that is needed in Computer Science in early years are already typical of curricula. Examples include basic numeracy and literacy skills, learning to classify and sort objects, understanding sequences of events, working with patterns in numbers and other symbols, becoming familiar with physical directions such as forward/left/right, and social competency to be able to follow and give instructions or identify the needs of another user.

5 Structuring the Curriculum

One of the constraints for curriculum design identified by Winch [15] is the need to introduce, early in the curriculum, all three major types of knowledge: concepts, propositions and know-how because these knowledge types are dependent on each other. One promising approach to addressing this constraint is a spiral curriculum, such as that developed in Poland [20] where at each level unified aims are addressed (see Table 2) but pedagogically the approach varies across three elements such that the first element is more important at lower levels and 2 and 3 become more important during progression:

1. problem situations, cooperative games, and puzzles that use concrete meaningful objects – discovering concepts
2. computational thinking about the objects and concepts – algorithms, solutions
3. programming

The concept of a spiral curriculum was put forward originally by Bruner [21] based on his cognitive theory in which in earlier stages of cognitive development manipulating real objects is important and later these may become more abstract representations. As the curriculum spirals upwards more complex concepts and approaches can be introduced. In line with Bruner's [21] proposals, benefits of such a spiral curriculum include: (1) reinforcement of key concepts and techniques each time the subject matter is revisited; (2) progression from simple concepts to more complex ones; (3) students can be encouraged to recap their previous knowledge and apply their knowledge to new problems and situation. This changing emphasis in a spiral curriculum can allow for a range of aspects of progression that are critical for Computer Science including: increasing difficulty of problems; enabling students to tackle more of the problem-solving process as they progress; consideration of the move from pictorial/block-based programming environments to text-based.

Table 2. Unified aims across all levels in computing curriculum in Poland [20]

Aim
1. Understanding and analysis of problems based on logical and abstract thinking, algorithmic thinking, and information representations
2. Programming and problem solving by using computers and other digital devices – designing algorithms and programs, organizing, searching and sharing information, using computer applications
3. Using computers, digital devices, and computer networks – principles of functioning of computers, digital devices, and computer networks, performing calculations and executing programs
4. Developing social competences – communication and cooperation, in particular in virtual environments, project based learning, taking various roles in group projects
5. Observing law and security principles and regulations – respecting privacy of personal information, intellectual property, data security, netiquette, and social norms, positive and negative impact of technology on culture, social life and security

6 Pedagogical and Assessment Challenges

While our discussion was focused on curriculum issues and it is beyond the scope of this paper to consider pedagogical and assessment challenges in depth, it is important that curriculum challenges are seen in the broader context of education. Specifically the curriculum is frequently depicted as in a triangular push-pull relationship with pedagogy and assessment in that both of these act as forces constraining or promoting curriculum change. Assessment was mentioned by many participants in the discussions as a constraint, particularly for more creative aspects of Computer Science that are typically harder to assess by traditional methods.

Implementing a curriculum focused on Computer Science was agreed to be particularly challenging in countries where the subject is being reintroduced and where there are not enough specialist-trained and experienced teachers and hence there is a lack of pedagogical expertise and a major professional development challenge. It is beyond the scope of this paper to discuss in depth the professional development needed to tackle these pedagogical challenges. Furthermore we acknowledge that factors leading to effective teacher professional development are difficult to identify and define and professional development is largely context dependent [see 22 for a review]. But in summary, our recommendations were to focus on teachers developing pedagogical content knowledge [23] which is much less well understood for Computer Science compared with other subject areas. Furthermore, we agreed on the importance of using technology resources to enhance or transform learning where appropriate and the importance of understanding the relationship between knowledge of technology use and pedagogical content knowledge [24]. An ongoing debate around the curriculum for Computer Science is the extent to which this curriculum must encompass enabling students to make good use of technologies. Learning Computer Science is not dependent on using the latest technologies and indeed the value of "unplugged activities" [25] for learning various difficult concepts in Computer Science is well recognised. Nevertheless good use of new technologies can transform learning and we believe that pedagogy for Computer Science should reflect appropriate use of technologies for achieving this transformation [24] and thus set an example for other curriculum areas.

The nature of Computer Science as both scientific and practical presents significant challenges for its implementation. The curriculum in Poland, for example, emphasises the importance of problem solving at all levels. In our discussions we achieved a consensus regarding the value of engaging students in tackling real-world problems in order to stimulate their intellectual curiosity and motivation [24]. However, we should not underestimate the challenges of implementing a curriculum that incorporates problem solving and computational thinking as key practical elements of Computer Science. Understanding of the importance of problem solving in the curriculum has had a long and difficult history [see for example Schoenfeld's reflections over many years 26]. Schoenfeld's work encompassed theory and practice of problem-solving generally but focused specifically on its implementation in Mathematics education, where problem-solving is recognised by many to be crucial. In spite of a strong focus on the importance of problem-solving, implementation in Mathematics curricula has been limited (ibid.) owing to: pedagogical challenges in teaching and managing open-ended problem-solving; difficulties assessing problem-solving skills especially in authentic contexts and identifying suitable problems for students to tackle.

7 Discussion and Conclusions

Key questions that emerged during our debate [4, 5] were:

1. What is the range of skills and understanding that should be developed in Computer Science?
2. Are such skills and understanding necessary for everyone? Should it be and remain compulsory?
3. At what age should Computer Science education commence?
4. How many computing languages or frameworks should a student be exposed to in the span of schooling from K-12?
5. How varied should these languages be? Should a variety of paradigms be explored?
6. How closely should the curriculum match computers available to schools and students?
7. What consideration in curriculum design should be given to emerging technologies such as quantum networks and optical computing?
8. What pedagogical approaches are likely to be appropriate, and how do they vary with age and other factors?

We have made some progress in answering Questions 1, 2, 3 and 8 but others remain to be examined. One of the strengths of the discussions that we have had to date are that they were not restricted to those engaged in Computer Science education but involved others who are committed to understanding the importance of digital technologies for learning but are more focused on digital literacy and the use of technologies for learning in other subjects. This has enabled us to gain greater insight into how Computer Science as a subject may be perceived and how we need to continue to make the case for Computer Science and consider its relationship to the rest of the curriculum. There remain, for example, many who regard Computer Science as a specialist subject that is accessible only to older or more capable students. Currently the curriculum in Israel exemplifies this approach. Furthermore, in the broader education community, the driver/mechanic analogy, a long-standing argument against Computer Science as a curriculum subject for all, is still often used. This argument suggests that cars are analogous to computers and that the majority of pupils need only to be able to use them rather than understand their working. In order to counter such arguments, we need to be aware of the rationales for Computer Science, as outlined in this paper, and to continue to research and develop pedagogical approaches and professional development that enables the promise of Computer Science as a curriculum subject to be realised.

References

1. Webb, M.E., Micheuz, P., Brinda, T., Overland, E., Malyn-Smith, J., Angeli, C., Kalas, I., Fluck, A., Syslo, M., Chtouki, Y.: From curriculum visions to computer science and computational thinking in the curriculum in practice. In: World Conference on Computers in Education (WCCE), Dublin, Ireland (2017)
2. Joint Informatics Europe and ACM Europe Working Group on Informatics Education: Informatics education: Europe cannot afford to miss the boat: Report of the joint Informatics Europe and ACM Europe Working Group on Informatics Education (2013)
3. The Royal Society: Shut down or restart? The way forward for computing in UK schools. The Royal Society (2012)
4. Wilson, C., Sudol, L.A., Stephenson, C., Stehlik, M.: Running on empty: the failure to teach K-12 computer science in the digital age. Association for Computing Machinery (ACM), Computer Science Teachers Association (CSTA) (2010)
5. Fluck, A., Webb, M.E., Cox, M., Angeli, C., Malyn-Smith, J., Voogt, J., Zagami, J.: Arguing for computer science in the school curriculum. Educ. Technol. Soc. **19**, 38–46 (2016)
6. Denning, P.J.: The profession of IT: computing is a natural science. Commun. ACM **50**, 13–18 (2007)
7. Computer Science Teachers Association (CSTA): CSTA K-12 Computer Science Standards (2017). https://www.csteachers.org/page/standards
8. Sahami, M., Roach, S., Cuadros-Vargas, E., LeBlanc, R.: ACM/IEEE-CS computer science curriculum 2013: reviewing the ironman report. In: Proceeding of the 44th ACM Technical Symposium on Computer Science Education, pp. 13–14. ACM, Denver (2013)
9. Webb, M.E., Fluck, A., Cox, M., Angeli-Valanides, C., Malyn-Smith, J., Voogt, J., Zagami, J.: Thematic working group 9: curriculum - advancing understanding of the roles of computer science/informatics in the curriculum. In: Lai, K.-W. (ed.) EDUsummIT 2015 Summary Report: Technology Advance Quality Learning for All, Bangkok, Thailand, pp. 60–69 (2015)
10. Adam-Bourdarios, C., Cowan, G., Germain, C., Guyon, I., Kegl, B., Rousseau, D.: The Higgs boson machine learning challenge. In: Proceedings of Machine Learning Research: Workshop on High-Energy Physics and Machine Learning and Conference Proceedings, vol. 42, pp. 19–55 (2015)

11. Salomon, G., Perkins, D.: Transfer of cognitive skills from programming: when and how? J. Educ. Comput. Res. **3**, 149–169 (1987)
12. Grover, S., Pea, R.: Computational thinking in K–12: a review of the state of the field. Educ. Res. **42**, 38–43 (2013)
13. Lye, S.Y., Koh, J.H.L.: Review on teaching and learning of computational thinking through programming: what is next for K-12? Comput. Hum. Behav. **41**, 51–61 (2014)
14. Webb, M.E., Davis, N., Bell, T., Katz, Y.J., Nicholas, R., Chambers, D.P., Sysło, M.M.: Computer science in K-12 school curricula of the 2lst century: why, what and when? Educ. Inf. Technol. **22**, 445–468 (2015)
15. Winch, C.: Curriculum design and epistemic ascent. J. Philos. Educ. **47**, 128–146 (2013)
16. Young, M.: Overcoming the crisis in curriculum theory: a knowledgebased approach. J. Curric. Stud. **45**, 101–118 (2013)
17. Seehorn, D., Carey, S., Fuschetto, B., Lee, I., Moix, D., O'Grady-Cunniff, D., Boucher Owens, B., Stephenson, C., Verno, A.: CSTA K–12 computer science standards. ACM/CSTA (2011)
18. Duncan, C., Bell, T., Tanimoto, S.: Should your 8-year-old learn coding? In: Proceedings of the 9th Workshop in Primary and Secondary Computing Education (WIPSCE 2015), pp. 60–69. ACM, New York (2015). https://doi.org/10.1145/2670757.2670774
19. Manches, A., Plowman, L.: Computing education in children's early years: a call for debate. Br. J. Educ. Technol. **48**, 191–201 (2017)
20. Sysło, M.M., Kwiatkowska, A.B.: Introducing a new computer science curriculum for all school levels in Poland. In: Brodnik, A., Vahrenhold, J. (eds.) ISSEP 2015. LNCS, vol. 9378, pp. 141–154. Springer, Cham (2015). https://doi.org/10.1007/978-3-319-25396-1_13
21. Bruner, J.S.: The Process of Education. Harvard University Press, Cambridge (1960)
22. Cordingley, P., Higgins, S., Greany, T., Buckler, N., Coles-Jordan, D., Crisp, B., Saunders, L., Coe, R.: Developing great teaching: lessons from the international reviews into effective professional development. Project Report, DU (2015)
23. Shulman, L.: Those who understand: knowledge growth in teaching. Educ. Res. **15**, 4–14 (1986)
24. Angeli, C., Voogt, J., Malyn-Smith, J., Webb, M.E., Fluck, A., Cox, M., Zagami, J.: A K-6 computational thinking curriculum framework: implications for teacher knowledge. Educ. Technol. Soc. **19**, 47–57 (2016)
25. Bell, T., Newton, H.: Unplugging computer science. In: Kadijevich, D.M., Angeli, C., Schulte, C. (eds.) Improving Computer Science Education, pp. 66–81. Routledge, New York, London (2013)
26. Schoenfeld, A.H.: Reflections on problem solving theory and practice. Math. Enthus. **10**, 9–34 (2013)

Basic Digital Education in Austria – One Step Further

Peter Micheuz(✉), Stefan Pasterk, and Andreas Bollin

Institute of Informatics Didactics, Alpen-Adria-University, Klagenfurt, Austria
{peter.micheuz, stefan.pasterk, andreas.bollin}@aau.at

Abstract. Based on a nearly thirty years long history to implement digital education in Austrian primary and lower secondary schools, this paper deals with the current development and strategies to encounter this challenge. After a literature review across national borders and some findings on different approaches in two different countries, a compressed historical view and exemplary empirical results from online-surveys describe the current Austrian situation. The paper closes with the outlines of the new curriculum "Basic Digital Education" and some remarks about it.

Keywords: Curriculum · Informatics · Digital literacy · Media literacy

1 Introduction

Up to now, digital education at primary and lower secondary level (grades 1–8) of Austrian schools is still to be seen as a patchwork lagging behind the requirements of a digital society in which all pupils should have equal access to "IT". About thirty years ago computers entered all secondary schools, with Informatics as an obligatory subject for upper secondary level. From the beginning on it was up to schools to offer ICT and Informatics education autonomously and non-obligatorily at lower grades.

In 2005, the situation was described like this [15].

- The digital gap between pupils at the end of lower secondary schools is unacceptably wide.
- Due to autonomy and inhomogeneous competences of teachers, the status of ICT/informatics differs extremely from school to school,
- Simplification and clarification of terminology in the context of ICT and Informatics are a matter of concern.
- There is a need for a reasonable framework which ensures also a certain level of digital literacy.
- Standardizing measures should be taken, so that pupils leaving lower secondary schools should have acquired a reasonable and clearly defined standard of digital and Informatics competence.

While the first two statements still hold true, resolving the other three requirements moves closer through promising top down actions by the Austrian Ministry of Education on a solid legal basis in form of a national curriculum. This year (2017) has the

A. Tatnall and M. Webb (Eds.): WCCE 2017, IFIP AICT 515, pp. 432–442, 2017.
https://doi.org/10.1007/978-3-319-74310-3_44

potential to go down in history as the year which marks the transition to accountability in form of a national curriculum for a new subject "Basic Digital Education", similar to the introduction of the new introduced subject Informatics in 1985 for all pupils in grade 9. Many single initiatives at local school level and grass root movements are about to get the long-awaited top-down support.

Currently, a draft curriculum for grades 5–8, building upon preliminary (inter)national work, has been devised. It will be piloted in 2017/18 within a recently constituted big Austrian network and a ministerial project of digitally advanced schools, called "eEducation" [16]. Provided that after a national election in autumn 2017 the political situation stays stable, the curriculum will be decreed by the Austrian Ministry of Education for all schools.

Every major project and political measure builds vertically on nationally and regionally grown structures and horizontally on comparable developments in other countries. After a short survey on international initiatives and a compressed look back into the short history of computers in Austrian schools, this paper closes with the presentation of the outlines of new curriculum and its constraints, followed by hinting at some challenges which lie ahead.

2 Looking Beyond National Borders

When looking beyond national borders, a lot of different models for education in digital and information technologies in elementary and secondary schools can be found. Following a report from the European Schoolnet [7] in 2015, several of the 21 participating European countries introduce digital technology related content in their national curriculum. In most cases, this content is part of curricula or educational standards for *Computer Science*, *Computing* or *Informatics* [7]. The Schoolnet report shows that the priorities for ICT skills concentrate on '*Digital Competence*' for 19 countries. Only 10 of the participating countries focus on '*Computing and Coding skills*' [7]. So, for most participating countries *Digital Competence* is a main goal to reach and can be understood as the 'confident, critical and creative use of ICT to achieve goals related to work, employability, learning, leisure, inclusion and/or participation in society' [9]. This definition was used in the DIGCOMP project to identify descriptors of digital competence in Europe [9], resulting in a framework that provides following five areas of digital competence:

1. Information: organize and analyze digital information
2. Communication: communicate and collaborate in digital environments
3. Content-Creation: create and edit new content including programs
4. Safety: safe use and protection of data
5. Problem-solving: identify digital needs and resources, make informed decisions on most appropriate digital tools according to the purpose or need, solve conceptual problems through digital means, creatively use technologies, solve technical problems, update own and other's competence [9].

After an update of this framework to DIGCOMP 2.0 in 2016, the first three areas were changed into *Information and data literacy* (instead of *Information*),

*Communication and collaboration (*instead of *Communication),* and *Digital content creation (*instead of *Content creation)* [10].

Besides this European framework, several countries introduced their own curriculum for digital education in primary and secondary schools, like, for example, England with the subject ‘Computing’ in 2014 [2]. Following Berry [5], the curriculum of the subject “Computing” [2] can be divided into the three aspects: *Computer Science (CS), Information Technology (IT),* and *Digital Literacy (DL).* Where the strand CS concentrates on ‘fundamental principles and concepts of computer science’ and first steps in programming, the strands IT and DL focus on the use (IT) and the ‘responsible, competent, confident and creative’ handling (DL) of information technology [5].

In Switzerland, the curriculum for primary and lower secondary education (called ‘Lehrplan 21’) was presented in 2014 and accepted by 21 of the 26 cantons. Each canton was able to adapt the original version of this curriculum [3]. It contains the subject ‘Medien und Informatik (Media and informatics)’ which starts in the first year of primary school. Where the media part focuses on the understanding and responsible use of media, in informatics the basic concepts of computer science and problem solving are included. Furthermore, the application competence should be fostered in the other subjects [3].

In a new curriculum for Informatics in Poland [11], presented in 2015, the subject is obligatory for primary and secondary education. The curriculum is a modification and extension of the former curriculum which also provided informatics on each education level. It includes unified aims defining following five knowledge areas, which are the same for each school level: *Understanding and analysis of problems*; *Programing and problem solving by using computers and other digital devices*; *Using computers, digital devices, and computer networks*; *Developing social competences*; and *Observing law and security principles and regulations* [11].

Looking at the USA, each state can have an own curriculum for computer science and ICT. As a proposal for teachers and curriculum developers, the CSTA (Computer Science Teachers Association) presented a model curriculum for K-12 computer science in 2003 [4], containing the use of technologies for learning, as well as topics like binary numbers, algorithms, and fundamental logic. In a next step the often-referenced K-12 Computer Science Standards of the CSTA [1] were developed. They are categorized into the five strands *Collaboration*; *Computational Thinking*; *Computing Practice and Programming*; *Computers and Communications Devices;* and *Community, Global, and Ethical Impacts*, which are very extensive and consider the use and the technical background of digital devices as well as programming skills. In 2016, these CS standards were revised, based on the in 2016 published K-12 Computer Science Framework [12,] and an interim version of new K-12 Computer Science Standards was published by the CSTA [8]. The framework includes seven core practices including computational thinking, which ‘describe the behaviors and ways of thinking that computationally literate students use to fully engage in today’s data-rich and interconnected world’ [12], and five core concepts, which ‘represent major content areas in the field of computer science’ [12]. The core practices are

1. Fostering and inclusive computing culture
2. Collaborating around computing

3. Recognizing and defining computational problems
4. Developing and using abstractions
5. Creating computational artifacts
6. Testing and refining computational artifacts
7. Communicating about computing.

In addition, the core concepts of the framework are Computing Systems; Networks and the Internet; Data and Analysis; Algorithms and Programming; and Impacts of Computing [12].

The Australian curriculum [6], introduced in 2015, includes two subjects *Design and Technologies* and *Digital Technologies* from primary to secondary education. *Design and Technologies* focuses on the impact of technologies on society and related design topics, whereas *Digital Technologies* covers the background and the use of information technology. Both subjects are divided into the two blocks *Knowledge and understanding* and *Processes and production skills*. In *Digital Technologies* the content areas *Digital systems* and *Representation of data* are part of the *Knowledge and understanding* block. The *Processes and production skills* block includes *Collecting, managing and analyzing data* and *Creating digital solutions by investigating and defining, generating and designing, producing and implementing, evaluating,* and *collaborating and managing* [6].

It seems that the structure and content of the curricula are well defined, but there is still room for improvement. During an ongoing project to analyze the quality of curricula [13] together with seven experts with didactical background, one is able to identify weakness in both, structure and content. Figure 1 visualizes the differences of the curricula from Switzerland (a) and Australia (b) by mapping their core competences and their relations for the first six school levels to a graph database and expressing the priorities for digital literacy or computer science topics. As the dark nodes represent skills concerning digital literacy, and the light nodes correspond to computer science skills, it can be seen, that the curriculum in Switzerland (a) focuses on digital literacy. Following the majority of the experts, eleven of the overall 44 skills can be matched to computer science.

Fig. 1. Curriculum from Switzerland (a) and Australia (b) represented as a graph

For comparison, the results from the Australian curriculum, as shown in Fig. 1(b), look a bit different. From overall 22 skills also eleven were matched to 'computer science'. This indicates a better balanced distribution of the topics, but with the provision that the decisions from the experts were not that clear, with one third of the matches being very close.

3 A Very Short History of Digital Education in Austria

This recent project and legal measure to implement a new curriculum for Basic Digital Education has a well-documented prehistory. After the very roots and single initiatives from 1970 on, the nationwide introduction of computers in schools at lower secondary level started from the period 1985–1990 on. This time can be denoted as an experimental one, with many computer pioneers among (programming) teachers. The last decade in the 20th century was characterized by networked computers, the beginning of the GUI era (1990–1995) followed by autonomy, the kickoff of the internet era (1995–2000), and the rise of application software at the expense of programming in Informatics lessons. During the first decade from 2000 to 2010, the term eLearning, accompanied practically by many (pilot) projects and (inter)national networks, emerged. At this time, educational standards have been introduced.

Due to the lack of a national curricula at primary and lower secondary level, ICT and Informatics developed very inhomogeneously throughout the country. This decline of digital education at this time was reinforced by a nationwide reduction of lessons in 2003 which made it almost impossible to implement ICT/Informatics lessons at the expense of other subjects.

A new era began with the development of the competence model 2011 [14] as depicted in Table 1. For the first time a holistic view on basic informatics education in Austria has been devised, leading to engagements of task forces which produced teaching and learning material as open educational resources [18]. The projects Digikomp4 for primary and Digikomp8 for lower secondary education can be seen as the building block of the new curriculum for Basic Digital Education (Digitale Grundbildung). The problem with every conceptual framework and even the offer of corresponding free teaching materials is its non-legally binding nature. Having never been evaluated nationally, the initiative Digikomp8 could not fulfill the requirements of executed educational standards and an attained curriculum for the majority of pupils.

Digikomp4 for primary level (grades 1–4), building on the same reference model as Digikomp8 (with 71 competences), but with less and age-appropriate 49 competences, has been published a little bit later [19]. Due to the special situation in primary schools (lack of particularly educated teachers and no legal anchoring in the curriculum) it has reached only a little selection of primary schools and pupils.

Table 1. Competence matrix for basic informatics education for Austria's primary and lower secondary level (K4/K8, 7–14 years)

		Competence levels		
		Basic	Extended	Special
Media reflexion related topics	1. Information technology, human and society			
	1.1. Impact of IT in Society			
	1.2. Responsibility in Using IT			
	1.3. Privacy and Data Security			
	1.4. Developments and Vocational Perspectives			
Digital media knowledge	2. Informatics systems			
	2.1. Technical Components and their Use			
	2.2. Design and Use of Personal Information Systems			
	2.3. Data Exchange in Networks			
	2.4. Human-Machine Interface			
Use and production of digital media	3. Software applications			
	3.1. Documentation, Publication and Presentation			
	3.2. Calculation and Visualization			
	3.3. Search, Selection and Organisation of Information			
	3.4. Communication and Cooperation			
Principles and computational thinking	4. Informatics concepts			
	4.1. Representation of Information			
	4.2. Structuring of Data			
	4.3. Automatization of Instructions			
	4.4. Coordination and Controlling of Processes			

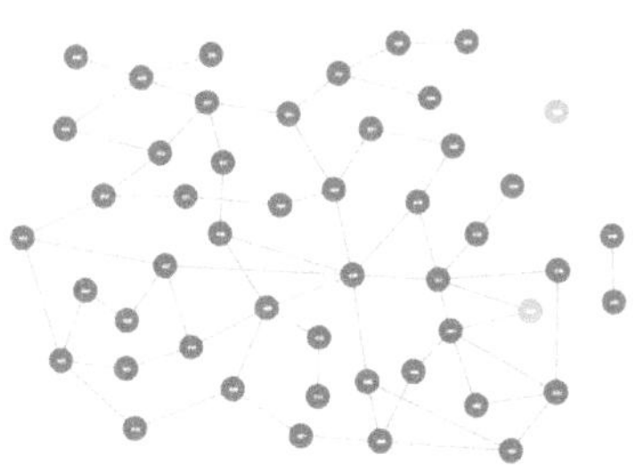

Fig. 2. Digikomp4 competency model represented as a graph

Figure 2 represents the competences and their relations in a graph, as it was done in the previous section with the curricula from Switzerland and Australia (Fig. 1). There was a 90% agreement from the experts that only two competences matched with computer science. Contrary to the proportion of computer science in the curricula of Australia and the geographically neighboring Switzerland, the Austrian competences at primary level are application oriented.

4 Some Findings from a Nationwide Empirical Research

Two nationwide online-surveys in form of online-questionnaires among teachers and teacher trainers, involved in digital education, have been conducted with an interval of one year at the end of 2015 and 2016. They mainly consisted of rating questions asking the survey respondents for their personal opinions to compare different items using a common scale. The response to the first survey 2015 was very good (424), whereas the response to the second one at the end of 2016 (127) can be regarded as satisfying. One reason for this significant decline in the response number is due to the fact that it aimed at expert teachers with a broader national overview and insight regarding the national digital sociotope.

The very first request in the survey 2015 was "Please rate the overall situation of Digital Education in Austria on a rating scale of 1–10, where 1 is 'very good' and 10 is 'very bad').

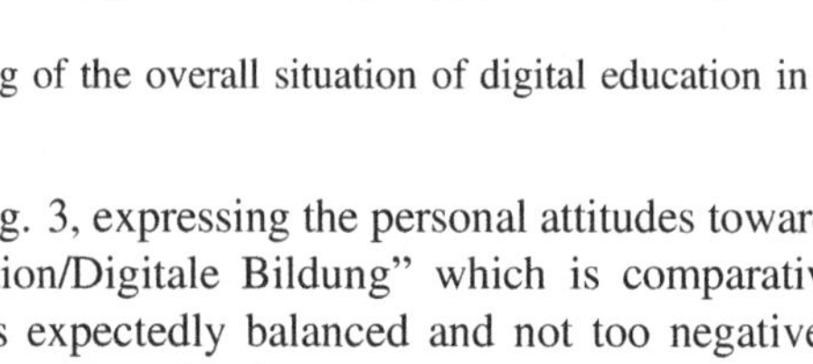

Fig. 3. Rating of the overall situation of digital education in Austria 2015

The diagram in Fig. 3, expressing the personal attitudes towards the comprehensive term "Digital Education/Digitale Bildung" which is comparatively new in German speaking countries, is expectedly balanced and not too negative, but with a striking local maximum at the scale value 8.

The figures in Table 2. are speaking for themselves. There is no doubt among expert teachers that Informatics contents should have its place in primary education. Though, further investigations are necessary about the perception of the role of Informatics within Digital Education. As Fig. 2 and Digikomp4 indicate, it can be assumed that for most Austrian teachers Informatics is mainly application driven.

Another object of further research is the impact of the ECDL, respectively its syllabus, in those schools where this certificate is offered. Since 2000, the ECDL plays a substantial and successful [17] role at lower secondary level. An overwhelming

Table 2. Cumulated exemplary results from the survey 2015

Primary Education	yes	rather yes	rather no	no	n.a.
Informatics content should be taught mandatorily.	102	106	69	39	25
Application competences should be mandatory.	126	107	59	31	21
Lower Secondary Education	yes	rather yes	rather no	no	n.a.
I know the project Digikomp8.	204	62	22	84	25
Its requirement can be taught without an interdependent subject.	50	79	103	62	92
An minimal standard should be obligatory.	258	104	11	4	20
A subject Digital Education in its own right is necessary.	222	90	37	28	20
Content issues at Lower Secondary Level	yes	rather yes	rather no	no	n.a.
Should all pupils learn typewriting?	225	99	46	22	6
The ECDL is gaining importance.	93	133	104	64	4
I could imagine an Austrian version "ECDL light".	134	112	58	82	11
Basics of programming should be taught obligatorily.	72	115	127	76	6
Maker-Movement (Physical Computing, Robotics, ..) for all?	54	110	146	63	22
Computational Thinking (Biber, ...) for all?	110	160	73	26	26
Suggested hours of weekly lessons of (Basic) Digital Education	zero	one	two	n.a.	
Grade 5	26	211	113	26	
Grade 6	22	208	119	25	
Grade 7	17	158	181	22	
Grade 8	16	150	185	23	

majority claims an independent subject (Basic) Digital Education. This implies that there is little confidence among the respondents that the demanding objectives of Digikomp8 can be reached solely by an integrative approach. Apparently a surprise is the mixed attitude towards programming. This can be explained by the low confidence of teachers and by the disappearing programming activities at lower secondary level since the 90-ties.

First findings from the recent survey in December 2016, with 127 respondents and a presumably less representativeness of the sample, are outlined here (Fig. 4).

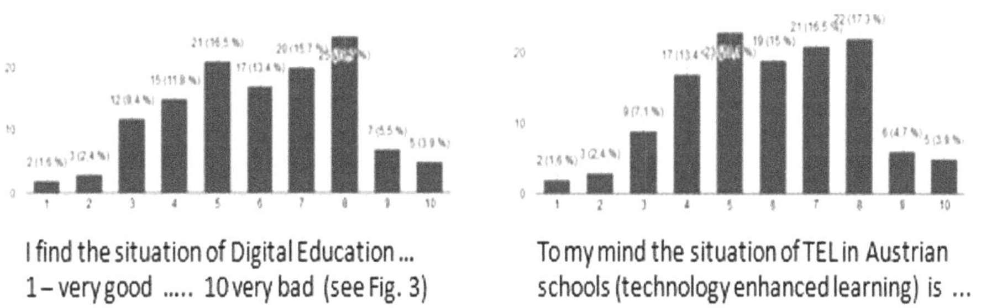

Fig. 4. Rating of the overall situation of digital education in Austria 2016 compared to the situation of digital technology in education (n = 127)

Compared to the rating of 2015, the survey in 2016 yields a slight shift to a more negative attitude, coincidentally with a peak also at the scale value 8 (rather bad).

The similarity of both diagrams is noticeable. It might be coincidental, but the presumption that even many Austrian expert teachers still struggle with the distinction between the new term Digital Education and digitally supported and augmented learning (TEL) (Fig. 5).

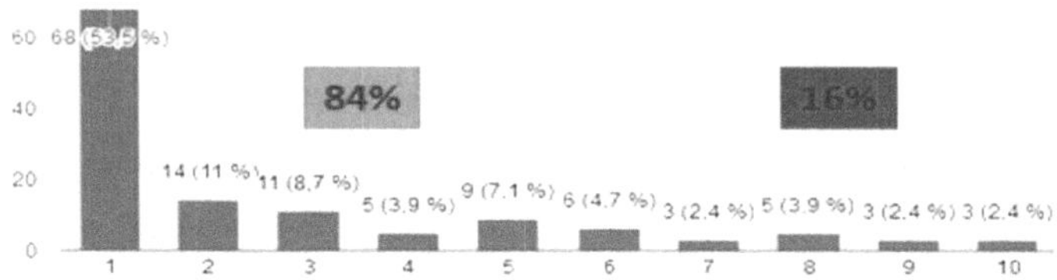

Fig. 5. Overwhelming claim for an independent subject

What is clearly evident resulting from both surveys, is the claim of a vast majority for a subject (Basic) Digital Education, in German: "Digitale Grundbildung". "Basic" bracketed means that the denotation of the new subject was still a secret when the survey has been conducted.

5 Towards a National Curriculum

As indicated above, "Basic Digital Education" is the new term for a new subject with a broad curriculum. But it remains, as all the years before, an option and it is still up to the schools to implement it in an independent specific school subject. If this is not possible due to organizational or personal reasons, the integrative approach within other existing subjects is recommended, in contrast to the opinions of a vast majority of experts.

In case of an independent subject, the amount of weekly hours will be between two and four within 120 mandatory weekly hours in four years of lower secondary education. Moreover, the subject has to be conducted as a mandatory exercise without grading. Schools can also offer mixed forms of mandatory and additional optional lessons. What is certain till now: There will be one curriculum for all four years of lower secondary education, encompassing eight main topics:

- Social Aspects of Media Change and Digitization
- Information-, Data- and Media Competence
- Operating Systems and Standard Applications
- Media Design
- Digital Communication and Social Media
- Security
- Technical Problem Solving
- Computational Thinking.

Obviously these topics stand for a very broad, but seen from particular viewpoints, not necessarily balanced curriculum. Therefore it is foreseeable that this wide spectrum, starting with a clear focus on media pedagogy and digital literacy, and ending up with Informatics in the disguise of Computational Thinking, will lead to controversial, but nonetheless fruitful, discussions among teachers and experts. Besides the content areas and its requirements expressed in detailed operationalised competences [20], there will be expectedly and hopefully also discussions about the accompanying legal conditions and constraints.

6 Concluding Remarks

In order to assure that all pupils will be demonstrably affected by the curriculum and its intended competences at the end of lower secondary education, there will be a quality assurance measure in form of an assessment, currently denoted as Digicheck8, representing quasi educational standards for the integrative or independent subject "Basic Digital Education".

It can be pointed out that the future national curriculum for this subject and the statutorily supported and intended change from too much arbitrariness to consolidation and accountability is basically desirable. With the measures indicated above, a first abstract and conceptual step in Austria is done, but the big challenges for a successful and concrete implementation lie ahead.

These challenges will consist of (still) conceptual, institutional, organizational and personal nature at many levels. In the view of digitally affine experts, this top down initiative was overdue and long-awaited. But nobody knows how the last but most important chain link, the schools, will react and cope with this new situation.

"That is the curse of our noble house: Striving hesitatingly on half ways to half action with half means. Yes or no, here is no middle road". This is a quote from the stage play "A Fratricidal Struggle in the House of Habsburgers", written by the well-known national Austrian poet Grillparzer who lived in the 19th century. Hopefully, this curse will be broken in the near future.

References

1. Seehorn, D., Carey, S., Fuschetto, B., Lee, I., Moix, D., O'Grady-Cunniff, D., Boucher Owens, B., Stephenson, C., Verno, A.: CSTA K–12 Computer Science Standards: Revised 2011. Technical report. ACM, New York, NY, USA (2011)
2. Curriculum England. https://www.gov.uk/government/publications/national-curriculum-in-england-computing-programmes-of-study/national-curriculum-in-england-computing-programmes-of-study#contents. Accessed 15 Feb 2017
3. Schweizer Lehrplan. http://www.lehrplan21.ch. Accessed 15 Feb 2017
4. Tucker, A.: A model curriculum for k–12 computer science: final report of the ACM K–12 task force curriculum committee. Technical report, New York, NY, USA (2003)
5. Berry, M.: Computing in the national curriculum – a guide for primary teachers. Computing at School (2013)
6. Australian Curriculum. http://www.australiancurriculum.edu.au/technologies/introduction

7. Balanskat, A., Engelhardt, K.: Computing our future. Computer programming and coding: priorities, school curricula and initiatives across Europe (2015). http://fcl.eun.org/documents/10180/14689/Computing+our+futurefinal.pdf/746e36b1-e1a6-4bf1-8105-ea27c0d2bbe0. Accessed 15 Feb 2017
8. CSTA. http://www.csteachers.org/?page=CSTA_Standards. Accessed 15 Feb 2017
9. Ferrari, A.: DIGCOMP: a framework for developing and understanding digital competence in Europe. Joint Res. Cent. Eur. Comm. (2013)
10. Vuorikari, R., Punie, Y., Gomez, S.C., Van den Brande, G.: DigComp 2.0: the digital competence framework for citizens. Update Phase 1: The Conceptual Reference Model. Luxembourg Publication Office of the European Union (2016)
11. Sysło, M.M., Kwiatkowska, A.B.: Introducing a new computer science curriculum for all school levels in Poland. In: Brodnik, A., Vahrenhold, J. (eds.) ISSEP 2015. LNCS, vol. 9378, pp. 141–154. Springer, Cham (2015). https://doi.org/10.1007/978-3-319-25396-1_13
12. K–12 computer science framework (2016). http://www.k12cs.org
13. University Klagenfurt. http://iid.aau.at/bin/view/Main/Projects. Accessed 15 Feb 2017
14. Micheuz, P.: A competence-oriented approach to basic informatics education in Austria. In: Kalaš, I., Mittermeir, R.T. (eds.) ISSEP 2011. LNCS, vol. 7013, pp. 43–55. Springer, Heidelberg (2011). https://doi.org/10.1007/978-3-642-24722-4_5
15. Micheuz, P.: The role of ICT and informatics in Austria's secondary academic schools. In: Mittermeir, R.T. (ed.) ISSEP 2005. LNCS, vol. 3422, pp. 166–177. Springer, Heidelberg (2005). https://doi.org/10.1007/978-3-540-31958-0_19
16. eEducation Project. http://www.eeducation.at. Accessed 15 Feb 2017
17. Karner, E., Prumetz, C.: 15 Jahre ECDL an Schulen in Österreich. In: Digitale Schule Österreich. OCG Schriftenreihe Wien (2013)
18. Narosy, T.: Kein kind ohne digitale Kompetenzen. In: Digitale Schule Österreich. OCG Schriftenreihe, Wien (2013)
19. Mulley, U., Zuliani, B.: Digitales Kompetenzmodell für die Volksschule. In: Digitale Schule Österreich. OCG Schriftenreihe, Wien (2013)
20. Curriculum. http://www.digitale-bildung.at/sekundarstufe-i. Accessed 15 Feb 2017

Experiential Learning: Beyond the Classroom and Connecting with the Industry

Waqar Haque(✉)

University of Northern British Columbia, Prince George, Canada
waqar.haque@unbc.ca

Abstract. To address dynamic needs of the industry, student learning must extend beyond the classroom. Considering the packed nature of traditional curriculum and logistics, incorporating new courses is challenging. A model is presented where the desired learning is acquired by engaging students in research partnerships, and without unduly extending the duration of their degree program. The success of this model has been demonstrated over many years by deployment of a variety of solutions for a diverse group of stakeholders, and an ever-growing demand for expansion. A few selected projects are presented in this paper to illustrate the skills acquired by students which include training in state-of-the-art technologies, creative thinking, research publications, and prospects for immediate hiring upon graduation. The benefits to faculty and industrial partners are also highlighted. Finally, the paper presents the challenges encountered which range from space, turnovers, transitioning, data access and perception of shadow IT. The ideas presented are applicable to all emerging areas.

Keywords: Experiential learning · Emerging ICT areas · Analytics Business intelligence

1 Introduction

The rapidly changing needs of the industry and desire to recruit students trained in state-of-the-art technologies raises pedagogical challenges for the academia. At the same time, students face recruitment challenges upon graduation when they discover that the conventional training during their academic pursuits does not align with industry needs. It is difficult to incorporate the dynamic emerging areas of computer science (CS) in the curriculum. The reasons are twofold: first, the CS curriculum is packed with traditional courses leaving very little room for electives; second, the field is moving too fast and the demands change too rapidly to be fulfilled through coursework. The process of introducing new courses requires several layers of approval and is not conducive to the changing needs of the industry. Some examples of the desirable areas of training are Business Intelligence (BI), advanced analytics, cloud computing, Internet of Things (IoT) and Business Process Management (BPM). Both BI and BPM focus on increasing business value through analysis and optimization.

A. Tatnall and M. Webb (Eds.): WCCE 2017, IFIP AICT 515, pp. 443–452, 2017.
https://doi.org/10.1007/978-3-319-74310-3_45

We have solved this problem by engaging community and industrial partners in collaborative projects which not only serve as proofs of concept, but have been successfully deployed in production mode. The projects provided pedagogical and financial benefits to the students, led to dissemination of results to research community, and opened avenues to increase business value within partner organizations. Some of the key challenges in undertaking these projects include availability of space, access to data, student turnover and resistance from the IT departments. In some healthcare related projects, privacy and confidentiality of data is also a key constraint and requires signing of non-disclosure agreements. In contrast, data for service-oriented projects is normally already in the public domain and does not require such clearances.

In this paper, we present some selected projects covering broad arenas including internal institutional tasks, conventional sectors such as healthcare, and non-conventional areas such as agriculture. The focus of these projects is on analytics, with or without the use of multi-dimensional Online Analytical Processing (OLAP) cubes. However, the ideas presented can be extended to other emerging areas as well.

2 Related Work

In rapidly evolving fields such as computer science, the academic institutions generally lag behind the industry needs. Many organizations therefore engage in in-house R&D and end up developing *de facto* standards in a race for the lead. A skill requirements review in the general field of information systems revealed that the "rapidly changing field requires the professional to continuously change as well" [1]. Analytics has become an increasingly strategic tool for companies to enhance their business value. A framework for integrated instruction of analytics, decision support and business intelligence using real cases with real data provides an opportunity for students to acquire the BI skills needed by companies [2]. The situation of ICT industry in EU and lack of ICT specialists trained in the required competences is presented in [3]. The authors clearly articulate a case for reengineering of the existing CS curriculum. A model curriculum has also been proposed to incorporate the emerging areas of business intelligence and business analytics [4]. This curriculum encompasses a hybrid academic domain of disciplines including statistics, management science, computer science and business information systems.

Academic institutions have tried to respond to industry needs in somewhat unstructured ways. Some have created new streams and programs whereas others have selectively integrated some areas into existing curriculum. These include BI, advanced analytics and automated business process management. Institutions have also resorted to offering certificates and diplomas through their Continuing Studies extensions. A comprehensive survey of Canadian and US schools is presented in [5].

3 Opportunities

The opportunities for students are broad, both within and outside of the academic institution. The limiting factor is generally space and time. The success of our approach has been demonstrated over a period spanning more than fifteen years. In this section, we present a few representative projects which have been successfully completed and deployed. The training provided through these projects span the general area of Business Intelligence (BI) including advanced analytics (Fig. 1). The students not only learn how to design interfaces, but also engage in fairly sophisticated backend design which includes integration, analysis through multi-dimensional queries, and reporting on a variety of metrics. In addition, they have used extensions such as ASP.NET wrappers for rendering reports, and developing cross-platform capabilities. Finally, understanding the process of requirements analysis and benefits of agile development comes as a very desirable aspect of training.

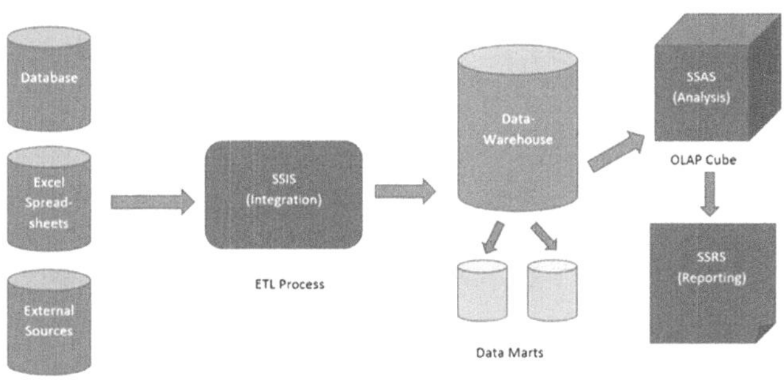

Fig. 1. BI modeling overview [6]

3.1 Industrial Collaborative Research Projects

A variety of industrial partners have been engaged ranging from silviculture and bioenergy to healthcare thus representing diverse requirements leading to evolution of creative techniques to deliver the unique objectives. The environment has also served as a platform for both students and potential employers to evaluate each other, resulting in recruitment prior to, or within days of, graduation.

A couple of representative projects completed using public domain data are related to health services delivery and availability of critical care services in geographically sparse areas. Healthcare organizations gather large volumes of data which is traditionally stored in legacy formats making it difficult to analyze or use effectively. The quality of this data is generally poor as it suffers from inconsistencies and lacks integrity. By applying BI techniques, we have been able to derive significant value from this data and made it available to broader audience through comprehensible and user-friendly interfaces (Fig. 2). The process started with developing an integration process to cleanse and import data from disparate sources into a data warehouse. A 12-dimensional OLAP cube was then built to allow slicing along multiple dimensions determined by various key performance indicators (KPIs) representing population and patient profiles, case mix groups and healthy community indicators. In addition to an extensive suite of standardized reports, capabilities for ad hoc reporting on facility comparison and availability of various service levels was also provided. This data visualization and ability to slice-and-dice data to desired granularity provided the key benefits: the ability to make informed decisions for optimal resource allocation, and enhanced patient care. The use of mapping tools, customized shape files and embedded objects further augmented the navigation (Fig. 3). Finally, web forms provide a mechanism for remote uploading of data and transparent processing of the cube in real-time. Access controls were implemented where necessary. The modular design left hooks for expansion without the need to rebuild the entire system.

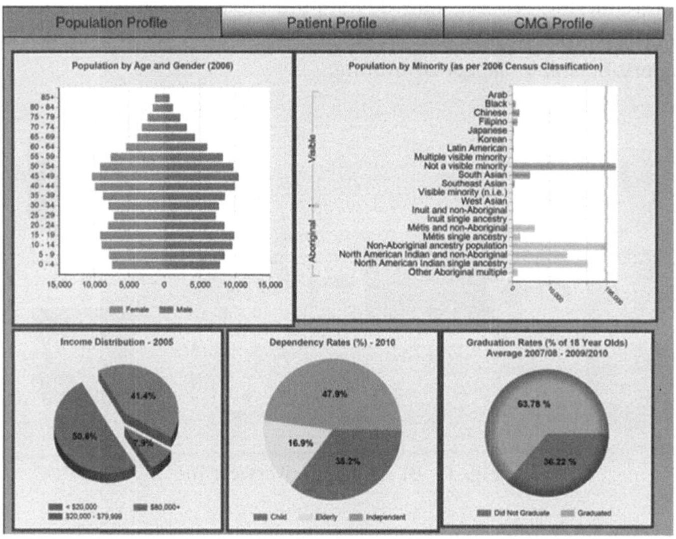

Fig. 2. Services main dashboard: population profile [10]

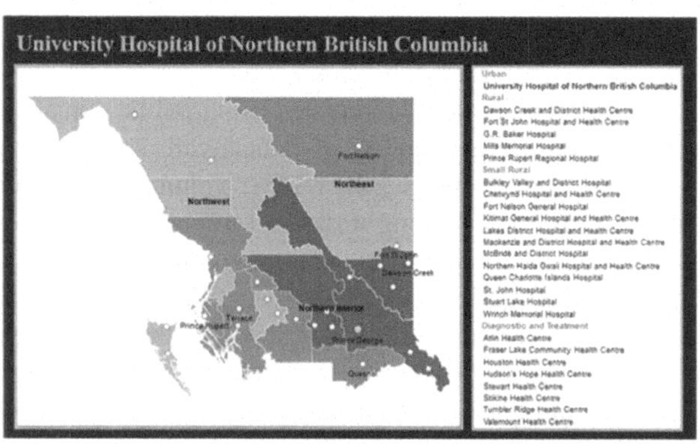

Fig. 3. Navigation map interface [7]

In many cases, patients suffer from medical conditions that can often be treated outside of a hospital setting. These conditions are commonly known as Ambulatory Care Sensitive Conditions (ACSC). The preventable hospitalizations can result in reduced healthcare costs and improved patient care. A BI model was developed to provide analytics based on highly customizable scenarios of population and medical records. The parameterized reports allowed selection of multiple dimensions simultaneously and were rendered in a matter of seconds. Figure 4 shows the main page from which intuitive navigation leads to other reports. This work was later extended to involve advanced analytics where predictive models were built to forecast 3–5 years in the future. Such information is very useful for reallocation of resources, if deemed necessary.

Often patients are transferred within facilities for several reasons. In such cases, the transfer operator must be able to objectively identify a destination which meets the

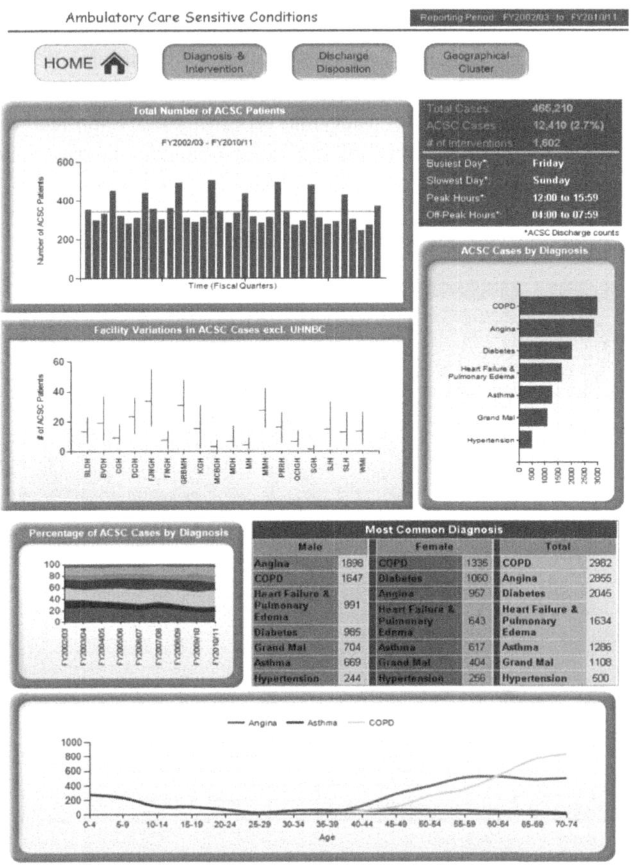

Fig. 4. ACSC - diagnosis grouping [8]

needs of a patient, within the constraints of facility's limitations. In order to facilitate an optimized and efficient patient transfer, a visual interface accessing a single data warehouse and using BI techniques was designed. The interface included map based navigation of the health authority as well as an interactive filtering mechanism to determine facilities meeting the selected criteria. These facilities are then presented to the user sorted by distance, time and available transportation modes (ground, air, water). The data visualization is backed by an intuitive data entry web form which safely constrains the data while ensuring consistency. The overall time required to identify the optimal destination for inter-facility transfers is reduced from hours to a few minutes with this interactive solution [7]. The solution is currently being expanded to include all health authorities in the province.

To demonstrate the use of business intelligence and analytics in non-conventional areas, we developed a model using data that was collected over a number of years for tracking plantation and monitoring stand development. The data existed as legacy reports in the form of simple tables, line charts and scatter graphs which did not provide any strategic or intuitive insights. Since the data was never collected for the purpose of analytics, it presented the typical challenges including inconsistencies, missing data, and incompatible formats. OLAP techniques were once again used to transform this data into an interactive dashboard for querying, reporting and visualization (Fig. 5) [9]. The proposed model has been used to link regenerated stands under various operational conditions with realistic long-term growth and yield predictions.

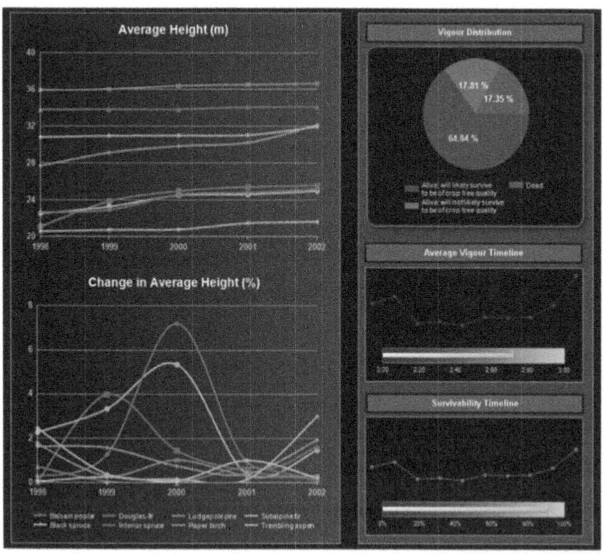

Fig. 5. Sample dashboard for vegetation management [9]

3.2 Internal Projects

The IT departments within academic institutions are overwhelmed with help desk and support activities. They rarely engage in state-of-the-art initiatives though the need for such projects is widespread. There are separate teams formed for institutional reporting using primitive methods such as spreadsheets and basic charts. This does not provide analytics for strategic objectives. This void can be covered by taking on proof of concept projects under the supervision of research faculty. Several projects have been completed over the last few years which resulted in direct training of a large number of undergraduate and graduate students. These projects have been in areas including enrolment management, workload assignments, tracking student progress, asset management, and automating complex tasks together with reporting.

Placements for nursing practicums has been a challenging task because of the frequency, volume and number of facilities spanning vast geographical areas. The existing practice involved extensive use of spreadsheets, whiteboards and phone calls. BI techniques were used to design a sophisticated dashboard (Fig. 6) which not only solved the placement problem, but also provided extensive reporting capabilities. In addition, a number of embedded controls were included to reduce errors such as oversubscribing and duplications. The system also auto-generated notifications for both students and coordinators. A suite of interactive web forms allows data to be entered by students (preferences), coordinators and managers. Historical data is also accessible for comparison purposes.

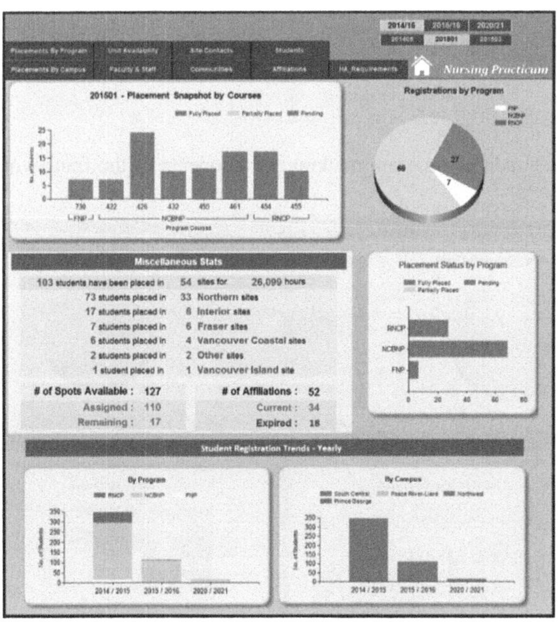

Fig. 6. Nursing placement – main dashboard [10]

While OLAP cubes are commonly used to deliver business intelligence, this may be an overkill in situations which do not require multi-layered drill downs, but still need multi-dimensional analysis and reporting. This was demonstrated through several projects where a combination of web interfaces and business intelligence tools were used while bypassing OLAP cubes. One of these applications was an interface to track progress of graduate students through their programs. The key components of such a system are shown in Fig. 7 whereas a snapshot of the top-level dashboard is shown in Fig. 8. This interface allows efficient rendering of reports from a business intelligence tool stack, in combination with web forms for data integration. The elimination of the middle layer resulted in significant performance enhancement, rapid application development, and created stable, user-friendly, low-maintenance platform which requires minimal operational support from the IT department.

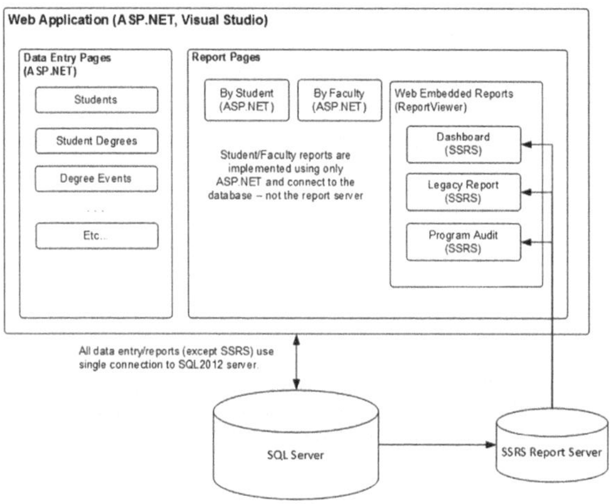

Fig. 7. Graduate program tracking: components of the framework [11]

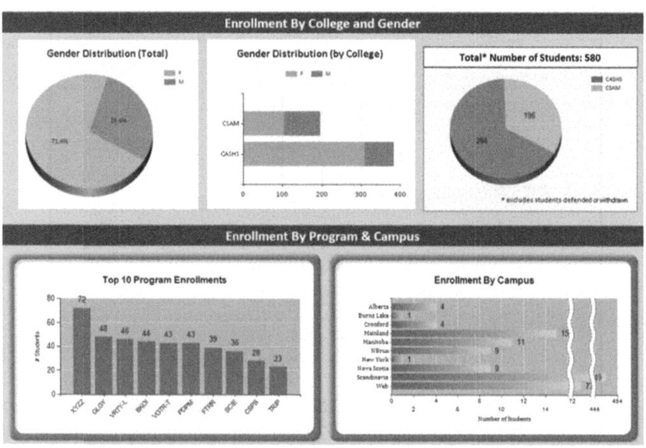

Fig. 8. Graduate enrolment snapshot [11]

4 Challenges

The success of the proposed model has been proven over a period spanning more than fifteen years. However, this did not come without challenges, both external and internal. When projects involve access to private and confidential data, arrangements should be made with the partners to anonymize the data and, in some cases, provide access to remote servers so that no data transfer is involved. These processes can be long and may need a champion in the partner organization to facilitate the process. Further, though the students are compensated when they work on these projects, there is no way to compete with the commercial rates. Thus, it is important to have informal anti-poaching arrangements with industrial partners as this is of mutual benefit for all involved. Internally, space and resources are an issue and it is important for the institution to recognize that this is a research initiative. Hosting of applications in the research lab should be avoided due to data confidentiality, licensing and support reasons. Selection of students is also important and a mix of both undergraduate and graduate students is essential. Overlapping teams should be structured keeping in mind that there will be continuous transition due to graduation. Students with business majors have also proven to be very effective in creating mocks and for frontend design. A technical review by partners must be conducted at an early stage to avoid any migration issues.

5 Conclusions

Despite a surge in unfilled positions, students graduating with a conventional degree in computer science face challenges in the labour market. Unlike Coop programs, experiential learning during the course of academic program prepares students for the real-world job market without extending the duration of their studies. The model is equally successful for both graduate and undergraduate students. The benefits are multi-faceted: for supervising faculty, new tools and techniques are developed for dissemination to research community, and research grants become relatively easy to acquire; for students, they are able to co-author papers, get trained in state-of-the-art technologies and are quickly recruited; for partners, they get projects completed cost effectively and in a timely manner - some of these projects would not even have gotten off the ground due to organizational priorities. At the same time, they are able to scout and hire students who are already trained on their platforms. It should be emphasized that training under this model does not come without challenges which include space, data access, continuity and occasional loss of talent.

References

1. Simon, D., Jackson, K.: A closer look at information systems graduate preparation and job needs: implications for higher education curriculum enhancements. World J. Educ. **3**(3), 52–62 (2013)

2. Gupta, B., Raja, U.: Teaching analytics, decision support, and business intelligence: challenges and trends. In: Iyer, L.S., Power, D.J. (eds.) Reshaping Society through Analytics, Collaboration, and Decision Support. AIS, vol. 18, pp. 205–209. Springer, Cham (2015). https://doi.org/10.1007/978-3-319-11575-7_14
3. Milosz, M., Lukasik, E.: Reengineering of computer science curriculum according to technology changes and market needs. In: IEEE Global Engineering Education Conference (EDUCON), Tallinn (2015)
4. Mitri, M., Palocsay, S.: Toward a model undergraduate curriculum for the emerging business intelligence and analytics discipline. Commun. Assoc. Inf. Syst. **37**(1), 31 (2015)
5. Haque, W.: Incorporating multidisciplinary emerging areas in CS curriculum: the pedagogical challenges. In: 21st Western Canadian Conference on Computing Education, Kamloops (2016)
6. Haque, W., Urquhart, B., Berg, E., Dhanoa, R.: Using business intelligence to analyze and share health system infrastructure data in a rural health authority. JMIR Med. Inform. **2**(2), e16 (2014). https://doi.org/10.2196/medinform.3590. https://medinform.jmir.org/2014/2/e16. PMID: 25599727. PMCID: 4288065
7. Haque, W., Derksen, B.A., Calado, D., Foster, L.: Using business intelligence for efficient inter-facility patient transfer. In: Information Technology and Communication in Health (ITCH), Victoria (2015)
8. Haque, W., Edwards, J.A.: Ambulatory care sensitive conditions: a business intelligence perspective. In: Advances in Health Informatics Conference, New York (2012)
9. Haque, W., Edwards, J., Belsham, E.: A decision analysis model for vegetation management. In: International Conference on Information and Communication Systems, Amman (2011)
10. Haque, W., Ahmad, D.W., Calado, D., Dhanoa, R., Samani, M.E.: Business intelligence enabled nursing practicum placements and reporting. J. Adv. Inf. Technol. **6**(3), 118–123 (2015)
11. Haque, W., Dhanoa, R.: A framework for reporting and analytics without OLAP cubes. In: Multidisciplinary Academic Conference on Education, Teaching and Learning (MAC-ETL), Prague (2015)

Social Demands in Ubiquitous Computing: Contexts for Tomorrow's Learning

Mareen Przybylla[1(✉)] and Ralf Romeike[2]

[1] University of Potsdam, Potsdam, Germany
przybyll@uni-potsdam.de
[2] Friedrich-Alexander-Universität Erlangen-Nürnberg, Erlangen, Germany

Abstract. We live in times of digital change, which manifests in the increasing pervasiveness of embedded and cyber-physical systems in our society. This change also needs to be reflected in education, as new knowledge and competencies become necessary to deal with everyday life challenges, for instance when estimating consequences of capturing, transmitting and evaluating sensor data in many devices and acting accordingly and responsibly. This article examines requirements that the digital society places on CS education. In our analysis, we identified numerous contexts, activities and knowledge areas relevant for students to cope with challenges of the digital world. Combined with content knowledge relevant in this domain, suitable phenomena and thus anchor points for teaching can be generated and, on this basis, specific learning scenarios can be developed that also consider general educative aims imposed by our society.

Keywords: Computer science · Education · Embedded systems
Ubiquitous computing · Social demands

1 Introduction and Motivation

Less and less technical developments of today contain classic computers with display, keyboard and mouse. We are predominantly surrounded by mobile devices and reactive systems that capture context variables with the aid of sensors and affect the physical world with actuators. Today, more than 98% of all microprocessors are integrated in technical devices such as pace makers, navigation systems or household devices [3]. We live in the digital world–a place where "information is available almost anywhere at almost any time, computer power is ubiquitous, communication of vast amounts of information is almost instantaneous" [10]. Thus, society puts demands on CS education: dealing with embedded systems requires new knowledge and competencies that cannot be acquired in traditional teaching. To allow future generations to participate in social discourse, to understand media coverage and to make informed decisions, it is essential to address the relevant aspects in the classroom. However, it is unclear what those demands and aspects are, especially with regard to ubiquitous computing. Thus, in this article we give an overview of relevant technical aspects in this field, analyze interview transcripts and documents that reflect the perspectives of different stakeholders in this domain to extract the social demands on computer science in school in

A. Tatnall and M. Webb (Eds.): WCCE 2017, IFIP AICT 515, pp. 453–462, 2017.
https://doi.org/10.1007/978-3-319-74310-3_46

terms of ubiquitous computing and embedded and cyber-physical systems. We discuss possible implications for the selection of appropriate content and contexts for teaching.

2 Phenomena of the Digital World: Ubiquitous Computing and Internet of Things

In the last decades computing systems have evolved according to the vision of ubiquitous computing pioneer Mark Weiser, who already predicted pervasive, efficient and invisible computers at the beginning of the 1990s [19]. Ubiquitous Computing nowadays is commonplace thanks to appropriate technologies. In the Internet of Things (IoT), "things" that contain embedded systems (ES) or cyber-physical systems (CPS), are networked with various services on the Internet. The IoT offers new possibilities for the generation of information by converging data of many things. The physical world merges with the virtual: integrating Internet services allows real-time analyses that are used to influence the real world. As a result of the constantly increasing diversity of information available on the Internet and things that are networked with people and processes, the IoT is evolving to eventually become the Internet of Everything (IoE) [4, p. 72].

ES combine hard- and software components, are embedded into a technical context and fulfil predefined tasks. They usually control, regulate or monitor a system continuously. For this purpose, in addition to possible user inputs and outputs, sensor data from the environment is recorded and commands are sent to actuators. ES often need to meet real-time requirements [3, 17]. CPS expand ES with network components for the communication of the subsystems among themselves and over the Internet [14, p. 4]. In CPS, connected ES monitor and control physical processes. This is usually done with control technology, where data from the environment influences calculation processes and vice versa. Control systems make a physical system's output track a desired reference input (e.g. cruise control, thermostat). Feed-forward systems compute a setting for the actuator based on a reference input. Feedback systems also monitor the error between the system output and the reference input and adjust it in response to this error. Control systems should track the reference input even with noise, model errors or disturbances. Thus, there are special metrics to be followed, e.g. stability, performance, disturbance rejection and robustness [18, pp. 246–257].

ES and CPS are the technological basis for many application areas, such as robotics, wearable computing or electronic textiles and disciplines, such as physical computing, interaction design or art that make use of these core technologies in different, often non-technical contexts. Depending on the field of application, different foci are set. Robots, for instance, quite often bring the challenge that their actions are dependent on their environment which is only known at the time of execution, especially when autonomous mobile robots are used in difficult terrain (e.g. space, sea or disaster areas). This makes it impossible to program all suitable action patterns in advance. Robots must therefore capture the environment with sensors, evaluate the data, and initiate appropriate actions depending on the environment variables [12, p. 2]. A typical requirement for such mobile robots is robustness, for instance in high or low temperature areas, in dusty environments or under water. Wearables, in contrast, need to be particularly small, light-weight and low in power consumption, which brings challenges to both, hard- and software design.

Although the application areas each specialize their products in different directions, there are many common properties and requirements. For example, in general a distinction is made between continuous time systems, which process signal streams, and discrete systems, which process event- or time-controlled discrete signals [14, p. 43f]. The design of ES and CPS comes with some technical challenges that occur repeatedly. These include dealing with concurrency in the physical world that needs to be sequentially organized in software, trade-offs between fast and less accurate or slower and more accurate programs, with the heterogeneity of the systems, their interactions and the data they process. Overall, the areas are interrelated and thus understanding certain concepts often requires prior knowledge from neighboring disciplines. The structure of the subject area depicted in Fig. 1 shows the different disciplines in the larger context and represents distinguishing features.

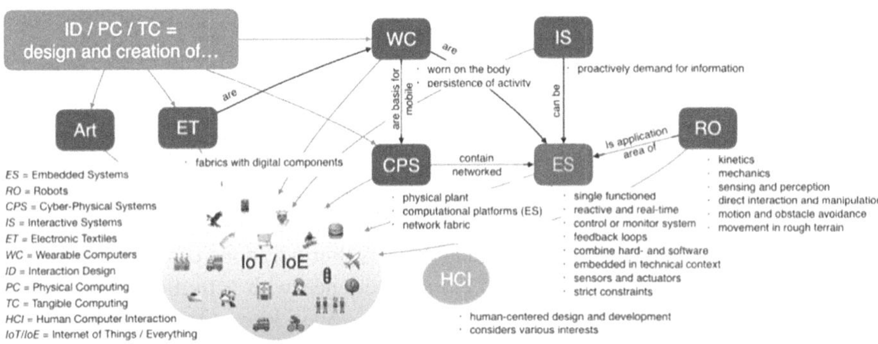

Fig. 1. Overview of different technologies in the Internet of Things

From an educational point-of-view, teaching should be oriented towards the competencies to be achieved, thus this purely content-related structure of the topic is not sufficient for teaching. However, the given overview can provide orientation in order to establish and secure necessary (prior) knowledge and make connections. This way competencies for the analysis, modelling and implementation of ubiquitous computing systems can be developed step by step. As the design and implementation of embedded systems is a great challenge that includes many steps, it is important to provide learners with appropriate contexts, and to investigate phenomena that promote the understanding of abstract content.

3 Analyzing Social Demands

The investigation of social demands within a thematic area helps to identify contexts that are relevant for students to cope with requirements that society puts on them in their everyday lives. This way, the significance of computer science for general education is underlined. It is important to realize and consider that social demands differ from setting to setting, even between schools in the same district or students of the same learning group under different circumstances [7]. Thus, if the analysis is not performed within a very specific context, it can only reflect general societal demands. Diethelm et al. [7] suggest interviewing stakeholders in education and analyzing constitutions, laws, curricula and standards.

3.1 Research Goals and Data Gathering

For analyzing the social demands and to find out how jobs, everyday life and education are effected by embedded and ubiquitous computing systems, we focused on perspectives by stakeholders in this domain that reflect different contexts and help to answer the following questions:

- In which areas are ubiquitous computing systems relevant in our society?
- What are areas in daily life where people encounter such systems?
- In which cases do people need to actively deal with these technologies?

Stakeholders are either active or passive: Active stakeholders are those, who are directly affected by the outcome of this research project, in our case students and teachers in secondary schools. Their perspectives are captured independently with the model of educational reconstruction for computer science education (MER-CSE, [11]). Results from research in this area show that we face some issues in computer science education: embedded, cyber-physical or interactive computing systems are not in students' focus, despite the ubiquity of such devices. Further, none of the students who took part in the study had any prior in-class-experience with activities around those technologies [16]. Also, teachers' prior knowledge is often low and many of them find working with sensors, actuators or microcontrollers intimidating in the beginning [17]. From teacher surveys, we learned that they are concerned about the balance between crafting and tinkering and the actual study of CS but they also see a lot of value in it because they assume that it boosts their students' motivation and creativity.

Passive stakeholders, on the other hand, influence school education from the outside. They form a society's beliefs and norms and thus define social demands that need to be considered. In the study described here, we focused on experts from industry and business, parents, educators and people in general. The aim of this investigation was to get an overview of the stakeholders' interests and demands that they place on CS education. We gained our data from interviews and diverse documents that represent the target groups' interests and conducted a qualitative content analysis of these data, which is based on the methodology of Mayring [15].

Experts from industry and business. We conducted stakeholder interviews with representatives from companies (e.g. Microsoft, Intel, NXP Semiconductors, Adata, Q-Technology) at the "embedded world" conference 2016. Among other questions we investigated their point-of-view on the social impacts of embedded and ubiquitous computing systems and the social demands that are connected to those systems. In short semi-structured interviews (5–15 min each), we interrogated the interviewees about general thoughts on ubiquitous computing and more specifically about their ideas for computer science education. The interviews were audio-recorded and then transcribed. In addition to the interviews, we analyzed a policy paper of the BITKOM[1] [3] and passages from a study about basics, applications and consequences of ubiquitous computing [9], which represent the interests of this target group and inform about the current state and future perspectives in the embedded sector.

Parents. To gain parents' expectations on education we analyzed a manifesto from the European Parents Association [8] and two documents from the German Federal Council of Parents: a resolution about self-determined life as a goal of education [5] and a press release on the requirements of digitization on the education system [6]. The Federal Council of Parents is an umbrella organization that represents the parents of about eight million children and adolescents in general and vocational schools in Germany.

Educators. The perspectives of educators are gathered with the analysis of four documents that are relevant internationally and specifically in Germany: In 2013, ACM and Informatics Europe issued a joint report of a working group of experts from academia and industry that reflect many countries' requirements [10]. The German Standing Conference of the Ministers of Education and Cultural Affairs (KMK) has published a strategy paper on education in the digital world [13] that contains many influential ideas and perspectives. Although the KMK has no legislative competence, its decisions are a consensus among the 16 federal states and thus often also lead to implementation in the different curricula. Similarly, the Educational standards published by the German Informatics Society (GI) [1, 2] formally are only recommendations, but find their way into schools in the long term and were hence included in our analysis.

People in General. We included a study of the office for technology assessment at the German Bundestag that represents many of the previously described stakeholders' perspectives [9]. Although this study was published in 2010 already, many aspects are still relevant. Some issues that were mentioned as future visions are reality today. Nevertheless, this study gives a complex overview of topics and especially basics, applications and consequences of ubiquitous computing for all people and diverse areas of everyone's lives. From this document, we also identified the perspectives of **laws** and **press**. Laws mirror society and have direct impact on CS education in schools. Press on the one hand reflects, and on the other hand also forms opinions and thus is influential both, as a mirror of society and in shaping it. Given that the press articles in the before-mentioned document were slightly outdated (published in 2005–2010), we also included more recent articles (published between 2014 and 2017) that were selected based on a keyword search (e.g. sensor, embedded systems, ubiquitous computing, Internet of things) in several German media databases[2]. We focused on German media, as we're primarily creating material for teachers and students in

[1] BITKOM: Digital Association of the German Information and Telecommunications Industry.

[2] ARD Mediathek, including ARD Online and broadcasting channels; Spiegel Online, TAZ, Die Welt, Computer Woche.

German schools. However, it can be assumed that the results apply to many Western-European countries, possibly with slight differences in the perception concerning ethical questions or when related to country-specific laws.

3.2 Data Analysis

In the analysis, we strove to gain a general overview of topics relevant in our society's discourse, thus we chose a qualitative approach. The overall aim of a qualitative content analysis depends on the context and may include to make statements about the subject matter or, e.g. when analyzing mass media, to find out about their effects on the public [15]. In our case, the aim is to identify requirements our society places on CS education, in particular schools, that come with the increasing pervasiveness of interactive and ubiquitous computing systems. As a first step, we analyzed the interview data. From the analysis goals, we derived the following coding system deductively:

- role of embedded and ubiquitous computing in society today
- role of embedded and ubiquitous computing in society in the future
- relevance of embedded and ubiquitous computing in everyday life
- ethical and social implications associated with ubiquitous computing
- aspects of ubiquitous computing that everyone should know about
- qualifications that applicants to jobs in this domain should have.

We identified 142 coding units (sentences and paragraphs of text) in our corpus and expanded the code system inductively based on the data, resulting in 63 codes (paraphrased coding units) that were then summarized into initial categories. These new categories describe the areas where ubiquitous computing is relevant, activities that are closely connected to these technologies, areas with ethical and social implications for and impact on society and general educative goals. These categories were then used for the analysis of the remaining material and refined throughout the process. The resulting category system is based on 271 codes and 1327 coding units and gives an overview of aspects relevant in our society from which social demands can be derived (Table 1).

3.3 Results and Interpretation

Our data is captured from different groups of stakeholders and reveals, for instance, that parents focus more on general educative aims, experts from industry and business mention many features of ubiquitous computing systems and their future relevance and press often discusses ethical and social implications of new technologies. For this work, however, we did not consider the single perspectives in detail, but instead combined the data to gain the bigger picture of general social demands relevant for teaching.

The analysis provided an extensive list of contexts, in which ubiquitous computing is relevant in our society, that are often overlapping. Additional categories were created to code activities as active or passive use of systems and to differentiate between today's reality and future visions. It is clearly visible in the data that especially in terms of identification and authentication there is a shift from past to future: while earlier and today, pin protected door locks, fingerprint scanners, RFID chipped cards or even retina scans require action by the user, future scenarios make use of contactless, unobtrusive methods such as face and gait recognition. This raises many questions concerning surveillance, data privacy and security, quite often discussed in the media and by people in general, but also reflected in laws and discussions about law changes. Also in other areas, such as health and medicine, passive use of devices is clearly dominant and equally often connected with concerns about possible profiling with personal data, surveillance or safety. The majority of concerns are connected to ethical questions, especially in medicine concerning informational self-determination and privacy, but also in the job sector: many people fear that humans are partially or fully replaced by machines (Table 2).

Table 1. Category system for the analysis of social demands

Relevance in society	Environment, smart home, traffic and transportation, health sector, work, clothing, shopping, economy, authorities, food industry, identification and authentication, marketing
Activities	Monitoring, prediction of future events, tracking the origin of goods, surveillance, profiling with personal data, support for ill and elderly, creative design, regulation and control, preventive action
Implications and impact	Pervasiveness of computing systems, data privacy, data security, system Dependency, intervening with individual autonomy, informational self-determination, consumer protection, safety, decision-making power of digital systems, digital divide
Education	Understand that everything can be programmed and controlled, at- tract all students alike, interdisciplinarity, involvement of pupils' experiences, basic principles and fundamental ideas, confidence in dealing with complexity, superficial goals (reasonability, responsibility, etc.), prepare students for the future, constructive production of artefacts, focus on competencies and skills

Despite users becoming more passive in those domains, future scenarios also show that ubiquitous computing systems will become even more pervasive also in everyday situations. No matter whether at home, in grocery stores, in the hospital or at work: everyone will have to deal with these technologies. Although most devices gather their data in the background, they are interactive and involve user actions. Thus, future visions show more active use of technologies than today in these areas.

This trend is also reflected in the general educative aims: according to the data, among other aims, to prepare them for the future and allow them to successfully participate in society, students need to understand that everything can be programmed and controlled. They need confidence in dealing with the complexity of technologies and to constructively produce artifacts instead of only consuming them. Basic principles and fundamental ideas should always be in focus and pupils' experience in everyday life should be considered in lesson planning (Table 3).

Table 2. Overview of frequent occurrences in code relations matrix

Code	Today	Future	Passive	Active	Concerns	Laws	Press	People	Parents	Educators	Industry
Concerns	6	16	27	4	0	8	26	39	1	2	3
Ethical/social implications	20	13	48	13	82	34	52	35	2	3	14
General education	5	1	2	11	2	2	0	11	11	65	35
Work sector	5	3	25	2	30	2	9	62	0	0	14
Transportation	25	22	24	24	3	0	0	28	0	0	6
Medicine	6	27	25	2	5	0	1	30	0	0	0
Health	25	32	32	4	11	1	7	38	0	0	3
Identification, authentication	20	13	16	8	3	0	3	23	0	0	0
Shopping	4	13	7	8	6	1	1	17	0	0	0
Smart home	24	13	18	10	3	0	21	21	0	0	4

Table 3. General educative aspects in ubiquitous computing

Code	Laws	Press	People	Parents	Educators	Industry
Understand that things can be programmed, controlled						X
Attract all students alike					X	X
Constructive production of artifacts					X	X
Involvement of pupils' experience				X	X	X
Interdisciplinarity					X	X
Basic principles and fundamental ideas	X		X		X	X
Confidence in dealing with complexity					X	X
Superficial goals (reasonability, responsibility, etc.)					X	X
Focus on competencies and skills			X	X	X	
Participation in future society	X			X	X	

The pervasiveness of ubiquitous computing systems in our society is reflected in about 200 different concrete contexts, activities and knowledge areas from 16 superordinate categories that are relevant for students to cope with the challenges of the digital world. The combination with content knowledge relevant in this subject area and to be taught in school results in a three-dimensional matrix. From this matrix, specific learning scenarios can be generated, not neglecting the findings on general educative aims (e. g. to attract all students alike, focus on competencies and skills or teach basic principles). Possible phenomena and thus anchor points for teaching could be generated as depicted in Fig. 2.

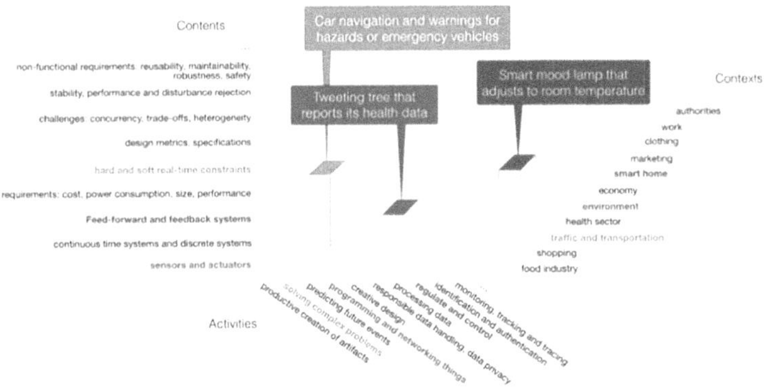

Fig. 2. Matrix of contents, contexts and activities

4 Conclusion

Dealing with ubiquitous computing systems, from a technical point of view, requires knowledge, skills and competencies that are less relevant or not present in dealing with transformational systems. Technical terminology has developed significantly over the last decades. Our results show that ES, CPS and similar technologies are relevant in all areas of our life and will become even more pervasive and relevant in the future. Thus, to ensure that everyone can cope with the challenges in our digital world, it is crucial to provide CS education that prepares students to participate in social discourse, to understand media coverage and to make informed judgments. Tomorrow's learning must not neglect the changes in our world and help clarify concerns, raise students' awareness of the risks and opportunities of modern technologies and built competencies so that they are able to customize and control their environment and to deal with new devices, systems and technologies with expertise and without fear. This work provides an empirically developed basis of contexts and activities from which phenomena and specific teaching scenarios can be developed that support modern and general educative computer science education.

References

1. Arbeitskreis Bildungsstandards der Gesellschaft für Informatik e.V.: Grundsätze und Standards für die Informatik in der Schule [Principles and standards for computer science in school], LOG IN 28 (150/151), supplement (2008)
2. Arbeitskreis Bildungsstandards SII der Gesellschaft für Informatik e.V.: Bildungsstandards Informatik für die Sekundarstufe II [Educational standards for secondary education] LOG IN 36 (183/184), supplement (2016)
3. BITKOM: Eingebettete Systeme–Ein strategisches Wachstumsfeld für Deutschland [Embedded Systems–A stratgic growth area for Germany]. http://www.bitkom.org/files/documents/EingebetteteSysteme_web.pdf. Accessed 26 July 2017

4. Bojanova, I., Hurlburt, G., Voas, J.: Imagineering an internet of anything. Computer **47**(6), 72–77 (2014)
5. Bundeselternrat: Selbstbestimmtes Leben als Ziel von Bildung–Was müssen unsere Kinder heute lernen? [Self-determined life as a goal of education–What do our children have to learn today?]. http://www.bundeselternrat.de/files/Dokumente/Resolutionen/2016/Bundeselternrat_Reso_Selbstbestimmtes_Leben_als_Ziel_von_Bildung20160424.pdf. Accessed 26 July 2017
6. Bundeselternrat: Digitalisierung/Individualisierung. [Digitization/Individualization]. https://bildungsklick.de/schule/meldung/digitalisierung-individualisierung/. Accessed 26 July 2017
7. Diethelm, I., Hubwieser, P., Klaus, R.: Students, teachers and phenomena: educational reconstruction for computer science education. In: Laakso, M.-J., McCartney, R. (eds.) Proceedings of Koli Calling 2012, pp. 164–173. ACM, New York (2012)
8. European Parents' Association: Manifesto (2015). http://euparents.eu/manifesto-2015/. Accessed 26 July 2017
9. Friedewald, M., Raabe, O., Georgieff, P., Koch, D.J.: Ubiquitäres Computing. [Ubiquitous Computing] Nomos Verlag, Berlin, Germany (2010)
10. Informatics Europe and ACM Europe Working Group on Informatics Education: Informatics Education: Europe Cannot Afford to Miss the Boat. Technical report (2013)
11. Grillenberger, A., Przybylla, M., Romeike, R.: Bringing CS innovations to the classroom using the model of educational reconstruction. In: Proceedings of ISSEP 2016, pp. 31–39. Münster, Germany (2016)
12. Hertzberg, J., Lingemann, K., Nüchter, A.: Mobile Roboter [Mobile Robots], vol. 7. Springer, Heidelberg (2012). https://doi.org/10.1007/978-3-642-01726-1
13. Kultusministerkonferenz: Bildung in der digitalen Welt [Education in the digital world], KMK, Berlin, Germany (2016)
14. Lee, E.A., Seshia, S.A.: Introduction to Embedded Systems - A Cyber-Physical Systems Approach, 2nd edn. MIT Press, Cambridge (2017)
15. Mayring, P.: Qualitative Content Analysis. Theoretical Foundation, Basic Procedures and Software Solution. Klagenfurt, Austria (2014). http://nbn-resolving.de/urn:nbn:de:0168-ssoar-395173. Accessed 26 July 2017
16. Przybylla, M., Romeike, R.: Overcoming issues with students' perceptions of informatics in everyday life and education with physical computing–suggestions for the enrichment of computer science classes. In: Gülbahar, Y., Karatas, E., Müge, A. (eds.) Proceedings of ISSEP 2014, pp. 9–20. Ankara University Press, Ankara (2014)
17. Przybylla, M., Romeike, R.: Teaching computer science teachers – a constructionist approach to professional development on physical computing. In: Sipitakiat, A., Tutiyaphuengprasert, N. (eds.) Proceedings of Constructionism 2016, pp. 265–274. Suksapattana Foundation, Bangkok (2016)
18. Vahid, F., Givargis, T.D.: Embedded System Design: A Unified Hardware/Software Introduction. Wiley, New York (2002)
19. Weiser, M.: Some computer science issues in ubiquitous computing. Commun. ACM **36**(7), 75–84 (1993)

Information Systems Curriculum in an Australian University: Past Developments and Future Directions

Arthur Tatnall(✉) and Stephen Burgess

Victoria University, Melbourne, Australia
{Arthur.Tatnall, Stephen.Burgess}@vu.edu.au

Abstract. In this paper we describe the development of Information Systems (IS) curricula in the Business Faculty of an Australian university over the last 40 years, but then look at how what has happened is likely to affect future developments. The paper looks at how curriculum content was added over the years when it covered what was considered, at the time, to be important new material. In many cases in later years this material became mainstream and so there was no need to include it in IS courses. An example of this is eCommerce which was an extremely important new area in the late 1990s that was developed into new IS subjects and new undergraduate and postgraduate degree courses. By the mid-2000s, however, everyone was using eCommerce and it was included in many other subject areas, making it no longer necessary to be included in IS courses and it disappeared. Finally we question what might happen to IS courses into the future.

Keywords: Information Systems · Business computing · Computer Science Higher Education · Australian universities · Curriculum · History

1 Introduction

This paper looks at how Information Systems (IS) curriculum developed in a Business Faculty over the last forty years in an Australian university. But one might ask: why is this important? The words of George Santayana [1]: *"Those who cannot remember the past are condemned to repeat it"* provide an answer and help us to understand why history is important. In this case, an important lesson of the past involves the reason for the rise and fall of a number of IS subject areas that covered what was considered to be important material at the time, but which later became mainstream and so not a necessary part of the IS curriculum. Our paper looks at the past, the present and postulates several scenarios for the future of IS courses.

2 Early Computing in Australia

Although Computer Science began in Australia's universities of the 1950s, courses in Information Systems (then called Business Computing) did not commence until the 1960s. In this paper we do not address Computer Science but only the development of Information Systems as part of Business degree courses.

A. Tatnall and M. Webb (Eds.): WCCE 2017, IFIP AICT 515, pp. 463–472, 2017.
https://doi.org/10.1007/978-3-319-74310-3_47

The CSIR Mk1 (CSIRAC) computer was built for the CSIRO[1] in the late 1940s and was Australia's first internally stored program computer, and (arguably) the world's fifth [2]. The fact that it was the CSIRO with its connections to the universities and to government that led the way into computing in Australia probably assisted in the early introduction of Computer Science courses into Australian universities [3].

In the late 1950s the Australian Government set out to computerise the operations of the Postmaster General's Department (PMG) and the Department of Defence and it can be argued that this means that the Government was the pacesetter in computing in Australia during the 1960s, and that in many ways the Commonwealth Public Service, rather than commerce in general, paved the way for the introduction of business computing in Australia.

This paper will discuss the beginnings, development and possible future of Information Systems courses at the university level in Australia by looking at these developments in one specific university: Victoria University, Melbourne.

3 The Beginnings of Computer Science and IS Curricula

Times change and most people now makes good use of mobile phones and the Internet, but twenty years ago these were just beginning to come into popular use. Sixty years ago a computer was something that few organisations could afford and any idea that people would use a computer at work or even have their own home computer was unthinkable. The advent, first of the mini-computer and later the PC changed everything and in the 1970s computers began to become accessible. Teaching about computers and their use then became important [4].

Computerising the operation of the Department of Defence and the Post Master General's Department created a massive requirement for trained computing personnel [5], but these could not be obtained from overseas as many other developed countries were also computerising government departments. This meant that they had to be trained locally [6]. The universities were then just trying to decide whether computing was a part of mathematics or should be considered as a new discipline [3, 4, 7] and their courses were quite theoretical and mathematical in nature. Consequently they showed little interest in providing applied courses to cover the establishment and operation of commercial and administrative computing applications [3].

To provide a temporary solution to this problem, in 1960 the Australian Government's Commonwealth Public Service Board set up its own: *Programmers in Training* (PIT) program [3] and it was this course, as we shall discuss later, that laid the way for Information Systems curriculum in Australia.

The PIT was seen as a "crash computing course" [5] of twelve weeks duration with the goal of alleviating the severe shortage of programmers and other computer professionals in Commonwealth Government departments [6]. The course covered the technical skills associated with computing: Computer Equipment and Techniques,

[1] Commonwealth Scientific and Industrial Research Organisation.

Computer Mathematics (Statistics), Programming, Systems Analysis and Design, but also the analytical skills required to design and/or modify systems. The course also had 24 weeks of on-the-job training [5, 8].

The Commonwealth Public Service Board continued running PIT courses until late in the 1960s when responsibility was transferred to the following Colleges of Advanced Education (CAEs) [3]: Caulfield Institute, Bendigo Institute, Canberra CAE and New South Wales Institute of Technology[2] [5].

These courses set the style for many of the Business Computing (Information Systems) courses later offered in Higher Education in Australia [5]. On the significance of the Commonwealth's initiatives to Higher Education, Pearcey [8: 120] notes that: "*In many of these institutions, teaching in computing started as a result of the staffing crisis that arose first from the Defence and PMG's projects*". These early CAE courses were typically based around subjects such as: Systems Analysis and Design, Database Design, Business Programming (typically done using languages such as COBOL or BASIC) and Systems Implementation. Many also had an introductory Computer Networking unit as well as one handling Computer Architecture. A few years later Footscray Institute of Technology began to offer similar courses.

4 Methodology

This study is about the historical beginnings, purpose and development of Information Systems courses at an Australian university and so the research techniques primarily used are those of Curriculum History and Case Study. According to Orlikowski and Baroudi [9], as IS research topics commonly involve the study of organisational systems a case study approach is often quite appropriate. Case study evidence can come from documents, archival records, interviews, direct observation, participant-observation or physical artefacts. In this quasi–historical case, evidence comes from several of these sources and in particular from participant-observation as both authors are long standing academics at Victoria University. The research methods employed can be seen to relate to studies in History [10, 11] and also in Curriculum History [12–14] which comprise both the analysis of documents and of oral narratives.

5 IS Curricula at Footscray Institute in the 1970s and 1980s

The institution that is now Victoria University was formed in the early 1990s from the merger of two formed Colleges of Advanced Education: Footscray Institute of Technology (FIT) and Western Institute (WI). Footscray Institute of Technology [15], formerly Footscray Technical College, was opened in 1916 and Western Institute in the 1980s. In 1991 they merged to form Victoria University (VU). We will begin by considering events at FIT in the 1980s.

[2] CAEs and Institutes of Technology were, in all but name, polytechnics.

Secretarial Studies and Office Automation were the first areas involving some form of computing to be introduced in the early 1970s with an *Associate Diploma in Secretarial Practice*. It was updated in the early 1980s *to* include: Word Processing, Office Automation, Use of Computer Technology and Electronic Mail.

In 1984 the new *Bachelor of Business: Information Management and Communication* [16] took its first students. The course was pioneering at the time in stressing that 'information is a critical organisational resource that must be managed effectively and efficiently', rather than one concentrating on 'pure computing' where a study of the technology involved was seen as the priority. Given its background, the course had an office automation/office systems flavour involving a study of office packages and how technology could address the systems life cycle.

At this time Moll and Flood [17] suggested that such courses should not be limited to one discipline, should prepare students with skills for tomorrow and should not be technology bound – their argument being that technological obsolescence occurred too quickly. Garrison [18] also noted that in addition to Office Automation, Information Management courses were emerging out of many disciplines such as the Library and Information Science, Business and Computer Science. Laverty and Sorg [19] identified computer-related knowledge and skills for people charged with the management of information resources as:

- Basic skills allowing use of the computer
- Ability to manage technology as an organisational resource
- Ability to implement IT policy: its promotion, implications of its use and an understanding of its impact on economic, political and the social climate.

As well as a major in Information Management, the degree course had a compulsory minor in more traditional computing areas – programming, systems analysis and systems development. Students were, however, encouraged to do a double major of both Information Management and Computing. At that stage the term 'Information Management' referred to recognition that the *information* that flowed into, out of and within an organisation was a resource that needed to be managed. The earlier office automation focus thus needed to be updated and so became Information Management.

Around this time, traditional Business Computing (later Information Systems) curricular was beginning to develop and most courses had a core of similar topics which were typically based around subjects related to systems analysis and design, database design, business programming (typically done using third generation such as BASIC, COBOL or Pascal) and systems implementation. Many of these courses also had an introductory computer networking unit which was probably the most technical and close to the discipline of Computer Science. An *Associate Diploma in Applied Science (Computing)* had been introduced in the late 1970s with Business input as well as from Applied Science in maths and statistics units.

By the late 1980s, there was growing support for the development of a computing course and the *Bachelor of Business (Information Technology) was launched with* two strands: *Information Management* and *Computing (Systems Development)*. Students were again encouraged to take subjects from both strands.

6 IS Curricula at Western Institute in the Late 1980s

Western Institute (WI) was a CAE newly formed in the mid-1980. In 1989 three courses were offered [20]: *Bachelor of Business (Office Administration and Technology), Bachelor of Business (Computing)* and *Associate Diploma of Applied Science (Computing)* – with emphasis on business applications.

In 1989 in order to offer an education in the fundamentals of computing to graduates of other discipline areas such as accounting, management, teaching and office administration, WI introduced the *Graduate Diploma in Business Computing*. The aim of this new post-graduate course was to offer people currently working in other careers the chance of moving to a career in computing and to offer those currently working with computers the chance to gain a professionally accepted qualification in this area. The course continued at VU after the merger.

7 Information Systems Curricula at VU from the 1990s – 2000

In 1992, WI and FIT merged to become Victoria University of Technology[3], which was one of a number of 'new generation' universities formed in Australia at this time by the 'Dawkins Reforms' [21]. One of the first areas to merge in the new university was the Department of Business Computing at WI and the Business Computing group at FIT (which had been located within the Department of Applied Economics). The new group became the Department of Business Computing. Before the merger FIT had concentrated on Information Management (with some Business Computing) while WI had taken a more traditional line in Business Computing. These streams needed to merge, and in the process several new areas emerged.

Whilst the separate degrees of the two former institutions continued for a few years, by the mid-1990s a new degree, the *B.Bus (Business Computing)* had been formed with two major streams, Computing and Information Management. This did not require much alteration to the previous units beyond some minor differences of opinion. For instance, at FIT Systems Analysis and Design was taught as two subjects while at WI the two units were taught as Systems Analysis and Systems Design. Whilst the WI model was selected, aspects of the FIT approach were incorporated. This course was delivered across five campuses of the university. A new offering was the *B.Bus (Computer Systems Support)*, which had some overlap with the generic faculty *B.Bus* degree, but also had some units that were offered to particularly target students wishing to work in the IT support services industry.

The merger of WI and FIT into a new university also provided the chance for the new department to offer postgraduate courses. Higher degree by research programs (Masters and PhDs) were offered from the outset and are still offered today. In the early 1990s the Faculty of Business introduced an MBA program which included a subject on: 'Management Information Systems' which aimed to provide general managers with all they needed to know about computing. A few years later a DBA (Doctor of

[3] Later renamed: Victoria University.

Business Administration) program (one year coursework and two years thesis) was introduced also containing an Information Systems subject. Each of these subjects progressed well in the MBA and DBA during the 1990s and early 2000s until the Faculty decided to discontinue them. The argument was that there was no longer any need to teach this material as most of it had become mainstream and students already understood as much about IS as they needed.

A key shift in focus in the second half of the 1990s was the Department of Business Computing changing its name to the School of Information Systems and so creating the *B.Bus (Information Systems)*. Another key shift which occurred late in the 1990s was an increased emphasis within the school on Enterprise Resource Planning (ERP) systems, championed by a particular staff member.

By the early 1990s many of the FIT staff involved in the information management units had left. At the time, one of this paper's authors took over coordination of the information management units, redesigned them from an office automation slant to concentrate more upon the information storage and retrieval aspects of the information life cycle – reflecting the typical approach taken by librarians in their version of information management. The catalyst for this was this author's completion of an *M.Bus (IT)* at RMIT University, a course which had a heavy librarianship focus. A key focus of the new units was the employment skills of students as 'information professionals'. The idea behind this was to develop students with skills that spanned a number of fields including: the technical skills of traditional computing personnel, an understanding of the concept of information as a resource to be managed within the organisation, understanding how IT could play a strategic role in the organisation and an ability to communicate with other professionals and with senior managers [22, 23]. At the same time the information management units were being redesigned, there were also some key changes on the computing side with the introduction of IT project management and the first visual programming languages.

Project Management is an important aspect of the work of any IT professional but it was not until the 1990s that university courses around the country began to reflect this due to the Australian Computer Society including IT Project Management in its Body of Knowledge for computer professionals [23, 24]. In 1994 a new undergraduate final year subject: Systems Implementation was introduced with a significant project management component. A postgraduate subject in IT Project Management was introduced several years later.

Systems Implementation also included database programming (in dBase IV) and the use of Visual Basic (VB) to create information system front-ends [25]. We chose VB as it was able to easily extract data from a variety of external sources.

8 IS Curriculum at VU from 2000 – the Present

In this period a number of significant new curriculum areas emerged, mainly due to the efforts of a small number of academic staff – and some disappeared. The way that this happened bears closely parallels the first stage of Layton's [14] model of curriculum development in which new subjects are seen to justify their existence on grounds of 'pertinence and utility'.

8.1 The Rise and Fall of Electronic Commerce

Towards the end of the 1990s an undergraduate electronic commerce degree was introduced as a new growth area for the university. In the postgraduate area several new e-commerce subjects were introduced in 2000 as increase in business importance of this topic was widely perceived [26, 27]. The new subjects were: Internet Commerce, Building Internet Commerce Systems, Internet Technologies in Business, Small Business Information and Internet Systems and Executive and Mobile Computing [28, 29]. A little later these subjects were combined into a Masters in e-Commerce and also became part of a combined Marketing/e-Commerce masters.

Not long after the 'dotcom' crash, however, student numbers began to drop and reduction in demand for e-business programs and a rationalisation of courses within the university resulted in their discontinuation. The Masters in e-Commerce was thus only offered in 2006 and Masters in e-Commerce/Marketing between 2003 and 2011. This decision was compounded as many of the 'e' aspects of Information Systems had by then become main-stream, and thus part of the main business curricula in Accounting, Management, Economics and other business areas.

8.2 Enterprise Resource Planning (ERP)

Around 2000 one of the School's academic staff members developed an interest in the German software company SAP's Enterprise Resource Planning software and soon convinced a number of his colleagues that ERP would be a worthwhile addition to the curriculum. It was first necessary, however, to have access to the software so he used his contacts to convince SAP to provide this. The ERP offerings have remained fairly consistent since the turn of the century, mainly in the postgraduate area and with a few units offered in the undergraduate program. Numbers for the postgraduate programs peaked around 2012, with some drop away since, but are still viable.

8.3 Consolidation of Offerings, 'Fly by Nighters' and a New Area

The 2000s saw the consolidation of the three undergraduate information systems offerings into one course and lack of interest in the *B.Bus (e-Commerce)* program lead to its discontinuation in 2011. In 2006, the Computer Systems Support program was repackaged and redesigned to become the *B.Bus (Computer Systems Management)* with an increased emphasis on management of IT support areas rather than just working in them. It was discontinued due to lack of numbers in 2013. The *B.Bus (Information Systems)* continued, but was repackaged and redesigned in 2014 as the *B.Bus (Information Systems Management)*. The program retained its emphasis on the core information systems units of Programming, Systems Analysis and Design and Database, as well as Information Systems Professional and IS Project Management units. The program remains in existence despite having significantly lower enrolled numbers when compared to the previous decade.

After many years of operation, the *Graduate Certificate and Graduate Diploma in Business Computing* were discontinued in 2008. The *M.Bus (Information Systems)* course was discontinued in 2013 due to low numbers after being the flagship post-graduate course for over a decade.

In 2006 two new masters' programs, which targeted more technical aspects of information systems were introduced, being the *M.Bus (Network Management)* and the *M.Bus (Network Application Integration)*. The aim of the network integration course was to concentrate upon the integration of business information systems both internally and with business partners. At the time, aspects of the design, development, implementation and management of this integration were encompassed under the term Enterprise Application Integration, the Network Management course examining information systems security, management of support services, and network administration. The course aimed to provide students the opportunity to gain a deeper understanding of these issues and the skills to manage in a commercial environment. The courses effectively had only one intake and were discontinued in 2008.

In 2015 as Business Analytics was seen as an important new area, the Information Systems area introduced its first new courses in nine years: the *Graduate Diploma* and *Masters in Business Analytics*. These courses aimed to train students for traditional business analyst roles in the modern age with new subjects related to the business analytics area, such as Business Analytics, Business Intelligence Systems and Predictive Analytics. It also shared some subjects with their counterparts in ERP. Some business analytics subjects are also offered as electives in the undergraduate program.

9 Conclusion: What of the Future?

We have described how the discipline of Information Systems developed, first in two Colleges of Advanced Education and then in the university created by their merger. During this 40 year period computing has changed dramatically from an area with a small number of Professional Experts to something that everyone now knows something about and makes use of every day. In IS curricula we have seen considerable change as a new curriculum area enters our courses in response to the development of new technologies and business applications and then disappears as this material enters the mainstream and is no longer necessary to be taught as a separate area. We have described a number of instances where this has occurred and, no doubt, there will be more.

The really interesting thing though, and something that must be unique to an area involving rapidly changing technology such as computing, is that from time to time IS course developers must discard much of their content and start again, largely from the beginning with new material [4]. We should now ask: *if we look back over the history of IS curriculum development, what lessons have we learned that we might avoid repeating*? Perhaps we should not be too quick to introduce a new course until we are sure that there is an industry need and a demand by students and that this will be long lasting. Perhaps we should pay more attention to how industry roles have developed over time with systems analysts becoming general business analysts and then moving into analytics, executive information systems becoming decision support systems and evolving into predictive analytics. Thus, not only do new areas need to be introduced, but existing roles and systems need to be updated through modification and adaptation to account for new approaches and technologies.

What does this mean for Information Systems departments? Some of the more technical aspects of Information System could merge with Computer Science while others will continue to enter the mainstream and become part of other business subjects. Will there even be a need for a separate discipline of Information Systems into the future? It will certainly be necessary for, perhaps a small number of people, to understand how to analyse business needs and how these could be solved using computing, but the actual construction of these systems in the future is likely to involve even less people than now. Will Information Systems departments continue to educate these people who will analyse business needs and commission the developments of new systems? Time will tell.

References

1. Santayana, G.: The Life of Reason. Charles Scribner's Sons, New York (1905)
2. McCann, D., Thorne, P.: The Last of the First - CSIRAC: Australia's First Computer. The University of Melbourne, Melbourne (2000)
3. Tatnall, A.: A Curriculum History of Business Computing in Victorian Tertiary Institutions from 1960–1985, in Education. Deakin University, Geelong (1993)
4. Tatnall, A.: Curriculum Cycles in the History of Information Systems in Australia. Heidelberg Press, Melbourne (2006)
5. Maynard, G.: Interview on the History of Business Computing, Melbourne (1990)
6. Tatnall, A.: Computer education and societal change: history of early courses in computing in universities and schools in Victoria. Inf. Technol. People **28**(4), 742–757 (2015)
7. Gries, D., Walker, T., Young, P.: The 1988 snowbird report: a discipline matures. Commun. ACM **32**(3), 294–297 (1989)
8. Pearcey, T.: A history of Australian computing. Melbourne, Chisholm Institute of Technology (1988)
9. Orlikowski, W.J., Baroudi, J.J.: Studying information technology in organizations: research approaches and assumptions. Inf. Syst. Res. **2**(1), 1–28 (1991)
10. Howell, M.C., Prevenier, W.: From Reliable Sources. An Introduction to Historical Methods. Cornell University Press, Ithaca (2001)
11. Mahoney, J., Rueschemeyer, D.: Comparative Historical Analysis in the Social Sciences. Cambridge University Press, Cambridge (2003)
12. Goodson, I.F. (ed.): International Perspectives in Curriculum History. Routledge, London (1988)
13. Franklin, B.M.: Curriculum history: its nature and boundaries. Curriculum Inquiry **7**(1), 67–79 (1977)
14. Layton, D.: Science as General Education. Trends in Educ. **25**, 11–15 (1972)
15. Rasmussen, C.: Poor Man's University. Footscray Institute of Technology, Melbourne (1989)
16. Footscray Institute of Technology: Handbook 1988 Footscray Institute of Technology. Footscray Institute of Technology, Melbourne (1988)
17. Moll, J.K., Flood, B.J.: Information science and information-related educational programs: their diversity and accreditation. J. Am. Soc. Inf. Sci. **39**, 318–322 (1988)
18. Garrison, G.: Challenges to information science education. J. Am. Soc. Inf. Sci. **39**(5), 362 (1988)

19. Laverty, E.P., Sorg, J.S.: Information technology and education for the public service. Int. J. Public Adm. **8**(4), 391–408 (1986)
20. Institute, W.: Western Institute 1989 Handbook. Western Institute, Melbourne (1989)
21. Dawkins, J.S.: Higher Education Policy Statement. AGPS, Canberra (1988)
22. Tatnall, A., Burgess, S.: Evolution of information systems curriculum in an australian university over the last twenty-five years. In: Tatnall, A., Jones, A. (eds.) WCCE 2009. IAICT, vol. 302, pp. 238–246. Springer, Heidelberg (2009). https://doi.org/10.1007/978-3-642-03115-1_25
23. Burgess, S.: Curriculum planning for information management, in business information technology. R. Melbourne Inst. Technol., Melbourne (1993)
24. Tatnall, A., Reyes, G.: Teaching IT project management to postgraduate business students: a practical approach. J. Inf. Technol. Educ. **4**, 153–166 (2005)
25. Davey, W., Tatnall, A.: Introducing object environments: cognitive difficulties. In: Software Education Conference: SRIG-ET 1994. IEEE Computer Society Press, Dunedin, New Zealand (1995)
26. Burgess, S., Tatnall, A.: Post graduate electronic commerce specialisations: an Australian university case study. In: Innovation Through Information Technology (IRMA). Idea Group Publishing, New Orleans, USA (2004)
27. Tatnall, A., Groom, C., Burgess, S.: Electronic commerce specialisations in MBAs: an Australian university case study. In: Informing Science and IT Education Conference. University College Cork, Cork, Ireland (2002)
28. Burgess, S., Tatnall, A., Darbyshire, P.: Teaching small business entrepreneurs about computers. In: EuroPME - Entrepreneurship: Building for the Future. Groupe ESC, Rennes Rennes, France (1999)
29. Tatnall, A., Burgess, S.: Experiences in building and using decision-support systems in postgraduate university courses. Interdisc. J. Inf. Knowl. Manag. **2**, 33–42 (2007)

A Survey of the Prior Programming Experience of Undergraduate Computing and Engineering Students in Ireland

Glenn Strong[1(✉)], Catherine Higgins[2], Nina Bresnihan[1], and Richard Millwood[1]

[1] Trinity College Dublin, Dublin, Ireland
{glenn.strong,nina.bresnihan, richard.millwood}@scss.tcd.ie
[2] Dublin Institute of Technology, Dublin, Ireland
catherine.higgins@dit.ie

Abstract. It has become apparent that increasing numbers of students arriving into undergraduate computing and engineering degree programmes in Irish 3rd-level institutions have prior experience of computer programming. As the extent of this prior exposure as well as its nature, origins, and usefulness is not known beyond anecdotal evidence, an annual survey of prior programming experience of freshman undergraduates who study programming as part of their degree has been designed and administered. This paper reports on the first two years of this survey in 2015 and 2016. It found that around one third had some prior experience of programming with nearly half of that group reporting a reasonable level of fluency in one or more languages. The authors expect that the effect of proposed changes to primary and 2nd-level curricula alongside the increasing popularity of informal programming clubs will be increasingly felt in coming years and therefore plan to continue and extend the survey in order to clarify the effect of such developments. The results should be of interest to 3rd-level educators in the planning of curriculum and teaching practice.

Keywords: Computer science education · Programming experience CS1

1 Introduction

In recent years, the academic community in Ireland has become aware that many students arriving at 3rd-level to sit computer science and engineering degree programmes do so with some prior exposure to programming. This is despite the fact that programming is not taught as a formal subject in the Leaving Certificate cycle and has only been made available since 2014 as part of an optional Junior Certificate short course in Coding [1][1]. However, outside of formal educational settings, there has been

[1] Note on the Irish education system: Primary corresponds to K1–K6 in the American system, and Second-level corresponds to K7–K12. The Junior Certificate is the stare examination taken at the end of the third year of second-level and the Leaving Certificate is the terminal state exam taken at the end of the K12-equivalent year.

A. Tatnall and M. Webb (Eds.): WCCE 2017, IFIP AICT 515, pp. 473–483, 2017.
https://doi.org/10.1007/978-3-319-74310-3_48

a surge of interest in learning to program as evidenced by the phenomenal success of the CoderDojo network of after-school programming clubs which since its foundation in 2011 has grown exponentially to include over 200 clubs across Ireland in January 2017 [2]. The impact of such initiatives on the intake into 3rd-level courses has yet to be assessed. The standard introductory programming course at 3rd-level assumes no prior knowledge of programming but, in this changing environment, this assumption needs to be questioned. Furthermore, with recent announcements that the National Council for Curriculum and Assessment is to consider approaches to introducing the teaching of programming in primary schools as well as a proposed introduction of Computer Science as a Leaving Certificate subject in 2018 [3], it is clear that 3rd-level institutions will need to adapt to cater for a new generation of students with prior programming experience. In this evolving context, the aim of the survey discussed here is to track the state of programming knowledge among freshman (first year undergraduates) and how this is changing over time thereby providing educators with an evidence-base for decisions about future curriculum design and teaching practice.

The structure of this paper is as follows: Sect. 2 reports related research while Sect. 3 gives a short overview of the research questions and the process used to collect data to answer these questions. Section 4 reports on the results gathered in the first two years of this survey and Sect. 5 concludes the paper with a discussion of the findings from this research, its future direction and the contribution it makes to the educational research and curriculum development for teaching programming.

2 Related Research

A review of related literature revealed that, while prior knowledge of programming among first year undergraduates has been investigated in previous studies, it has generally not been the primary focus of the research. Such studies have investigated the effects of prior knowledge on such things as confidence levels [4], problem solving [5] and gender balance [8] with previous programming experience often being cited as a predictor of programming success [6, 7]. Interestingly, studies have shown that it is not prior knowledge of programming concepts alone but student self-efficacy, or their self-perception of their programming ability that has the strongest correlation with programming performance [9, 10]. Krpan et al.'s investigation into the correlation between students' success in introductory programming and mathematical courses included an analysis of student expectations and success rates in introductory programming courses at the Faculty of Science, University of Split over three years. They found that early failure to understand basic programming concepts affects students' confidence and leads to increased drop-out rates [11].

The background of Computer Science freshmen across two Finnish universities, was investigated in 2011 and 2012 [12]. Differing levels of prior programming experience were found between the two institutions (62% and 38%), with the university with the more selective entrance criteria having the higher percentage. It is worth noting that between 43% and 63% of those with experience gained it through formal studies, an opportunity not currently available to most Irish undergraduates.

Data relating to the prior experience of over 900 students at the Eidgenössische Technische Hochschule (ETH) Zurich was collected over seven years from 2003 and gathered from 77 students from University of York in 2008 [13]. During this time Computer Science was an optional subject not universally available in either Switzerland or the UK at primary or 2nd level, yet in both institutions, prior experience was high, running at a stable level of 78%–84% across the 7 years. Interestingly, only 16%–25% gained their experience at school, with most reporting self-study as the source. The authors note that generalisation of their results may be limited to other universities with similar admission regulations and students who studied in a comparable school system and recommend that research be broadened to more universities and countries. Indeed, no research on collating data relating to students' prior knowledge of programming at a national or international level was found during our literature search and the survey discussed here is believed to be the first to attempt to do so on a national level.

3 Research Question and Data Collection

This research project aims to find out what programming knowledge and experience students have before commencing undergraduate degree programmes with a programming component in Irish 3rd-level institutions. It also explores how this exposure affects their experience of programming during their freshman year and how this picture is changing over time.

To gain answers to these questions, it was decided to undertake a repeated cross-sectional study using an annual survey. This paper reports on the first two years of results from that activity. The survey population is freshman students undertaking a third level, undergraduate degree programme in Ireland which involves the studying of programming in first year. Such programmes are typically computer science and engineering programmes. The decision was made to target students in the latter part of the second semester of their freshman year so they could make a judgement with regard to the impact of their prior experience on their current studies. While the overwhelming majority of the survey population would have undergone their second-level education in Ireland, we note that as of the 2014/2015 academic year approximately 10% of students in Irish higher education are "international" students [14]. We expect that a number of these students would have experienced some level of formal exposure to programming in their previous education.

An online survey was deemed to be the most suitable data collection instrument as this enabled easy collection of standardised data from a geographically distributed sample. The benefits of this process were deemed to outweigh our concerns about any bias resulting from the self-reporting nature of the responses. Ethical approval was sought and granted by the appropriate ethical committee with Google Forms being the platform currently used by the researchers to administer and maintain the survey.

Rather than contact the target respondents directly it was decided that a higher response rate would be likely if they were recruited by teaching staff in their own institutions. Contact was made with appropriate personnel nationwide to ask for their collaboration in introducing the goal of the survey and forwarding it to their students.

In return, the researchers furnish each participating institution with their raw student data as well as a copy of the annual report of analysed results.

In 2015, a pilot study was run between two 3rd-level institutions in Dublin in order to validate the survey design and gather some baseline data. In this pilot, categories of questions were developed to understand the profile of the student population in terms of age, gender and programme of study; to ascertain if students had prior experience; to understand the languages learned with the level of fluency and finally to examine the impact of the experience on students' current studies. The pilot survey was issued to students in both institutions across all 4 years of relevant programmes (students were also asked to identify their year of study as part of the survey, allowing us to make direct comparisons year-by-year). Based on responses to the pilot, the survey was subsequently updated to include two extra categories of questions which examined the source of the student experience as well as their reflections regarding the usefulness of the experience.

From 2016, invitations were issued to 3rd-level institutions nationwide aimed exclusively at freshman students with 8 institutions agreeing to participate which resulted in a sample of n = 321 respondents. The aim of the researchers is to continue to grow the institution and participant levels on an annual basis so the generalisability of trends and patterns identified in the years going forward continues to increase. The current design of the survey has 6 categories of questions with a mix of closed multiple choice and open short answer questions producing 32 questions in total. Category 1 examines the profile of the population by asking respondents for personal information such as 3rd-level institution attended, age, gender, and degree programme. Category 2 has a singular focus on asking if respondents have prior experience. For those with experience, there is a further 4 sections. Category 3 examines the nature of their experience in terms of the language(s) learned and the degree of fluency in the language(s). Category 4 examines the origins of their experience from a school, club, online and self-taught perspective. Category 5 examines aspects of their experience that students signal they found particularly helpful in growing their knowledge of programming and finally Category 6 examines how useful students find their prior experience to be in their current freshman studies.

3.1 Data Validity

The total population size is only available for two thirds of the group surveyed, which precludes calculating confidence for our overall results, a deficit that will be addressed in future surveys. Where accurate information on cohort size is available, from three institutions (n = 222, population = 651), we calculate a confidence interval of ±5.34, at a confidence level of 95%. Our overall results do not differ significantly from the results obtained (i.e., they lie within the confidence interval reported) when only considering this restricted set of the population, nevertheless we must be cautious in interpreting the overall results as a result of this weakness.

Some respondents chose not to indicate which institution they were attending, making it impossible to include them in these figures; a requirement of the study's ethical approval was that no question be compulsory making such occasional gaps in the data inevitable. Where it has been possible to uniquely infer a student's institution from their stated course of study we have done so.

With respect to other threats to validity, we note that having students self-assess their level of confidence and ability, rather than applying an objective test, may introduce some bias, though it is not clear in which direction this may lie.

4 Results and Analysis

4.1 Participants

As the 2015 participants included all 4 years of a programme, we restricted our analysis of the 2015 data to the 122 freshman students, to give a truer basis for comparison. These figures are laid out in Table 1:

Table 1. Participant details

Year	Total	Male	Female	Age 18–22	Age 22+
2015 (n = 122)	122	72%	28%	92%	8%
2016 (n = 321)	321	76%	24%	76%	24%

While only around 25% of respondents are female across both years of the study, this is in fact a slight overrepresentation in the survey as enrolment figures for full-time honours degrees for 2014/2015 for females are a mere 14.9% for computing degrees and 18.1% for Engineering degrees [14]. The reason for the substantial jump in the mature student rate from 2015 to 2016 is unknown.

4.2 Programming Experience

The data of most interest was the percentage of students who self-identified as having programming experience. Of the 321 students who responded to the 2016 survey, **66%** indicated that they had **no** prior exposure to programming with **34.2%** indicating they had some experience prior to the start of their 3rd-level course. These figures broadly reflect those from the 2015 pilot survey where **63%** of freshman students (n = 120) indicated they had no prior experience. A Chi-squared test showed no significant difference between the two survey results (P = 0.938).

Students were also asked to self-report their prior level of fluency in programming. The 2016 cohort reported having a much stronger level of fluency than the 2015 respondents (see Fig. 1 for figures and an explanation of fluency levels).

A Chi-squared test was performed to confirm the significance (P = 0.0176). Reasons for the stronger reported fluency in the 2016 cohort is not apparent from the survey data but it will be interesting to see if this trend continues in the years ahead and to ascertain possible reasons for this increase.

Comparing these results to the results of the ETH Zurich study [13] where 78%–84% of respondents reported prior experience highlights the relatively low level of experience of Irish students at the outset of their 3rd-level study. We believe this is most

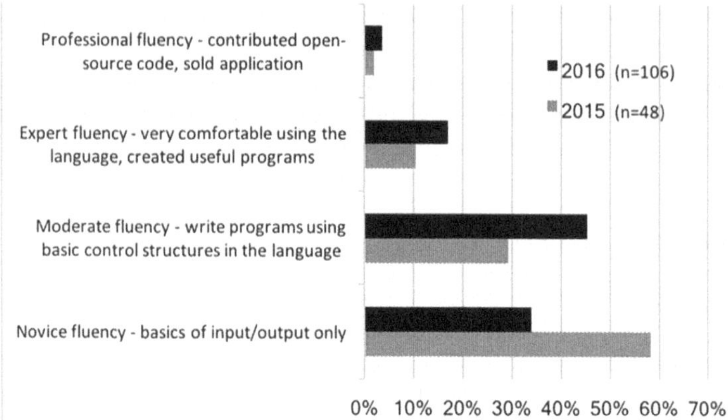

Fig. 1. Level of fluency from 2015 and 2016

likely due to the majority of students coming directly from Irish second-level schools where programming is not yet widely taught. Equally interesting was the level of fluency reported which suggested that for the students who did have experience their previous studies were often deep and considered.

4.3 Programming Languages

Students who reported having some programming experience were then asked to indicate which languages they had some experience with. In 2015 this was presented as multiple choice list (with an "other" option), while in 2016 students were instead presented with an open question giving respondents freedom to indicate the range of languages they had experienced. The two years' responses are presented in Table 2.

Table 2. Programming languages experienced prior to 3rd-level

Language	2015 freshmen (n = 48)	2016 (n = 106)
C, C++, C#	33%	40%
HTML	60%	28%
Java	44%	59%
JavaScript	23%	17%
Other	0%	22%
PHP	0%	12%
Python	25%	33%
Scratch	38%	1%
Basic variants	4%	14%

Students have clearly engaged with a wide variety of languages which is an indicator of the diversity and range of courses on offer. As an aside, the almost complete absence of the educational language "Scratch" in the 2016 results is striking. We would speculate that this is due to the change to the open-question format in the 2016 survey causing students to omit Scratch from their answers based on a perception of what constitutes a "real" programming language.

4.4 Helpfulness of Experience

Respondents were asked to report on how (or not) their prior programming experience helped them in their freshman year of studying programming. The question was presented as an open-question prompting a varied response. Interestingly, 15% of respondents in 2015 and 10% in 2016 indicated that their prior experience didn't help at all. The analysis of the responses given by the remaining respondents who did report an impact produced the following broad categories:

- A head start boosted confidence helping students transition to 3rd-level.
- Not struggling with the basic concepts allowed for deeper learning to occur.
- Understanding fundamental concepts helped in adapting to new languages.
- More receptive to understanding complex concepts.
- More time could be spent on studying other modules.

As we might expect, prior exposure to programming concepts is considered helpful when dealing with introductory programming modules. Interestingly, the first group that emerged doesn't relate directly to the conceptual knowledge and skills gained from prior experience but instead focuses on the affective impact of having such knowledge particularly in the area of confidence levels and receptiveness to new learning. This underlines the importance of educators adopting pedagogical approaches that support the growth of confidence in learners. Given the diversity of programming tools and skills encountered, it's perhaps not surprising that familiarity with the core concepts of programming had a significant positive impact. Since many introductory programming modules focus on trying to impart these core skills, students who have a head start reported that they can focus purely on advanced constructs or even on other modules.

In 2016 only, respondents were asked, again using an open question, which parts of their prior experience were the most useful to them overall. 35% reported that nothing helped them. This could mean that they either didn't find their experience useful or they were unable to articulate or remember any particular aspects they found useful. The remaining respondents' responses were grouped into the categories listed in Fig. 2.

Over a quarter of respondents indicated that while their experience was useful, nothing specific stood out as having helped them. With the remaining responses, the most frequently cited helpful activities were time spent on projects or practice (19%) and specific online or print resources (15%) notably Codecademy and YouTube.

The fact that a substantial number of participants were unwilling (or unable) to identify individual sources of their experience as being helpful could indicate that nothing at all, or no single specific aspect was helpful. However, alternative readings could suggest that students either had difficulty in reflecting on its effect or that their overall experience - rather than specific experiences - was helpful. This question will need careful redesign in future iterations to assist students answer more accurately without biasing and guiding their responses.

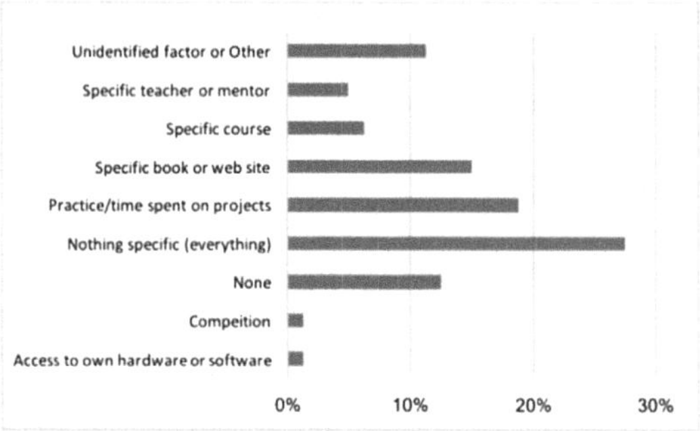

Fig. 2. Sources of useful prior experience - 2016 (n = 80)

4.5 Origins of Experience

In 2016, participants with prior experience were asked a series of questions to gain insight into its origins. These were categorized into school, club, online and self-directed learning with respondents also having an opportunity to indicate any other sources of their experience. This is a particularly interesting question in the Irish context where programming has not been widely available as a formal school subject and grassroots organisations like CoderDojo report considerable activity. Most respondents reported multiple sources for their experience.

School Activities: 27% indicated that they had participated in programming activities through school. These activities were identified as short summer classes, transition year courses (a one year programme in Irish second-level schools with no formal exams prior to beginning the two year terminal examination), elective classes, preparation for programming competitions, and as a formal part of school curriculum (international students). The duration of these activities ranged from 1 day to 2 years.

Club Activities: 13% of respondents reported participation in clubs or groups outside of school. Of those, 36% had attended CoderDojo; 27% were involved with other computer clubs; 19% were involved with 3rd-level access and youth programmes with the remaining 18% citing adult education courses.

Online Activities: Reported participation in online courses (including courses that they may not have finished) was 42%. The most common sites used were Codecademy (46%), non-specified tutorial sites (27%) and YouTube (7%) with other specified sites each representing just over 2%.

Self-directed Learning: When asked if they had engaged with any self-directed learning such as books or building projects, 63% answered in the affirmative with the majority of those citing projects that they had designed and developed. These included games (41%), websites (22%), web applications (17%), Arduino/Raspberry Pi projects (17%) and general business applications (3%). The time spent on these projects varied significantly from a couple of hours to a couple of years with the average amount reported as approximately 40 h.

Other Sources of Experience: 30% of respondents indicated they had other sources of experience. These included post-2nd-level school courses that were not diplomas or degrees (43%), previous 3rd-level courses (23%), previous employment (13%) with the remaining 21% not specified.

When examining the origins of prior experience, it was not unexpected, given the lack of formal inclusion of programming in Irish schools' curricula, that a high number (73%) of respondents gained their experience outside of school. Indeed, what was surprising was the extent and range of extra courses run by some schools both as part of their day-to-day curriculum and as extra short courses after school. The percentage of 13% of students participating in clubs/groups would appear to be low when compared to the activity that is school based (27%). This is despite the high profile of CoderDojo but may well be due to the relative infancy of this club, founded in 2011, and we would expect this number to increase in the future in line with the increasing participation and growth of dojos in Ireland. However, this is only speculative analysis and data gathered in the years going forward will allow more concrete patterns of participation in clubs to emerge. At present it is clear that most non-online computing activities undertaken by students are via school.

Not unexpectedly, there is a relatively high number of students undertaking online courses with Codecademy being the clear leader. The most popular languages being learned online are the web development scripting languages and Python. While there is no indicator in the survey regarding the reasons why students chose those languages, having an understanding of popular online programming paradigms could provide assistance both in understanding prior experience and also in the generation of online courses for distance education at 3rd-level.

5 Discussion

When examining the profile of freshman students in any discipline, there is always diversity in terms of age, background and general experience. This is a factor that 3rd-level educators have always had to take into consideration when designing courses and choosing appropriate pedagogical approaches. With computer science primary degrees having the highest rate of non-progression in Ireland (varying between universities (15%) and institutes of technology (26%) [15]) it is clearly important that the nature and impact of that previous experience be more fully understood so that introductory courses be made more relevant and appealing to students.

While Ireland has not as yet introduced formal computer science or programming as mainstream subjects in schools, it has become apparent to educators that a growing number of students are already presenting in Irish 3rd-level institutions with prior programming experience. From the results of the survey presented in this paper, it can be seen that roughly a third of those surveyed have had some exposure to programming. To date, a lot of that experience is, necessarily, from self-directed and online study but a surprising amount stems from schools which emerged as an important driver and facilitator for encouraging students into their first steps in programming. Non-school clubs such as CoderDojo have grown in numbers and popularity since their foundation in 2011, however their effect in Ireland cannot be seen as yet in the 3rd-level population. Together with the mooted introduction of programming through the new mathematics curriculum at primary level and the introduction of computer science as a Leaving Certificate subject from September 2018, it is clear that the nature and extent of the prior programming experience of incoming undergraduates will be subject to enormous change over the coming decade.

The early results of this study, while limited in their scope, can provide an indication of the current situation as well as a baseline from which to evaluate the inevitable further changes in our student profile. The authors will continue to expand the reach of this survey and administer it annually in order to track these changes and see how they impact student interest and experience in programming going forward. Given the shortage of comparable national studies from other countries, it is difficult to compare these results against international standards. However, given the growing interest in computer science and programming at school level worldwide and the resulting increase in the skills and knowledge of incoming 3rd-level students, it is expected that research and interest in this area will grow. We would argue that this survey will lead to a better understanding of student experience prior to their arrival at 3rd-level and help to provide an evidence-base for decisions about future curriculum design and teaching practice, consequently providing some contribution to student retention and competency levels.

Acknowledgments. The authors would like to thank our colleagues at various institutions in Ireland who have circulated the survey to their students.

References

1. National Council for Curriculum and Assessment: JuniorCycle. ie - Short Courses. http://www.juniorcycle.ie/Curriculum/Short-Courses
2. N.A.: CoderDojo Zen. https://zen.coderdojo.com/
3. Department of Education and Skills: Action Plan for Education 2017 (2017)
4. Macleod, H., Patterson, J.: A survey of undergraduate technology use and attitudes. University of Edinburgh (2012). https://doi.org/10.7488/ds/97
5. Chen, T.-Y., Lewandowski, G., McCartney, R., Sanders, K., Simon, B.: Commonsense computing: using student sorting abilities to improve instruction. In: ACM SIGCSE Bulletin, pp. 276–280. ACM (2007)
6. Madigan, E.M., Goodfellow, M., Stone, J.A.: Gender, perceptions, and reality: technological literacy among first-year students. In: Presented at the ACM SIGCSE Bulletin (2007)
7. Hagan, D., Markham, S.: Does it help to have some programming experience before beginning a computing degree program? In: Proceedings of the 5th Annual SIGCSE/SIGCUE ITiCSE Conference on Innovation and Technology in Computer Science Education, pp. 25–28. ACM, New York (2000)
8. Wilson, B.C.: A study of factors promoting success in computer science including gender differences. Comput. Sci. Educ. **12**, 141–164 (2002)
9. Bergin, S., Reilly, R.: Programming: factors that influence success. In: ACM SIGCSE Bulletin, vol. 37, no. 1, pp. 411–415 (2005)

10. Wilson, B.C., Shrock, S.: Contributing to success in an introductory computer science course: a study of twelve factors. In: ACM SIGCSE Bulletin, vol. 33, no. 1, pp. 184–188 (2001)
11. Krpan, D., Mladenović, S., Rosić, M.: Undergraduate programming courses, students' perception and success. Proc.-Soc. Behav. Sci. **174**, 3868–3872 (2015)
12. Kinnunen, P., Marttila-Kontio, M., Pesonen, E.: Getting to know computer science freshmen. In: Proceedings of the 13th Koli Calling International Conference on Computing Education Research, pp. 59–66. ACM, New York (2013)
13. Pedroni, M., Oriol, M., Meyer, B.: The prior experience of entering CS students. ETH, Department of Computer Science (2011)
14. Higher Education Authority: Student Enrollment Statistics 2014–2015. http://www.hea.ie/node/1557
15. Higher Education Authority: A Study of Progression in Irish Higher Education 2012/13 to 2013/14 (2016)

Measuring Learners' Interest in Computing (Education): Development of an Instrument and First Results

Torsten Brinda[1(✉)], David Tobinski[2], and Stefan Schwinem[1]

[1] Computing Education Research Group, University of Duisburg-Essen, Essen, Germany
torsten.brinda@uni-due.de, stefan.schwinem@stud.uni-due.de
[2] Cognitive and Educational Psychology, University of Duisburg-Essen, Essen, Germany
david.tobinski@uni-due.de

Abstract. So far, there is hardly any empirical research on the question of what raises or influences the interest of school learners in computer science or computing education. Aspects to be considered are for example pedagogical decisions of the teacher concerning contexts, phenomena, situations, or concepts to which a lesson or a lesson sequence refers, planned learner activities and many others. This paper analyses a model for describing interest in physics on its transferability to computer science, reports about the development of an online questionnaire for investigating the computing-related interests of school learners and gives results of a first empirical pilot study (based on $N = 141$ datasets). Based on the participants' answers concerning socio-demographical aspects, the computing interest of different groups of learners was analyzed. A higher level of computing interest was found at male pupils, learners who indicated that they were striving for a computing-related job, that computing was their favorite school subject, or that they had good or very good school marks in mathematics or computing.

Keywords: Learners' interest · Computing interest · Secondary education Questionnaire · Empirical study · Explorative study

1 Introduction

Among other things, school education shall be directed to "the development of the child's personality, talents and mental and physical abilities to their fullest potential" [1]. This includes the development of *interests*, perhaps even long-term domain interests, which may lead to a professional career in the particular area after graduation from school in the future. The pedagogical-psychological literature (e.g. [2, 3]) assumes that interest as an element of the learning potential influences the activities of learners and, finally, together with other factors, affects their competencies and personality development. Because of the importance of interest in the design of teaching-learning processes, the description, modelling and development of interest has already been

A. Tatnall and M. Webb (Eds.): WCCE 2017, IFIP AICT 515, pp. 484–493, 2017.
https://doi.org/10.1007/978-3-319-74310-3_49

investigated intensively, e.g. in the fields of educational and natural sciences. Krapp and Prenzel give an overview of the research field in the area of pedagogical psychology [4]. According to them, interest is a multidimensional, psychological construct directed to a particular object whose operational definition requires cognitive and emotional categories. Interest can arise from the interaction of an individual with its environment and is influenced by his or her values and feelings. Individual interest, which is anchored in the personality structure of the individual, and situational interest generated by external factors can be distinguished. From a school perspective, teachers would like to see learners to be interested in their lessons and the course of lessons as well as in the addressed concepts and activities. The goal of generating or maintaining interest in mathematics, computing, science or technology is also of interest for many countries and leads worldwide to various educational initiatives, such as www.stemedcoalition.org, www.stemnet.org.uk or www.mintzukunftschaffen.de, because the STEM business field (science – technology – engineering – mathematics) is regarded as very important for the economic development.

Since interest in computer science or computing as a school subject have so far hardly been empirically investigated, this paper aims to contribute to its description and investigation. So, the rest of this paper is structured as follows: in Sect. 2, we analyze a model for structuring interest in physics for its transferability to computer science. In Sect. 3, we describe the development and the structure of our questionnaire for investigating computing interests, followed by results of a first pilot study we carried out in 2016 in Sect. 4. The paper ends with conclusions and outlook in Sect. 5. A detailed documentation of the study can be found in [5].

2 Structuring Computing Interest

An important work in the field was carried out in the subject physics. In the so-called *IPN*[1] *interest study in physics*, learners' interest in the school subject and the academic discipline physics were measured and analyzed in different grade levels of lower secondary education with an extensive questionnaire over a longer period of time [6]. This study was based on a three-dimensional interest model with the dimensions *concepts*, *contexts* and *activities*. On this basis, the study investigated the prior knowledge and interest in various topics of the school subject physics as well as in different sub-areas of the academic discipline and the learners' interest in learning more about it. The sub-areas were sketched by means of a short text in order to give learners, who did not yet have any or no physics lessons on the respective topic, the possibility to answer the questions. In addition, leisure and future job interests were measured on the basis of questions about media usage during leisure time as well as by discussion topics in the circle of friends.

In an international study on the *Relevance of Science Education (ROSE)* [7] among other things, ranking lists of the most interesting and uninteresting topics were created – from computer science perspective, the finding that the topic "How computers work"

[1] Leibnitz Institute for Science and Mathematics Education, Kiel, Germany.

was the third-most interesting one for boys in this science-related survey is especially recognizable. Further areas of interest related to computer science were not reported.

For computer science, there is a study on "student wishes in computer science" [8], which is closer related to the focus of the paper at hand – also carried out at the IPN. The wishes of pupils concerning computing education at school were investigated based on the computing curriculum of the federal state of Schleswig-Holstein (Germany) valid at the time of the study as well as on the recommendations for educational standards for lower secondary computing education of the German Informatics Association (GI) [9]. The topological structure of computing interest (as in the IPN interest study in physics) was not investigated.

This leads to the question: What would be possible facets of computing interest? For this purpose, the structure model used in physics is subsequently examined with regard to its suitability for the description of computing interest.

Relevant concretizations of the two dimensions *concepts* and *activities* provide the *content* and *process fields*, as they are, for example, defined in the educational standards for computing education in lower and upper secondary education of the GI [9, 10], as well as in computing curricula of Germany's federal states (e.g. [11]). A similar structure can also be found, for example, in the K12 Computer Science Framework, which was developed in cooperation of ACM, https://code.org/, CSTA and others (see https://k12cs.org/). This work distinguishes between the *concepts* "computing systems", "networks and the internet", "data and analysis", "algorithms and programming" as well as "impacts of computing" and the *practices* "fostering an inclusive computing culture", "collaborating around computing", "recognizing and defining computational problems", "developing and using abstractions", "creating computational artefacts", "testing and refining computational artefacts" and "communicating about computing". Computing interest can develop in terms of computing concepts as well as in terms of computing activities such as "coding" or "programming".

There is also various research on the dimension of *contexts*, which details this in terms of computer science. On the website of the German project "computer science in context" (www.informatik-im-kontext.de, see also [12]) there are several examples of possible computing contexts, such as "intelligent houses" and "social networks". The aim of relating lessons to contexts is to link different aspects of a subject in a larger overall perspective, but also to show learners how the competencies to be acquired relate to their everyday lives. Starting point of school lessons can be, for example, certain everyday situations with a connection to computer science, which can then serve to open up the larger context. In connection with such situations, various phenomena of computer science may occur [13], which may require explanation and which can initiate questions and research interests. This way, everyday situations and computing phenomena can generate interest.

Another area that could be investigated with regard to computing interests is the media usage behaviour of learners. According to the annual German JIM (youths – information – multimedia) studies, it can be assumed that nearly all young people have access to smartphones [14], as well as to digital devices of a wide range of other categories. The goal to use digital media competently, but also to understand and to help shape the "digital" world, is a core statement of overall concepts for "education in the digital networked world" (e.g. [15, 16]). Digital media such as the MIT

AppInventor (appinventor.mit.edu) enable shaping through app development in a simple, visual way. Digital media of a different kinds can create interest of pupils by themselves, by related computing phenomena [13] or by embedding them in subordinate contexts [12]. Since digital media from the point of view of computer science are either computing systems (e.g. a learning app, an eBook reader) or digital representations of information (e.g. a learning video, an eBook), there is no need to extend the above-mentioned structure model here. In the course of the discussion about education in the digital networked world, it was argued that systems, phenomena, artefacts and contexts of the digital world should be analyzed from an application-oriented, from a technological and from a socio-cultural perspective – in order to enable full participation in view of understanding as well as the ability to contribute. The application-oriented perspective can already be found in the structural model in two places: as "using" as possible activity as well as with regard to the "application object", a computing system, which is a possible subject concept. The technological perspective is formed by computing concepts and activities and is thus also included. Finally, the socio-cultural perspective can be found in the content field "Informatics, man, and society" [9] and/or "Impacts of Computing" (https://k12cs.org/), where everyday contexts are the starting point for further consideration.

In conclusion, there is much evidence that the structural model used in the IPN interest study in physics could also be viable for computer science.

3 Investigating Interest in Computing

The above considerations were the starting point for the development of an online questionnaire for the exploratory investigation of computing interest and its piloting in some groups of learners of different school forms [5], as will be described next.

3.1 Structure of the Questionnaire

The decision for an online questionnaire was made in order to be able to reach a potentially larger group of participants, essentially regardless of location. The structure of the questionnaire was orientated at the IPN interest study in physics [6], computing interest was analogously differentiated in interest in the school subject and the academic discipline. A translated version of the questionnaire is available at http://udue.de/csinterest. At first, the participants were asked how many semesters they have already had computing as a school subject or whether they intended to select the subject in the future and thereby differentiated.

Those who have or had taken the subject were asked for their *interest in computing as a subject*. For this purpose, an instrument for the subject social sciences [17] was adapted to computing. With this instrument, students' attitudes towards the subject are measured using a four-level Likert scale from "strongly agree" to "strongly disagree". This scale has also been used in further questions, the decision for four levels was taken to encourage the participants to a decision [18]. Statements to be rated in this section were e.g. "It is fun for me to deal with computer science" or "Computer science helps me to develop as a person". The pedagogical design of the lesson was disregarded here.

These items were followed by a block on the *decision to take computing classes* in the past or the future. Also with a four-level Likert scale different answer options could be rated here, such as "because I would like to help myself with problems with my smartphone, tablet or computer" or "because I want to know how I can encounter dangers on the Internet, which target my data and my privacy".

The following section provided statements on the *importance of computer science in their own leisure time*, concerning e.g. their own research interests, discussions in the family or friends' circle with a relation to computing, as well as their active pursuing of computing topics in journals or media reports. In order to be able to adapt the following questions in the best possible way to the respective age group, the participants' current grade level as well as the type of their school were questioned next.

In the next section, the participants were asked about their interest in certain computing-related *contexts and situations*. Contexts and situations used for the study were derived based on theory: already tested contexts of "Computer science in context" [12] were used as well as information about the media usage behavior as reported in the KIM and JIM studies [14, 19]. In this case, learners in lower and upper secondary education were given common and separate items. Examples used were "attack by malware on the computer", "friendship recommendations in social networks" (both lower secondary education), "computer games", "mobile devices" (all participants), "home automation" (upper secondary education), and others. In each case, the learners were first asked about their prior knowledge (four-level response from "very much" to "very little" and about their interest to look on the respective situation or context from an application-oriented, technological, socio-cultural and creating perspective [15]. Related items referred to the learners' interest "how to create computer games", "how social networks function internally", "what effects the distribution of malware might have" or "how to use search engines properly". Furthermore, the participants were questioned whether the respective topic had already been dealt with in the classroom, as well as for the extent to which their interest was induced by computing education at school, the media, their circle of friends, plans for a future job or their own leisure activities.

The last section consisted of statements on various *concepts and activities* within computing education, which were collected from a choice of curricular documents [9, 11, 20]. Among other things, the participants were asked for their interest to plan programs, to know how hard- and software work together, how the discipline computer science develops, or how to use computing terms correctly. The questionnaire ended with sociodemographic questions about age, sex, their latest marks in mathematics and computer science (three-level: very good to good, average, rather bad), their favourite school subject and their future career plans. Pre-test investigations showed that it took about 30 min to answer the questionnaire.

3.2 Data Collection and Evaluation

The online questionnaire was created using the "LimeSurvey" software (www.limesurvey.org). An invitation letter with an explanation of the planned study, a pdf version of the questionnaire as well as a link to the online version were distributed via existing e-mail lists for computing teachers in the German federal states of

Baden-Wurttemberg, North Rhine-Westphalia, and Rhineland-Palatinate. Furthermore, some regional schools with personal contacts of the authors were also included. The data collection phase took place in the second half of June 2016. A total of 172 datasets were collected, of which 18 were incomplete. In addition, 13 records had to be excluded from the evaluation because of obviously nonsensical answers, so that the sample had a total size of $N = 141$.

The evaluation was carried out using the statistical software IBM SPSS v. 22 for the production of descriptive statistics as well as for the comparison of the interests of different groups of persons (separated by gender, favourite subject computer science, computer-related job wishes, assignment to lower or upper secondary education, (very) good marks in mathematics, (very) good marks in computing. For this, among other things, the "Mann-Whitney-U-Test" [21] appropriate for ordinal data was used.

4 Results of a First Pilot Study

4.1 Descriptive Statistics

In the section concerning *subject interest* six out of eight items were answered between 56% and 73% with "totally agree" or "agree". Percentages given in the following always are the sum of the values of the approving or rejecting categories. The participants expressed a generally positive attitude towards computing. However, nearly 60% of the respondents said that it is (rather) true that computer science is indifferent to them. The majority of respondents (57%) rejected (positive) statements regarding a positive effect of dealing with computer science on their own personality development.

Concerning their *decision on taking computing classes*, items were rather approved, which focused on help for self-help (55%), the understanding of computer science concepts (58%), or the acquisition of software application competencies (54%). Statements about dangers on the Internet, study or career decisions, experiences of siblings, friends or relatives active in the field of computer science, or expected advantages for other school subjects were (mostly) rejected or given a mixed picture.

Furthermore, *dealing with computer science in their everyday lives* was apparently of secondary importance for the participants – all respective items were (rather) rejected by 60% to 86% of the participants.

Concerning *situations and contexts*, a differentiated picture emerged: learners in *lower secondary education* ($n = 73$) rated dealing with malicious software (on the average of the sum of all assigned positive statements: 57%), computer games (62%) as well as smartphones and tablets (53%) from the afore mentioned pedagogical perspectives (see Sect. 2) as (rather) interesting, dealing with word processing (respectively negative statements: 60%) as well as social networks (54%) but of (rather) little interest. Their previous knowledge had no recognizable influence on these ratings: the participants rated their prior knowledge concerning word processing (76%), computer games (66%) and smartphones and tablets (75%) as (rather) high, their knowledge concerning the other contexts as rather low. Explicitly asked for factors affecting their interest, the participants' answers showed that an assumed importance of word processing for potential future careers (53%) and concerning computer games its relevance in their circles of friends (66%) as well as their interest in this field as a leisure activity (59%) had a positive effect on their interest. That such interest would have been induced by computing education at school or media reports was clearly rejected – this also applies analogously for the participants of *upper secondary education*. These participants ($n = 68$) rated their interest in the contexts computer games (average of the sum of all the associated positive statements: 66%), search engines (55%), clouds (51%), smartphones and tablets (62%), and home automation (48%; about 8% of the participants did not answer here, in the other contexts only about 1% to 3%) as (rather) high, only a few items related to the application-oriented and the socio-cultural perspective (contexts search engines, clouds, house automation) showed an undecided or slightly negative picture. In these areas, the participants said they had (rather) little prior knowledge. There is a need for further research here to investigate, whether there is a correlation. Explicitly asked for factors influencing their interest, again only few aspects very rated positively. Leisure interests with computer games (54%), relevance in their circle of friends (69%) and leisure interests (73%) with search engines. Although the participants rather agreed with the statement that it would be interesting to them to learn more about the internal functioning and the creation of search engines, it remains open at this point to which aspects their leisure/friends' circle interests relate. It would also be conceivable here that web-based searches on topics of their own interest using search engines were meant.

Asked for different *concepts and activities* of computing education, the following picture was found in lower secondary education: modelling and implementing algorithms and programs for solving problems – either alone or in cooperation with others –, understanding the functioning of computing systems as well as the correct usage of computing terms were evaluated as (rather) interesting, statements referring to socio-cultural aspects of computing, e.g. concerning secure passwords, behavior in social networks and the development of computer science as a discipline, were rated as (rather) little interesting. The same tendency was found in the group of the participants of upper secondary education. However, the software development process and software development in teams were considered as rather uninteresting, the creation of multimedia products (audio/video) was rated indifferently.

4.2 Selected Differences Between Groups of Persons

In the field of *interest in computing* there were clear deviations in the approval values for different groups of participants. For example, male pupils tended to agree with the items more than female pupils, in particular with the items "I like computer science" as well as "I like computer science mainly because of the interesting topics". Participants with computing as their favourite subject agreed stronger with the items "I like to learn about computer science", "It is fun for me to deal with computer science" as well as "It is of great personal importance to me to learn something about computer science" than participants with another favourite subject. For all eight items the differences were significant. Furthermore, computing career wishes, the assignment to lower secondary education as well as a (very) good mark in computer science or mathematics led to a stronger approval.

There were no significant gender differences between the *"reasons for the choice to take computing classes"*. A favourite subject computing, a computing-related job wish and a (very) good mark in mathematics or computer science led to a higher degree of approval than in the other subgroup.

In the section on *computer science in everyday life* the gender had only a medium effect on the response behaviour, although significant differences showed up: the males tended to agree with the items more than the females. The effect of the secondary level allocation was also low, with participants from the lower secondary level tending to agree more. In the other comparisons, there were significant differences especially in the items "When I get to know a new topic related to computer science at school, I try to find out more about it.", "I talk to my family about subjects related to computer science." as well as in "I speak in my circle of friends about subjects related to computer science.". There were higher levels of consent from learners with a favourite subject computer science, computer-related career plans and assignment to lower secondary education. (Very) good mathematics and computer science marks led to higher levels of approval in all questions of this section. In the case of better mathematics marks the interest in learning about computing was significantly higher. In the case of better results in computing, the difference for the item "I read in professional journals about computer science" was also significant.

In the group of participants from lower secondary education differences in interest showed up concerning the *situations and contexts* relating to computer games and word processing systems. The male participants more strongly agreed to be interested in a consideration of computer games from a technical as well as a creating perspective. This also applies to the learners with higher rated computing skills; but the interest in the technical perspective was somewhat higher among the other participants. The learners with favourite subject computer science also agreed more strongly to be interested in dealing with computer games from a creating perspective. This also applies to learners with better-assessed computing marks; the interest of the other participants in the technical perspective was partly higher though. The learners with favourite subject computer science also agreed more strongly. Mathematics marks and a desire for a computing career had only a significant influence concerning the context "word processing": a computing-related job wish led to an overall stronger approval. Furthermore, the interest in learning the productive usage of word processing systems was significantly higher in the case of better mathematics marks.

There were also differences in upper secondary education. In the field of computer games, males rated their respective prior knowledge significantly higher than females. Learners with a favorite subject computer science were more interested in dealing with computer games from all four perspectives than learners with other favorite subjects. There were no significant differences with regard to the learners' career plans. Learners with a better assessment of their computing marks were significantly more interested in the consideration of all situations and contexts from a technological perspective than their classmates with a weaker assessment.

5 Conclusion and Outlook

If one's own real-world interest was in the foreground, a higher proportion of learners answered the corresponding items positively. Objects, which were of no great importance in the learners' everyday lives, were also of less interest to them. Socio-cultural aspects – in contrast to technological and application-related ones – met with little interest. Learners in lower secondary education were generally more interested than learners in upper secondary education. A more pronounced interest was also found among learners with a computing-related career plan, favorite subject computer science and (very) good last mark in mathematics or computing. Regarding gender, the assessment of interest was often not significantly different. Furthermore, there was a relatively low interest among the participants in dealing with computer science topics during leisure time, unless a personal benefit was evident (usage of mobiles or search engines).

As another result, the study provides an instrument for assessing computing interest, which has been tested once in a pilot study and which should be refined in future work. The selection of situations and contexts needs further development, as should the statements on concepts and activities be varied more systematically according to the structure model presented in Sect. 2. It would be desirable to learn more about the interests of pupils in future in order to be able to take them more into account in didactic decisions. The rather small interest in socio-cultural aspects in this study should lead to the examination and, if necessary, the revision of the assigned items, and to the realization that an interesting instruction can be particularly important here.

As a conclusion for practice in future computer science courses, it should be taken into account that the topics and activities should meet the interests of the students. It must be obvious to them that the topics are relevant to their personal life and useful to them today, but also in the future – not only for their careers, but also for their everyday activities.

References

1. United Nations: Convention on the rights of the child. Adopted and opened for signature, ratification and accession by general assembly resolution 44/25 of 20 November 1989; entry into force 2 September 1990, in accordance with article 49 (1989). http://www.ohchr.org/EN/ProfessionalInterest/Pages/CRC.aspx
2. Helmke, A.: Unterrichtsqualität und Lehrerprofessionalität. Diagnose, Evaluation und Verbesserung des Unterrichts. Kallmeyer/Klett, Seelze-Velber (2012)
3. Kunter, M., Trautwein, U.: Psychologie des Unterrichts. Schöningh, Paderborn (2013)
4. Krapp, A., Prenzel, M.: Research on interest in science: theories, methods, and findings. Int. J. Sci. Educ. **33**(1), 27–50 (2011)
5. Schwinem, S.: Schülerinteresse im Informatikunterricht. Master thesis. University of Duisburg-Essen/Germany, Faculty of Business Administration and Economics (2016). (in German)
6. Häußler, P.: Measuring students' interest in physics – design and results of a cross-sectional study in the Federal Republic of Germany. Int. J. Sci. Educ. **9**(1), 79–92 (1987)

7. Holstermann, N., Bögeholz, S.: Interesse von Jungen und Mädchen an naturwissenschaftlichen Themen am Ende der Sekundarstufe I. Zeitschrift für Didaktik der Naturwissenschaften **13**, 71–86 (2007). (in German)
8. Barthel, H.: Informatikunterricht. Wünsche und Erwartungen von Schülerinnen und Schülern. Dissertation. University of Kiel, Germany, Department of Philosophy (2010). (in German)
9. Brinda, T., Puhlmann, H., Schulte, C.: Bridging ICT and CS – educational standards for computer science in lower secondary education. In: ACM (ed.) Proceedings of the 2009 ACM SIGCSE Annual Conference on Innovation and Technology in Computer Science Education, pp. 288–292. ACM Press, New York (2009)
10. German Informatics Association: Educational Standards for Computing in Upper Secondary Education (2016). http://www.informatikstandards.de/docs/Bildungsstandards_SII.pdf. (in German)
11. Ministry of School and Further Education of North Rhine-Westphalia/Germany: Core curriculum for computing in upper secondary education (2013). http://www.schulentwicklung.nrw.de/lehrplaene/upload/klp_SII/if/KLP_GOSt_Informatik.pdf. (in German)
12. Diethelm, I., Hildebrandt, C., Krekeler, L.: Implementation of computer science in context – a research perspective regarding teacher-training. In: Proceeding of the Koli Calling Conference, pp. 97–100 (2009)
13. Humbert, L., Puhlmann, H.: Essential ingredients of literacy in informatics. In: Magenheim, J., Schubert, S. (eds.) Informatics and Student Assessment. Concepts of Empirical Research and Standardisation of Measurement in the Area of Didactics of Informatics, Köllen, Bonn, pp. 65–76 (2004)
14. Medienpädagogischer Forschungsverbund Südwest: JIM-Studie 2015. Jugend, Information, (Multi-)Media. Basisuntersuchung zum Medienumgang 12- bis 19-Jähriger (2015). http://www.mpfs.de/fileadmin/JIM-pdf15/JIM_2015.pdf. (in German)
15. Brinda, T., Diethelm, I., Gemulla, R., Romeike, R., Schöning, J., Schulte, C., et al.: Dagstuhl Declaration: Education in the Digital Networked World (2016). https://www.gi.de/fileadmin/redaktion/Themen/dagstuhl-erklaerung-bildung-in-der-digitalen-welt-2016.pdf. (in German)
16. Brinda, T.: Declaration of the Department of "Computing and Education/Computing Education" of the German Informatics Association concerning the Strategy of the German Ministries of Cultural Affairs on "Education in Digital World" (2016). https://fb-iad.gi.de/fileadmin/stellungnahmen/gi-fb-iad-stellungnahme-kmk-strategie-digitale-bildung.pdf. (in German)
17. Ferdinand, H.: Entwicklung von Fachinteresse: Längsschnittstudie zu Interessenverläufen und Determinanten positiver Entwicklung in der Schule. Waxmann, Münster (2014). (in German)
18. Bühner, M.: Einführung in die Test- und Fragebogenkonstruktion. Pearson Studium, Munich/Boston (2011). (in German)
19. Medienpädagogischer Forschungsverbund Südwest: KIM-Studie 2014. Kinder + Medien, Computer + Internet. Basisuntersuchung zum Medienumgang 6- bis 13-Jähriger (2014). http://www.mpfs.de/fileadmin/KIM-pdf14/KIM14.pdf. (in German)
20. Computer Science Teachers Association (ed.): CS Standards Crosswalk with CSTA K-12 Computer Science Standards for State/District/Course Standards (2011). http://csta.acm.org/Curriculum/sub/K12Standards.html
21. Rasch, B., Friese, M., Hofmann, W., Naumann, E.: Quantitative Methoden 2: Einführung in die Statistik für Psychologen und Sozialwissenschaftler. Springer, Heidelberg (2014). https://doi.org/10.1007/978-3-662-43548-9. (in German)

Computing Camps for Girls – A First-Time Experience at the University of Limerick

Clare McInerney[1(✉)], Anna-Lena Lamprecht[2], and Tiziana Margaria[1,3]

[1] Lero – The Irish Software Research Centre, University of Limerick, Limerick, Ireland
Clare.mcinerney@lero.ie, Tiziana.Margaria@ul.ie
[2] Department of Information and Computing Sciences, Utrecht University, Utrecht, The Netherlands
a.l.lamprecht@uu.nl
[3] Department of Computer Science and Information Systems, University of Limerick, Limerick, Ireland

Abstract. Increasing the number of females in ICT-related university courses has been a major concern for several years. In 2015, we offered a girls-only computing summer camp for the first time, as a new component in our education and outreach activities to foster students' interest in our discipline. In this paper, we describe the motivation for the camp and how we designed the program, and we report our experiences and survey findings from the first two editions of the camp. They can provide guidance for planning further events targeting females, and help to integrate awareness about underrepresentation of females in other activities.

Keywords: Computer science education · Computational thinking Modelling · Programming · Women in STEM

1 Introduction

According to the latest national enrolment statistics (for the academic year 2014–2015)[1], of all students enrolled in Information and Computer Technology (ICT) full time undergraduate courses in all Universities and Institutes of Technologies in Ireland, 85% were males and 15% females. In our university, the University of Limerick, females represented 16% full time undergraduate enrolments for ICT courses and males 84%. Increasing the number of females in these courses has been a major concern for several years, and has recently become even more important in the light of the Athena SWAN[2] accreditation processes at our university.

A recent Google report titled "Women Who Choose Computer Science - What Really Matters" [1], identifies the following top four influencing factors to whether or not a young woman decided to pursue a Computer Science Degree:

---

[1] http://www.hea.ie/node/1557.
[2] http://www.ecu.ac.uk/equality-charters/athena-swan/.

A. Tatnall and M. Webb (Eds.): WCCE 2017, IFIP AICT 515, pp. 494–505, 2017.
https://doi.org/10.1007/978-3-319-74310-3_50

1. **Social encouragement** is having positive reinforcement of computer science from family and peers.
2. **Self-perception** is having an interest in puzzles and problem solving and a belief that these skills can be translated into a successful career.
3. **Academic exposure** is the availability of and opportunity to participate in computer science work.
4. **Career perception** is the familiarity with/perception of computer science as a career with diverse applications and a broad potential for positive societal impact.

In a similar Accenture report on "Powering economic growth; Attracting more young women into science and technology" [2], key barriers to women in the STEM field included that negative stereotypes persist, that STEM is perceived more suitable for boys, that parents, while being the main influencers, lack information on STEM career options, that information about STEM careers is fragmented, and that there is a disconnect between industry skills needs and subject choices in school. A recent literature review [3] on research about the impact of pre-college computing activities on choices of major furthermore emphasizes that females who participate in outreach activities are more likely to go for a computing degree [4–7].

As part of our education and outreach initiatives, we have been running summer computing camps for both post-primary boys and girls since 2010. These camps consist of three days each, with half-day sessions on different technologies. 20% females participated in the camps since 2012. While we were aware of the success of other institutions running summer camps for females and the challenges of underrepresentation of females in computer science [8–11], it was not something our institution had offered. In 2015 we received a Google RISE Award[3] to run summer camps specifically for girls. As the only recipient of this international award in our country, it helped us raise awareness about the underrepresentation of females in computing within our research centre and to highlight the need to increase female participation in our camps, and it enabled us to organise and run female-only camps free of charge. We devised new programme content for a girls-only camp, designed to address the influencing factors and barriers highlighted in the reports mentioned above. As well as incorporating a new set of tools that focus on logic and computational thinking [12] rather than on coding, so that no prior programming experience was required, we also invited (female) industry speakers and academics from the university to present to the students. Overall feedback from the camp suggests participants enjoyed the experience and also learned a lot about the field of computing. The insights gained from the surveys enable us to more easily plan further events and activities targeting females and integrate awareness about underrepresentation of females in other events and activities we run.

In this paper we describe the new programme and how we ran the camp (Sect. 2), and discuss the experiences of the 41 students that attended the camps and findings from the accompanying surveys (Sect. 3). Section 4 concludes the paper.

[3] https://edu.google.com/resources/programs/google-rise-awards/.

2 Overview of the Summer Camp

We ran two three-day camps for post-primary girls aged 14 and up during the summer of 2015 at the University of Limerick. We advertised the camps in May in local newspapers, online and social media and through our contacts in local schools. Table 1 outlines the schedule for the three days, with different colours marking the main components of the programme: The development of game strategies for the ChainReaction board game (blue), invited speakers (red), a robotics session (green) and presentations (yellow). The following describes these components in more detail.

Table 1. Camp schedule

	Day 1	Day 2	Day 3
10:00-10:30	Registration, pre-survey	Strategy Development/ Improvement	Preparation of Presentation Slides
10:30-11:15	Introduction to ChainReaction		
11:15-11:30	Break	Break	Break
11:30-12:15	Exploring ChainReaction on paper	Strategy Development/ Improvement	Final tournament, discussion of results
12:15-12:45			Finalisation of presentation slides
12:45-13:30	Lunch	Lunch	Lunch
13:30-14:15	Invited Speaker	Invited Speaker	Invited Speaker
14:15-15:15	Introduction to jABC	Robotics session	Presentations
15:15-16:00			Post-survey, closing

2.1 Game Strategies for ChainReaction (Blue)

The modelling of executable strategies for a board game, ChainReaction, was a major component of the programme (blue sections in the table). Games typically make attractive course topics for students of all ages [13, 14], and game development allows students to experience various aspects of software development, by systematically exploring the mechanics of a game.

ChainReaction[4] is a strategy game for two players, who play against each other on a special 6×5 board, both trying to initiate chain reactions of atoms to conquer the whole board and win the game (see e.g. the "Introduction to ChainReaction" page[5] for a detailed description of the rules). The development of the game strategies to be followed by a computer player takes place in a specially prepared version of the jABC modelling framework [15], which supports the intuitive, graphical development of flow-graph structures to define the behaviour of a system. Figure 1 gives an impression of how the modelling of ChainReaction strategies with the jABC works: The component library on the left contains the building blocks from which the strategies are

[4] http://chainreaction.freewarepoint.de.

[5] https://hope.scce.info/chainreaction/.

assembled. The strategies focus on defining how the score for a cell on the board is to be computed. The framework then evaluates the strategies for all cells and places the next atom into the cell with the highest score (or, if there are multiple cells with the same highest score, randomly choosing one of them).

The framework, which is very similar to the successful jABC version for the modelling of game strategies for the more popular ConnectFour board game [16], combines an easily accessible application domain with a quick sense of achievement: The first game strategies are typically ready to run after a 30-min introduction to the modelling tool. Students can then work on incrementally improving this starting strategy. They also get immediate feedback about the quality of the results by playing against their own strategies or by letting the strategy play against other computer players. As such, it provides a very motivational framework and a fun and lightweight learning-by-doing way to acquire and practice computational thinking skills.

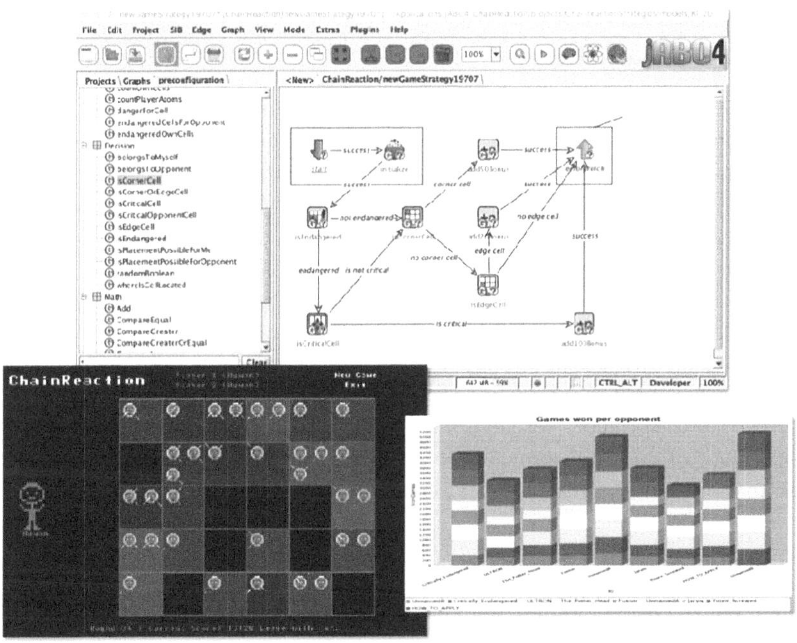

Fig. 1. The ChainReaction game, modelling of ChainReaction strategies with jABC, and results of a tournament played between nine strategies.

In the first camp session, we introduced the participants only to the basic ChainReaction game and gave them some time to play and familiarize themselves with it. The girls paired up on one computer for this exercise, and we let them work together in these pairs for the rest of the camp.

The next session was designed to foster more strategic thinking about the game. The task for the girls was to write down – simply on paper – how they had actually played the game, that is, which strategy they had followed to decide where to place their atoms. We then let the groups exchange strategies on paper, and each group tried to play strictly according to what the other group had written down. In a very entertaining way, this demonstrated the importance of formulating precise and unambiguous instructions.

In the last session of the first day, we introduced the modelling tool and taught students how to model and execute their first simple ChainReaction strategy. The remainder of this session and the ChainReaction sessions on Day 2 were focused on the development and improvement of game strategies. At various intervals we provided the girls with additional hints and suggestions to help them improve their strategies, which became quite sophisticated towards the end of the second day.

In the last ChainReaction session, on the third day, every group had to select and submit their final strategy, and we ran a final tournament with all strategies playing against each other to determine the best one. The bar chart in Fig. 1 (lower right) shows the results of a tournament of nine strategies.

2.2 Invited Speakers (Red)

The camps were held on campus at the University of Limerick so that the participants had the opportunity to experience the academic environment. Invited speakers from both academia and industry provided further insights into what it means to become and to be an IT professional. On the first day of the camp, the Head of the Computer Science Department talked to the girls. She described each of the available courses in detail, outlined the challenges that students face in their first year in college, but also the benefits of completing a computer science course. Regarding career progression, we invited industry speakers for Day 2 and Day 3 to give short presentations to the students based on their personal career experiences. Speakers included employees from Dell, Intel and Google. All invited speakers were women and, more importantly, did not correspond to common stereotypes about IT professionals. Recent research shows the importance of non-stereotypical role models when attempting to convey to girls or women that they can be successful in STEM fields [17].

2.3 Robotics Session (Green)

The afternoon session of Day 2 introduced the students to robotics. While the effectiveness of using robots, over a year-long period, in encouraging students to select computer science as a field of study is negative [18, 19] we considered the use of robots in a short session as a fun and attractive example of an area of computing. The students explored robot programming using a NAO robot and a LEGO Mindstorms kit.

The NAO robot[6] is a 58-cm tall humanoid robot that can easily be programmed via the block-based Choreographe interface[7]. Students were broken up into groups of 6-8

[6] https://www.aldebaran.com/en/humanoid-robot/nao-robot.

[7] http://doc.aldebaran.com/1-14/software/choregraphe/index.html.

and each group had access to a NAO robot for 45 min. They used Choreographe to program the robot, and made him, for example, speak, dance and do push-ups.

The LEGO Mindstorms[8] kits contain both hardware and software components with which small robots can be assembled and programmed. The students were given a basic demonstration of the use of different sensors (touch, light, and distance), and then had some time to experiment with them.

Equipped with smartphones and tablet computers, the girls also took a lot of pictures and video clips during this session, especially of the NAO robot in action. Thus, although this short session did not go into any detail of robotics and used mainly predefined functionality, it contributed a lot to a positive experience and good memories of the camp, even for those who did not feel confident with the strategy development in the jABC tool.

2.4 Presentations (Yellow)

The fourth component of the camp programme was presentations. The girls were asked to give presentations about the game strategies they had developed and about their experiences in the camp. In the morning of the last day, they had time to prepare PowerPoint slides. Notably, they were already familiar with the software, and creating colourful presentations with pictures and animations was easy and enjoyable for the group. The presentations were delivered in the last session of the camp, just before the closing and awards ceremony. In addition to practicing presentation skills, this part of the programme served the purpose of letting everybody see what the other groups had done, and what the perceived highlights of the camp were from the girls' perspective.

3 Survey Results

In order to assess the impact of the summer camp, we administered surveys at the beginning and at the end of the camp. We used the pre and post surveys developed by "Georgia Computes!" at Georgia Institute of Technology [20] with some modifications in order to address the top four influencing factors on whether or not a young woman decides to pursue a degree in Computer Science as described earlier. The surveys comprised three major parts: At the beginning of the camp we asked the girls about their prior computing experiences. These questions address social encouragement, and self-perception factors. Another set of questions, on different aspects of their attitude towards computing, was asked both before and after the camp, so that we could compare the answers pre-camp and post-camp. These questions address self-perception and career perception factors. The third set of questions was on the camp itself, and also asked at the end. These questions address academic exposure and career perception factors. We present and discuss selected results from the surveys in this section. They are based on the answers from 41 girls who participated in the 2015 summer camps.

[8] http://www.lego.com/en-us/mindstorms/?domainredir=mindstorms.lego.com.

3.1 Pre-survey: Prior Computing Experiences (Social Encouragement/Self Perception)

Computing is offered optionally in schools in Ireland. If schools are offering "computers", what is taught in schools varies widely. 77% of our camp participants attend schools that offer computer classes. Content for these classes included HTML/Web Design, ECDL, browsing the web, typing, Scratch, GIMP and Microsoft Word and Excel. At the start of the camp, 26% of the participants stated that they had written a computer program before, while 51% stated they did not, and 23% did not know if they had (see Fig. 2, left).

We can compare the data for the girls-only camps with data for the summer camps that we have been running for boys and girls since 2012 (see Fig. 2, centre).

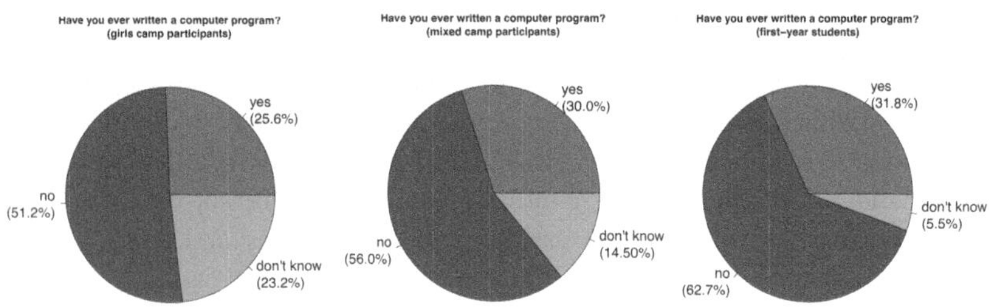

Fig. 2. "Have you ever written a computer program?" (left: girls camp participants, centre: mixed camp participants, right: CS first-year students 2016/17)"

Data gathered over the course of four years shows that 56% of camp participants had never written a computer program before, 14% did not know if they had, and 30% had written a computer program before. This indicates that prior computing experiences of students attending girls-only camps versus mixed camps do not vary widely in our institution. At the beginning of the last autumn semester, we also asked the computer science first-year students (110 students) to answer this question. As Fig. 2 (right) shows, 63% stated that they had never written a computer program before, 32% said they had, and 5% did not know. This suggests that generally the computer science knowledge at the time of leaving school is not much different from early secondary school level. This is also reflected in the finding that only 11% of the first-year students reported that they had a computer science course at school.

In terms of social encouragement, 58% of the girls agreed and strongly agreed that they are encouraged by their families to use computers. 70% agreed and strongly agreed that their friends like using computers. While this means that the majority of the girls find themselves in an environment that is positive towards computing and using computers, there is also a considerable percentage that does not get this form of social encouragement.

3.2 Pre- and Post-survey: Attitude Towards Computing (Self-perception/Career Perception)

Regarding students' self-perception of computing, we can see an increase in students agreeing and strongly agreeing that they are good at computing by the end of the 3-day camp (see Fig. 3, left). The number of students that are in between regarding this statement has decreased between the pre and post surveys. The students' perceived ability to know how to program computers also increased between pre and post survey (see Fig. 3, right).

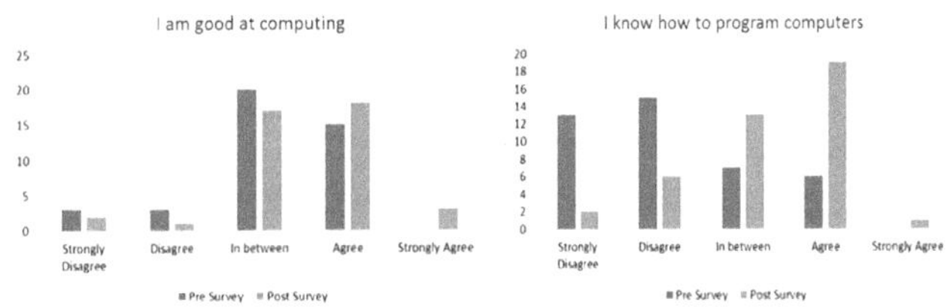

Fig. 3. "I am good at computing." and "I know how to program computers." pre and post camp.

In our post survey, 95% agreed and strongly agreed that they know more about computing as a job because of the camp. Also the students' interest in computing as a career increased during the camp (see Fig. 4, left). In terms of whether students were considering doing a computer science related course at third level there was an increase in the participants strongly agreeing with this statement by the end of the camp (see Fig. 4, right). Of course, most of the participants came to the camp already with or because of a positive disposition towards computing as a subject and/or job, so the high levels of agreement do not necessarily reflect the average attitude of girls in this age group. However, we know from the survey that some of the girls were also sent to the camp by their parents, presumably those that expressed disagreement to the statements related to interest, but the level of disagreement was lower after the camp.

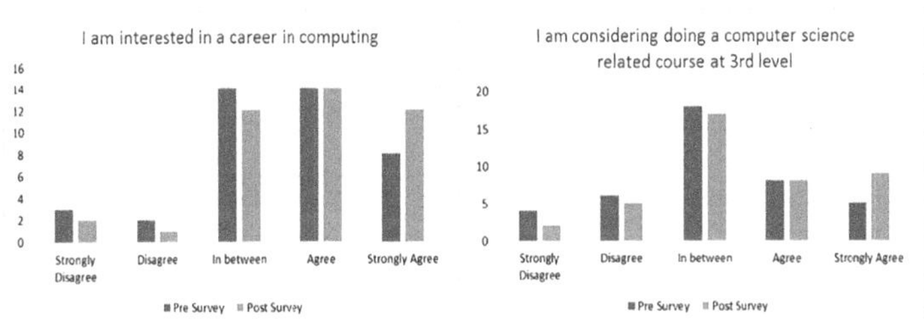

Fig. 4. "I am interested in a career in computing." and "I am considering doing a computer science related course at 3rd level." pre and post camp.

As mentioned earlier, computing is not currently offered in a formal way at upper secondary school level in Ireland. One of the questions we asked the students after the camp was if a computing/computer science leaving certificate subject was available in their schools, would they choose it. 87% said yes. A recent government report, the Action Plan for Education 2017[9], outlines government plans to introduce Computer Science as a subject at senior cycle in 2018. This is an exciting development and we look forward to summer camp students having the opportunity to pursue their passion in school.

In terms of students' perceptions of ability of males and females to do computing we asked students if they agreed with the statement "Women can do computing". There was no significant change between pre and post survey. 93% strongly agreed with the statement pre and post. 7% agreed in the pre survey. 5% agreed and 2% were in between for the post survey. When we asked students if they agreed with the statement "Men can do computing", 90% strongly agreed and 7% agreed with this statement in pre and post survey. We asked the computer science first-year students (see above) similar attitude questions, and obtained very similar results. This indicates that secondary school students see males and females as equally capable of mastering computer science, and hence gender seems not to be perceived as the factor that prohibits learning the subject.

3.3 Post-survey: Camp Experience (Academic Exposure/Career Perception)

After the camp, we asked the participants to rate their camp experience and to tell us what they liked best about it and why, what they liked least and why, and what changes they would make to make it better. The latter was asked in the form of open free-text questions, and indeed they showed a great variety of opinions and gave us good feedback about how the girls had experienced the camp.

Regarding what the participants liked best about the camp, the different components (ChainReaction workshop, invited talks, robotics session, and presentations) were mentioned almost equally often. Several answers also emphasized social aspects of the camp, like the good atmosphere, friendly people and new friends (two examples are: *"I liked the fact that I got to meet new friends and I also got to improve my computing skills"* and *"I liked the way the people working here are so friendly and so helpful").* 78% of students agreed and strongly agreed with the statement "I made new friends at this camp". In fact, 15% of students mentioned "friends" or "friendly" in their responses to what they liked best about the camp. This compares with 3% citing "friends" or "friendly" from our mixed camps. One female participant in our mixed camps said: *"I love the experience and the people even though we were split up in to groups and I was the only girl in the group I still made friends."* Interestingly, when this student was asked about what she liked least about the mixed camps she said: *"I didn't dislike most things the only thing I would change is putting at least one other girl*

[9] http://www.education.ie/en/Publications/Corporate-Reports/Strategy-Statement/Action-Plan-for-Education-2017.pdf.

into the group that I was in." This suggests that the young girls simply might feel uncomfortable being the only female in a group, and female-only or better balanced mixed-gender groups make them feel more comfortable.

The answers to the question what they liked least were a bit more diverse. From the four main components of the camp, only the invited talks were mentioned frequently, however predominantly by students who also stated that they had already attended similar presentations and that there was a lot of repetition for them. Many answers to this question pointed to organisational aspects, like the days being too short, too long or starting too early, and also the sandwiches that were provided for lunch were mentioned several times here. While we will certainly consider changing the latter for next editions of the camp, the former comments seem to be more a question of personal preferences and will be difficult to perfect for everybody.

Many answers to the question about changes to the camp were in fact "nothing", but there were also some concrete suggestions. For example, several participants said they would like a longer camp (like a week), and to include more "real coding" into the program. Other frequent wishes included more variety in the program (for instance by including more outdoor activities or exercises on fast typing), less talks, and something different for lunch. We are going to take these suggestions into account for the next camps.

4 Conclusion

Based on the participants' responses to the questionnaires we feel confident in saying that the girls-only camp was a very positive experience for them. Students' self-perception that they are good at computing and their perceived ability to know how to program increased by the end of the 3-day camp. In terms of the perception of computing as a career, participants knew more and were more positive about the field as a result of the camp. The answers to the survey questions also align well with our own impression that the students had an enjoyable time, while at the same time confirming that they learned a lot. The enthusiasm of the students can also be viewed in this video that was created from footage shot by the students on the last day of the camp.[10]

The Google RISE funding award for the girls-only camp has enabled us to raise awareness about underrepresentation of females in particular and we will continue to plan and run activities for females again in the future. We are going to use similar tools and technologies, but other aspects such as food choices, timing allocated to talks, and inclusion of outdoor activities may be tweaked based on survey feedback.

Specifically targeting females is however only one of many projects that our research centre is involved in to encourage an interest in computing from primary through secondary and into third level. Other initiatives include running (mixed-gender) events during TechWeek, EU Code Week, Hour of Code, Science Week, Smart Futures, the national Scratch competition and the Junior Cycle Short Course in Coding.

[10] https://www.youtube.com/watch?v=EzBXqouzd8k.

Colleagues at another institution of our research centre registered interest in our summer camps in particular and they ran an Information Systems Innovation Workshop in 2016. During the camp, participants designed and built a prototype of a mobile application learning skills in innovation, design, problem solving, application development, business analysis, teamwork and collaboration. Feedback from this camp was similarly very positive.

Acknowledgments. This work was supported with the financial support of the Science Foundation Ireland grant 13/RC/2094 and co-funded under the European Regional Development Fund through the Southern & Eastern Regional Operational Programme to Lero - the Irish Software Research Centre (www.lero.ie). We would like to acknowledge the support of Google RISE funding.

References

1. Google: Women Who Choose Computer Science - What Really Matters (2014). https://docs.google.com/file/d/0B-E2rcvhnlQ_a1Q4VUxWQ2dtTHM/edit. Accessed 21 Aug 2017
2. Accenture: Powering economic growth; attracting more young women into science and technology (2014). https://www.accenture.com/ie-en/~/media/Accenture/Conversion-Assets/DotCom/Documents/Global/PDF/Industries_14/Accenture-STEM-Powering-Economic-Growth.pdf. Accessed 21 Aug 2017
3. McGill, M.M., Decker, A., Settle, A.: Undergraduate students' perceptions of the impact of pre-college computing activities on choices of major. Trans. Comput. Educ. **16**(4), 1–33 (2016)
4. Crutchfield, O.S.L., et al.: Berkeley foundation for opportunities in information technology: a decade of broadening participation. Trans. Comput. Educ. **11**(3), 1–24 (2011)
5. Doerschuk, P., Liu, J., Mann, J.: INSPIRED broadening participation in computing: most successful strategies and lessons learned. In: 2010 IEEE Frontiers in Education Conference (FIE) (2010)
6. Dahlberg, T., et al.: The STARS alliance: viable strategies for broadening participation in computing. Trans. Comput. Educ. **11**(3), 1–25 (2011)
7. Guzdial, M., et al.: A statewide survey on computing education pathways and influences: factors in broadening participation in computing. In: Proceedings of the Ninth Annual International Conference on International Computing Education Research, pp. 143–150. ACM, Auckland (2012)
8. Adams, J.C.: Alice, middle schoolers & the imaginary worlds camps. SIGCSE Bull. **39**(1), 307–311 (2007)
9. Webb, H.C., Rosson, M.B.: Exploring careers while learning Alice 3D: a summer camp for middle school girls. In: Proceedings of the 42nd ACM Technical Symposium on Computer Science Education, pp. 377–382. ACM, Dallas (2011)
10. Burge, J.E., et al.: Girls on the go: a CS summer camp to attract and inspire female high school students. In: Proceeding of the 44th ACM Technical Symposium on Computer Science Education, pp. 615–620. ACM, Denver (2013)
11. Margolis, J.: Unlocking the clubhouse: a decade later and now what? In: Proceeding of the 44th ACM Technical Symposium on Computer Science Education, pp. 9–10. ACM, Denver (2013)
12. Wing, J.M.: Computational thinking. Commun. ACM **49**(3), 33–35 (2006)

13. Roscoe, J.F., et al.: Teaching computational thinking by playing games and building robots. In: 2014 International Conference on Interactive Technologies and Games (iTAG 2014), pp. 9–12 (2014)
14. Mladenovic, S., Krpan, D., Mladenovic, M.: Using games to help novices embrace programming: from elementary to higher education. Int. J. Eng. Educ. **32**(1), 521–531 (2016)
15. Steffen, B., Margaria, T., Nagel, R., Jörges, S., Kubczak, C.: Model-driven development with the jABC. In: Bin, E., Ziv, A., Ur, S. (eds.) HVC 2006. LNCS, vol. 4383, pp. 92–108. Springer, Heidelberg (2007). https://doi.org/10.1007/978-3-540-70889-6_7
16. Margaria, T., Jörges, S., Bakera, M.: Test your strategy: graphical construction of strategies for connect-four. In: IEEE International Conference on Engineering of Complex Computer Systems (2009)
17. Cheryan, S., et al.: Do female and male role models who embody STEM stereotypes hinder women's anticipated success in STEM? Soc. Psychol. Pers. Sci. **2**(6), 656–664 (2011)
18. McNally, M., et al.: Do lego mindstorms robots have a future in CS education? SIGCSE Bull. **38**(1), 61–62 (2006)
19. Fagin, B.S., Merkle, L.: Quantitative analysis of the effects of robots on introductory Computer Science education. J. Educ. Resour. Comput. **2**(4), 2 (2002)
20. Ericson, B., McKlin, T.: Effective and sustainable computing summer camps. In: Proceedings of the 43rd ACM Technical Symposium on Computer Science Education, pp. 289–294. ACM, Raleigh (2012)

How Can We Make Computing Lessons More Inclusive?

Chris Shelton(✉)

Institute of Education, University of Chichester, Chichester, UK
c.shelton@chi.ac.uk

Abstract. Whilst there is a substantial body of research that shows how Information and Communications Technologies (ICTs) can support schools and teachers to make their classrooms more inclusive, there is a need for more evidence describing how best to ensure that the teaching of computing itself is inclusive. This paper reports on a literature review of inclusive education in school computing lessons. It identifies a number of inclusive practices, including ensuring a relevant and authentic curriculum that focuses on depth of understanding, promoting culturally relevant tasks, and ensuring an inclusive environment that challenges bias. The review also identifies a need for much more research into what constitutes an inclusive computing classroom.

Keywords: Schools · Computing · Computer science education
Inclusion · Pedagogy

1 Introduction

According to UNESCO [1], inclusion is "a process of addressing and responding to the diversity of needs of all children, youth and adults through increasing participation in learning, cultures and communities, and reducing and eliminating exclusion within and from education" (p. 8). An inclusive school is therefore one which modifies its "content, approaches, structures and strategies" (p. 9) to better educate all children.

While early debates about inclusion focused on whether pupils should be educated in mainstream schools or alternative 'special' provision [2], over time, understandings of inclusion have broadened away from the location of schooling to address a wide range of pupil characteristics, including, but not limited to: race, class, gender, language, cultural and social differences. Ainscow et al. [3] suggest that inclusion is an approach to education based on inclusive values (including equity, participation, compassion, respect of diversity, sustainability and entitlement).

School pupils are not a homogenous group [4] and there is now a substantial body of research that shows how the most effective uses of Information and Communications Technologies (ICTs) can support schools and teachers to make their classrooms more inclusive (see, for example, Seale [5]). However, while much research on use of ICT for inclusion is relevant to all teachers, there are still gaps in the evidence of how best to ensure that computing lessons are inclusive. Given the concern over low participation rates in Higher Education and the later years of secondary computing, there is a need for specific research that investigates how inclusive school teaching of computing

A. Tatnall and M. Webb (Eds.): WCCE 2017, IFIP AICT 515, pp. 506–514, 2017.
https://doi.org/10.1007/978-3-319-74310-3_51

is and how this might be improved. This is vital as there is evidence that digital literacy is highly influenced by inequalities outside of school [4] and that a lack of access and skills forces individuals and groups to becoming uncritical consumers of digital texts [6].

Therefore, this literature review was intended to survey the current literature regarding inclusive computing education in schools to identify both aspects of effective practice and areas for further research.

2 Method

The aim of this project was to conduct a literature review of research focusing on inclusive computing teaching in schools. There were three criteria for inclusion in the review:

(1) The text must be concerned with school level education
(2) The text must focus on the teaching of computing or computer science (rather than the use of technology across the curriculum)
(3) The text must focus on one or more issues of inclusion.

In order to find sources for the review, three databases were searched: ERIC (eric.ed.gov), Web of Science (including the Social Sciences Citation Index (SSCI) and Conference Proceedings Citation Index – Social Science and Humanities (CPCI-SSH)) and the ACM Digital Library Guide to Computing Literature. The ACM database contains both full-text and citation data regarding computer science research as well as social science research and therefore an adapted search strategy was required for this database. The searches were conducted in January 2017. Three categories of search terms were required to ensure that the three criteria were met:

(1) To ensure that all texts were focussed on school level education, the terms searched for were: "primary", "secondary", "elementary", "school" or "K-12". For the ACM database, the terms "school" and "primary" were excluded as they returned texts relating to Higher Education and/or Computer Science.
(2) To ensure that all texts were focussed on the teaching of computing, the following terms were used: "computing", "teaching IT", "teaching ICT", "teaching information technology", "teaching information communication technology", "computer science", "computer programming", "digital literacy" and "informatics". Other terms considered but not used included "coding" (this gave irrelevant results due to the use of coding as a term to describe the analysis of research data), "programming" (frequently used to refer to the design of special education intervention programmes) and variations of "IT" (these led to several thousand papers many of which were about the use of technology to teach across the curriculum). This search term was not required for the ACM database as all texts were related to computing in some form.
(3) To ensure the texts focus on issues of inclusion, the terms "inclusive" or "inclusion" were used. (Where allowable, the wildcard inclus* was used.)

The initial searches resulted in 329 possible sources. The abstracts of all texts identified by these searches were read and assessed against the three criteria. This resulted in 29 relevant publications. The relatively high rate of ineligible publications reflects the multiple meanings of the search terms (Table 1).

Table 1. Summary of search results

Database	Potential sources	Sources meeting criteria
ERIC	33	10
SSCI/CPCI-SSH	127	7
ACM	169	12

3 Results and Discussion

The papers identified through this review identify several specific inclusion issues: gender, diversity, special educational needs, attainment, and economic disadvantage. While these issues are reported separately below and the majority of papers had a clear focus on just one of these, some papers acknowledged that these issues intersect. However, none of the papers attempted to provide a comprehensive description or analysis of inclusive computing teaching or pedagogy.

Gender

The most commonly discussed inclusion topic was gender. There is clear evidence that females are significantly underrepresented in computing (both in employment and in the proportion taking higher qualifications) [7]. Ashcraft et al. provides a comprehensive literature review of the research into underrepresentation of females in computing [7]. This review shows that girls' perceptions, interests, confidence and career decisions are influenced by many factors and categorises these factors as formal/informal education, peer influences, families and community influences and media influences. Of particular relevance for this review are the sections pertaining to formal education where Ashcraft et al. identify issues of curriculum and pedagogy.

In terms of curriculum, Ashcraft et al. suggest that girls may often hold perceptions that the computing curriculum is irrelevant to them. They suggest that computing has often been taught in the abstract rather than addressing how computing can help to address real-life problems. This abstract curriculum also reinforces views of computing as a "lonely, isolated, machine-focused set of tasks" (p. 21).

The review highlights the work of Lasen [8] that compares the views of school girls who chose or did not choose to take advanced ICT options. Both those who chose these courses and those who did not expressed "an aversion to programming" with those who took the courses attracted to the creative aspects of the subjects (such as multimedia and web design) and enjoying authentic, problem based tasks. The view that girls do not opt for computing subjects because they do not value them is also expressed by Downes and Looker [9].

This suggests that a computing curriculum needs to be designed to incorporate and connect to real-life problems. It should also address some of the other areas that influence pupil perceptions, for example, by incorporating lessons on or discussions of media representations of computing.

Another curriculum issue identified by Ashcraft et al. is a focus on breadth of coverage and speed rather than depth and fluency. A computing curriculum that is focussed on speed and competence at isolated tasks can negatively affect pupils who prefer to study more deeply [7]. They suggest that computing curricula should focus on fluency – activities that transfer or can be applied in other contexts.

One suggestion proposed as a way of engaging girls has been a curriculum based around computer games. However, Osunde et al. [10] have identified that teenage boys and girls prefer games with different features (e.g. graphical style, storyline, number of players). While Robertson [11] provides an example of a game making project that was enjoyed by students but did not address the gender gap and even indicated that pupils were "less likely to like computing, or want to find out more about the subject after taking part in the project" (p. 37).

The second set of issues relate to pedagogy and Ashcraft et al. suggest that hands-on activities, collaborative work, and project-based learning are important to motivate and include girls. They suggest that active, practical work retains pupils' interest and help to make computing relevant while improving fluency. Similarly, Corneliussen, and Prøitz [12] suggest that school computing curricula need to adopt the playfulness with technology found in after school code clubs in order to include girls.

Ashcraft et al. also suggest that there is evidence that the use of collaborative learning activities have positive effects for girls, including increased persistence in the face of problems. However, they claim that teachers tend to privilege independent work and sometimes even discourage group-work.

It is also important to ensure that the classroom environment promotes suitable role models and avoids stereotypical displays (Ashcraft et al. mention environments referencing science fiction and displaying computer parts as being less appealing for girls [7]). Coupal [13] highlights the importance of paying attention to power relationships in school and Ashcraft et al. suggest that teachers need to pay attention to classroom interactions to ensure pupils receive reliable feedback and avoid pupils judging themselves based on their speed of work rather than depth of understanding.

Ashcraft et al. also suggest that teachers need to be aware of the potential for unconscious bias regarding who will be most likely to succeed in computing and warns against mistaking prior experience for innate ability. As Downes and Looker [9] note, ability and value beliefs are gendered. Fisher and Cox [14] note that programming contests use assessment methods that are biased towards males, (e.g. through time constraints, question topics, etc.) and this may have implications for multiple choice assessments in schools.

Diversity

Ladner and Israel [15] point out that in the USA, pupils of school age are ethnically diverse with less than 50% of the population white and 15% of students having a disability. This highlights the need for teachers to "be able to implement pedagogies that promote learning and engagement for diverse learners" (p. 27). Iqbal et al. [16]

note that there has been limited research into minority ethnic pupils' experiences of computing in the UK. In their study, "pupils suggested they were more engaged when teachers tried to overcome the disconnection with pupils' social context outside of school" (p. 1297).

Ladner and Israel suggest that one potential approach to including diverse learners is "culturally responsive computing education". This is described by Eglash et al. [17] as a set of approaches which merge computational thinking with cultural practices. This might include demonstrating the sophisticated mathematical or computational practices found in pupils' cultural heritage; using culturally authentic characters as sprites when teaching Scratch; or engaging in projects related to culturally relevant problems or issues.

Promoting culturally relevant activities is suitable for all ages of school pupils. Lotherington and Chow [18] describe how very young pupils created culturally relevant multimedia versions of the traditional tale, Goldilocks, thus developing digital literacy skills in a culturally diverse way. While Pirbhai-Illich et al. [6] show that high school students in alternative education provision can create multimedia texts reflecting their culture.

Special Educational Needs

Pupils with Special Educational Needs are also at risk of exclusion from computing lessons. Ladner and Israel [15] identify three aspects of exclusion: teachers' attitudes/expectations; pedagogical approaches; and accessibility.

Teachers' attitudes can have a negative impact on pupils' achievement in computing if they hold lower expectations of a pupil because of their particular needs. Ladner and Israel suggest that this may "create an unconscious bias that the student cannot learn computer science" (p. 27). In contrast, Echeveste [19] shows that this is not necessarily the case and observed that "students labeled as special ed worked steadily on programming tasks performing sometimes better than their peers" (p. 359). However, Echeveste does not explain why this might be or if particular features of the tasks or pedagogy supported this.

For pupils with certain Special Educational Needs, specific resources or approaches are required to enable them to access the curriculum. For example, pupils with visual impairment remain underrepresented in higher education computing [20]. In recent years, there has been a huge rise in the use of block-based programming languages, e.g. Scratch, particularly to introduce computing to pupils. While there are numerous benefits to such languages, they are not accessible for pupils with visual impairments [21]. In an outreach robotics program for secondary pupils with visual impairments, inclusive practices that would be appropriate for all subjects (e.g. use of braille, allowing pupils time to orient themselves to the space, etc.) were supplemented by practices that were specific to computing: the use of a text based language, fully commented source code and a screen reader set to read all punctuation [20]. Together these supported pupils to solve complex challenges. Another approach is that of Papazafiropulos et al. [22] who used 3D printing to produce accessible resources to teach visually impaired pupils computer science concepts (e.g. data structures). They found that the resources they created were also successful with sighted pupils and had potential to be used in inclusive classrooms.

Attainment

In any computing class, there will also be differences in pupils' level of attainment in computing. These differences may relate to other aspects of inclusion. For example, Hatlevik and Christophersen [23] suggest that some of the differences between pupils' digital competence relate to their cultural capital and home language. Others note that perceptions and beliefs about ability are often biased and gendered [9].

Even when differences of attainment are identified, teachers may not be equipped to ensure that the work they set is at the correct level of challenge for pupils. As Dagiene and Stupuriene [24] note, the experience of question authors for the Bebras computing competition has shown that experts do not evaluate accurately the difficulty and complexity of the tasks they set for different age groups.

It is noticeable that none of the reviewed papers fully addressed how teachers can support the wide range of attainment that might be expected in a school computing class. There is clearly scope for adapting the inclusive pedagogical approaches used successfully in many other subjects [25] and for researchers to engage with work on pupil mindsets and alternatives to ability grouping and setting. For example, through setting a range of different learning challenges that demonstrate progression in the aspect of computing being taught, children can select for themselves the task that is at the most appropriate level for them [26].

Economic disadvantage

Few of the reviewed papers specifically addressed ways of including pupils who have less access to technology because of economic disadvantage. As Ashcraft et al. noted above, attainment in computing may have more to do with prior experience than any 'natural' ability and Iqbal et al. [16] show that insufficient access to technology can be related to the socio-cultural learning contexts of minority groups. Thus, inequalities are compounded with this limited access having a more acute impact for pupils who are already disadvantaged in other ways.

There are examples of specific actions taken to address digital exclusion. Thomaz et al. [27] demonstrate how practical activities with robotics motivated and enriched the learning of digitally excluded pupils in Brazil. These activities demonstrated several features of pedagogy identified by researchers looking at other areas of inclusion, for example, using practical activities and valuing collaboration.

4 Conclusions

This review found research relating to a number of inclusion issues, in particular, gender, diversity, special educational needs, attainment and economic disadvantage. However, the number of papers found was relatively small due to the use of the search terms "inclusion" and "inclusive". It is clear that there are other studies relating to each of the five areas above that do not use these terms and so do not appear in this review, for example, there was little reference to research that considers the experiences of pupils with autism learning computing, or parental influences on young peoples' participation in computing. The gaps in the review are indicative of the way that research in each of these areas has remained separate from the wider educational literature on inclusion and inclusive pedagogies or even to the literature on the use of ICT for inclusion. The review has shown that there is insufficient research that synthesises these different strands and provides the guidance that teachers need to ensure that their computing lessons are truly inclusive for all pupils.

That is not to say that researchers do not recognise the need for work that addresses the full range of inclusion issues and particularly focuses on those who are disadvantaged in multiple ways. In fact, Ashcraft et al. [7] suggests that a crucial next step in efforts to diversify computing is "future research that takes a more in-depth look at intersections of race, gender, class, ability, and sexuality" (p. 5).

Notwithstanding these limitations, the review has identified some common practices that have potential to further the inclusion of underrepresented and disadvantaged groups by improving the school computing curriculum, teachers' pedagogy and individual attitudes. Firstly, there is a need to ensure that the school computing curriculum is relevant and authentic. Rudd [28] demonstrates how recent changes to the ICT curriculum in England reflect ideological and neo-liberal political positions which could lead to computer science being constructed as a selective and elitist subject. In contrast, he argues the need for a curriculum and practices that promote greater social justice and equity. Such a curriculum must be designed so that it is valued by pupils and addresses issues that are important to them. One such approach is to focus computing lessons on developing 'computational participation' which Kafai and Burke propose as an extension of the concept of computational thinking to include personal expression and social participation [29]. Approaches to computing should emphasise deep fluency rather than superficial understanding and speed and highlight the social aspects of computing rather than reinforce stereotypes of the lone, isolated programmer. For example, Holbert demonstrates how creating artefacts for others may help to align computing with values of connectedness [30]. This can be complemented by "culturally responsive computing" approaches that purposefully value and engage with aspects of pupils' culture or go further and actively promote critical reflection and engagement with issues of exclusion, disadvantage and power relationships (see, for example, the work of Lee and Soep [31]).

Such a curriculum should be taught through inclusive pedagogical approaches that allow children to engage in meaningful practical tasks in a welcoming environment. Teachers should encourage collaboration and pay attention to potential unconscious bias and how interactions within the classroom may promote or reinforce stereotypical behaviour.

In terms of future research, there is a need for a more comprehensive review of each of the five themes identified here that draws on the wider literature of inclusive practice and applies this to computing. It is also clear that many studies of inclusion in computing have been situated in informal or outreach activities rather than inclusive mainstream classrooms. As Kafai and Burke point out, extra-curricular activities compete with pupils' other interests and will never reach all of the pupils who may benefit from them [29]. Therefore, schools have a vital role to play in ensuring all pupils have an inclusive experience of computing and researchers have an important role in supporting this by researching computing practices in more formal settings.

References

1. UNESCO: Policy Guidelines on Inclusion in Education. UNESCO, Paris (2009)
2. Frederickson, N., Cline, T.: Special Educational Needs, Inclusion and Diversity, 2nd edn. Open University Press, Maidenhead (2009)
3. Ainscow, M., Booth, T., Dyson, A.: Improving Schools, Developing Inclusion. Routledge, London (2006)
4. Meneses, J., Momino, J.M.: Putting digital literacy in practice: how schools contribute to digital inclusion in the network society. Inf. Soc. **26**(3), 197–208 (2010)
5. Seale, J.: Digital Inclusion: A Research Briefing by the Technology-Enhanced Learning Phase of the Teaching and Learning Research Programme. London Knowledge Lab, London (2010). http://www.tlrp.org/docs/DigitalInclusion.pdf
6. Pirbhai-Illich, F., Nat Turner, K.C., Austin, T.Y.: Using digital technologies to address aboriginal adolescents' education. Multicult. Educ. Technol. J. **3**(2), 144–162 (2009)
7. Ashcraft, C.S., Eger, E., Friend, M.M.: Girls in IT. In: NCWIT (2013)
8. Lasen, M.: Education and career pathways in information communication technology: what are schoolgirls saying? Comput. Educ. **54**(4), 1117–1126 (2010)
9. Downes, T., Looker, D.: Factors that influence students' plans to take computing and information technology subjects in senior secondary school. Comput. Sci. Educ. **21**(2), 175–199 (2011)
10. Osunde, J., et al.: An investigation of digital games features that appeal to young females and males. In: Munkvold, R., Kolas, L. (eds.) Proceedings of the 9th European Conference on Games Based Learning (2015)
11. Robertson, J.: The influence of a game-making project on male and female learners' attitudes to computing. Comput. Sci. Educ. **23**(1), 58–83 (2013)
12. Corneliussen, H.G., Prøitz, L.: Kids Code in a rural village in Norway: could code clubs be a new arena for increasing girls' digital interest and competence? Inf. Commun. Soc. **19**(1), 95–110 (2015)
13. Coupal, L.V.: Computer-based technologies and the social construction of gendered identities: an ethnography of the power/knowledge relations of schooling. Ph.D. thesis (2003)
14. Fisher, M., Cox, A.: Gender and programming contests: mitigating exclusionary practices. Inform. Educ. **5**(1), 1–16 (2006)
15. Ladner, R.E., Israel, M.: For all in computer science for all. Commun. ACM **59**(9), 26–28 (2016)
16. Iqbal, J., et al.: The face of digital literacy for Muslim teenage girls: a comparative study of Bradford Muslim girl schools. Int. J. Incl. Educ. **18**(12), 1283–1303 (2014)
17. Eglash, R., Gilbert, J.E., Foster, E.: Toward culturally responsive computing education. Commun. ACM **56**(7), 33 (2013)
18. Lotherington, H., Chow, S.: Rewriting "Goldilocks" in the urban, multicultural elementary school. Read. Teach. **60**(3), 244–252 (2006)
19. Echeveste, M.E.: Challenges of introducing computer science into the traditional grammar of K-12 schooling. In: Proceedings of the 2016 ACM Conference on Innovation and Technology in Computer Science Education, ITiCSE 2016, p. 359 (2016)
20. Ludi, S., Reichlmayr, T.: Developing inclusive outreach activities for students with visual impairments. In: SIGCSE 2008: Proceedings of the 39th ACM Technical Symposium on Computer Science Education, pp. 439–443 (2008)
21. Ludi, S., Reichlmayr, T.: The use of robotics to promote computing to pre-college students with visual impairments. ACM Trans. Comput. Educ. **11**(3), 1–20 (2011)

22. Papazafiropulos, N., Fanucci, L., Leporini, B., Pelagatti, S., Roncella, R.: Haptic models of arrays through 3D printing for computer science education. In: Miesenberger, K., Bühler, C., Penaz, P. (eds.) ICCHP 2016. LNCS, vol. 9758, pp. 491–498. Springer, Cham (2016). https://doi.org/10.1007/978-3-319-41264-1_67
23. Hatlevik, O.E., Christophersen, K.-A.: Digital competence at the beginning of upper secondary school: identifying factors explaining digital inclusion. Comput. Educ. **63**, 240–247 (2013)
24. Dagiene, V., Stupuriene, G.: Bebras - a sustainable community building model for the concept based learning of informatics and computational thinking. Inform. Educ. **15**(1), 25–44 (2016)
25. Florian, L.: Conceptualising inclusive pedagogy: the inclusive pedagogical approach in action. In: Deppeler, J.M., Loreman, T., Smith, R., Florian, L. (eds.) Inclusive Pedagogy Across the Curriculum (International Perspectives on Inclusive Education), vol. 7, pp. 11–24. Emerald Group Publishing Limited, Bingley (2015)
26. Shelton, C.: Beyond lesson recipes: first steps towards a repertoire for teaching primary computing. In: Proceedings of Constructionism, Bangkok (2016)
27. Thomaz, S., et al.: RoboEduc: a pedagogical tool to support educational robotics. In: 39th ASEE/IEEE Frontiers in Education Conference (2009)
28. Rudd, T.: The ideological construction of a new form of digital exclusion: computer science as latin or total deus ex machina? J. Crit. Educ. Policy Stud. **11**(3), 287–305 (2013)
29. Kafai, Y.B., Burke, Q.: Connected Code: Why Children Need to Learn Programming. MIT Press, Boston (2014)
30. Holbert, N.: Leveraging cultural values and "ways of knowing" to increase diversity in maker activities. Int. J. Child-Comput. Interact. **9–10**, 33–39 (2016)
31. Lee, C.H., Soep, E.: None but ourselves can free our minds: critical computational literacy as a pedagogy of resistance. Equity Excell. Educ. **49**(4), 480–492 (2016)

Educational Support on Computing and Informatics as Means of Empowering Disadvantaged Young People in Developed Countries

Toshinori Saito(✉)

Graduate School of Practitioners in Education, Seisa University, Yokohama, Kanagawa, Japan
t-saito@gred.seisa.ac.jp

Abstract. The paper discusses a research into civil empowerment in a developed country through promoting learning opportunities of computing and informatics based on a question as follows: What kind of possibility and limitation can be found in educational support on computing and informatics as a means of empowerment and social inclusion of socially disadvantaged youths in developed countries? For the question, following action research methodology, the author had joined a group's activity of helping social participation of disadvantaged youths in a mid-sized city in Japan and engaged in supporting learning computing. We found that creative aspects of computing had involved the youths into autonomous learning of computing; however, their expanded capacities of computing hadn't obviously been converted into their motivation for social participation. It suggests that more holistic support enabling them to find the meaning of learning computing in context should be designed and practiced for their further empowerment.

Keywords: Computing and informatics · Socially disadvantaged learners
Educational support · Social inclusion · Empowerment

1 Introduction

Global disemination of information and communication technologies (ICTs) was supposed to lead to development and reinforcement of global democracy [1]. However, despite the global disemination of ICTs, realization of equitable enjoyment of its benefit is still seen problematic. Instead of promoting democratic values through the disemination of ICTs, the digital divide has been reported emerging and widening [2].

Accordingly, in pursuit of the framework for approaching the digital divide especially in developed country's setting, the paper presents a discussion on civil empowerment and social inclusion through promoting learning opportunities of computing and informatics. The discussion is based on a research project in progress conducted in a small-scaled support group for students with school absenteeism and socially withdrawn youths [3, 4]. The group is placed in a mid-sized provincial city in Japan.

A. Tatnall and M. Webb (Eds.): WCCE 2017, IFIP AICT 515, pp. 515–524, 2017.
https://doi.org/10.1007/978-3-319-74310-3_52

The purpose of the research is to advance understanding of the significance of promoting learning opportunities of computing and informatics in terms of civil empowerment and social inclusion. The research was conducted in accordance with the research question as follows:

- What kind of possibility and limitation can be found in educational support on computing and informatics for socially disadvantaged youths in developed countries as a means of empowerment and social inclusion?

2 Relevant Literatures

Concerning the discussion on tackling of the digital divide, the focus of discussion has now moved from achieving equal access to ICTs with providing physical infrastructures toward delivering equitable opportunities for citizens to enjoy substantial improvement of well-being through the empowerment on technology use [2, 5, 6]. Empirical researches on the digital divide have revealed the factors that may affect citizens' disparity not only in access but also in use of ICTs, namely, race, ethnicity, gender, class, educational background, and other factors relating to the socioeconomic situations [7–11]. These factors commonly reflect social, economical, cultural, and historical circumstances of the society, which may form the background of the disparity between the 'haves' and the 'have nots' among citizens.

Results of the prior research have also led to the shared recognition that approaching the digital divide should be based on the conception of empowerment, which is directed toward fostering human capacities for living well thorough making good use of ICTs [12–15]. The conception of empowerment as a basis for tackling the digital divide can be applied to the situation not only in developing countries but also in developed countries, since it is common for both of the countries to have social structures reproducing socially disadvantaged members at risk of being excluded from informatized situation of the society [16]. In terms of the empowerment for such members in a society, the problem of digital divide can be understood intrinsically as a subset of so-called social exclusion, which is asking for the promotion of equitable opportunities for digital participations [17]. This means it is crucial to construct a blueprint of social inclusion into informatized societies under the circumstance of the globalized digital divide.

The research question shown above is informed with the outcome of preceding research on information and communication technologies for development (ICT4D). Many of the literatures on ICT4D insist on the indirectness between ICTs as technological input and enhancement of the residents' well-being as its output. Through the research on ICT development for rural communities in Bolivia, Gigler [12, 14, 18] emphasized that no direct relations had been found between improved ICT access and enhanced socio-economic development. In addition, using the notion of 'catalyst', Gigler argued the significance of 'intermediary organizations' in converting ICT access into 'meaningful use' of ICTs through educational support for the rural poor citizens. With the model of the ICT4D value chain, Heeks [19, 20] also argued the indirect relationship between ICT infrastructure and development impacts, which indicated the

ICT access should be seen as merely a 'starting point in understanding ICT's contribution to development' [20].

The problem of the indirectness between ICT access and enhancement of residents' well-being is supposed to be common toward the developed countries where ICT diffusion has mostly been completed. This indirectness is basically affected by the social structure reflecting inequality and inequity in obtaining learning opportunity of computing and informatics, which is seen not only in developing countries but in developed countries (e.g. [8]). Though the state of basic literacy is generally better in developed countries, the distribution of learning opportunities to convert ICT access into meaningful use of ICTs is still left to be insufficient (e.g. [21]).

Furthermore, the research question is basically asking about the roles of computing and informatics education on the disadvantaged citizens' empowerment in informatized societies. The preceding arguments [22–24] have shown the roles of such education in introducing fundamental concepts of computing and informatics and in expanding human capacities necessary to utilize ICTs effectively for various purposes. The arguments also have reported that expanding such capacities enabled people to produce systematic ways of problem-solving with ICTs and to create representations reflecting their own ideas. The role in expanding career choice with the enhancement of computing skills has also been discussed in some literatures (e.g. [23, 25]). There is, in addition, an argument which illustrates the educational role in promoting democratic participation, being considered as a basis of public education, through encouraging creating programs to contribute to others in the society [26].

However, the role of computing and informatics education hasn't been investigated and discussed adequately yet, especially in terms of empowering disadvantaged citizens living in informatized developed countries. We believe that such investigation and discussion will add an alternative view of computing and informatics education's contribution toward the realization of digital equity.

3 Methodologies

To explore the research question, the author joined a group's activity to help rehabilitation and social participation of the pupils and students with school absenteeism and the youths who had experienced socially withdrawal. The group was placed in a mid-sized provincial city in Japan. The group's size had varied during the research period, however, there were around 5 to 10 young people with 2 to 5 staff members including part time supporters. The author acted as a part time member mainly to support such youths in getting familiar with computing and in learning something about computing and informatics. As a data collection the author had made a series of text descriptions with some pictures and movies in the field, that was the author thought as field notes, noting events and occurrences, dialogues with group's participants, findings and interpretations, and reflections on every session during the research period. The data were analyzed into important themes and issues in accordance with the research question. This process was supplemented with further observations and dialogues in the field.

The research was conducted in May 2015, after a period of pilot study in the same field from December 2013 to January 2014, and still continues at present. This paper reports the findings based on the analysis of the field notes taken from May 2015 to March 2017. During the period, we, the author and the young people in the group, had been involved in learning introductions of computing and informatics with several practices, such as making games, teaching elderly people programming with Scratch, and constructing a programmable robot called MugBot[1].

The research followed the basic conceptions of action research as a participatory research methodology. Action research is explained as an approach "that enables people to find effective solutions to problems they confront in their everyday lives" [27] by collaborative commitment toward real social problems for a group of people that are relevant to the problems. In this methodology, the researcher is not merely an objective observer but a member who actively participate in the process of problem-solving. Moreover, the research process is interpreted as a process seeking for positive social change based on democratic values [28]. The author applied the conceptions of action research for the research question called for practical engagement in an educational support project practiced in a real context of a developed country.

4 Findings

4.1 The Possibility of Educational Support on Computing and Informatics

Firstly, we will examine the findings which suggest the possibility of educational support on computing and informatics as a means of empowerment and social inclusion of the youths in the group.

While joining the group's activity the author had met certain amount of young people who were at various range of the ages (from elementary pupils to late 20's). Among them the author had built a continuous relationship with two young people who were supported in the group for their rehabilitations. Both of them were male of late 20's had experienced the status of social withdrawal in years past and hadn't have any opportunity of regular employment (in the paper they are named as "M01" and "M02" for anonymization).

Based on the reflection and interpretation of the involvement with them, which had been noted in the field notes and other visual materials, the author found these suggestions shown below relating to the possibility of educational support on computing and informatics.

- With some triggers (e.g. suggestions on the joy of making games with programming, the way of obtaining teaching materials and other useful information in the

[1] MugBot is a nonproprietary open source social robot originally designed by Koike Laboratory in Tokyo Metropolitan University. http://www.mugbot.com.

web, and the annual event on Scratch programming) brought by the author, they got interested in using computers in more creative ways and autonomously engaged in learning computing.
- They were also motivated to learn introductory part of informatics and succeeded in finding the joy of learning it.
- During the period that they were learning and practicing computing and informatics in the group, they enjoyed the chances to communicate with others (e.g. support staffs, other young participants, neighboring residents participated as volunteer supporter, and the pupils and students of the schools around) for their capacities of computing and informatics.

For instance, the author had noted in the field notes the circumstance in which the group members' had decided to engage in constructing MugBot. It shows how the members' emerging interests into creative aspects of computing had involved them into learning computing:

– Excerpt 1: *Though my suggestion being one of the causes for them (includes M01, M02, and two other staffs of the group) to start the activity of making MugBot, more directly it has started by their own decision made after the participation of "Scratch Day in Tokyo 2016", at which they visited the booth presenting MugBot and felt very interesting with it.*[2]

Actually, after that, M01 and M02 had begun to construct a unit of MugBot in early September of 2016 and kept their effort to complete all of the process of construction. Then they finally succeeded in completing the construction and controlling all of the basic functions (blinking eyes of LED, voicing given text data, and moving its head according to given programs) in late December. While they were engaged in it, they supposed to learn controlling devices with programs and had experienced constructing an example of network system, which requires basic understanding of the Internet Protocol, merely with a textbook and other resources they found themselves. Very occasionally, the author gave advices when they seemed to get into difficulties that might be beyond their capacities.

Moreover, their capacities of computing and informatics had become a cause of generating new communication with others visited their working space. For instance, when the group accepted two students of a junior high school located near the group's space for the students' work experience program in the school, M01 had autonomously attempted to introduce making programs with Scratch toward the students. To the author's eyes the students' time for work experience program seemed to become more meaningful and more pleasurable for it. The author described this incident in the field notes as shown below:

– Excerpt 2: (1) *I (the author) left how the progression (of introducing programming to the students) should be to M01's judge. Then M01 took an introductory*

[2] It is extracted from the field notes written in 25th August 2016. The whole part of the field notes is written in Japanese and all of the quoted parts in this paper are English translation of the original field notes.

algorithm book and handed it to the students. (2) *M01 sat besides the students and sometimes gave suggestions to them. One of the students showed a smile on his face.* (3) *The way M01 introduced programming to the students can apparently be interpreted as an inclusion for the students into the culture of programming (suppose there is something like that).*[3]

4.2 Limitations of Educational Support on Computing and Informatics

The author also found these suggestions, as a result of the reflection on the field notes, concerning limitations of educational support on computing and informatics.

- The young people's expanded capacities of computing and informatics didn't seem to expand obviously their motivation for making use of such capacities for their social participation to improve their personal situation in the surrounding society.
- Their motivation for making use of such capacities to improve circumstances of the community they belonged to also didn't manifest itself in their behavior.
- It seemed difficult for the group members (including the support staffs) to convert efficiently such capacities they had made into the group's competence.

With regard to the first and the second points, there is a description of the author's consideration over an incident happened in the field:

– Excerpt 3: *As we have seen in today's practice, the aim (of the practice) 'creating programs which can afford someone a certain level of convenience' itself is substantially social in terms of supposing a real context by considering 'someone' and 'a certain level of convenience'. Moreover, the activity of 'making a process of a task more efficient (or offering a pleasure to someone) by creating a program' is unavoidably a social practice because it needs a setting of others (or a self as an object in the context of society). The reason why M01 consistently tells 'I have no interest in doing it' or 'I am not good at doing it' seems to reflect his strong refusal of engaging in the activity that requires being social.*[4]

The incident based on the consideration above was that M01 showed negative attitude toward the author's offer of creating a program based on his own or the group's needs of computing. M01 was quite positive when he had leaned and reproduced programs according to some situation-settings given by the textbooks. In addition, M01 seemed to have enjoyed learning an introductory level of informatics with making programs according to the instruction in the textbooks. However, M01 had consistently expressed his indifference to create something which could be a solution for 'real problems' concerning his personal or the group's daily activities making use of his capacity of computing.

The third point had related to the limitation of the members' participation in the educational support. The group was mainly managed by two core staffs, who were the manager and the co-manager of the group, with the help of several volunteer staffs

[3] All of the quoted part is from the field notes written in 19th January 2017.

[4] The quoted part is from the field notes written in 16th Februaly 2017.

(M01 had changed his position in the group from a supported member toward a volunteer stuff during the research period. He had been virtually supported in his social participation while working as a volunteer stuff). In the author's view, they had had a shortage in staffs for the amount of their tasks, which made it difficult to involve themselves into the practice of computing and informatics as much as they could develop their own educational support programs by themselves.

Concerning the supported members, the author and the staffs (especially M01 and the manager of the group) had provided various occasions for them to encounter the practice of computing, mainly with Scratch programming as an introduction. And actually, many of them seemed to be interested in practicing computing. However, the membership of the supported members had not been stable because of their participation in the group was basically left to their own circumstances, which were sometimes too complicated socially and personally to keep attending the practice.

5 Discussion and Conclusion

We finally propose following suggestions obtained regarding the possibility of educational support on computing and informatics based on the findings of the field research. The suggestions are that (1) such support can expand the mode of disadvantaged youths' daily use of ICT facilities; (2) it also can derive their desire for personal challenges of autonomous expansion of their computing capacity; (3) it can enlarge the youths' communication opportunities with others around. Concerning the suggestion (1), the youths in the observed group had successfully learned to enjoy utilizing ICT facilities in more creative ways with programming whereas they at first had very limited idea to utilize them because of their limited learning opportunity for the personal and social circumstances. Concerning the suggestion (2), promotion of the autonomous behavior in learning computing had commonly been observed in both M01 and M02's usual practices during the research period. Concerning the suggestion (3), such communication opportunities were observed among them with the staff members, volunteer supporters, other youths in the group, visiting residents, and so forth, which had occurred in the context of computing practices.

On the other hand, we have to propose following suggestions regarding the limitations of the educational support based on the findings. The suggestions are that (1) such support cannot turn disadvantaged youths' expanded capacities of computing directly into the ideas of applying it toward real problem solving activities in social situations; (2) it also cannot enhance the youths' motivation for utilizing their computing capacities into strengthening their connections with societies around; (3) it cannot function without continuous help of volunteer supporters who have computing capacities and are ready for work with practitioners in the field. Concerning the suggestion (1), both M01 and M02 had consistently shown quite reserved attitudes to engage in solving problems relating to the group's activities utilizing their computing capacities. Concerning the suggestion (2), on M01 and M02's case, strengthening of the connections with societies in this term had potentially contained seeking jobs, attempting to learn in higher education, creating the group's new activity to contribute toward neighboring communities, and so force. In the research period any obvious incidents relating to these hadn't be observed. Concerning the suggestion (3), it should be noted that, as far as the reported research period, most part of the educational support in the group had maintained mainly with the author's participation.

The obtained suggestions lead two conclusions. One is that, premising collaboration of the practitioners of both computing and social participation support backgrounds, educational support on computing and informatics for disadvantaged youths in developed country has a certain potential of expanding their choice of meaningful use of ICTs with deriving autonomous participation in computing practices. This conclusion is consistent with the recent tendency of digital divide research which emphasizes the gap of 'meaningful use' rather than 'physical access' as a key factor of approaching inequitable circumstances of ICT use (e.g. [17, 29]). Moreover, this conclusion corresponds with an ICT4D's evaluation framework, the 'Choice Framework' proposed by Kleine [30], which argues the significance of small case development studies on ICTs' role of expanding freedom of residents' choice as empowerment [20].

Another is that, the educational support cannot be the solo factor to encourage them in their social participation through utilizing their computing capacities. We suppose that there will be a limitation within such educational support in terms of empowerment for social participation if computing and informatics are to be taught and learned merely as a value-free decontextualized knowledge by the learners. In other words, potential of the educational support to overcome the indirectness between ICT access and enhancement of residents' well-being should be understood restrictedly for the present. This is consistent with the indication made by Gigler [14] that "improving the access to resources for the poor, for instance providing access to girls' education or access to ICTs only represents a potential for enhancing their capabilities and thus does not automatically have to lead to positive outcomes on empowerment."

Nevertheless, this does not mean educational support on computing and informatics is absolutely unsuitable for the empowerment of disadvantaged youths' social participation since there is room for improvement in its pedagogical design to link the supported youths with the context of surrounding societies through utilizing computing capacities. From the author's viewpoint, the shown limitation rather signifies a demand for the educational support designed based on more social and contextual conceptions that can afford the supported youths an idea (or ideas) about engaging with societies utilizing their computing capacities. In this direction, Schultz's literature [26] will be one of the bases to pursue the possibility of computing education in the light of learner's social participation.

The educational support will continue for the purpose of investigating further affect on the youths and also on the group's activity. Therefore the author presents some insights derived as recommendations for the continuous educational support; practices in the support should be designed considering involving the youths into computing in context so as to make more opportunities to link their capacities toward real needs of computing; the 'real needs' for computing capacities should be explored under the dialogical relationship among the youths, the practitioners, and the researcher; for the pursuit of sustainable support, an institutional framework to include the support group into decent computing culture should be explored. In other words, more holistic support, containing some active problem-solving projects utilizing computing capacities for instance, that enables the supported youths to find the meaning of learning computing in context should be explored and practiced for further empowerment.

Acknowledgments. The author would like to thank all of the members of the support group who kindly gave the opportunity to conduct the field sessions. The research was supported by JSPS KAKENHI Grant Number 16K01136.

References

1. Ferdinand, P.: The internet democracy democratization. Democratization **7**(1), 1–17 (2000)
2. Revenaugh, M.: Beyond the digital divide: pathways to equity. Technol. Learn. **1**, 38–50 (2000)
3. Tateno, M., Park, T.W., Kato, T.A., Umene-Nakano, W., Saito, T.: Hikikomori as a possible clinical term in psychiatry: a questionnaire survey. BMC Psychiatry. **12**, 169 (2012)
4. Tajan, N.: Japanese post-modern social renouncers: an exploratory study of the narratives of Hikikomori subjects. Subjectivity **8**, 283–304 (2015)
5. Warschauer, M.: Reconceptualizing the digital divide. First Monday **7**(7) (2002). https://doi.org/10.5210/fm.v7i7.967
6. Warschauer, M.: Technology and equity in schooling: deconstructing the digital divide. Educ. Policy. **18**, 562–588 (2004)
7. Clark, C., Gorski, P.: Multicultural education and the digital divide: focus on socioeconomic class background. Multicult. Perspect. **4**, 25–36 (2002)
8. Kvasny, L.: Cultural (re) production of digital inequality in a US community technology initiative. Inf. Commun. Soc. **9**, 160–181 (2006)
9. Gudmundsdottir, G.: From digital divide to digital equity: learners' ICT competence in four primary schools in Cape Town, South Africa. Int. J. Educ. Dev. ICT **6**, 84–105 (2010)
10. Ritzhaupt, A., Liu, F.: Differences in student information and communication technology literacy based on socio-economic status, ethnicity, and gender: evidence of a digital divide. J. Res. Technol. Educ. **45**, 291–307 (2013)
11. Willis, S., Tranter, B.: Beyond the "digital divide": internet diffusion and inequality in Australia. J. Sociol. **42**, 43–59 (2006)
12. Gigler, B.-S.: Including the Excluded- Can ICTs empower poor communities? Towards an alternative evaluation framework based on the capability approach. In: 4th International Conference on the Capability Approach, vol. 5, no. 7, September 2004. University of Pavia, Italy (2004)
13. Johnstone, J.: Technology as empowerment: a capability approach to computer ethics. Ethics Inf. Technol. **9**, 73–87 (2007)
14. Gigler, B.-S.: Informational Capabilities - The Missing Link for the Impact of ICT on Development (2011). https://doi.org/10.2139/ssrn.2191594
15. Simsek, E., Simsek, A.: New literacies for digital citizenship. Contemp. Educ. Technol. **4**, 126–137 (2013)
16. Selwyn, N.: Reconsidering political and popular understandings of the digital divide. New Media Soc. **6**, 341–362 (2004)
17. Wei, L., Hindman, D.B.: Does the digital divide matter more? Comparing the effects of new media and old media use on the education-based knowledge gap. Mass Commun. Soc. **14**, 216–235 (2011)
18. Gigler, B.: Poverty, inequality and human development of indigenous peoples in Bolivia (2009)

19. Heeks, R., Molla, A.: Impact assessment of ICT-for-Development projects: a compendium of approaches. University of Manchester, Manchester (2009)
20. Heeks, R.: Do information and communication technologies (ICTs) contribute to development? J. Int. Dev. **22**, 625–640 (2010)
21. European Commission: The International Computer and Information Literacy Study (ICILS) : Main Findings and Implications for Education Policies in Europe (2014). http://ec.europa.eu/dgs/education_culture/repository/education/library/study/2014/ec-icils_en.pdf
22. Resnick, M., Flanagan, M., Kelleher, C., MacLaurin, M., Ohshima, Y., Perlin, K., Torres, R.: Growing up programming democratizing the creation of dynamic, interactive media. In: CHI EA 2009 Proceedings of the 27th International Conference Extended Abstracts on Human Factors in Computing Systems, 4–9 April 2009, Boston, Massachusetts, USA. pp. 3293–3296 (2009)
23. Hromkovič, J., Steffen, B.: Why teaching informatics in schools is as important as teaching mathematics and natural sciences. In: Kalaš, I., Mittermeir, Roland T. (eds.) ISSEP 2011. LNCS, vol. 7013, pp. 21–30. Springer, Heidelberg (2011). https://doi.org/10.1007/978-3-642-24722-4_3
24. Sysło, M.M., Kwiatkowska, A.B.: Informatics for all high school students. In: Diethelm, I., Mittermeir, Roland T. (eds.) ISSEP 2013. LNCS, vol. 7780, pp. 43–56. Springer, Heidelberg (2013). https://doi.org/10.1007/978-3-642-36617-8_4
25. Seehorn, D., Carey, S., Fuschetto, B., Lee, I., Moix, D., O'Grady-Cunniff, D., Owens, B.B., Stephenson, C.: CSTA K -12 Computer Science Standards: Revised 2011. Academic Press, Cambridge (2011)
26. Schulte, C.: Reflections on the role of Programming in primary and secondary computing education. In: Proceedings of the 8th Workshop in Primary and Secondary Computing Education, WiPSE 2013, pp. 17–24. ACM (2013)
27. Stringer, E.T.: Action research. Sage Publications, Thousand Oaks (2013). p. 1
28. Brydon-Miller, M., Greenwood, D., Maguire, P.: Why action research? Action Res. **1**(1), 9–28 (2003). https://doi.org/10.1177/14767503030011002
29. Warschauer, M.: Technology and social inclusion: rethinking the digital divide, p. 216. MIT Press, Cambridge (2003)
30. Kleine, D.: ICT4What? – using the choice framework to operationalise the capability approach to development. J. Int. Dev. **22**, 674–692 (2010)

Smartwalk: Computer Science on the Schoolyard

Michael Weigend(✉)

Holzkamp Gesamtschule Witten, Witten, Germany
mw@creative-informatics.de

Abstract. Smartwalk is a playful enrichment activity for sixth- or seventh-graders on computer science. It takes place outside on the schoolyard. The basic idea is to do things that Generation Z-kids usually do with their mobile devices in a different (metaphorical) way using the physical environment outside on the schoolyard. The goal is to make aware of computer sciences concepts adopted in smartphone apps and to promote the acquisition of computational thinking.

Keywords: Computational thinking · Mobile device
Computer science concepts · Media education

1 Media Education and Computer Science

In many western countries, high school students – the Generation Z – are comfortable with digital technology from young age. For example, 83% of German children in the age of 12 to 13 own a smartphone with internet connectivity and most of them are members of social networks [1]. However, there is some scepticism among parents and teachers regarding the proper use of digital devices. Based on the results of his study on 300.000 smartphone users, Alexander Markowetz warns that we are in danger of a "digital burnout" [2]. Especially young people get interrupted too often by a ringing cell phone. This leads to a loss of joy and productivity. Frequent use of digital technology does not necessarily imply information literacy. This is why there is a tendency at schools to include media education in the curriculum. Media skills are taught either within a dedicated subject (like computer science) or elements of media education are distributed on several traditional subjects: image processing in art lessons, data visualization in mathematics lessons, presentations in Science lessons etc. The Smartwalk activity is considered to be a "stand alone" element of media education, which does not require any specific pre-knowledge and can therefore be allocated to any subject. It is designed for a certain environment – the schoolyard of some German high school – but it can easily be adapted to any schoolyard. In contrast to activities practicing the efficient and responsible usage of digital technology (media literacy), Smartwalk focuses on the computer science background. There are basically two main goals:

(1) The participants get an idea of computer science concepts that are adopted in software on mobile devices.
(2) They develop computational thinking.

A. Tatnall and M. Webb (Eds.): WCCE 2017, IFIP AICT 515, pp. 525–535, 2017.
https://doi.org/10.1007/978-3-319-74310-3_53

The basic idea of Smartwalk is to do things that Generation Z-kids usually do with their mobile devices in a different (metaphorical) way outside in fresh air. For example they publish a statement similar to a SnapChat posting by putting a sticky note to a wall. They create "Land Art" artifacts somewhere on the schoolyard and make them accessible to the public by publishing the title and a URL-like address. Other topics covered by Smartwalk are augmented reality (adopted for example in Pokémon Go), image recognition and navigation.

Smartwalk takes two lessons (90 min). The class (grade 6 or 7, ages 11 to 13) is divided in small "mission teams" of four persons. Each team gets a mission plan containing directions where to go and challenges that have to be solved at certain locations. Some of the locations are specified by a photo and/or coordinates on a map and thus easy to find. The teams can start at different entry points and then follow a common path. They try to solve as many tasks as possible during the given time. At the end there are at least ten minutes of evaluation and reflection.

2 Task Design

Smartwalk is a computer science activity without computers. For this Bell, Witten and Fellows have coined the term "computer science unplugged" and meanwhile there are several collections of "unplugged" activities illustrating computer science concepts [3–5]. Especially to mention is the big reservoir of quiz tasks provided by the Bebras International Challenge on Informatics and Computational Thinking (http://www.bebras.org). One rule for the design of a Bebras task is that it must contain all information necessary to solve it. Another rule is that it must be solvable in two or three minutes. Smartwalk challenges are similar to Bebras tasks. The main difference is that they are intensely connected to the real life environment. Part of the information, which is necessary for solving a task, is not just given but must be found by interacting with the physical environment. The children walk around, get exhausted, observe carefully and co-operate with class mates. Smartwalk has elements of an experience-oriented setting. The idea is to make it more exciting for children. One has to consider that activities related to computational thinking may not sound very interesting to young people. For example, according to the ROSE study (Relevance of Science Education) "searching for structure" seems to be one of most boring item for fifteen years old students in Germany and other European countries [6]. Aversions of this kind are barriers that have to be overcome, when it is about motivating young people to go into informatics. Kurt Hahn, the inventor of the "outward bound" movement, argues that only in unusual and somewhat adventurous situations people are open to try new ways of thinking and acting [7].

3 Fostering Computational Thinking

As Jeanette Wing defines in 2006, "computational thinking represents a universally applicable attitude and skill set everyone, not just computer scientists, would be eager to learn and use" [8, p. 33]. Based on an analysis of relevant literature, Selby and

Woollard identify five basic facets of computational thinking: Abstraction, decomposition, evaluation, algorithmic thinking and generalization [9]. This section presents a few tasks from the Smartwalk activity illustrating how to foster some of these skills in an outdoor setting.

3.1 Abstraction

Computer programming includes abstraction. The programmer considers only those aspects of a phenomenon which are relevant for the purpose of the project and ignores unimportant details (from Latin abstrahere "to drag away"). In computer science the usage of metaphors and formal languages are two means of abstraction. [10] suggest that a metaphorical term is a prototype of a category. Therefore the metaphorical meaning is more abstract than the literal meaning. Based on this idea they define levels of abstraction. The more abstract an expression the more facets of the literal meaning are missing in the metaphoric meaning. Psycholinguists define metaphorical thinking as a transfer of knowledge from a familiar source domain to target domain. Conceptual metaphors are "vehicles" carrying the learners to new knowledge beyond their intellectual horizons [11]. In programming, conceptual metaphors are used on several levels of abstraction. Well known high level metaphors are "World Wide Web" or the "scan line" in algorithmic geometry. Data structures or standard classes like stacks and queues are metaphors projecting knowledge about physical collections onto the domain of data processing. For example, a physical stack of plates supports certain access-operations: You can only remove the top plate (pop) and put a new plate on top of the stack (push).

In the following task a metaphor is used to define a structure consisting of one object in the middle and several objects of a different type around it (Fig. 1).
Challenge 7: Find a thing, which is similar to the image.

Fig. 1. Dancing around a maypole at a Renaissance faire in Tuxedo Park (photo: public domain)

The image on the left hand side of Fig. 2 depicts the expected solution. But a manhole cover, (which actually exists at a different location on the schoolyard) also corresponds to the maypole dancing.

Fig. 2. Two different objects corresponding to the same metaphor

Another technique of abstraction in computer programming obviously is the use of a formal language for describing structures. The following task uses the Python notation of tuples to describe a sequence of objects:

Challenge 3: At the wall there are several objects with the structure (0, 1, 0, 0, 1, 0). What is the purpose of these objects?

Fig. 3. A window protection with two types of bars

The expected solution is shown in Fig. 3. The tuple is an abstraction of a window protection consisting of two different types of bars. The number 0 represents a straight bar and the number 1 represents a twisted bar.

3.2 Algorithms

An algorithm is a precise description of activity that leads to a certain goal. Every computer program is an algorithm. Creating and understanding algorithms is one of the core competences of computer scientist. The Smartwalk mission plan contains directions to certain places on the schoolyard. These are algorithms, mostly consisting of linear sequences of commands like "walk 50 steps straight on". They may also contain control structures with complex conditions like "Walk along the wall until you are standing beside two vertical wires." Algorithms can also be used to identify a static structure, as in the following task.

Challenge 8: Look around and find a thing, which has been constructed this way:

```
go forward 200 cm
repeat 4 times:
    turn right 30°
    go forward 30 cm
```

Figure 4 depicts the solution.

Fig. 4. Air ventilation pipe

Algorithms are an integral part of software that children use in their everyday life. The behaviour of a product as well as the ways how to use it is defined by algorithms. For example, a SnapChat message is not just a media but it has some kind of behaviour that is defined by an algorithm. It vanishes after some time. In challenge 11 the Smartwalkers create postings with a lifetime (Fig. 5).

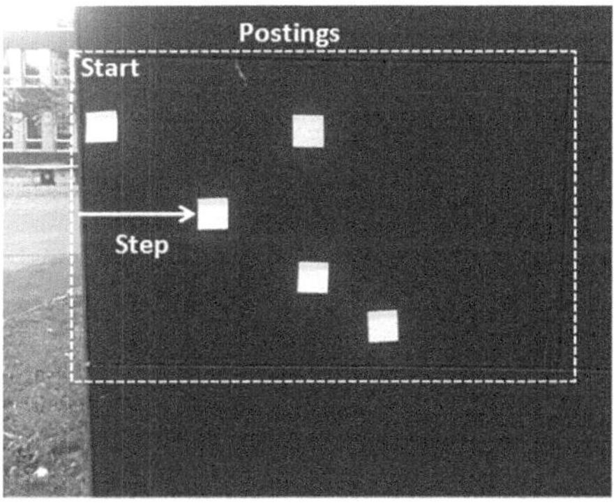

Fig. 5. A wall for posting poems

- *Find the wall depicted on the photo.*
- *Write a poem (two lines) on a sticky note and put it at the left side of the "Postings"-area.*
- *Read two or three postings that are already sticking at the wall. After you have read a posting move it for one step to the right.*
- *Remove the postings that have left the "Postings"-area.*

3.3 Decomposition

In the context of computer programming the term decomposition means breaking down a large problem into smaller chunks that are easier to handle. Like abstraction, decomposition is a means to cope with complexity. In object oriented programming decomposition takes place during the design of a system, when the developer creates a class diagram representing the whole project. The following tasks are simple examples of decomposition in everyday life.

Challenge 6: Look around. There is a thing with this structure:

```
((plastic, plastic, plastic), (metal, metal))
```

Figure 6 shows the solution.

Fig. 6. A bench on the schoolyard

The following task is more abstract since it does not use meaningful names. On the other hand it is more explicit because it introduces names for the parts of the whole aggregate.

Challenge 5: Follow the way and look down.
Find something that has structure B, which is described in the box.

```
A = (a, a, a, a, a, a, a) B = (A, A)
```

Draw an a.

Figure 7 shows the object that is expected to be found: a drain. The model is a nested tuple. Object B is a tuple containing two objects A, which consist of seven objects a each. Thus, the Smartwalkers are expected to draw an elongated hole.

Fig. 7. A drain on the ground

3.4 Generalisation

Generalisation means to deduce a general principle from examples. In the following challenge generalisation is adopted to figure out the addressing technique (Fig. 8).

Challenge 9: Some areas on the schoolyard have identifiers that are explained in the satellite photo. In the area with the identifier `science.1` *there is a small tree.*

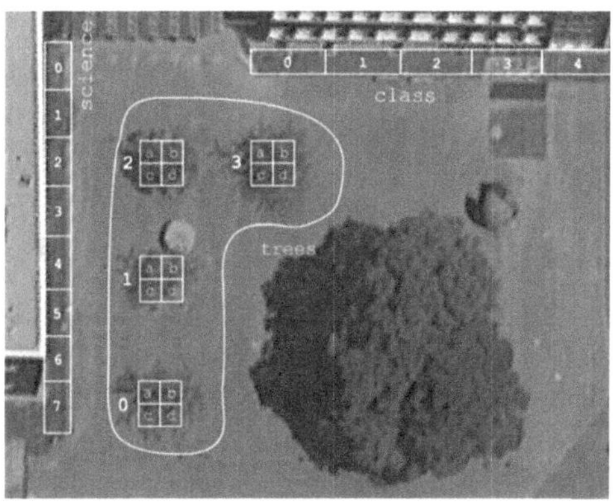

Fig. 8. URL-like addresses of areas on a schoolyard

(a) *What kind of sports equipment is close to area trees.1.b?*
(b) *Tell the identifier of the area, where there is a manhole cover (photo).*

Note that understanding the given example and solving the tasks requires exploring the physical environment and finding the mentioned objects (small tree, sports equipment, manhole cover).

4 Evaluation

Smartwalk was performed with 48 students (age 11 to 13 from grades 6 and 7) at a German high school in autumn 2016 (24 girls, 14 boys, 10 did not tell their gender). Each four-persons mission team was accompanied by a tutor. These were students from a pedagogy class (age 18 to 20), who already had some experience with similar enrichment activities [12]. They had solved all tasks before, and had discussed the underlying CS concepts. Some of the tasks were considered to be rather difficult. So the pedagogy students developed scaffolding hints that do not reveal the solution (according to the Montessori motto "Help me to do it myself").

At the end of the mission the tutors asked the younger students to rate the tasks. They sat together and discussed in what way the challenges were connected to computer science. As a start a tutor presented some concepts or digital techniques and asked the young participants to allocate corresponding challenges. Example:

"The digital camera in your smartphone can recognize faces on an image. The camera app explores the shapes in the image and when it finds a certain pattern, it draws a rectangle or circle around it which you can see on the display. A simple pattern of a human face is a smiley consisting of two dark spots (the eyes) and a curved line below (the mouth). This is just an example. Many computer programs use simple patterns of real things. Which challenges were about recognizing a pattern?"

Table 1 shows some results. It displays for each challenge the average ratings and the percentage of students, who considered this challenge to be related to a certain concept or technology:

- CT: Computer technology in general
- A: Addresses like URLs in the WWW
- AR: Augmented Reality like in Pokémon Go
- Nav: Navigation like in guiding systems
- Pat: Recognizing patterns like the pattern of a face, which is recognized by camera software
- Sna: Publishing images like in SnapChat.

For each concept or technology the students could mark at most three corresponding challenges. The students rated the attractiveness of a challenge (item *Attract*) by numbers from 1 (very good) to 6 (very poor). The item *Success* indicates how well the participants solved a task. The value is the average of group tutors' ratings (percentage of maximum points). A "mission team" could earn between 0 and 3 points for a challenge, depending on how much help they got from their tutor.

Ratings show that most students loved the Smartwalk. Participants' statements during the reflection at the end suggest that the experience of success and insight makes a challenge attractive ("I like this task because I was able to understand and to solve it"). In contrast to results of the ROSE study [6], structure-oriented tasks (3, 6) were rated as rather attractive.

From a computer scientist's point of view all challenges are related to computer technology (CT) in some way. The challenges listed in Table 1 are ordered according to their overall correspondence to CT from the perspective of the young Smartwalkers. Challenges highly related to CT contained these elements:

- Create something and publish it (10: 42%, 11: 26%)
- A tuple, formally describing the structure of a real thing (5: 34%, 3: 24%)
- URL-like addresses (10: 42%, 9: 35%).

Table 1. Students' ratings of Smartwalk challenge (n = 48, average age 11.9 years)

Challenge	Rating
(10) Pick a rectangular area on the satellite photo. Create a small Land Art artefact on this area using materials like stones or wood that is lying around. Create a title for your artefact. Write title and identifier according to the satellite photo on a sticky note and put it on the door (see photo)	CT: 42%, A: 37%, AR: 26%, Nav: 32%, Pat: 16%, Snap: 29%, Attract: 2.0, Success: 87%
(9) On a satellite photo, rectangular areas on the school yard are identified by strings. In area sience.1 there is a small tree. (a) What kind of sports equipment is close to area trees.1.b? (b) Tell the identifier of the area, where there is a manhole cover (photo)	CT: 35%, A: 38%, AR: 23%, Nav: 30%, Pat: 30%, Snap: 10%, Attract: 2.4, Success: 92%
(5) Follow the way and look down. Find an object with structure B according to `A = (a, a, a, a, a, a, a), B = (A, A)`	CT: 34%, A: 43%, AR: 0%, Nav: 20%, Pat: 43%, Snap: 3%, Attract: 2.7, Success: 70%
(11) Write a poem on a sticky note and put it at a certain spot at a wall (identified by a photo). Read a few poems written by other persons. After having read a poem, move it for 20 cm to the right. If it has crossed the right border, remove it from the wall	CT: 26%, A: 37%, AR: 12%, Nav: 19%, Pat: 9%, Snap: 56%, Attract: 1.9, Success: 92%
(3) Go to a place identified by coordinates on the map. Find an object with structure `(0, 1, 0, 0, 1, 0)`	CT: 24%, A: 6%, AR: 18%, Nav: 15%, Pat: 63%, Snap: 12%, Attract: 1.7, Success: 88%
(8) Go to a place using coordinates on the map. Find an object that can be constructed that way: `go forward 200 cm`...	CT: 19%, A: 9%, AR: 19%, Nav: 78%, Pat: 13%, Snap: 9%, Attract: 2.9, Success: 83%
(6) Go to a place using coordinates and a map. Find an object with this structure: `((plastic, plastic, plastic), (metal, metal))`	CT: 17%, A: 21%, AR: 7%, Nav: 24%, Pat: 59%, Snap: 3%, Attract: 2.1, Success: 90%
(4) Find a place following directions and using coordinates and a map. Identify an object on a photo which does not exist in reality	CT: 16%, A: 8%, AR: 66%, Nav: 13%, Pat: 39%, Snap: 26%, Attract: 1.9, Success: 100%
(7) Go to a place using coordinates and a map. Find an object with the same structure as a scene on a photo (people dancing around a maypole)	CT: 15%, A: 27%, AR: 36%, Nav: 6%, Pat: 48%, Snap: 21%, Attract: 2.4, Success: 77%
(2) Find an object on the school yard following written directions and looking up the coordinates of this object on a map	CT: 11%, A: 29%, AR: 22%, Nav: 79%, Pat: 7%, Snap: 11%, Attract: 1.8, Success: 93%
(1) Go to a place using a photo and coordinates. Find an object on a photo which does not exist at this place.	CT: 3%, A: 23%, AR: 55%, Nav: 20%, Pat: 38%, Snap: 30%, Attract: 2.3, Success: 87%

In some cases the young participants were able to apply the presented CS concepts, when discussing the challenges. They related "Augmented Reality" to challenges that require identifying non-existent objects (4: 66%, 1: 55%). Challenges which contained tuples describing real objects were related to pattern recognition (3: 63%, 6: 59%, 5: 43%)

Challenge 8 includes a LOGO-like program that describes the shape of a ventilation pipe. Instead of stating a correspondence with pattern-recognition (13%) most students related this problem to navigation (78%). This reflects the intuitive understanding of the LOGO-Turtle commands. Statements like `go forward 200 cm` are easy to understand because they are from the knowledge domain of navigation, which is familiar to 12 years old children.

5 Conclusion

Outdoor activities on Computer Science - like Smartwalk - help students to get a new perspective on digital devices they use all day. Since the tasks can be designed to be self-contained (no pre-knowledge necessary), they can be integrated in a media education curriculum for everybody. Experience-oriented outdoor activities can also be enrichment in a regular computer science class that focuses on programming. Creating programs is a constructive process. The motivation for working on the project is the expectation that we have a nice product at the end. This is the philosophy of Constructionism (Papert, Resnick). Create a digital artifact, share it and discover "big ideas" during the process [12]. An experience-oriented outdoor activity like Smartwalk follows a different approach. The idea is to inspire children to look at the world from a different perspective – the perspective of a computer scientist. Instead of producing (taking the role of an artist or engineer), it is about trying out, reflecting and discussing concepts used in digital technology (taking the role of a philosopher).

References

1. Medienpädagogischer Forschungsverbund Südwest KIM-Studie 2014. Stuttgart (2015). https://www.mpfs.de/fileadmin/files/Studien/KIM/2014/KIM_Studie_2014.pdf
2. Markowetz, A.: Digitaler Burnout. Knaur Verlag, Munich (2015)
3. Gallenbacher, J.: Abenteuer Informatik. IT zum Anfassen. Spektrum Akademischer Verlag (2006)
4. Bell, T.C., Witten, I.H., Fellows, M.R.: Computer science unplugged: off-line activities and games for all ages (1998)
5. Bell, T., Alexander, J., Freeman, I., Grimley, M.: Computer science unplugged: school students doing real computing without computers. New Zealand J. Appl. Comput. Inf. Technol. **13**(1), 20–29 (2009)
6. Sjøberg, S., Schreiner, C.: The ROSE Project: An Overview and Key Findings. University of Oslo, Oslo (2010). pp. 1–31
7. Ziegenspeck, J.: Erlebnispädagogik: Entwicklungen und Trends. Spektrum Freizeit **18**(1), 51–58 (1996)
8. Wing, J.M.: Computational thinking. Commun. ACM **49**(3), 33–35 (2006)

9. Selby, C., Woollard, J.: Computational thinking: the developing definition. (2013). https://core.ac.uk/download/pdf/17189251.pdf
10. Torreano, L.A., Cacciari, C., Glucksberg, S.: When dogs can fly: level of abstraction as a cue to metaphorical use of verbs. Metaphor Symbol **20**(4), 259–274 (2005)
11. Lakoff, G., Núnez, R.E.: The metaphorical structure of mathematics: sketching out cognitive foundations for a mind-based mathematics. In: Lyn, D. (ed.) Mathematical Reasoning. Analogies, Metaphors, and Images. Lawrence Erlbaum Associates, Publishers, Mahwah, London (1997)
12. Papert, S.: Mindstorms: Children, Computers, and Powerful Ideas. Basic Books Inc, New York (1980)

Informatics Teachers' Self-efficacy - A Survey Instrument and First Results

Claudia Hildebrandt(✉)

Computer Science Education Research Group, University of Oldenburg, Oldenburg, Germany
claudia.hildebrandt@uni-oldenburg.de

Abstract. The general concept of self-efficacy is based on the individual's own perception of being capable to handle challenging professional situations, for example in the fields of scientific knowledge, pedagogic expertise and conflict management. By means of existing literature, a questionnaire has been created to measure different aspects of self-efficacy in German informatics teachers as well as professional overload. Completed questionnaires of 58 informatics teachers have been analysed to investigate their perceived general self-efficacy and their informatics-specific self-efficacy. The results suggest that the majority of the surveyed teachers have a relatively high self-perceived overall self-efficacy and don't feel professionally overloaded. In contrast to other studies, this investigation determines no correlations between informatics teacher's general self-efficacy and their ratings of professional overload. However, there is only evidence for medium negative coherence between informatics teacher's self-efficacy in a very subject-specific area of informatics and professional overload.

Keywords: Self-efficacy · Social cognitive theory · Teachers' self-efficacy Computer science education · Empirical study

1 Introduction and Motivation

Teachers must meet several very different expectations: e.g. structuring teaching lessons properly regarding educational content with consideration of didactical elements to increase student's motivation, offering differentiated support and showing assertiveness not only during conflict situations. To accomplish these methodical-didactical, professional and pedagogical requirements, a high level of individual belief in own capabilities, the so-called expectation of self-efficacy, is necessary. The perceived self-efficacy is known to influence perception, motivation and performance as well as acting habits [4]. Following this approach, this paper is focused on the theoretical background of the self-efficacy theory and its importance in the school field (cf. Sect. 2). Specifically, professional overload, the individual teacher's self-efficacy and informatics-specific self-efficacy, particularly in the area of automated processes, are investigated and considered in the following structure. In Sect. 3 the research issues are described and a description of the applied constructs is given. Furthermore, the designed questionnaire

A. Tatnall and M. Webb (Eds.): WCCE 2017, IFIP AICT 515, pp. 536–546, 2017.
https://doi.org/10.1007/978-3-319-74310-3_54

and its utilisation for the collection of quantitative data are introduced in Sect. 4. The preliminary results, which refer to the research questions, are outlined in Sect. 5.

2 Background and Related Work

The scientific foundation for the present work is the concept of self-efficacy, which was developed in the context of clinical psychology by Bandura [2] in the 1970s. This concept has gained in importance within several recent studies of empirical educational research [17]. Bandura defined self-efficacy as the belief about one's own capabilities to organize and execute a certain task. Furthermore, Bandura assumed that "expectations of personal efficacy determine whether coping behaviour will be initiated, how much effort will be expended, and how long it will be sustained in the face of obstacles and aversive experiences" [2, p. 191]. Efficacy beliefs, which are defined as the "beliefs in one's capabilities to organize and execute the courses of action required to manage prospective situations" [3, p. 2], affect the thoughts, feelings, personal motivation and actions. These beliefs may contribute significantly to attainments and human motivation [3, p. 3]. Following the explanations by Bandura, the **individual self-efficacy of teachers** is defined as the conviction and expectation of being able to use one's own abilities and resources to handle specific challenging professional situations successfully.

This concept of individual self-efficacy of teachers is to distinguish from their individual self-concept: "In very broad terms, self-concept is a person's perception of himself" [16, p. 411]. Both constructs, self-concept and self-efficacy, are similar in cases of the centrality of perceived competence in construct definition, whereby mastery experience serves as main information source as well as social comparisons, and appraisals. To assess the constructs of self-concepts, contextual information is negligible, whereas when self-efficacy is determined the achievement of specific goals within given circumstances is substantial. The assumption of a teacher of being able to teach e.g. certain sorting algorithms in a student-orientated way, is a self-efficacy expectation, but gives no declaration about the competence of the teacher to convey every kind of algorithm in this way (self-concept). Further differences and information concerning self-efficacy and self-concept can be found in [6].

The results from the self-efficacy research of the last 40 years suggest that a teacher's high level of occupation-specific self-efficacy corresponds positively with the quality of classroom processes (instructional support, classroom organisation, emotional support), with students' academic adjustment (academic achievement, student motivation) and, not least with the teacher's well-being ([4, pp. 240–243], [17]). Gibson and Dembo [9], who investigated elementary school teachers, found that teachers with a high sense of instructional efficacy and strong beliefs in their ability to promote learning, devote more classroom time to academic activities, provide students, who encounter difficulties, with the guidance they need to succeed, praise their academic accomplishments, and create master experiences for their students. In contrast, teachers with a low perceived efficacy and self-doubts about their instructional efficacy spend more time on non-academic pastimes, readily give up on difficult students, criticize them for their failures, and construct classroom environments that are likely to undermine students' judgments of their abilities and their cognitive development time.

In a German pilot experiment at ten schools from 1995–1998 a common goal was to increase the level of self-efficacy among students and teachers. It was shown that a teacher's high degree of vocational-specific self-efficacy had a positive health effect and could be considered as a preventative factor for example against the burn-out syndrome [14, 15].

The number of the research projects on factors that influence the teacher's self-efficacy in daily school life is limited [8, p. 9f]. By considering the collected data of 50 elementary and secondary school teachers, Santos and Pedro [13] concluded that ICT[1]-training presents significantly positive effects on teachers' level of computers self-efficacy and the level of ICT use in classrooms. In a longitudinal study, Holzberger et al. investigated how teacher's self-efficacy may be related to instructional quality. Amongst other things, they found that an increase in self-efficacy relates to experiences of success in the classroom [10]. From 2003 to 2008, during the model project, at independent schools in North Rhine-Westphalia, Germany, Gebauer investigated determinants of the teachers' self-efficacy beliefs. One of her central conclusions was that the teacher's affective and emotional current state shows the strongest and most stable correlation to their self-efficacy beliefs. Therefore, this current state is an essential source to acquire the belief in one's self-efficacy in a teacher's everyday school life. Her scales for measuring job satisfaction and the situation of the working atmosphere serve as indicators of this source - the affective and emotional state [8, p. 139]. Following this approach, professional overload is one investigated indicator in this survey.

3 Research Questions

Based on Bandura's theory of self-efficacy, this survey may help to investigate different forms of teachers' self-efficacy. It is intended to compare the obtained results with the results of the study of [15], who investigated individual teacher's self-efficacy in different types of teachers. The main research questions are the following:

1. How do informatics teachers rate their individual self-efficacy as a teacher and their professional overload compared to the results of Schwarzer/Jerusalem [15]?
2. How do teachers rate their individual teacher's self-efficacy in the subject informatics and their individual teacher's self-efficacy in the subject area automated processes as well as their general subjective teaching competence in informatics (their self-concept in teaching informatics in general) and in automated processes (their self-concept in teaching automated processes) at the beginning of a further teacher training?
3. To what extent do individual teacher's self-efficacy, general informatics-specific self-efficacy, subject-specific self-efficacy in automated processes, professional overload, general teaching competences in informatics and teaching competence in automated processes correlate?

[1] Information and Communication Technologies (ICT).

3.1 Definitions of Constructs

To gain information about the teachers' perceptions the following constructs are used:

Individual teacher's self-efficacy: This construct measures the teacher's belief to master a general challenging professional situation with the help of own capabilities and resources. For example, the success in creating learning environments to develop students' cognitive competences bases, according to Bandura [4, p. 240], not only on the talent, but also on the self-efficacy.

General informatics-specific self-efficacy: The construct includes the belief of a teacher to master general informatics-specific and challenging professional situations with the help of his/her capabilities and resources. Certain aspects that belong to the educational contribution of the subject informatics to the general education can be recorded with this construct.

Subject-specific self-efficacy: The construct is based on the belief of a teacher to master informatics-specific challenging professional situations with own capabilities and resources. In this investigation only the area of automated processes is considered. **Automated processes** contain autonomously working technical systems, which change their states with the aid of an information processing unit. For instance, this area includes the construction and implementation of a robot as a simple informatics system. This system controls the actuators with sensors and processing components. The step-by-step formulated instructions should be implemented as an algorithm.

Professional overload: This construct reflects the perceived occupational strain of a teacher in general.

An overview of the constructs, their reliability and exemplary items can be found in Table 1.

Table 1. Overview of the constructs, number of items n and Cronbach's Alpha α

Construct	n	α	Example items
Individual teacher's self-efficacy	10	0.752	I know that I can keep in good contact with the parents even in challenging situations (WIRKLEHR_02). I am sure that I can deal with the students' individual problems very well (WIRKLEHR_04).
General informatics-specific self-efficacy	8	0.884	I know that my informatics lessons enable the students to handle informatics systems reflectively and responsibly.
Subject-specific self-efficacy (automated processes)	5	0.866	I know that I am able to impart students the competence to develop an algorithm to control a simple informatics system.
Professional overload	6	0.740	I often feel overburdened (BEL_09). I often have a bad conscience towards the students (BEL_12).

4 Research Method

4.1 The Measurement Instrument

This chapter describes the development of the questionnaire. In a first step, all items of the defined characteristics were determined. In the selection of the constructs' items *individual teacher's self-efficacy* and *professional overload* already existing scales were used. The items have been adopted nearly unchanged from Schwarzer and Jerusalem [15]. Their individual teacher's self-efficacy included areas with different competence requirements of teachers like social interactions with students, parents, colleagues, and coping with stressful professional situations [15, p. 60]. Minor changes have been implemented to some items: "I can enforce changes within the model project over sceptical colleagues." was changed into "I can enforce changes within the school-internal curriculum over sceptical colleagues." (WIRKLEHR_10). One of Gebauer's results was that the affective and emotional state is a dominant source in order to acquire the belief in one's own self-efficacy as a teacher (see Sect. 2, [8, p. 139]) in everyday school life. Therefore, professional overload is one investigated indicator. The scale for professional overload has been adopted from [15, p. 73]. The outcomes of Schwarzer's and Jerusalem's first data collection with 273 teachers are relatively old. However, more recent data for these constructs are not available. Consequently, the results of Schwarzer and Jerusalem are compared with the ones described here.

In the development of the constructs *general informatics-specific self-efficacy* and *subject-specific self-efficacy* the indicators' requirements analysis was done under consideration of the core curriculum for informatics for the classes 5 to 10 of all secondary school types in Lower Saxony from August 2014 [12]. With a compact measuring instrument, the general informatics-specific self-efficacy has been collected. It embraces the contribution to education, which the subject informatics must fulfil. For example, "Even though I make efforts, I fail in students gaining systematic and product-independent basic knowledge" (WIRKLEHR_07, negative polarised item). Thus, a certain level of content validity is guaranteed. The development of the *subject-specific self-efficacy scale* (here for the area automated processes) was implemented as in the aforementioned way. The construct consists of items which define the individual assessment of success in teaching students certain learning area specific competences, such as the development of an algorithm to control an informatics system [12, p. 22f]. The topic-specific dealing with students was taken into account, for instance, whether the teachers feel capable to get students interested in new projects within the area of automated processes.

Eventually, the examination of the constructs (see above) was done via items. These items have been structured as a Likert scale system [11, p. 77f] ranging from "strong disagreement" (1) to "strong agreement" (6). However, Schwarzer and Jerusalem [15] used a four-level and a five-level scale, respectively. The analysis of Beierlein et al. [5, p. 10] showed that the four-level scale lacked a differentiability of answers in the upper area of the scale. To counteract this problem and the central tendency to the middle, they suggest a six-level scale, which was chosen for this exploration. A certain number of items (not less than three) form a construct.

In addition to that, the teacher questionnaire comprises two important single items, which investigate the level of the subjective self-concept of the general teaching competency in the subject informatics, and of the subjective self-concept of the teaching competency in the area automated processes. The items are tested in the same way as described above, ranging from "very low = 1" to "very high = 6". The item self-concept of ability in informatics includes the self-awareness of competence. Consequently, we can compare the level of the different types of self-efficacy with the subjectively perceived degree of self-concept.

Answers on Likert scales are typically ordinally-scaled. However, for this analysis we use the Likert scale as an interval scale, because the answers, the numerical markers [11, p. 78], on our Likert scale are equidistantly displayed. Test participants should recognize the various possible answers as being equidistant. Furthermore, the results of statistical tests are falsified only marginally by the interpretation of ordinally scaled data as interval scaled data [11, p. 69]. This fact is confirmed by Allerbeck [1]. To see how far a group of test items can be taken as measurement of individual variables (here: constructs), we use Cronbach's Alpha-coefficient. The Cronbach's Alpha value was established between 0.7 and 1 (see Table 1), and so the constructs can be used.

4.2 Planning and Implementation

Until now, data collection has been taking place in the context of further teacher training, before and after five one-day to three-day in-service training programs in November 2016 as well as January, February and March of 2017. They have been attended by 58 teachers (13 female, 45 male) so far. Paper questionnaires have been used to collect data within the framework of empirical research. The following results relate to the surveys a priori to the training programs. The age range has been between 26 to 63 years. As for school types the Oberschule has been represented 34 times, the other teachers belong to either comprehensive school (seven), Realschule (six), Gymnasium (six), Hauptschule (two), schools for children with learning difficulties (two), or primary school (one). More than half of the participating teachers teach at middle schools and haven't studied computer science. They usually gain their competence to teach informatics through in-service training or autodidactically acquired know-how.

5 First Results

Research question 1 deals with individual teacher's self-efficacy and the professional overload factor before the in-service training. The results are shown in Tables 2 and 3. After linear transformations the item mean values from Schwarzer and Jerusalem [15] m_{SJ} have been transformed into m_{SJtrans}, which are based on a six-level scale. Here, the obtained data are compared with the first results from [15, p. 73]. Their first data collection with 273 participants took place in January of 1996 (see Sect. 2). The comparison of the data from both investigations before the programs is realised with a one-sample test. The items' mean-values of [15] are compared to each corresponding item value of the study described here. The results show that six out of the ten item values of teacher's individual self-efficacy, WIRKLEHR_01, -_02, -_04, -_05, -_07, -_09, differ significantly from the mean-values coming from previous data ($p < 0.05$). Therefore, the informatics teacher rate six self-efficacy items remarkably higher than in the previous study. In study, reported in this paper, the informatics teachers rate the self-efficacy item "I know that I will succeed in teaching the matter relevant for the examination even to the problematic students." (WIRKLEHR_01) considerably higher, 1.15 on average on a scale of 1–6. These results suggest the assumption that the investigated teachers have a relatively high individual teacher's self-efficacy. But these findings, which have originated by comparing the different data sets, show only tendencies. Further investigations of teachers of different subjects are now essential to support these findings, because the data of [15] are older and based on a four-level scale.

Table 2. Item mean values of individual teacher's self-efficacy of the first survey from [15, p. 61] ($\boldsymbol{m_{SJ}}$, N = 273) and of here described survey ($\boldsymbol{m}$, N = 58) as well as standard deviations $\boldsymbol{\sigma}$

Exemplary items	m_{SJ} (scale: 1–4)	m_{SJtrans} (scale: 1–6)	m (scale: 1–6)	$m - m_{SJtrans}$
WIRKLEHR_01	2.34 (σ: 0.73)	**3.23**	**4.40** (σ: 0.83)	**+1.17**
WIRKLEHR_02	2.97 (σ: 0.74)	4.28	4.73 (σ: 0.78)	+0.45
WIRKLEHR_04	2.76 (σ: 0.79)	3.93	4.78 (σ: 0.76)	+0.85
WIRKLEHR_05	2.87 (σ: 0.78)	4.12	4.53 (σ: 1.10)	+0.41
WIRKLEHR_07$_{\mathrm{reversed}}$	2.73 (σ: 0.85)	3.88	4.35 (σ: 0.95)	+0.47
WIRKLEHR_09	3.03 (σ: 0.74)	4.38	4.91 (σ: 0.75)	+0.53

The item mean values of teacher's professional overload present that the informatics teachers partly feel considerably less overwhelmed. Following the results of the one-sample test, one finds out that two out of the six item values of this construct (BEL_9 and BEL_12) differ significantly from the mean-values coming from previous data ($p < 0.05$). In a nutshell, the average of the item mean-values of the informatics teachers here are 2.74 and of the other teachers 2.93 on a scale reaching from 1 (equates to no professional overload) to 6 (equates to a high professional overload). This average difference is statistically not significant. This suggests that the teachers may feel marginally not professionally overloaded. However, item mean values of BEL_15 ("The time pressure I work under is too heavy.") and BEL_02 ("In my job the challenge is permanently too much to handle.") are relatively high. This may be explained by the fact that nearly all teachers haven't studied the subject informatics and have attained their qualification to teach this subject through self-study or/and further education programs. So, they may spend more extra time on their professional qualification than other teachers, and thus may have a partly higher perceived load. This phenomenon certainly requires more investigation in further research.

Table 3. Item mean values of professional overload of the first survey from [15, p. 73] ($\boldsymbol{m_{SJ}}$, N = 273) and of here described survey ($\boldsymbol{m}$, N = 58) as well as standard deviations $\boldsymbol{\sigma}$

Exemplary items	m_{SJ} (scale: 1–5)	$m_{SJtrans}$ (scale: 1–6)	m (scale: 1–6)	$m - m_{SJtrans}$
BEL_02	2.77 (σ: 0.98)	3.21	3.36 (σ: 1.12)	+0.15
BEL_09	2.36 (σ: 0.96)	2.70	2.40 (σ: 0.94)	−0.30
BEL_12	2.17 (σ: 0.83)	2.46	2.02 (σ: 0.95)	−0.45
BEL_15	3.10 (σ: 1.13)	3.63	3.47 (σ: 1.17)	−0.16

To answer the **second research question** the results of Table 4 should be considered. One can see that the mean values of the general informatics-specific self-efficacy, the subject-specific self-efficacy in automated processes and the general teaching competence in informatics are higher than the general teaching competence in the specific field of automated processes. The level of subjective competence assessments in automated processes (mean value: 3.33) is significantly lower than the one of self-efficacy beliefs in this area (mean value: 4.10). Thus, the teachers have trust in themselves to master informatics specific challenges with the help of their capabilities although they don't consider their teaching competences in a specific area as high. Further investigation is needed to show if there are changes in the self-efficacy and teaching competence in informatics after further training and if there are gender specific differences.

Table 4. Scale and item mean values

Construct/item	Mean value (scale: 1–6)
General informatics-specific self-efficacy	4.33 (σ: 0.79)
Subject-specific self-efficacy in automated processes	4.10 (σ: 1.03)
General teaching competence in informatics	4.13 (σ: 0.99)
General teaching competence in automated processes	3.33 (σ: 1.16)

The **third research question** is concerned with the correlation between the different constructs (see Table 5). We can describe the strength of the non-parametric Spearman's correlation using the guide that Evans [7, p. 146] suggests for the absolute value of r. Consequently, the correlation Table 5 shows that there are weak (0.20–0.39), moderate (0.40–0.59) and strong (0.60–0.79) significant correlations between most of the constructs. For example, a correlation value of r = 0.643 would be a "strong positive correlation". These results support past investigations showing a correlation between self-efficacy and self-concept (see Sect. 2), whereas in this investigation the general informatics-specific self-efficacy does not correlate significantly with the teaching competence in automated processes. Contrary to our expectations, the perception of the professional overload seems only related to the construct subject-specific self-efficacy in automated processes and teaching competence in automated processes. This outcome contradicts the results of [8, 14]. The results of

Gebauer's inquiry lead to the conclusion that the individual teacher's self-efficacy also correlates with professional overload (see Sect. 2, [8, p. 139]) in a negative way. For example, this relation can be found in [14] (correlations around $r = -0.50$). People who feel overworked in their jobs have less motivation to face new or difficult challenges. Additionally, further investigations with more participants are necessary to support the current findings. For all correlations it must be noted that due to missing data the different analyses are undertaken with responses varying from 36 to 56 participants.

Table 5. Correlations regarding the different constructs (*$p < 0.05$, **$p < 0.01$, other correlations are non-significant)

	Individual teacher's SE[a]	General informatics-specific SE	Subject-specific SE in AP[b]	Teaching competence in informatics	Teaching competence in AP
Individual teacher's SE	1.000				
General informatics-specific SE	**0.476****	1.000			
Subject-specific SE in AP	**0.387****	0.260	1.000		
Teaching competence in informatics	**0.297***	**0.643****	**0.442****	1.000	
Teaching competence in AP	**0.373****	0.296	**0.618****	**0.403****	1.000
Professional overload	−0.115	−0.223	**−0.393****	−0.214	**−0.355****

[a]Self-efficacy is abbreviated as "SE".
[b]Automated processes is abbreviated as "AP".

6 Conclusion

One important research result is that the informatics teachers perceive that the job is challenging and much to handle (item mean value: 3.36) and the time pressure they work under is heavy (item mean value: 3.47), but their teaching self-efficacy (construct mean value: 4.54) and their general informatics-specific self-efficacy (construct mean value: 4.33) are relatively high. Consequently, I assume that they might be able to spend more extra time, than other teachers, on improving their professional qualifications before they feel too overworked. Therefore, one should offer the chance to participate in in-service training programs (one day to three days training). In the process, the themes and levels (beginner and advanced teachers) should be taken into account to avoid teachers feeling overburdened. This is one way to enable many teachers at secondary schools, who teach informatics as non-specialists, to improve their qualification in teaching the subject informatics. Then these teachers can provide their students even better with sustainable skills to deal with information technology responsibly. Further on, it must be investigated whether in-service training programs (one to three days) influence the level of teacher's self-efficacy. And if so, the factors which make training programs work successfully must be found out. This is an important aspect, because teachers with a high level of teacher's self-efficacy influence the quality of classroom processes in a very positive way (cf. Sect. 2).

References

1. Allerbeck, K.R.: Messniveau und Analyseverfahren - Das Problem strittiger Intervallskalen. Zeitschrift für Soziologie **7**(3), 199–214 (1978)
2. Bandura, A.: Self-efficacy: toward a unifying theory of behavioral change. Psychol. Rev. **84** (2), 191–215 (1977)
3. Bandura, A.: Exercise of personal and collective efficacy in changing societies. In: Bandura, A. (ed.) Self-efficacy in Changing Societies, pp. 1–45. Cambridge University Press, New York (1995)
4. Bandura, A.: Self-Efficacy: The Exercise of Control. Freeman, New York (1997)
5. Beierlein, C., Kovaleva, A., Kemper, C.J., Rammstedt, B.: Ein Messinstrument zur Erfassung subjektiver Kompetenzerwartungen: Allgemeine Selbstwirksamkeit Kurzskala (ASKU). GESIS, Mannheim (2012)
6. Bong, M., Skaalvik, E.M.: Academic self-concept and self-efficacy: how different are they really? Edu. Psychol. Rev. **15**(1), 17–30 (2003)
7. Evans, J.D.: Straightforward Statistics for the Behavioral Sciences. Brooks/Cole Publishing, Pacific Grove (1996)
8. Gebauer, M.M.: Determinanten der Selbstwirksamkeitsüberzeugung von Lehrenden: Schulischer Berufsalltag an Gymnasien und Hauptschulen. Springer VS, Wiesbaden (2013). https://doi.org/10.1007/978-3-658-00613-6
9. Gibson, S., Dembo, M.H.: Teacher efficacy: a construct validation. J. Educ. Psychol. **76**(4), 569–582 (1984)
10. Holzberger, D., Philipp, A., Kunter, M.: How teachers' self-efficacy is related to instructional quality: a longitudinal analysis. J. Educ. Psychol. **105**(3), 774–786 (2013)
11. Hussy, W., Schreier, M., Echterhoff, G.: Forschungsmethoden in Psychologie und Sozialwissenschaften für Bachelor, 2nd edn. Springer, Heidelberg (2013). https://doi.org/10.1007/978-3-642-34362-9
12. Niedersächsisches Kultusministerium: Kerncurriculum für die Schulformen des Sekundarbereichs I Schuljahrgänge 5–10 Informatik. Unidruck, Hannover (2014)
13. Santos, A., Pedro, N.: The relationship between teachers' training, personal sense of efficacy and ICT integration: analysing its strength and stability. In: ICICTE 2012 Proceedings of International Conference on Information Communication Technologies in Education, pp. 343–354. ICICTE, Rhodes (2012)
14. Schmitz, G.S., Schwarzer, R.: Selbstwirksamkeitserwartung von Lehrern: Längsschnittbefunde mit einem neuen Instrument. Zeitschrift für Pädagogische Psychologie **14**, 12–25 (2000)
15. Schwarzer, R., Jerusalem, M.: Skalen zur Erfassung von Lehrer-und Schülermerkmalen. Dokumentation der psychometrischen Verfahren im Rahmen der Wissenschaftlichen Begleitung des Modellversuchs Selbstwirksame Schulen. Freie Universität Berlin, Berlin (1999)

16. Shavelson, R.J., Hubner, J.J., Stanton, G.C.: Self-concept: validation of construct interpretations. Rev. Educ. Res. **46**(3), 407–441 (1976)
17. Zee, M., Koomen, H.M.Y.: Teacher self-efficacy and its effects on classroom processes, student academic adjustment, and teacher well-being: a synthesis of 40 years of research. Rev. Educ. Res. **86**(4), 981–1015 (2016)

Utilizing the Repertory Grid Method to Investigate Learners' Perceptions of Computer Science Concepts

Nils Pancratz(✉) and Ira Diethelm

Department of Computing Science,
University of Oldenburg, Oldenburg, Germany
nils.pancratz@uni-oldenburg.de

Abstract. When it comes to studying learners' perceptions, the most common methods range from arranged questionnaires to carefully structured interviews. While the former are arguably inadequate to understand learners' perceptions correctly due to the lack of response, the latter lack the ability to flexibly focus on interesting points during the interviews. Since the importance of learners' perceptions is well-known and many Computer Science concepts are not covered yet, we want to introduce a technique from the field of social psychology and apply it to the domain of Computer Science Education. With our field report on "Utilizing the Repertory Grid Method to Investigate Learners' Perceptions of Computer Science Concepts" we want to encourage this qualitative approach in this field. We present our application of this method in order to study five 11- to 13-year-old secondary school students' conceptions of the Internet and the corresponding IT devices. It turns out that the technique is a promising alternative when it comes to studying learners' perceptions indeed.

Keywords: Learners' perceptions · Repertory Grid Method
Personal Construct Psychology · Computer Science Education

1 Introduction and Motivation

It is quite important to know learners' perceptions of Computer Science (CS) concepts to plan and design CS courses. But even though the special role that students' perspectives play for the design and arrangement of CS lessons and courses has been pointed out in the model of educational reconstruction for Computer Science Education (CSE) in 2012 [1], there is still a lot of work to do in this field, since perceptions of many CS concepts are not investigated yet.

But how do researchers get information on students' conceptions usually? The common methods (cf. Sect. 1.2) range from questionnaires to structured interviews, which are two ways bringing their own disadvantages like the lack of response or the wanting flexibility. The Repertory Grid Method[1] (RGM) combines their advantages: The assessors are allowed to use their own vocabulary; thus a comparability of various

[1] The procedure is called *Method* by some authors while others name it *Technique*. At this point we want to indicate that we use both terms interchangeably in this paper.

A. Tatnall and M. Webb (Eds.): WCCE 2017, IFIP AICT 515, pp. 547–556, 2017.
https://doi.org/10.1007/978-3-319-74310-3_55

Repertory Grid Interviews is warranted by providing the elements of the grid (cf. Sect. 2). It is also possible to flexibly focus on interesting points during the interviews using the RGM.

We chose to study students' conceptions of the Internet since there is already a great amount of information on how children and teenagers think the Internet works (cf. Sects. 1.2 and 3.3). This enables us to discuss whether or not this method is capable of studying learners' perceptions because we are able to compare our results to previous studies (cf. Sect. 3.3). We introduce the basics and the possibilities of the RGM and briefly present the design and the results of our study in the following, to finally discuss the suitability of this technique for the purpose of elaborating learners' perceptions.

1.1 Kelly's Personal Construct Psychology

The Personal Construct Psychology (PCP) came into existence as an answer to the critique on the decisive psychological concepts in the 1940's and 1950's. Its founder, the American psychologist Kelly, presented his theory in his major work "The psychology of Personal Constructs" for the first time in 1955 [2]. One of his main points is that we as human beings develop our own theories and "come to understand the world [...] by erecting a personally organized system of [...] constructs of experienced events" [3]. He argues "that we make sense out of our world by simultaneously noting likenesses and differences" [4]. The systematically organized constructs then are "our way of distinguishing similarity from difference" [3]. "They are linked, related and integrated into a complex hierarchical structure or system containing many sub-systems. Through our system of [...] constructs we are able to predict and control our [...] world. Thus they are our guidelines for living" [3].

The Repertory Grid Method (RGM) that is introduced in the following Sect. 2 allows us "to elicit personal constructs and examine the relationships between them within a specific domain" [3].

1.2 Related Work and Our Goals

Most researchers get information on learners' perceptions of CS concepts using standardized or (semi-)structured Interviews [5–7] or questionnaires [8, 9]. Only little work in this field is making use of more 'exotic' methods like drawings e.g. [9, 10]. A common approach to get information on the way learners view on CS is through the methodology of *Grounded Theory* [11–13].

However, in this paper we want to introduce the Repertory Grid Method (RGM), which has already been used in a few didactic studies and investigations of childrens' perceptions successfully. Lengnink and Prediger applied the method in a qualitative evaluation study of a pre-service teacher course "to explore teacher students' individual conceptions about learning and teaching mathematics" [14] for example. Williams used the technique "to describe the informal models of the limit concept held by two college calculus students" [15]. Baxter, Jack and Schröder used the RGM "to elicit constructs from 23 children aged between 8 and 11 years of age relating to their perceptions of eight common vegetables" [16].

Although the work mentioned represents only an excerpt of the available didactic publications that utilize the RGM, we do not know of any authors that applied it to the domain of CSE yet. This leads us to the aim of our study, which is mainly not to confirm learners' views already carved out by other authors, but to look into the suitability of the RGM for this purpose and to encourage this qualitative approach in this field.

2 Methodology

2.1 Origins of the Repertory Grid Technique

The most common Personal Construct Psychology (PCP) method is the "Role Construct Repertory Test". It is no standardized test with a set procedure in its usual sense, but a structured interview [3]. In the 1980's the RGM was increasingly growing in popularity after 30 years of existence [3]. The benefits that result from the grid interviews providing structured data despite being flexible and open for the personal constructs of the interviewees "encouraged many people [of the most different fields of work] to design and develop their own applications" [17]. Thereby the basic idea of Repertory Tests is to "elicit personal constructs and examine the relationships between them within a specific domain" [3], by structuring the conversation.

Since Kelly's basic work, the evolution of the RGM generated a multitude of different variations [3]. Nonetheless, this thoroughly suits Kelly's mind: In his opinion the RGM is an open and variable method. However, all the Repertory Grid Interviews have in common that the interviewees are asked to differentiate between objects of their experience (elements) and that these differentiations (constructs) are then recorded in a data grid. Within the single procedures the preparation, post-processing and evaluation vary considerably [18].

2.2 Modifications of the Technique

As already mentioned there is no particular RGM. However, all the corresponding studies share the fact that the subjects are asked to differentiate between various elements. Thereby these – mostly up to twelve[2] [17] – elements can range from important persons within the radius of the interviewed person to material things such as chocolate bars, "flowers in the garden, the meals of the day or other aspects of life that are important to the person" [4]. So there is no restriction in the choice of elements. Furthermore, the elements can be obtained by different strategies: They are either elaborated together with the interviewee during the conversation or completely provided by the investigator. Even a mixed strategy, where some of the elements or a pool or area of interests is provided and others are generated by the interviewee, is possible [3, 17].

[2] Here it has to be pointed out that Repertory Grids are typically not capable of considering more than approx. twelve elements.

Groups of elements are chosen by the interviewer and provided to the interviewee to gain the so called constructs [3]. While it is the proband's task to think about how the presented elements are similar to and different from one another, the attributes describing similarities and differences are denominating the constructs.

The most common method of gaining constructs is the so called *triad method*, since a construct at least has to be build out of one similarity relation between two elements and a dissimilarity relation between those two elements and the third one according to Kelly's dichotomy corollary [2].

"But since one is eliciting constructs already established in the person's repertoire there is no reason why three elements need to be used" [4]. So, the *dyad method*, where only two elements are given when comparing them, often is applied when working with children or other persons that are overstrained with the task of comparing groups of three elements [4].

The combinations of elements to be compared are usually gathered by randomly drawing two or three elements. Therefore, the elements need to be homogeneous, so that it would not carry weight, if single elements did appear in none of the triads, while others were consulted more often [17]. During the Repertory Grid Interview, the interviewer usefully ensures that the elements occur equally. Furthermore, it is even possible to decide "which combinations will bring out the greatest contrast in the elements available" [17].

As for the elements, even for the constructs "quite a literature has developed over the question whether or not supplied or provided constructs give the same answers as do elicited constructs" [4]. But since it is our goal to detect students' perceptions of IT topics we will not go into detail of this alternative.

2.3 Analysis and Interpretation of Repertory Grids and the Importance of Explanations During Repertory Grid Interviews

Easterby-Smith points out "that the interpretation of grid data is very much an art and not a technology" [17]. It is also a common misconception "that it cannot be analyzed adequately without a computer" [17]. While he refers to *correlation matrices* as the most common technique for manual analysis, he reminds that computer analysis "does not add anything to the information available in a grid, nor does it provide any indication of the meaning of a grid; it simply reduces the amount of work required for interpretation by summarizing and condensing the data available" [17]. An interesting alternative to factor or cluster analysis was used by Lengnink and Prediger: They visualized the structures of their grids in *line diagrams* to make the logical structures explicit [14]. We wanted to briefly name these two possibilities, because we applied them in our study (cf. Sect. 3.2).

Originally the RGM was thought of as a structured interview, in which the interviewees shall provide information about their subjective meanings of the reviewed elements [18]. Not only Kelly but also the authors of the following decades completely lose sight of the detailed conversation that needs to develop when elaborating personal constructs [18], though he must have been aware of the interview situation of this technique right from the beginning. Kelly almost by the way mentions a crucial requirement when it comes to understanding people's personal constructs: the explanations of the terms used by the subjects. But the only thing you learn from Kelly about how such explanations look like and how they come off is that referring to this somehow the interviewers' skills matter [18]. While it might have been completely self-evident to him, that a simple retrieval of terms belonging together on its own has nothing to do with understanding other people's personal constructs, many scientists worked off such lists of terms, looked at that as an application of the Repertory Grid Technique, and published their work after him [18]. Instead of that it is essential to attend to the explanations, comments and statements the subjects make while elaborating constructs and to consult these explanations in the analysis of the interviews.

2.4 Developing the Repertory Grid Interviews for this Particular CSE Study

At the beginning of the interviews for this study the elements were provided by the investigator to guarantee a comparability of the interviews among each other. If a set of elements is provided, it is important to ensure that these elements "provide representative coverage of the area to be investigated" [17]. Once the Repertory Grid Technique is used to gain information about learners' views on the Internet it means that the elements have to conform to the framework of terms that are needed to describe the functionality of the Internet scientifically. At the same time these elements should represent the phenomena and artifacts that teenagers associate the Internet with. Considering these aspects, the following twelve elements were chosen for this Repertory Grid study: *the Internet, (my) computer, server, web page, IP address, e-mail, cable, Google, data, router, (data) packet, (chat) application.* Before the actual interviews started these elements were printed on index cards to guarantee an optimal flow of the interviews.

Since this study mainly wants to examine whether the RGM is appropriate for investigating learners' views, we decided to design two variations of the method, that differ in the way the constructs are gained:

1. In the *first variation* the order of comparisons of elements (e.g. first compare the triad (my) computer, cable, the Internet then compare the triad router, IP address, server and so on) is determined.
2. In the *second variation* the subject is asked to sort the index cards first of all, so that elements belonging together lie on one pile. After that the proband has to assemble commonalities in the single piles, which then set the constructs. While the construct poles result directly from the descriptions of commonalities in the elements of the single piles, the contrast poles then have to be asked for ("What is the opposite of this characteristic?") in a second step.

3 Results

3.1 Execution of this Investigation

Within the framework of this study five male students at eleven to thirteen years that participated in a voluntary "robotics" study group at a northern German secondary school were interviewed. Because of the students' voluntary participation in the study group we can assume an over-average interest in topics around computers and their functionalities. In addition to that all of them mention their daily usage of the Internet for mainly social (social media) or entertaining (online games) purposes.

Variation 1 was conducted by three students while two students participated in Repertory Grid Interviews based on variation 2 (cf. Sect. 2.4). At the beginning of the interviews an introductory example on chocolate bars, which was inspired by a market research[3] and impressively shows the variety of possible applications of the technique, was worked through with the interviewees each time. Thereby, the sample was adjusted according to the actual variation of the procedure. The individual interviews lasted between 30 and 50 min. During the process of planning the interviews the possibility of switching from the triad to the dyad method was retained, as long as the relevant interviewee is overstrained with the task of comparing three elements (cf. Sect. 2.3).

All of the interviews were recorded to be able to go into substantial statements of the subjects during the evaluation of the interviews. Figure 1 shows an exemplary Repertory Grid as it was worked out during one of the interviews that were led in the context of this study.

✔	(my) computer	cable	the Internet	router	IP adress	server	website	Google	(chat) application	e-mail	data	(data) packet	✘
touchable	·✔	·✔	·✘	✔	✘	✘	✘	✘	✘	✘	✘	✘	not touchable
is fixed / you can't choose one	✘	✘	✔	·✔	·✘	·✔	✘	✔	✘	✘	✘	✘	can be chosen
I have one at home	·✔	✔	·✘	✔	✘	·✔	✘	✘	✘	✘	✘	✘	global
is a website	✘	✘	✘	✘	✘	✘	·✘	·✔	·✔	✔	✘	✘	general term
is necessary to go online	·✔	·✘	–	·✔	✘	✔	✘	✘	✘	✘	✘	✘	is unnecessary to go online
you can operate various digital functions on it	✔	✘	✔	✔	✔	✔	·✔	✔	✔	·✔	✔	✔	you can operate no digital functions on it
you can type something in	✔	✘	✔	✘	✔	✘	✔	·✔	✔	·✔	✔	✔	you can't type anything in
needs electricity	✔	·✔	✔	✔	✔	✔	·✔	✔	✔	✔	✔	✔	also works without electricity
is an application	✘	✘	✔	✘	✘	✘	✔	·✔	·✔	✔	✘	✘	is no application
consists of data	✔	✘	✔	✔	✔	✔	✔	✔	✔	✔	·✔	·✔	doesn't consist of data
therein data is stored	·✔	✘	✔	✔	✔	✔	✔	✔	✔	✔	·✔	✔	therein no data is stored

Fig. 1. An exemplary Repertory Grid as it was worked out during one of the interviews that were led in the context of this study. This particular Repertory Grid comes from variation 1 of the method. The dots indicate the triad or pair of elements that led to the particular construct. Students' quotes were translated from German.

[3] In 1989 McEwan and Thomson studied chocolate-bar consumers preferences applying the Repertory Grid Technique [19].

3.2 Evaluating the Repertory Grid Interviews

The participants of this investigation were actively prompted to deal with their cognitive organization structures by finding similarities and differences between the provided elements. Thereby the explanations that were vehemently called for provide the basis of the learners' views on the Internet that were identified in this study. However, the actual Repertory Grids might move into background as each interview progressed, though the organization structures of the grids are still reflected in the students' explanations. In order to evaluate the interviews, we listened back to the audio tracks, transcribed meaningful passages and then wrote down the mentioned perceptions while keeping an eye on the original Repertory Grids.

We created correlation matrices and line diagrams from the Repertory Grids but saw no mentionable advantage. Especially the advantage of line diagrams only seems to work, if the subjects are directly confronted with them during the interviews.

3.3 A Comparison of the Perceptions of the Internet We Won in this Study and the Results of Other Works

Comparing the single interviews with one another we found out that everyone of the five participants of this study holds concise misconceptions of servers, IP addresses and Google. In this paper we want to focus on these three aspects and summarize them briefly due to the lack of space.

Servers: The subjects of our study were of the mind that servers generally are not touchable and that they are something purely virtual. They consider servers as a possibility to play online games with friends and they are completely not aware of them being the central elements of the Internet. Correspondingly the model of a single, central computer that runs the whole Internet has already been worked out in an older study [5]. One of our participant's visualization of servers as "huge hay bales" of cables with numerous crossroads is similar to a model that was also elaborated in the mentioned paper: In this particular model markers on the Internet show where to go next [5].

IP addresses: While some of the participants of this study believe that Google is responsible for finding the IP address belonging to the query, others consider that IP addresses are used in combination with self-selected passwords to log in to various websites. There is reason to suspect that the former simply mix up IP and URL addresses or that they even use both abbreviations synonymously. The latter likely mix IP addresses up with user names. Again, parallels between the results of this study and previous ones can be found: It has already been attested that the majority of pupils indeed is sensible of the need for a one-time address on the Internet although many students believe that such an addressing could be realized by proper (user) names [5].

Google: 60% of the subjects explained that Google is the first thing you get to automatically when connecting to the Internet. Furthermore, it is quite striking that two students even are of the opinion that Google would provide the IP addresses of other websites. Another student explains, that he gets to other websites by putting their names into Google's search field. These are results that seem to be plausible since they have been worked out by others, too [6].

One basic similarity is the functional, application-oriented view on the Internet that all of the interviewed students share: They mainly describe what you can do on the Internet and more scarcely wherefore or even how. Furthermore, the impression unfolds that all of the five students obviously never asked themselves how single processes on the Internet work and that they just as recently as they were asked to find similarities and differences during the Repertory Grid Interviews developed their own theories to this. Again, this fact has been elaborated by Seifert et al. [6] before.

4 Discussion

The results of this study mainly were not surprising and we could confirm many perceptions that other authors already worked out using common techniques like interviews. In addition to that some conceptions were elaborated that have not been studied by other authors yet but seem to be conclusive. Basically it can already be recapped at this point that Repertory Grids are definitely suitable for gaining information on learners' views on CS concepts. In the following Sect. 4.1 we want to point out the advantages and disadvantages we saw in using the RGM for our purpose.

4.1 Advantages of Using the Repertory Grid Method Instead of Other Instruments

The interviewees were permanently asked to wonder about their thoughts on their subjective organization structures because of the demanded comparisons of the elements. In this regard it would be interesting to look into the method when it is adapted in a way that two persons can be interviewed at once. Then two students had to respond to each other to come to an agreement about the characteristics of the elements. But basically the individual interviews made it possible to gain insights into the world of ideas of the students, by asking them to explain their choices. We do not recommend using the most original variation of the RGM to gain information on learners' views after our pre-tests though (cf. Sect. 2.3) because letting the subjects elaborate the elements by themselves by naming things they connect with the Internet complicates the later comparisons probably due to a lack of comparability. Both of the variations that were used in this study (cf. Sect. 2.4) have their own advantages and disadvantages: Thus the "motivational barrier" that results from the task of sorting the elements to piles of similar ones is a disadvantage of variation 2, since both students that took part in this variation of the study stopped carving out constructs after they completed each pile by only naming one characteristic shared by elements of the pile. However, it seemed as if the task of sorting piles and afterwards finding characteristics (variation 2) was a lot easier for the children than variation 1, where they had to compare triads that were given by the interviewer. The initial classification of elements belonging together (as it is the case with variation 2) results in a structural order that is not manipulated by a previously determined order of elements (as is the case with variation 1). Using the first variation it is in fact possible for students to avoid elements being compared with one another, which prevents the researcher from drawing conclusions about students' perceptions. But you cannot completely ignore the fact that the interviewees are challenged with the task of comparing elements they are unfamiliar with, which is indeed the huge disadvantage of variation 1. Accordingly, two of three students that participated in variation 1 of the study were overstrained being asked to compare triads of elements. When working with children it is obviously a lot easier to simply ask them to find similarities, which provides variation 2 with an advantage over variation 1. However, the task had to be formulated a lot more precisely, so that the interviewees do not carve out only as many constructs as they find piles of elements. Practically, the task could be expressed as sorting the cards several times according to various criteria.

Finally, the Repertory Grid Interviews enabled us to get a detailed insight into the learners' perceptions of the CS concepts investigated, by carving out similarities and differences between the elements. In conclusion Repertory Grids are suitable for qualitative analysis of students' perspectives indeed. The only disadvantage that we saw was the difficulty of finding meaningful terms for the constructs. The students had no problems working out similarities and differences at all, but they had a hard time to describe these constructs with short terms for the grid. And that is why the explanations during the Repertory Grid interviews are the important basis for the perception analysis. For the evaluation process, the grids originally worked out move into background.

5 Conclusion

It has been this study's aim to adapt the RGM with the objective of investigating learners' views on the functionality of the Internet and then to discuss the effectiveness of this method for this particular application purpose. The students' perceptions that were elaborated in this study and mainly have also been worked out by the authors of previous investigations already prove that it is actually possible to use this method for qualitative research on students' perceptions. However, this method is as time-consuming as the more original research methods (cf. Sect. 1.2) and the evaluation also is as tedious. Thus there is no advantage regarding the duration of execution and analysis. In addition to that most of the times it is hard for the subject and the interviewer to come to an agreement about expressing the constructs as precisely yet concisely as possible. Therefore, it is often hard to find out what the subject wanted to express by only looking at the constructs written on the log sheet. That is why it is so important to record the interviews on tape to be able to refer to decisive explanations that turned out to be the crucial source of information in this study when it comes to elaborate perceptions.

Finally the RGM does not necessarily enjoy such great popularity because of the possibility to perform numerous calculations on grids or to visualize relationships in line diagrams. It is rather the researchers' task to work out similarities and differences that forces participants to actively deal with their perceptions and concepts and to express them properly. We wanted to present our way of designing Repertory Grid Interviews to study learners' views on the functionality of the Internet and hopefully encourage you to use the RGM as a skeleton for the interviews of your future plans on studying learners' conceptions. For us the method worked out as a promising approach.

References

1. Diethelm, I., Hubwieser, P., Klaus, R.: Students, teachers and phenomena: educational reconstruction for computer science education. In: Proceedings of the 12th Koli Calling International Conference on Computing Education Research, pp. 164–173. ACM (2012)
2. Kelly, G.A.: The Psychology of Personal Constructs. Norton, New York (1955)
3. Beail, N.: Repertory Grid Technique and Personal Constructs: Applications in Clinical and Educational Settings. Croom Helm, London (1985)
4. Fransella, F., Bannister, D.: A Manual for Repertory Grid Technique. Academic Press, London (1977)
5. Diethelm, I., Wilken, H., Zumbrägel, S.: An investigation of secondary school students' conceptions on how the internet works. In: Proceedings of the 12th Koli Calling International Conference on Computing Education Research, pp. 67–73. ACM (2012)
6. Seifert, O., Sauck, T., Schwarzbach, M., Lerch, C., Weinert, M., Knobelsdorf, M.: Ich glaube, Google ist so was wie eine Vorhalle des internets. In: 15th Informatik erweitert Horizonte, INFOS 2013. GI-Fachtagung Informatik und Schule, Kiel, Germany, pp. 45–56 (2013)
7. Hammond, M., Rogers, P.: An investigation of children's conceptualisation of computers and how they work. Educ. Inf. Technol. **12**(1), 3–15 (2007)
8. Borowski, C., Diethelm, I., Wilken, H.: What children ask about computers, the internet, robots, mobiles, games etc. In: Proceedings of the 11th Workshop in Primary and Secondary Computing Education (WiPSCE 2016), pp. 72–75. ACM, New York (2016)
9. Papastergiou, M.: Students' mental models of the internet and their didactical exploitation in informatics education. Educ. Inf. Technol. **10**(4), 341–360 (2005)
10. Dinet, J., Kitajima, M.: "Draw me the web": impact of mental model of the Web on information search performance of young users. In: Riveill, M. (ed.) IHM, pp. 1–7. ACM (2011)
11. Strauss, A., Corbin, J.M.: Grounded Theory in Practice. Sage, Beverly Hills (1997)
12. Hewner, M.: Undergraduate conceptions of the field of computer science. In: Proceedings of the Ninth Annual International ACM Conference on International Computing Education Research (ICER 2013), pp. 107–114. ACM, New York (2013)
13. Rücker, M.T., Pinkwart, N.: The things that belong: a grounded theory study of student categorizations of complex technical artifacts. Int. J. Technol. Des. Educ. **27**, 1–20 (2017)
14. Lengnink, K., Prediger, S.: Development of the personal constructs about mathematical tasks – a qualitative study using repertory grid methodology. In: Proceedings of the 27th Annual Meeting of the International Group for the Psychology of Mathematics Education (PME), Hawaii, pp. 39–46 (2003)
15. Williams, S.R.: Predications of the limit concept: an application of repertory grids. J. Res. Math. Educ. **32**(4), 341–367 (2001)
16. Baxter, I.A., Jack, F.R., Schröder, M.J.: The use of repertory grid method to elicit perceptual data from primary school children. Food Qual. Prefer. **9**(1–2), 73–80 (1998)
17. Easterby-Smith, M.: The design, analysis and interpretation of repertory grids. Int. J. Man Mach. Stud. **13**(1), 3–24 (1980)
18. Fromm, M.: Repertory Grid Methodik. Dt.-Studien-Verl., Weinheim (1995)
19. McEwan, J.A., Thomson, D.M.: The repertory grid method and preference mapping in market research: a case study on chocolate confectionery. Food Qual. Prefer. **1**(2), 59–68 (1989)

What Teachers and Students Know About Data Management

Andreas Grillenberger(✉) and Ralf Romeike

Friedrich-Alexander-Universität Erlangen-Nürnberg, Erlangen, Germany
{andreas.grillenberger, ralf.romeike}@fau.de

Abstract. Data management is a highly innovative field of CS, which evolved from the original field databases in the last years. With the ongoing developments, several topics from this field, such as cloud computing, large data collections or data analyses, pervade our daily lives. Although more and more students and teachers come in contact with data management topics and need to develop competencies in this field, current CS education typically does not sufficiently address them. Yet, both students and teachers already have experience with certain aspects of data management and may have built up knowledge and perceptions, which need to be considered in CS teaching. Hence, in a qualitative study, we investigated the attitudes and prior knowledge of teachers on several data management topics and explored students' knowledge in this field.

Keywords: Data management · Knowledge · Experiences · Teachers Students

1 Introduction

In recent years, new requirements and technologies led to the formation of *data management* as a new field of CS, in particular due to continuously increasing amounts of data being stored and analyzed. Although it is highly relevant in CS today and becomes increasingly pervasive in everyone's daily lives, secondary CS education sets its focus predominantly on other fields of CS. Nowadays, in lessons on data-oriented topics, there is a clear emphasis on databases and database-related aspects, while other parts of data management are typically left out [6]. Considering data management topics in CS education can enrich current teaching and opens up various new possibilities, in particular because they are not only interesting from a scientific perspective, but also exemplary for the ongoing developments in CS. They also support the development of competencies that everyone needs for responsibly handling their own and others' personal data [7]. Consequently, more and more curricula and educational standards introduce topics such as data analysis, security and privacy (cf. e.g. [3]). Our experience shows that students and teachers are generally interested in topics related to big data and data management and that they regard competencies in this field as essential.

There is strong agreement that, besides central principles, also the prior knowledge of teachers and students should be considered when bringing new topics to school

A. Tatnall and M. Webb (Eds.): WCCE 2017, IFIP AICT 515, pp. 557–566, 2017.
https://doi.org/10.1007/978-3-319-74310-3_56

(cf. e.g. [5]). Hence, we describe two investigations: First, we examine teachers' content knowledge about and attitudes towards typical data management topics, as well as the challenges they see for teaching. Second, in order to gain insight into students' experience, we describe an exploratory analysis of their knowledge in this field.

2 Data Management from a CS Perspective

In the last 10 to 15 years, *data management* has evolved from the field databases. A central topic in this field is *big data*, which deals with storing and analyzing large amounts of highly varied data as fast as possible (cf. e.g. [8]). With the increasing relevance of correlation-based data analyses ("data mining"), new requirements are imposed on data management systems, for example the need to store data distributed on multiple servers because of the high volumes. At the same time, ensuring a high velocity requires minimizing the amount of communication between the servers involved. Hence, various new systems and technologies have emerged and became important areas of data management research, for example non-relational *NoSQL databases*, *in-memory databases* or *cloud computing*. Correspondingly, new and highly innovative methods, approaches and principles were developed and became important to CS. Aside its relevance in CS research, the significance of data management topics in our daily lives has also massively increased: Nowadays, everyone uses various technologies based on data management techniques, comes into contact with metadata, stores data, protects and shares it and reads news about data-related topics, such as extensive data analyses by companies or intelligence agencies.

3 Related Work

Despite the significant developments in data management, hardly any research in this field, but also related to databases and data in general has been conducted in CS education research since database teaching was established in the early 1990s. Even in recent years, only occasional approaches were described, e.g. on introducing big data at high school [2]. In a qualitative analysis of curricula and teaching standards, we identified the gap between current CS education and the scientific perspective on this field [6], which in particular affects newer aspects of data management. Also, we already identified several key competencies everyone needs for handling data in everyday life, for example that students need to "*understand the consequences of synchronizing data and deal with synchronization conflicts*" [7].

Despite the importance of this field, students' and teachers' knowledge about and attitudes towards data management and the traditional topic databases, have not been investigated yet. Typically, research concerning students' perspectives assesses their preconceptions (e.g. [5]): For example, Diethelm et al. [4] presented an approach for identifying contexts relevant for the students by using the miracle question method. In studies on teachers' perspectives, their knowledge and attitudes are often considered by investigating their content knowledge or pedagogical content knowledge, which, together with the general pedagogical knowledge, are central for teaching [10].

For example, in the context of developing teacher training, Mesaroş and Diethelm [9] surveyed teachers in order to discover their ideas about lesson planning on specific topics.

4 Teachers' Content Knowledge and Attitudes

4.1 Aims

The investigation of teachers' perspectives on data management has various possible foci, e.g. their motivation, attitudes, content and/or pedagogical content knowledge or their experience with these topics. As data management is rather new to CS education, we expect that they have no teaching experience yet. Hence, in this study we concentrate on the following questions:

What do teachers know about data management topics (content knowledge)?
Which topics do they consider interesting for their teaching?
Which challenges do they expect when including data management topics in their teaching?

Based on previous feedback from teachers, our hypothesis is that they have only limited knowledge about data management, except for traditional aspects such as databases and data modelling. Additionally, we assume that the complexity of the topics and a lack of suitable software could be seen as significant obstacles for CS teaching in this field.

4.2 Survey Method and Implementation

For investigating these questions, we surveyed 53 teachers prior to three teacher training workshops using questionnaires. We decided for this method, because the goal was not to get deep insight; instead, we wanted to get an overview of the teachers' knowledge, interest and expected challenges when including this topic in teaching. The participants were from three German federal states (36 from Bavaria, 17 from the Berlin/Brandenburg area) and different types of secondary schools. Among the teachers, 31 were master teachers in CS at their respective schools.

In the questionnaires, we presented the teachers a list of data management topics, which were selected in an empirical analysis of widely accepted literature on data management in previous work. This list is shown along with the results in Table 1. On each of these topics, we asked the teachers the following questions:

1. How do you rate your knowledge about each of the topics?
   four point Likert scale from "unknown" to "detailed knowledge"
2. How interesting do you consider each topic for your teaching?
   four point Likert scale from "not interesting" to "very interesting"
3. Which challenges do you expect in lessons on this topic?
   options: insufficient own knowledge, missing tools, topic is too complex.

4.3 Results and Interpretation

Before analyzing the results, we cleaned the data: When the answer to the first question stated that the topic is unknown, the answers to the other questions were not considered, as answering these is not possible without knowing about the topic. The data was then aggregated by calculating median and mode measures as well as the mean deviation from the median (MD) for every question and topic. As the dimensions of our questions are on an ordinal scale, these measures are appropriate for aggregating the data. The complete results are shown in Table 1.

In general, the teachers state to have limited knowledge about the presented data management topics, but have already heard of most of them. This is the case even for teachers who consider data management topics interesting. Despite this, they estimated their knowledge about *relational databases* as rather detailed, while about other topics that are already considered in school, such as *data analysis*, *data encryption* or *metadata,* they supposed to have basic knowledge. For topics that are typically left out in current CS education, such as *distributed databases*, *big data* and *data mining*, they stated to have only little knowledge. One exception is *cloud storage*, on which they estimate their knowledge as basic. Merely three topics were unknown to them: the *CAP theorem*, the *ACID* and *BASE paradigms*[1]. For 13 of the 19 topics, the MD is below or at 0.25, while for all others it is at least below 0.5. Hence, most results show a relatively high consensus among the participants.

While the teachers rate *data security*, *data privacy* and *threats of automatic data processing* as very interesting for their teaching, they consider rather technology-oriented terms such as *non-relational* and *distributed databases*, *open data* or the underlying principles as less interesting. Yet, in general, most data management topics were rated rather interesting for teaching. Most of the answers have a high MD and hence a wide spread in the answers: with a closer look at the results, it becomes clear that most topics were rated as being very interesting by several teachers and at the same time as hardly interesting by others.

When including data management topics in their teaching, most teachers see the primary challenge in their insufficient knowledge. This and the results from the first question show a strong need for materials and teacher training that helps to build up this knowledge. In addition, teachers also see a challenge in missing tools that are suitable for CS teaching. Yet, in general, they do not expect to encounter any problems with the complexity of these topics, which may be influenced by their limited knowledge.

Resulting from these data, we can assume that although the participants of the workshops were generally interested in data management, they have only limited knowledge in this field. This is the case even for teachers who are master teachers at their respective schools. Hence, our results show a clear need for further education of CS teachers in data management topics.

[1] The *ACID paradigm* describes the four central characteristics of traditional databases, **a**tomicity, **c**onsistency, **i**solation and **d**urability. The *BASE paradigm* is central to non-relational databases, which are **b**asically **a**vailable, **s**oft-state, **e**ventually consistent. The *CAP theorem* concludes, that **c**onsistency, **a**vailability and **p**artition tolernace, cannot be achieved at the same time in a data management system [1].

Table 1. Results of the teacher questionnaire

	Knowledge 0 = unknown 1 = little knowledge 2 = basic knowledge 3 = detailed knowledge				Estimated interest 0 = not interesting 1 = hardly interesting 2 = rather interesting 3 = very interesting				Challenges % of teachers		
	# answers	Mode	Median	MD	# answers	Mode	Median	MD	Insufficient knowledge	Missing tools	Complexity
Relational databases	53	3	3	0.43	53	3	2	0.58	1.9	11.3	7.5
NoSQL/non-relational databases	52	1	1	0.02	33	1	1	0.39	49.1	11.3	11.3
Distributed databases	52	1	1	0.15	34	1	1	0.50	41.5	15.1	11.3
Cloud storage	53	2	2	0.11	49	2	2	0.12	30.2	20.8	1.9
Cloud computing	51	1	1	0.45	44	2	2	0.02	35.8	28.3	11.3
Data analysis	51	2	2	0.25	44	2	2	0.14	18.9	24.5	5.7
Data mining	52	1	1	0.10	37	2	2	0.16	49.1	18.9	7.5
Big data	51	1	1	0.27	38	2	2	0.16	39.6	24.5	9.4
Open data	51	1	1	0.22	23	1	2	0.74	37.7	11.3	1.9
Data encryption	53	2	2	0.11	50	3	3	0.50	13.2	18.9	11.3
Data modeling	52	2	2	0.23	49	3	2	0.69	11.3	3.8	3.8
Function of search engines	51	2	2	0.31	45	2	2	0.20	18.9	17.0	1.9
CAP theorem	51	0	0	0.14	3	1	1	0.00	47.2	0.0	0.0
ACID paradigm	51	0	0	0.39	6	1	2	0.50	37.7	0.0	0.0
BASE paradigm	51	0	0	0.12	4	1	1	0.00	45.3	0.0	0.0
Meta data	51	1	1	0.45	36	2	2	0.22	32.1	17.0	3.8
Data security (e.g. backup)	52	2	2	0.15	46	3	2	0.74	11.3	9.4	0.0
Data privacy	53	2	2	0.21	50	3	3	0.46	11.3	17.0	1.9
Threats of automatic data processing	51	2	2	0.02	48	3	3	0.60	7.5	22.6	3.8

5 Students' Knowledge and Experience

5.1 Aims

For school teaching, the students' prior knowledge about and experience with a topic are an important basis to build upon. Although data management is hardly represented in CS lessons, it is reasonable to assume that due to the ubiquity of these topics (and related technologies), students acquire some knowledge and gain experience e.g. through using smartphones and the Internet or by managing their personal data on computers. Exploring their knowledge in this field can thus help to get insight into how students come into contact with data management topics. Hence, our main question for the investigation is: *What do students know about specific topics of data management?*

5.2 Survey Method and Implementation

For exploring their knowledge, we surveyed 42 Bavarian students using questionnaires in extra-curricular settings. Among them, 38 are from higher secondary schools ("Gymnasium") and four from an intermediate secondary school ("Realschule"). Most students already came into contact with relational databases and data modeling. Yet, in school teaching other aspects of data management have hardly been considered. To explore the students' knowledge about data management, we asked them questions on:

1. Which knowledge do students have concerning the purpose and use of databases and data analyses?
2. Which metadata do students expect to be captured in situations from their daily life (taking photos with the smartphone, surfing the web)?
3. Which data do students estimate as valuable enough to create backups? How do they create backups?

The topics of the first question were selected because they are on the one hand central to data management, but also typical topics of secondary CS teaching (databases) or at least strongly related to current teaching (data analyses). Hence, we expected them to have at least little knowledge about these topics. In order to assess this knowledge, we presented them several statements (e.g. *"In databases, all data must be stored consistently"*, *"Metadata is often more interesting than the original data"*), for which they should decide whether they are correct or not. For the second question type, two situations related to the production and use of metadata were described (taking a photo with a smartphone, surfing the web), for which they should decide which metadata from a given list are stored/transmitted along with the original data. While in the first situation metadata is fairly obvious to students, in the second case students probably have not come into contact with it. Thus, the questions can give insight into whether the students are aware of metadata being stored, about what kind of information they think can be transmitted, and about their estimation of the extent of such data. The third question type refers to one exemplary topic of data management strongly related to the students' daily life and gives insight into how valuable data is for the students: The creation of backups requires various considerations, for example selecting appropriate backup media (e.g. by creating backups on external drives or thumb drives or synchronizing their data with the cloud), deciding whether full or incremental backups are to be created, how long data is being stored and also which data to backup.

5.3 Results and Interpretation

All statements that the students could tick were treated as sub questions, for which the number of students who checked them was counted. The question on backups was treated separately, since it was the only one with free text answers: For this, we extracted all responses and counted the respective number of answers. The results of all questions are shown in Table 2.

The results from the first question show that students have very vague knowledge concerning databases and data analyses. Although most of them have already attended lessons on databases, there is hardly any difference between the answers on questions related to typical topics of teaching and such that typically cannot be answered with school knowledge. About 38% of the students know that data analyses may be used for finding additional information that is not obviously contained in the original data, nearly 55% know that metadata is often more interesting than the original data. This suggests that they have already heard of these topics in daily life, e.g. in news reports

Table 2. Results of the student questionnaire

		# answers
Q1	*Databases & data analyses*	
1.1	In databases, all data must be stored in a consistent way	12 (28.6%)
1.2	Only 5 users can use a database at the same time	1 (2.4%)
1.3	Each database is stored on an own server	9 (21.4%)
1.4	Cloud services typically use databases	25 (59.5%)
1.5	Data analyses always last very long	6 (14.3%)
1.6	Small amounts of data should be preferred as analyzing them is faster	19 (45.2%)
1.7	When analyzing large amounts of data, only few information can be found	6 (14.3%)
1.8	By data analyses, it is possible to find more information on users than contained in the original data	16 (38.1%)
1.9	Large amounts of data can hardly be analyzed	6 (14.3%)
1.10	Meta data are often more interesting than the original data	23 (54.8%)
Q2	*Meta data of smartphone photos*	
2.1	Date/time	41 (97.6%)
2.2	GPS location	25 (59.5%)
2.3	Names of persons shown on the photo	3 (7.1%)
2.4	Description of the photo	3 (7.1%)
2.5	Name of the photographer	3 (7.1%)
2.6	Information on the camera	25 (59.5%)
Q3	*Meta data when accessing web sites*	
3.1	Referring URL	21 (50%)
3.2	Browser name	32 (76.2%)
3.3	Operating system	22 (52.4%)
3.4	GPS location	15 (35.7%)
3.5	Name of user	7 (16.7%)
3.6	Names of several installed programs	5 (11.9%)
3.7	Mail address of user	10 (23.8%)
3.8	Interests of user	13 (31%)
3.9	Unique user ID	8 (19%)
3.10	Stationary or mobile device	26 (61.9%)
3.11	Screen resolution	3 (7.1%)
3.12	Language	22 (52.4%)
3.13	Country	33 (78.6%)
3.14	Age of user	2 (4.8%)
Q4	*Backup*	
4.1	Regular creation of backups on e.g. thumb drives	31 (73.8%)
4.2	Synchronization with cloud	16 (38.1%)
4.3	My data are not valuable enough	7 (16.7%)
4.4	Did not yet think about that	3 (7.1%)

(continued)

Table 2. (*continued*)

		# answers
4.5	Data being backuped:	
4.5.1	Photos	22 (52.4%)
4.5.2	Documents	6 (14.3%)
4.5.3	Videos	14 (33.3%)
4.5.4	School-related files	2 (4.8%)
4.5.5	Savegames	1 (2.4%)
4.5.6	Applications	1 (2.4%)
4.5.7	Application data	3 (7.1%)
4.5.8	Music	4 (9.5%)
4.5.9	Contacts	4 (9.5%)

on analyses of shopping habits at large online shops. About 45% of the students support the statement that small amounts of data should be preferred for analysis purposes, because analyzing them is faster, which suggests that their knowledge about data analyses is only superficial. In general, the results indicate that the participants of the survey have a basic but also very diverse knowledge about data analyses.

The second question give an impression about students' knowledge about metadata in two different contexts: Most of them know that date and time are captured when taking a photo with their smartphone. Also, about 60% know that the GPS location are stored along with the picture, as well as information about the camera/phone with which the photo was taken. Most students were correct in assuming that names of persons or a description of the photo are typically not stored automatically. On the second situation we described to them, surfing the web, a majority of the students assumed that the web server gets to know the client's web browser, about 78% expect that the user's country can be discovered and only 52% think the same applies to language and operating system. While several students underestimate the amount of metadata and thus do not expect the programs installed or the screen resolution to be disclosed, others overestimate the possibilities and even assume that web sites automatically get the user's mail address or information their interests.

These results show that they are generally aware that additional data may be collected when using devices like their smartphone, which is explicable as they encounter such data regularly. Yet, when metadata are created rather in the background, despite knowing the basic concept, fewer students are aware of the creation of such data and can estimate their extent. These results are in particular interesting for CS teaching, as it clearly shows that the students relate to the topic metadata in their daily life and have built up knowledge prior to data management lessons.

The question about backups gives insight into how important personal data is for students and how they protect it. Nearly 88% stated that they create backups regularly: 74% use external media such as thumb drives for this purpose, while 38.1% synchronize data to the cloud and about 29% use both methods. The others, nearly 17%, do not create any backups. Among those, the majority thinks that their data is not valuable enough, while three students stated that they did not even think about creating backups.

Thus, in general the results show that their data is valuable for students and hence they want to protect it. The most important data is photos (52%) and videos (33%), followed by documents (14%).

Summarizing, the results show that students have already heard of several aspects of databases, data analyses and metadata. They are using at least two different approaches for data backup and probably take advantage of metadata stored along with photos. This confirms our hypothesis that they have prior knowledge about data management topics that should not be neglected when planning lessons. Particular topics on which they have wrong or incomplete conceptions, need to be addressed in data management teaching in order to foster a deeper understanding of such topics that are strongly related to their daily life.

6 Conclusion

Our teacher questionnaires clearly show that professional development opportunities on data management topics should be provided for teachers: Although they show significant interest and in some cases tried to incorporate data management topics in their teaching, they generally consider their own knowledge as insufficient. Thus, continuous professional development is deemed an important task. Despite their lack of knowledge, the participants do not expect that data management topics are too complex for secondary school teaching. Prior to the teacher training workshops, several teachers told us that they could not grasp this large field, as it included too many aspects that are unknown to them. Nevertheless, they also see the topics as motivating and interesting for themselves and their students. The discussions following the subsequent workshop have reinforced this impression.

While students come in contact with metadata of photos and thus know about them, they are not aware of which data is disclosed when surfing the web. Also, they have strategies concerning how to store and backup their own data. So, concerning the students' results, we conclude that there is rudimentary knowledge about data management topics, which teaching could build upon. Yet, they only have a vague understanding of the use and possibilities of data management topics. Generally-spoken, their knowledge is not sufficient for recognizing the ubiquity of data management and in particular for understanding influences on their daily lives. Students regularly encounter phenomena related to data management, for example when synchronization errors occur while using cloud storage services. However, their knowledge is typically not sufficient for understanding the reasons of these problems, for preventing them, and for deciding how to solve such conflicts.

For supporting students' understanding of phenomena and consequences related to data management, CS education needs to further emphasize this field. In addition to basic knowledge about the concepts and principles, competencies need to be fostered that are necessary for understanding the public discourse on topics such as data storage and data analyses, for estimating and circumventing threats as well as for self-determined and responsible handling their own and others' personal data. On the other hand, the teachers' results emphasize the need for professional development opportunities and show clear starting points for developing appropriate materials in this field.

In conclusion, for giving further guidelines on how to bring CS education to school, the results shown in this paper are a clear basis, but there is a strong need for further research.

References

1. Brewer, E.: CAP twelve years later: how the "rules" have changed. Computer **45**(2), 23–29 (2012)
2. Buffum, P.S., Martinez-Arocho, A.G., Frankosky, M.H., Rodriguez, F.J., Wiebe, E.N., Boyer, K.E.: CS principles goes to middle school. In: Dougherty, J.D., Nagel, K. (eds.) Proceedings of the 45th ACM Technical Symposium on Computer Science Education, pp. 151–156. ACM, New York (2014)
3. CSTA Standards Taskforce: (Interim) CSTA K-12 Computer Science Standards. CSTA/ACM, New York (2016)
4. Diethelm, I., Borowski, C., Weber, T.: Identifying relevant CS contexts using the miracle question. In: Schulte, C., Suhonen, J. (eds.) Proceedings of the 10th Koli Calling International Conference on Computing Education Research, pp. 74–75. ACM, New York (2010)
5. Diethelm, I., Hubwieser, P., Klaus, R.: Students, teachers and phenomena: educational reconstruction for computer science education. In: Laakso, M.-J., McCartney, R. (eds.) Proceedings of the 12th Koli Calling International Conference on Computing Education Research, pp. 164–173. ACM, New York (2012)
6. Grillenberger, A., Romeike, R.: A comparison of the field data management and its representation in secondary CS curricula. In: Schulte, C., Caspersen, M.E., Gal-Ezer, J. (eds.) Proceedings of the 9th Workshop in Primary and Secondary Computing Education, pp. 29–36. ACM, New York (2014)
7. Grillenberger, A., Romeike, R.: Teaching data management: key competencies and opportunities. In: Brinda, T., Reynolds, N., Romeike, R., Schwill, A. (eds.) KEYCIT 2014: Key Competencies in Informatics and ICT, pp. 133–150. Universitätsverlag Potsdam, Potsdam (2014)
8. Laney, D.: 3D Data Management: Controlling Data Volume, Velocity, and Variety. META Group, Stamford (2001)
9. Mesaroş, A.-M., Diethelm, I.: Ways of planning lessons on the topic of networks and the internet. In: Knobelsdorf, M., Romeike, R. (eds.) Proceedings of the 7th Workshop in Primary and Secondary Computing Education, pp. 70–73. ACM, New York (2012)
10. Shulman, L.S.: Those who understand: knowledge growth in teaching. Educ. Res. **15**(2), 4–14 (1986)

Defining Procedures in Early Computing Education

Ivan Kalas[1,2(✉)] and Laura Benton[2]

[1] Department of Informatics Education,
Comenius University, Bratislava, Slovakia
kalas@fmph.uniba.sk
[2] UCL Knowledge Lab, UCL Institute of Education, London, UK
l.benton@ucl.ac.uk

Abstract. From the early years of educational programming researchers considered procedural abstraction a key instrument of computational thinking and tried to understand the cognitive difficulties encountered through this concept. Defining procedures is promoted in renewed computing curricula in several countries. And yet, it is rarely acknowledged by more recent educational research. In this paper, we consider the fact that the delayed implementation of a mechanism for building procedures (known as *definitions*) within Scratch, a widely used programming environment for children, may have negatively impacted the focus within curricular content on this powerful idea. In our research, which is a part of a broader ScratchMaths (SM) research project, we set out to explore which factors play a role in upper primary pupils understanding and utilizing the concept of defining procedures as a common and inherent instrument of their programming. We present our observations from the project design schools and demonstrate how they guided the development of our *SM pedagogic strategy for definitions*.

Keywords: Primary computing education · Procedure · Abstraction
ScratchMaths

1 Background

Computer scientists have recognised the power of defining a *procedure* since the early days of computer programming in the late 1950s, technically defining its role as offering "a single point of reference for some small goal or task that the developer or programmer can trigger by invoking the procedure itself" [1]. Later, whilst studying the idea of a computational process in the 1980s, Abelson et al. [2] in their seminal writing identified three basic mechanisms of a programming language, including *the means of abstraction* by which compound elements can be named and manipulated as units[1], i.e. "… the means that the [programming] language provides for combining simple ideas to form more complex ideas" [ibid].

[1] The other two mechanisms being primitive expressions and the means of combination.

A. Tatnall and M. Webb (Eds.): WCCE 2017, IFIP AICT 515, pp. 567–578, 2017.
https://doi.org/10.1007/978-3-319-74310-3_57

In the early years of educational programming, within the context of Logo programming Papert [3] proposed the metaphor of "teaching the Turtle a new word" to represent the process of programming a computer. In 1974 Perlman, inspired by Papert, tried to implement the concept of procedure in a tangible programming interface for preschool children in her Tortis Slot Machine, see [4–6]. Through this work she started considering the *cognitive difficulties* behind some aspects of programming [5, p. 4] after observing children becoming overwhelmed when introduced to multiple new concepts through her system.

For Papert, turtle geometry provided an excellent opportunity to practice "the art of splitting difficulties" [3, p. 64], for example through drawing a house by splitting it into two parts – a square and triangle. He proposed that a Logo procedure can become something named, manipulated and recognised; terming it "an object to think with".

Since the early 1980s the mechanism of defining new procedures (in different forms) has been implemented in many programming environments for novice programmers, including children[2] and this is promoted through renewed computing curricula in several countries highlighting the power of abstraction and procedure. For example, Computing at School (CAS) in the UK [7] characterises procedure as a mechanism of abstraction, an instrument of generalisation, a pattern to be used to control complexity by sharing common features, and suggests "these abstractions may be deeply nested, layer upon layer" [ibid, p. 11]. CAS recommends that as well as *using procedures* pupils should become proficient in *creating new abstractions* of their own.

1.1 Defining Procedures in Research Literature

Within the Logo culture of 1980s and 1990s, researchers frequently examined the *procedural thinking* of the learners, but their studies often point to some inherent difficulties with the notion of procedure, see e.g. [8–10]. Pea et al. [10] observed that most of the pupils involved in their study in the early 1980s did not spontaneously accept programming practices such as "… structured planned approaches to procedure composition, use of conditional or recursive structures" [ibid p. 211].

Despite the legacy of being difficult and not naturally exploited by children as an everyday instrument in their programming, Logo educators and researchers have always considered procedural abstraction to be one of the most 'powerful ideas' of computing education. However, this is rarely acknowledged by more recent educational research.

Most of the research projects looking at the learning of computer science and computing concepts focus on *variables*, *loops*, *conditions* and *control structures*, *message passing* or *concurrency*, often not mentioning definitions at all. For example Meerbaum-Salant et al. [11] study how Scratch can be used to teach computer science, focusing on 'standard' key concepts, but not on defining new blocks. Similarly, Ouahbi

---

[2] Such as Karel the Robot (1981), Solo (1983), Boxer (1986), Roamer (1989), Show and Tell (1990), Turingal (1991) among others, see e.g. [4].

et al. [12] study how novices learn basic programming concepts by creating games but do not include definitions of new blocks in their observations.

Vaníček [13] identifies several potential risks in the emerging Scratch programming practices of the student-teachers, including unnecessarily long scripts. However, defining new blocks is not considered among the instruments to cope with that risk.

Futschek and Moschitz [14] explore a transition from a playful programming environment with tangible objects to a virtual Scratch environment and identify five basic computational concepts which should be present in learning scenarios with the aim to develop early algorithmic thinking, abstraction being one of them. They suggest that learners should experience a transition from perceiving a basic virtual command as an abstraction of a basic tangible action to perceiving a command as an abstraction of a compound (constructed) action.

1.2 Defining Procedures in Scratch

The Scratch programming environment has become an icon of the recent widespread interest of schools around the world in computing education for every pupil. It is a visual programming environment that allows users "to learn programming while working on personally meaningful projects such as animated stories and games" [15].

Brennan and Resnick [16] explain that in Scratch abstraction is employed at multiple levels "from the initial work of conceptualizing the problem to translating the concept into individual sprites and stacks of code". However, the previous version of Scratch (1.4) had no means to employ abstraction by defining new procedures. In 2010 Maloney et al. [15] wrote:

"Early versions of Scratch had a mechanism for creating procedures. In early field tests, however, many users were confused by procedures since they seemed very similar to broadcasts – both involved associating a name with a collection of commands. In the interest of simplicity and minimalism, procedures were removed from the language before Scratch was officially released…"[3].

More recently in Scratch 2.0 (released in 2013) the functionality for defining procedures was implemented as the **Make a Block** operation (see Fig. 1).

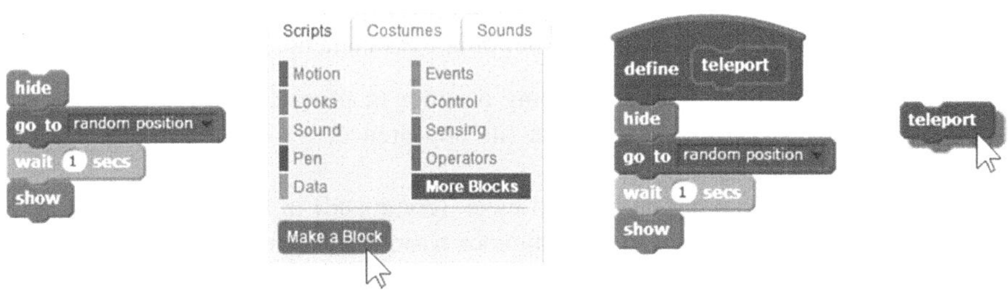

Fig. 1. In Scratch the define hat block is attached to a script, thus defining a new block (Color figure online)

[3] Later on we probe this observation through our own experience with the SM schools.

2 Procedural Abstraction Within ScratchMaths

The research reported within this paper is a part of a broader project, ScratchMaths (SM), which aims to explore connections between developing computational and mathematical thinking in the upper primary age pupils[4] in England [17, 18]. In the project we have iteratively designed detailed curriculum materials for computing lessons in years 5 and 6, which are currently being trialled in 50+ primary schools across the country. The intervention consists of six modules (three per year), with each module consisting of a series of activities organised within investigations (with accompanying classroom resources). The first three modules focused more on introducing key computing concepts (sequencing, repetition, algorithm, debugging, abstraction, initialisation, randomness, conditions, expressions, broadcasting), with links to mathematics made implicitly and the remaining three modules explicitly focused on particularly challenging mathematical concepts (place value, ratio and proportion, coordinates and geometry). Each year of the intervention included a two-day professional development program for class teachers, which was intended to introduce the 'big ideas' of the SM curriculum as well as the pedagogical approach to delivering the intervention. Through the research conducted as part of this project, we seek to better understand the *construct of procedural abstraction* in early computing education.

In their new framework for studying computational thinking, Brennan and Resnick [16] identify three key dimensions: *computational concepts* (like sequences, loops, events etc.), *computational practices* (like testing, debugging, reusing, remixing etc.) and *computational perspectives* (about the world around us). In our research we extend their first dimension into *computational constructs,* which comprise *computational concepts* (like procedural abstraction in this case) and *computational procedures* associated with the practice of the learners to exploit the concept.

2.1 SM Pedagogic Strategy for Definitions

Through the design of the SM intervention we recognise five implicit stages in developing the construct of procedural abstraction:

(1) **Perceiving a script[5] as an object to work and think with:** One of the key SM design principles is systematically building the distinction between:

- *direct manipulation*, e.g. dragging a sprite (a programmable object) by the mouse or switching its costume (its appearence) by clicking on a different costume in the list.
- *direct drive*, clicking an isolated block (command) in the scripting area, thus getting an immediate and unambiguous basic reaction, e.g. clicking **move −50 steps** block would make a sprite move backwards 50 steps.
- *computational drive*, building and using a script as a representation of the compound future behaviour of a sprite e.g. by clicking it in the scripting area.

[4] I.e. aged 9–11 years.

[5] In Scratch a stack of blocks snapped together, a piece of program.

Typically it is only later that a script (a behaviour) is turned into a complete reaction to a certain event through the addition of a hat block[6], e.g. **when this sprite clicked** or **when green flag clicked**.

By adopting this distinction pupils start perceiving scripts (with no hat blocks, see the lower left script in Fig. 2) as *patterns of actions*[7], representations of partial or complete *behaviours*, as objects to build, explore, modify, and use (i.e. as objects to think with) and possibly abstract later. In our intervention we incorporate activities developing this approach as a preliminary phase for developing procedural abstraction.

(2) **Giving a name to a script.** When a useful script has been built it can be given a name (Fig. 2-right). Within our SM pedagogical framework [17] we encourage pupils to follow the procedure: (i) build a script, debug and use it, (ii) give it a name, i.e. attach a new **define** hat block to the script, (iii) keep the define script (the definition), and (iv) use the new block as a shortcut instead, as a name of that pattern of action – using the defined block in isolation (in the direct drive mode), then within a script (in the computational drive).

In SM Module 1 pupils define more new blocks for creating different visual patterns and combine them in short scripts to draw complex circular patterns. While doing that, in line with our pedagogical framework we suggest class discussion points to *explain* and *exchange* ideas such as: *How did you teach a sprite a new command? Why did you make new blocks? How did it help your programming, thinking, and problem solving? What name did you give your new block and why?*

(3) **Working with new blocks (own and provided):** Pupils repeat the same process of making new blocks as useful shortcuts for previously built and used scripts in several contexts, to draw different compositions, e.g. a tower, a house, a swarm of colour dots etc. Gradually, they also start using their own new blocks to build more compound definitions (called nested definitions).

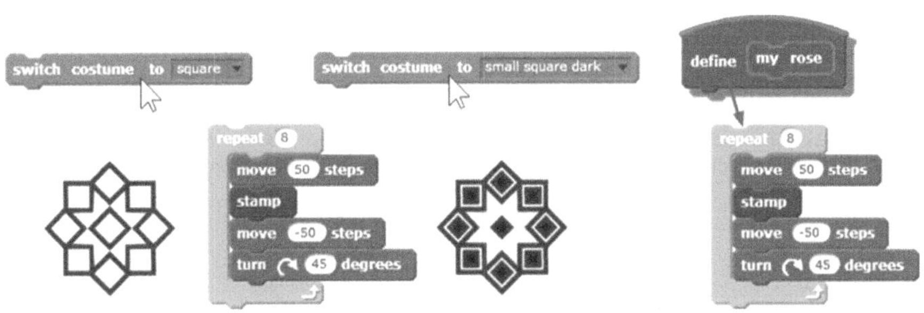

Fig. 2. Naming a useful script – i.e. certain *pattern of action* (Color figure online)

[6] The topmost block to start a script, e.g. **when this sprite clicked** hat block.

[7] In the context of SM Module 1, *patterns of actions* are procedural representations of the corresponding *visual patterns*.

Pupils also use new blocks created by the SM designers and available within specific 'starter' projects using within the modules, e.g. **set random pen size** (see Fig. 3), within their own scripts.

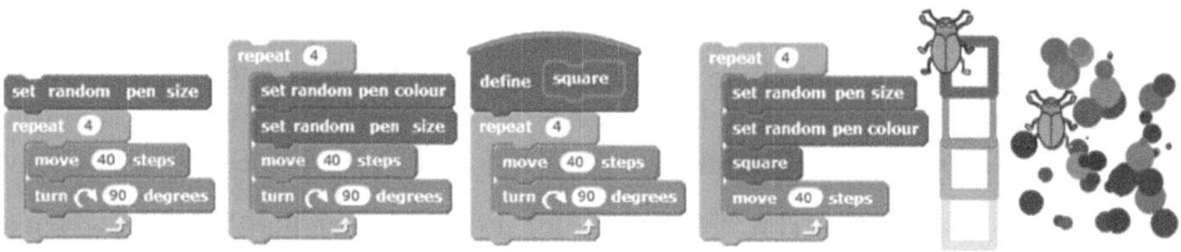

Fig. 3. Defining, using and modifying new blocks in different contexts (Color figure online)

(4) **Customising and duplicating definitions.** In the SM intervention there are contexts (situations) which require pupils to modify the behaviour of the pre-defined new blocks. They discover the "hidden" definitions[8], explore the input values to their **pick random... to...** operator blocks and modify them so that the defined blocks suit their design plan.

In another context, when working with multiple sprites, pupils also discover that each definition belongs to only one particular sprite[9] and that they need to copy or reconstruct it for use with other sprites.

(5) **Generalising definitions by indirect parameter.** Pupils use the **ask/answer** pair of blocks, first using **answer** as an input to simple scripts, later also in the definitions of their own blocks as their *indirect parameter*, (Fig. 4-left). Once they need to refer to several previous answers, variables are introduced and subsequently used in scripts and definitions (Fig. 4-right).

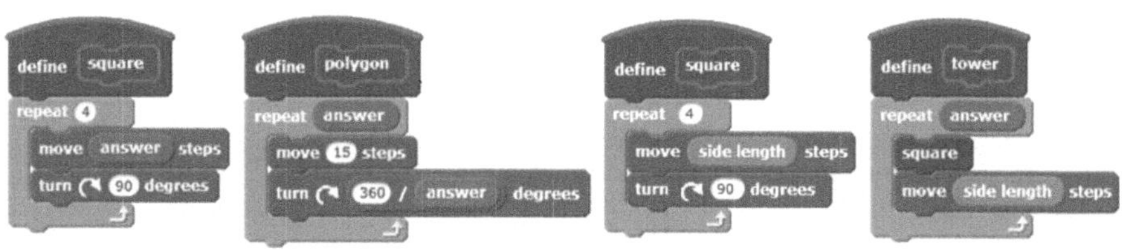

Fig. 4. Definitions generalised by using answer and variables as *indirect parameters* (Color figure online)

3 Method

In developing the SM intervention, we followed a design research process to iteratively design the curriculum content and learning progression [17]. This involved drafting learning activities and subsequently trialling them with classes of pupils in one of four

---

[8] Their definitions are so far "hidden" from view on the far right of the scripting area.

[9] Or to the stage, for completeness.

'design' schools (primary schools in London). One to three SM researchers observed the lessons, took detailed notes as well as collected pupils' Scratch projects. The researchers then discussed together the observations and outcomes of each lesson, which informed the following redesign of the learning activity.

Within this paper, we focus on two specific research questions, which we explored through our design process:

RQ1: *Which factors play a role in (upper primary) pupils' understanding and choosing to utilize within their own programs the construct of procedural abstraction?*

RQ2: *Which computational procedures need to be mastered to support pupils' understanding and exploiting procedural abstraction (i.e. defining and using new blocks in Scratch)?*

3.1 Analysis

During the prototyping phase of the design research process each iteration of the curriculum content was trialled in three to five classes of the design schools, (between January 2015 and July 2016) with one or two researchers observing the lessons and collecting the Scratch projects. All activities were trialled in at least one school, with any activities that required modifications then retrialled in the same class (where substantial changes had been made) or a different class/school (where more minor refinements had been made). Further refinements were also made as a result of feedback received during the professional development sessions conducted with class teachers prior to trialling the final intervention within a wider group of schools. During this phase we focused on the systematic and coherent integration of procedural abstraction in all six modules of the intervention.

In this paper, we focus on analysing collected observations and projects from the perspective of the construct of procedural abstraction. Firstly we conducted a content analysis on the Scratch projects collected in several design schools during one Module 2 activity (partway through the year 5 curriculum), requiring pupils to define and use a block to draw a square, to identify the common initial issues or misconceptions the pupils encounter when learning about definitions (Research Lesson 1).

Secondly we conducted a content analysis on the Scratch projects collected during a 90 min lesson in one design school which took place at the very end of the design research phase (after the trial of the year 6 content) to assess the pupils' understanding of the key constructs of the SM intervention (Research Lesson 2). This analysis was intended to identify the choices made by pupils with regard to the use of definitions within an open task following the SM intervention.

3.2 Initial Issues and Misconceptions

We identified three key issues in pupils' initial *building* and *use* of definitions during Research Lesson 1. Below we describe these issues and describe how they are addressed within our SM pedagogic strategy for definitions, which were subsequently promoted by researchers in classrooms later in the design research process. For example when defining a new block for drawing a square of the side length of 40, pupils:

i. did not attach the **define square** hat block to the script – new block **square** itself would then have "no behaviour" as it had no define script, i.e. no definition. *We advocate that teachers should encourage pupils to firstly build a script (stage 1) and then give it a name by creating a new block and attaching the hat block (stage 2).*
ii. attached the **define square** hat block to the define script, however later started "stealing" the blocks from their define script, as if once having been defined, Scratch would simply "remember the definition". *We suggest that teachers should encourage pupils to get into the routine of moving the define script to the right of the scripts area out of the way once they are happy with it and then not touching it (unless they intentionally decide to modify it).*
iii. attached the **define square** hat block to the define script, however continued building another **repeat 4 move 40 turn right 90 degrees** script whenever they needed to draw a square, instead of using the new **square** block as a name of that *pattern of action. We propose that teachers should encourage pupils to use their new blocks in isolation (stage 2) and then to use within different scripts (stage 3).*

3.3 Use of Definitions After SM Intervention

During Research Lesson 2 the teacher first demonstrated the final behaviour in the full screen mode – so that pupils could not see the scripts of the model solution. When the (Beetle) sprite was clicked it asked how many houses it should draw and then drew a row of randomly sized and coloured houses. This could be repeated several times thus creating a hamlet, see Fig. 5.

Fig. 5. Picturesque hamlet, the final assignment in a design school (Color figure online)

The class then as a group (in front of the interactive whiteboard) discussed the activity, steps and possible strategies, dealing with questions such as: *How many houses did the Beetle draw in one row and why? Do they all have the same side length? How are they positioned? How would the Beetle draw a house and a row of houses? Does the Beetle choose a side length, how does it remember that value while drawing a house? How will the Beetle learn how many houses to draw?* Pupils were not prompted to define their own new blocks.

A starter Scratch project was provided, with the Beetle sprite, a simple setup script (to clear the stage etc.), the **side length** variable already created, a pre-defined block **set random pen size colour shade** and two isolated blocks in the scripting area: **set side length to 0** and the **side length** reporter block.

Initial discussion took 15 min. Pupils were then divided into mixed ability pairs or threes by the teacher. Teams worked on their projects independently for 70 min with a short break, the teacher providing only limited guidance. There were 23 pupils in the class, and we collected 9 projects (which represented the work of 21 pupils), hereafter referred to as P1 to P9.

Our content analysis of the *nesting structure* of definitions within the projects was then conducted focusing on:

(a) the definitions of new blocks and whether a new block is being used (nested) inside another definition – i.e. whether pupils achieved stage 3 of the SM pedagogic strategy for definitions.
(b) whether the indirect parameters are properly implemented in the definitions – the **answer** block and the **side length** variable – that is, whether pupils achieved stage 5 of our strategy.

Figure 6 presents the projects' nesting structure in the following way: the topmost triangular block represents the overall behaviour (solution), usually the **when this sprite clicked** script. Each circle represents a definition, the positioning corresponds to nesting, i.e. using a new block inside another definition. For example, in P1 a block for drawing a **house** was defined, then used in the definition of a block to draw a **row of houses**, which is then used in the overall behaviour of the sprite. Sometimes the **house** block itself was defined by using another new block in it, usually a **square** (in P5) or a **square** and a **triangle** (in P6).

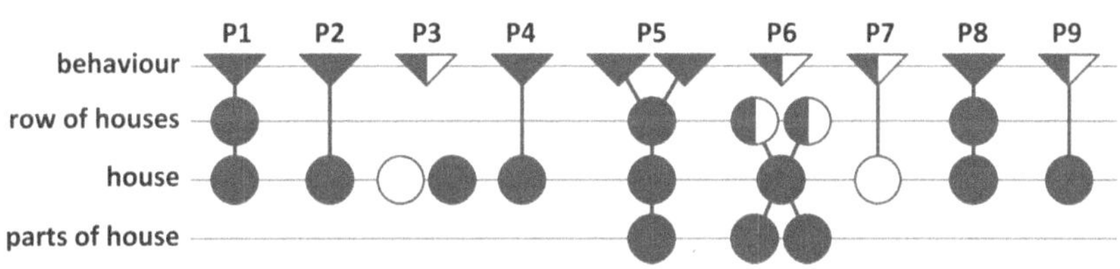

Fig. 6. Nesting analysis of the definitions in the projects

A circle or a triangle in Fig. 6 is filled, semi-filled or empty, depending on whether the definition correctly, partially or incorrectly[10] works with the indirect parameter i.e. **answer** or **side length**, the most advanced (stage 5) definition type in the SM curriculum.

[10] Including not using it at all.

4 Discussion

Despite some initial issues/misconceptions of definitions, our findings show that paying close attention to repeatedly exploring and explaining the practice of *building a script, giving it a name, keeping the definition and using new block as a shortcut* helped to reduce observed misconceptions and encouraged pupils to choose for themselves to utilise the power of definitions within their own scripts. Our pedagogic approach allowed pupils to automatize this computational procedure in different contexts, before creating a situation when pupils needed to get back to the define script and modify it.

Although back in 2010 Maloney et al. [15] reported certain confusion of definitions and broadcasts, we have not observed this within our research. It may be due to two factors: In the SM pedagogic framework [17] we strive to encourage pupils to work with (incomplete) scripts as (partial) representations of action or behaviours. A hat block is usually added only later, as an instrument to clarify how this behaviour will be activated. From the first module pupils add the **define** hat block to some scripts to give them name. Much later, in the third module (in year 5) they start using some scripts as reactions to receiving a message.

Through our nesting analysis of the pupils' final assignment, see Fig. 6, we looked at whether making new blocks has been adopted by the learners as an instrument to cope with complexity. We noted that every team made at least one new block and 5 of 9 teams made two or more new blocks (up to five). Two teams nested their definition in two levels, 2 teams even in three levels. We also noted that 8 teams correctly or partially correctly worked with the indirect parameter(s) in their scripts thus achieving stage 5 of the SM pedagogic strategy for definitions.

Through our content analysis we also identified that definitions of new procedures play **different roles** in the SM intervention:

- *Aggregating basic commands into one*: when several basic commands are simply attached together, with new command often carrying the names of its 'atoms', e.g. **set random pen size colour shade** or **dot stamp jump**.
- *Extending the language:* (in the sense of Abelson et al. [2]) when a new command gives a name to a compound reaction or behaviour, thus building a higher layer of the means of expression – abstracting from the detail, e.g. **house** or **teleport**.
- *Transforming the language:* when a basic command is 'replaced' by a new one to be used instead, e.g. replacing **move 20 steps** by a new block **move one tile**.
- *'Patching' the language*: when new block 'completes' the same layer of the means of expression as offered by other basic blocks – extending the language in a 'horizontal way'. This may lead to more consistent code, see Fig. 7 which illustrates the definition of such block – **previous costume**.

Fig. 7. *Patching the language.* While next costume is a standard block, 'symmetrical' previous costume block can be defined to highlight the analogy. (Color figure online)

5 Conclusion

Although several designers updated their Scratch 1.4 materials to illustrate definitions, rarely is this construct integrated and systematically exploited as a truly powerful idea. In the SM intervention, the thread of developing procedural abstraction winds through all six modules, through five implicit stages. In our research we acknowledge the importance of the role that definitions play in developing early computational thinking, facilitating [19] **decomposition** (by creating a structure, breaking down a problem), **abstraction** (by hiding detail), and **generalisation** (by highlighting certain patterns of action and encouraging to use them later in different contexts). Our experiences in the context of the SM intervention validate the importance of exploiting a tool with affordances that support pupils in building definitions, but also the importance of employing a pedagogic strategy that systematically develops all computational processes associated with the practice of the learners to exploit this concept.

Acknowledgments. The authors would like to thank the other SM project team members Richard Noss, Celia Hoyles, Piers Saunders, Johanna Carvajal and Dave Pratt, the Education Endowment Foundation for funding this work, and also all the teachers and pupils from our design schools for their invaluable contributions to the design and development of the SM intervention.

References

1. Technopedia: What does procedure mean. www.technopedia.com
2. Abelson, H., Sussman, G.J., Sussman, J.: Structure and Interpretation of Computer Programs. The MIT Press, Cambridge (1985). 657 p.
3. Papert, S.: Mindstorms. Children, Computers, and Powerful Ideas. Basic Books, New York (1980). 230 p.
4. Kelleher, C., Pausch, R.: Lowering the barriers to programming: a taxonomy of programming environments and languages for novice programmers. ACM Comput. Surv. (CSUR) **37**(2), 83–137 (2005)
5. Morgado, L., Cruz, M., Kahn, K.: Radia Perlman – a pioneer of young children computer programming. Current Developments in Technology-Assisted Education, pp. 1903–1908. Formatex (2006)
6. Perlman, R.: Using Computer Technology to Provide a Creative Learning Environment for Preschool Children. AI Memo 360. MIT, Cambridge (1976). 32 p.

7. Computing at School Working Group: Computer science: a curriculum for schools (2012). www.computingatschool.org.uk/data/uploads/ComputingCurric.pdf
8. Hillel, J.: The notion of variable in the context of turtle graphics. In: Hoyles, C., Noss, R. (eds.) Learning Mathematics and Logo, pp. 11–36. The MIT Press, Cambridge (1992)
9. Leron, U.: Some problems in children's logo learning. In: Proceedings of the 7th International Conference for the psychology of Mathematics Education, Israel, pp. 346–351 (1983)
10. Pea, R.D., et al.: Logo and the development of thinking skills. In: Chen, M., Paisley, W. (eds.) Children and Microcomputers Research on the Newest Medium, pp. 193–212. Sage, Newcastle upon Tyne (1985)
11. Meerbaum-Salant, O., Armoni, M., Ben-Ari, M.M.: Learning computer science concepts with Scratch. Comput. Sci. Educ. **23**(3), 239–264 (2013)
12. Ouahbi, I., et al.: Learning basic programming concepts by creating games with Scratch programming environment. Procedia - Soc. Behav. Sci. **191**, 1479–1482 (2015)
13. Vaníček, J.: Programming in Scratch using inquiry-based approach. In: Brodnik, A., Vahrenhold, J. (eds.) ISSEP 2015. LNCS, vol. 9378, pp. 82–93. Springer, Cham (2015). https://doi.org/10.1007/978-3-319-25396-1_8
14. Futschek, G., Moschitz, J.: Learning algorithmic thinking with tangible objects eases transition to computer programming. In: Kalaš, I., Mittermeir, Roland T. (eds.) ISSEP 2011. LNCS, vol. 7013, pp. 155–164. Springer, Heidelberg (2011). https://doi.org/10.1007/978-3-642-24722-4_14
15. Maloney, J., Resnick, M., Rusk, N., Silverman, B., Eastmond, E.: The Scratch programming language and environment. ACM Trans. Comput. Educ. **10**(4), 15 (2010). Article 16
16. Brennan, K., Resnick, M.: New frameworks for studying and assessing the development of computational thinking. In: Proceedings of the 2012 Annual Meeting of the American Educational Research Association, Vancouver, Canada (2012)
17. Benton, L., Hoyles, C., Kalas, I., Noss, R.: Bridging primary programming and mathematics: some findings of design research in England. Digit. Exp. Math. Educ. **3**, 115–138 (2017). https://doi.org/10.1007/s40751-017-0028-x
18. Benton, L., Hoyles, C., Kalas, I., Noss, R.: Building mathematical knowledge with programming: insights from the ScratchMaths project. In: Constructionism 2016, Bangkok, pp. 25–32 (2016)
19. Guttag, J.V.: Introduction to Computation and Programming Using Python. The MIT Press, Cambridge (2013). 298 p.

Involving Everyone: Coding and Decoding Languages

Therese Keane[1(✉)], Monica Williams[2], Christina Chalmers[3], and Marie Boden[4]

[1] Department of Education, Swinburne University of Technology, Melbourne, Australia
tkeane@swin.edu.au
[2] Association of Independent Schools of South Australia, Adelaide, Australia
williamsm@ais.sa.edu.au
[3] Faculty of Education, Queensland University of Technology, Brisbane, Australia
c.chalmers@qut.edu.au
[4] School of IT and Electrical Engineering, University of Queensland, Brisbane, Australia
marieb@itee.uq.edu.au

Abstract. Through the use of humanoid robots, a rural school in South Australia has included both Aboriginal and non-Aboriginal people in embedding the "sleeping" language of the traditional owners of the land (the Narungga people) into the classroom. Aboriginal and non-Aboriginal students worked with virtual and real humanoid robots to develop in parallel both their programming skills and their understanding of the Narungga language and culture. This research is part of a larger three-year study investigating the impact of humanoid robots on students' learning and engagement and draws on questionnaires, interviews and journals from the educators. The study demonstrated how pride and interest in Aboriginal culture can be partially reclaimed using these inclusive and adaptive technologies. Simultaneously, students and educators were learning two languages; the coding language required to program the robot and the Narungga language.

Keywords: Programming · Humanoid robots · Aboriginal students Language and culture

1 Introduction

Humanoid robots and programming were introduced to a rural school in South Australia with the intention to use technology to connect students with the local indigenous culture. Historically, the Australian Aboriginal and Torres Strait Islander people have been alienated from their traditional culture, firstly as a result of British colonial practices in the nineteenth century and then subsequent Australian Government policies. Post-colonisation, most of the 350 Aboriginal and Torres Strait Islander nations were forced from their lands and Government policies made it difficult to engage with their language and culture. Almost two centuries later, Aboriginal children on the Yorke Peninsula know little about the culture of their people and do not speak or know

A. Tatnall and M. Webb (Eds.): WCCE 2017, IFIP AICT 515, pp. 579–588, 2017.
https://doi.org/10.1007/978-3-319-74310-3_58

their Aboriginal language. With limited knowledge of their cultural identity and a traumatic post-colonial history, students do not have a pride in their Aboriginal identity that is befitting of the children, of one of the oldest living cultures in the world.

The Kindergarten - Year 9 school in this study has 240 students, 22% are Aboriginal students. The traditional owners of the Yorke Peninsula are the Narungga people and many of the students at the school in this study have Narungga heritage. The school acknowledged the injustice that has been done to the Aboriginal peoples and wanted to find a way to work in a partnership with the local Aboriginal community to reconnect these students to their heritage. For six years, dictionaries for the Narungga language laid unused at the school. What brought the dictionaries to life was the integration with digital technologies, through the use of humanoid robots and through the authentic learning of the Narungga language.

This research project reconnected the Aboriginal students, and non-Aboriginal students, with the language and culture of the traditional owners of the land on which the school was built. With the vision of the principal and three educators, this rural school involved their local community in using adaptive technology to build deeper understanding and respect between communities. By working in partnership with the local Aboriginal community and the one fluent speaker, the school re-invigorated interest in the language, which had been dormant for generations. The learning that happened in the school was a result of a unique partnership between the Association of Independent Schools of South Australia (AISSA), the school, and the local Aboriginal community. The educators, students, and the AISSA shared their learning of two languages; the local Aboriginal language of Narungga and digital programming, with their wider communities.

2 Literature Review

The interest in educational robotics has seen its popularity grow [1, 2]. For over a quarter of a century, many initiatives, courses and competitions have been developed in the context of educational robotics, however the introduction of humanoid robots is relatively new to schools. More needs to be known about how humanoid robots can have a positive impact on students' learning and motivation [3].

It has been argued that educational robots are one of the best problem-solving tools to assist students develop knowledge and skills required for the 21st century [4, 5]. Asking questions, working together, problem solving, and thinking critically and creativity are seen as essential for the 21st century. These 21st century skills, also known as the 4Cs, have been identified as critical thinking, collaboration. communication, and creativity [6–8]. Keane et al. stated that appropriate situations need to be created to allow students to develop a mastery of the 4Cs. Students can engage in critical thinking with robots by investigating problems [9].

The use of humanoid robotics affords an environment where students can solve real life problems or conduct experiments, based on their interests, and their skill level. This type of environment according to Alimisis [10] engages "students' curiosity and initiate motivation." Students are more likely to persevere with problems whilst engaged in robotics activities that require them to analyze and synthesize and come up with new and creative ways to find solutions, collaborate with their peers, and communicate their learning. Other uses of educational robotics such as the telling of stories, can be considered an alternative pathway to engaging with educational robots [11].

The humanoid robot used in schools are pre-assembled and take the shape of a human form with two arms, two legs, a body and a head. The robot sensors and movements emulate human interactions, such as sight, sound, touch and social behaviours which can be programmed through drag and drop software or through Python code.

In this study, humanoid robots and programming were introduced to students in a rural school with the intention to use technology to reconnect students with their Indigenous language and culture. Robots can act as a bridge in enabling students to understand humans [12]; and in this study, to understand the Narungga language and culture. Thorpe and Galassi [13] believed that digital technologies have been an enabler for Indigenous people by providing a means for their cultural heritage to be "digitally returned and brought together for community use." Technologies, embedded in culturally responsive pedagogies that link the Aboriginal home culture and school culture, have been shown to improve engagement and learning within Indigenous students in STEM subjects [14]. In this case study where students are learning to program a humanoid robot, they are developing 21st century skills within a framework of Indigenous interests, cultures and languages, and strengthening the connection between school, home and country.

3 Background Information About the Project

The Association of Independent Schools South Australia (AISSA) purchased two NAO humanoid robots (Pink and Thomas) to use in independent schools in South Australia. For three years, the AISSA regularly invited all of its 96 member schools to submit a proposal outlining how the school intended to incorporate the robot into student learning. Interested principals approached educators and together they forwarded an expression of interest to participate in the study. The AISSA allocated the robots to successful schools for a period of time ranging from 8 weeks and up to 6 months. The university researchers were not part of the selection process, and their involvement commenced once the robot had completed its time in a school. Before the humanoid robot was deployed, the AISSA offered two days of professional learning to the participating teacher/s from the school. The professional learning outlined the project aims, emerging themes from the research, and was designed to also support educators to program and code the robot. During the workshops educators were encouraged to consider their pedagogical approaches and data collection that would provide them with insights into students' learning.

4 Method

In this project, a humanoid robot (Pink) was deployed into a rural school in South Australia for a period of six months. This paper (second year of the study), is part of a wider 3-year multiple case study research project that investigates the use of humanoid robots in different school settings. Each school was considered as a separate case study from the perspective of the "qualitative or naturalistic research paradigm" [15]. As the investigation was focused on description and investigation rather than on cause and effect, the research focus was on the impact humanoid robots have on learning and engagement in the classroom. The case study approach was chosen for a number of reasons; it was important to understand what was being done by educators and students, the depth of the student learning, and the classroom context. In this paper, we will be focusing on one school and how they unified difficult, complex, and sensitive issues with technology and programming with the intention of involving everyone at the school and strengthening their community.

4.1 Sample

A humanoid robot was deployed for 6 months in a Kindergarten- Year 9 school. The principal and three teaching staff were directly involved in this project. These four educators came from a variety of learning contexts, had varying years of teaching experience and represented a range of learning areas. They also had varying capabilities, attitudes, skills, and confidence with regards to using technology. The four staff at this school wanted to know if the humanoid robot could be a catalyst for offering Aboriginal students a greater sense of pride in their culture and if the technology could create a more inclusive school community, by strengthening relationships and respect between the Aboriginal and non-Aboriginal members. The following Table 1 provides a breakdown of the participants:

Table 1. Breakdown of participants

Name	Year level/role	# Aboriginal students	# Non aboriginal students
Educator A	Year 1 and 2	6	0
Educator B	Year 3	2	16
Educator C	Year 4	9	20
Educator D	Principal	53	187

4.2 Sources of Data

Data collection methods included questionnaire, semi-structured interviews, classroom videos, student work samples and reflective journals.

The questionnaire consisted of 24 questions and was delivered electronically to participants at the conclusion of the robot's deployment. The questionnaire was mainly qualitative in nature and involved a series of open-ended response questions. The questions explored the teachers experience of using the robot in their teaching and their perceptions of student learning. The participants were also asked to identify structural and organizational considerations that needed to be addressed when using the humanoid robot.

The reflective journals used in this study provided participants with the means to move beyond focusing on skill development in digital technologies by providing scope for challenging existing beliefs and about pedagogical practices that promote deep student learning [16]; about how their class engaged and interacted with the robot; the benefits for students; and any frustrations and concerns that occurred with the technology. Participants were asked to reflect on the following:

- How do the students in your class engage and interact with the robot?
- How was the robot used in your classroom?
- How has the robot been beneficial for students' understanding of technology?
- Did you have any concerns or frustrations with the technology?
- What suggestions do you have for other teachers trying to integrate humanoid robots with the Australian Curriculum?
- Can you provide samples of activities that you did in your classes and comment on whether these activities were successful or not?

Semi-structured interviewing was used in this study for the purpose of collecting educators' responses for this research. During the interviews, educators were encouraged to discuss their experience working with the humanoid robot in the classroom. These questions were derived from the reflective journal to clarify and further explore information provided by the teachers in their reflective journal.

5 Data and Results

The collected responses from the educators in this case study were analysed and the results aligned with the 4plus4 Model developed from the emerging themes from the first year of the study [4]. This model was developed by investigating how humanoid robots integrated into the classroom and the common themes that emerged, such as curiosity, challenge, collaboration, communication, critical thinking, creative thinking, computational thinking and coding.

Whilst the 4plus4 Model was created after analysing the data from the first year of case studies, the researchers wanted to know whether this model could be applied to this specific school. Even though, the students were learning to program, which in some respects was no different to other schools the robot was deployed in, this one had complex overlays which made it distinctive. This robotic project was designed to show respect to the Narungga people and provided a vehicle for the school community to appreciate the culture of the traditional owners of the land on which the school sits. The 4plus4 Model highlights how students can achieve success in computational thinking and coding by incorporating the 21st century fluencies; collaboration, communication, critical thinking and creative thinking (4Cs) and combining their natural curiosity in solving complex challenges.

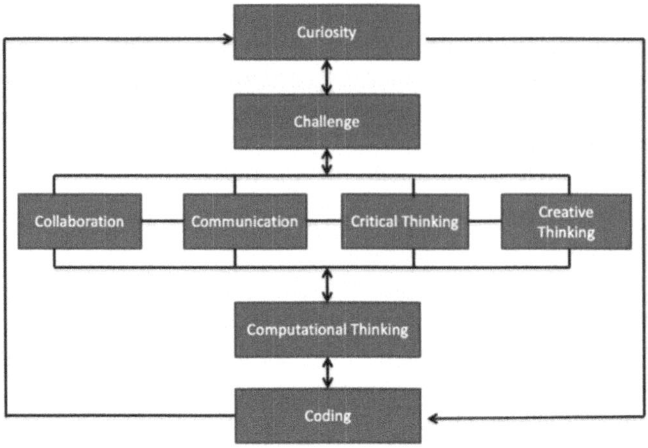

Fig. 1. The 4plus4 model in Fig. 1 identifies eight themes including curiosity, challenge, collaboration, communication, critical thinking, creative thinking, computational thinking and coding.

5.1 Curiosity

Curiosity was a pivotal theme evident in both educators and students who engaged with the humanoid robot. Technology must also be easy to use, ubiquitous, linked to real-world problem solving, and involve deep learning. Curiosity incorporates the constructs of interest and engagement and involves students attempting to solve their own questions, suggesting possible relationships and identifying factors that could influence the situation [17].

Curiosity about the humanoid robot was identified by the educators as an important motivational factor that underpinned the acceptance of the robot in the classroom. In this study, it was evident that students were curious when they intentionally sought out additional information to work with the robot so they could explore more advanced programming. Students' interactions with the robots were fueled by the students' curiosity about their new robot friend: the students are driven by a desire to see [the humanoid robot] do 'cool' things. So, they actively try to push the boundaries. Their inquisitive nature and the endless possibilities… with [the humanoid robot] meant that the students should never get bored. [Educator B]

5.2 Challenge

Curiosity was enhanced by the complexity of the challenge and this led to further curiosity. The challenge presented a subset of problems which required the students to find a unique solution. For example, when students were learning to program the robot, they needed to firstly learn to speak the Narungga language as well as learn to program the robot using Choregraphe (the proprietary software). They discovered that the robot could not pronounce the Narungga words when they were typed into the programming language. Therefore, the students started using the phonetic spelling of the words.

Classroom teachers claimed that deep learning occurred as students began to work on problems that challenged them to think differently. For example, Educator C provided an example of deep learning in his classroom:

> I was thinking about how much deeper the learning has gone, for instance trying to get the language coded into the robot, we played around with recording voice first of all,…that was not working to well so then we thought, about how else we can do it, and we ended up typing the words in and so we did that first of all and of course they did not pronounce properly. …then going back to the individual sounds and then decoding how they can reproduce those different sounds using different letter combinations.

Students were highly aspirational in the design of their projects and pursued ideas that had higher degrees of difficulty than their teacher had set. Motivated by the challenge, students were engaged in problem solving with the humanoid robot. There was evidence that there were multiple ways students were challenged by the programming activities: the robots provided an opportunity for differentiated, self-directed learning to take place; the visual programming software (Choregraphe) used to program the humanoid robot provided a range of entry points for students; and the challenge of the complex open-ended learning tasks permitted students to create programs that stretched their intellect while remaining within their zone of proximal development [18].

5.3 Collaboration, Communication, Creativity and Critical Thinking

The participants identified collaboration, communication, creativity, and critical thinking as four skills their students developed whilst working with the humanoid robot. These skills, grouped together are also known as 21st century skills [5–8, 19]. This study found that both educators and students were able to communicate their ideas and understanding, therefore creating a more collaborative classroom. The educators reported that students engaged with creative and critical thinking whilst they were focused on completing their robot programs. Students were critically evaluating ideas and refining them to accommodate their expanding coding skills to constantly improve the functionality of the humanoid robot.

This was demonstrated in the classroom when students developed their programming ideas into actuality through individual and collaborative problem-solving. As students' ideas and coding skills developed so did their confidence levels and this was evident when they pursued increasingly complex programming concepts and successfully mastered them.

5.4 Computational Thinking

According to Wing [20], "computational thinking involves solving problems, designing systems, and understanding human behaviour, by drawing on the concepts fundamental to computer science." Wing [21] proposed that computational thinking would enable students to use abstraction, algorithmic and recursive thinking, pattern-matching, and logical thinking in order to solve complex problems. These skills were evident in this study as Educator A stated:

> [There was] lots of problem solving with my group… Working out how to get Pink to say Narungga words correctly and adjusting our spelling to suit, trying different things with object recognition, to try and get it to work, trying to solve problems when getting Pink to touch her knees.

The educators identified a number of skills that students adopted related to computational thinking including: problem decomposition, algorithmic thinking, problem solving, and testing and debugging. Using the computational thinking skills students were able to use the humanoid robot to develop new ways of thinking about problems, particularly in relation to how to use the robot's software and hardware to embed the Narungga language and culture. The students represented their solutions as computational steps and algorithms.

5.5 Coding/Programming

The educators in the study reported that the humanoid robot sparked students' interest in coding and robotics. The students' curiosity in engaging with the humanoid robot extended to using the humanoid robot's drag and drop programming software. The students programmed the robot using its proprietary software (Choregraphe) loaded onto a computer. Once the students completed the coding sequence on the computer, the program was then uploaded to the robot. Students in Year 1 and 2 programmed visual recognition and facial recognition movements and the Year 4 students synchronised the robot's movements and actions, through programming. Teacher A remarked on how quickly her Year 1 and 2 students embraced coding the robot.

As the students' confidence in engaging with the robot increased, they tried more complex programming and were more willing to take risks. Students further developed their coding skills as they experimented with the programming software.

The educators in this school recognised the importance of coding and robotics for their students' future and the far-reaching opportunities to integrate this technology in ways that build respect and understanding between cultures:

> This has not only engaged our students; it has engaged our staff as well. It has given them encouragement in what they have seen from the students to keep progressing with the [Narungga] language as well as the digital side of things. [Educator D]

More than anything, this project has confirmed for this school that their vision is to be an innovative school that utilises coding as part of the inclusive and adaptive technologies to connect in authentic ways with their Aboriginal and non-Aboriginal communities.

6 Discussion and Conclusion

This research paper is part of a larger three-year study investigating the impact that humanoid robots have on student learning and engagement. It was apparent from the four educator's perspectives, that the students were deeply engaged with learning about the local Aboriginal language and culture through the use of a humanoid robot. What is intriguing about this case study, is that the complexity, the authenticity, and the purpose created a conducive and accepting environment whereby the students were learning the language and culture of the Narungga people – the traditional owners of the land. The students were learning the language and culture of a dormant and sleeping language, whilst simultaneously learning a programming language by communicating instructions to a humanoid robot.

Both languages, (Narungga and the programming language) were unfamiliar to students and the educators. It was considered a steep learning curve to learn and understand two different ways of communicating – both old and new, however, the school was determined to ensure the involvement of the wider community, the educators, and students. There was considerable trust shown by all involved, to be able to breathe new life into a dormant language using cutting-edge technology, was a precarious project that was considered successful by the principal and the educators involved. The Aboriginal and non-Aboriginal students who participated in the study had reported new sense of pride in the language of the traditional owners of the land and significantly, the success of this project was dependent upon the support of the local Aboriginal community, in particular the Narungga people.

While our findings confirm previous research that robotics technology engaged students in learning, the use of humanoid robots in the classroom has been recent. Using the 4plus4 Model to analyse the data collected highlighted how humanoid robots can develop 21st century skills of creativity, critical thinking, communication, and collaboration along with coding and computational thinking skills. Curiosity was also evident due to the engaging nature of the technology. This curiosity was enhanced by the challenge of solving complex open-ended learning tasks. Students were able to achieve success with coding by using computational thinking skills. The students developed a deeper understanding of coding as they experimented with the software engaging in real-world tasks that re-invigorated a 'sleeping' Aboriginal language. Educators reported that the complexity and sophistication of computational thinking and coding surpassed their expectations and made them see their Aboriginal and non-Aboriginal students in new and different ways. This finding challenges not only long held assumptions about students and their learning potential, but also the pedagogy, the very beliefs that educators have about their learners in the area of digital technologies, and the strategies and methodologies that promote deep learning.

References

1. Alimisis, D.: Educational robotics: open questions and new challenges. Themes Sci. Technol. Educ. **6**(1), 63–71 (2013)
2. Somyürek, S.: An effective educational tool: Construction kits for fun and meaningful learning. Int. J. Technol. Des. Educ. **25**(1), 25–41 (2015)
3. Chang, C.-W., Lee, J.-H., Chao, P.-Y., Wang, C.-Y., Chen, G.-D.: Exploring the possibility of using humanoid robots as instructional tools for teaching a second language in primary school. Educ. Technol. Soc. **13**(2), 13–24 (2010)
4. Keane, T., Chalmers, C., Williams, M., Boden, M.: The impact of humanoid robots on students' computational thinking. In: Australian Computers in Education Conference 2016, pp. 93–103 (2016)

5. Eguchi, A.: What is educational robotics? Theories behind it and practical implementation. In: Society for Information Technology and Teacher Education International Conference, pp. 4006–4014. AACE (2010)
6. University of Melbourne: http://atc21s.org/index.php/about/what-are-21st-century-skills/
7. Keane, T., Keane, W.F., Blicblau, A.S.: Beyond traditional literacy: learning and transformative practices using ICT. Educ. Inf. Technol. **21**(4), 769–781 (2016)
8. MCEETYA: Melbourne Declaration on Educational Goals for Young Australians. Curriculum Corporation (2008)
9. Savard, A., Freiman, V.: Investigating complexity to assess student learning from a robotics-based task. Digit. Experien. Math. Educ. **2**(2), 93–114 (2016)
10. Alimisis, D.: Robotics in education and education in robotics: shifting focus from technology to pedagogy. In: Proceedings of the 3rd International Conference on Robotics in Education, pp. 7–14 (2012)
11. Rusk, N., Resnick, M., Berg, R., Pezalla-Granlund, M.: New pathways into robotics: strategies for broadening participation. J. Sci. Educ. Technol. **17**(1), 59–69 (2008)
12. Mubin, O., Stevens, C.J., Shahid, S., Al Mahmud, A., Dong, J.-J.: A review of the applicability of robots in education. J. Technol. Educ. Learn. **1**, 1–7 (2013)
13. Thorpe, K., Galassi, M.: Rediscovering indigenous languages: the role and impact of libraries and archives in cultural revitalisation. Aust. Acad. Res. Libr. **45**(2), 81–100 (2014)
14. McKinley, E.: STEM and indigenous students. In: Research Conference 2016 - Improving STEM Learning - What will it take? pp. 64–68. Australian Council for Educational Research, Brisbane Convention and Exhibition Centre (2016)
15. Merriam, S.B.: Case Study Research in Education. Jossey-Bass, San Francisco (1988)
16. Koszalka, T.A.: Reflection as a critical component of the technology adoption process. ERIC Doc. Reprod. Serv. ED **480**, 237 (2003)
17. Arnone, M.P., Small, R.V., Chauncey, S.A., McKenna, H.P.: Curiosity, interest and engagement in technology-pervasive learning environments: a new research agenda. Educ. Technol. Res. Dev. **59**(2), 181–198 (2011)
18. Vygotsky, L.: Thought and language. MIT Press, Cambridge (1962). Published originally in Russian in 1934
19. http://www.amanet.org/organizations/2010-survey-critical-skills.aspx
20. Wing, J.M.: Computational thinking and thinking about computing. Philos. Trans. Roy. Soc. Lond. A Math. Phys. Eng. Sci. **366**(1881), 3717–3725 (2008)
21. Wing, J.M.: Computational thinking. Commun. ACM **49**(3), 33–35 (2006)

Constructive Interaction on Collaborative Programming: Case Study for Grade 6 Students Group

Sayaka Tohyama[1(✉)], Yoshiaki Matsuzawa[2], Shohei Yokoyama[1], Teppei Koguchi[1], and Yugo Takeuchi[1]

[1] Shizuoka University, 3-5-1 Johoku, Naka-ku, Hamamatsu-shi, Shizuoka, Japan
toyama.sayaka@shizuoka.ac.jp
[2] Aoyama Gakuin University, 5-10-1 Fuchinobe, Chuo-ku, Sagamihara-shi, Kanagawa, Japan

Abstract. Recent learning sciences have revealed some of the mechanisms of how people learn through interactions in collaborative educational settings. In this research, we tried to capture the nature of constructive interaction by in-depth qualitative analysis of the discourse in a programming learning environment. The analyzed group was comprised of three female students, all in the sixth grade, who engaged in making an animation using Scratch. However, they had trouble with their object modelling during the task. Through their problem-solving procedure, the students attempted externalizations of their solution ideas, and these interactions promoted their understanding of the problem through the iterative process of each individual. Working collaboratively, the three students used various procedures to solve their shared object-modelling problems.

Keywords: Collaborative learning · Programming · Computational thinking K–12 · Constructive interaction

1 Introduction

Computing education with "Computational Thinking" [1] is not only growing as a research field but is also being addressed as a political and common issue all over the world [2]. To develop computing competencies during the early stage of citizens' lives, many countries start compulsory programming education in grades K–12. They have been discussing what should be taught [3, 4] as Computational Thinking at this level for all citizens living in a 21st century knowledge-based society.

There is a consensus between researchers that the movement of computing education is a revival of the 1980s programing education conducted using Logo [5]. The origin of programming education with Logo by Papert, who coined the term "computational thinking" [6], was not primarily intended to develop programming skills but to open a new method of learning mathematics through programming. By preparing situated environments, children could construct their ideas by directly operating them in a situated world [7]. Kay expanded the application of the idea from mathematics to

A. Tatnall and M. Webb (Eds.): WCCE 2017, IFIP AICT 515, pp. 589–598, 2017.
https://doi.org/10.1007/978-3-319-74310-3_59

various other disciplines [8]—he called it "dynamic media"—in which programming is considered basic literacy in a computing society where citizens are using computers as meta media [9]. This dream was inherited to the latest programming environments for kids, Scratch, which is the direct successor of Squeak and Logo.

Many works exploring the effects of programming education with Logo were done by cognitive science researchers in the '80s and '90s. At that time, synonyms for computational thinking included powerful thinking or higher order problem-solving skills, with the key issue being whether programming experiences developed such skills. While we assume "programming" to be a cyclic process comprised of modelling, planning, coding, and the evaluation (debugging) process, it is considered a complex, ill-structured task. As expert programmers can integrate the knowledge of generic algorithm-construction and that of programming language [10], they are assumed to possess high cognitive skills. Actually, they showed a higher level of generic problem-solving skills, such as the decomposition or inferring of problems [11]. Accordingly, programming was expected to develop one's cognitive skills.

Despite the limited numbers, there are a few works that show evidence of developing transferrable competencies through programming. Lawler succeeded in illustrating the development process of a 6-year-old child's cognitive strategy for calculation through Logo programming experiences [12], albeit within the limitations of single-subject research. Clements and Gullo conducted an experimental study between a CAI and a programming group. The results supported that the programming experiences developed students' creative-thinking, reflectivity, and cognitive skills [13].

However, many reports have appeared to show some results that contradict the expectation of programming education. In particular, Pea and Kurland [14, 15] criticized developing transferrable cognitive skills by programming, based on their results. Webb et al. tackled analyzing the problem-solving strategies in a group programming process [16, 17]. Pair of children (aged 11–14) learned programming using BASIC. Although the results were not negative, they did not succeed in finding clear evidence of advancing children's planning skills.

This issue in programming education has been controversial since the 1980s, as discussed above; however, there has been remarkably little research conducted after 2000. Consequently, we remain at the 1980s level of discussion in the cognitive study of programming education, despite the improvement of the programming environment [18] and studies from cognitive science and the "learning sciences".

From these points of view, firstly, we suggest the use of Scratch. Scratch, is a visualized programming environment that is broadly used by practitioners and researchers in programming workshops. Scratch may better enhance students' focus on higher level problem-solving than the text coding. Secondly, we focused on collaborative learning. For this reason, the handbook of collaborative learning was published [19], and PISA started an assessment of collaborative problem solving in 2015 [20]. From the trend of collaborative learning, Constructive Interaction (CI) [21] is a key reason for our choice of a collaborative setting in this study. Not only is the CI analysis method capable of revealing an iterative, progressive problem-solving process, but participants deepened their own understandings when CI occurred in their discussions. Miyake pointed out that CI is well produced if the participants externalize their own understandings and the depths of their understandings differed. In this paper, the key suggestion is that there are levels of understanding, and the difference in these levels helps the participants deepen their understanding.

We intend to contribute to the pursuit of a modern version of Webb's work [16, 17] using the viewpoints of Miyake's work [21]. Webb's paper discussed concerns about familiarity with and the students' typing skills as reasons for why they could not observe quality interactions. Higher-level problem-solving interactions can be expected if we add CI points of view.

Toward the goal of clarifying the mechanism for problem solving in programming, we attempted a qualitative analysis of collaborative programming that enhances the externalization of the participants' different levels of understanding using Scratch.

2 Method

2.1 Programming Workshop

We held a one-day collaborative programming workshop for elementary school students. The participants were 16 sixth-grade students who responded to the request for participation issued at Hamamatsu Elementary School, which is attached to the Faculty of Education, Shizuoka University (8 boys, 8 girls; 4 of the students had no programming experience). We conducted the workshop at the school, on August 9, 2016, using iPads. We installed the app "Pyonkee" on the iPads and distributed one iPad to each student.

Based on constructionism, we designed the workshop so as to encourage students to express their creative ideas in their own ways. We avoided a training design that focuses solely on fostering accurate and impressive coding skills.

To encourage collaborative programming, we asked the students to form teams and to produce a single work from each team. We allowed the students to form their teams themselves. The students formed five three-person, unisex teams.

Table 1 shows the flow of the workshop. We first conducted a preliminary questionnaire survey (four-point scale) to ascertain the students' programming experience, their impressions of programming, and their attitudes toward collaborative learning. Next, each team produced a storyboard design sheet for the program to externalize their work designs, and the teams presented their diagrams to each other. The team members then wrote a program to implement what they envisaged on their team's storyboard design sheet. Finally, the teams presented their programs to each other and completed a feedback questionnaire. The feedback questionnaire was identical in content to the preliminary questionnaire (see Table 1).

We recorded the students' activities in the workshop using a video camera and audio recorder. During the programming process, we projected the screen content of the students' iPads onto a projector using Apple TV and recorded the projected images using a video camera.

Table 1. Timetable of the workshop

Time	Contents
10:00–10:50	Preliminary questionnaire, guidance
11:00–12:00	Drawing storyboard design sheet
13:00–15:15	Programming
15:15–15:45	Presentation
15:45–15:55	Feedback questionnaire

2.2 Programming Environment: Pyonkee

Figure 1 shows Pyonkee's operation screen. It works in almost the same manner as Scratch. Scratch is an environment for object-oriented programming in which users can issue motion instructions to objects (an example of an object is the character at the top right of Fig. 1). Pyonkee allows users to create a range of works, including moving picture shows and shooter games. In Pyonkee, the protagonist and his/her environment (the ground, the sky, etc.) are treated as "objects." Multiple objects can move correspondingly. If we use two objects, they will impact each other using "message-passing." The programs are written by selecting pre-prepared blocks of code and arranging them into as many combinations as desired.

Pyonkee also allows users to create objects as backgrounds (the stage). In Pyonkee, the entire stage is treated as a single object.

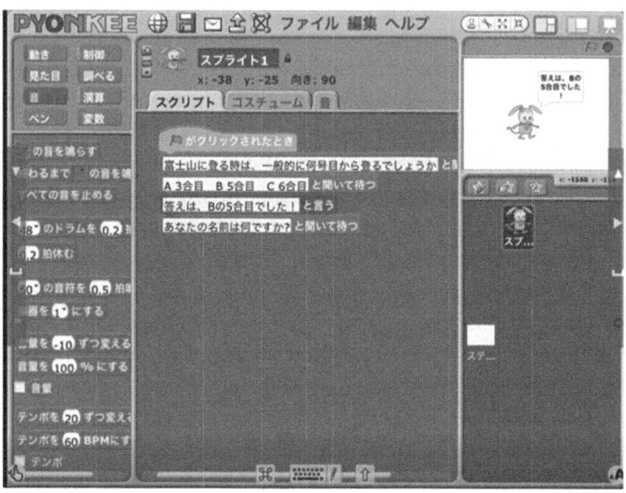

Fig. 1. Pyonkee

2.3 Analytical Sample

Of the children who participated in the workshop, we focused on one of the five groups. There were three girls in this group (X, Y, and Z). In the questionnaires, these three girls exhibited a different trend than those of the other teams. Specifically, the girls' average score for the question, "Does programming feature in your daily life?" improved by 1.5 points in the feedback survey compared to the preliminary survey (change in the overall mean score for this question was 0.2 points).

These girls had participated in a previous programming workshop that we conducted. X conducted most of the programming operations on the iPad without any suggestions from the supervisors or the other girls (Y and Z).

2.4 Analytical Method

To analyze the girls' activity qualitatively, we transcribed their discourse and operations on the iPad. We split the discourse into 236 utterances made by mouth, and we wrote each utterance into lines of the transcript.

The girls' programming progress culminated in the completion of their program according to their storyboard design sheet (see Fig. 2). They told the story of a climbing experience during school camp. The storyboard design sheet comprised three situations: the protagonist started climbing, it started to rain mid-climb, and the protagonist slipped on muddy tracks while climbing.

2.5 Focused Situation

We focused on the third situation (the protagonist slipped) because it required using the message-passing technique to depict the protagonist, rain, and ground simultaneously. The girls took about 40 min to complete their program.

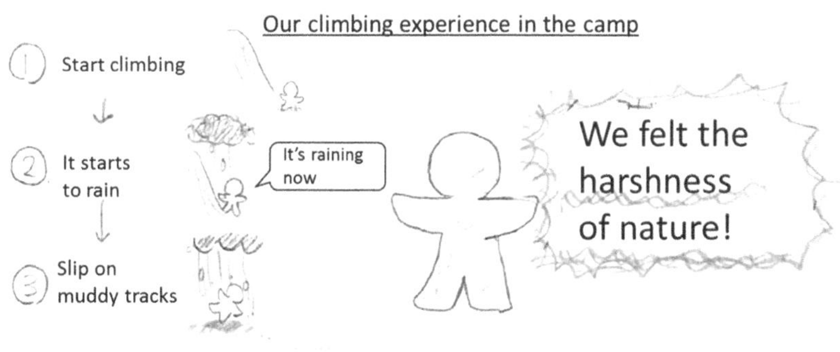

Fig. 2. Storyboard design sheet designed by X, Y and Z

2.6 Levels

We defined "levels" to depict how the girls' programming completion levels raised on the third situation qualitatively. To distinguish each level, we checked the existence of objects, separation between each object, and appropriateness of rotations of each object. Five levels were defined, and a higher number of levels indicate a higher state of program completion. Level 1 showed only the protagonist; Level 2 included all of the objects but not appropriate rotation of the rain and the ground because they were not separated from the protagonist; Level 3 did not include the ground; Level 4 had all of the objects, but the ground was not separated from the protagonist; and Level 5 showed the third situation perfectly.

2.7 Phases

According to time series, we divided the girls' transcript into "phases" to summarize their activities. We separated the phases based on which level was focused on by each girl. We did not consider whether their program had been completed or not because we focused on the girls' viewpoints. The transcript was split into 27 phases.

Table 2. Levels of the girls' programming (✓ means the object exists, +means correct rotation of the object, - means incorrect rotation of the object)

Levels	execution results	protagonist	ground	rain	protagonist	ground	rain
1		✓			+		
2		✓	✓	✓	+	-	-
3		✓		✓	+		+
4		✓	✓	✓	+	-	+
5		✓	✓	✓	+	+	+

3 Results

3.1 Summary

First of all, the girls began trying the command of rotation (see Level 1 in Table 2). Then, they depicted the protagonist, the ground, and the rain, as if these three were one object, and gave commands such as "turn 30 degrees." As a result, they failed to get the protagonist to turn independently from the background (see Level 2 in Table 2). The girls discussed why the protagonist and the ground turned, and eventually they were able to separate the protagonist from the background.

In the activity, the girls showed different trends. X initially remained at Level 1, and then moved between levels 1 and 5. Y was alongside X from Phases 8 to 20. Z mainly focused on Level 5 and did not say much. We will show these trends in Fig. 3.

3.2 Detailed Analysis

Referring to Table 2, we analyzed the utterances and programming actions of X, Y, and Z and plotted the results of this analysis onto a graph (see Fig. 3). We divided the above phases into four scenes according to their activity trends to create an outline. The orange circles in Fig. 3 indicate that programming was executed in that phase.

Scene 1: X struggled by herself (Phases 1–6)

X was separated from Y and Z. Y and Z repeatedly explained the desired program motion (Level 5) as depicted in their storyboard design sheet. X attempted to implement their ideas using Pyonkee. However, she failed to make a complete program for the desired motion, and Y and Z conveyed their opinions.

Scene 2: X and Y shared the problem (Phases 7–12)

X raised an issue with Y in the form of a question, saying "Hey Y? There's something that doesn't work." She then made the following Level 5 utterance: "We should not put the background in when the protagonist is climbing; the background should only be there when the protagonist is slipping" (Phase 9, Level 5). Y responded: "So I guess it should just be the protagonist that moves?" (Phase 10, Level 5). X then restated her utterance, saying, "We should only put the background in here (when the protagonist is slipping)" (Phase 12, Level 5). However, these ideas were not incorporated into the program during this scene.

Meanwhile, Z was focusing more on the background than on the protagonist. She reminded the others about the background, saying, "I want the background to be rain" (Phase 11, Level 3).

Scene 3: X and Y compromised (Phases 13–20)

Despite Z's reminder, X modified the program in such a way that the protagonist alone slipped (no ground). This was not the result that even X intended. Y again pointed out that the execution result differed from the storyboard design sheet. Then, Y joined X in the iPad operation, and they collaborated to erase the ground from the protagonist object (Phases 14–18).

After some discussion between X and Y—with X around Level 2 and Y around Level 5—they edited the program so that the protagonist slipped along the ground in the rain (Level 3). Even though the program was incomplete, X and Y expressed satisfaction with this result to Z, saying, "Not bad, is it?" (Phases 19 and 20).

Scene 4: Clarified the Goal (Phase 21–27)

Z, who was acting as a monitor from Phases 1 to 21, pointed out that there was still a discrepancy between the program and the storyboard design sheet: "When the protagonist slips, there needs to be ground there; without any ground, I cannot understand that the protagonist has slipped on a muddy track!" In response, X drew ground beneath the protagonist, but the ground also turned along with the protagonist. Y disagreed with the results because the ground should be flat. In an attempt to correct this fault, X erased the ground beneath the protagonist. Then, Z intervened again, saying "Now there's no ground… you got rid of the ground? Why did you do that?" In response, X drew the ground as a background, which means the protagonist was separated from the ground. Consequently, they completed a program that matched their storyboard design sheet.

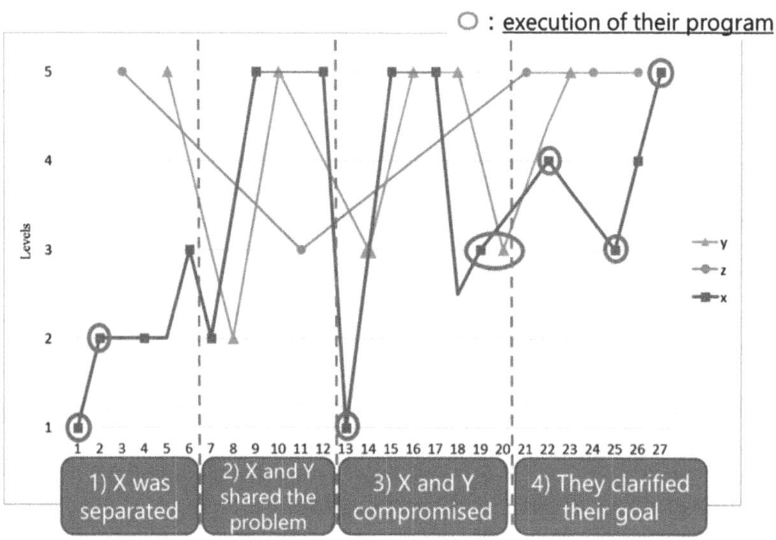

Fig. 3. Levels of the girls' viewpoints in each phase

4 Discussion

In conclusion, CI was observed because the completeness of the program was eventually getting higher through the discussion between the task-doer (X) and the monitors (Y, Z). The girls gradually noticed their problems by observing the execution results, solved their problems by discussing them with each other, and eventually raised the program's completion level. These problems were not identified by the task-doer (X) but by the monitors (Y and Z).

As we showed in the example of the discussion, collaborative programming is effective in avoiding the downsizing of goals to match what the learners can do. A statement such as, "There we are. I think it's complete now," which we observed in the third scene, is far from rare in a Constructionism-based workshop. In that case, collaborators (often monitors) deny downsizing because the monitor still strives to complete the program as planned. The monitor then contributes to raising their program's completion level.

Programming has the potential to foster in children a tenacious learning attitude. However, such a learning attitude would never take root if the learner gives up, as in the above example, and sets their sights on a lower goal. From that point of view, collaborative programming has the potential to elevate the activity of programming and to foster children's creativity. Based on this perspective, the process analysis that we conducted in this study might serve as a measure for assessing children's collaborative programming processes.

5 Conclusion and Future Directions

According to our analysis, it is possible to identify the challenges and difficulties children face in programming. The girls encountered difficulties even though they were only distinguishing (not coding) the objects in our analysis. Furthermore, even after separating the ground and rain from the protagonist, the girls still had to undergo a number of trial-and-error iterations. We think that the reason that the girls raised their completion level of their program is that they continued their endeavor from the viewpoint of asking, "Why has it gone wrong?"

In the example, there were a number of problems that needed to be resolved in order to complete the program. Most often, the person who identified these problems was not the one who engaged directly in the problem-solving operations (who in this case was X), but it was rather the person who closely observed the problem-solver's work (in this case, Y and Z). According to Shirouzu et al. [22], monitors are better at observing the task objectively than is a task-doer. Kent argued that pair programming improves productivity [23]. This is probably because the strategy of having a task-doer and monitor exchange opinions from their respective positions works effectively.

As the mechanism of CI, a single person notices ambiguous points in his/her thinking when another person asks questions. These questions encourage the task-doer to reconsider the matter in order to resolve such ambiguity, and it encourages him or her to achieve a deeper understanding. In a sense, programming has the potential to enhance the mechanism of CI because it requires the externalization of one's thinking.

A limitation of this study is that the analysis focused only on one team. In the future, we intend to create an assessment method for evaluating teams that produce different kinds of work and to use this method for evaluating the workshop.

Acknowledgments. This study received funding from Shizuoka University's Takayanagi Memorial Future Technology Creation Fund and a JSPS Grant-in-Aid for Scientific Research (KAKENHI; No. 26280129, 17K17786). In addition, we were able to implement the study owing to the support of Koji Tominaga, a teacher at Hamamatsu Elementary School, attached to the Faculty of Education, Shizuoka University. We would like to express our sincere appreciation to him.

References

1. Wing, J.: Computational thinking and thinking about computing. Philos. Trans. Roy. Soc. A **366**, 3717–3725 (2008)
2. Bocconi, S., Chioccariello, A., Dettori, G., Ferrari, A., Engelhardt, K.: Developing computational thinking in compulsory education-implications for policy and practice (No. JRC104188). Joint Research Centre (Seville site) (2016)
3. Lye, S., Koh, J.: Review on teaching and learning of computational thinking through programming: what is next for K-12? Comput. Hum. Behav. **41**, 51–61 (2014)
4. Barr, V., Stephenson, C.: Bringing computational thinking to K-12: what is involved and what is the role of the computer science education community? ACM Inroads **2**(1), 48–54 (2011)
5. Tedre, M., Denning, P.: The long quest for computational thinking. In: Proceedings of the 16th Koli Calling Conference on Computing Education Research, pp. 120–129 (2016)
6. Papert, S.: Mindstorms: Children, Computers, and Powerful Ideas. Basic Books, New York (1980)
7. Papert, S.: Situating Constructionism. In: Harel, I., Papert, S. (ed.) Construtionism, pp. 1–12 (1991)
8. Papert, S.: Perestroika and epistemological politics. In: Harel, I., Papert, S. (eds.) Construtionism, pp. 13–28 (1991)
9. Kay, A., Goldberg, A.: Personal dynamic media. Computer **10**(3), 31–41 (1977)
10. Nickerson, R.S.: Computer programming as a vehicle for teaching thinking skills. Think. J. Philos. Child. **4**, 42–48 (1982)
11. Hayes-Roth, B., Hayes-Roth, F.A.: A cognitive model of planning. Cogn. Sci. **3**, 275–310 (1979)
12. Lawler, R.W.: The progressive construction of mind. Cogn. Sci. **5**, 1–30 (1981)
13. Clements, D.H., Gullo, D.F.: Effects of computer programming on young children's cognition. J. Educ. Psychol. **76**(6), 1051–1058 (1984)
14. Pea, R.: Logo programming and problem solving. Paper Presented at Symposium of American Educational Research Association (1983)
15. Pea, R., Kurland, D.: On the cognitive effects of learning computer programming. New Ideas Psychol. **2**(2), 137–168 (1984)
16. Webb, N.M.: Microcomputer learning in small groups: cognitive requirements and group processes. J. Educ. Psychol. **76**, 1076–1088 (1984)
17. Webb, N.M., Ender, P., Lewis, S.: Problem-solving strategies and group processes in small groups learning computer programming. Am. Educ. Res. J. **23**(2), 243–261 (1986)
18. Brennen, K., Resnick, M.: New frameworks for studying and assessing the development of computational thinking. In: Annual Meeting of the American Educational Research Association (2012)
19. Hmelo-Silver, C.E., Chinn, C.A., Chan, C.K.K., O'donnell, A., (eds.): The International Handbook of Collaborative Learning. Routledge, New York (2013)
20. OECD: PISA 2015 Collaborative Problem Solving Framework. OECD Publishing (2013)
21. Miyake, N.: Constructive interaction and the iterative process of understanding. Cogn. Sci. **10**(2), 151–177 (1986)
22. Shirouzu, H., Miyake, N., Masukawa, H.: Cognitively active externalization for situated reflection. Cogn. Sci. **26**(4), 469–501 (2002)
23. Beck, K., Andres, C.: Extreme Programming Explained: Embrace Change, 2nd edn. Addison-Wesley Professional, Boston (2004)

A Software Development Process for Freshman Undergraduate Students

Catherine Higgins(✉), Fredrick Mtenzi, Ciaran O'Leary, Orla Hanratty, and Claire McAvinia

Dublin Institute of Technology, Aungier St., Dublin 2, Ireland
{catherine.higgins, fredrick.mtenzi, ciaran.oleary, orla.hanratty, claire.mcavinia}@dit.ie

Abstract. This conceptual paper presents work which is part of an ongoing research project into the design of a software development process aimed at freshman, undergraduate computing students. The process of how to plan and develop a solution is a topic that is addressed very lightly in many freshman, undergraduate courses which can leave novices open to developing habit-forming, maladaptive cognitive practices. The conceptual software development process described in this paper has a learning process at its core which centres on declarative knowledge (in the form of threshold concepts) and procedural knowledge (in the form of computational thinking skills) scaffolding freshman software development from initial planning through to final solution. The process - known as Computational Analysis and Design Engineered Thinking (CADET) - aims to support the structured development of both software and student self-efficacy.

Keywords: Introductory software development process
Computational thinking · Threshold concepts

1 Introduction

A software development process is a mechanism which informs a software developer of the steps and stages involved in developing quality software from initial analysis to final design and implementation [1]. Even though there are many software development processes available for experienced developers, very little work has been carried out on developing appropriate processes for freshman, 3rd level learners [2]. This lack of appropriate software development processes presents a vacuum for educators which means that software analysis and design is typically taught very informally and implicitly on introductory courses at 3rd level with an emphasis instead on teaching a programming language [3–6]. Unless they are guided to do otherwise, novices will often jump straight into implementing some aspect of a solution without any planning because they can find it difficult to separate ideas for solutions from the implementation of those ideas [7, 8]. This can lead to novices adopting maladaptive cognitive practices in software development, particularly surface practices (e.g. coding by rote learning)

A. Tatnall and M. Webb (Eds.): WCCE 2017, IFIP AICT 515, pp. 599–608, 2017.
https://doi.org/10.1007/978-3-319-74310-3_60

which can be very difficult to unlearn and can ultimately prohibit student progression in the acquisition of software development skills [9]. It has also been found that problems in designing software solutions can persist even to graduation [10]. Therefore, it follows that if a software development process is incorporated explicitly in an appropriate way into introductory courses to scaffold students in software development, this could limit the development of such maladaptive practices.

This paper describes a conceptual and dynamic software development process which has been devised for undergraduate freshman learners. Section 2 describes related research while Sect. 3 gives a short overview of the framework on which the process is based. Section 4 describes the factors that guided the operationalision of the framework into a software development process. Section 5 describes the process and Sect. 6 concludes the paper with a discussion of the contribution this paper makes to software engineering educational research.

2 Related Research

There has been a wealth of research over many decades into software development education within the context of improving retention and development proficiency at 3rd level. Research has focused on many areas such as reviewing the choice of programming languages and paradigms suitable for novice learners with a wide variety of languages suggested from commercial, textual languages through to visual block-based languages [11]; the development of visualisation tools to create a diagrammatic overview of the notional machine as a user traces through programs and algorithms [12, 13]; and the use of game based learning as a basis for learning programming and game construction [14, 15].

Research that specifically looks at software development processes for introductory courses at 3rd level have a tendency to focus attention on a particular stage of the development process. Examples are the STREAM process [2] which focuses on design in an object oriented environment; the P^3F framework [16] with a focus on software design and arming novice designers with expert strategies; a programming process by Hu et al. [17] which focuses on generating goals and plans and converting those into a coded solution via a visual block-based programming language; POPT [18] which has a focus on supporting software testing; and Morgado and Barbosa's process [19] which aims to support students from problem presentation to the development of a solution though the use of template forms coupled with an instructor supplied prototype. The process described in this paper is similar to Morgado and Barboso's process in that it aims to support all stages of developing software but the focus here is based on the provision of a process that can grow with students' experience. The process is not tied to any particular programming paradigm but its use is assumed to be in the context of imperative, commercial programming languages which are commonly taught at 3rd level [20].

3 Computational Analysis and Design Engineered Thinking (CADET) Framework

Prior to the development of a software development process, it was important to formulate a framework on which the process will be based. The role of this framework is to guide the context and content of the resulting software development process. The first issue that required attention was in understanding the context in which the software development process would be used. This is an environment where freshman undergraduate students typically have little or no programming experience and are learning how to develop software solutions in a systematic fashion. This brought up an interesting question – should students be taught how to program first and then be introduced to a software development process or should programming concepts and skills be taught as part of a process? This research takes the latter view as teaching students how to program independently of process runs the risk of students developing poor development habits that become ingrained by the time they learn a process. Therefore, the software development process is scaffolded so that it inherently encompasses a learning process which can slowly fade as students gain expertise of developmental concepts, practices and grow their self-efficacy. The relationship between learning process and software development process is visualised in Fig. 1 where the 4 stages of competence model [21] is used to timeline the progression of learning.

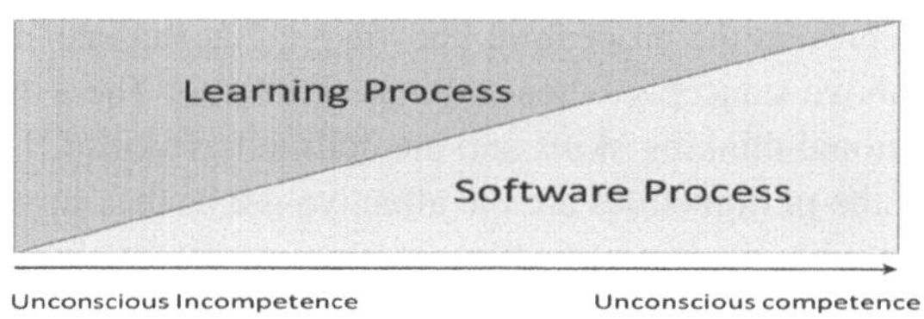

Fig. 1. From learning process to software development process (Source: Author)

Initially, the learner is categorised as an unconscious incompetent who doesn't know what they need to know so the software development process is heavily scaffolded as a learning process where students are guided to use the software development process to solve a suite of problems that are appropriate to each stage of their learning. By the time the user has gained experience of the foundational developmental concepts and practices, the scaffolding of the learning process will be removed to allow the learner continue to use the software development process in solving new and more complex problems as they expand their learning and continue their journey towards becoming unconscious competents.

Once the context of the environment was understood, a conceptual framework was devised and developed in order to fully identify the components and activities in the learning process. The full details of the background, rationale for - and development of - the framework can be found in reference [22]. A diagrammatic overview of the framework is given in Fig. 2.

Concepts (threshold stages)	Practices (CT skills)	Perspectives (affective issues)
TC1. State and Sequential Flow TC2. Non-Sequential Flow Control TC3. Modularity TC4. Object Behaviour	CT1. Abstraction CT2. Data Representation CT3. Decomposition CT4. Evaluation of solutions (Testing, Debugging, Critiquing) CT5. Pattern recognition CT6. Generating Algorithms (modelling and simulation)	AI1. Self-Efficacy

Fig. 2. The CADET framework (Source: Author)

In summary, the **concepts** represent the declarative knowledge that students need in order to be able to understand and use programming constructs. These concepts are categorised as four threshold concepts stages [18]. *TC1 State and Sequential Flow* involves gaining an understanding of "simple" data items (e.g. characters, numbers and strings) and how their state changes when sequential actions are carried out on them. *TC2 Non-sequential Flow Control* keeps the focus on state but adds complexity to this idea by presenting more complex actions such as iteration and how these actions affect state and flow control. *TC3 Modularity* introduces modularity and how that affects state and especially flow control. Finally, *TC4 Object Behaviour* - which is optional and is only used in an object-oriented environment - examines the idea of objects and the connection between state and behaviour and how objects interact and activate each other's behaviour.

The **practices** represent the procedural knowledge that students need in order to be able to apply the above concepts when solving problems. These practices are categorised as computational thinking skills and are codified as skills CT1–CT6 in column 2 of Fig. 2. Finally, the **perspectives** are the affective issues that impact learning which are considered to be embodied in self-efficacy.

This framework marries current research into threshold concepts, computational thinking and affective learning to produce a framework that supports declarative knowledge (threshold concepts), procedural knowledge (computational thinking) and affective learning issues [18]. Learning these knowledge areas is facilitated by instruction and by repeatedly solving problems using Pólya's problem solving model [23] which has been adapted to suit the context of this research [18]. The framework (and subsequent process) is known as computational analysis and design engineered thinking (CADET).

4 Operationalisation of Framework to Process

As part of the operationalisation and development of the framework into a software development process, current best practice in both the teaching of software development and in software development processes for professional developers is considered for inclusion into the process.

4.1 Best Practice in Teaching Software Development

There are two basic approaches to teaching software development – top-down and bottom up. The top-down stepwise refinement approach originated in the 1970s by Wirth [24] and involves breaking down a problem into a series of levels with tasks. One advantage of the top-down approach is that a high-level overview of the solution is first constructed which can then be slowly broken down into its constituent parts. However, critics of top-down design state that it involves creating a monolithic design where coding cannot begin until the design is fully complete [25]. The bottom-up approach starts from a finely granulated specification of the problem which is generated by identifying and implementing the smallest tasks. These tasks are then combined to form larger tasks with this successive amalgamation of smaller tasks into larger tasks continuing until the entire solution is implemented. A very high level view of the solution is not available at the start of the process which can prove problematic for novices who typically find it difficult to reassemble tasks back into a full solution [26].

In comparing expert developers to novices, experts have a breadth first, top down approach to formulating solutions whereas novices tend to have a depth first, bottom up approach where they focus on specific aspects of the problem [26, 27]. However, as noted above, novices can then find it difficult to re-integrate the different parts of the problem into a final solution and may revert to trial and error approaches to find something that works [26]. On the other hand, experts use strategies based on their experience to avoid trial and error [16] which suggests that novices need to be supplied with scaffolded strategies to help them problem solve as they gain experience.

This research suggests a hybrid approach - between top down and bottom up development - as an attempt to keep novices focused on the big picture while allowing them to use a depth first approach. This approach has been coined by this researcher as a "*design down, code up*" approach where solutions are visually designed by students in a scaffolded, top down fashion; code is produced for low level designs which gives feedback to the students who are then supported in combining these tasks to effectively code up to a final solution.

In the context of applying an appropriate learning theory, research into computer science education has several successes using constructivist and constructionist theory [28–30]. Social constructivism occurs when learning is perceived as an active process and where individual knowledge is constructed through solving problems in a collaborative exercise. This theory forms the basis of the development process described in this paper as the students will carry out extensive problem solving to construct their own individual knowledge and will engage in Vygotsky's theory of the "more able other" [31] by participating in paired development and in articulating solutions to the class cohort. Therefore, the learning process for this software development process has been designed with the aim of facilitating constructivist learning.

4.2 Best Practice in Software Development Processes

As well as ensuring that best practice in the teaching of software development is incorporated into the software development process described in this paper, it is also important to consider and include current best practice in existing software development processes. One way of incorporating best practice is to align this process with the philosophy of verifiably successful software development processes. Given that most modern software development projects use Agile processes [32], this is the category of process chosen to represent best practice. Kastl et al. [33] has demonstrated how the philosophy and general characteristics of Agile processes can be adapted as a guide for best practice. This means that the core characteristics that govern all Agile processes will be used to guide the operation of this process. These characteristics include the use of iterative and incremental development, adaptive modelling, refactoring of development artefacts and paired programming.

5 Computational Analysis and Design Engineered Thinking (CADET) Software Development Process

The software development process operates as a 4 stage problem solving model based on an adapted version of Pólya's model as described in the CADET framework [22]. The four stages of the model are *1. Understand the problem, 2. Break into tasks, 3. Design and Code, 4. Evaluate solution and learning*. During the learning process stage, learners will work in pairs and will be taught the threshold concept stages which make up the declarative knowledge. This learning aspect of the software development process is represented as a ladder of learning where each concept is ordered and is a prerequisite to learning the next concept. Each concept is taught via instruction and the computational thinking skills required to ustilise the concept are acquired by solving a suite of problems using the 4 stage adapted problem solving model which is supported by an Agile philosophy. Each stage of the problem solving model will use a subset of computational thinking skills. The process is summerised in Fig. 3.

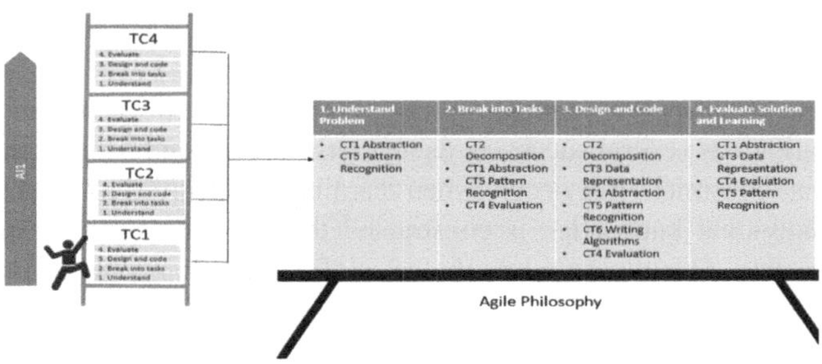

Fig. 3. CADET software development process (Source: Author)

When all 4 threshold concept stages have been taught and practiced, students will continue to use the 4 stage problem solving model with associated computational thinking practices as the basis for the software development process. The software development process is augmented by a support tool which will provide a platform to provide learners with problems to solve as well as diagrammatic tools to support their analysis, design and reflective work. While it is expected that student's self-efficacy will grow and wane as they attempt to solve problems, it is hoped that the scaffolded environment based on social constructivist learning will allow the student's self-efficacy to generally grow in tandem with their knowledge (identified as A1 in the vertical arrow beside the ladder of learning in Fig. 3). This will be measured by student reflection. Each of the 4 stages of the problem solving model are now described in more detail.

1. *Understand the problem* - Using the support tool, learners will be invited to articulate their understanding of either a problem that they have provided or a problem that is provided to them as part of the learning process stage. This articulation of understanding is achieved by employing the computational thinking skills of *functional abstraction* to generate a high-level summary of the problem and *pattern recognition* to see if the problem is similar to any previous problems that the learner may have solved. This high level summary is recorded in the support tool.
2. *Break into tasks* - This stage employs *decomposition* to convert the high-level summary and specification from stage 1 into an intermediate set of constituent tasks and to further refine those tasks into more basic tasks if required. In order to make this stage visual, the tool supports students brainstorming candidate tasks using a mind map where their problem summary is the central task. Mind mapping has been shown to be successful in helping learners to brainstorm and specifically in analysing software solutions [34]. The map will be refined into ordered tasks and subtasks. The support tool will facilitate leaners to utilise *abstraction* to visually trace backwards and forwards from the high-level summary from stage 1 into this stage to ensure consistency between the stages. *Pattern recognition* will be employed by learners to identify any tasks that have been used in previous problems and colour coding will be employed to identify any complex tasks that need to be designed.
3. *Design and Code* - This stage employs *decomposition* to take a task and generate an algorithm represented as a flow chart (or optionally a class diagram if operating in an object oriented paradigm) for the task. This stage also involves *data representation* and *algorithm writing* to represent the computational steps needed to represent a task solution as a flowchart with a level of detail to make it easy for the task to be converted into program code. All tasks will be designed, coded and evaluated in an iterative manner until correct and then reintegrated into a growing final product. The support tool will facilitate leaners to visually utilise *abstraction* to oscillate between tasks identified in the mind map and any associated designs and code to ensure consistent mapping between stages.
4. *Evaluate Solution and Learning* - This stage allows learners to reflect on their solution from start to finish and employ abstraction to zoom in and out of the solution to understand it at the various functional and data abstraction levels. The support tool will prompt learners to employ critiquing mechanisms to see if any aspect of the solution could have benefited from using analysis, design or coding artefacts from previous problems or if the solution can be optimized by identifying any duplication. Learners will be required to reflect on and articulate their learning.

When the process is being employed solely as a software development process, learners will be able to use both the process and associated support tool by providing their own specification for a problem and working through each of the above stages to systematically develop their final solution.

6 Discussion

Despite the acknowledged importance of using software development processes both in the software industry and in education, this research has identified a gap in software engineering education in the provision of appropriate software development processes for freshman, undergraduate computing students in a context where learners predominately have no prior programming experience. One reason for this gap is due to the problematic nature of teaching software processes to novices. A software development process gives guidance to developers in the development of software solutions from analysis through to final product but for commercial processes, it is assumed that the developer has pre-existing programming knowledge. This makes the use of such processes difficult for educators of introductory software development courses and produces a conundrum in how to support students in the use of development processes in the absence of programming knowledge. In such an environment, it is natural that the focus of such courses will gravitate towards the teaching of programming concepts first with the topic of development process coming later in the course or in later years. The problem with such a strategy is that it allows students to potentially develop maladaptive cognitive practices which can prohibit student progression in such courses.

This paper aims to contribute to this gap by presenting a conceptual software development process which utilities the affordances of computational thinking to create a software development process that encompasses a learning process. The process combines current research into computational thinking as a problem solving process underpinned by the focus of threshold concepts and an Agile philosophy to support students learning how to develop software solutions from problem specification through to the final tested product. The aim of the process is to provide scaffolding to students as they learn how to develop software in a systematic fashion. It is the contention of this research that the provision of such a process could provide a structured and scaffolded environment to directly address the maladaptive cognitive habits that students often form and find hard to unlearn. The next stage of this research will involve the development of a support tool and the deployment and evaluation of the software development process.

References

1. Boehm, B.: A view of 20th and 21st century software engineering. In: Proceedings of the 28th International Conference on Software Engineering. ACM (2006)
2. Caspersen, M.E., Kolling, M.: STREAM: a first programming process. Trans. Comput. Educ. **9**(1), 1–29 (2009)

3. Kazimoglu, C., Kiernan, M., Bacon, L., MacKinnon, L.: Developing a game model for computational thinking and learning traditional programming through game-play. In: Sanchez, J., Zhang, K. (eds.), pp. 1378–1386. AACE, Chesapeake (2010)
4. Liu, C.-C., Cheng, Y.-B., Huang, C.-W.: The effect of simulation games on the learning of computational problem solving. Comput. Educ. **57**(3), 1907–1918 (2011)
5. Suo, X.: Toward more effective strategies in teaching programming for novice students. In: 2012 IEEE International Conference on Teaching, Assessment and Learning for Engineering (TALE), p. T2A-1 (2012)
6. Coffey, J.W.: Relationship between design and programming skills in an advanced computer programming class. J. Comput. Sci. Coll. **30**(5), 39–45 (2015)
7. Kokotovich, V.: Problem analysis and thinking tools: an empirical study of non-hierarchical mind mapping. Des. Stud. **29**(1), 49–69 (2008)
8. Fornaro, R.J., Heil, M.R., Tharp, A.L.: What clients want - what students do: reflections on ten years of sponsored senior design projects. In: 19th Conference on Software Engineering Education and Training (CSEET 2006), pp. 226–236 (2006)
9. Huang, T.-C., Shu, Y., Chen, C.-C., Chen, M.-Y.: The development of an innovative programming teaching framework for modifying students' maladaptive learning pattern. Int. J. Inf. Educ. Technol. **3**(6), 591 (2013)
10. Loftus, C., Thomas, L., Zander, C.: Can graduating students design: revisited. In: Proceedings of the 42nd ACM Technical Symposium on Computer Science Education. ACM, Dallas (2011)
11. Pears, A., Seidman, S., Malmi, L., Mannila, L., Adams, E., Bennedsen, J., Devlin, M., Paterson, J.: A survey of literature on the teaching of introductory programming. ACM SIGCSE Bull. **39**(2), 19 (2007)
12. Guo, P.J.: Online python tutor: embeddable web-based program visualization for cs education. In: Proceeding of the 44th ACM Technical Symposium on Computer Science Education. ACM (2013)
13. Gautier, M., Wrobel-Dautcourt, B.: artEoz-dynamic program visualization. In: ISSEP 2016, p. 70 (2016)
14. Mozelius, P., Shabalina, O., Malliarakis, C., Tomos, F., Miller, C., Turner, D.: Let the students contruct their own fun and knowledge-learning to program by building computer games. In: European Conference on Games Based Learning. Academic Conferences International Limited (2013)
15. Trevathan, M., Peters, M., Willis, J., Sansing, L.: Serious games classroom implementation: teacher perspectives and student learning outcomes. In: Society for Information Technology and Teacher Education International Conference (2016)
16. Wright, D.R.: Inoculating novice software designers with expert design strategies. In: Proceedings of the American Society for Engineering Education. American Society for Engineering Education (2012)
17. Hu, M., Winikoff, M., Cranefield, S.: A process for novice programming using goals and plans. In: Proceedings of the Fifteenth Australasian Computing Education Conference, vol. 136. Australian Computer Society, Inc., Adelaide (2013)
18. Neto, V.L., Coelho, R., Leite, L., Guerrero, D.S., Mendon, A.P.: POPT: a problem-oriented programming and testing approach for novice students. In: Proceedings of the 2013 International Conference on Software Engineering. IEEE Press, San Francisco (2013)
19. Morgado, C., Barbosa, F.: A structured approach to problem solving in CS1. In: Proceedings of the 17th ACM Annual Conference on Innovation and Technology in Computer Science Education. ACM, Haifa (2012)
20. Siegfried, R.M., Greco, D., Miceli, N., Siegfried, J.: Whatever happened to Richard Reid's list of first programming languages? J. Inf. Syst. Educ. **10**(4), 7 (2012)

21. Maslow, A.H., Frager, R., Fadiman, J., McReynolds, C., Cox, R.: Motivation and Personality, vol. 2. Harper & Row, New York (1970)
22. Higgins, C., Mtenzi, F., O'Leary, C., Hanratty, O., McAvinia, C.: A conceptual framework for a software development process based on computational thinking. In: 11th International Technology, Education and Development Conference, Valencia, Spain (2017, in Print)
23. Polya, G.: How To Solve It, 2nd edn. Princeton University Press, Princeton (1957)
24. Wirth, N.: Program development by stepwise refinement. Commun. ACM **14**(4), 221–227 (1971)
25. Pizka, M., Bauer, A.: A brief top-down and bottom-up philosophy on software evolution. In: 2004 Proceedings of the 7th International Workshop on Principles of Software Evolution. IEEE (2004)
26. Liikkanen, L.A., Perttula, M.: Exploring problem decomposition in conceptual design among novice designers. Des. Stud. **30**(1), 38–59 (2009)
27. Robins, A., Rountree, J., Rountree, N.: Learning and teaching programming: a review and discussion. Comput. Sci. Educ. **13**(2), 137–172 (2003)
28. Abelson, H., DiSessa, A.A.: Turtle Geometry: The Computer as a Medium for Exploring Mathematics. MIT press, Cambridge (1986)
29. Resnick, M., Maloney, J., Monroy-Hernandez, A., Rusk, N., Eastmond, E., Brennan, K., Millner, A., Rosenbaum, E., Silver, J., Silverman, B., Kafai, Y.: Scratch: programming for all. Commun. ACM **52**(11), 60–67 (2009)
30. Thevathayan, C., Hamilton, M.: Supporting diverse novice programming cohorts through flexible and incremental visual constructivist pathways. In: Proceedings of the 2015 ACM Conference on Innovation and Technology in Computer Science Education. ACM (2015)
31. Vygotsky, L.: Interaction between learning and development. Read. Dev. Child. **23**(3), 34–41 (1978)
32. Bustard, D., Wilkie, G., Greer, D.: The maturation of agile software development principles and practice: observations on successive industrial studies in 2010 and 2012. In: 2013 20th IEEE International Conference and Workshops on the Engineering of Computer Based Systems (ECBS). IEEE (2013)
33. Kastl, P., Kiesmüller, U., Romeike, R.: Starting out with projects: experiences with agile software development in high schools. In: Proceedings of the 11th Workshop in Primary and Secondary Computing Education. ACM (2016)
34. Li, C.L., Yang, L.P., Wang, W.: Application of mind mapping to improve the teaching effect of Java program design course. In: Computing, Control, Information and Education Engineering: Proceedings of the 2015 Second International Conference on Computer, Intelligent and Education Technology (CICET 2015), 11–12 April 2015, Guilin, PR China. CRC Press (2015)

Agile Development in Software Engineering Instruction

Jaana Holvikivi(✉) and Peter Hjort

Metropolia University of Applied Sciences, Helsinki, Finland
{jaana.holvikivi,peter.hjort}@metropolia.fi

Abstract. Agile methods are replacing former, highly systematic project management practices in software development. Many studies have shown that agile methods are already mainstream in the software industry. Academia has incorporated these changes in development practices into education rather reluctantly. Much of higher education still depends on very traditional teaching practices and conventional curricula. In this paper, we describe a series of efforts to bring the agile world fully to ICT education, and discuss results for students and teachers alike. Agile methods can be taught, and moreover, they can also be part of the teaching toolkit. Teachers of agile courses face certain personality requirements: they need to be able to tolerate uncertainty and to be professionally proficient because of demands for flexibility and quick adjustment. The results of using agile methods as course structure, as well as agile planning of course content in small instructor teams have been successful.

Keywords: Agile methods · ICT education · Collaboration practices
Project based learning · Scrum

1 Introduction

Agile software development has replaced former, highly systematic project management practices in many areas of the software industry. Many studies have shown that agile methods are already mainstream in the industry [1, 2]. However, the incorporation of the tremendous changes to development practices have entered academic education rather slowly. Much of higher education still depends on very traditional teaching practices and conventional curricula. First efforts to include agile methods to higher education were made more than a decade ago [3], and currently, courses on agile development are widely offered as part of software engineering curricula [4–6]. However, actual use of agile methods as educational practices is less common but a widespread use is probably on the brink of breakthrough [7]. Agile development can be applied in many kinds of project-based learning courses by replacing traditional project management with flexible practices and by replacing formal meetings with scrum meetings [8].

Collaborative problem solving and project-based learning are considered central methods to educate present day engineering students, because they simulate challenges that the students will face in professional work, such as open ended assignments,

A. Tatnall and M. Webb (Eds.): WCCE 2017, IFIP AICT 515, pp. 609–618, 2017.
https://doi.org/10.1007/978-3-319-74310-3_61

uncertainty and coordination of collaborative efforts [9]. Numerous implementations of project-based learning have been reported in various countries in recent years [10–12].

Currently, education at the Metropolia University of Applied Sciences in Helsinki aims at developing the knowledge, skills, ethics, communication, and emotional components of the professional expertise required to meet the need for highly integrated competence in present day working environments. Dialogue with companies has revealed that ICT education had failed to fully respond to the new requirements in the software industry [13]. Demands from companies increasingly stress capabilities for collaboration, efficient team work and professional communication. Therefore, a curriculum reform was implemented in 2014. Project-based methods were included into most modules in the new curriculum. Additionally, the concepts of progressive inquiry [14] and problem-based learning were applied in course design. The aim was to change the studies in a way that makes entering the information technology profession a natural and exciting process regardless of student background.

In this paper, we describe a series of efforts to bring the agile world fully to the education, and discuss the results in culturally diverse groups. First, we explain trials of new practices, and then how they were extended to the entire software engineering curriculum. We discuss the results based on large amount of feedback and interview data among students and teaching staff.

2 Background

2.1 A Preliminary Case: Swengi - A New Interface for a Mobile Version of a Daily Newspaper

The initial trial was organized as a simulated work placement for a group of students. A large Finnish newspaper wanted to attract young audiences to their tablet version. The development of tablet and mobile versions of the newspaper had thus far been centered around iPhone and iPad versions, which were quite popular. However, the paper was mainly read by middle-aged and older, well-educated urban citizens. As the use of Android devices is more common among the younger target audience, they were assumed to need a specifically designed user interface. The client was looking for fresh ideas for the user interface, and how to customize the offer of content especially for students. The task was organized as an experimental project, no monetary transactions were involved, and no functional product was expected.

The work was organized as an agile project, which emulated real workplace conditions. 14 students participated by working full time as interns in a designated office space inside the school building during three months. The project group held regular scrum meetings every morning where teachers participated as needed. In a scrum meeting, all participants stand up and explain briefly what they have done since the last meeting, what they intend to do next, and what kinds of problems they face. The students were requested to create user studies in an early phase of the project and after the first prototype was completed.

The idea was to offer a working life experience that teaches project management and team working skills in a simulated workplace setting, in addition to technical skills.

Moreover, students started understanding what making a commercial product entails, and how user needs are incorporated in design. The scrum development project was a new method for the participants. In the beginning, the group held scrum meetings every day in the morning. Teachers were involved in the beginning to show the method, set up time sheets for work, and comment on student achievements and plans. Three weeks later, teachers let the team divide into technical and user interface groups that were self-regulating. Students were allowed to decide how often they need scrum meetings, and stopped holding them daily. Soon they noticed that having fewer meetings did not facilitate the process. A similar result has been detected with other inexperienced developer teams [15].

The main result was a prototype of the application. Its design went through a couple of changes based on the reassessment by the team and client comments. In fact, the final design was unconventional enough to surprise the client. Later, some of those ideas were even implemented in the actual product.

Student self-evaluation was done continuously in scrum-meetings. Very soon it turned out that students reported rather mechanically their progress but actual self-reflection was superficial. This finding is not surprising in the light of our current university procedures where self-reflection is not systematically required or practiced. Another finding was the lack of detail in reflection and reporting. These are typical shortcomings in a technical university. They need to be addressed in curriculum development, so that self-evaluation becomes an inherent part of the study process [16].

In the closing session of the project, students were asked to answer the question "What did I learn?" The answers included many technical skills, such as Android, cursor control, and JSON. Most importantly, team work skills were seen as a major result of the internship. Students also noted their improvement in multicultural skills as the team consisted of Indian, Nepalese, Italian, Finnish, Pakistani and Vietnamese students. Additionally, they mentioned communication skills, scrum and project skills, presentation skills and English, and finally, stress management. What was not mentioned in student answers but could be observed by the teachers, was enhanced user experience understanding, user research methods, and actual design skills. Interestingly, they went unnoticed by students, even though the user survey that they conducted as well as user observations had a strong impact on the final solution. Probably this happened because the setup of the project was product-centered, which directed the concentration towards technology.

2.2 Students

The student groups in the international undergraduate information technology degree programme at the Metropolia University of Applied Sciences consist of 48–60 engineering students from a variety of nationalities, the majority of students in recent years being young Asian men from Vietnam and Nepal, but including a varied mix of other nationalities as well, particularly from Eastern Europe. In the first year, international students study separately from Finnish students, but in the second year, they begin to study together with Finnish nationals. The students are divided into smaller study groups (30–40 students) according to their major, which usually has for each study module five teachers from different professional disciplines such as mathematics, software, media engineering, and communication skills. Even though the majority of students come from a high school or secondary school background, some of them also have previous university studies in their own country. One of the main problems with international study groups has been the slow integration to the university environment and adoption of appropriate study habits [16]. It was anticipated that participation in team work and projects would bring them closer and create a cohesive study community [17].

2.3 Curriculum Reform and Agile Study Modules

The university remodelled the entire curriculum for the academic year 2014–15. In the information technology education, the first study year is now divided into four 15 ECTS modules. Each module has a theme that introduces the different subjects students can major in: networks, programming and web-development, electronic devices, and object-oriented programming. The project in each module is supported by a varying amount of basic and theoretical studies such as mathematics and physics. The first module, a project-based orientation course enables students to acquire basic knowledge of the study environment together. The course also helps students build a social network. Consequently, they have other modules that consist of individual work and projects of different sizes.

Even though the main aim of the curriculum reform was to create large modules of 15 ECTS credits that consisted of projects, the practice has not been uniform within the modules. Actually, the modules implemented according to the new curriculum structure have various designs and arrangements for teaching. Each theme has an instructor team of 5 or 6 teachers who have a considerable degree of freedom when planning the implementation. Therefore, the ways that subjects are integrated varies a lot. The actual implementations could be classified as follows:

1. *Separated parts.* The implementations of some courses actually consist of almost separate parts. Some instructor teams simply decided to continue their earlier courses under a new umbrella, and the 15 ECTS module is divided into three disconnected parts worth of 5 ECTS each that are assessed separately.
2. *Partially integrated module.* Many implementations have a separate unit for mathematics and/or physics, but the professional content is mainly unified, even though media and programming tools or laboratory measurements are taught separately. Usually, however, there is a common project for students. The evaluation consists of several components that are summarized together.
3. *Integrated module.* Apart from the separate science classes, all professional and language content (communication skills) is integrated, and teachers collaborate in theoretical subjects and project work. Deliverables such as presentations and project documentation are assessed both on substance and communication aspects. Some types of lessons usually have more than one teacher present. Also during student team presentations most teachers attend, give feedback and evaluate together.

The integrated modules that are described in this paper and that applied agile approach, are Orientation and Games (programming) in the first year (2014 and 2015 implementations), Application Development Methods in the second year (2016 and

2017 implementations), and Software Business Start-up in the third year (2016). They were largely similar in design, lead by nearly the same teacher teams who applied agile practices in the planning of instruction.

The Orientation module had weekly assignments, most of which were completed in small teams. There were no permanent teams for the whole module.

The Games module was actually an introduction to Java programming. In the beginning of the module, students attended some lectures in programming, and completed a large number of programming assignments in a MOOC setting. The MOOC (massive open online course) was provided by the University of Helsinki. Additionally, students completed a game project during those 8 weeks. After the setup of teams in the second week, teams held weekly scrum meetings, and they were required to use kanban (Trello) for task management. In this module, the composition of teams was constrained in a way that single-nationality teams were not allowed. Earlier experiences have shown that single-nationality teams slow down the cultural adaptation process as well as leading to less successful projects [16]. On the other hand, multicultural teams teach important skills for the future of international students.

The Application Development Methods module in the second year contained a mix of Finnish and international software engineering students. As the name implies, the module concentrated on software project management skills. The lectures covered some conventional project management, a number of development tools, and user-centered design. The technical skills included setting up a Java server, creating a responsive client-side, using github and REST API, and usability testing tools. Other methods that the students were already familiar with included Trello and scrum meetings. As regular scrum meetings were not compulsory, some teams skipped most of them.

The Software Business Start-up module was conducted in the beginning of the third study year. The module built on the skills that had been acquired earlier including git version control, weekly scrum meetings, voluntary use of kanban and other agile tools. Some new technical skills were introduced, namely the so-called MEAN stack that contains node.js and noSQL databases, and use of Heroku server. Student teams were allowed to assemble freely, but the team size was limited to four.

3 Research and Methods

The main results that have been proven until now are the study results. These students have not graduated yet, and therefore no data on their competences in the industry are available. For analysis of the outcomes, we collected student writings, conducted student and teacher interviews, conducted several surveys, and used feedback questionnaires. Data about the modules was also collected through field ethnography and participant observation [18, 19]. One team of educators (including some of the authors of this paper) took field notes of classroom practices, held numerous discussions on the successes and failures of pedagogical interventions, and videotaped a couple of classroom and planning sessions [20]. The study can be characterized as an explanatory building case study [21] where qualitative and descriptive methods are applied in data collection and analysis.

4 Results

4.1 Findings

The ECTS credit accumulation was investigated by examining how many students stayed on track with their studies, completing the expected 30 credits in the two study periods of the first semester. As can be seen from the figures, the number of students attaining at least 30 ECTS increased from 17% in 2013 to over 80% in the years 2014 and 2015 in the international groups (Table 1). This indicates a very successful start of the studies compared to earlier years.

Table 1. Course completions of international study groups in IT

	2012 n = 74	2013 n = 76	2014 n = 45	2015 n = 48
1–14 ECTS credits	23%	14%	0%	2%
15–29 ECTS credits	46%	68%	20%	8%
30–>	31%	17%	80%	90%

Moreover, the completion rate of modules in successive studies was also very satisfactory. The composition of student groups varied between modules depending on their choice of major, and some Finnish students joined the groups, which explains the variation of student numbers in Table 2.

Table 2. The success rate of SE students in the agile modules

Module	Students	Passed	%	Average grade
Games 1	24	22	92%	4.05
Games 2	27	26	96%	3.59
Application Development methods	41	34	83%	3.42
Software business startup	35	32	91%	3.50

The grades are on scale of 1–5, which means that an average above 4 is very good. The latest module, Software Business Start-up, showed an increasing ability of the students to apply agile development methods. Students needed no more instruction in the basic practices, and their mode of work was geared towards agile work. In the first module with scrum, namely Games, students experienced considerable anxiety, which they reported in the feedback. Even though the Software start-up module had the least distinctly defined goals, the uncertainty of the outcome was taken as granted by the students. In that module, students were asked to brainstorm their business ideas, and teams were built around the most inspiring ideas. As a surprise to teachers, some Asian students actually appeared to have earlier start-up experience from their own countries. The cross-cultural comparison of Nepalese and Finnish experiences brought up certain similarities and some differences between business cultures, which transpired as an additional learning outcome for all. Very obviously, student ability to tolerate uncertainty increased from one module to the next.

4.2 Results of Collaboration

In order to measure collaboration in the classroom, a small survey was conducted with 40 first year students after the second study module called Games. The module contained an introduction to programming using a MOOC on Java language [22], after which the students undertook a team project to develop a text-based adventure game. In addition, the course included 20% mathematics and 10% practice in web development. The amount of team work was designed to be about 50% of the total. Students were asked "What helped you most to learn in this course?" with options "Teachers", "Team-mates", "Other students" and "MOOC". The results are shown in Table 3.

Table 3. Contributors to study success in one module (%)

	Teachers	Team	Others	MOOC	*Share of individual study*
Average	19	34	12	34	*50*
Standard deviation	13	20	13	24	*20*
Max	50	60	40	85	*80*
Min	5	1	0	0	*18*

This result quite clearly confirms the observation that teacher contribution to actual work was conceived as small by the students. The role of teachers appeared more as facilitators and enablers of the study, even though actual teacher presence in the classroom was high and lectures were given regularly. The informal setting in the classroom where students sit in round tables probably made lectures appear more like discussion sessions than actual lectures. Nevertheless, the schedule of the course and the materials and assignments were prepared in advance.

The answers to the second question "What was the share (%) of your own study to your achievements (asides from team work)?" are shown in the same Table 3 in the column "Share of individual study". The variation in student perception of their own efforts was here large, as well. We can conclude that the course was not teacher-centred despite the continuous teacher presence in the classroom. The aim of students taking charge of their own learning was unarguably achieved. Other questions in this small survey were open. Many commented on the team work, which was deemed important and useful though they found it difficult to reconcile different opinions and control the process. Team work divided opinions as it caused small conflicts and frustrations, even though students agreed that it is an important skill for working life.

The students were also asked to indicate who helped them and who were the students that received help form them. As can be detected from Fig. 1, the mutual helping networks extended beyond team members. Teams can be observed as triads, but many nodes such as A, C, and G, have multiple connections. They are the best programmers whose advice was often sought by students outside of their teams. The average number of helping relations was 4.7, which exceeds the team size of 3.

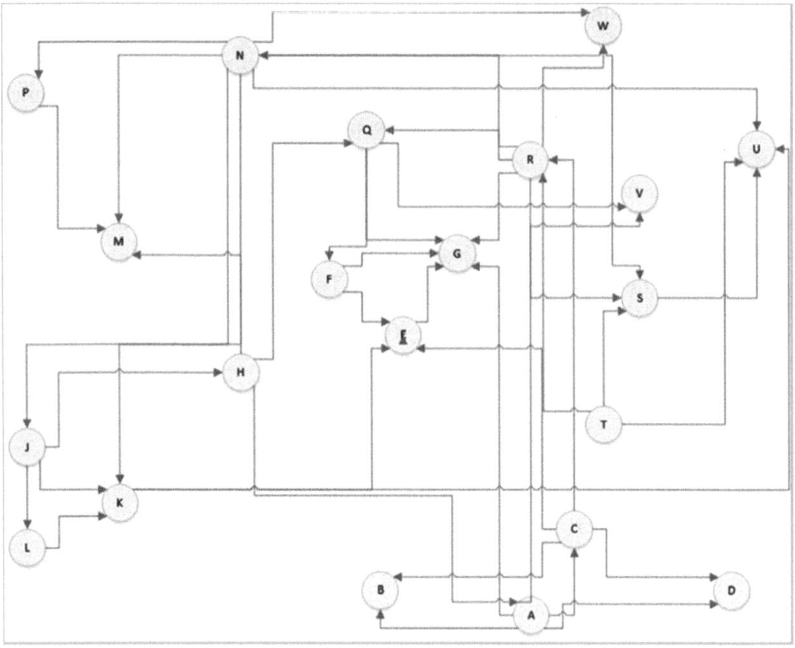

Fig. 1. Collaboration networks in one Games module group

5 Conclusion

Based on earlier studies and literature reporting teaching of agile courses, the promising outcomes of this study are not surprising. However, it remains unclear whether negative cases have been reported to the same extent as positive outcomes. As far as agile working methods have been studied in multicultural groups [4], or in courses on software business [23], our results are compatible. Nevertheless, the results of this study extend beyond agile courses, as in the present case, agile work has been expanded to the entire curriculum. Not only the subject of study, but the methods of teachers in course design and implementation, have applied agile ideas. The modules were not defined in much detail in advance, instead, the planning was flexible and done in small increments during the implementation [24]. In case of heterogeneous student groups, this allowed more freedom in the realization.

The method requires that teachers have an open mind and are ready to face uncertainty. Teachers need to have enough professional experience and confidence when they start collaboration in this format. Moreover, in our case the presence of one teacher from a different cultural background (India, as opposed to other Finnish teachers) increased credibility of the method among third world students. The results would encourage other universities to consider experimenting with agile teaching.

References

1. Kropp, M., Meier, A., Biddle, R.: Teaching agile collaboration skills in the classroom. In: IEEE 29th International Conference on Software Engineering Education and Training (2016)
2. Laanti, M., Salo, O., Abrahamsson, P.: Agile methods rapidly replacing traditional methods at Nokia: a survey of opinions on agile transformation. Inf. Softw. Technol. **53**, 276–290 (2011)
3. Rico, D.F, Sayani, H.H.: Use of agile methods in software engineering education. In: Agile Conference, AGILE 2009 (2009)
4. Paasivaara, M., Blincoe, K., Lassenius, C., Damian, D., Sheoran, J., Harrison, F., Chhabra, P., Yussuf, A., Isotalo, V.: Learning global agile software engineering using same-site and cross-site teams. In: 2015 IEEE/ACM 37th IEEE International Conference on Software Engineering, pp. 285–294 (2015)
5. Mahnic, V.: A capstone course on agile software development using scrum. IEEE Trans. Educ. **55**(1), 99–106 (2012)
6. Devedžić, V., Milenkovic, S.R.: Teaching agile software development: a case study. IEEE Trans. Educ. **54**(2), 273–278 (2011)
7. Gannod, G., Troy, D.A., Luczaj, J.E., Rover, D.T.: Agile way of educating. In: IEEE Workshop Proposal 2015 (2015)
8. Longmuß, J., Höhne, B.P., Bräutigam, S., Oberländer, A., Schindler, F.: Agile learning: bridging the gap between industry and university. A model approach to embedded learning and competence development for the future workforce. In: The Proceedings of 44th Annual SEFI Conference (2016)
9. Crawley, E.F., Malmqvist, J., Östlund, S., Brodeur, D.R.: Rethinking Engineering Education: The CDIO Approach. Springer, New York (2007). https://doi.org/10.1007/978-0-387-38290-6
10. Marjoram, T.: An introduction to the organization of the profession. In: Engineering: Issues, Challenges and Opportunities for Development. UNESCO, Paris, pp. 135–136 (2010)
11. Dalsgaard, F., Du, X., Kolmos, A.: Innovative application of a new PBL model to interdisciplinary and intercultural projects. Int. J. Electr. Eng. Educ. **47**, 174–188 (2010)
12. Kolmos, A., Dahms, M., Du, X.: Problem-based learning. In: Engineering: Issues, Challenges and Opportunities for Development. UNESCO, Paris, pp. 334–340 (2010)
13. Holvikivi, J., Lakkala, M., Muukkonen, H.: Introducing collaborative practices to undergraduate studies. In: Brinda, T., Mavengere, N., Haukijärvi, I., Lewin, C., Passey, D. (eds.) SaITE 2016. IAICT, vol. 493, pp. 47–55. Springer, Cham (2016). https://doi.org/10.1007/978-3-319-54687-2_5
14. Paavola, S., Hakkarainen, K.: Trialogical approach for knowledge creation. In: Tan, S.C., So, H.J., Yeo, J. (eds.) Knowledge Creation in Education. EIS, pp. 53–73. Springer, Singapore (2014). https://doi.org/10.1007/978-981-287-047-6_4
15. Kropp, M., Meier, A., Perellano, G.: Experience report of teaching agile collaboration and values: agile software development in large student teams. In: IEEE 29th International Conference on Software Engineering Education and Training (2016)
16. Holvikivi, J.: Culture and cognition in information technology education. SimLab Publications, Dissertation series 5, Espoo, Finland (2009)
17. Hjort, P., Holvikivi, J., Vesikivi, P., Lukkarinen, S.: Student collaboration and independence from day one in higher education. In: The Proceedings of the 43rd Annual SEFI Conference, Orléans, France (2015)
18. Spradley, J.P.: Participant Observation. Thomson Learning, Boston (1980)

19. Green, J., Bloome, D.: Ethnography and ethnographers of and in education: a situated perspective. In: Flood, J., Heath, S.B., Lapp, D. (eds.) Handbook of Research on Teaching Literacy Through the Communicative and Visual Arts, pp. 181–202. Macmillan Publishers, New York (1997)
20. Vesikivi, P., Hjort, P., Lakkala, M., Holvikivi, J., Lukkarinen, S.: Adoption of a new project - based learning (PBL) curriculum in information technology. In: The Proceedings of the 43rd Annual SEFI Conference, Orléans, France (2015)
21. Yin, R.K.: Case Study Research: Design and Methods, 5th edn. SAGE Publications, Thousand Oaks (2014)
22. Eckerdal, A., Kinnunen, P., Thota, N., Nylén, A., Sheard, J., Malmi, L.: Teaching and learning with MOOCs: computing academics' perspectives and engagement. In: Proceedings of the 2014 Conference on Innovation and Technology in Computer Science Education. ACM Press, Uppsala (2014)
23. Read, A., Derrick, D.C., Ligon, G.S.: Developing entrepreneurial skills in IT courses: the role of agile software development practices in producing successful student initiated products. In: 47th Hawaii International Conference on System Science, pp. 201–209 (2014)
24. Vesikivi, P., Lakkala, M., Holvikivi, J., Lukkarinen, S.: Teacher collaboration in IT project courses: resistance and success. In: SEFI 2016 Annual Conference, Tampere (2016)

A Demonstration of Evidence-Based Action Research Using Information Dashboard in Introductory Programming Education

Yoshiaki Matsuzawa[1(✉)], Yoshiki Tanaka[2], Tomoya Kitani[2], and Sanshiro Sakai[2]

[1] Aoyama Gakuin University, Tokyo, Japan
matsuzawa@si.aoyama.ac.jp
[2] Shizuoka University, Shizuoka, Japan

Abstract. In this paper, we demonstrated an evidence-based action research in an introductory programming class with the use of an information dashboard which provides coding metrics to visualize students' engagement of their assignments. The information dashboard was designed for teachers to improve their classroom teaching using the same coding metrics which was verified in our previous research [9]. The system was equipped with a cross-filter functionality for exploring the entire classroom metrics. Accordingly, teachers can easily conduct a temporal analysis, an across-year comparison, and a cross metrics analysis. We examined the system for the improvement of the 5th year course using a dataset from the past four years from a non-CS introductory programming course at a university. Qualitative analysis was conducted using the discourse between teachers and teaching assistants with the proposed dashboard. The results showed that the system succeeded in promoting discourse, which included a clearer understanding of the class and its improvement, such as teaching method, assignments, or of students' behavior.

Keywords: Programming education · Information dashboard
Learning analytics · Action research

1 Introduction

Twenty-first century knowledge societies and the commonality of information and communication technologies in societies have been pushing for a fundamental reform in education [1]. This request will greatly affect learning management in the informatics field, with a shift from teaching how to use applications to "computing" - creating and designing a new problem solution with computational thinking [2]. This new assessment method for the programming education is significant for research in this field [3, 4].

The issue of definition and its assessment has been a long quest [5]. Recent technologies are enabling us to collect fine-grained massive logs in educational situations by an automated way. Using the terms of educational data mining or learning analytics, a new assessment method using the collected data has been anticipated even in programming education [6]. The first generation of research in the 2000s was limited to simple analysis such as compilation error occurrences profiles analysis (e.g. [7]),

A. Tatnall and M. Webb (Eds.): WCCE 2017, IFIP AICT 515, pp. 619–629, 2017.
https://doi.org/10.1007/978-3-319-74310-3_62

although recently fine-grained log analysis has increasingly revealed the actual efforts for student assignments [8], or measuring the impact of block-based language [9].

Prior studies have highlighted the difficulty of reproducing/replicating research results in this field [6]. There is general difficulty in human subject studies, as controversial discussions are still ongoing in programming education research [10, 11]. We should continue the pursuit of research toward the goal of the elucidating the nature of programming education. Simultaneously, the environment for analysis using the collected dataset should be developed in order to improve actual classroom learning.

Towards this end, we proposed an information dashboard for teachers to improve their introductory programming classroom. The tool was designed to help teachers' action research to improve the teaching/learning environment, especially in the case of classes that are repeatedly conducted over a relatively long period of time (imagine the 2nd year course of the subject will be improved by the data of the 1st year course).

The academic contributions of this paper contain three aspects. First is the design of the dashboard, which is based on our previous research, and enable teachers to effectively ascertain the unique learning issues in their respective classrooms. In addition, as we use the latest web technology, teachers can easily access the dashboard and explore it using a filtering functionality. The second contribution is the application of the dashboard to actual classroom environments. Teachers tried to make improvements for 5th year course using the dashboard which shows the former 4 years' data-set. The third contribution is our study methodology. All of the sessions containing the detailed discussions of the teachers and assistants with the dashboard were recorded and in-depth qualitative analyses for each session were carried out.

2 Related Work

As discussed in the previous section, the recorded data in the actual programming session and proposed method of analyzing the recorded data are a common research approach within this field. For example, Toll et al. [8] proposed four categories to be classified by the granularity of the recorded logs. The categories include Compilations, Text change, Active Use, and Time in Tool. Jadud's compilation analysis [7] is categorized as the Compilation level, and Matsuzawa's compile error visualization [12] can be categorized at the level as well.

ClockIt [13] and Retina [14] are categorized as the Text change level. Comparing this approach through focusing on teacher usage of the visualizations, ClockIt is designed for a single student. Retina is designed for both students and teachers; however, the teacher's view shows the detailed errors for each student. There are limitations in the ability for conducting action research to improve an entire class.

Helminen et al. [15] and PPV [16] are tools to display the replay of programming sessions using fine-grained typing logs. The purpose of these tools is to perform an in-depth analysis of each individual student. Alammary et al. [17] advocated a "Smart Lab". A dashboard is a system for teachers to visualize the students "seats map" and shows the status of each student. This kind of tool is considered useful for ascertaining the progress of student assignments in real-time. But its use is questionable toward the improvement of an entire class or curriculum.

In the field of software engineering, Johnson and Zhang [18] proposed a dashboard system. They used the metaphor of a medical ICU (Intensive Care Unit). The proposed system shows a commit (code) telemetry which visualizes the current status using the metrics used in the software engineering field.

Heig et al. [19] advocated a suite of visualization tools to show the usage of the learning management system and attempted to detect the student behavior patterns. The data they used were the access logs of a learning management system. Although differing from our research, the visualization of a heat map for each student has some resemblance to our tool.

Student performance in undergraduate programming classes has been studied using paper exams. Lister et al. [20] reported on reading and tracing skills for multi-regional university students. Ford [21] tried to assess the achievement of their classes incorporating tests used in cognitive studies in programming [10]. Results showed that only 50% of students understood class assignments, so they attempted to improve this aspect of their classroom. This is quite a remarkable result as a form of evidence-based action research within programming education.

3 Information Dashboard

This section will provide a brief description of the information dashboard which is designed for teachers to improve an introductory programming class, by providing coding metrics [9] to show the engagement of students in their assignments. The whole view of the dashboard is shown below in Fig. 1. According to Few [22], an information dashboard can be defined as follows:

> *A dashboard is a visual display of the most important information needed to achieve one or more objectives; consolidated and arranged on a single screen so the information can be monitored at a glance.*

The main objective of this study is to improve an introductory-level programming classroom. All the visualization graphs are laid out in an HD (1920 × 1080 pixels) screen, which provides teachers with a glance view of all the coding metrics. The purpose of the dashboard is not for real-time "monitoring", but to promote teacher "exploration" of the data over a relatively long period of time (weekly, monthly, or yearly). Hence, the dashboard design resembles an "accumulated" view rather than a general telemetry system, which promotes understanding of the summary in a short time.

The logs of student computer operations were collected by the previously proposed framework [16], and the system computes the coding metrics: working time, LOC (lines of code), compile error correction time, and block editor usage ratio. The metrics are computed for each unit of assignment x student. Brief explanations of each graph in Fig. 1 are described as follows:

1. Pie graphs show the years and weeks. A user can filter by clicking this part.
2. A scatter plot shows the relationship between two selected coding metrics.
3. Five line charts are shown for each of the 5 coding metrics, which are arranged with the assignments ordered chronologically. Each colored line shows a different year.
4. A box plot shows the distribution of students for a selected coding metric.

5. A histogram shows the distribution of a particular selected assignment.
6. Tiled representations provide a graduation analysis environment as used in our previous research [9].

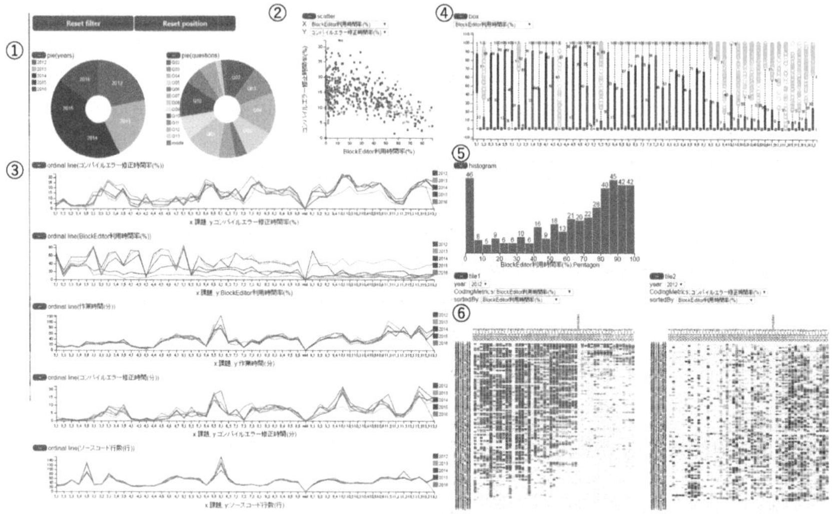

Fig. 1. Proposed information dashboard (Color figure online)

The system was implemented on the web with Javascript, with the user being able to use a browser to see the dashboard. The libraries of d3.js, dc.js, and crossfilter.js were used in the implementation; accordingly, the system is equipped with cross-filter functionality for exploring the entire classroom metrics. Teachers can easily conduct a temporal analysis or cross-year comparison.

4 Research Method

4.1 Research Questions

We conducted an evaluation of the dashboard in an actual class setting. The research questions of the evaluation generally focused on whether or not we would be able to achieve the objectives of the dashboard design:

RQ1: Can the dashboard facilitate among teachers productive discussions for the goal of improving the quality of introductory programming classes? Can this be entirely performed by using coding metrics visualized on the dashboard?
RQ2: While RQ1 is supported, how does it work? What can be facilitated as discoveries or actual ideas by users for improvements in their classrooms?

4.2 Education Environment Descriptions

The introductory programming course was designed for liberal arts students, as opposed to computer science students. Therefore, the main objective of the course was to develop a better understanding of task-oriented programming. The objective was independent from any programming language, although Java language was used in the actual environment. Approximately 100 students participated annually in the course, which was administered by two teachers and six teaching assistants.

4.3 Use of the Dashboard and Analyzed Discourse

We evaluated the dashboard at teaching staff meetings which were held weekly for the purpose of classroom management. Two teachers and six teaching assistants participated in the meetings, and their discussions focused on reflecting on the previous week's class and management methods for the next class. The evaluation was conducted in a 2016 course management meeting using the proposed dashboard on a shared projection screen, which showed the prior four years' data plus additional data up until the previous meeting.

All discussion sessions were recorded using a camcorder, and seven cases were selected (as described on Sect. 5.1) in which the discussants used the dashboard in their discussions to conduct in-depth qualitative analysis.

4.4 Coding Method

We conducted two types of analyses for the seven discourse cases. An example of the two analyses is shown in Fig. 2. As for RQ1: to confirm the dashboard properly works,

Case4, Scene1: Preparation for the 11th week class

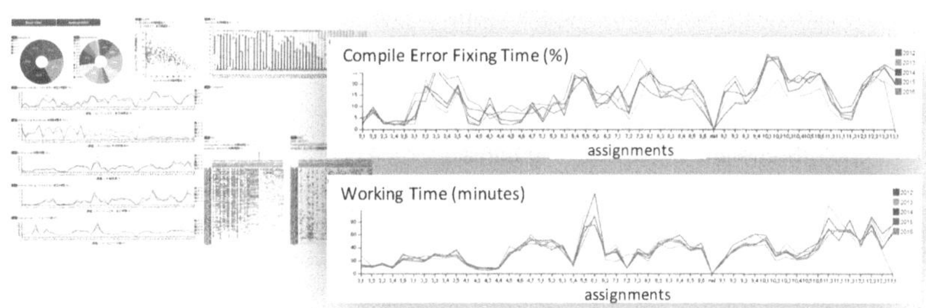

Reply#	Discussant	Reply	
1	TA3	The next week will be 11th. Students did not take compile errors fixing in the 11th week 's assignments.	
2	TA2	It's reasonable, because students will face many opportunities to run program, but..	
3	TA3	The week's compile error fixing time is low in every year, but in terms of working time...	Across-year Comparison
4	Teacher2	Can I confirm that are we talking about the next week's class.	Mentioning Quantity
5	TA3	Yes, we are. There are many assignments for students, students took much working time while comparing with other weeks'.	
6	Teacher2	Okay, consequently which is the best instruction for the week? A debug mode in the programming environment may be used to solve this problem....	Educational Discovery
7	TA3	We didn't use it before, but we may try to use a debugger	Idea for Improvement
8	TA1	I agree with it.	
9	TA3	As the topic of the week is GUI (recursion), studnets can trace their code one by one by using a debugger, it should work. It clealy guides where is the problem. Though it is not easy to fix the problem if they find the problem.	

Fig. 2. An example of the coding method used in the qualitative analysis of the discourse using the proposed dashboard (Color figure online)

we inspected the relationships between the discourse and usage of the dashboard. As shown in Fig. 2, the arrows reveal the relationships, each indicating an underlined sentence where an arrow starts from and mentions the part of the dashboard the arrow points to.

Table 1. The coding scheme for RQ2: how does the dashboard promote productive discussions for teachers?

Coding category	Brief definition	Representative example(s)
Across-year comparison	A discussant is talking about an across-year comparison using particular parts of the dashboard, by comparing two lines, or using filtering functionality	- This year's shape of line is opposite to the previous years' - The maximum of LOC in middle assignment was around 300 until 2013, but this year...
Mentioning quantity	A discussant is mentioning to a quantitative data which indicated in a particular part of the dashboard	- This 20% means approximately 1 of 5 students used block editor... - To my surprise, there is a student who wrote 12000+ lines in assignment...
Educational discovery	A discussant (or whole group) found the new fact or ide for educational situation including students behaviors. Tacit knowledge which is observed by teaching staff in classroom was clearly supported or unsupported by data which is shared between teaching staff as explicit knowledge	- This student accomplished really hard work to draw his favor figure - We can confirm the negative correlation between working tin and compile error fixing time, though its obvious
Idea for improvement	A discussant suggested or proposed an idea for improvement of educational situation, such as difficulty assignment, method of instruction, teaching	- This assignment can be split into two or three small steps because... - A debug mode I5 in the programming environment may be us to solve this problem...

As for RQ2: how the dashboard promotes productive discussions for teachers, we created a coding scheme as shown in Table 1. The coding categories are comprised of Across-year Comparison, Mentioning Quality, Educational Discovery, and Idea for Improvement. The four categories are colored as shown in the legend in Fig. 2, with the coded parts in the discourse highlighted in each color.

The analysis for entire discourse was performed by a single rater, who also served as a teaching assistant and participated in the teaching staff meetings. The second rater performed independently for 4 of 7 cases (57%) of the discourse. The interrater reliability was 73%, conflicts are resolved by a raters' discussion.

5 Results

5.1 Short Descriptions of Each Case

Case 1: Effects of reordering assignments

The teaching staff discussed what the obstacles were for why students in previous courses required a longer time in completing their assignments. The teachers hypothesized that the problem was caused by the ordering of assignments, so that the teachers tried to reorder the assignments for the current year. A week later, the teachers could confirm there was improvement, as the dashboard indicated the actual working time was reduced by nearly 10 min. They also discovered that there were some students who exhibited a longer compile error correction time, particularly in the target assignment, later confirming one of the reasons was their low usage of BlockEditor.

Case 2: Compile error correction time and its improvement

One teacher had felt it was difficult to maintain student motivation in some assignments in which the average compile error correction time was indicated as being longer. The teaching team isolated the type of assignments, and then realized that students tended to compile once after writing the whole program. A few suggestions were given for how to improve the situation, including dividing the assignment into some smaller steps, or teaching students to compile progressively one by one for each small part.

Case 3: Working time and maximum lines of codes

Midterm assignment: a task to create their own GUI contents (Game or other interactive contents) was discussed. The average working time was approximately five hours, with a maximum time of over 25 h. The result was unexpectedly long in a positive way. The maximum code size was 16,000+. It was negatively evaluated because the teachers considered it was caused by copying without thinking of the abstraction of the algorithm.

Case 4: Characteristics of the assignment and improvement of instruction

The dashboard indicated a particular week's characteristics: students worked long, but took a short time to compile error corrections. The topic of the week was recursion. The team concluded to promote student use of a debugger to trace their code.

Case 5: Working time outside of classroom

The team tried to estimate how long students worked outside of classroom time. As the working time of each assignment was 40 min, the working time outside was estimated to be one hour. The team discussed the estimation's validity for education.

Case 6: Correlation between several coding metrics

Correlations between several coding metrics were analyzed in the discussion. For example, the fact there was no correlation between working time and lines of code was an unexpected result. After the discussion about the reason for the result, teachers reached a consensus that the assigned common tasks were well-structured, and the code size could be estimated within a common solution.

Case 7: BlockEditor usage of the 2016 year's course
Similar analyses to those of BlockEditor's research [9] were discussed. During the current year there were a few compulsory assignments using BlockEditor, although the results indicated a low BlockEditor usage ratio even during the early weeks of the course. Whereas during the prior years the usage ratios of BlockEditor were shown to also be high during the latter weeks of the course. The team also confirmed several other facts: students selected BlockEditor to reduce compile error corrections, or there were no significant differences in working time and LOC between BlockEditor users and non-users.

5.2 Results of Qualitative Analysis

Based on the results of the qualitative analysis of seven cases, we created a heat-map to visualize the coverage of used graphs on the dashboard. The heat-map is shown in Fig. 3. In the figure, the used graphs in the discussion of each case are highlighted in transparent red.

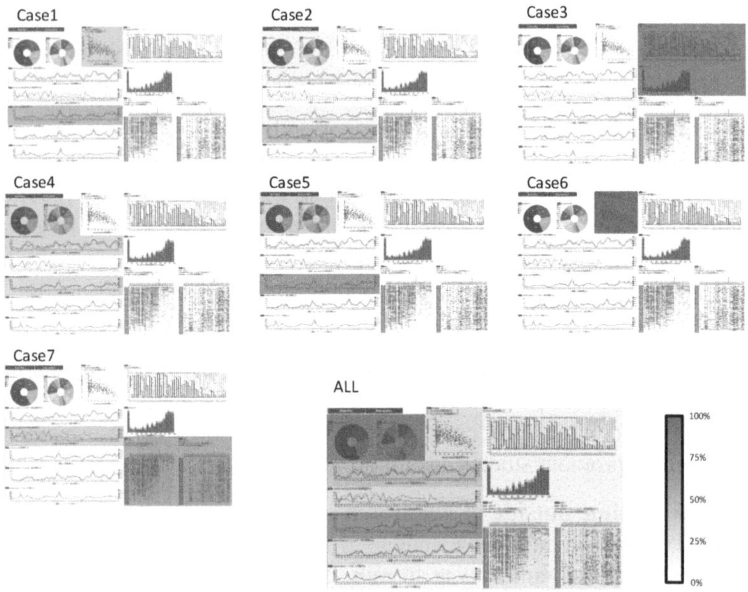

Fig. 3. A heat-map representing the coverage of graph-usage in each case. ALL shows the coverage by summing up all seven cases (Color figure online)

The depth of transparency red in Fig. 3 shows the percentage of usage, which is calculated by the frequencies of arrows in the discourse (Fig. 2). The heat-map of ALL indicates the graphs used in all seven cases, which is calculated by the number of cases in which the graph was used.

Table 2. The results of analysis for RQ2: how does the dashboard promote productive discussion for teachers?

	Across-year comparison	Mentioning quantity	Educational discovery	Idea for improvement
Casel: effects of reordering assignments	3	2	3	0
Case2: compile error fixing time in the class and its improvement	0	0	2	2
Case3: corrrelation between working time and maximum lines of codes	3	13	4	0
Case4: characteristics of particular assignment and improvement of its instruction	0	0	2	1
Case5: working time on outside classroom	0	2	1	0
Case6: correlation between several coding metrics	0	0	2	0
Case7: block-editor usage of this year's class	1	4	5	0
Total	7	21	19	3

The results of the analysis using the described coding scheme (as shown in Table 1) are shown in Table 2. We could confirm that the four coding categories can be seen in most cases broadly. Essentially, many educational discoveries were identified using the dashboard, and the phenomenon is supported by the descriptions of each case described in Sect. 5.1. Although the number of Ideas for Improvement was not particularly high if compared with the other categories, these were ideas supported by the facts discovered in the Educational Discovery category.

6 Discussion

RQ1 asked "Can the dashboard facilitate teachers' productive discussion to improve introductory programming classroom? And is it able to be performed by using coding metrics visualized in the dashboard?" The results were generally positive: we could examine 100% of the coverage by use of the graphs in the seven cases by the heat-map, which were effectively used in the discourse on improving the classes. The filtering functionality was also used in 6 out of 7 cases. To be specific in each case, the use of line charts of coding metrics was popular, and the other boxplot or tile representations were used when users needed to use specific data to explore deeper facts in the classroom.

RQ2 asked "While RQ1 is supported, how does it work? And what can be facilitated as discoveries or actual ideas by users for improvements of their classroom?" A surprising result revealed by the qualitative analysis was that 19 Educational Discoveries were coded in all of the seven cases. We define Educational Discovery not only as finding a new fact or idea in an educational situation, but by whether or not the tacit knowledge observed in the classroom was clearly supported. The results indicate that evidence-based facts can be shared between teaching staff as explicit knowledge. Furthermore, misunderstandings of the classroom environment can be fixed through this process. We strongly believe that a progressive, iterative, and continuous improvement of classrooms can be attained through this process.

Acknowledgments. This work was supported by JSPS KAKENHI Grant Numbers 25730203, 26280129.

References

1. Griffin, P., McGaw, B., Care, E. (eds.): Assessment and Teaching of 21st Century Skills. Springer, New York (2012). https://doi.org/10.1007/978-94-007-2324-5
2. Wing, J.: Computational thinking and thinking about computing. Philos. Trans. R. Soc. A **366**, 3717–3725 (2008)
3. Brennan, K., Resnick, M.: New frameworks for studying and assessing the development of computational thinking. In: Annual American Educational Research Association Meeting (2012)
4. Lye, S., Koh, J.: Review on teaching and learning of computational thinking through programming: what is next for K-12? Comput. Hum. Behav. **41**, 51–61 (2014)
5. Tedre, M., Denning, P.: The long quest for computational thinking. In: Proceedings of the 16th Koli Calling Conference on Computing Education Research, pp. 120–129 (2016)
6. Ihantola, P., Vihavainen, A., Ahadi, A., Butler, M., Börstler, J., Edwards, S., Isohanni, E., Korhonen, A., Petersen, A., Rivers, K., Rubio, M., Sheard, J., Skuupas, B., Spacco, J., Szabo, C., Toll, D.: Educational data mining and learning analytics in programming: literature review and case studies. In: ITiCSE WGR 2016, pp. 41–63 (2015)
7. Jadud, M.: Methods and tools for exploring novice compilation behaviour. In: Proceedings of the Second International Workshop on Computing Education Research ICER 2006, pp. 73–84 (2006)
8. Toll, D., Olsson, T., Ericsson, M., Wingkvist, A.: Fine-grained recording of student programming sessions to improve teaching and time estimations. Int. J. Eng. Educ. **32**(3A), 1069–1077 (2016)
9. Matsuzawa, Y., Tanaka, Y., Sakai, S.: Measuring an impact of block-based language in introductory programming. In: Brinda, T., Mavengere, N., Haukijärvi, I., Lewin, C., Passey, D. (eds.) SaITE 2016. IAICT, vol. 493, pp. 16–25. Springer, Cham (2016). https://doi.org/10.1007/978-3-319-54687-2_2
10. Dehnadi, S.: A cognitive study of learning to program in introductory programming courses. Ph.D. thesis, Middlesex University (2009)
11. Lung, J., Aranda J., Easterbrook, S., Wilson, G.: On the difficulty of replicating human subject studies in software engineering. In: ICSE 2008, p. 191 (2008)

12. Matsuzawa, Y., Hirao, M., Sakai, S.: Compile error collection viewer: visualization of compile error correction history for self-assessment in programming education. Int. J. Eng. Educ. **32**(3A), 1117–1127 (2016)
13. Norris, C., Barry, F., Fenwick, J., Reid, K., Rountree, J.: ClockIt: collecting quantitative data on how beginning software developers really work. In: ITiCSE 2008, pp. 37–41 (2008)
14. Murphy, C., Kaiser, G., Loveland, K, Hasan, S.: Retina: helping students and instructors based on observed programming activities. In: SIGCSE 2009, pp. 178–182 (2009)
15. Helminen, J., Ihantola, P., Karavirta, V.: Recording and analyzing in-browser programming sessions. In: Koli Calling 2013, pp. 13–22 (2013)
16. Matsuzawa, Y., Okada, K., Sakai, S.: Programming process visualizer: a proposal of the tool for students to observer their programming process. In: Proceedings of the ITiCSE 2013, pp. 46–51 (2013)
17. Alammary, A., Carbone, A., Sheard, J.: Implementation of a smart lab for teachers of novice programmers. In: Proceeding ACE 2012 Proceedings of the Fourteenth Australasian Computing Education Conference, pp. 121–130 (2012)
18. Johnson, P., Zhang, S.: We need more coverage, stat! Classroom experience with the software ICU. In: 3rd International Symposium on Empirical Software Engineering and Management, pp. 168–178 (2009)
19. Haig, T., Falkner, K., Falkner, N.: Visualisation of learning management system usage for detecting student behaviour patterns. In: Proceedings of the Fifteenth Australasian Computing Education Conference, ACE 2013, pp. 107–115 (2013)
20. Lister, R., Adams, E., Fitzgerald, S., Fone, W., Hamer, J., Lindholm, M., McCartney, R., Mostrom, J., Sanders, K., Seppala, O., Simon, B., Thomas, L.: A multi-national study of reading and tracing skills in novice programmers. In: SIGCSE 2004, pp. 119–150 (2004)
21. Ford, M., Venema, S.: Assessing the success of an introductory programming course. J. Inf. Technol. Educ. **9**, 133–145 (2010)
22. Few, S.: Information Dashboard Design: Displaying Data for At-a-Glance Monitoring. O'Reilly Media, Newton (2006)

Understanding the Differences Between Novice and Expert Programmers in Memorizing Source Code

Matthias Kramer[1(✉)], Mike Barkmin[1], David Tobinski[2], and Torsten Brinda[1]

[1] Didactics of Informatics, University of Duisburg-Essen, Essen, Germany
{matthias.kramer,mike.barkmin, torsten.brinda}@uni-due.de
[2] Cognitive and Educational Psychology, University of Duisburg-Essen, Essen, Germany
david.tobinski@uni-due.de

Abstract. This study investigates the difference between novice and expert programmers in memorizing source code. The categorization was based on a questionnaire, which measured the self-estimated programming experience. An instrument for assessing the ability to memorize source code was developed. Also, well-known cognitive tests for measuring working memory capacity and attention were used, based on the work of Kellog and Hayes. Forty-two participants transcribed items which were hidden initially but could be revealed by the participants at will. We recorded all keystrokes, counted the lookups and measured the lookup time. The results suggest that experts could memorize more source code at once, because they used fewer lookups and less lookup time. By investigating the items in more detail, we found that it is possible that experts memorize short source codes in semantic entities, whereas novice programmers memorize them line by line. Because our experts were significantly better in the performed memory capacity tests, our findings must be viewed with caution. Therefore, there is a definite need to investigate the correlation between working memory and self-estimated programming experience.

Keywords: Assessment · Object-oriented programming · Working memory
Programming experience

1 Introduction

The identification and empirical validation of competency structures have been one of the core topics in German educational research during the last few years, see [1, 2]. Fueled in addition by the results of international comparative studies such as PISA[1], TIMSS and PIRLS[2] the German educational system had to undergo a rigorous restructuring process [3] from an input oriented and teacher centered system to an output

[1] See https://www.oecd.org/pisa/.
[2] See http://timss.bc.edu/.

A. Tatnall and M. Webb (Eds.): WCCE 2017, IFIP AICT 515, pp. 630–639, 2017.
https://doi.org/10.1007/978-3-319-74310-3_63

oriented and learner centered system. Instead of concentrating on the specific content to teach, the focus shifted to the skills and abilities that learners need to solve problems in a specific situation. These skills and abilities are typically described with the term *competency*. A precise definition was given by Weinert and can be found in [4].

During this shift, a priority programme[3] of the German national science foundation, the DFG, was initiated. The research areas covered several educational fields and ranged from the theoretical derivation of competencies and their gathering in competency models up to practical implications for people who work in the educational field [5]. The approaches in the numerous sub-projects were the basis for our project COMMOOP which deals with the determination and empirical validation of competencies from beginners in the area of object-oriented programming (OOP). The process of literature-based derivation as well as a first resulting version of the competency model is documented in [6]. First assessment results for the competency facets of recognizing object-oriented syntax elements in given source code can be found in [7].

These results already gave first hints, that beginners identify syntax elements based on taught code conventions, such as position of elements in the code or upper/lower case of letters but not on a semantic level. Based on these results and referring to the results of Adelson [8] we assume that programming experts have internalized the programming syntax. Hence, we hypothesize that they mentally compile given code structures into semantic entities and memorize the working algorithm behind while beginners tend to memorize syntactic elements. To confirm this hypothesis, we conducted a test where we asked participants to reproduce given code. Furthermore, we investigated the influence of the working memory to examine the contributions of "natural" memorization abilities. Referring to our competency model, this test assesses competency facets *Syntax and Semantics* from the competency dimension *Mastering Representation* in conjunction with the cognitive process of *Remembering*. In Sect. 2 we give an overview on the theoretical work on the concept of working memory in the field of cognitive psychology as well as research results with similar settings. Section 3 includes the description of the test instrument and the items included there. A presentation of the results of a first test is given in Sect. 4, followed by a discussion in Sect. 5 and an outlook for further work in Sect. 6.

2 Background and Related Work

Basic processes such as editing a natural language text may require some cognitive systems. For example, Kellog [9] assumed, that specific parts of the working memory are used in such processes. Hayes [10] independently proposed a broader model of the role of working memory in writing natural language texts, which also shows the interaction between an individual and a task environment. He divided the task environment into two interacting components – the social environment and the physical environment. The individual was categorized into motivation, cognitive processes, long-term memory and working memory, which also interact with each other. Although programming languages

[3] See http://kompetenzmodelle.dipf.de/en/.

are formal languages, the model gave us an indication on which interactions could happen during the process of writing source code. Because we used this model as a reference for a transcription task, which only involved reproducing source code, the task environment and the motivation/affect component were not relevant for our study and hence we reduced the model by taking only the individual component in account.

Therefore, we reduced the model, by only considering long-term memory, working memory and cognitive processes (see Fig. 1) and translated the components. The cognitive process "text interpretation" was translated to "code analyzing" and "text production" to "code production". Long-term memory components were replaced with "OOP knowledge and skills" and "mastering representations" as proposed in our competency structure model [6]. Due to our aforementioned interest in code reproduction, we were specifically interested in assessing the participant's working memory. Hayes derived the working memory component from Baddeley's and Hitch's model [11], which consists of the following four parts:

1. Phonological loop/memory (stores phonological information, such as a telephone number, and prevents its decay by continuously refreshing it in a rehearsal loop)
2. Visuo-spatial (visual/spatial) sketchpad (stores visual and spatial information, such as the arrangement of chairs in a room)
3. Semantic memory/episodic buffer (contains information that combine phonological, visual, and spatial information)
4. Central executive (controls the attention and therefore filters unnecessary information and coordinates cognitive tasks).

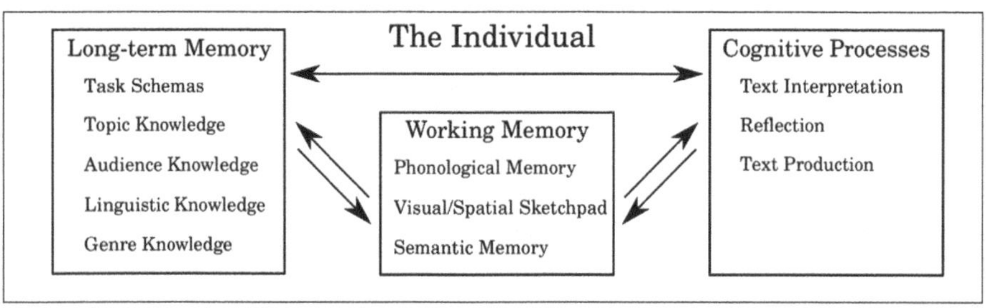

Fig. 1. Reduced Hayes-Flower-model (Source: [10], p. 4)

In the last decades, there have been several studies to show the interaction of these components in various contexts. In 1965, de Groot [12] conducted a study with master chess players, which proved that they only need five seconds to study a midgame board to reproduce it with 90% accuracy. Chase and Simon [13] reproduced the study and found that, master chess players memorized attacking and defending formations, rather than individual pieces. Thus, they could reproduce the board with a much higher accuracy than normal chess players. Adelson [7] used the results of de Groot and Chase and Simon to test if this phenomenon occurs in programming related tasks as well. In Adelson's experiment novice and expert programmers were shown sixteen randomly ordered lines of Polymorphic Programming Language source code, which they should remember and later recall. By testing five novices and five experts, Adelson found that experts are more likely to remember a higher number of source code lines. This study also investigated why experts are more capable of memorizing the source code lines. Adelson found, that novice programmers tried to memorize the source code in syntactic categories. Experts, however, tried to memorize it in semantic categories. So, Adelson concluded that with more expertise, the categories, which are used to remember source code, are getting more complex.

This paper attempts to combine Adelson's and de Groot's ideas by changing the amount of code given at a time. We wanted to find out, if the same behavior as described by Adelson occurs, when the subjects get to view the full source code at once like de Groot's experiment. Moreover, our purpose was to extend the existing research by taking a psychological perspective into regard. We therefore designed a study in which the subjects do not only run through programming tasks but also through tests from the domain of the cognitive psychology.

3 Methodology

In this study, most of the participants were tested using well-known cognitive tests to measure the attention ability and working memory capacity. They also transcribed natural language texts and source codes to tests if there is a difference between expert and novice programmers. The complete test design is described in Sect. 3.1, followed by an explanation on how we constructed the items in Sect. 3.2 and an overview of our participants is given in Sect. 3.3.

3.1 Design

To identify a correlation between the performance in memorizing and reproducing source code and programming experience, we proceeded in two steps.

In the first step, we gathered four well-reviewed cognitive tests to measure the attention ability and working memory capacity of the subjects. One of the most prominent tools for assessing the visual-spatial sketchpad is the Corsi block-tapping-test [14]. It is originally executed on a wooden board with blocks on it, but for our study we used a computer-based version to better control the experimenter artifact. For relating our results with the ones of Brunetti et al. [15], who already developed and tested an e-Corsi test in 2014, we took their description as a draft for our implementation. For further measuring of the working memory, we used two modules of the intelligence structure test I-S-T 2000R [16]. One of them is used to measure the ability to memorize verbal expression (capacity of the phonological loop), whereas the other focused on figural objects (capacity of the visuo-spatial sketchpad). To quantify the attention of the subjects (central executive), we used the d2 test of attention [17], which measures the selective and sustained attention and visual scanning speed.

In the second step, we tested the ability to memorize and reproduce source code. For that purpose, we asked the subjects to transcribe text. First, the content was presented on the left side of the screen and should be transcribed to a text area on the right side of the same screen. This was used to calculate the typing speed (keystrokes per seconds) of the subjects. Afterwards, the content was hidden but could be revealed by the participants on their own demand. To prevent the subjects from cheating by taking notes or a picture, the text was only revealed if the keys <CTRL> and <ALT> and a mouse button were pressed. A pre-test has shown, that we cannot require a 100% match, because in some cases misspellings or transpositions of two nearby characters were hard to find and have resulted in a much longer time required to process an item. Therefore, we used the Levenshtein-distance [18] to determine how similar a subject's text and the correct one was. The algorithm calculates the minimum distance between two strings. The minimum distance is defined as the smallest number of deletions, insertions and reversals that will transform a string A into a string B. After another test, we found, that 95% similarity (one minus current Levenshtein-distance divided by Levenshtein-distance with an empty string) was a good threshold. The subjects were informed on the current similarity of their text with the correct one, by showing a process indicator above the text area. It changed its color to green, when the threshold was reached to indicate that the subject can submit his/her work. During each keystroke, we have saved the respective key, the time and the Levenshtein-distance. We also saved each period when the hidden text was revealed and concealed again. Keeping in mind this format could have been unknown to the subjects, we implemented test items for the hidden and for the visible content tasks.

The pre-tests already gave us the hint that both parts of the test (assessment of the several parts of the working memory as well as reproducing source code) could respectively be finished in about 30 min, so that the whole test didn't take up more time than 60 min altogether. After these tests were completed, the subjects were asked to give further information on their programming experience in a questionnaire. Five items were constructed using the results of Siegmund et al. [19], who researched the correlation between questionnaires used in other researches and performance in solving program-comprehension tasks. They have found that self-estimation indicates programming experience well.

3.2 Item Construction

For the hidden content task three groups of three items were constructed. Each group contained a source code with a class structure, a source code with an algorithm and a natural text. These should be comparable to each other in the dimension of character count and complexity. For the items of group 1 see Fig. 2.

Items of group 2 consists of a class "Datei" composed of two attributes, a constructor and a setter, a text about "Lettland" and an algorithm "einruecken" to indent a

```
public class Haus {
  private int nummer;
  private String farbe;

  public void
   streiche(String farbe) {
    this.farbe = farbe;
  }
}
```

```
Lettland ist ein
Staat im Osten von
Europa. Er liegt an
der Ostsee und
gehört zu den
baltischen Staaten.
Die beiden anderen
sind Estland und
Litauen.
```

```
boolean istVielfaches(int
    zahl, int vielfaches) {
  if(vielfaches % zahl ==
      0){
    return true;
  } else {
    return false;
  }
}
```

Fig. 2. Item group 1

given string by using a symbol. The last group contained an item with a class "Vieleck" and a subclass "Dreieck", a text about "Allerheiligen" and an algorithm "istPrimzahl" to test if a number is prime. Therefore, we calculated the complexity of the classes with the weighted class complexity (WCC) by Misra and Adewumi [20]. We have chosen this complexity metric, because it uses a cognitive weight for basic control structures to calculate a method complexity (MC), which we used for the algorithms.

The complexity of the texts was calculated by using a readability index, which indicates how easy it is to read the text. It should be mentioned, that understanding the text is not considered. Because the readability is dependent on the grammar of the language, we used special readability indexes for German, namely the Flesh-Reading-Ease for German (FRE) [21], based on the original Flesh-Reading-Ease [22], which calculates the readability in values between 0 and 100 (lower = more difficult to read), and the "Wiener-Sachtext-Formel" (WSF) [23], which calculates the readability in school years between 4 and 15 (higher = more difficult to read). We took these two, because they make slightly different assumptions of what is difficult to read. By respecting both we can argue, that our chosen texts got increasingly more complex to read in every aspect.

These considerations resulted in three groups. The first group contains items with the lowest character count and complexity. The last group contains items with the highest character count and complexity compared to the others (Table 1).

Table 1. Item groups

Group	Class		Text			Algorithm	
	Chars	WCC	Chars	FRE	WSF	Chars	MC
Group 1	147	3	149	79	5	146	2
Group 2	219	5	206	69	8	214	4
Group 3	237	7	221	49	10	244	8

For the visible content task, we constructed two items, one text and one algorithm, which were comparable in character count and complexity to the items of group 3.

3.3 Participants

Forty-two students were recruited for this study. Thirty of them studied in a field related to computer science and had at least finished an introduction course for object-oriented programming. Of this group, six had a bachelor's degree and two a master's degrees. The remaining students studied something unrelated to computer science. One third of the sample size were female.

4 Results

We have used the recorded keystrokes and lookup times to analyze the difference between novice and experts for each item. Therefore, we have divided the group into novice and experts by using the median of the sum of the programming experience items of the questionnaire. This is allowed, because the internal consistency of the five items was excellent (cronbach's alpha = 0.96). The maximum score possible was 50, the lowest 5 and the median 29.

The typing speed and error rate (percentage of <Del> and <Backspace>) of the subjects showed no significant correlation with the programming experience. The performance of the subjects in the Corsi block-tapping-test did not significantly correlated with our measures. The d2 test only correlated with the last item of our test (r = 0.37, p-value = 0.0248).

4.1 Lookup Count

We found, that a higher score in the working memory test correlated with the difference in lookup count in many of our items (see Table 2). Also, the programming experience correlated with all items expect Class2. Therefore, we tested if we could find group differences between novice and experts by executing a Mann-Whitney U test analysis. We used this test, because our data was not normally distributed which we found out by using the Kolmogorow-Smirnow-test.

Table 2. Correlation between lookup count, working memory and programming experience (IST-F = I-S-T 2000R figural, IST-V = I-S-T 2000R verbal, PE = programming experience)

	Class1	Algo1	Class2	Algo2	Class3	Algo3
IST-F	0.42*	0.46**	0.13	0.10	0.47**	0.39*
IST-V	0.47**	0.36*	−0.01	0.25	0.48**	0.69***
PE	0.52***	0.73***	0.28	0.22	0.33*	0.43*

Note: *p < .05; **p < .01; ***p < .001

The U test analysis showed, that the difference in lookup count between the normal text and the source codes was significantly higher for the novice than for the experts in the items of the first group (class: W = 91, p-value = 0.0015, algorithm: W = 61, p-value = 0.001). The mean lookup count of novices was 2.47 units higher for the class item and 3.24 units higher for the algorithm one than for the lookup count of the first normal text. Experts had a mean lookup count difference of −0.40 for the class item and 0.40 for the algorithm one. The lookup count difference in class item of the third group was significantly (W = 104, p-value = 0.045) higher for the novice (4.24) then for the experts (2.4). The algorithmic item and second group showed no significance (p-values between 0.27 and 0.75) in this regard.

4.2 Lookup Time

The programming experience correlated significantly with Class1, Algo1, Class2, Algo3. The verbal working memory test only correlated with Class2 and the figural working memory test only correlated with Algo3 (see Table 3).

Table 3. Correlation between lookup time, working memory and programming experience (IST-F = I-S-T 2000R figural, IST-V = I-S-T 2000R verbal, PE = programming experience)

	Class1	Algo1	Class2	Algo2	Class3	Algo3
IST-F	0.40*	0.43**	0.18	−0.03	0.27	0.38*
IST-V	0.15	0.20	0.07	0.03	0.11	0.41*
PE	0.53***	0.71***	0.39*	0.24	0.22	0.38*

Note: *p < .05; **p < .01; ***p < .001

Table 4 shows the results of the U test analysis. There was a significant difference between experts and novices regarding the lookup time difference in items Class1, Algo1 and Class3.

Table 4. U test results. Lookup time difference between experts and novices.

	Class1	Algo1	Class2	Algo2	Class3	Algo3
Experts	2.01	3.05	8.64	−7.54	−4.64	−8.58
Novices	−6.30	−7.89	0.30	−12.83	−9.60	−18.50
W	73***	55***	116	140	96*	120

Note: *p < .05; **p < .01; ***p < .001

4.3 Working Memory

Because general working memory capacity could influence our results, we also tested on group difference in regard to the I-S-T 2000R verbal and figural score. Only in figural working memory we could find a significant difference (IST-V: W = 132, p-value = 0.212, IST-F: W = 81, p-value = 0.006), hence our experts had a better working memory capacity in this regard.

5 Discussion

It was hypothesized that expert programmers would memorize the working algorithm or class structure, while novices would tend to memorize syntactic elements. The results of this study indicate that this might be true. We have found that the lookup count difference between novices and experts was significantly different but only for the items of the first group and for the item Class3. A possible explanation for this might be that with increasing length and complexity the experts were not able to recognize the underlying class structure or algorithm. Therefore, they might have needed to memorize the source code line by line as novices needed to do.

We also found that experts needed fewer lookups for the first class item but more lookups for the first algorithm than for the first normal text. An implication of this is the possibility that experts remember classes easier than algorithms. This evidence is also supported by the U test analysis of the lookup time difference. We have found that the lookup time difference between novices and experts was significantly different for the same items. It can thus be suggested that expert programmers are more familiar with the syntax of the programming language and therefore do not need to remember all syntactic elements which leads to less lookup time. It is also notable that expert programmers looked at the items of the first less than they looked at the normal text. Whereas the class items of the third group was looked at more than the normal text. This finding also suggests that experts memorize shorter source codes on a semantic level, therefore they needed less lookup time. However, when the source codes got increasingly longer and more complex expert programmers might only benefit from their familiarity in the syntax of the programming language. Therefore, it makes sense that the longest and most complex algorithm showed no difference between experts and novices. Hence our results are in line with Adelson's [8] but a note of caution is due here since our experts had a significantly better working memory capacity than our novices. This could have influenced our results.

6 Conclusion

This study has identified that expert programmers are better in memorizing source code than novices. We also have found that expert programmers performed differently when presented long and complex source code than short and less complex source codes. These results support the idea that expert programmers memorize source code in semantic entities, whereas novice programmers memorize source code in syntactical entities as found by Adelson [8]. One source of weakness in this study which could have affected our results was the significant difference in working memory capacity between novices and experts. This issue of the correlation between working memory capacity and programming experience is an intriguing one which could be usefully explored in further research. There is, therefore, a definite need for conducting a similar study as presented in this paper, when the correlation between memory capacity and programming experience is clearer.

References

1. Klieme, E., Hartig, J., Rauch, D.: The concept of competence in educational contexts. Assess. Competencies Educ. Contexts. 3–22 (2008)
2. Koeppen, K., Hartig, J., Klieme, E., Leutner, D.: Current issues in competence modeling and assessment. Zeitschrift für Psychologie/J. Psychol. **216**(2), 61–73 (2008)
3. Martens, K., Niemann, D.: When do numbers count? The differential impact of the PISA rating and ranking on education policy in Germany and the US. Ger. Polit. **22**(3), 314–332 (2013)
4. Weinert, F.E.: Concept of competence: a conceptual clarification. In: Rychen, D., Salganik, S., Hersh, L. (eds.) Defining and Selecting Key Competencies. Hogrefe & Huber Publishers, Ashland (2001)
5. Leutner, D., Fleischer, J., Grünkorn, J., Klieme, E. (eds.): Competence Assessment in Education. MEMA. Springer, Cham (2017). https://doi.org/10.1007/978-3-319-50030-0
6. Kramer, M.; Hubwieser, P.; Brinda, T.: A competency structure model of object-oriented programming. In: 2016 International Conference on Learning and Teaching in Computing and Engineering (LaTICE), pp. 1–8. IEEE (2016)

7. Kramer, M., Tobinski, D., Brinda, T.: On the way to a test instrument for object-oriented programming competencies. In: Proceedings of the 16th Koli Calling International Conference on Computing Education Research, pp. 145–149. ACM (2016)
8. Adelson, B.: Problem solving and the development of abstract categories in programming languages. Mem. Cogn. **9**(4), 422–433 (1981)
9. Kellog, R.T.: A model of working memory in writing. Cogn. Demands Writ.: Process. Capacity Working Mem. Text Prod. 57–71. Amsterdam University Press (1996)
10. Hayes, J.R.: A new framework for understanding cognition and affect in writing. In: Perspectives on writing: Research, theory, and practice, p. 6 (1996)
11. Baddeley, A.D., Hitch, G.: Working memory. Psychol. Learn. Motiv. **8**, 47–89 (1974)
12. de Groot, A.: Thought and Choice in Chess. De Gruyter, Berlin (2014)
13. Chase, W.G., Simon, H.A.: Perception in chess. Cogn. Psychol. **4**(1), 55–81 (1973)
14. Corsi, P.: Human Memory and the Medial Temporal Region of the Brain. McGill University, Montréal (1972)
15. Brunetti, R., Gatto, C.D., Delogu, F.: eCorsi: Implementation and testing of the corsi block-tapping task for digital tablets. Front. Psychol. **5** (2014)
16. Beauducel, A.: Intelligence Structure Test: IST. Hogrefe, Oxford (2009)
17. Bates, M.E., Lemay, E.P.: The d2 test of attention: construct validity and extensions in scoring techniques. J. Int. Neuropsychological Soc. **10**(3), 392–400 (2004)
18. Levenshtein, V.: Binary codes capable of correcting deletions, insertions reversals. Sov. Phys. Dokl. **10**, 707 (1966)
19. Siegmund, J., Kästner, C., Liebig, J., Apel, S., Hanenberg, S.: Measuring and modeling programming experience. Empirical Softw. Eng. **19**(5), 1299–1334 (2014)
20. Misra, S., Adewumi, A.: Object-oriented cognitive complexity measures. In: Handbook of Research on Innovations in Systems and Software Engineering. IGI Global, Hershey (2015)
21. Amstad, T.: Wie verständlich sind unsere Zeitungen? University of Zurich (1978)
22. Flesch, R.: A new readability yardstick. J. Appl. Psychol. **32**(3), 221–233 (1948)
23. Bamberger, R.: Lesen - verstehen - lernen - schreiben: die Schwierigkeitsstufen von Texten in deutscher Sprache. Jugend und Volk [u.a.]. Wien (1984)

Student Retention: Towards Defining Measures for Improved Quality of Teaching and Learning in the First Year of Computer Science Studies

Bernhard Standl(✉), Elisabeth Wetzinger, and Gerald Futschek

Institute of Software Technology and Interactive Systems,
TU Wien, Vienna, Austria
{bernhard.standl,elisabeth.wetzinger,
gerald.futschek}@ifs.tuwien.ac.at

Abstract. At the Faculty of Computer Science at the TU Wien, Vienna, Austria, the studies of computer science (CS) face two issues in the first year: a gender gap and a high student dropout rate. In order to tackle these problems, the faculty has set up a project called *START Informatics* to analyse the status quo, to identify potential pitfalls, to take actions and to develop measures to improve the quality of the first year of CS studies. Therefore, we will first examine the current situation in teaching with a mixed methods approach comprising lecture observations, student and teacher interviews and a large-scale questionnaire for first year students. As a result, the objective of the project is to describe recommendations and measures to improve the learning and teaching experience with a focus on student retention and potential gender issues.

Keywords: Student retention · Gender gap · Quality in teaching
Didactics

1 Introduction

In our efforts to improve quality in the first year of CS studies, we identified two challenges: first, the gender gap, as only 20% of beginners are women and even less (15%) graduate, and second, the high dropout rate of more than 50% which is predominant in the first year of CS studies [6]. In this paper, we present a recently launched project carried out at the TU Wien, Vienna, Austria, which aims at improving teaching and learning during the first year of CS and business informatics studies focusing on student retention and gender issues, called *START Informatics*. Therefore, we first conducted a literature research in order to identify related universities that had similar problems and analysed their successful approaches. Based on these insights, we put the focus to the above mentioned two core issues and subsequently described research questions and designed a research process to identify the status quo of the first-year studies, from the students', the teachers' and external perspectives. As a result, we will be developing measures to improve the first-year studies aiming at

A. Tatnall and M. Webb (Eds.): WCCE 2017, IFIP AICT 515, pp. 640–647, 2017.
https://doi.org/10.1007/978-3-319-74310-3_64

gender equality and a higher retention rate: a didactical framework with tools for lecturers and a MOOC course as example how those approaches can be applied in practice.

1.1 Related Work

Increasing student retention and closing the gender gap are ongoing challenges for universities in particular in STEM studies. In order to master these challenges, many different activities have been done and different approaches were identified. It often turned out, that large student groups and problems resulting from this are frequent reasons for students' dissatisfaction: For instance, Derboven et al. mention in [1] that students often experience being afraid of asking questions in front of other students which might seem too easy to them, and describe it as a factor for a negative learning environment. They reported further, that students mentioned that they had to learn things they were not able to relate to and saw no relation to a practical application. Günther describes in [2] that organizational issues as finding lecture rooms, or registering for seminars also can be challenges for students. Again, Derboven et al. suggest in [1] how engineering studies can be made more attractive to students. They propose to provide students room for asking any related questions during lectures and in small learning groups. A beneficial learning climate in introductory computer science classes, where students feel comfortable in, leads very likely to better student performances what again can reduce the dropout rate [8]. Günther mentions in [2] similar issues that students *could be afraid to ask a question in front of a larger group*, and suggests to offer different channels, such as learning forums or small learning groups. A similar idea describes Hauch in [3] with providing small learning groups especially before exams. Hauch further states in [3] that students have different learning styles that should be considered in teaching. Such differentiated learning could be organized as small student learning groups or in pairs, which again is beneficial for social and interpersonal aspects. Swail et al. focus in [4] on a *Commitment to Educational Goals and the Institution* which can be a factor to increase the number of graduates if all persons including all departments, administration, faculty, staff, and students are part of such new concept. Again, Hauch sees in [3] that organizational modifications as optimizing the students' schedules can lead to an improved learning experience. As measures to encounter dropouts, Derboven et al. propose in [1] to improve the pedagogical quality of teaching and the organization of lectures. In [5] Sampietro et al. describe, that future female students are rather interested in technical studies if the faculty represents itself more in a way that attracts female students by emphasizing on diversity, sustainability, social- and soft-skills. Furthermore, they state that female students frequently identify themselves more with the studies if they see successful female role models during their studies, such as lecturers, guest lecturers or successful female graduates from their University.

In Hauch [3] it is further described that women often prefer to learn in women-only groups on- and off-line. Comparing the success of measures implemented by institutions, such as CMU (Carnegie Mellon School of Computer Science) or HMC (Harvey Mudd College) as described in [7], to the status quo at our faculty, we see significant potential for improving the overall quality by implementing changes in the didactical practice and for providing measurements to evaluate the effects of the interventions. In summarizing these related findings, we set the focus in our project first on the identification of current students' learning experiences and the evaluation of teaching practice as well as the development and implementation of actions required to design a framework for an improved practice in teaching and learning at our Faculty. Considering this, our mission is to take action for all students from all backgrounds and gender to make a smooth transition from high school to university possible.

1.2 Research Questions

Considering this, our research focus can be tailored to research questions as described below. However, they are not closed for the research process but rather frame our field of research, which emerged from the literature research and our individual research interests: *(1) Which pedagogical and organizational action steps are required to improve the quality of the first year of studies? (2) How to introduce measures for a gender sensitive first year of studies? (3) Which material, methods, tools, tasks and other supportive teaching material can help to support such experience?* In order to answer these questions, the project is structured as described in the next section.

2 Project Structure

In addition, to organizational improvements, we have learned that pedagogical measures can help to decrease the dropout rate and to retain female students. Hence, the project has three goals: First, the collection of evidence as base for the evaluation of quality in first year in CS studies by analysing courses, materials, and international best practices. Second, the development of measures and recommendations for first year teaching in CS studies by describing didactical teacher-guidelines and recommendations. Finally, the development of a MOOC course for introductory programming to be implemented in the transition phase right before the beginning of the studies. The MOOC course will take into account lessons learned during the field research and the research outcome as mentioned above.

2.1 Research Design

The complexity of assessing the quality of teaching and learning requires a combination of different instruments and approaches to retrieve an objective and valid view on the field. Therefore, the mixed research approach triangulates data from different research instruments to get the view on teaching and learning from different perspectives. First, the students' view and their experiences during the first year of studies builds the most important part of the data collection. Furthermore, we also include the teachers' perspectives and an external view on the system. Beyond focusing at first years teaching from different angles, we are also considering experiences others made so far as mentioned in the related work section above.

2.2 Research Instruments

In order to integrate the research design with different perspectives in the field, we have applied qualitative and quantitative research instruments, as it is shown in the Table 1 below.

Table 1. Research instruments

Instrument	Data collected	Group
Questionnaire (Pre-/Post)	Students' beliefs/experiences	1st year students
Group discussion	Students' experiences	1st year students
Observation of courses	View on teaching practice	1st year courses
Interview with teachers	Teachers' experiences made	Lecturers
Best practice workshop	View to outside	International experts

For identifying the changes in experiences, we conducted one survey at the beginning of the first term and a follow up survey at the beginning of the second term. We also asked freshmen students and lecturers in interviews to talk openly about positive and negative experiences they made and what suggestions they have for improving the first year of CS studies.

Each of these instruments provides data to obtain an objective view of the current state of the first semester teaching/learning experience. Our research plan, see Fig. 1, visualizes, that the accumulated data and insights will provide a base for answering our research questions and for creating well-grounded actions in practice.

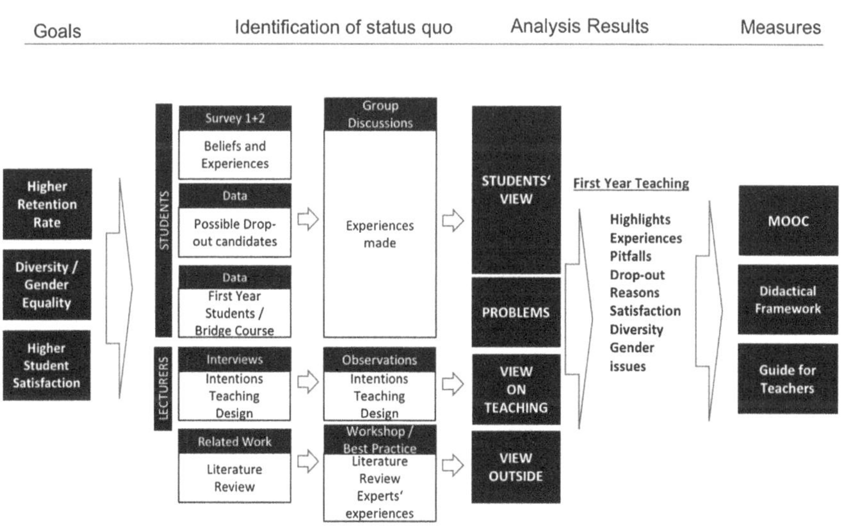

Fig. 1. Research plan

3 Actions Planned

Based on the outcomes of the literature research and of the evaluations of the current teaching and learning practices as well as from researching international best practices, we will define recommendations for our CS faculty. So far, we have outlined actions that will be accomplished in course of the 2-year project time:

1. A *MOOC (Massive Open Online Course)* to enhance the existing course "Introduction to Programming", which is compulsory for all first-year students of computer science and business informatics and challenges most of the students, depending on their level of prior knowledge. Pre-university programming skills are usually obtained at secondary schools. In order to smoothen the transition from school to university, our faculty already offers a bridging course for computer programming that is set before the first term starts. To reach even more students we will develop and offer an openly accessible MOOC on introductory programming. Although the development of this MOOC is still in the conceptual phase we suppose, that the MOOC could support the coding newbies and offer a technological bridge to the introductory course of the first semester. In particular, we assume that a MOOC in the transition phase between school and college can help to lower barriers for students without a technical pre-education and to address future female students by introducing programming in an attractive way. This was already integrated in the field of mathematics for smoothening the transition phase from school to university [9]. This assumption is in particular based on experiences described in related literature mentioned above, that a beneficial learning climate and an improved organization of a lecture can contribute positively. As we have designed our MOOC based on lecture designs, content and experiences we made in our existing successful bridging courses for freshmen students, which are limited to a certain number of students, we are convinced, that an additional MOOC course can offer learning experiences for even a larger student audience.
2. A *didactical framework* for teaching computer science aimed at increasing the quality of teaching and learning as well as higher student retention during the first year. This model considers our research outcomes and experiences we made during the project. It will include:

A guide for lecturers to adjust their lesson organization in respect of our outcomes for a higher student motivation, retention rate and learning success. This will include for example a *golden thread* approach as a crucial measure to improve the students' satisfaction and learning success, which is harmonizing similarities in content across first year courses. Our *golden thread approach* is an organizational and methodical-pedagogical approach to improve the students' learning experience and has two dimensions. In one dimension, the golden thread approach is supposed to provide organizational consistency for students. This means, there should be no barriers for finding class registration details, lecture notes or lecture videos, knowing examination requirements, and other kind of organizational issues. In the pedagogical dimension, the golden thread approach means consistency in content and teaching. Lecture content is easier graspable across all first-year lectures, if they relate to each other. In order to provide students a comprehensive picture of computer science content in different areas, it is required for lecturers to be aware of what is taught in other lectures in order to relate to each other. Hence, our golden thread approach aims at optimizing, rearranging and modifying existing structures in a way as to improve the teaching-/and learning-organization experience. This also includes measures for increasing gender equality aimed at increasing number of female students in CS studies and retaining them. Those will be measures such as community building, team work or presenting successful women in technology jobs as role models.

4 First Results

Corresponding to our research design, we have distributed 235 questionnaires at the beginning and the end of the first term to first-year students. Through defining individual codes, we were also able to match 91 of the filled questionnaires. Despite the low number of successfully matched questionnaires, still first results give insights in the students' confidence of study choice (Fig. 2).

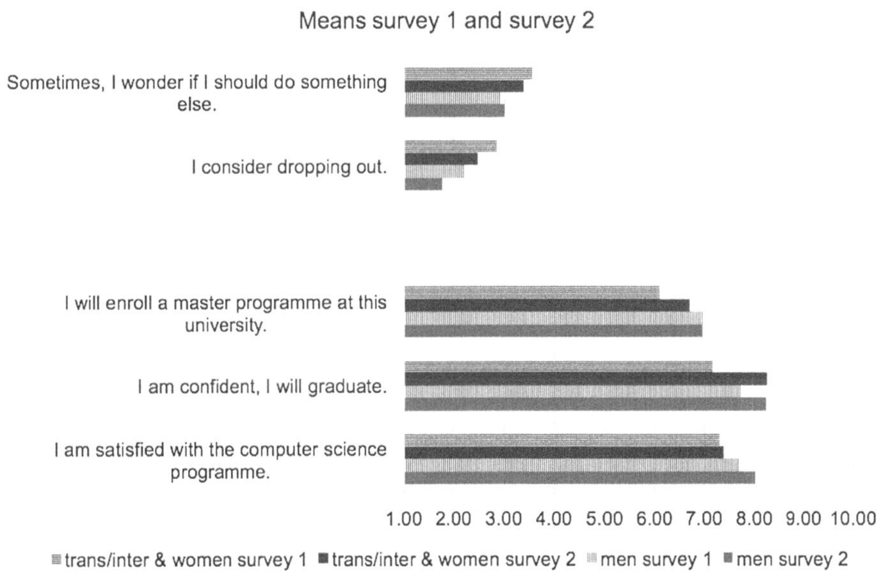

Fig. 2. Example data of student survey: Confidence in study choice (*1 = not at all... 10 = absolutely sure*)

Compared to the means of the responses in survey 1 the participants in survey 2 seem to be more confident about graduating and pursuing a master degree than those in survey one. This is indicated by higher affirmation to the statements "I am satisfied with the computer science programme", "I am confident, I will graduate" and "I will enrol a master programme at this university" as well as a weaker acceptance of the statements

"Sometimes I wonder if I should do something else" and "I consider dropping out" in survey 2 compared to survey 1.

First results of qualitative interview data underline the hypothesis that good teaching practice is a key-factor of student satisfaction. We also have observed that existing methods are perceived as good but the didactical implementation needs some improvement. In some large lectures with over 500 students in the lecture hall, a second lecturer supports the primary lecturer by managing students' questions. This has been recognized as very useful and beneficial. The golden thread approach has already been identified partly as lecture content overlaps.

Details of data we have collected in interviews and discussions also give insights in the current situation. One lecturer described his course as easy to step-in:

> *"...we start quite rudimentarily, have no prerequisites in the course. As far as the knowledge of the students is concerned."*

While another lecturer from another first-year course identified difficulties for beginners:

> *"It is easy to see that the people who come without experience are quite overwhelmed."*

But also sees problems in students' self-picture of their knowledge:

> *"...there are also people who totally overestimate themselves."*

> *"...They have no idea how a computer works."*

On the other hand, a student mentioned in an interview, that he has realized that the course on "Introduction to Programming" in fact starts out easy, but this changes over time:

> *"...At first very easy entry into programming and then the level increases very fast."*

In the group discussion, a student underlined, that there is possibly too much content to learn for one term.

> *"...who is able to learn how to code within the period of half a year has my deepest respect!"*

Another student stated in the interview, that discussions during lectures frequently fail:

> *"...I often try to participate in the discussion, but then there is no discussion developing."*

These first results indicate, that there exist already good structures for learning and teaching at our University but there is also still space to improve respectively rearrange existing methods and procedures.

5 Conclusion

This paper introduced a project named *START Informatics* at the TU Vienna which aims at developing an approach to increase student satisfaction in order to increase student retention in CS studies. We presented a brief literature review and described our motivation to carry out this project as well as the structure of the research project. First results of the data analysis show that there already exist activities at our Faculty, which have potential to improve the quality of the first year. For instance, additional lecturers assisting in large lectures, video streams and video recordings of lectures, and lecture content available on the university learning platforms. Nevertheless, there is still a need to improve the situation in many places: Above all, our planned didactic guideline can contribute to the optimization of existing processes and introduce new measures, especially for coordinating and arranging learning/teaching processes. The introduction of a MOOC is also a concrete implementation of our findings and forms a key action in improving the first year of studies in computer science concerning programming. Next steps in this project will be the collection of further data and the analysis of it in order to draw first conclusions and insights for further investigations. At the same time, we develop the MOOC course and describe the recommendations and the teaching guide including the golden thread approach.

References

1. Derboven, W., Winkler, G.: Ingenieurwissenschaftliche Studiengänge attraktiver gestalten. Springer, Heidelberg (2010). https://doi.org/10.1007/978-3-642-00558-9
2. Günther, E.A.: The ideal student (PhD Thesis) (2016)
3. Hauch, G.: Das Technikstudium aus der Sicht von Frauen und Männern. TEquality – Technik. Gender.Equality (2007)
4. Swail, W.S., Redd, K.E., Perna, L.W.: Retaining minority students in higher education: a framework for success. ASHE-ERIC Higher Education Report No. 2. School of Education and Human Development, The George Washington University, Washington, D.C. (2003)
5. Sampietro, T.W., Ramsauer, N.: Gendergerechte technische Fachhochschulstudiengänge: Ein Entwicklungsprojekt in den Studiengängen Elektrotechnik, Unternehmensinformatik und Biotechnologie der Zürcher Hochschule für Angewandte Wissenschaften. Beiträge zur nachhaltigen Entwicklung; 9. Winterthur: ZHAW Zürcher Hochschule für Angewandte Wissenschaften (2008). https://doi.org/10.21256/zhaw-114. ISBN 978-3-905745-18-4
6. Günther, E., Koeszegi, S.T.: Gender counts?! Analysis of student dropout at Vienna University of Technology. In: Béraud, A., Godfroy, A.S., Michel, J. (eds.) GIEE 2011: Gender and Interdisciplinary Education for Engineers, pp. 439–453. SensePublishers, Rotterdam (2012). https://doi.org/10.1007/978-94-6091-982-4_32
7. Alvarado, C., Zachary D.: Women in CS: an evaluation of three promising practices. In Proceedings of the 41st ACM Technical Symposium on Computer Science Education. ACM (2010)
8. Alvarado, C., Lee, C.B., Gillespie, G.: New CS1 pedagogies and curriculum, the same success factors? In: Proceedings of the 45th ACM Computer Science Symposium on Computer Science Education - SIGCSE 2014, pp. 379–384 (2014)
9. Daza, V., Makriyannis, N., Riera, C.: MOOC attack: closing the gap between pre-university and university mathematics. Open Learn. J. open Distance e-learning **28**(3), 227–238 (2013)

How to Implement Computing Education for All – Discussion of Alternative Organisational Models

Torsten Brinda(✉)

Computing Education Research Group, University of Duisburg-Essen, Essen, Germany
torsten.brinda@uni-due.de

Abstract. In the context of the implementation of computing education for all school students, different implementation models are proposed and discussed: integration of computer science concepts and competencies into existing school subjects, establishment of a separate computing subject, offers of workshops and projects in schools, and out-of-school activities. Within the context of this position paper, the afore-mentioned implementation variants are discussed and evaluated.

Keywords: Computing education · Integration · Mandatory subject

1 Introduction

The progressive imprinting of our life- and work environments by means of digitalization and the resulting, pressing challenges of personal, social and economic nature make it necessary for educational policy to respond to these challenges by further development of school education. It is noteworthy that the choice of compulsory school subjects in most countries remained essentially unchanged since the time before digitalization. Students learn several languages in order to be able to read and to write and to be prepared for the challenges of increasing internationalization. They deal with mathematics in order to understand and calculate quantitative facts. They get to know the aesthetics of musical and artistic artefacts to understand them and to discover and develop a potential talent in this area. The same applies to the social and natural sciences. Personal insights concerning interest or even talent are also possible because pupils have to take – to a certain extent – compulsory components in these areas and thus are led to processes of understanding, analysis and creation in the particular subject. With regard to aspects concerning the world characterized by digitalization, often only electoral offers (optional subjects, working groups, etc.) are provided and it is thereby left to the self-responsibility of the pupils to ascertain themselves whether they would be interested and could be successful in this field. In view of the challenges faced by digitalization, it is necessary that all pupils become adequately computing-literate in order to also understand this part of the world surrounding them and to be prepared for active participation to extend comparable to other subjects [1]. There are different approaches to implementing computing education for school students, which are discussed in the following section.

A. Tatnall and M. Webb (Eds.): WCCE 2017, IFIP AICT 515, pp. 648–652, 2017.
https://doi.org/10.1007/978-3-319-74310-3_65

2 Discussion of Organizational Models of Computing Education

2.1 Integration into Existing Subjects

There are a number of questions concerning the integration of new learning objectives into existing school subjects while leaving the available teaching time unchanged. The teachers of the respective subjects must be prepared to integrate computing competencies or have to be motivatable in an extrinsic manner. Furthermore, they must be able to acquire the necessary competencies by themselves or with the help of others to such an extent that they can competently prepare and give own lessons. Large-scale international studies on the integration of digital media into school subjects showed that this approach has not been successful in the past (e.g. [2]). It is thus left to chance in the respective field, which competencies the learners will acquire, which is problematic with regard to ensuring equal opportunities for all of them. The binding nature of competencies could be increased by using the outcome-related control mechanisms of the respective school administration (e.g. educational standards, centralized learning-level surveys, centralized exams). This could help counteract unfavorable developments. Since the individual school is usually only reached every several years by central learning surveys, demonstrable changes – even against the will of individual teachers – are, however, a lengthy process. In the case of integration into other subjects, media and computing competencies would then have to be assessed in this way, school-internal curricula including these competencies would have to be designed and maintained for standardization. What has apparently already been a challenge for the use of digital media, which was not mastered successfully in a broad way, should be almost hopeless in the case of computing concepts despite the possible inclusion of output control. While the integration of digital media requires "only" their intelligible and didactically reflected application from the particular subject perspective and "only" is an extension of the tools available for teaching certain competencies, it is still about teaching and learning in the respective subject. An inclusion of computer science concepts requires a completely new, unfamiliar perspective. This is not to deny that a large number of teachers of other subjects are already including computing concepts and competencies in their respective subjects or support extracurricular offers. This is generally positive, provided that it is done in a technically competent way, but it is essentially determined by the motivation, the specific qualifications and the commitment of these persons and it may be more than doubted that a large number of teachers of other subjects would develop enough enthusiasm for that, especially in the light of the fact that they have deliberately opted for their respective subjects. Furthermore, no systematic statement can be made about the computing qualification of these teachers and the extent to which the objectives of computing education are pursued and achieved.

In order to obtain an adequate view of computer science, teacher education study programmes in Germany require passing modules taken from the fields of programming, algorithms and data structures, modelling, software engineering, databases, computer networks, operating systems, computer architecture, formal languages and automata, impacts of computing, and computing education [3] – in short, a complete computer science teaching degree study, which would have to be studied as an additional subject. A reduced selection of individual modules, however, only reveals individual aspects; the underlying principles and the design of computing systems, their impacts on society and the teaching of corresponding concepts are only revealed in the completeness. The inclusion of new competencies in an existing subject with the same time for instruction also inevitably raises the question of what other content should be reduced. While the inclusion of digital media would only lead to a different media-based teaching-learning process, the inclusion of computing competencies (as described in curricular recommendations, e.g. k12cs.org) would in fact necessarily lead to the analysis of which of the host-subject's concepts and competencies should be reduced. In this respect the same question arises here, which also needs to be answered in the case of a mandatory subject.

2.2 A Separate (Mandatory) Subject for Computing Education

According to Fluck et al. [4] the reasons for a (mandatory) computing subject are essentially social, cultural and economic. From a social point of view, it is desirable to enable young people to participate actively in society also from a technological perspective and not only to turn them into passive consumers of technology. This also includes recognizing and promoting the new technical possibilities with regard to their potential to increase productivity. Media and tools have often served as enhancers of human skills (see [5], p. 6–8). A hammer reinforces the possibilities of the hand, a vehicle that of the legs, through texts arise new possibilities of self-expression and thought. In future, many people will get into contact with programming in their private lives as well as in their jobs and even program to a certain extent – but without being or becoming a software developer. The aim of "learning to program" is not to enable everybody to program systems such as MS Office or Facebook, as "learning to write" does not necessarily lead to writing an 800-page world bestseller book in the future – but it is a prerequisite. Computing-literate people can express themselves more comprehensively, that is also by means of computer science, and thus obtain further possibilities for action, which contributes to an increase in their productivity potential. On the other hand, uninformed decisions lead to social costs through lost productivity. All those who are qualified can, as well-informed citizens, decide by themselves which role they want to take in society – from user to creator everything is possible. From a cultural perspective, it is about empowering people to actively co-shape cultural change and not simply accept it as given and to adapt their lives accordingly. From an economic point of view, there is a great demand for specialists in the ICT sector both in Germany and abroad. In order to make and keep the respective country internationally competitive in a world increasingly characterized by computer science (see [4]), it is necessary to open up young people more than previously also professional career paths in this area. This requires that more pupils acquire competencies in the field of computer science, learn about the discipline in analogy to others represented in the school and can develop self-confidence and interest in it. The international perspective shows that computing competencies are becoming mandatory in more and more countries (e.g. [1]).

Furthermore, a separate subject offers the possibility to systematize, structure and network the technical concepts by placing them in an overall picture. Teachers, who have not studied computer science as a subject, cannot take responsibility for this, because, even if they have received a basic qualification in computer science, they can only have a very limited view of the discipline. In this context, a comparison with the school subject related to mother tongue, e.g. German language, is helpful. German language is used in all except for foreign language classes in Germany. Nevertheless, in German classes, the language itself is not only analysed, but also artefacts are produced in order to be not only a "consumer", but also a "creator" (i.e. a writer) of German language artefacts oneself. In order to promote reading in an understanding way, lessons deal, for example, with syntactical and grammatical aspects and examine the structure and special characteristics of typical text categories (e.g. authors' intentions). Furthermore, texts of different categories are produced (e.g. essays, discussions, definitions). This results in a stepwise construction of the systematics in the subject German combined with a domain-specific application of German language in (almost) all other subjects. This analogy can be well applied to the argument here. Working with digital media in other subjects also provides specific links to computer science, e.g. the functioning of semiconductors in physics, audio compression processes in music. A computing subject builds a systematic structure analogously to the language subject above, and can thus integrate cross-references to subject-specific aspects in an overall picture. This promotes the development of corresponding knowledge structures of the learners. The host-subjects' teaching staff, who have not studied computer science, cannot take responsibility for this, because they lack the necessary disciplinary overview of computer science. In this respect, both the integration and a separate subject are required.

Against an elective subject it is argued that their offering and choice are strongly dependent on local contexts and discussions taking place in them. By means of optional respectively optional compulsory subjects, continuous work and systematic competence development is not possible for all pupils.

2.3 School Working Groups/Projects

Working groups or projects enable pupils to pursue individual interests and to deepen themselves in these areas. This is fundamentally welcome and a valuable tool for the design of learning processes at school. However, this approach is unsuitable for developing competencies, which all students of a generation should develop in the same quality, since the prerequisite would be a gapless offer of corresponding working groups or projects and the competency acquisition would have to be systematically enabled and assessed. This would be the same as a mandatory school subject.

2.4 Out-of-School Activities

Outreach activities of various kinds enable pupils to get to know selected ideas of computer science in temporary workshops. Due to the time constraints and the locally different availability of such offers, neither a systematic competency development nor equality of opportunity can be achieved for all learners.

3 Conclusions

Since educational policy sometimes seems to avoid to answer the question, where the required lesson time for a new mandatory subject should come from, the concepts and competencies of this field are often either abstractly delegated for integration into all or a choice of other subjects, or totally discarded. In the case of teaching and learning with digital media in all subjects, broad integration was not yet successful, so it seems even less achievable in the case of computer science concepts and competencies. Furthermore, the goal of integrating computer science in all subjects leads to a de-professionalization of the profession of computing teachers, since it could then be concluded that every teacher can and would like to take over the respective tasks in addition to his or her own ones and that no particular study is needed for that. This can only lead to either no systematic computing education at all, or one only at a professional level, which can be supported by a large number of teachers – it would be surprising, if this level would exceed that of primary education significantly. Since the recruitment of teachers is essentially controlled by school subjects, a separate mandatory computing subject seems to be without alternative at the present time.

To this end, all countries should develop a plan for the computing competencies that all learners should acquire in the future, and by which time this should be implemented in which way in the school system.

References

1. Hubwieser, P., Giannakos, M.N., Berges, M., Brinda, T., Diethelm, I., Magenheim, J., Pal, Y., Jackova, J., Jasute, E.: A global snapshot of computer science education in K-12 schools. In: Proceedings of the 2015 ITiCSE on Working Group Reports (ITICSE-WGR 2015), pp. 65–83. ACM, New York (2015). http://dx.doi.org/10.1145/2858796.2858799
2. Plomp, T., Anderson, R.E., Law, N., Quale, A. (eds.): Cross-National Information and Communication Technology: Policies and Practices in Education. Information Age Publishing, Charlotte (2009)
3. Secretary of the Standing Conference of the Ministers of Education and Cultural Affairs of the Federal Countries of Germany (ed.): Ländergemeinsame inhaltliche Anforderungen für die Fachwissenschaften und Fachdidaktiken in der Lehrerbildung. Beschluss der Kultusministerkonferenz vom 16.10.2008 i. d. F. vom 06.10.2016 (2016). (in German), http://www.kmk.org/fileadmin/Dateien/veroeffentlichungen_beschluesse/2008/2008_10_16-Fachprofile-Lehrerbildung.pdf
4. Fluck, A., Webb, M., Cox, M., Angeli, C., Malyn-Smith, J., Voogt, J., Zagami, J.: Arguing for computer science in the school curriculum. J. Educ. Technol. Soc. **19**(3), 38–46 (2016)
5. Guzdial, M.: Learner-centered design of computing education: research on computing for everyone. Synth. Lect. Hum.-Centered Inf. **8**(6), 1–165 (2015)

Education in the Digital Networked World

Torsten Brinda[1(✉)] and Ira Diethelm[2]

[1] Computing Education Research Group, University of Duisburg-Essen, Essen, Germany
torsten.brinda@uni-due.de
[2] Computing Education Research Group, University of Oldenburg, Oldenburg, Germany
ira.diethelm@uni-oldenburg.de

Abstract. The steadily advancing digitalization of our world requires that educational systems adequately prepare everybody for the resulting challenges. Different actors in educational systems often see the solution either in digital media education, or computing education. This position paper presents a combined model – the so-called "Dagstuhl triangle", which was developed in collaboration of about 30 computer scientists, computing and media education researchers, teachers, and representatives from IT companies and foundations.

Keywords: Computing education · Media education · Digital education K12

1 Introduction

Digital change, which affects our entire society, culture and economy, is shaped by people who are qualified in computer science, persons who have either completed vocational training or a university degree in computer science or who have acquired such competencies by themselves. These people develop new devices and device categories, associated operating systems, as well as applications and apps for a variety of purposes, not just personal needs. By providing AppStores developers of large operating systems (such as Windows, macOS, iOS, Android, Linux) have created infrastructures and distribution channels, which in principle enable everyone to implement and make available software solutions to problems of any kind. The ICT economy, which drives the world's change through digitization and thus plays a key role in shaping social and work-related processes, has been "complaining" internationally about a shortage of skilled workers – according to forecasts, this deficit could lead to e.g. 120,000 missing academics by the year 2030 in Germany alone[1].

The developments of the past years have shown that the progress of digitalization and automation is by no means a short-term phenomenon, rather steadily advancing and that new device categories, applications and application scenarios are constantly being developed. Although the term "digitization" dominates the description and discussion of phenomena and artefacts, corresponding innovations have also been described as "new media", "modern information and communication technologies" or

[1] http://www.it-business.de/fachkraeftemangel-spitzt-sich-zu-a-541910/.

A. Tatnall and M. Webb (Eds.): WCCE 2017, IFIP AICT 515, pp. 653–657, 2017.
https://doi.org/10.1007/978-3-319-74310-3_66

more broadly, as computing systems before. An end to these innovations and technological developments is not in sight. The concrete systems (applications and devices) are subject to a constant change (in particular by new versions with modified user interfaces) and disappearing off sight, while the underlying technical concepts of computer science are time-stable. Many of the above-mentioned systems and applications can, in principle, be used as teaching media for certain technical contexts, but not all. However, all of these systems are based on certain basic principles of computer science, which include, but are not limited to, terms such as encoding and modelling of information, algorithms, data structures, programming and network communication.

2 Educational Perspectives on the Digital Networked World

Advancements in digitalization make young people get in contact with a wide range of computing systems. As a result, they develop mental models of their structure and working principles. These self-constructed models do not always correspond to the scientific ones: they often are incomplete, partly correct, faulty. So far, only a few empirical findings on the everyday conceptions of pupils in the field of computer science (e.g. [2, 3]) are available. However, understanding the world and co-shaping it requires correct models, which must be developed in school by teachers with appropriate professional competence. But what is needed to really understand the "digital world"? How can this be characterized without a long list of normative settings of content or competencies?

In the so-called *Dagstuhl declaration* on "Education in the Digital Networked World" [1] (in short: "digital education") it was argued that in comprehensively oriented education the phenomena, artefacts, systems and situations of the "digital world" encountered and perceived by students must be regarded from three different perspectives: the *structural perspective*, the *social-cultural perspective* and the *application-oriented perspective*, see Fig. 1. This means: from an *application-oriented perspective*, the question should be answered how and when specific systems and tools are used for which purposes, in a *socio-cultural perspective* the effects and interactions between system, individual and society are examined and the consideration of systems "from within" from a *structural perspective* provides insight into how special and typical systems (in principle) are internally structured and how they function. All are needed to provide sustainable education as a solid ground for a "digital society".

The approach values existing views such as *user training*, *media education* and *computing education* and has the intention of integrating these views into a coherent overall concept. In order to comprehensively understand all the above-mentioned facets and thus to contribute to the construction of a coherent image of the learners with regard to the "digital world", a corresponding intake of all the mentioned perspectives is necessary. Interestingly, already in 1983 an IFIP working group for elementary education stated that "the aim of elementary education is to help every child reach his/her full human potential and to achieve social, emotional, and mental maturity. When computers are introduced into schools, we should be concerned about three levels of use – the technical level (how and when to use them), the understanding level (why they bring about the results they do) and the reflective level (the personal and societal values involved in using them)" [4]. In order to enable learners for active participation in and shaping of the "digital world" with others, these perspectives should again be taken up from a creating point of view as well. From an *application-oriented perspective*, it is then possible to question how tasks or problems of everyday life can be performed resp. solved using existing systems. From a *socio-cultural perspective*, it is considered how interactions between systems, individuals and society can be shaped, and finally, from a *structural point of view*, it is investigated how systems for the solution of problems can be developed, that is, systematically planned and subsequently programmed. The Dagstuhl triangle (see Fig. 1) provides an overall model for digital education, i.e. learning *about* the "digital world". It explicitly includes the use of computer systems as teaching tools in all disciplines, but goes far beyond that by including computing competences, which make active participation also from a technical point of view possible.

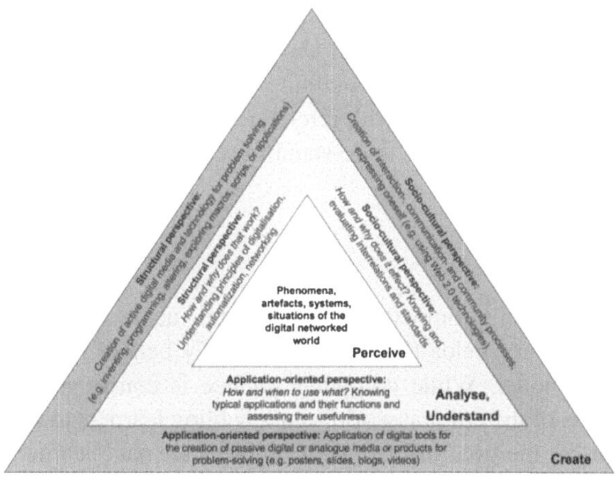

Fig. 1. Educational perspectives on the digital networked world ("Dagstuhl perspectives")

Public discussions on the value and the incorporation of computing competences into education show that various actors have a wide-ranging understanding of the terminology, which differs considerably from scientific definitions (e.g. [5]). For example, the term "informatics" is also used by some actors for the use of digital media in educational processes, as well as for user qualification regarding standard software, others associate aspects of computer administration or programming with this term. Even if computer-based systems are involved, computer science is a scientific discipline. Some actors also occasionally demand that "algorithms" or "data structures" should be integrated into school and use these terms as representatives of the discipline [6]. Even though these concepts are of great importance within the discipline, they are however hardly learnable in an isolated way that would lead to systematic development of an individuals' computing competences. A similar approach would be in mathematics to deal with just the function or – or even only – with the set concept. Both concepts are disciplinarily central, but there are other important concepts, such as the concept of probability, which in turn refers to the concepts function and set.

Computer science is the science of the systematic processing of information, in particular the automatic processing with the help of computers. It deals with the principles and procedures underlying the understanding and modelling of automatic information processing including modelling and distributing via networks and its application in the development of computing systems [7] and is an academic discipline [8, p. 3]. In the Anglo-American language area, the underlying cognitive processes are referred to as "Computational Thinking" [9], a way of thinking that goes beyond hardware and software and provides a framework to analyse systems and problems.

In this context, the question is sometimes raised as to why knowledge about computer science is necessary, if the aim is "only" the competent use of computer systems and no corresponding professional career in the field of computer science is pursued. This question could be applied in the same way to all other school subjects, for example: Why must one be able to interpret poems, if one does not want to become a poet? Why do you have to learn mental arithmetic, if you can use a pocket calculator later? Why do you have to analyse the physique of animals in detail, if you do not want to become a veterinarian? etc. Through the discipline-specific ways of creating a separate approach to the respective discipline results. All the above questions can therefore be answered, for example, with reference to overall educational goals, such as "participation" and resp. or "world understanding".

3 Conclusions

The teaching of computing competences and digital media education are, therefore, essentially complementary fields that can substantially benefit from each other in the sense of the above model. While computer science is concerned with teaching the underlying principles of the "digital world" and enabling learners to actively participate in the "digital world", the goal of media education is to make learners competent and reflected users of existing IT systems [8, p. 4]. Both aspects are important and central to education in the "digital world". Even if advertisements propagate that there is "an app for everything", we have to prepare young people for a world that does not yet exist, involving technologies that have not yet been invented, and that present technical and ethical challenges of which we are not yet aware [8, p. 3]. Comprehensive education must therefore also look at digitalization from a computing perspective as a subject of instruction. Various national approaches have already been developed and implemented [10]. Overall concepts of education in the digital age should therefore integrate all the above-mentioned perspectives and come to the conclusion that *not either digital literacy or computing education* is the solution for the needs of the digital age – it is the adequate *combination of both*, as summarized in the Dagstuhl declaration [1]:

1. Education in the digital networked world must be taken into consideration from a structural, socio-cultural and application-oriented perspective.
2. A separate learning area (e.g. a mandatory school subject) must be set up in schools, in which the basic concepts and competences for the orientation in the digital networked world are acquired.
3. In addition, it is task of all subjects to integrate and implement digital literacy.

4. Digital education in the above-mentioned learning area as well as within the other subjects must be carried out continuously across all school levels for all pupils following a spiral curriculum.
5. An accordingly well-founded teacher training in the related sciences of computer science and media education is essential for this. This means:
   a. A study component within teacher education, which includes concepts and competencies from the fields of computer science and media education, has to be established.
   b. All related sciences must meet the challenge and conduct further research and develop concepts for digital education.
   c. Comprehensive training and further education for teachers from the above-mentioned perspectives must be set up in the short term.

References

1. Brinda, T., Diethelm, I., Gemulla, R., Romeike, R., Schöning, J., Schulte, C., et al.: Bildung in der digitalen vernetzten Welt – Dagstuhl Erklärung (2016). (in German). https://www.gi.de/aktuelles/meldungen/detailansicht/article/dagstuhl-erklaerung-bildung-in-der-digitalen-vernetzten-welt.html
2. Diethelm, I., Wilken, H., Zumbrägel, S.: An investigation of secondary school students' conceptions on how the internet works. In: Proceedings of the 12th Koli Calling International Conference on Computing Education Research, pp. 67–73. ACM, New York (2012)
3. Rücker, M.T., Pinkwart, N.: Review and discussion of children's conceptions of computers. J. Sci. Educ. Technol. **25**(2), 274–283 (2016)
4. Tinsley, J.D., Tagg, E.D. (eds.): Informatics in elementary education. In: Proceedings of the IFIP WG 3.1 Working Conference on Informatics in Elementary Education. Elsevier, Amsterdam (1984)
5. Institut für Bildung in der Informationsgesellschaft gGmbH: Stakeholder-Studie zum Bundestagsbeschluss. Durch Stärkung der Digitalen Bildung Medienkompetenz fördern und digitale Spaltung überwinden (2016). (in German). http://www.ibi.tu-berlin.de/images/161013_IBIStudie_Digitale_Bildung_BT-Beschluss_Langfassung.pdf
6. Secretary of the Standing Conference of the Ministers of Education and Cultural Affairs of the Federal Countries of Germany: Bildung in der digitalen Welt. Strategie der Kultusministerkonferenz (2016). (in German). https://www.kmk.org/fileadmin/Dateien/pdf/PresseUndAktuelles/2016/Bildung_digitale_Welt_Webversion.pdf
7. German Informatics Association (ed.): Was ist Informatik? (2005). (in German). https://www.gi.de/themen/was-ist-informatik.html
8. Computing at School Working Group: Computer Science – A Curriculum for Schools (2012). https://www.computingatschool.org.uk/data/uploads/ComputingCurric.pdf
9. Wing, J.M.: Computational thinking. Commun. ACM **49**(3), 33–35 (2006)
10. Hubwieser, P., Giannakos, M.N., Berges, M., Brinda, T., Diethelm, I., Magenheim, J., Pal, Y., Jackova, J., Jasute, E.: A global snapshot of computer science education in K-12 schools. In: Proceedings of the 2015 ITiCSE on Working Group Reports (ITICSE-WGR 2015), pp. 65–83. ACM, New York (2015). http://dx.doi.org/10.1145/2858796.2858799

Activation of Computer Science Teachers in Slovenia

Andrej Brodnik[1,2(✉)], Matija Lokar[3], and Nataša Mori[1]

[1] Faculty of Computer and Information Science, University of Ljubljana, Ljubljana, Slovenia
{andrej.brodnik,natasa.mori}@fri.uni-lj.si
[2] Department of Information Science and Technology, University of Primorska, Koper, Slovenia
[3] Faculty of Mathematics and Physics, University of Ljubljana, Ljubljana, Slovenia
matija.lokar@fmf.uni-lj.si

Abstract. The paper describes an approach of improving Slovenian Computer Science Education in general secondary school by forming an active and sustainable Computer Science Community of Practice (CS CoP). In project NAPOJ three systems teachers use in teaching programming are combined: CS e-textbook, LMS Moodle and TOMO, automatic assessment system for learning programming. Group of master teachers were selected, who prepared the initial set of in-class resources and material at a half a week workshop. This was followed by the regional workshops for other CS teachers throughout the Slovenia and run by master teachers. Development of CoP was observed and analyzed through various data gathering tools, such as questionnaires, discussions and observations, and preliminary results are highlighted.

Keywords: Community of practice · Programming · Master teachers
Teaching resources · General secondary school

1 Introduction

Computer Science (CS) is taught in Slovenian general secondary school in the first year as a mandatory and in the later three years as an elective subject. Fortunately, the valid curriculum is written very openly, covering all four years and giving teachers quite some freedom in choosing the topics. Through this openness we aimed to improve general secondary school's CS education [1]. The first step was to introduce a new e-textbook [2] and some changes in the national examination process (Matura). There has been quite a lot of concern and anxiety among the teachers about the requirements these changes would bring to their teaching. Through interviews with them, following discussion in Forums, discussion at various teacher's related events, and through personal contacts we found out that teachers as one of their main concerns feel insecurity of how to approach teaching programming. They also had an impression of lacking the teaching resources. As reported in [3–9], a possible answer to such concerns is a Community of practice (CoP). In this paper we report on intervention in

A. Tatnall and M. Webb (Eds.): WCCE 2017, IFIP AICT 515, pp. 658–662, 2017.
https://doi.org/10.1007/978-3-319-74310-3_67

which we established CoP among the Slovenian CS teachers to increase their teaching confidence and consequently improve student's knowledge of programming.

The paper is organized as follows: first, the general theory behind CoP is highlighted, then our project is presented in more detail and some of our experiences are listed, the paper is then concluded with our thoughts.

2 Communities of Practice

As CS is a relatively new discipline in K-12 education we face many challenges related to the way CS is taught. In many schools teachers feel isolated [6], which combined with a lack of confidence is also reported in [8]. To overcome the feeling of isolation we can introduce CoP. In [9] the following definition is given: "CoP are groups of people who share a concern or a passion for something they do and learn how to do it better as they interact regularly". An important part of CoP, besides sharing the interest, is that the members are practitioners sharing experience, stories, tools, and ways of addressing problems. Fincher and Tenenberg [10, 11] created the Disciplinary Commons project, which invites a group of computing educators within the same discipline to meet monthly during an academic year in order to share, reflect upon, and document their teaching. Ni et al. [6] report how this approach has been useful in establishing a community to support high school (HS) CS teachers. One of their most important results was that teachers reported they were able to build a sense of belonging to a community. Participation in community activities helped them to validate their work and build confidence in themselves as HS CS teachers. A successful CoP can be observed within Computing At School (CAS) movement in Great Britain. As reported in [8], CAS has a particular focus on supporting teachers to deliver the new curriculum in the classroom, with confidence and enthusiasm, through building local CoP.

3 NAPOJ Project

NAPOJ (potion) stands for *Design of Teaching Algorithms and Programming and Establishing a Community* (translated from Slovenian). It is a far-reaching idea to establish a community of Slovenian K12 teachers of CS, starting with a general secondary schools (*Gymnasia*).

3.1 Goal

The primary goal was to establish an active and sustainable CS teacher CoP and provide it with the necessary initial material and tools. A slightly narrower aim has been to produce and share resources as well as to document and share knowledge about teaching and student learning in introductory programming courses.

We mostly tried to address the feeling of teachers that they have not enough knowledge to approach introductory programming and to show them that through active participation within CoP they would gain confidence they feel they are lacking.

The first of three steps was to integrate several resources teachers use in teaching programming. The second step was a hands-on workshop for CS master teachers, where an initial set of in-class material was prepared. In the third step master teachers ran their local workshops for all CS teachers, covering whole Slovenia. With regional workshops, we wanted to give master teachers the opportunity not only to adjust the workshops to the needs of the local communities but also to establish stronger contacts.

3.2 Framework

The target group were all Slovenian Gymnasia CS teachers. The model of Master Teachers was followed. Master Teachers (cf. [8]) are teachers with expertise in CS as well as with skills necessary to impart this to other teachers. This model focuses on local, face-to-face, peer-to-peer delivery. Master Teachers run regional professional development sessions and offer support to their local community of teachers. This way on one side we lower the cost, but even more importantly enable face-to-face and peer-to-peer delivery to all teachers. In our case, candidates for master teachers were selected individually and 14 of them became CS master teachers.

One of the project's goals was to prepare the learning and CoP environment by integrating three systems. The main platform used for resources and interaction among teachers is a Moodle LMS, where the resources are stored following the chapters in the e-textbook [2]. The Moodle LMS also includes forums and other activities, where teachers can collaborate by interacting, exchanging experience and discussing CS education. The LMS platform is complemented by the CS e-textbook and TOMO, an automatic assessment system environment for learning programming [12].

3.3 Some Evaluation and Results

We were observing the development of the community behaviour from the very beginning. Several surveys for teachers (for master teachers as well as for attendants of regional workshops) were conducted through online questionnaires and discussions. The master teachers' activity was also measured via their online participation. For each milestone the data were collected as follows:

1. **Face-to-face meeting with candidates for master teachers** (*June 2016*): (i) Online questionnaire and discussion after the meeting, and (ii) Activity (in integrated online system).
2. **Online meeting with candidates for master teachers** (*June 2016*): (i) Online questionnaire before the meeting, (ii) Discussion after the meeting, and (iii) Activity.
3. **Workshop for master teachers** (*August 2016*): (i) Online questionnaire before the workshop, (ii) Programming assignment and online questionnaire about the assignment, (iii) Observation, (iv) Discussion after the workshop, and (v) Activity.
4. **Regional workshops for teachers** (*November 2016 – January 2017*): (i) Online questionnaire before the workshop, (ii) after the workshop, and (iii) Activity.

We observed that the participants (master teachers as well as participants in regional workshops) had done most of the activities Wenger mentions in [9, 13] as the building blocks of a successful CoP. Those activities were problem solving, requests for information, seeking experience, reusing assets, coordination, and strategy, building an argument, growing confidence, discussing developments, documenting projects, visits, mapping knowledge and identifying gaps. During this half-year period, most of the myths about CoP mentioned in [9], were also encountered. In a forthcoming paper, we will discuss how we coped with those myths.

3.4 Questionnaires and Observations

All three of the questionnaires used before the milestones had similar sections: besides the demographic questions, also questions about the content of CS course, attitude towards CS and teacher's self-evaluation. The differences were only in the section, which was intended for the specific milestone. We got data from all 14 Master Teachers and from 27 teachers who attended regional workshops. They represent a good sample of Slovenian teachers as we have 53 Gymnasia with approximately 70 teachers of CS.

The data gathered covers broader aspects as those reported in this paper and had to be analyzed further. To observe our main goal – establishment of an active CoP – an important part of the questionnaires were the questions about the teacher's motivation in programming and their self-confidence. We asked them if they like to code (95.2% said yes), and if they thought they are good coders. Interestingly, the opinion between master teachers and teachers at regional workshop was exactly the opposite, although they all completed short programming test without a problem. Master teachers thought they were quite good coders (7.7% very good, 30.8% good and 61.5% in the middle), while other teachers were more pessimistic (18.2% good, 54.5% in the middle, 18.2% bad and 9.1% very bad).

After the first meeting, we asked questions about the community in general, whether it would succeed to establish an active one and what should be done at their local school to improve the CS course. We were positively surprised about the optimism of all teachers regarding the development of community and the resources. However, they were still worried about the students' motivation for programming.

During the workshop, different aspects of socializing were observed, where the most important and efficient way of mutual introducing and forming groups was a team building section.

Finally yet importantly, we asked them what they liked about the master teachers idea, and one teacher explicitly said, "I like the fact that the resources are made by the teachers who actually teach in class."

4 Conclusion

We are planning to gather the remaining data, while improving and widening the community. We cannot overlook the teachers missing self-confidence, which needs to be addressed properly. Furthermore, there is still a room for improvement in gathering the data and further activation of community, but we were very pleased with optimism and enthusiasm teachers showed and the amount of resources they already shared.

Acknowledgement. The project was funded by Google, with Computer Science for High School (CS4HS) 2016 award.

References

1. Mori, N., Brodnik, A., Lokar, M.: Development of CS curriculum for secondary schools through changes in external examination and textbooks. In: Proceedings of the IFIP TC3 Joint Conference Stakeholders and Information Technology in Education, p. 58. University of Minho, Guimares (2016)
2. Mori, N., Lokar, M.: A new interactive computer science textbook in Slovenia. In: Brodnik, A., Tort, F. (eds.) ISSEP 2016. LNCS, vol. 9973, pp. 167–178. Springer, Cham (2016). https://doi.org/10.1007/978-3-319-46747-4_14
3. Chalmers, L., Keown, P.: Communities of practice and professional development. Int. J. Lifelong Educ. **2**(25), 139–156 (2006)
4. Corso, M., Giacobbe, A.: Building communities of practice that work: a case study based research. In: The Sixth European Conference on Organizational Knowledge, Learning, and Capabilities, pp. 17–19. Bentley College, Waltham (2005)
5. CUREE: Centre for the use of research evidence in education: Understanding what enables high quality professional learning (a report on the research evidence). http://www.curee.co.uk/files/publication/[site-timestamp]/CUREE-Report.pdf. Accessed 3 Mar 2017
6. Ni, L., Guzdial, M., Tew, A. E., Morrison, B., Galanos, R.: Building a community to support HS CS teachers: the disciplinary commons for computing educators. In: Proceedings of the 42nd ACM Technical Symposium on Computer Science Education (SIGCSE 2011), pp. 553–558. ACM (2011)
7. Sentance, S., Humphreys, S.: Online vs face-to-face engagement of computing teachers for their professional development needs. In: Brodnik, A., Vahrenhold, J. (eds.) ISSEP 2015. LNCS, vol. 9378, pp. 69–81. Springer, Cham (2015). https://doi.org/10.1007/978-3-319-25396-1_7
8. Sentance, S., Humphreys, S., Dorling, M.: The network of teaching excellence in CS and master teachers. In: Proceedings of the 9th Workshop in Primary and Secondary Computing Education, pp. 80–88. ACM (2014)
9. Wenger-Trayner, E., Wenger-Trayner, B.: Introduction to Communities of Practice. A Brief Overview of the Concept and its Uses. Wenger-Trayner (2015)
10. Fincher, S., Tenenberg, J.: Warren's question. In: Proceedings of the Third International Computing Education Research Workshop, pp. 51–60. ACM (2007)
11. Tenenberg, J., Fincher, S.: Opening the door of the computer science classroom: the disciplinary commons. In: Proceedings of the 38th SIGCSE Technical Symposium on Computer Science Education, pp. 514–518. ACM (2007)
12. Lokar, M., Pretnar, M.: Tomo, automatic assessment system environment for learning programming (2015). https://www.projekt-tomo.si. Accessed 3 Mar 2017
13. Wenger, E.: Communities of Practice. Cambridge University Press, Cambridge (1998)

Computational Thinking in Primary Schools: Theory and Causal Models

Christine Bescherer(✉) and Andreas Fest

Ludwigsburg University of Education, Ludwigsburg, Germany
{bescherer,fest}@ph-ludwigsburg.de

Abstract. During a one-year-subproject, student teachers develop and pilot learning scenarios and materials in mathematics classrooms for third and fourth graders fostering 'Computational Thinking'. To evaluate these interventions regarding the impact on the student teachers as well as the schoolchildren 'impact models' are used. These models based on program impact theory will be continuously refined to converge to a 'proof of the success' of the project.

Keywords: Computational thinking in primary schools
Half-baked microworlds · Evaluation theory · Impact models

1 Introduction

The project 'Digital Learning in Primary Schools Stuttgart/Ludwigsburg' ('Digitales Lernen in der Grundschule Stuttgart/Ludwigsburg' dileg-SL) at the Ludwigsburg University of Education is funded by Deutsche Telekom Stiftung. It aims at the development of digital learning scenarios at primary schools. Beneath the productive and critical exposure to digital media in different contexts and subjects like German and English language, biology, music, physical education, another important objective is the development of primary schoolchildren's basic competencies in computer science and algorithmic thinking.

Student teachers learn in a special seminar about 'computational thinking' themselves and then develop learning scenarios to foster algorithmic and computer science related competencies in mathematics classrooms for third or fourth grade. These student teachers will test their scenarios in 3rd and 4th grade classrooms and reflect on their experience.

Projects like this where classroom related, rather complex learning scenarios are developed and implemented always pose the problem how to show they are successful. The number of student teachers and primary schoolchildren are here too small to allow sophisticated quantitative research statistics. In addition, in this case because of the structure of the project an experimental design is not possible either. So how to evaluate the learning scenarios or to describe and even measure the impact? Further, questions like whether there are different impacts for different groups (i.e. girls/boys or low/high computer use) also need to be answered.

The whole project dileg-SL started in 2016 and the special seminar in math teacher education referred to will take place from October 2017 until July 2018 (two semesters). The schoolchildren will have use of iPads and/or Convertibles supplied by the university.

A. Tatnall and M. Webb (Eds.): WCCE 2017, IFIP AICT 515, pp. 663–667, 2017.
https://doi.org/10.1007/978-3-319-74310-3_68

2 Theoretical Background

The theoretical background covers the teaching and learning of computer science and algorithmic thinking in (primary) schools as well as program impact theory. In this paper the aspects of media pedagogy are not discussed even though they play a major role in the umbrella project.

2.1 Computational Thinking/FITness

'Computational thinking' is a rather inflationary used concept, which is still not well defined. Wing [1] describes 'conceptualization' and 'thinking on multiple levels of abstraction' as important aspects of computational thinking. Grover and Pea [2] give in their review of the state of the field on computational thinking in K-12 the following list as widely accepted elements of computational thinking

- 'Abstractions and pattern generalizations (including models and simulations)
- Systematic processing of information
- Symbol systems and representations
- Algorithmic notions of flow of control
- Structured problem decomposition (modularizing)
- Iterative, recursive, and parallel thinking
- Conditional logic
- Efficiency and performance constraints
- Debugging and systematic error detection' [2, p. 39/40].

Obviously, these elements cover very different levels of knowledge: there are some factual knowledge (i.e. conditional logic, efficiency and performance constraints), some are basic concepts of computer science thinking (i.e. algorithmic notions of flow of control or iterative, recursive, and parallel thinking) as well as typical procedures computer scientists use (like modelling and simulation, modularization, debugging and systematic error detection). Therefore, these elements are not a list to go through step by step to learn computational thinking, rather the factual knowledge and basic concepts should be understood and deepened by working like a typical computer scientist.

An older definition of what is necessary to be 'FIT' in using IT is the 'Fluency with Information Technology' ('FITness') concept [3] from 1999. There the authors define three kinds of knowledge: contemporary skills, foundational concepts, and intellectual capabilities. Further, they stated the role of programming in becoming 'fit' with information technology. Programming and mathematics learning in primary school have a long tradition [4]. Gadanidis et al. [5] describe a concept for introducing computational thinking in primary mathematics classrooms where grade 1 pupils experience several aspects of computational thinking.

During the ScratchMath project a 'framework for action' to bring together primary programming and mathematics was developed by Benton et al. [6]. It consists of the

'5Es' – 'explore', 'explain', 'envisage', 'exchange' and 'bridgE' which scaffold the design of learning scenarios combining programming and math learning.

2.2 Half-Baked Microworlds

Writing program code on the empty screen is demotivating or not following learning theories like constructivism. Primary schoolchildren are not supposed to become experts in programming 'full grown' computer languages but they should experience how computers work and develop basic concepts. Later in secondary schools, they can build their computer science skills and competencies based on these fundamental exposures.

Therefore, learning scenarios based on educational theories like Seymour Papert's microworlds [4] qualify for the project. Another suitable concept are different levels of worked examples with either intentional mistakes or cloze which learners have to identify and fill out [8]. Learning with worked examples has been successful for learning mathematical concepts [9] and could similarly work while learning programming. A combination of these learning scenarios are the half-baked microworlds proposed by Kynigos [10].

Kynigos understands half-baked microworlds 'designed to facilitate communication between researchers, technicians, teachers and students as they become engaged in changing them' [10, p. 335].

2.3 Program Impact Theory

'Program Theory-Driven Evaluation Science is the systematic use of substantive knowledge about the phenomena under investigation and scientific methods to improve, to produce knowledge and feedback about, and to determine the merit, worth, and significance of evaluands such as social, educational, health, community, and organizational programs.' [11, p. 7] One way of measuring the success of a pedagogical intervention is to set up a 'casual model', which gives the statistical correlations between different input- and output-factors. This would implicate that there is a measurable cause with correlation and high effect size, which in small-scale real classroom settings is often just not possible.

To develop, to describe and to communicate the impact(s) of a program or a complex learning scenario impact models [12] are used. Impact models do not describe cause and effect, but they allow closing in on an empirical and well-founded causal relationship.

An impact model fitting to classroom interventions usually consist of theoretical input – activities/learning scenarios – expected or measured outcome(s) (Fig. 1). As the project develops further this initial model will be iteratively refined with every new finding. The series of improved impact models show the impact of the project work thus converging to a conclusive argument. This is not an analytical or empirical proof but it comes close to one.

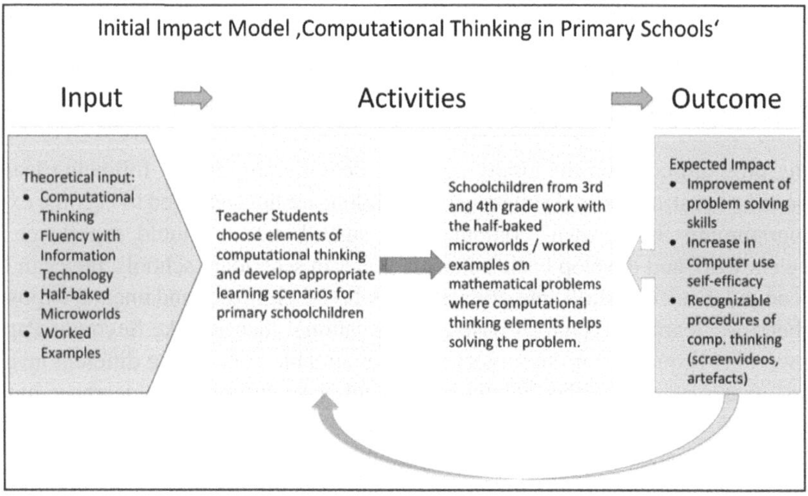

Fig. 1. Initial impact model

3 Methods and Implementation

In the project, the student teachers will work in the seminar with half-baked microworlds as well as worked examples to learn about the elements of computational thinking. In the second half of the semester, they will develop analogues scenarios for the schoolchildren in 3rd and 4th grade. These scenarios will be used in real classrooms in a primary school with a special focus on media education close to the university. Afterwards the student teachers will reflect on the teaching experience according to previously discussed hypotheses.

To see whether a rather complex project involving different target groups like student teachers and schoolchildren works at all or to determine for which subgroups it fits better different ways of measuring or research approaches can be used. Since only a small numbers of participants will take part in the project and an experimental design is not possible we decided to work with impact models of the program theory evaluation approach.

One of the measures beside the artefacts the student teachers and the pupils will produce (i.e. Logo or Scratch programs, descriptions of the learning scenarios, worksheets,…) computer use self-efficacy questionnaires will be used to determine whether there are pre-post-differences. Figure 1 shows the initial causal model for the subproject described in this paper, which will be refined further during the project.

4 Outlook and Summary

The seminar and the piloting in the primary school will start in October 2017. Until then the half-baked microworlds, the worked examples for the student teachers, the questionnaires and preparations for the analysis of the artefacts and the screen videos will be developed. This paper gives an idea about the theoretical input and the planed methods including an initial impact model according to program theory evaluation science.

Acknowledgments. The authors would like to thank the Deutsche Telekom Stiftung (https://www.telekom-stiftung.de/en) for financing the project.

References

1. Wing, J.M.: Computational thinking. Commun. ACM **49**(3), 33–35 (2006)
2. Grover, S., Pea, R.: Computational thinking in K–12 a review of the state of the field. Educ. Res. **42**(1), 38–43 (2013)
3. National Research Council: Being Fluent with Information Technology. National Academies Press, Washington (1999)
4. Benton, L., Hoyles, C., Kalas, I., Noss, R.: Bridging primary programming and mathematics: some findings of design research in England. Digit. Exp. Math. Educ. **3**, 115–138 (2017)
5. Gadanidis, G., Hughes, J.M., Minniti, L., White, B.J.: Computational thinking, grade 1 students and the binomial theorem. Digit. Exp. Math. Educ. **3**, 77–96 (2017)
6. Benton, L., Hoyles, C., Kalas, I., Noss, R.: Building mathematical knowledge with programming: insights from the ScratchMaths project. In: Conference Proceedings Constructionism in Action 2016, pp. 25–32 (2016)
7. Papert, S.: Teaching children thinking. J. Struct. Lang. **4**, 219–229 (1975)
8. Renkl, A.: Worked-out examples: instructional explanations support learning by self-explanations. Learn. Instr. **12**(5), 529–556 (2002)
9. Scherrmann, A.: Learning with worked examples – how does it work in a real classroom setting? In: Proceedings 10th Congress of European Research in Mathematics Education (2017). https://keynote.conference-services.net/resources/444/5118/pdf/CERME10_0322.pdf, Accessed 30 Aug 2017
10. Kynigos, C.: Half-baked logo microworlds as boundary objects in integrated design. Inform. Educ. – Int. J. **6**(2), 335–359 (2007)
11. Donaldson, S.I.: Program Theory-Driven Evaluation Science: Strategies and Applications. Routledge, London (2012)
12. Rogers, P.J.: Causal models in program theory evaluation. New Dir. Eval. **87**, 47–55 (2000)

Author Index

The manufacturer's authorised representative in the EU is Springer Nature Customer Service Centre GmbH, Europaplatz 3, 69115 Heidelberg, Germany. If you have any concerns regarding our products, please contact ProductSafety@springernature.com

Printed and bound by CPI Group (UK) Ltd, Croydon, CR0 4YY
05/10/2026
02228125-0020